AMERICAN PO
INDEX
VOLUME 2

AMERICAN POETRY INDEX

An Author, Title and Subject Index to Poetry by Americans in Single-Author Collections

VOLUME 2 • 1983

Prepared by
THE EDITORIAL BOARD
GRANGER BOOK CO.

GRANGER BOOK CO.
Great Neck, New York

International Standard Book Number 0-89609-241-0
International Standard Serial Number 0741-3165
Library of Congress Catalog Number 83-81682

Manufactured in the U.S.A.

CONTENTS

PREFACE   vii

EXPLANATORY NOTES   ix

LIST OF COLLECTIONS INDEXED   xi

AUTHOR AND TITLE INDEX   1

DIRECTORY OF PUBLISHERS   383

PREFACE

The AMERICAN POETRY INDEX has been created to provide access to poems in single-author collections which are not indexed anywhere. Standard poetry indexes analyze anthologies only.

With this new reference tool, the over 10,000 American poems published each year in book form will be located and identified in one source. Moreover, the systematic listing of each year's poetical output, including that of even the smallest presses, will contribute to the chronicling of American poetic history.

The AMERICAN POETRY INDEX will be published annually, analyzing the poetry collections of the prior year. Being cumulative, each edition will be a permanent volume. Volume 1, the inaugural volume, indexes 192 collections published in 1981 and 1982. Volume 2 accesses collections published in 1983.

EXPLANATORY NOTES

Each collection indexed is identified and referred to by a key number. The complete title of the collection, its key number, and other publishing information is contained in the List of Collections section which follows. Each poem of each collection is indexed by author, title, and subject.

Works containing prose and poetry are analyzed for poetry only. Collaborative works are treated as single-author collections with the main author entry accessed by the first named poet.

As many of the publishers of the collections indexed are small and may not be generally known, a Directory of Publishers is included at the back of the book.

Entries. Entries are by author, title, and subject. Each entry is complete in itself and each contains the key number (the last item in each entry) assigned to identify the collection indexed. Cross-reference between entries is therefore not required.

Arrangement. The filing is alphabetical word by word. Articles at the beginning of titles are retained but disregarded in the alphabeting. The alphabeting is stringently applied: all words are listed as spelled, including abbreviations.

Publication Dates. Determination of book publication dates is often a parlous matter. For the purposes of this index, copyright dates are generally, but not conclusively, determinative.

LIST OF COLLECTIONS INDEXED

Numbers 1-190 appeared in Volume I of AMERICAN POETRY INDEX for collections published in 1981-82.

191. **ACKER, Kathy**. Hello, I'm Erica Jong. (1982) Contact II
192. **ADCOCK, Betty**. Nettles. (1983) Louisiana State University
193. **AKILLAN, Michael H.** The eating of names. (1983) Ashod
194. **ANBIAN, Robert**. Bohemian airs and other kefs. (1982) Night Horn
195. **ANDERSON, Gene**. Coyote space. (1983) Holmgangers
196. **ANDREWS, Jenne**. Reunion. (1983) Lynx House
197. **ANGLUND, Joan Walsh**. The circle of the spirit. (1983) Random House
198. **APPLEWHITE, James**. Foreseeing the journey. (1983) Louisiana State University
199. **BAILIE, Anne**. In the soul's riptide. (1982) Chantry
200. **BARAKA, Amiri**. Reggae or not. (1981) Contact II
201. **BARKER, John F.** So I have been. (1983) Golden Quill
202. **BECKER, Robin**. Backtalk. (1982) Alice James Books
203. **BERSSENBRUGGE, Mei-Mei**. The heat bird. (1983) Burning Deck
204. **BERSSENBRUGGE, Mei-Mei**. Pack rat sieve. (1983) Contact II
205. **BIGGS, Margaret Key**. Petals from the womanflower. (1983) Adastra
206. **BLACK, Patsie**. Tapestry, a fine spun grace and mercy. (1982) Multnomah
207. **BLASING, Randy**. The particles. (1983) Cooper Beech
208. **BLESSING, Richard**. Poems and stories. (1983) Dragon Gate
209. **BLY, Robert**. The man in the black coat turns. (1983) Penguin
210. **BOEHRINGER, Marie Daerr**. Everyday miracles (1983) Golden Quill
211. **BOGAR, Rosa**. Black woman sorrow. (1983) Guild Press
212. **BOOKER, Stephen Todd**. Waves & license. (1983) Greenfield Review
213. **BOSS, Laura**. Stripping. (1982) Chantry
214. **BRANDI, John**. Rite for the beautification of all beings. (1983) Toothpaste
215. **BRITTS, Maurice W.** I will survive. (1982) Guild Press
216. **BRUCE, Debra**. Pure daughter. (1983) University of Arkansas
217. **BRYAN, Sharon**. Salt air. (1983) Wesleyan University
218. **BURKE, Theta**. Loving who you are, where you are. (1982) Delafield
219. **BURSK, Christopher**. Place of residence. (1983) Sparrow
220. **CHEATWOOD, Kiarri T-H.** Psalms of redemption. (1983) Lotus
221. **CHISHOLM, Scott**. Desperate affections. (1982) State Street
222. **CLAMPITT, Amy**. The kingfisher. (1983) Knopf
223. **CODRESCU, Andrei**. Selected poems, 1970-1980. (1983) Sun
224. **COLBY, Joan**. How the sky begins to fall. (1982) Spoon River
225. **COLEMAN, Wanda**. Imagoes. (1983) Black Sparrow
226. **CREWS, Judson**. The clock of moss. (1983) Ahsahta
227. **DAVIDSON, Alice Joyce**. Reflections of love. (1983) Revell
228. **DAVIS, PAUL**. A bright defiance and other poems. (1983) Patrice
229. **DERRICOTTE, Toi**. Natural birth. (1983) Crossing
230. **DETRO, Gene**. When all the wild summer. (1983) Holmgangers
231. **DIXON, Melvin**. Change of territory. (1983) University of Kentucky
232. **DODGE, Mary Mapes**. Mary Anne. (1983) Lothrop, Lee and Shepard
233. **DOVICKI, A.** The morning after midnight. (1983) Iron
234. **DuBOIS, Rochelle**. Timelapse. (1983) Lunchroom
235. **EASTHAM, Scott**. Paradise & Ezra Pound. (1983) University Press of America
236. **EATON, Charles Edward**. The thing king. (1983) Cornwall
237. **EIGNER, Larry**. Waters, places, a time. (1983) Black Sparrow
238. **EKLUND, George**. Gone west of sunrise highway. (1982) Bearstone
239. **EMANUEL, James A.** The broken bowl. (1983) Lotus
240. **ESHLEMAN, Clayton**. Fracture. (1983) Black Sparrow
241. **EVERHARD, Jim**. Cute. (1982) Gay Sunshine
242. **FELDMAN, Irving**. Teach me, dear sister. (1983) Penguin
243. **FERRIL, Thomas Hornsby**. Anvil of roses. (1983) Ahsahta

244. FISHER, Aileen. Rabbits, rabbits. (1983) Harper
245. FISHER, Harrison. UHFO. (1982) Diana's
246. FISHMAN, Sam. The restless mind. (1982) Lyle Stuart
247. FLEMING, Ray. Diplomatic relations. (1982) Lotus
248. FRANK, Jacqueline. No one took a country from me. (1982) Alice James
249. FROST, Carol. The fearful child. (1983) Ithaca House
250. FROST, Robert. North of Boston. (1977, current edition 1983) Dodd, Mead
251. FULLER, R. Buckminster. Intuition. (1983) Impact
252. GALARZA, Ernesto. Kodachromes in rhyme. (1982) University of Notre Dame
253. GIBB, Robert. The names of the earth in summer. (1983) Stone Country
254. GIDLOW, Elsa. Sapphic songs. (1982) Naiad
255. GILBERT, Sandra. The summer kitchen. (1983) Heyeck
256. GILLAN, Maria. Flowers from the tree of night. (1981) Chantry
257. GILLILAND, Mary. Gathering fire. (1982) Ithaca House
258. GILLIS, Everett A. Far beyond distance. (1981) Pisces
259. GIZZI, Michael. Species of intoxication. (1983) Burning Deck
259A. GLUCK, Louise. First Born. (1983) Ecco
260. GODFREY, John. Dabble: poems 1966-1980. (1982) Full Court
261. GOLDBARTH, Albert. Original light. (1983) Ontario Review, dist. Persea
262. GOLDBERGER, Iefke. The catch. (1982) Sol
263. GOLDEN, Evelyn. Glimpses. (1983) Dragon's Teeth
264. GOODMAN, Miriam. Signal-noise. (1982) Alice James
265. GREEN, Rose Basile. Songs of ourselves. (1982) Cornwall
266. GRENFELL, Cynthia. Stone run: tidings. (1983) Sunstone
267. GULLANS, Charles. A diatribe to Dr. Steele. (1982) Symposium
268. HANKLA, Cathryn. Phenomena. (1983) University of Missouri
269. HARJO, Joy. She had some horses. (1983) Thunder's Mouth
270. HAWKES, John. The bestowal. (1983) Sparrow
271. HAZEN, Rachel A. Words ready for music. (1983) Branden
272. HEMINGWAY, Ernest. Complete poems. (1979, current edition, 1983) University of Nebraska
273. HINRICHSEN, Dennis. The attraction of heavenly bodies. (1983) Wesleyan University
274. HOLLIS, Jocelyn. Vietnam poets II. (1983) American Poetry Press
275. HONIG, Edwin. Interrupted praise. (1983) Scarecrow
276. HOWARD, Mitchell. Always seeking the edge. (1982) Amphibian
277. HUDSON, Marc. Afterlight. (1983) University of Massachusetts
278. HUMES, Harry. Winter weeds. (1983) University of Missouri
279. HUNT, Connie. Reaching (1983) Pulsar
280. INEZ, Colette. Eight minutes from the sun. (1983) Saturday Press
281. IORIO, James. Journeys. (1983) Golden Quill
282. JAMES, David. Surface streets. (1981) Applezaba
283. JANSSEN, Martha. Silent scream. (1983) Fortress
284. JOHN, Da Free. Crazy Da must sing, inclined to his weaker side. (1982) Dawn Horse
285. JOLLY, Erin. Golden eyelids. (1983) Golden Quill
286. JONES, Gayl. The hermit-woman. (1983) Lotus
287. KALLET, Marilyn. In the great night. (1981) Ithaca
288. KAMINSKY, Marc. A table with people. (1981) Sun
289. KELLY, Robert. Under words. (1983) Black Sparrow
290. KENNEDY, X.J. Did Adam name the vinegarroon? (1982) Godine
291. KENNY, Maurice. The smell of slaughter. (1982) Blue Cloud
292. KHATCHADOURIAN, Haig. Shadows to time. (1983) Ashod
293. KIRK, Norman Andrew. Panda zoo. (1983) Bitterroot-West
294. KLOSS, Phillips. Selected poems. (1983) Sunstone
295. KNAUTH, Stephen. Night-fishing on Irish Buffalo Creek. (1982) Ithaca
296. KNOTT, Bill. Becos (1983) Random House
297. KOCH, Kenneth. Days and nights. (1982) Random House
298. KOWIT, Steve. Cutting our loses. (1982) Contact II
299. KOWIT, Steve. Lurid confessions. (1983) Carpenter
300. KUZMA, Greg. Everyday life. (1983) Spoon River

LIST OF COLLECTIONS INDEXED

301. LATTIMORE, Richmond. Continuing conclusions. (1983) Louisiana State University
302. LENGYEL, Cornel. Late news from Adam's acres. (1983) Dragon's Teeth
303. LIFSHIN, Lyn. Madonna who shifts for herself. (1983) Applezaba
304. LOBEL, Arnold. The book of pigericks. (1983) Harper
305. LOHMANN, Jeanne. Steadying the landscape. (1982) Lohmann
306. LUMPKIN, Kirk. Co-hearing. (1983) Zyga
307. LUX, Thomas. Tarantulas on the lifebouy. (1983) Ampersand
308. MAGORIAN, James. Taxidermy lessons. (1982) Black Oak
309. MAGORIAN, James. The Walden Pond caper. (1983) Black Oak
310. MALANGA, Gerard. This will kill that. (1983) Black Sparrow
311. MARGOLIS, Gary. The day we will stand here. (1983) University of Georgia
312. MARZ, Roy. The island maker. (1982) Ithaca
313. MAURA, SISTER What we women know (1980, current edition 1983) Black Sparrow
314. MAYES, Frances. The arts of fire. (1982) Heyeck
315. McGRATH, Thomas. Echoes inside the labyrinth. (1983) Thunder's Mouth
316. McKUEN, Rod. The sound of solitude. (1983) Harper
317. McPHERSON, Sandra. Patron happiness. (1983) Ecco
318. MERRILL, James. Santorini: stopping the leak. (1982) Metacom
319. MILES, Josephine. Collected poems, 1930-83. (1983) University of Illinois
320. MILLER, May. The ransomed wait. (1983) Lotus
321. MILLS, Jr, Ralph J. March light. (1983) Sparrow
322. MOFFI, Larry. A simple progression. (1982) Ampersand
323. MOORE, Richard. The education of a mouse. (1983) Countryman
324. MORETTI, Josephine B. Love is where. (1982) Golden Quill
325. MORGAN, Robin. Depth perception. (1982) Anchor/Doubleday
326. MORRIS, Herbert. Peru. (1983) Harper
327. MORRISON, Madison. Light. (1983) Working Week
328. MORRISON, Madison. O. (1982) Working Week
329. MORROW, Bradford. Posthumes. (1982) Cadmus
330. MURDOCH, Royal. The disrobing. (1982) Gay Sunshine
331. NELSON, Rodney, Thor's home. (1983) Holmgangers
332. NEWTON, Alice Spohn. Have a cup of bygones. (1983) Golden Quill
333. NEWTON, Alice Spohn. My song of many loves. (1982) Golden Quill
334. NOEL, Linda. Where you first saw the eyes of the coyote. (1983) Strawberry
335. OANDASAN, William. A branch of California redwood. (1981) University of California
336. OATES, Joyce Carol. Invisible woman. (1982) Ontario Review, dist. Persea
337. OLSON, Charles. The Maximus poems. (1983) University of California
338. ORMEROD, Jan. Rhymes around the day. (1983) Lothrop
339. ORTH, Ghita. The music of what happens. (1982) Saturday Press
340. OSBEY, Brenda Marie. Ceremony for Minneconjoux. (1983) University of Kentucky
341. PAWLOWSKI, Robert. The seven sacraments and other poems. (1982) Flower Mound
342. PENZI, James. Scenes in bk & wh (1982) Contact II
343. PETERS, Robert. What Dillinger meant to me. (1983) Sea Horse
344. PETROSKY, Anthony. Jurgis Petraskas. (1983) Louisiana State University
345. PICK, Michael Robert. Childhood, namhood, manhood. (1982) Pizzuto
346. PIERCY, Marge. Stone, paper, knife. (1983) Knopf
347. POE, Edgar Allan. The unabridged Edgar Allan Poe. (1983) Running Press
—   POUND, EZRA. See #235
348. PRELUTSKY, Jack. It's Valentine's Day. (1983) Greenwillow
349. PRELUTSKY, Jack. Zoo doings. (1983) Greenwillow
350. REED, John. The complete poetry of John Reed. (1983) University Press of America
351. REVELL, Donald. From the abandoned cities. (1983) Harper
352. RHODES, James R. Poems. (1982) Mellen
353. RICH, Adrienne. Sources. (1983) Heyeck
354. RIVERS, J.W. Proud and on my feet. (1983) University of Georgia
355. ROKWAHO. Covers. (1982) Strawberry
356. RUGO, Marieve. Fields of vision. (1983) University of Alabama

357. **SANDY, Stephen**. Riding to Greylock. (1983) Random House
358. **SAUNDERS, Sally Love**. Fresh bread. (1982) Golden Quill
359. **SCHECTER, Ruth Lisa**. Speedway. (1983) Chantry
360. **SCHEVILL, James Erwin**. The American fantasies. (1983) Swallow
361. **SCHNEIDER, Franz**. The roof of stone. (1982) Temporal Acuity
362. **SEARS, Donald A**. The Magellan heart. (1982) Harian
363. **SHAPIRO, David**. To an idea. (1983) Overlook
364. **SILVER-LILLYWHITE, Eileen**. All that autumn. (1983) Ithaca
365. **SIMMERMAN, Jim**. Home. (1983) Dragon Gate
366. **SLEIGH, Tom**. After one. (1983) Houghton
367. **SMITH, Dave**. In the house of the judge. (1983) Harper
368. **SMITH, TOM**. Singing the middle ages. (1982) Countryman
369. **SNODGRASS, W.D. (William DeWitt)**. Heart's needle. (1983) Knopf
370. **SOLLOV, Jacques**. Gold of the stars. (1983) White Eagle
371. **SOLLOV, Jacques**. Reborn again in the kingdom. (1982) White Eagle
372. **SONG, Cathy**. Picture bride. (1983) Yale University
373. **STAFFORD, William**. A glass face in the rain. (1982) Harper
374. **STEELE, Timothy**. The prudent heart. (1983) Symposium
375. **STOCK, Susan**. Early morning through the door. (1983) Holmgangers
376. **STOLOFF, Carolyn**. A spool of blue. (1983) Scarecrow
377. **STRYK, Lucien**. Cherries. (1983) Ampersand
378. **TALL, Deborah**. Ninth life. (1982) Ithaca
379. **TATE, James**. Constant defender. (1983) Ecco
380. **TEDLOCK, Ernest**. Told by the weather. (1983) Holmgangers
381. **TICHY, Susan**. The hands in exile. (1983) Random House
382. **TICKLE, Phyllis A**. Selections. (1983) Erasmus
383. **TRIEM, Eve**. Midsummer rites. (1982) Seal
384. **TURNER, Alberta T**. A belfry of knees. (1983) University of Alabama
385. **TURNER, Thomas Noel**. Hillbilly night afore Christmas. (1983) Pelican
386. **USHER, Harlan**. The grownups' Mother Goose. (1983) Ell Ell
387. **VINZ, Mark**. Climbing the stairs. (1983) Spoon River
388. **VIOLI, Paul**. Splurge. (1981) Sun
389. **WAGNER, Anneliese**. Hand work. (1983) Saturday Press
390. **WAGONER, David**. First light. (1983) Little
391. **WAKOSKI, Diane**. The lady who drove me to the airport. (1982) Metacom
392. **WALDROP, Keith**. The space of half an hour. (1983) Burning Deck
393. **WALLENSTEIN, Barry**. Roller Coaster kid, & other poems. (1982) T.Y. Crowell.
394. **WANN, David**. Log rhythms. (1983) North Atlantic
395. **WARREN, Robert Penn**. Chief Joseph of the Nez Perce. (1983) Random House
396. **WHITE, James L.**The salt ecstasies. (1982) Graywolf
397. **WILLIAMS, S. Bradford, Jr.** Caress softly thy love. (1982) Copper Orchid
398. **WILLIAMS, S. Bradford, Jr.** Sunshine grows the day. (1983) Copper Orchid
399. **WILLIAMS, Miller**. The boys on their bony mules. (1983) Louisiana State University
400. **WILSON, Keith**. Stone roses. (1983) Utah State University
401. **WILSON, Robert L**. Practicing for death. (1983) Golden Quill
402. **WRIGHT, C.D.** Translations of the gospel back into tongues. (1982) State University of New York
403. **WRIGHT, James**. The temple in Nimes. (1982) Metacom
404. **YAU, John**. Corpse and mirror. (1983) Holt

A priori. David Wann. 394
A-glitter with radiance. Rachel
    A. Hazen. 271
A distant day. Evelyn Golden. 263
The **aardvark**. Jack Prelutsky. 349
Aardvarks
    The aardvark. Jack Prelutsky.
    349
Abandoned airfield, 1977. Joyce
    Carol Oates. 336
Abattoir. Frances Mayes. 314
Abortion
    The abortion: words for a young
    woman. Jeanne Lohmann. 305
Abortion. See also Death -
    Prenatal

          . .
The **abortion**: words for a young
    woman. Jeanne Lohmann. 305
About God & things. Wanda
    Coleman. 225
About our lips. Mary Gilliland.
    257
About photography. Andrei
    Codrescu. 223
About the time. Rod McKuen. 316
Above a dry pool. Larry Moffi.
    322
Above Moraine Park. Marc Hudson.
    277
"**Above** the head of John Day's
    pasture land." Charles Olson.
    337
Abraham
    The first subdivider. Cornel
    Lengyel. 302
Abraham, without papers. Norman
    Andrew Kirk. 293
Abrak. Robert Kelly. 289
Absalom. Thomas Hornsby Ferril.
    243
Absence. Anneliese Wagner. 389
Absence. See Separation

Absences. William Stafford. 373
Absinthe
    Geneva. Michael Gizzi. 259
Absolute man. Josephine Miles.
    319
Absolute zero in the brain. Marge
    Piercy. 346
Absolution. Rod McKuen. 316
The **abstract** man encounters the
    adjutant, sels. Edwin Honig.
    275
The **abstract** nude. Roy Marz. 312
Abstraction no. 1. James Torio.
    281
The **abuses** of New York. Mitchell
    Howard. 276

Academic circles. Ray Fleming.
    247
Academic fowl. Cornel Lengyel.
    302
Acceptance. Evelyn Golden. 263
Acceptance. Connie Hunt. 279
Accident, from a Wajda movie.
    James A. Emanuel. 239
Accidents
    Accident, from a Wajda movie.
    James A. Emanuel. 239
    The disaster plan. Joan Colby.
    224
    Easter. Cathryn Hankla. 268
    "The force." Larry Eigner. 237
    Night accident. Robert Peters.
    343
    Second variation on Corpse and
    mirror. John Yau. 404
    Surviving the wreck. Betty
    Adcock. 192
    Who was killed in the car. Greg
    Kuzma. 300
Accommodations. Miriam Goodman.
    264
The **account** book of B Ellery.
    Charles Olson. 337
The **accountings**. Albert
    Goldbarth. 261
Acker, Kathy
    Hello, I'm Erica Jong. 191
Acoma. William Oandasan. 335
Acoma mesa. William Stafford. 373
Acoma, New Mexico
    Acoma. William Oandasan. 335
Acrobats
    High-wire artist. Joyce Carol
    Oates. 336
    Il salto mortale. Marieve Rugo.
    356
    The last of the Wallendas.
    Stephen Sandy. 357
Acrophobia. Ghita Orth. 339
Across a bridge. Anne Bailie. 199
Across the board. Ernest
    Hemingway. 272
An **acrostic**. Edgar Allan Poe. 347
Act V. Josephine Miles. 319
Acting and Actors
    Psychodrama. James Magorian. 308
    Who's afraid of Maurice
    Schwartz? Ruth Lisa Schechter.
    359
Acute memory. Martha Janssen. 283
Adam and Eve
    The first eviction. Cornel
    Lengyel. 302
    A hereditary ailment. Cornel
    Lengyel. 302
    Paradise lost and found. Sam

Fishman. 246
Roots. Sister Maura. 313
They. Irving Feldman. 242
Adam's fault. Cornel Lengyel. 302
Adams, Henry
Effort for distraction.
Josephine Miles. 319
Adams, Thomas
The Chiclets paragraphs. Paul
Violi. 388
Adcock, Betty
Afternoon, playing on a bed. 192
Asthma, 1948. 192
Blind singer. 192
Box-camera snapshot. 192
The clouded leopards of Cambodia
and Viet Nam. 192
The Elizabeth poems. 192
The farm. 192
Fishing. 192
From the dunked clown at the
carnival. 192
Front porch. 192
Hand made. 192
Lines on a poet's face. 192
Luxor. 192
Mineral. 192
Note for the birdwatchers of the
sublime. 192
One street. 192
One year. 192
Poetry workshop in a maximum
security reform school. 192
Redlands journey. 192
Repetition. 192
Roller rink. 192
South woods in October, with the
spiders of memory. 192
Surviving the wreck. 192
The swan story. 192
To my father, killed in a
hunting accident. 192
To Sylvia, grown daughter. 192
Topsail island. 192
Traveling, 1950. 192
Twentieth anniversary. 192
Two words. 192
Witness. 192
Add your love to my love. Alice
Joyce Davidson. 227
*Added to/making a republic.
Charles Olson. 337
"Addicts progress from
saturation." Josephine Miles.
319
Adding padding. Josephine B.
Moretti. 324
Adirondacks. Scott Chisholm. 221
The admonitions. Jenne Andrews.
196

Adolescence. Eileen
Silver-Lillywite. 364
Adolescence. Martha Janssen. 283
Adolescence
Adolescence. Eileen
Silver-Lillywite. 364
Adolescence. Martha Janssen. 283
The adolescents. Everett A.
Gillis. 258
Senior prom. James Magorian. 309
Sixteen. Martha Janssen. 283
Thirteen. Martha Janssen. 283
An adolescent girl. Carol Frost.
249
"An adolescent room." Madison
Morrison. 327
The adolescents. Everett A.
Gillis. 258
Adopted daughter. Sharon Bryan.
217
Adoption
Madonna. James R. Rhodes. 352
Room for more. Iefke Goldberger.
262
Three with a boat on Pine Lake.
Iefke Goldberger. 262
Advent. John F. Barker. 201
Adventurers
End of the picaro. Stephen
Sandy. 357
Advertising
Mr. Martin in the advertising
agency. James Schevill. 360
Pelleas and Melisande. Josephine
Miles. 319
Advice
Baghdad. Michael Gizzi. 259
The candy lady. Laura Boss. 213
For travelers on the sabbath.
Cornel Lengyel. 302
Fulfillment. Connie Hunt. 279
Lessons. Wanda Coleman. 225
A modern version of Polonius'
advice. Ernest Hemingway. 272
"My son." Michael Robert Pick.
345
The non-swimmer advises his
nephew about the beach. J.W.
Rivers. 354
The road ahead. Maurice W.
Britts. 215
Uncle Max leaves for Rumania.
J.W. Rivers. 354
Uncle Max steeps young
Culpepper... J.W. Rivers. 354
Advice to a son. Ernest
Hemingway. 272
Advice to older marrieds.
Josephine B. Moretti. 324
Advice to the lovelorn. Cornel

Lengyel. 302

Aeneid, The
    Creusa, the wife. May Miller.
       320
Aerial act. David Wagoner. 390
Aerobatics
    Aerial act. David Wagoner. 390
Aesthete's complaint. Donald
      Revell. 351
Aesthetic distance. Miller
      Williams. 399
The **affinities** of Orpheus, sels.
      Edwin Honig. 275
Affirmation. Alice Joyce
      Davidson. 227
Affirmation. George Eklund. 238
Affirmations. Maria Gillan. 256
Africa
    Dark continent. Robert A. Sears.
      362
    French club - Kano. Robert A.
      Sears. 362
    Going to Africa. Melvin Dixon.
      231
    On, Africa. Rosa Bogar. 211
    Out of Africa. Robert A. Sears.
      362
    These three. Ruth Lisa
      Schechter. 359
    Tour guide: La Maison des
      Esclaves. Melvin Dixon. 231
    Wapa club. Robert A. Sears. 362
After. Stephen Sandy. 357
After a governmental purge. Anne
      Bailie. 199
After an illness. Phyllis A.
      Tickle. 382
After apple-picking. Robert
      Frost. 250
After arguing against the
      contention that art... William
      Stafford. 373
After leaving you. Eileen
      Silver-Lillywite. 364
After making love. Robin Becker.
      202
After Marie. Marilyn Kallet. 287
After one. Thomas R. Sleigh. 366
After reading parts of Mother
      Goose to a friend's children.
      Jenne Andrews. 196
After running, for Peter. Mary
      Gilliland. 257
After sleep. Jim Everhard. 241
After some verses by Morvaen Le
      Gaelique & Paul Verlaine.
      Kenneth Koch. 297
After terror... Joyce Carol
      Oates. 336
After the Anglican communion.

Jenne Andrews. 196
After the dying. Ghita Orth. 339
After the high school graduation,
      1944. David Wagoner. 390
After the hotwave. Eileen
      Silver-Lillywite. 364
After the letter. Edwin Honig.
      275
After the poem. Wanda Coleman.
      225
After the poem (2). Wanda
      Coleman. 225
After the rain. Tefke Goldberger.
      262
After the reading. Herbert
      Morris. 326
After the revolution. David
      James. 282
After the separation papers had
      been signed. Laura Boss. 213
After the separation. Edwin
      Honig. 275
After the war (I). John Yau. 404
After the war (II). John Yau. 404
After the war (III). John Yau.
      404
After the war (IV). John Yau. 404
After Tijuana: the pool. Randy
      Blasing. 207
After Villon: the dead ladies.
      Tom Smith. 368
"After violence the." Madison
      Morrison. 327
After waking from my nap.
      Christopher Bursk. 219
After work. Wanda Coleman. 225
After-hours acrobatics. Rod
      McKuen. 316
After "after apple-picking."
      Larry Moffi. 322
After a southern visit. Jeanne
      Lohmann. 305
After all these years. Jeanne
      Lohmann. 305
After gossip. Sister Maura. 313
"After I come home from the
      meeting with friends."
      Josephine Miles. 319
"After noon I lie down."
      Josephine Miles. 319
"After the storm was over."
      Charles Olson. 337
After this, sea. Josephine Miles.
      319
After/words. Ruth Lisa Schechter.
      359
Afterall, the children. Norman
      Andrew Kirk. 293
Afterglow. May Miller. 320
Afterlight. Marc Hudson. 277

Afternoon. David Wann. 394

Afternoon of the faun. James
    Torio. 281

Afternoon social. Phyllis A.
    Tickle. 382

Afternoon walk. Josephine Miles.
    319

Afternoon, playing on a bed.
    Betty Adcock. 192

Afterwards. Royal Murdoch. 330

Again, Van Gogh. George Eklund.
    238

Against meaning. Andrei Codrescu.
    223

Against the weather. Marilyn
    Kallet. 287

Agates
    Fire agate, fr. Gem show.
        Everett A. Gillis. 258

The age demanded. Ernest
    Hemingway. 272

Age is not what we are but where
    we have been in time. Everett
    A. Gillis. 258

The age of silence... James
    Schevill. 360

Age. See Middle Age, Old Age,
    Youth

Agent orange. Evelyn Golden. 263

"Aggre-/gates.". Larry Eigner.
    237

Aggressor. Josephine Miles. 319

Aging
    Age is not what we are but where
        we have been in time. Everett
        A. Gillis. 258
    Albert Feinstein. Irving
        Feldman. 242
    At the light I saw Pam. Frances
        Mayes. 314
    The avocado connection. Charles
        Edward Eaton. 236
    Beach boy. Josephine B. Moretti.
        324
    Cell damage. George Eklund. 238
    Daisy fields, enchanted forests.
        Richmond Lattimore. 301
    Dirge. Lucien Stryk. 377
    Drift. C.D. Wright. 402
    Experience. Anne Bailie. 199
    Explanations. Josephine B.
        Moretti. 324
    The final virtue. May Miller.
        320
    For Bill who passed on with the
        summer. Mary Gilliland. 257
    Form and actuality. Richmond
        Lattimore. 301
    Gone. Ralph J., Jr. Mills. 321

Growing in grace. Alice Joyce
    Davidson. 227

Harvest song. Cornel Lengyel.
    302

A harvest. Mark Vinz. 387

Horoscope. James Magorian. 308

How old are you? Josephine B.
    Moretti. 324

"I fear to take a step;along the
    edge." Josephine Miles. 319

In search of a second dawn.
    Margaret Key Biggs. 205

A lament for Willie Wyler. James
    Torio. 281

Lesefruchte. Richmond Lattimore.
    301

The lines of living. Laura Boss.
    213

Making old bones. Alberta
    Turner. 384

Masks in 1980 for age 60. James
    Schevill. 360

Me. Josephine B. Moretti. 324

Middle aged wife. Josephine B.
    Moretti. 324

Near four. Ralph J., Jr. Mills.
    321

Night song. Ralph J., Jr. Mills.
    321

No more, no more. Sam Fishman.
    246

The oldest story. Bill Knott.
    296

On not being the youngest wife
    at the Shop-Rite. Laura Boss.
    213

The queue. Steve Kowit. 299

Recluse. Mark Vinz. 387

Returning. James L. White. 396

Short memory. Josephine B.
    Moretti. 324

Sliding scales. Richmond
    Lattimore. 301

Song. Thomas McGrath. 315

A song for the queen. Jeanne
    Lohmann. 305

Song of a dark pine morning.
    Maria Gillan. 256

To what's-her-name. Irving
    Feldman. 242

The trembling of the veil.
    Thomas McGrath. 315

Who, me? I'm fine. Marie Daerr
    Boehringer. 210

The world. Kenneth Koch. 297

The aging poet writes of the
    continuing evidence of his...
    Sister Maura. 313

Agnew, Spiro T.
    The reincarnation of Spirow T.

Agnew. James Magorian. 309
Agreement
   Saying yes. Connie Hunt. 279
Ah, my soul. Patsie Black. 206
AI nostri. Rose Basile Green. 265
Aim. Josephine Miles. 319
Air. Larry Eigner. 237
Air
   In air. Josephine Miles. 319
Air burial. Harry Humes. 278
The air clears, after. Mary
   Gilliland. 257
Air for air. Stephen Sandy. 357
Air Travel
   Arrival. Rose Basile Green. 265
   As seen from an airplane. Sally
      Love Saunders. 358
   Aspiration. Rose Basile Green.
      265
   Crossing over. James Applewhite.
      198
   Delay. Josephine Miles. 319
   Ecstasy of flight. Joyce Carol
      Oates. 336
   The first prayer of angles.
      Cathryn Hankla. 268
   Going by jet. Eve Triem. 383
   "High piled/clouds." Larry
      Eigner. 237
   "If connections are." Madison
      Morrison. 327
   Iron age flying. James
      Applewhite. 198
   It looks a war. Paul Davis. 228
   Jet lag. James Torio. 281
   The late flight. William
      Stafford. 373
   O. Madison Morrison. 328
   Pearl. Josephine Miles. 319
   Remembering the man. Miller
      Williams. 399
   Scene from an airplane. Sally
      Love Saunders. 358
   Takeoff. Deborah Tall. 378
   The terminal. James Applewhite.
      198
   Travelers. Josephine Miles. 319
   White bear. Joy Harjo. 269
   "With the bill of a cap."
      Madison Morrison. 327
   Words to persons who find
      themselves feeling small.
      Mitchell Howard. 276
Air Warfare
   The game-master explains the
      rules of the game for
      bombings. James Schevill. 360
   In the sleep of reason. Thomas
      McGrath. 315
Airplanes. See Aviation

Akillian, Michael
   Another poem about colored
      leaves. 193
   Ascent. 193
   The eating of names. 193
   Four quotes that didn't make the
      bible. 193
   Harbor. 193
   Her kitchen. 193
   In winter. 193
   The jumper. 193
   Leaving. 193
   The life course. 193
   Like any great forest. 193
   Oak against bleak sky. 193
   The painting. 193
   Perkin's cove. 193
   Progressive dinner. 193
   Segovia playing. 193
   Self portrait. 193
   The service. 193
   The song. 193
   The tennis match. 193
   Trilogy. 193
   Walk by a cemetery wall. 193
   Water's edge. 193
   The work of the soul. 193
Al Aaraaf. Edgar Allan Poe. 347
Al Haji Nuhu takes a fourth wife.
   Robert A. Sears. 362
Alain LeRoy Locke. May Miller.
   320
Alaska. Sally Love Saunders. 358
Alaska
   Alaska. Sally Love Saunders. 358
   "Alaska, the state of secrets."
      Sally Love Saunders. 358
   "Alaskan tundra misses." Sally
      Love Saunders. 358
   Cloudy day in Alaska. Sally Love
      Saunders. 358
   "Columbian Glacier." Sally Love
      Saunders. 358
   Prince Williams Sound. Sally
      Love Saunders. 358
"Alaska, the state of secrets."
   Sally Love Saunders. 358
"Alaskan tundra misses." Sally
   Love Saunders. 358
Albemarle. Donald Revell. 351
Albert. Robert Peters. 343
Albert Feinstein. Irving Feldman.
   242
Alberta. Andrei Codrescu. 223
Alberta Abrams fishes for mullet.
   J.W. Rivers. 354
Albinos
   They call them 'The Starlings.'
      Paul Violi. 388

Album. Josephine Miles. 319
Alcatraz (island)
    A woman staring through a
    telescope at Alcatraz. James
    Schevill. 360
Alchemy. Joseph Penzi. 342
Alcohol. See Drinks and Drinking

Aleppo. Micnael Gizzi. 259
Alexander. Jacques Sollov. 370
Alexander the Great
    Alexander. Jacques Sollov. 370
Alice's brilliance. Andrei
    Codrescu. 223
Alien. Gnita Orth. 339
Alienation
    A hairline fracture. Amy
    Clampitt. 222
    "Our vulnerability." Theta
    Burke. 218
    Outsiders. Elsa Gidlow. 254
The aliens. Robert L. Wilson. 401
The aliens. Marilyn Kallet. 287
Alighting. Alice Joyce Davidson.
    227
Alive. Joy Harjo. 269
Alkest, property of M. Valerius;
    and Nicolas Flamel. Albert
    Goldbarth. 261
"All armies are the same." Ernest
    Hemingway. 272
All Hallows in Lucy. Phyllis A.
    Tickle. 382
All is one. Connie Hunt. 279
All literature. Marilyn Kallet.
    287
"All night long." Charles Olson.
    337
"All of the fine mist from our
    soles." Sally Love Saunders.
    358
"All parts/are necessary/to the
    circle." Joan Walsh Anglund.
    197
All Saints' Day
    Woman at midnight. Phyllis A.
    Tickle. 382
All that autumn. Eileen
    Silver-Lillywite. 364
"All the names are already
    written." Da Free John. 284
All the nights the house slept
    through. Edwin Honig. 275
"All the stories never told."
    Theta Burke. 218
All things are one, said
    Empodocles... Colette Inez.
    280
All wars are holy. Andrei
    Codrescu. 223

All's well. James R. Rhodes. 352
All-nite donuts. Albert
    Goldbarth. 261
The all-stars. Irving Feldman.
    242
All farewells. Elsa Gidlow. 254
"All matter/standing." Larry
    Eigner. 237
"All of the joy." A. Dovichi. 233
All's fair. James A. Emanuel. 239
All-the heart's song. Kirk
    Lumpkin. 306
All hallow. Josephine Miles. 319
All hallow's eve. Gerard Malanga.
    310
All men are Gemini. Roy Marz. 312
All my life I've heard about
    many. Charles Olson. 337
All that is necessary. Jeanne
    Lohmann. 305
Alla breve loving. C.D. Wright.
    402
Alley. David Wann. 394
Alleys. Sandra McPherson. 317
Alleys. See Roads and Trails

"The alligator.". Charles Olson.
    337
Alligators
    Looking for alligators. Jeanne
    Lohmann. 305
Almaden road. Ernesto Galarza.
    252
Almonds
    Now let us examine the almond.
    David Wann. 394
"An almost empty tube." Sally
    Love Saunders. 358
Alone. Edgar Allan Poe. 347
Alone. Martha Janssen. 283
Alone (to-). Edgar Allan Poe. 347
Alone inside. Rachel A. Hazen.
    271
"Alone is the consitions of
    bliss." Da Free John. 284
"Alone now/together." A. Dovichi.
    233
Alone on a blanket. Lyn Lifshin.
    303
Along the Garonne. Colette Inez.
    280
Along the Hudson. Maurice Kenny.
    291
Along the Katsura walk. Ruth Lisa
    Schechter. 359
Along the street. William
    Oandasan. 335
"Along the street where we used
    to stop for bread." Josephine
    Miles. 319

Along the way. Mark Vinz. 387
"Along these sidewalks." Madison
    Morrison. 327
"Along walls." Larry Eigner. 237
Along with youth. Ernest
    Hemingway. 272
Aloning. James R. Rhodes. 352
Aloof. Martha Janssen. 283
Alp. Thomas R. Sleigh. 366
Alpenglow. Patsie Black. 206
Alps
    With family below Albion Basin.
        Sharon Bryan. 217
Altar cross. Patsie Black. 206
Alternative lifestyle. Ray
    Fleming. 247
Altitude. Susan Tichy. 381
Alvaro's resurrection machine.
    Jenne Andrews. 196
Always open. Ralph J., Jr. Mills.
    321
Always we walk through unknown
    people. James Schevill. 360
Alyce Bianco. Sally Love
    Saunders. 358
Amabo, mea dulcis ipsithilla.
    Steve Kowit. 299
Amaranth and Moly. Amy Clampitt.
    222
The amateurs. Roy Marz. 312
An ambassador from the future.
    Mitchell Howard. 276
Ambition
    A goal. Alice Joyce Davidson.
        227
    The history of it. Bradford
        Morrow. 329
    Portrait of a man rising in his
        profession. Charles Edward
        Eaton. 236
    Upward mobility. Connie Hunt.
        279
Ambivalence
    The enemies of cold water.
        Gerard Malanga. 310
Ambrose Remy. Stephen Knauth. 295
America. Alice Joyce Davidson.
    227
America. Eileen Silver-Lillywite.
    364
America 1918. John Reed. 350
America, all singing. Rose Basile
    Green. 265
Americadians. Rose Basile Green.
    265
American baroque. Mitchell
    Howard. 276
American beauties. Harrison
    Fisher. 245
American beauties. Eileen

    Silver-Lillywite. 364
American belles. Harrison Fisher.
    245
An American expressed. Charles
    Edward Eaton. 236
The American field. Stephen
    Knauth. 295
American genesis. Phyllis A.
    Tickle. 382
American gigantism: Gutzon
    Borglum at Mt. Rushmore. James
    Schevill. 360
The American girl. Harrison
    Fisher. 245
The American literary conference.
    Keith Wilson. 400
American men. Marc Kaminsky. 288
American Revolution
    Deed. Josephine Miles. 319
    Soundscape. Rose Basile Green.
        265
    Washington's man. Paul Davis.
        228
Americans to Europeans. Rose
    Basile Green. 265
Amherst songs. Ralph J., Jr.
    Mills. 321
Amherst, Massachusetts
    Amherst songs. Ralph J., Jr.
        Mills. 321
Amicus Curiae. Jeanne Lohmann.
    305
Amnesia. Cynthia Grenfell. 266
Amnesia. Stephen Knauth. 295
"Among a hundred mirrors."
    Michael Robert Pick. 345
Among cattle. Dennis Hinrichsen.
    273
Among dark hills. Robert L.
    Wilson. 401
Among many to decide. Paul Davis.
    228
Among the craggy rocks. Judson
    Crews. 226
Among the maybes, sels. Robert A.
    Sears. 362
"Among the maybes." Robert A.
    Sears. 362
Among wild oats. Ernesto Galarza.
    252
The amputee. Charles Edward
    Eaton. 236
Amsterdam, student round-up.
    Tefke Goldberger. 262
Amusement Parks
    Roller coaster kid. Barry
        Wallenstein. 393
An I for an I. Tefke Goldberger.
    262
Anagoge for an island. Thomas

Hornsby Ferril. 243
The **analyst's** report on his
    convalescent patient. Franz
    Schneider. 361
Analytic hymn. Robert Kelly. 289
Ananke. Gerard Malanga. 310
Anatolia. Paul Violi. 388
Anatomy
    Bone structure. Richmond
        Lattimore. 301
Anatomy of a mirror. Anne Bailie.
    199
Anaximander
    "Aristotle & Augustine." Charles
        Olson. 337
Anbian, Robert
    Bohemian airs. 194
    Coda. 194
    The dying man's shame. 194
    Element of the act. 194
    Hiemal watch. 194
    Inverted sunday. 194
    Night's beard. 194
    Oceanology. 194
    Old woman. 194
    Poem for an ex-schoolgirl. 194
    Postcard from a voyage. 194
    Real estate. 194
    Sea watch. 194
    Spatial relations. 194
    Two photographs for a
        non-existent album. 194
Ancestors. Dennis Hinrichsen. 273
Ancestors. Edwin Honig. 275
Ancestry. See Heritage

Anchorage. Joy Harjo. 269
Anchorage. Sally Love Saunders.
    358
Anchorage. Ghita Orth. 339
Anchorage, Alaska
    Anchorage. Joy Harjo. 269
    Anchorage. Sally Love Saunders.
        358
And. Albert Goldbarth. 261
And after. Josephine Miles. 319
"**And** did you know." Robert A.
    Sears. 362
"**And** everything the author
    knows." Ernest Hemingway. 272
And for Jenny. Rachel A. Hazen.
    271
"**And** in the preface..." Albert
    Goldbarth. 261
And melancholy. Charles Olson.
    337
And nobody cries. Rachel A.
    Hazen. 271
"**And** now Farley is going to
    sing..." Albert Goldbarth. 261

"**And** now let all the ships come
    in." Charles Olson. 337
And now, the others. Rachel A.
    Hazen. 271
And so on. Sam Fishman. 246
And the songs of life's joy...,
    sels. S. Bradford Williams
    (Jr.). 398
"**And** then the old woman." Michael
    Robert Pick. 345
And yet-. John Reed. 350
"**And** you, Pa." Michael Robert
    Pick. 345
And you? James R. Rhodes. 352
And-a-one-2-3-.. Stephen Todd
    Booker. 212
"**And/so** it ends/quickly." A.
    Dovichi. 233
"**And/with** the passing/of time."
    A. Dovichi. 233
And: a funeral hymn for Ernest
    Hemingway. James Schevill. 360
&. Andrei Codrescu. 223
Anderson, Gene
    Breaking up. 195
    Buddhist meditation while
        fertilizing. 195
    Coyote bone. 195
    Coyote lovesong. 195
    The creosote bush. 195
    Death of the old orange orchard.
        195
    Desert rose. 195
    Fall garden: 1. 195
    Fall garden: 2. 195
    Golden eagle. 195
    Grandparents and grandchildren.
        195
    Hamsa: in memoriam. 195
    High blood pressure. 195
    Jordan River. 195
    Learning to bake bread. 195
    The meadowlark. 195
    Meetings in October. 195
    No name. 195
    The Olive Mountain coyote pack.
        195
    Owling. 195
    Seventeen years ending. 195
    Sky coyote loses the year's
        gambling game for rain. 195
    Strange vision after divorce.
        195
    Symbiosis. 195
    Through the gate. 195
    A walk with my children. 195
    Worshipping Kali in the San
        Bernardino Mountains. 195
    Year of the dog. 195
Andrea Mendoza is aboard the

train from Durango. J.W.
Rivers. 354
Andrew's cyclones. James A.
Emanuel. 239
Andrews, Jenne
The admonitions. 196
After reading parts of Mother
Goose to a friend's children.
196
After the Anglican communion.
196
Alvaro's resurrection machine.
196
An atrocity, a sunset. 196
Canticle: tightening. 196
A criminology. 196
Dark latitude. 196
A dream of salt. 196
Exultations in late summer. 196
Forecast. 196
Home. 196
If there were only this music.
196
In dreams, a violinist. 196
In pursuit of the family. 196
In Rome. 196
The life in common. 196
The love of horses. 196
Love on the farm. 196
New Mexico territory. 196
Palm Sunday debriefing. 196
Reunion. 196
Running on Ramsey Hill. 196
The swim. 196
A telling. 196
There were estuaries. 196
The uses of sunday's music. 196
Waiting in paradise for Adam to
come back from the city. 196
We hear the whisper of the
perfect. 196
Why this loving is better. 196
Andros. John F. Barker. 201
Anemones. Maurice Kenny. 291
Anenecuilco: the Pueblo speaks.
J.W. Rivers. 354
Angel baby. Wanda Coleman. 225
The angel of - Alberta Turner.
384
The angel of the dialectic.
Robert Kelly. 289
The angel passes over. Larry
Moffi. 322
The angel track. James Schevill.
360
"Angelic youth." Larry Eigner.
237
Angelou, Maya
You've touched me. Connie Hunt.
279

Angels. Anthony Petrosky. 344
Angels
Crimes. Andrei Codrescu. 223
Israfel. Edgar Allan Poe. 347
Just another evening esse.
Bradford Morrow. 329
"On the outskirts of London..."
Albert Goldbarth. 261
"The angels came... and there was
loveliness." Joan Walsh
Anglund. 197
Angels of ascent. Melvin Dixon.
231
Angelus. Haig Khatchadourian. 292
Anger. Martha Janssen. 283
Anger
Anger. Martha Janssen. 283
Esterhazy shakes his fist at the
Sunday sky. J.W. Rivers. 354
Goodbye. Josephine Miles. 319
Heartbeat. Joy Harjo. 269
"Heating up I boil mad." Michael
Robert Pick. 345
"If the wall of your anger."
Theta Burke. 218
In the face of anger. Jacqueline
Frank. 248
"Long years ago." Theta Burke.
218
The quiet, angry man. George
Eklund. 238
Riot. Josephine Miles. 319
Some nasty business. Mitchell
Howard. 276
"Sometimes I get lost." Michael
Robert Pick. 345
Symbiosis. Connie Hunt. 279
Violence. Gerard Malanga. 310
"A whitened fist." Theta Burke.
218
Anglund, Joan Walsh
"All parts/are necessary/to the
circle." 197
"The angels came... and there
was loveliness." 197
"Because/the sun dips/its bright
face/beneath the horizon." 197
"The candle does not know/...
and yet its flame." 197
"The circle/has no beginning."
197
"Do not ask/... but listen." 197
"Do not desire the way/for the
way/is yours." 197
"Holding hands/we are a
circle/...of the spirit." 197
"I have come/to tell you/of the
way." 197
"One tree/holds/a hundred
birds." 197

"Only the open gate/can
    receive." 197
"Release/...and you will
    receive." 197
"Shadows.../doubt is a shadow."
    197
"spirit is not the flesh." 197
"The spirit is still." 197
"The spirit is the unseen
    circle/within." 197
"The spirit that speaks through
    you/is as the light." 197
"There is no question." 197
"The waters teach us/the sands
    teach us/the winds speak." 197
"The way waits/... and we must
    walk it." 197
"We are as a closed eye/...that
    will not see." 197
"We live in the body/... but we
    are not of the body." 197
"We see but part/of the circle."
    197
"Why fear death?" 197
"Within the spinning of
    events/...which is time." 197
"Within/our letting go/is the
    seed/of our receiving." 197
"The word/has been spoken/why
    need we speak it/again?" 197
Anima. Deborah Tall. 378
Animal cracker box. Eileen
    Silver-Lillywite. 364
Animals
    Augusta thinks through a
        definition. Carolyn Stoloff.
        376
    Beyond the clearing. James A.
        Emanuel. 239
    Dead animals. Harry Humes. 278
    The deep shade. Robert
        Pawlowski. 341
    This jeweled beast: a fable.
        Everett A. Gillis. 258
    Slow motion. Amy Clampitt. 222
    Unexplained absences. Sandra
        McPherson. 317
    The wild creatures of my
        childhood. Kirk Lumpkin. 306
Animals = Extinct
    Archeopteryx. X.J. Kennedy. 290
    Long gone. Jack Prelutsky. 349
    Tyrannosaur. X.J. Kennedy. 290
Animals = Fictitious
    Hippogriff. X.J. Kennedy. 290
Animals in groups. Barry
    Wallenstein. 393
Animaux. Donald Revell. 351
Anna, I am here to leave you.
    Gary Margolis. 311

Annabel Lee. Edgar Allan Poe. 347
Annanda's talk with Buddha. Gary
    Margolis. 311
The annealing. Marge Piercy. 346
Anniversary. Deborah Tall. 378
Anniversary song. Phyllis A.
    Tickle. 382
Anniversary sonnet. Stephen
    Sandy. 357
The anniversary. Amy Clampitt.
    222
The annunciations. Roy Marz. 312
The anointing. Sandra McPherson.
    317
Anomaly. Elsa Gidlow. 254
Anorexia Nervosa
    Madonna anorexia nervosa. Lyn
        Lifshin. 303
Another. Joyce Carol Oates. 336
Another. Edwin Honig. 275
Another backward stripper
    madonna. Lyn Lifshin. 303
Another chance. Miriam Goodman.
    264
Another day. Thomas McGrath. 315
Another March. Edwin Honig. 275
Another me. Connie Hunt. 279
Another Orpheus. Edwin Honig. 275
"Another plane is/gas..." Larry
    Eigner. 237
Another poem about colored
    leaves. Michael Akillian. 193
Another posthuem. Bradford
    Morrow. 329
Another question. Josephine B.
    Moretti. 324
Another spring. Maria Gillan. 256
Another thought. Sam Fishman. 246
Another view. Deborah Tall. 378
An answer for my daughter. Ghita
    Orth. 339
Answering thr past. Cathryn
    Hankla. 268
Answers
    Hot mountain poem. Gene Detro.
        230
    "Our answers/are a part of our
        questions." Theta Burke. 218
Ant. Barry Wallenstein. 393
"Antagonist and/agonist..."
    Madison Morrison. 327
Anthem. Rose Basile Green. 265
Anthropological sonnet. Mitchell
    Howard. 276
Anthropologist. Mark Vinz. 387
Anthropology. David James. 282
Anticipating. William Stafford.
    373
Anticipating murder. Wanda
    Coleman. 225

Antique tree ornaments.
    Christopher Bursk. 219
Antiquing. Robert A. Sears. 362
Antiquity
    "Existed/3000/BC?" Charles
    Olson. 337
Antonic Gomic (at Monument Park
    in Yugoslavia). James A.
    Emanuel. 239
Ants
    Among the craggy rocks. Judson
    Crews. 226
    Ant. Barry Wallenstein. 393
Anxiety. Rochelle DuBois. 234
Anxiety
    Anxiety. Rochelle DuBois. 234
    Driver saying. Josephine Miles.
    319
    Hanging on. Iefke Goldberger.
    262
    In danger of drowning.
    Jacqueline Frank. 248
    "The party host." Madison
    Morrison. 327
    Snakes. Wanda Coleman. 225
    Square hole day. Mary Gilliland.
    257
    A timebomb inside. Rochelle
    DuBois. 234
    Torque. William Stafford. 373
    Up-tight. James R. Rhodes. 352
Any day now you will return. John
    Yau. 404
Any day of the week:a Sunday
    text. Thomas McGrath. 315
Any letters today? Josephine B.
    Moretti. 324
Anything. James R. Rhodes. 352
Anything but murder. Jim
    Evernard. 241
"Apart from branches in
    courtyards and small stones."
    Josephine Miles. 319
Apartment. Josephine Miles. 319
Apartment complex manager getting
    the low-down on... James
    Magorian. 309
Apathy
    The people, us. James R. Rhodes.
    352
Apathy award. James Magorian. 308
Apennines (mountains), Italy
    In the Apennines. Franz
    Schneider. 361
Apes
    Some further observations. Paul
    Violi. 388
Apocalyptic poetry. Anne Bailie.
    199
Apocaylpse in me. Mitchell

Howard. 276
Apollinaire, Guillaume
    The book, fr. The green step.
    Kenneth Koch. 297
Apology for a sudden voyage.
    Scott Chisholm. 221
An apology to the groundhog.
    Mitchell Howard. 276
Appalachia
    Hillbilly night before
    Christmas. Thomas Noel Turner.
    385
Apparition of the duck. Clayton
    Eshleman. 240
Appetite and terror on the wide
    white sands of...Florida.
    Joyce Carol Oates. 336
The apple tree. Robert Gibb. 253
Apple Trees
    After "after apple-picking."
    Larry Moffi. 322
    Passions of the flowering apple.
    Gary Margolis. 311
    This chill air. Stephen Sandy.
    357
    Through the ice tree. Harry
    Humes. 278
    Toward paradise. Thomas McGrath.
    315
Apple, the family love and
    asshole. James Schevill. 360
Apples
    After apple-picking. Robert
    Frost. 250
    The apple tree. Robert Gibb. 253
    Discussing apples. Elsa Gidlow.
    254
    "Flock of birds." Larry Eigner.
    237
    "Followed his sow to apples."
    Charles Olson. 337
    Joysome apples. Alice Spohn
    Newton. 332
    Three apparitions. Carol Frost.
    249
    Throwing the apple. Scott
    Chisholm. 221
Applewhite, James
    At the university: to William
    Blackburn. 198
    Attending chapel. 198
    Beyond the romantic destination.
    198
    Blackberries. 198
    Blood ties: for Jan. 198
    Breasts in the sun. 198
    A broken lake. 198
    A capsized boat. 198
    Crossing over. 198
    The diamond in shadow. 198

First by the sea. 198
Forseeing the journey. 198
Grandfather Noah. 198
Heroic discoverer. 198
History's library. 198
Iron age flying. 198
The lumber mill fire. 198
A map of simplicities. 198
The mortal heroes. 198
Notes from a journal by the
    river. 198
Passing the marquee in
    Maysville. 198
The ravine. 198
Red wing hawk. 198
Rheumatic fever. 198
Rooms named mercy. 198
The scene. 198
Science fiction. 198
Southland drive-in. 198
The station. 198
Summer was ending. 198
The terminal. 198
That which is. 198
Trying to drive away from the
    past. 198
Two at the fair. 198
View from a tower. 198
The visitor. 198
White lake. 198
Appointment in doctor's office.
    Josephine Miles. 319
Approach. Josephine Miles. 319
Approaching Dover. May Miller.
    320
Approaching Troy. Randy Blasing.
    207
April. Ralph J., Jr. Mills. 321
April. John Reed. 350
April
    April. John Reed. 350
    April Thanksgiving. Marie Daerr
        Boehringer. 210
    False spring: late snow. Dave
        Smith. 367
    Green April. Robert L. Wilson.
        401
    Now that April's here. Josephine
        Miles. 319
    Spring song. Cornel Lengyel. 302
    Three pieces. Ralph J., Jr.
        Mills. 321
    When April. Stephen Sandy. 357
April 7, 1967 John F. Barker. 201
April in Hollywood. Wanda
    Coleman. 225
April inventory. W.D. (William De
    Witt) Snodgrass. 369
April parade. May Miller. 320
April people. Rod McKuen. 316

April Thanksgiving. Marie Daerr
    Boehringer. 210
April today main street. Charles
    Olson. 337
"The apron off the." Madison
    Morrison. 327
Aquarium. Ruth Lisa Schechter.
    359
Arabs
    The town of the summer palace.
        Deborah Tall. 378
Arabs. See also Women - Arab

Aranjuez. Michael Gizzi. 259
Arbus, Diane
    In praise of a photograph by
        Diane Arbus... James Schevill.
        360
The arc-welder's blue. James L.
    White. 396
The arcade's discourse on method.
    Clayton Eshleman. 240
Arcadia - River Ladon. Michael
    Gizzi. 259
Arch. Stephen Sandy. 357
Arch. Alberta Turner. 384
"The arch is." Madison Morrison.
    327
The archaeologist. Carolyn
    Stoloff. 376
Archaeology
    The archaeologist. Carolyn
        Stoloff. 376
    To the north. Carolyn Stoloff.
        376
Archeopteryx. X.J. Kennedy. 290
The archer. Robert Kelly. 289
Archibald MacLeish. Greg Kuzma.
    300
Architectural visions. Charles
    Edward Eaton. 236
Architecture. Andrei Codrescu.
    223
Architecture and Architects
    Scenes from the life of Boullee.
        John Yau. 404
Arden. Michael Gizzi. 259
"Are you/from this earth?" A.
    Dovichi. 233
Argument for parting. Miriam
    Goodman. 264
The argument. John F. Barker. 201
Ariel view. Robin Morgan. 325
"Aristotle & Augustine." Charles
    Olson. 337
Arizona
    Tucson, Arizona. Frances Mayes.
        314
Ark
    Waiting their turn. Gary

Margolis. 311
Arkansas night. Robert L. Wilson.
    401
The armadillo. Jack Prelutsky.
    349
Armadillos
    The armadillo. Jack Prelutsky.
    349
Armageddon. Michael Gizzi. 259
Armchair traveler. Josephine B.
    Moretti. 324
Armies
    "All armies are the same."
    Ernest Hemingway. 272
    The army. Jocelyn Hollis. 274
The arming of the bomb. Jocelyn
    Hollis. 274
Armistice Day. See Veterans Day

Arms. Martha Janssen. 283
Army, American
    On resumption of the military
    draft. Thomas Lux. 307
Army, Italian
    Riparto d'assalto. Ernest
    Hemingway. 272
The army. Jocelyn Hollis. 274
Arnold Arboretum. Michael Gizzi.
    259
Around you, your house. William
    Stafford. 373
The arrangement. Debra Bruce. 216
"Arrested on drunk driving."
    Michael Robert Pick. 345
Arrival. Marie Daerr Boehringer.
    210
Arrival. Rose Basile Green. 265
Arrival at St. George. Carolyn
    Stoloff. 376
Ars poetica. Frances Mayes. 314
Ars poetica. Everett A. Gillis.
    258
"Arsiero, Asiago." Ernest
    Hemingway. 272
Art. Rochelle DuBois. 234
Art
    Art. Rochelle DuBois. 234
    Art gallery closing time.
    Josephine Miles. 319
    "The art world." Madison
    Morrison. 327
    The exchange. Margaret Key
    Biggs. 205
    The gift of pain. Roy Marz. 312
    Higher criticism. Thomas
    McGrath. 315
    The importance of artists'
    biographies. Albert Goldbarth.
    261
    It was the tender way. Paul

Davis. 228
    "The lunching/art world."
    Madison Morrison. 327
Art and society. Kenneth Koch.
    297
An art called gothonic. Charles
    Olson. 337
Art gallery closing time.
    Josephine Miles. 319
An art of summer. Edwin Honig.
    275
The art of surrender. David
    Wagoner. 390
"The art world." Madison
    Morrison. 327
Arthur Bremer blues. Andrei
    Codrescu. 223
Articulation of the ruby
    bracelet. Charles Edward
    Eaton. 236
Artillery. Susan Tichy. 381
Artini's kitchen. Bradford
    Morrow. 329
The artist of escape: Houdini.
    James Schevill. 360
The artist. Elsa Gidlow. 254
Artists anonymous. Charles Edward
    Eaton. 236
"As a four-year-old." Sally Love
    Saunders. 358
As a great prince. Edwin Honig.
    275
As a man thinketh. Phillips
    Kloss. 294
As at the cathedral, the young
    man. Paul Davis. 228
"As Cabeza de Vaca..." Charles
    Olson. 337
As comes the day. Alice Spohn
    Newton. 332
"As difference blends into
    identity." Josephine Miles.
    319
As gentle rain. Alice Spohn
    Newton. 332
"As I leave him." Madison
    Morrison. 327
As I live and I feel. S. Bradford
    Williams (Jr.). 398
"As I love you." Michael Robert
    Pick. 345
"As I stand, he." Madison
    Morrison. 327
"As I study at." Madison
    Morrison. 327
As if. Marilyn Kallet. 287
As is. Patsie Black. 206
As of Parsonses or Fishermans
    Field... Charles Olson. 337
As seen from an airplane. Sally

Love Saunders. 358
As the hand goes. Carolyn Stoloff. 376
"As the light descended." Edwin Honig. 275
"As the soft white." Sally Love Saunders. 358
As though I didn't know. Carolyn Stoloff. 376
As usual. Elsa Gidlow. 254
"As we human beings search for life in clues." Michael Robert Pick. 345
As we sit in the garden, early and late. Cynthia Grenfell. 266
"As we would have it." Edwin Honig. 275
As who knows, so goes. John Godfrey. 260
"As you give what you need." Theta Burke. 218
As you think. Alice Joyce Davidson. 227
Ascending scale. Marge Piercy. 346
Ascension. Ghita Orth. 339
Ascent. Michael Akillian. 193
Ash Wednesday. Maria Gillan. 256
Ashenfoot, Herbert
Confidential data on the loyalty investigation... James Schevill. 360
Ashes, ashes, all fall down. Marge Piercy. 346
Ask Sindbad. Stephen Todd Booker. 212
Aspects of time. Richmond Lattimore. 301
Asphalt paving contractor taking a dead parakeet to... James Magorian. 309
Aspiration. Rose Basile Green. 265
Assassination. John F. Barker. 201
The assassination. Norman Andrew Kirk. 293
Assassinations and Assassins
Arthur Bremer blues. Andrei Codrescu. 223
The assassination. Norman Andrew Kirk. 293
Public servant. Christopher Bursk. 219
The violence and glory of the American spirit. James Schevill. 360
"The assistant offers." Madison Morrison. 327
Assistant professor of juxtapositions granted tenure... James Magorian. 309
Assorted short poems. Bill Knott. 296
Assumption, The
"He who addresses you." Kenneth Koch. 297
Asters
Purple aster. Debra Bruce. 216
Purple aster. Mary Gilliland. 257
Asthma, 1948. Betty Adcock. 192
The astonished listener hears the radio... James Schevill. 360
Astral roulette. John Godfrey. 260
"Astride/the Chabot/fault." Charles Olson. 337
The astrological houses. Rochelle DuBois. 234
Astronomy and Astronomers
Calculation. Josephine Miles. 319
Nadirs. Josephine Miles. 319
On eliminating the astronomer from photographs of gases. Marilyn Kallet. 287
At a Quaker meeting a man arose and spoke of love. James Schevill. 360
At an open window. George Eklund. 238
At Berkeley Park. Marc Hudson. 277
At dawn. Susan Tichy. 381
"At dusk I pull in." Madison Morrison. 327
At Eve's house. Margaret Key Biggs. 205
At Frost's farm in Derry, New Hampshire. James Schevill. 360
At home. Andrei Codrescu. 223
At home. Sam Fishman. 246
At Keflavik. Marc Hudson. 277
At last, the secret. Alice Spohn Newton. 332
At Mergellina. Anne Bailie. 199
At night. Barry Wallenstein. 393
At night. Kenneth Koch. 297
"At night I lay with you." Ernest Hemingway. 272
At night in the high mountains. Carolyn Stoloff. 376
"At our best we did outrageous things." Robert A. Sears. 362
At Peaks Island. Stephen Sandy. 357
At Penn's Landing, Philadelphia, Pa. Jocelyn Hollis. 274

At Plymouth Rock. James Schevill.
    360
At seventeen. Jacqueline Frank.
    248
At Suthurstrond. Marc Hudson. 277
At Sutter's grave: Lititz, PA.
    Robert Gibb. 253
"At ten of six I plead." Madison
    Morrison. 327
"At that price." Madison
    Morrison. 327
At that time. Maurice Kenny. 291
At the Ballard Locks. Richard
    Blessing. 208
At the border. Herbert Morris.
    326
'At the boundry of the mighty
    world.' Charles Olson. 337
At the Chateau de Villegenis that
    summer. Herbert Morris. 326
At the church of Elijah Lovejoy.
    Paul Davis. 228
'At the corner of Muck and Myer.'
    Paul Violi. 388
At the counter. Josephine Miles.
    319
At the drive-in. Debra Bruce. 216
At the edge of the glacier.
    Thomas McGrath. 315
At the falls: a birthday picture.
    William Stafford. 373
"At the fish market we walked
    back and forth." Kenneth Koch.
    297
At the gravesite. Dennis
    Hinrichsen. 273
At the hotel where the long dark
    begins. Herbert Morris. 326
At the jazz club he comes on a
    ghost. Wanda Coleman. 225
At the land's end. Ray Fleming.
    247
At the light I saw Pam. Frances
    Mayes. 314
At the Mexican border. James
    Schevill. 360
At the museum. Jeanne Lohmann.
    305
At the museum this week. Bill
    Knott. 296
At the park dance. W.D. (William
    De Witt) Snodgrass. 369
At the record hop. Wanda Coleman.
    225
At the same time. James R.
    Rhodes. 352
At the tomb of the unknown
    soldier. Robert Pawlowski. 341
At the university: to William
    Blackburn. James Applewhite.
    198
At the up-town window. George
    Eklund. 238
At the Wailing Wall. Susan Tichy.
    381
At the Western Wall. Ghita Orth.
    339
At the White House, Washington,
    D.C., 1973 James Schevill. 360
At the Woodstock cemetery.
    Carolyn Stoloff. 376
At thirty-nine. Robert Pawlowski.
    341
At vital statistics. Wanda
    Coleman. 225
Atheism
    The grounds keeper. James Iorio.
    281
Athena. Debra Bruce. 216
Athens
    To the dead. David Shapiro. 363
Athletic verse, sels. Ernest
    Hemingway. 272
Atlas. John Godfrey. 260
The atom and the poet. Phillips
    Kloss. 294
Atomic Bomb
    The arming of the bomb. Jocelyn
    Hollis. 274
    The atom and the poet. Phillips
    Kloss. 294
    Atomic detente. James R. Rhodes.
    352
    Before thunder struck. Ruth Lisa
    Schechter. 359
    The future of jazz. David Wann.
    394
    In the theater of the absurd.
    James Schevill. 360
    Nowhere. May Miller. 320
    Savants. Lucien Stryk. 377
    Walking to Dewato. Marc Hudson.
    277
Atomic detente. James R. Rhodes.
    352
Atoms unlimited. David Wann. 394
An atrocity, a sunset. Jenne
    Andrews. 196
Attachments. Ruth Lisa Schechter.
    359
Attempt to spell, incantate and
    annoy. Andrei Codrescu. 223
Attempted kidnapping. Robert L.
    Wilson. 401
Attempting to make lyrics of my
    lovers. Carolyn Stoloff. 376
Attending chapel. James
    Applewhite. 198
Attila
    No timid sawyer. Harrison

Fisher. 245

Au bout du temps. Andrei
    Codrescu. 223
Aubade. Robert Gibb. 253
Aubade. Phyllis A. Tickle. 382
Aubade. Robert Pawlowski. 341
Aubade of an early homo sapiens.
    Carol Frost. 249
An aubade. Timothy Steele. 374
An auburn girl has. Madison
    Morrison. 327
Auctions
    Livestock auction. James
        Magorian. 309
Auden, W.H.
    Just another smack. Irving
        Feldman. 242
An audiovisual glimpse of
    Cabarrus County, North
    Carolina. Stephen Knauth. 295
Audition. John Godfrey. 260
Auguries. Robert Kelly. 289
August. Gary Margolis. 311
August
    August nocturne. Stephen Knauth.
        295
    Blackberry weather. Robert A.
        Sears. 362
August assignment. Marie Daerr
    Boehringer. 210
August islands. Rod McKuen. 316
August nocturne. Stephen Knauth.
    295
Augusta at the shore. Carolyn
    Stoloff. 376
Augusta berates a wayward moon.
    Carolyn Stoloff. 376
Augusta discusses carrots, their
    meaning and use. Carolyn
    Stoloff. 376
Augusta discusses some of her
    best known roles. Carolyn
    Stoloff. 376
Augusta receives a communication
    concerning a bill. Carolyn
    Stoloff. 376
Augusta speaks about the first
    manifestation of the dead...
    Carolyn Stoloff. 376
Augusta summons Easter. Carolyn
    Stoloff. 376
Augusta tells how she chose a
    profession. Carolyn Stoloff.
    376
Augusta tells the milkman.
    Carolyn Stoloff. 376
Augusta thinks through a
    definition. Carolyn Stoloff.
    376
Augusta's 'Think-positive' song.

Carolyn Stoloff. 376
Augusta's confrontation with her
    landlady. Carolyn Stoloff. 376
Augusta's little nose song.
    Carolyn Stoloff. 376
Augusta's morning meditation.
    Carolyn Stoloff. 376
Augustine, Saint
    Dream I am St. Augustine. Susan
        Tichy. 381
    St. Augustine's prayer to God,
        the Father. Franz Schneider.
        361
Aunt. Robert Peters. 343
Aunts
    Aunt. Robert Peters. 343
    Kent Circle song. Charles Olson.
        337
    Raking leaves. Debra Bruce. 216
Aureole. James R. Rhodes. 352
The aurignacian summation.
    Clayton Eshleman. 240
Aurore. John Reed. 350
The austere place. Carolyn
    Stoloff. 376
Austerlitz, New York
    Upstate. Paul Violi. 388
The Austin tower. Stephen Sandy.
    357
Australia
    Australian gold. Rod McKuen. 316
    Cloud Valley. Rod McKuen. 316
    Down under. Rod McKuen. 316
    Elizabeth Bay evening. Rod
        McKuen. 316
Australian gold. Rod McKuen. 316
Author of 'American ornithology'
    sketches a bird... David
    Wagoner. 390
The author says goodbye to his
    hero. David Wagoner. 390
Author's acknowledgment. Connie
    Hunt. 279
Author's forward. Stephen Todd
    Booker. 212
"The authority of Cape Ann."
    Charles Olson. 337
Autistic child, no longer child.
    Joyce Carol Oates. 336
Auto-Eroticism
    Payment. Christopher Bursk. 219
    Woods. Robert Peters. 343
Auto-portrait at 1/5th. Gerard
    Malanga. 310
Autobiographies
    What happened. Marieve Rugo. 356
Autobiography. Dennis Hinrichsen.
    273
Autograph. Randy Blasing. 207
Automobile Racing

The racer's widow. Louise Gluck.
    259A
Automobiles
    "At dusk I pull in." Madison
        Morrison. 327
    Beaver's first car. Alice Spohn
        Newton. 333
    "A car in the garage." Madison
        Morrison. 327
    Car-shopper's guide. Marie Daerr
        Boehringer. 210
    Cat. Josephine Miles. 319
    Death of a Buick. Larry Moffi.
        322
    Delivery guaranteed. Marie Daerr
        Boehringer. 210
    Double trouble. Marie Daerr
        Boehringer. 210
    The drive. Miriam Goodman. 264
    A fable for animals. James A.
        Emanuel. 239
    "The fog holds." Larry Eigner.
        237
    4-wheeler, with. Stephen Todd
        Booker. 212
    "The/frosted car." Larry Eigner.
        237
    Graham-paige. Josephine Miles.
        319
    Grandpa and the Model T Ford.
        Alice Spohn Newton. 333
    I live for my car. Wanda
        Coleman. 225
    I'm trading in my car today.
        Laura Boss. 213
    Industrial park from the air.
        Miriam Goodman. 264
    Intersection. Carolyn Stoloff.
        376
    "The intersection." Larry
        Eigner. 237
    Joyrider. James Schevill. 360
    "The little man, who." Madison
        Morrison. 327
    Lone. Josephine Miles. 319
    Low. Larry Eigner. 237
    "A man from the South." Madison
        Morrison. 327
    "The mechanic/with dirty hands."
        Madison Morrison. 327
    Night driving, New Year's Eve.
        Joyce Carol Oates. 336
    On speed. Wanda Coleman. 225
    Outer drive. Edwin Honig. 275
    Pedestrian viewpoint. Marie
        Daerr Boehringer. 210
    Photographic plate, partly
        spidered, Hampton Roads...
        Dave Smith. 367
    Required reading. Marie Daerr

    Boehringer. 210
    Rush-hour ramblings. Marie Daerr
        Boehringer. 210
    "Someone's in touch." Madison
        Morrison. 327
    Southside. Mark Vinz. 387
    Steer strait. Marie Daerr
        Boehringer. 210
    Wheel zeal. Josephine B.
        Moretti. 324
Automobiles. See also Gasoline
    Stations

Autopsies
    The satchel. Stephen Todd
        Booker. 212
Autumn. Franz Schneider. 361
Autumn
    Autumn. Franz Schneider. 361
    Autumn arrival. Marie Daerr
        Boehringer. 210
    Autumn ball. Alice Joyce
        Davidson. 227
    Autumn dancers. Robert L.
        Wilson. 401
    Autumn music. Barry Wallenstein.
        393
    Autumn plea. Robert L. Wilson.
        401
    Autumn song. Sandra Gilbert. 255
    Autumn's prophecy. Evelyn
        Golden. 263
    Bittersweet brown. James R.
        Rhodes. 352
    Blue flowers. Albert Goldbarth.
        261
    The climate of your plans.
        Miriam Goodman. 264
    An episode for reflection. John
        F. Barker. 201
    Fall. John F. Barker. 201
    Fall. Robert L. Wilson. 401
    Fall guise. Richmond Lattimore.
        301
    Fall song. Cornel Lengyel. 302
    A fall song. Ralph J., Jr.
        Mills. 321
    Fargo fall. Rodney Nelson. 331
    Forecast. Marie Daerr
        Boehringer. 210
    Frost. Carol Frost. 249
    The garden in ruins. Harry
        Humes. 278
    Gnomon. Thomas Hornsby Ferril.
        243
    A harmony. John F. Barker. 201
    Holding on. Robert L. Wilson.
        401
    Love poem. Jacqueline Frank. 248
    More than a season. Marie Daerr

Boehringer. 210
Mornings in fall. Randy Blasing. 207
Needlepoint in Autumn. Charles Edward Eaton. 236
No two hands the same. Robert L. Wilson. 401
North Carolina life cycle. Stephen Knauth. 295
October. Susan Tichy. 381
October. John Reed. 350
October. Bill Knott. 296
Response. Marie Daerr Boehringer. 210
September afternoon. Marie Daerr Boehringer. 210
September in the park. W.D. (William De Witt) Snodgrass. 369
Song/for Franklin Brainard. Ralph J., Jr. Mills. 321
Speech. Edwin Honig. 275
Tantara! Tantara! Thomas McGrath. 315
Two poems. Ralph J., Jr. Mills. 321
Autumn apology. Carol Frost. 249
Autumn arrival. Marie Daerr Boehringer. 210
Autumn ball. Alice Joyce Davidson. 227
Autumn dancers. Robert L. Wilson. 401
Autumn leaves. Josephine B. Moretti. 324
Autumn month. Gary Margolis. 311
Autumn music. Barry Wallenstein. 393
Autumn picnic. Josephine B. Moretti. 324
Autumn plea. Robert L. Wilson. 401
Autumn song. Sandra Gilbert. 255
Autumn words. Maria Gillan. 256
Autumn's prophecy. Evelyn Golden. 263
Autumnal. Josephine Miles. 319
"The avatar's done." Madison Morrison. 327
Avenal. Ernesto Galarza. 252
Avenues. See Roads and Trails

Aviation
Abandoned airfield, 1977. Joyce Carol Oates. 336
Alvaro's resurrection machine. Jenne Andrews. 196
Ascent. Michael Akillian. 193
A flying machine. Alice Spohn Newton. 333

The jet engine. Sandra McPherson. 317
"The jets jet." Larry Eigner. 237
Machines. Lucien Stryk. 377
Avila, Spain
Outside Avila's walls. Carolyn Stoloff. 376
The avocado connection. Charles Edward Eaton. 236
Awakening. Maria Gillan. 256
The award for the best argument of the year in Omaha. James Magorian. 309
Awareness. Marie Daerr Boehringer. 210
Away. Josephine Miles. 319
The ax-helve. Robert Frost. 250
Axes
Adirondacks. Scott Chisholm. 221
Axetime autumn. Scott Chisholm. 221
Aztec love song. John Yau. 404

"B. Ellery." Charles Olson. 337
Babies
After. Stephen Sandy. 357
"Charlie is a giant size." Sally Love Saunders. 358
First steps. Mary Gilliland. 257
For an infant whose heart stopped for eleven minutes. Carol Frost. 249
Is this my love? Robert Pawlowski. 341
Maidens fair. Harrison Fisher. 245
My cousin in April. Louise Gluck. 259A
The presentation. Toi Derricote. 229
Rooms named mercy. James Applewhite. 198
The sitter moves. Gary Margolis. 311
Toddler under glass. Clayton Eshleman. 240
Young man with infant. Stephen Sandy. 357
Baby. Joyce Carol Oates. 336
Baby picture, circa 1932. Stephen Knauth. 295
Babylon. Michael Gizzi. 259
Bachelor belles. Harrison Fisher. 245
Back. Gary Margolis. 311
Back in an hour. John Godfrey.

260

The back of Antelope Island.
    Sharon Bryan. 217
The back-door ghost. Mitchell
    Howard. 276
Back country. Joyce Carol Oates.
    336
The back pockets of love. Marge
    Piercy. 346
Background. Robert A. Sears. 362
Backs (body)
    Preventive medicine. Marie Daerr
        Boehringer. 210
Backtracking. David Wagoner. 390
Backwards. Joy Harjo. 269
Backwards stripping madonna. Lyn
    Lifshin. 303
The backyard. Michael Gizzi. 259
Bad. Wanda Coleman. 225
Bad grounds. C.D. Wright. 402
The bad uncle. David Wagoner. 390
Baden-baden. Michael Gizzi. 259
Badly-gored explorer reading
    poetry at a debutante party.
    James Magorian. 309
Baghdad. Michael Gizzi. 259
Bagnio di Viareggio. Robert A.
    Sears. 362
Bah! Sheep! Harlan Usher. 386
Bailie, Anne
    Across a bridge. 199
    After a governmental purge. 199
    Anatomy of a mirror. 199
    Apocalyptic poetry. 199
    At Mergellina. 199
    Behind: the summer. 199
    Camp-songs. 199
    Deja vu. 199
    Elegy for soldiers. 199
    Elegy from a dark country. 199
    Encounter with sirens. 199
    Escape into autumn. 199
    Experience. 199
    Fear. 199
    Fourth dimension. 199
    High road from Naples. 199
    Lazarus. 199
    The length of your absence. 199
    Metal and stone. 199
    Momoyama. 199
    Notes on Venice. 199
    On the edge of knowledge. 199
    On the election of a president.
        199
    On the great wheel. 199
    Ophelia's last soliloquy. 199
    Postcard from Provence. 199
    Remembrance of summers past. 199
    Silk scroll. 199
    Skyscraper. 199

    Song of the shrubs. 199
    St. John and the angel. 199
    Stages of chilhood. 199
    The term's end. 199
    Terminal sickness. 199
    t3 fears in triptych. 199
    Van Gogh's "The Starry Night"
        199
    Winter voyage. 199
    Wisconsin village. 199
    Yellow leaves. 199
"Bailyn shows sharp rise."
    Charles Olson. 337
Baja California, Mexico
    Baja trip. David James. 282
Baja trip. David James. 282
The baker. Gary Margolis. 311
Baking and Bakers
    Spell against weather. Joan
        Colby. 224
Bakke's law, or lateral movement.
    Ray Fleming. 247
Bal des ardents. Donald Revell.
    351
Balance. Stephen Sandy. 357
Bald woman needs no title. Mary
    Gilliland. 257
Baldness
    Once when I was walking up the
        stairs. Anthony Petrosky. 344
Bali
    When the world was steady. David
        James. 282
Ballad of Claudine. Sam Fishman.
    246
Ballad of the typist. Andrei
    Codrescu. 223
Ballade. Erin Jolly. 285
Ballade for a canoeist. Harry
    Humes. 278
Ballet. Jacques Sollov. 371
Ballet
    I'd trade these words. James L.
        White. 396
Balloon sleeves and velvet, the
    century turned. Colette Inez.
    280
Balloons
    Old Barry, the balloon seller.
        James Schevill. 360
Balms. Amy Clampitt. 222
Band of essayists trapped in a
    box canyon by bitter... James
    Magorian. 309
Band-I-Amir
    The seven lakes of Band-I-Amir.
        Kirk Lumpkin. 306
Bandages. James A. Emanuel. 239
Baptism. Robert Pawlowski. 341
Baptism

Baptism. Robert Pawlowski. 341
Baraka (LeRoi Jones), Amiri
   Class struggle in music (1). 200
   Class struggle in music (2). 200
   Reggae or not! 200
Barbara. Rosa Bogar. 211
"Barbara Ellis, ramp." Charles
   Olson. 337
Barbary Coast. Michael Gizzi. 259
Barbecues
   Barbeque. Larry Moffi. 322
Barbed Wire
   The woodlot. Amy Clampitt. 222
Barbeque. Larry Moffi. 322
Barbers
   Speciality barber in
     beast-heads. James Schevill.
     360
Bards of the golden west.
   Phillips Kloss. 294
Barefoot realization. David
   Wann. 394
Bargaining. Susan Tichy. 381
Barge. Josephine Miles. 319
Baring friendship. Mary
   Gilliland. 257
Barker, John F.
   Advent. 201
   Andros. 201
   April 7, 1967 201
   The argument. 201
   Assassination. 201
   Belated spring. 201
   Bound. 201
   The bus. 201
   Casualty report. 201
   Civil liberty. 201
   The crucifixion. 201
   The crusted earth. 201
   Cyprus. 201
   Danny. 201
   An episode for reflection. 201
   Fall. 201
   Forgiveness. 201
   Fraternite. 201
   Garcon. 201
   Garmisch-Partenkirchen. 201
   The grail. 201
   A harmony. 201
   Heritage. 201
   Homo Sapiens. 201
   A hundred years ago. 201
   Ida Maria. 201
   In memory of a man. 201
   L'envoi. 201
   La cite de Carcassonne. 201
   The lacquer box. 201
   Left hand view. 201
   Lines written for June. 201
   Lines written for Mrs. Hagood.

     201
   Loudoun. 201
   The mask. 201
   May madness. 201
   Mount Everest. 201
   N11/22/63. 201
   A November afternoon. 201
   The old wives. 201
   On a high hill. 201
   The open fire. 201
   Pax vobiscum. 201
   The prayer wheel. 201
   The quilt. 201
   Requiescat. 201
   A seldom wind. 201
   Simplicity. 201
   Sir Winston. 201
   The south. 201
The **baron** of bulk. James
   Schevill. 360
Barricade. Josephine Miles. 319
Bars and Barrooms
   Dramas of the rose. James
     Schevill. 360
   The newsboy enters the bar.
     James Schevill. 360
   Saint Augustine. John Godfrey.
     260
Barth, Richmond
   Richmond Barthe: meeting in
     Lyon. Melvin Dixon. 231
Baseball
   The all-stars. Irving Feldman.
     242
   The astonished listener hears
     the radio... James Schevill.
     360
   Callahan Park Field, Bradford,
     Pennsylvania. Richard
     Blessing. 208
   Hardball. J.W. Rivers. 354
   "Local boy shines in relief."
     Larry Moffi. 322
   Lousy in center field. James
     Tate. 379
   Minor league batting champion.
     James Magorian. 309
   Mitts and gloves. Bill Knott.
     296
   No batter. Carol Frost. 249
   Notes for a lecture. Larry
     Moffi. 322
   Opening day of the world series.
     James Magorian. 309
   The opening game. Ernest
     Hemingway. 272
   Rooter. Josephine Miles. 319
   Shutout. Mitchell Howard. 276
   The uses of New York. Mitchell
     Howard. 276

Bashir was my name. James
        Schevill. 360
Basketball
    "Basketball players." Madison
        Morrison. 327
    Hypnotist and Bird. Gary
        Margolis. 311
    "On the same fall." Madison
        Morrison. 327
"Basketball players." Madison
        Morrison. 327
Bath time. Martha Janssen. 283
The bathers. Irving Feldman. 242
Baths and Bathing
    Bath time. Martha Janssen. 283
    "I find myself now." Madison
        Morrison. 327
    Relinquishing. Ghita Orth. 339
    Saturday night bath. Alice Spohn
        Newton. 333
    War games in the bath.
        Christopher Bursk. 219
Bats. Dave Smith. 367
Bats
    Bats. Dave Smith. 367
Battery. Robin Morgan. 325
The battle of Coppenhagen. Ernest
        Hemingway. 272
Bauchi bird. Robert A. Sears. 362
"Baying dogs." Michael Robert
        Pick. 345
Bayou water. Ernesto Galarza. 252
Bayous
    Bayou water. Ernesto Galarza.
        252
Be my muse. Kirk Lumpkin. 306
Be nice to Bonny. Alice Spohn
        Newton. 332
Be or be not. James R. Rhodes.
        352
Beach boy. Josephine B. Moretti.
        324
Beach glass. Amy Clampitt. 222
Beach idyll. Franz Schneider. 361
Beach in Sebastopol, California.
        Andrei Codrescu. 223
The beach of time. Alice Joyce
        Davidson. 227
Beach party given by T.
        Snaughnessy for the sisters.
        Josephine Miles. 319
Beach story. Josephine B.
        Moretti. 324
Beaded turtle. Maurice Kenny. 291
Beans
    Four portraits of beans. David
        James. 282
Bear gulch: home place. Franz
        Schneider. 361
Beard-growing contest. James

        Magorian. 309
Bearing it. Carolyn Stoloff. 376
Bears
    The black bear. Jack Prelutsky.
        349
    Escape of a polar bear from the
        city zoo. James Torio. 281
    Gypsy bears. Keith Wilson. 400
    The polar bear. Jack Prelutsky.
        349
Beast. Stephen Knauth. 295
The beaten one. Rachel A. Hazen.
        271
Beatrice. Alice Spohn Newton. 333
Beauties. Harrison Fisher. 245
The beautiful and lovely face.
        Greg Kuzma. 300
Beautiful stranger. Jacques
        Sollov. 370
The beautiful urinals of Paris.
        C.D. Wright. 402
Beauty. Irving Feldman. 242
Beauty
    Al Aaraaf. Edgar Allan Poe. 347
    Alice's brilliance. Andrei
        Codrescu. 223
    Ballet. Jacques Sollov. 371
    Beauty queen. Jacques Sollov.
        370
    Caring with care. Alice Spohn
        Newton. 332
    City love. John Godfrey. 260
    Dissipation. Norman Andrew Kirk.
        293
    Encounters. Ernesto Galarza. 252
    Evening: matters. Bradford
        Morrow. 329
    The eyes of a girl. Jacques
        Sollov. 370
    "I've seen the halyards of the
        sun." Michael Robert Pick. 345
    If only you could see. Rosa
        Bogar. 211
    Ikebana. Cathy Song. 372
    Incredible day. Connie Hunt. 279
    The lesson. Sam Fishman. 246
    Mirror, mirror, fr. Mirror
        suite. Everett A. Gillis. 258
    Mysterious star! Edgar Allan
        Poe. 347
    Promise. Marie Daerr Boehringer.
        210
    The pure light. Jacques Sollov.
        371
    The purple sun. Jacques Sollov.
        371
    "Silent memories trickle down a
        stream." Michael Robert Pick.
        345
    Spinner. Jim Simmerman. 365

The telling. Sam Fishman. 246
"Those who are beautiful."
    Robert Kelly. 289
To Helen ("Thy beauty is to
    me"). Edgar Allan Poe. 347
To Helen (I saw thee once...).
    Edgar Allan Poe. 347
White lady. Norman Andrew Kirk.
    293
White rose. Jacques Sollov. 370
Beauty and sadness. Cathy Song.
    372
Beauty queen. Jacques Sollov. 370
Beaver's first car. Alice Sponn
    Newton. 333
Beaver, my love. Alice Spohn
    Newton. 332
Beaver, Oklahoma
    Beaver, my love. Alice Sponn
        Newton. 332
The beaver. Jack Prelutsky. 349
Beavers
    The beaver. Jack Prelutsky. 349
"Because a sailor's pockets."
    Carolyn Stoloff. 376
Because radio is a relic. Larry
    Moffi. 322
"Because things inside/felt so
    tenuous and uncertain." Theta
    Burke. 218
"Because/the sun dips/its bright
    face/beneath the horizon."
    Joan Walsh Anglund. 197
Becker, Robin
    After making love. 202
    Berkshire County journal. 202
    Captivities. 202
    The Chinese lunar calendar
        horoscope. 202
    Configuration. 202
    The conversion of the Jews. 202
    Creative writing. 202
    Documentary. 202
    Dreaming. 202
    The echolaliac. 202
    Family album. 202
    For Sarah, home after a weekend
        in the country. 202
    Ghazal: the impasse. 202
    A good education. 202
    Great expectations. 202
    Hockey season. 202
    Illinois winter. 202
    The immigrant's story. 202
    In conversation. 202
    Letters to Michael. 202
    A long distance. 202
    Maple sugaring. 202
    Morning poem. 202
    North. 202

Old women and hills. 202
On being literal-minded. 202
On not being able to imagine the
    future. 202
Phone call at 1 am. 202
Posing for the photographer. 202
Prairie. 202
Quabbin Reservoir. 202
Rose's poem. 202
Sailmaker's palm. 202
Sideshow. 202
The sketchbook. 202
Someone else's children. 202
Studies from life. 202
Such an alliance. 202
Tourists in Italy. 202
Training the dog to come. 202
Vermont/January. 202
When friends leave. 202
Winter in Lincoln Park
    Conservatory. 202
Women in love. 202
Bedridden. Christopher Bursk. 219
Beds
    Gardens. Jeanne Lohmann. 305
    In bed. Kenneth Koch. 297
    The new bed. Jacqueline Frank.
        248
Bedtime
    "Diddle, diddle, dumpling." Jan
        Ormerod. 338
    "Go to bed late." Jan Ormerod.
        338
    "Niddledy, noddledy, to and
        fro." Jan Ormerod. 338
    "Up to the wooden hill." Jan
        Ormerod. 338
Bedtime question. Alice Joyce
    Davidson. 227
Bedtime story. James Magorian.
    308
Bedtime story. Mark Vinz. 387
Bee. X.J. Kennedy. 290
The bee, the bubble, the lovely
    thought. Stephen Todd Booker.
    212
Beech Trees
    Beeches. Ralph J., Jr. Mills.
        321
    November through a giant copper
        beech. Edwin Honig. 275
Beeches. Ralph J., Jr. Mills. 321
Beer
    Trinc. Thomas McGrath. 315
Bees. Jack Prelutsky. 349
Bees
    Autumn picnic. Josephine B.
        Moretti. 324
    Bee. X.J. Kennedy. 290
    Bees. Jack Prelutsky. 349

23

Berssenbrugge, Mei-Mei

Belly dancing. James R. Rhodes. 352

Carpenter bees. Robert Gibb. 253

The flower. David Wagoner. 390

Go away little bee! Josephine B. Moretti. 324

Mine is the other. Gary Margolis. 311

Zzzzz. X.J. Kennedy. 290

Beethoven's Polish birthday. Gary Margolis. 311

Beethoven, Ludwig van
Beethoven, Opus 111. Amy Clampitt. 222

Beethoven, Opus 111. Amy Clampitt. 222

Beets. Sandra Gilbert. 255

Beets
Beets. Sandra Gilbert. 255
Breakfast. Josephine Miles. 319

Before. Josephine Miles. 319

Before. Albert Goldbarth. 261

Before meat. Alberta Turner. 384

Before thunder struck. Ruth Lisa Schechter. 359

"Before we could begin our life." Robert A. Sears. 362

Beggars
American men. Marc Kaminsky. 288

"Begin a/mid things." Larry Eigner. 237

Begin again. Thomas Hornsby Ferril. 243

Beginning again. Rod McKuen. 316

The beginning of the end. Randy Blasing. 207

Beginning over. Jeanne Lohmann. 305

The beginning. Sister Maura. 313

The beginnings (facts). Charles Olson. 337

Behavior modification. Martha Janssen. 283

Behind the starched light. Carolyn Stoloff. 376

Behind: the summer. Anne Bailie. 199

Being. Connie Hunt. 279

Being a soldier. Herbert Morris. 326

Being left. Marge Piercy. 346

"Being near dinner time." Madison Morrison. 327

Being somebody. Edwin Honig. 275

Belated spring. John F. Barker. 201

Belfast. Donald Revell. 351

The Belfast swallows. Roy Marz. 312

Belgium

Out of the frame. Colette Inez. 280

Belief. Josephine Miles. 319

Believing. Connie Hunt. 279

Bell. Josephine Miles. 319

Bells
The bells. Edgar Allan Poe. 347
In time of praise. Jacqueline Frank. 248

The bells. Edgar Allan Poe. 347

Belly dancing. James R. Rhodes. 352

A bench to bear. James A. Emanuel. 239

Beneath the friable moon. Bradford Morrow. 329

Beneath the snowy trees. Aileen Fisher. 244

Benediction. Susan Tichy. 381

Benediction. James R. Rhodes. 352

Benediction for my daughters. Anneliese Wagner. 389

The Bengal tiger. Jack Prelutsky. 349

Benjamin, Walter
The night sky and to Walter Benjamin. David Shapiro. 363

Bennet. George Eklund. 238

Bent tones. C.D. Wright. 402

Benumbed. Robert L. Wilson. 401

Bequest. Marie Daerr Boehringer. 210

Berceuse. Amy Clampitt. 222

Bergerac, Cyrano de
Cyrano de Bergerac. Ernesto Galarza. 252

Berkshire County journal. Robin Becker. 202

Berlin, Germany
Ecstasy of boredom at the Berlin Wall. Joyce Carol Oates. 336
Hotel Steinplatz, Berlin, December 25 (1966). Charles Olson. 337

Bermuda
Arrival at St. George. Carolyn Stoloff. 376
Bermuda notebook. Carolyn Stoloff. 376

Bermuda notebook. Carolyn Stoloff. 376

Berry, Duc de
Marginal employment. Amy Clampitt. 222

Berryman, John (about)
Forlorn dream song. Richmond Lattimore. 301

Berssenbrugge, Mei-Mei
Farolita. 203
The heat bird. 203

Pack rat sieve. 203, 204
Ricochet off water. 203
The best fullback in
    Transylvania. James Magorian.
    309
The best side of me. Andrei
    Codrescu. 223
The best slow dancer. David
    Wagoner. 390
Bestiary, sels. Tom Smith. 368
The bestowal. John Hawkes. 270
Betrayal. Eileen
    Silver-Lillywite. 364
Betrayal. Joyce Carol Oates. 336
Betrayals. Maria Gillan. 256
"Between Cruiser & Plato..."
    Charles Olson. 337
"Between two birches." Robert
    Kelly. 289
Bewitched visit. Elsa Gidlow. 254
Beyond. Patsie Black. 206
Beyond limits. May Miller. 320
Beyond the clearing. James A.
    Emanuel. 239
Beyond the mountain. Rachel A.
    Hazen. 271
Beyond the parallel lines.
    Carolyn Stoloff. 376
Beyond the red river. Thomas
    McGrath. 315
Beyond the romantic destination.
    James Applewhite. 198
Beyond time, sels. Rochelle
    DuBois. 234
Bi-lingual. Andrei Codrescu. 223
Bibbiena. Robert A. Sears. 362
Bible - Satire
    Four quotes that didn't make the
    bible. Michael Akillian. 193
Bibliographer. Josephine Miles.
    319
Bicycles
    "I will set out from." Madison
    Morrison. 327
    Prairie path. Joan Colby. 224
The big empty. Wanda Coleman. 225
Big sheep knocks you about.
    Sharon Bryan. 217
Big-time wrestling. Dennis
    Hinrichsen. 273
Big bird seen hanging with blue
    legs... Robert L. Wilson. 401
Big daddy. Paul Violi. 388
The big dance on the hill. Ernest
    Hemingway. 272
Biggs, Margaret Key
    At Eve's house. 205
    Calico caribes. 205
    The couple. 205
    Earth music. 205

The exchange. 205
From the womanflower. 205
Girl under streetlight. 205
In search of a second dawn. 205
Seasoned. 205
Stern warning. 205
Under the mushroom. 205
Woman untouched. 205
Bikini man. Ernesto Galarza. 252
Billboard. Erin Jolly. 285
Billings, William
    How to create music by William
    Billings. James Schevill. 360
Billy "balloon" Laura Boss. 213
Binding by striking. Robert
    Kelly. 289
The biographers of solitude.
    Irving Feldman. 242
Biographical note on Ms Goose.
    Harlan Usher. 386
Biology lesson. Robert Peters.
    343
Birch Trees
    "Between two birches." Robert
    Kelly. 289
Bird. Albert Goldbarth. 261
Bird feeder. Harry Humes. 278
The bird flew off. Elsa Gidlow.
    254
The bird is God. Roy Marz. 312
Bird of night. Ernest Hemingway.
    272
Bird, flower, child. Joan Colby.
    224
Bird, Larry
    Hypnotist and Bird. Gary
    Margolis. 311
"A bird/bath a cloud." Larry
    Eigner. 237
The bird. Joseph Penzi. 342
The bird. Greg Kuzma. 300
Birds
    Bauchi bird. Robert A. Sears.
    362
    Big bird seen hanging with blue
    legs... Robert L. Wilson. 401
    The bird. Joseph Penzi. 342
    The buzzard. Roy Marz. 312
    Camouflage. Amy Clampitt. 222
    A dark moor bird. James Wright.
    403
    Earthbird. David Wagoner. 390
    'The face of the precipice is
    black with lovers' Thomas
    McGrath. 315
    Flights. Joan Colby. 224
    From a trilogy of birds. Andrei
    Codrescu. 223
    A girl's life & other pictures.
    Harrison Fisher. 245

"Head full/of birds..." Larry
    Eigner. 237
The heat bird. Mei-Mei
    Berssenbrugge. 203
Juncos feeding. Marie Daerr
    Boehringer. 210
"A mark on paper." Robert Kelly.
    289
May. Greg Kuzma. 300
The one indigenous bird. Larry
    Moffi. 322
Quetzal. X.J. Kennedy. 290
Red bird in a white tree.
    Marieve Rugo. 356
Scarecrow: the road to Toulouse.
    James A. Emanuel. 239
Singers. Tom Smith. 368
Spring '44. Josephine Miles. 319
"The sun solid." Larry Eigner.
    237
"Swirling tinsel veils."
    Rokwaho. 355
"To open your ears." Larry
    Eigner. 237
Troubleshooting. William
    Stafford. 373
"The two lights in/unison..."
    Larry Eigner. 237
"When Sanders brings feed to his
    chickens,some sparrows."
    Josephine Miles. 319
Why birds sing. Tom Smith. 368
Woodpile whistler. Ernesto
    Galarza. 252
Birds = Legendary
    Roc. X.J. Kennedy. 290
The birds. Greg Kuzma. 300
Birth
    Birth song: in the wing seat, at
        night. Edwin Honig. 275
    Childbirth. Judson Crews. 226
    Cottonmouth country. Louise
        Gluck. 259A
    Delivery. Toi Derricote. 229
    Doctor. Robert Peters. 343
    The egg. Louise Gluck. 259A
    The egg. Jack Prelutsky. 349
    For Rebecca on a Sunday morning
        in the spring. Phyllis A.
        Tickle. 382
    From something, nothing. Marge
        Piercy. 346
    Giving birth. Wanda Coleman. 225
    Helen Todd : My birthname.
        Sandra McPherson. 317
    January. Cathy Song. 372
    Litanies. Maria Gillan. 256
    Maternity. Toi Derricote. 229
    Naming. Gnita Orth. 339
    Nativity. Stephen Sandy. 357

Nativity. Edwin Honig. 275
Night call. James Torio. 281
Obedience of the corpse. C.D.
    Wright. 402
Postpartum blue. Stephen Sandy.
    357
So born. May Miller. 320
Sweet Mama Wanda tells fortunes
    for a price (2). Wanda
    Coleman. 225
10:29.t. Toi Derricote. 229
Transition. Toi Derricote. 229
Utrecht. Michael Gizzi. 259
Birth of the blues. Miller
    Williams. 399
Birth song: in the wing seat, at
    night. Edwin Honig. 275
Birthday. Anneliese Wagner. 389
Birthday bouquet. Alice Joyce
    Davidson. 227
Birthday party. Robert Peters.
    343
Birthdays
    At the falls: a birthday
        picture. William Stafford. 373
    Birthday. Anneliese Wagner. 389
    Birthday bouquet. Alice Joyce
        Davidson. 227
    Celebration. Sister Maura. 313
    Happy birthday and lettuce.
        James Magorian. 309
    "I will be thirty one years."
        Michael Robert Pick. 345
    On a birthday. Ralph J., Jr.
        Mills. 321
Birthmarks. Cathy Song. 372
Bisbane's flower. Bradford
    Morrow. 329
Biscayne Bay. Ernesto Galarza.
    252
Bishop's rock. Deborah Tall. 378
Bishop, Elizabeth
    For Elizabeth Bishop. Sandra
        McPherson. 317
    Poem about breath. David
        Wagoner. 390
Bison
    O buffalo, buffalo. Stephen Todd
        Booker. 212
A bit of me. Rachel A. Hazen. 271
Bitter cherry. David Wagoner. 390
Bitter light. Mary Gilliland. 257
Bitter orange village. Randy
    Blasing. 207
Bitterness. Martha Janssen. 283
Bittersweet brown. James R.
    Rhodes. 352
Biz. James R. Rhodes. 352
Bk ii chapter 37. Charles Olson.
    337

Black. Rosa Bogar. 211
Black angel. Jim Simmerman. 365
The black bear. Jack Prelutsky.
    349
The black cottage. Robert Frost.
    250
"Black ebony shiny slug." Sally
    Love Saunders. 358
Black is the color. Roy Marz. 312
Black Muslim boy in a hospital.
    James A. Emanuel. 239
The black room. Joy Harjo. 269
Black soap. Sandra McPherson. 317
Black square/white field. David
    James. 282
Black, Patsie
    Ah, my soul. 206
    Alpenglow. 206
    Altar cross. 206
    As is. 206
    Beyond. 206
    Bridge of return. 206
    Calvary. 206
    Canto. 206
    "Cogito ergo sum." 206
    Daybreak. 206
    Deliverance. 206
    Desideratum. 206
    Duet. 206
    Eleventh hour. 206
    Epiphany. 206
    An etching. 206
    Exodus. 206
    Free. 206
    Friend me a friend. 206
    Gabbatha. 206
    Home-sick. 206
    Invocation. 206
    Maran'atha. 206
    Metamorphosis. 206
    A night to remember. 206
    Now. 206
    Ode to Trinity. 206
    Pas-de-deux. 206
    Peacock feathers. 206
    Prayer. 206
    R.S.V.P. 206
    Rejoice. 206
    Rightside up. 206
    The sawdust trail. 206
    Sighted. 206
    Silent grows a loveliness. 206
    Someone ought to cry. 206
    Somewhere. 206
    Spaceship earth. 206
    Tapestry. 206
    Tell me a rainbow of sacrifice.
        206
    Tell me a rainbow of
        celebration. 206
    Thursday. 206
    Windows of the world. 206
Black-ass poem after talking to
    Pamela Churchill. Ernest
    Hemingway. 272
Black shoes. Carolyn Stoloff. 376
Black/white. Cynthia Grenfell.
    266
Blackberries. James Applewhite.
    198
Blackberry weather. Robert A.
    Sears. 362
"Blackening ebbtide." Edwin
    Honig. 275
Blair, Mac (about)
    News of your death. Thomas
        McGrath. 315
[Blank verse.]. Ernest
    Hemingway. 272
Blasing, Randy
    After Tijuana: the pool. 207
    Approaching Troy. 207
    Autograph. 207
    The beginning of the end. 207
    Bitter orange village. 207
    Blue Point. 207
    Chill. 207
    Cybele: a fragment. 207
    Earthling. 207
    Foreign waters. 207
    Gilgamesh visits Ephesus. 207
    Home ground. 207
    Insight. 207
    The keys. 207
    Last day in Istanbul. 207
    Little Compton. 207
    Mornings in fall. 207
    Mountain man. 207
    Narragansett snow dance. 207
    Near East Aubade. 207
    On the rocks at forty. 207
    One March. 207
    Orange blossom trail. 207
    Orange freeway. 207
    Over drinks. 207
    The particles. 207
    Persephone's descent. 207
    Quatrains. 207
    Railroad road. 207
    Ramazan at New Phocaea. 207
    Smoke valley equinox. 207
    Sundown song. 207
    Trinity. 207
    Walking on water. 207
    Xmas day with Miss Universe. 207
    Zenith. 207
Blazes. C.D. Wright. 402
Blazes in the night. Alice Spohn
    Newton. 333
Blazing accusation. May Miller.

320
"Bleak dismal stark glazed eyes."
     Michael Robert Pick. 345
Blenheim, Battle of
     Spanish succession. Richmond
          Lattimore. 301
Blessed Martin. Maurice W.
     Britts. 215
Blessing, Richard
     At the Ballard Locks. 208
     Callahan Park Field, Bradford,
          Pennsylvania. 208
     Comeback. 208
     Counting backward. 208
     Hawk-man. 208
     Homecoming. 208
     Late news. 208
     On first looking into Norton's
          Anthology of Poetry (Revised)
          208
     Scott. 208
     Seizure. 208
     Semi-private. 208
     State of women. 208
     Subtraction. 208
     Sundowner. 208
     Tumor. 208
A blessing. Jim Simmerman. 365
Blessings of the day. Rod McKuen.
     316
Blind Leon's escape. Stephen
     Knauth. 295
The blind man. Roy Marz. 312
The blind men and the
     disillusioned elephant. James
     Magorian. 308
Blind sight. James R. Rhodes. 352
Blind singer. Betty Adcock. 192
Blindness
     The blind man. Roy Marz. 312
     Going blind: the woman's voice.
          Anthony Petrosky. 344
     One time. William Stafford. 373
Bliss. Alberta Turner. 384
Blizzard. Colette Inez. 280
Blocks. Josephine Miles. 319
"The blond dresser." Madison
     Morrison. 327
Blond, carlight. John Godfrey.
     260
Blondes and brunettes. Jim
     Everhard. 241
Blood
     Blood relations. Richmond
          Lattimore. 301
     "Someone, an engineer, told a
          confab of wires." Josephine
          Miles. 319
The blood buoy. Charles Edward
     Eaton. 236

'"Blood is thicker than water.'"
     Ernest Hemingway. 272
Blood red nail polish madonna.
     Lyn Lifshin. 303
Blood relations. Richmond
     Lattimore. 301
Blood ties: for Jan. James
     Applewhite. 198
Blood wedding. Scott Chisholm.
     221
Blood's the only secret. James A.
     Emanuel. 239
Blood-remembering. Ghita Orth.
     339
Bloodworms. J.W. Rivers. 354
The bloody harvest. George
     Eklund. 238
Bloom. Josephine Miles. 319
Bloomsday sermon. Mitchell
     Howard. 276
"The blow is creation." Charles
     Olson. 337
Blue. Wanda Coleman. 225
Blue (color)
     An American expressed. Charles
          Edward Eaton. 236
     Blue. Wanda Coleman. 225
     Toward Senesqua. Ruth Lisa
          Schechter. 359
Blue and white lines after
     O'Keefe. Cathy Song. 372
A blue chicken. Mary Gilliland.
     257
Blue flowers. Albert Goldbarth.
     261
Blue lantern. Cathy Song. 372
The blue light. Jacques Sollov.
     370
"Blue meal." Da Free John. 284
Blue mountain. Debra Bruce. 216
Blue movies. Steve Kowit. 299
The blue pajamas. Charles Edward
     Eaton. 236
Blue Point. Randy Blasing. 207
Blue song sung in room of torrid
     goodbyes. Wanda Coleman. 225
Blue spill. James Tate. 379
The blue tablecloth. Roy Marz.
     312
Blue tapestry. Ruth Lisa
     Schechter. 359
The blue, the dead one. Donald
     Revell. 351
Blueberries. Robert Frost. 250
Blueberries. Dennis Hinrichsen.
     273
Bluebird houses. James Tate. 379
Bluejays. Jeanne Lohmann. 305
Blueprint to forever. Alice Spohn
     Newton. 332

Blues (jazz music)
    Fingering the jagged grains.
        Melvin Dixon. 231
    Music. Martha Janssen. 283
    She who sang the blues. Stephen
        Todd Booker. 212
    Sweet singing blues. Everett A.
        Gillis. 258
Blues (jazz music). See also Jazz
    Music

"The blues and lights." Da Free
    John. 284
Blues are American haikus. Andrei
    Codrescu. 223
Bly, Robert
    A bouquet of ten roses. 209
    The convict and his radio. 209
    Crazy Carlson's meadow. 209
    The dried sturgeon. 209
    Eleven o'clock at night. 209
    Fifty males sitting together.
        209
    Finding an old ant mansion. 209
    For my son Noah, ten years old.
        209
    Four ways of knowledge. 209
    The grief of men. 209
    Kennedy's inauguration. 209
    Kneeling down to look into a
        culvert. 209
    A meditation on philosophy. 209
    Morning Pablo Neruda. 209
    My father's wedding 1924. 209
    The prodigal son. 209
    A sacrifice in the orchard. 209
    The ship's captain looking over
        the rail. 209
    Snowbanks north of the house.
        209
    Visiting Emily Dickinson's grave
        with Robert Francis. 209
    Visiting the Farallones. 209
    What the fox agreed to do. 209
    Words rising. 209
    Written at Mule Hollow, Utah.
        209
Bly, Robert (about)
    Totems (I). Thomas McGrath. 315
The boa-constrictor. Erin Jolly.
    285
Boat building at midnight. Dave
    Smith. 367
Boats and Boating
    Boat building at midnight. Dave
        Smith. 367
    Bohlin 1. Charles Olson. 337
    Bohlin 2. Charles Olson. 337
    A capsized boat. James
        Applewhite. 198

Cashes. Charles Olson. 337
"How peaceful to ride in the
    arms." Sally Love Saunders.
    358
Itinerant. Ghita Orth. 339
Mooring. Deborah Tall. 378
Newport, 1930. Herbert Morris.
    326
Old men sailing the Baltic. Ray
    Fleming. 247
Riverboat. Stephen Sandy. 357
Riverboat. Robert Kelly. 289
The rowers. Eileen
    Silver-Lillywite. 364
The ship (Translated being La
    paquebot). Ernest Hemingway.
    272
Tyrian businesses. Charles
    Olson. 337
"The boats' lights in the
    dawn..." Charles Olson. 337
Bobo Baoule. Melvin Dixon. 231
Bodega, goodbye. Edwin Honig. 275
Bodies of water. Charles Edward
    Eaton. 236
"Bodily kindness is common;though
    some." Josephine Miles. 319
Body (human)
    The amputee. Charles Edward
        Eaton. 236
    As who knows, so goes. John
        Godfrey. 260
    Body blues. Andrei Codrescu. 223
    Compensatory. Ghita Orth. 339
    The day of the body, sels. Carol
        Frost. 249
    Flesh. Marieve Rugo. 356
    Flesh tones. Richmond Lattimore.
        301
    "The heart and soul." Madison
        Morrison. 327
    The muscle. Charles Edward
        Eaton. 236
    My body. Martha Janssen. 283
    Parts of the body. Christopher
        Bursk. 219
    Sheep. Josephine Miles. 319
    Strange duality. Evelyn Golden.
        263
    "The way waits/... and we must
        walk it." Joan Walsh Anglund.
        197
    We, the churches. Kirk Lumpkin.
        306
Body blues. Andrei Codrescu. 223
Boehringer, Marie Daerr
    April Thanksgiving. 210
    Arrival. 210
    August assignment. 210
    Autumn arrival. 210

Awareness. 210
Bequest. 210
Bridge builder. 210
By your leaf. 210
Can't beet it. 210
Candlelight service. 210
Captive. 210
Car-shopper's guide. 210
Change of climate. 210
Christmas Eve carol. 210
Christmas homecomings. 210
City lilac. 210
Closing song. 210
Cocktail-party puzzler. 210
Confession. 210
Contrast. 210
Convinced. 210
Cover. 210
Day in February. 210
Decision. 210
Delivery guaranteed. 210
Diary aus Deutschland. 210
Dieter's due. 210
Dip trip. 210
Double trouble. 210
Edibility test. 210
Encore. 210
Evensong. 210
Everyday miracles. 210
Forecast. 210
Frenzied forecast. 210
Fulfillment. 210
Green April. 210
Ho hum. 210
Identity. 210
In charge. 210
It's a snap. 210
It's snow fun. 210
Juncos feeding. 210
June garden. 210
June miracle. 210
A kind of magic. 210
Lemonade stand. 210
Life styles. 210
Mannerly memo. 210
Mealtime moocher. 210
Misnomer. 210
Mom's September song. 210
More than a season. 210
Motor matter. 210
Nap time. 210
New garden. 210
Ninety-year-old. 210
No return. 210
Old year's farewell. 210
On the face of it. 210
Parental puzzlement. 210
Pedestrian viewpoint. 210
Perennial necessity. 210
Petition. 210

Phenomenon. 210
Pill problem. 210
Postal protest. 210
Pre-morning moment. 210
Preventive medicine. 210
Promise. 210
Puzzle. 210
Renewal. 210
Required reading. 210
Response. 210
Roadside reflection. 210
Rush-hour ramblings. 210
September afternoon. 210
Serenity. 210
Snow-time success. 210
Some springs. 210
Spring song. 210
Steer strait. 210
Summer: small town. 210
Tasty triumph. 210
This hill. 210
This time of year. 210
Triumph. 210
Victory. 210
Village square: July. 210
Weather-wise. 210
Weather insurance. 210
Who, me? I'm fine. 210
Wild garden. 210
Winter wait. 210
With thanks to time. 210
Year's turn. 210
Bogar, Rosa
Barbara. 211
Black. 211
Conception. 211
Contented. 211
Day into night. 211
Dear Mom. 211
He's surely blessing you. 211
Hey, young folks. 211
I care. 211
I elevate my mind. 211
I painted a picture. 211
I see me. 211
I want to know you. 211
If. 211
If only you could see. 211
In a daze. 211
In memory of Donny Hathaway. 211
In memory of Mahalia Jackson.
    211
In memory of Minnie Ripperton.
    211
Just me. 211
The killing. 211
Letter from a son. 211
Lover will you come? 211
Messages in the wind. 211
The mountain in you. 211

My people. 211
A new kind of man. 211
Night into day. 211
Now I know why. 211
Oh, Africa. 211
The old man and the morning bus. 211
Pass me not. 211
The rare flower. 211
Real peace. 211
Rosa. 211
Scattered dreams. 211
Society. 211
Talent. 211
Together again. 211
The way I feel. 211
We are so far apart. 211
What am I to do? 211
When love is gone. 211
Who am I? 211
Who will it be? 211
With child. 211
You fed me well. 211
Young eyes. 211
Your friend. 211
Bohemian airs. Robert Anbian. 194
Bonlin 1. Charles Olson. 337
Bohlin 2. Charles Olson. 337
The boilerman. James Schevill. 360
Bomb, bullet or arrow. Phillips Kloss. 294
Bombay. Josephine Miles. 319
Bombay, India
    Bombay. Josephine Miles. 319
"Bona Dea..." Charles Olson. 337
Bonaparte. Jacques Sollov. 370
Bone breaker. George Eklund. 238
Bone structure. Richmond Lattimore. 301
The bone walkers, post world war three underground dream. Colette Inez. 280
The bones of my ribs. Judson Crews. 226
Bones. See Anatomy

Bonsai. Charles Edward Eaton. 236
"The book says 'Record.'" Madison Morrison. 327
The book, fr. The green step. Kenneth Koch. 297
Booker, Stephen Todd
    And-a-one-2-3-. 212
    Ask Sindbad. 212
    Author's forward. 212
    The bee, the bubble, the lovely thought. 212
    Buddy - in and not in arms. 212
    The childling. 212

Composition. 212
Contraband s.o.s. 212
Cram session. 212
Daniel's ship. 212
De chroof. 212
The dragons of Machinato. 212
Flash. 212
4-wheeler, with. 212
Freedom, freedom, freedom-hosiery. 212
The genesis of the egg. 212
"Gods no matter how huge." 212
The helper. 212
"The hummingbird is a docile woodpecker." 212
I marvel at this comic creature. 212
The insomnia of Oscar Keinemann. 212
License. 212
Like abortion haikus. 212
Like Ester. 212
Like girder haikus. 212
Look away/look away. 212
Losing tickets underfoot. 212
Lynched. 212
Matrix. 212
Muddy bootheels click to attention. 212
New York. 212
The night of the censustakers. 212
No fig. 212
O buffalo, buffalo. 212
The oath. 212
On April 24th 1981. 212
On Jan. 10th 1981, the nite. 212
On Jan. 17th 1980 212
On Jan. 4th 1981 212
On March 30th 1981. 212
A pair of intuitive dogs. 212
Paperweight escape. 212
Pigfish. 212
A poem. 212
The power of redderrick. 212
Promises. 212
The races at murderloin downs. 212
The room. 212
Rubberband. 212
Running. 212
The satchel. 212
Satisfied. 212
Seminary. 212
She who sang the blues. 212
Sunflower. 212
Them capybaras of alabac. 212
Tigers, tygers, and tigres. 212
To kick an epic tail. 212
Today. 212

Tremorhands. 212
The Ukiah arcade/p.o. box 3838.
  212
Us. 212
Versus. 212
Waves. 212
Books. Andrei Codrescu. 223
Books and Reading
  American beauties. Harrison
    Fisher. 245
  American belles. Harrison
    Fisher. 245
  Balms. Amy Clampitt. 222
  Bibliographer. Josephine Miles.
    319
  Books. Andrei Codrescu. 223
  Curriculum. Bradford Morrow. 329
  Eberheim. Irving Feldman. 242
  Elegy for the twenty-four
    shelves of books. David
    Wagoner. 390
  A garden of girls. Harrison
    Fisher. 245
  "The grey man works." Madison
    Morrison. 327
  Hammock reading, fr. Nostalgia
    poems. Robert A. Sears. 362
  The Harrison Fisher book.
    Harrison Fisher. 245
  Harrison Fisher girls. Harrison
    Fisher. 245
  "I am W.B., and." Madison
    Morrison. 327
  Now wait-. William Stafford. 373
  Other me's. Alice Spohn Newton.
    332
  A pause for a fine phrase. James
    A. Emanuel. 239
  Philobiblian. Sharon Bryan. 217
  Pictures in color. Harrison
    Fisher. 245
  Reading late by a simple light.
    Harry Humes. 278
  The refugee and his library.
    James Schevill. 360
  A tentative welcome to readers.
    William Stafford. 373
  To the page. David Shapiro. 363
  Unlimited timeouts. Ray Fleming.
    247
  What's wrong? James Schevill.
    360
  Woman at window. Everett A.
    Gillis. 258
**Books and Reading. See also Comic
  Books**

Boots and Shoes
  Black shoes. Carolyn Stoloff.
    376
  Little boots. Josephine B.
    Moretti. 324
  Lucy Robinson. Robert Peters.
    343
  Obeservation. Josephine B.
    Moretti. 324
  Red shoes in the rain. May
    Miller. 320
  Sale. Josephine Miles. 319
  Shopping for shoes. Carolyn
    Stoloff. 376
Borders. Marieve Rugo. 356
Borders
  At the Mexican border. James
    Schevill. 360
Boredom. Joyce Carol Oates. 336
Boredom
  Inside silence. Rod McKuen. 316
  "Only in my fantasies." Sally
    Love Saunders. 358
  Slump. Paul Violi. 388
Borges sang. Marilyn Kallet. 287
Borges, Jorge Luis
  Borges sang. Marilyn Kallet. 287
  Recognition of the tigers. Ruth
    Lisa Schechter. 359
Borglum, Gutzon
  American gigantism: Gutzon
    Borglum at Mt. Rushmore. James
    Schevill. 360
Boss of darkness. C.D. Wright.
  402
Boss, Laura
  After the separation papers had
    been signed. 213
  Billy "balloon" 213
  Calendar days, yellow page
    nights. 213
  The candy lady. 213
  A Doll's House revisited. 213
  Driving to the 10Am PCC reading.
    213
  Each morning at four. 213
  Each new dress you've never
    seen. 213
  Exchange. 213
  For now. 213
  I am my father's daughter. 213
  I live my life by three minute
    phone calls. 213
  I'm squeezed somewhere in his
    appointment book. 213
  I'm trading in my car today. 213
  It's the Passaic poetry reading
    tonight. 213
  The ladie's locker room at the
    Concord. 213
  The lines of living. 213
  Long distance. 213
  My analyst told me. 213

My ringless fingers on the
    steering wheel tell the story.
    213
The night I read my poetry at
    the Paterson Library. 213
The night my son packed for
    college. 213
Not waving but drowning. 213
On board the QE2 213
On my father's side. 213
On not being the youngest wife
    at the Shop-Rite. 213
Protector. 213
Separated. 213
Sitting in the doctor's office
    the next day. 213
Tonight is the coldest night of
    the year. 213
Turn on. 213
What hit me in the newspaper
    article. 213
Bossie. Alice Spohn Newton. 332
Boston
    O. Madison Morrison. 328
    The twist. Charles Olson. 337
Botanical nomenclature. Amy
    Clampitt. 222
Botany. Josephine Miles. 319
"Bottled up for days..." Charles
    Olson. 337
"The bottom/backward.". Charles
    Olson. 337
Boullee, Etienne-Louis
    Scenes from the life of Boullee.
    John Yau. 404
Bouncing vision of the commuter.
    James Schevill. 360
Bound. John F. Barker. 201
Bounty. Ghita Orth. 339
A bouquet of ten roses. Robert
    Bly. 209
Bourgeoisie
    Any day of the week:a Sunday
    text. Thomas McGrath. 315
Bovary, Madame Emma
    Madame Bovary falls on my head.
    Mary Gilliland. 257
The Bowery of dreams. Clayton
    Eshleman. 240
Box-camera snapshot. Betty
    Adcock. 192
The box. Connie Hunt. 279
Boxed to go. Alice Spohn Newton.
    333
"Boxes of old tattered photos."
    Michael Robert Pick. 345
Boxing. See Fights and Fighting

Boy blue. Harlan Usher. 386
Boy buried on Sunday. Roy Marz.
    312
Boy in a pit. Cornel Lengyel. 302
The boy next door. Eileen
    Silver-Lillywite. 364
Boy watching a light-bulb death
    in a country town. James
    Schevill. 360
A boy, a dog, a deer. Robert A.
    Sears. 362
Boyhood country creek. Maurice
    Kenny. 291
Boys. See Youth

Brace. Alberta Turner. 384
Bracelets
    Articulation of the ruby
    bracelet. Charles Edward
    Eaton. 236
    Spaces we leave empty. Cathy
    Song. 372
Brad and Tade's song. S. Bradford
    Williams (Jr.). 398
Brahman. Jacques Sollov. 371
Brain
    Brain on the beach. Phillips
    Kloss. 294
    Dream. Andrei Codrescu. 223
    The haunted palace. Edgar Allan
    Poe. 347
    Tumor. Richard Blessing. 208
Brain and mind. R. Buckminster
    Fuller. 251
Brain on the beach. Phillips
    Kloss. 294
Braintree. Michael Gizzi. 259
Brake-down. Josephine B. Moretti.
    324
Brandi, John
    Rite for the beautification of
    all beings. 214
"Brang that thing out." Charles
    Olson. 337
Brazil
    At the hotel where the long dark
    begins. Herbert Morris. 326
"Break the dogfight." Larry
    Eigner. 237
Breakage. Ghita Orth. 339
Breakaway. Marieve Rugo. 356
Breakfast. Josephine Miles. 319
Breakfast. David Wann. 394
"Breaking down my own being."
    Michael Robert Pick. 345
Breaking the ice again. Larry
    Moffi. 322
Breaking the spell. Jeanne
    Lohmann. 305
"Breaking through trees." Michael
    Robert Pick. 345
Breaking up. Gene Anderson. 195

Breakthrough. Paul Davis. 228
Breasts
    Bust lust on the bus or horny on
      muni. Kirk Lumpkin. 306
Breasts in the sun. James
    Applewhite. 198
A breath of winter. Robert L.
    Wilson. 401
Breath test. David Wagoner. 390
Breathless interlude. Ernesto
    Galarza. 252
The breeze and the day. Maurice
    W. Britts. 215
Breuil, Henri
    Through Breuil's eyes. Clayton
      Eshleman. 240
Briar rose. Marilyn Kallet. 287
A bribed referee. James Magorian.
    309
Bridal ballad. Edgar Allan Poe.
    347
Bridal piece. Louise Gluck. 259A
Bridal veil. Sally Love Saunders.
    358
Bridal Veil Falls in Yosemite
    Valley. Evelyn Golden. 263
Bridge builder. Marie Daerr
    Boehringer. 210
Bridge climbing. Robert Peters.
    343
Bridge of abandonment. Stephen
    Sandy. 357
Bridge of return. Patsie Black.
    206
Bridge to eternity. Alice Spohn
    Newton. 333
Bridges. May Miller. 320
Bridges
    Bridge climbing. Robert Peters.
      343
    Bridges. May Miller. 320
    The burning of bridges. David
      James. 282
    Ponte a Poppi. Robert A. Sears.
      362
Brief. Debra Bruce. 216
A brief introduction. Jim
    Simmerman. 365
Brief is beautiful. Cornel
    Lengyel. 302
Brief item. John Yau. 404
Brief lives. Sister Maura. 313
Brief thaw. Ralph J., Jr. Mills.
    321
Briefe an Maxwell Perkins. Gerard
    Malanga. 310
A bright defiance. Paul Davis.
    228
Bright hope. Alice Joyce
    Davidson. 227

Brighter places. Judson Crews.
    226
"Brilliance/shooting stars
    erupt." Michael Robert Pick.
    345
Brim. Josephine Miles. 319
The British in Africa. Albert
    Goldbarth. 261
In brittle molds of love. John
    Godfrey. 260
Britts, Maurice W.
    Blessed Martin. 215
    The breeze and the day. 215
    Cynthia. 215
    A design of choice. 215
    Despair. 215
    The dream and the reality. 215
    The dream of life. 215
    Dreams. 215
    Ego sum via, veritas et vita.
      215
    football game/The. 215
    For those yet unborn. 215
    Homesickness. 215
    Hope. 215
    Hymn to childhood. 215
    I kiss your cold silent lips.
      215
    I will survive. 215
    Invincible force. 215
    Lilacs on Mother's Day. 215
    Marital dilemma. 215
    My hope for the future. 215
    My wish. 215
    Nobody cares. 215
    Nowhere is a lonely, lonely
      place. 215
    Ode to the trees of Lebanon. 215
    The old things. 215
    Our response to death. 215
    Pain. 215
    Part of America's pride. 215
    A plea. 215
    Poor Bill. 215
    A prayer for a share. 215
    The road ahead. 215
    The score. 215
    Setting the pace. 215
    Sharon. 215
    Shut windows. 215
    Star of life. 215
    Strange lady. 215
    Sunset and stars. 215
    Survival blue. 215
    A thought. 215
    To my birthday girl. 215
    What do you do with a wasted
      life? 215
    What is love? 215
    Why do I love you? 215

Wind at my window. 215
The winds of March. 215
Brochure. Paul Violi. 388
Broke up. Wanda Coleman. 225
A **broken** arm. Alice Spohn Newton. 333
The **broken** bowl. James A. Emanuel. 239
"**Broken** cement." Larry Eigner. 237
A **broken** house. Marc Kaminsky. 288
A **broken** lake. James Applewhite. 198
Broken off by the music. John Yau. 404
The **broken-field** runner through age. James Schevill. 360
Bronte Sisters, The
Charlotte to Emily. Roy Marz. 312
Bronzed baby shoes. James Magorian. 309
Bronzed by frost. Mary Gilliland. 257
The **brook**, fr. The green step. Kenneth Koch. 297
Brookhaven, New York
Wildies of Burnett Lane. Maurice Kenny. 291
Brooklyn
Fulton Street. George Eklund. 238
The silo burns in Brooklyn. George Eklund. 238
Sonnet ("Snow falls exclusively for the voice to mount.") John Godfrey. 260
Brooklyn Botanic Garden. Michael Gizzi. 259
Brooklyn, Iowa, and west. Josephine Miles. 319
Brooks and Streams
The brook, fr. The green step. Kenneth Koch. 297
The green step, sels. Kenneth Koch. 297
Standing in Barr creek. David Wagoner. 390
West-running brook. Robert Frost. 250
Brother's farewell. Rose Basile Green. 265
Brother's unfinished business. James Tate. 379
Brotherhood
The brothers. Sam Fishman. 246
The chosen. Maria Gillan. 256
The Congress creed (the Eucharistic Congress...) Rose

Basile Green. 265
Ensemble. Rose Basile Green. 265
One song is sung. Alice Joyce Davidson. 227
A prayer for a share. Maurice W. Britts. 215
Brothers and Sisters
American beauties. Eileen Silver-Lillywite. 364
At the gravesite. Dennis Hinrichsen. 273
Autistic child, no longer child. Joyce Carol Oates. 336
Brother's farewell. Rose Basile Green. 265
Brother's unfinished business. James Tate. 379
Edward's birthday. Rod McKuen. 316
Elegy for my brother. Jacqueline Frank. 248
Five years old. James Tate. 379
For my brother. Cathy Song. 372
For my sister. Debra Bruce. 216
His mind ceases. Carol Frost. 249
Hurtling ahead to nowhere. Eileen Silver-Lillywite. 364
The invisible brother. Jim Everhard. 241
Mindy. Susan Stock. 375
My brother Edward. Rod McKuen. 316
My brother's hands. Jim Simmerman. 365
My brother, my stranger. Maria Gillan. 256
"No longer would he have to run." Edwin Honig. 275
Pontoons. C.D. Wright. 402
Remembering brother Bob. William Stafford. 373
Silverpoint. Louise Gluck. 259A
The sisters. Roy Marz. 312
Songs of the only child. Ghita Orth. 339
Teach me, dear sister. Irving Feldman. 242
The **brothers.** Sam Fishman. 246
Brown, John
Harper's Ferry. Steve Kowit. 298, 299
Browne, Sir Thomas
Another posthuem. Bradford Morrow. 329
Bruce, Debra
The arrangement. 216
At the drive-in. 216
Athena. 216
Blue mountain. 216

Brief. 216
Crossing the lawn. 216
A curious erotic custom. 216
Days. 216
Disney. 216
Divorced men. 216
Divorced women. 216
Dr. Martin's day off. 216
Elegy for cliches. 216
Epistemology. 216
Fasting. 216
Fear of love. 216
First ticket. 216
For bad grandmother and Betty
    Bumhead. 216
For my sister. 216
For the boy reading Playboy. 216
Fortune cookies. 216
Helen and me. 216
Hey baby. 216
I haven't been able to get
    anything done since I met you.
    216
In season. 216
In your house, the museum. 216
Insomnia. 216
Medusa. 216
My father's house. 216
Native language. 216
The other woman. 216
Our Lady of Angel's sight saving
    class. 216
Perspective. 216
Philomela's tapestry. 216
The photograph. 216
Purple aster. 216
Raking leaves. 216
Reasons for living. 216
Snowshoes. 216
Spring cleaning. 216
The storm. 216
Winter in Norfolk, Virginia. 216
Witches' winter. 216
You said. 216
Brussels Sprouts
    The Brussels sprouts. Sandra
        Gilbert. 255
The Brussels sprouts. Sandra
    Gilbert. 255
"The brute man." Madison
    Morrison. 327
Bryan, Sharon
    Adopted daughter. 217
    The back of Antelope Island. 217
    Big sheep knocks you about. 217
    Common prayer. 217
    Corner lot. 217
    Deception pass, fr. Salt Air.
        217
    Desdemona's throat. 217

Going back. 217
The Great Salt Lake. 217
Hokusai's 'Wild Horses.' 217
Hollandaise. 217
Ile des monts deserts, fr. Salt
    Air. 217
Learning the elements. 217
New kitchen. 217
The ocean floor as it would look
    without water, fr. Salt Air.
    217
One basket. 217
Philobiblian. 217
Root-bound. 217
Salt air. 217
The same river twice. 217
Seeing it. 217
A S17th century New England
    house. 217
Sleeping with the light on. 217
Use capricious in a sentence.
    217
Vermont: passing the time. 217
Viewing the body. 217
What to answer. 217
What to say. 217
With family below Albion Basin.
    217
Bryant, Louise
    A letter to Louise. John Reed.
        350
Buchenwald: the beginnings.
    Evelyn Golden. 263
"Bucking and rolling,the ship
    bent." Josephine Miles. 319
Budapest, Hungary
    Christmas Eve, 1980. J.W.
        Rivers. 354
Buddha and Buddhism
    Annanda's talk with Buddha. Gary
        Margolis. 311
    The Buddhist car. James
        Schevill. 360
    Former bank examiner feigning
        sleep in a monastery in Tibet.
        James Magorian. 309
    Tantrik X-ray. Clayton Eshleman.
        240
The Buddhist car. James Schevill.
    360
Buddhist meditation while
    fertilizing. Gene Anderson.
    195
Buddy - in and not in arms.
    Stephen Todd Booker. 212
"Buds unfurl the grace of life."
    Michael Robert Pick. 345
Buffalo man. James Schevill. 360
Building. James R. Rhodes. 352
Building a snowperson. James

Magorian. 308
Building houses. Dave Smith. 367
Buildings and Builders
   An art called gothonic. Charles
      Olson. 337
   Building. James R. Rhodes. 352
   Building houses. Dave Smith. 367
   Vinebrook Plaza demolition.
      Miriam Goodman. 264
Bulgy eyes. Aileen Fisher. 244
The **bull shooter.** Phyllis A.
   Tickle. 382
Bullfighting
   In the Plaza de Toros. David
      Wagoner. 390
   The poem is by Maera. Ernest
      Hemingway. 272
Buonarotti to his public and God.
   Roy Marz. 312
Buonarotti to Vittoria Colonna.
   Roy Marz. 312
Buoys
   The blood buoy. Charles Edward
      Eaton. 236
The **bur.** Roy Marz. 312
Bureau. Josephine Miles. 319
Bureau 2. Josephine Miles. 319
The **bureau.** Carolyn Stoloff. 376
Bureaucracy
   Bureau. Josephine Miles. 319
   Bureau 2. Josephine Miles. 319
Burglars. Wanda Coleman. 225
Burglary. Phyllis A. Tickle. 382
Burial. Robert Peters. 343
Burials. See Funerals

Burke, Theta
   "All the stories never told."
      218
   "As you give what you need." 218
   "Because things inside/felt so
      tenuous and uncertain." 218
   "Concrete actions." 218
   "Early needs/unmet," 218
   "Fidelity to one's soul." 218
   "Freedom/is the coming of
      one/unto himself." 218
   "From inner battle he has come."
      218
   "He died/shoveling snow." 218
   "He who had seemed/to seek
      battle." 218
   "How can one/who has always
      heard." 218
   "How quickly/the fire of joy."
      218
   "I am truly vulnerable." 218
   "I am/(not because I do)." 218
   "Ideal soil/makes for shallow
      roots." 218

   "If I ask of you/what I would
      give." 218
   "If the wall of your anger." 218
   "Is it possible/for one to come
      unto." 218
   "Long years ago." 218
   "Love sees." 218
   "Love/once felt." 218
   "Misunderstandings." 218
   "A moment of high excitement."
      218
   "One attuned to the spirit." 218
   "One never intends/to be
      selfish." 218
   "One reached out/in her need."
      218
   "Our answers/are a part of our
      questions." 218
   "Our vulnerability." 218
   "Pain/phsyical or emotional."
      218
   "The pains of life and love."
      218
   "Scattered bits." 218
   "She affirmed herself." 218
   "She tried to do/just as they'd
      say." 218
   "So often/she seemed to speak
      too quickly." 218
   "Someone would say/we are
      responsible." 218
   "Somewhere/in some yesterday."
      218
   "Speak not to others." 218
   Speaking and reaching, sels. 218
   "There's a lonely part," 218
   "Those times when I can feel no
      hope." 218
   "Through the inside dark," 218
   Through the searching, sels. 218
   "To resist one's self." 218
   Toward integrity, sels. 218
   "Treasures and pains." 218
   "We are each/a piece of a great
      puzzle." 218
   "We cling to/and espouse a
      creed." 218
   "We make heroes of some." 218
   "When a spider begins/to spin
      his web." 218
   "When I am not." 218
   "When I fear to speak." 218
   "When I'm lost and alone." 218
   "When one acts toward another."
      218
   "When the fire is low." 218
   "When the soul reaches the
      level." 218
   "A whitened fist." 218
   "With a heavy heart." 218

"With no love to feel." 218
"Witnin you/lie the answers."
    218
"You get a cold." 218
"Your love." 218
Burlesque. Royal Murdoch. 330
The burlesque queen. James A.
    Emanuel. 239
Burlesquer's song. Bradford
    Morrow. 329
Burning. Robert Peters. 343
The burning child. Amy Clampitt.
    222
Burning leaves: the spinster. Tom
    Smith. 368
Burning leaves: the groom. Tom
    Smitn. 368
The burning of bridges. David
    James. 282
The burning wards of Meadowbrook.
    Colette Inez. 280
A burning:a poem in nine parts.
    Frances Mayes. 314
Burningly cold. Norman Andrew
    Kirk. 293
Burrow. Miriam Goodman. 264
Bursk, Christopher
    After waking from my nap. 219
    Antique tree ornaments. 219
    Bedridden. 219
    Chores. 219
    The death of a small beast. 219
    First aid at 4 a.m. 219
    First job. 219
    Ill at fifteen. 219
    Lies. 219
    "Lord I believe. Help me in my
        unbelief." 219
    The morning's mail. 219
    'Neither fish nor fowle.' 219
    An ordinary man. 219
    Parts of the body. 219
    Payment. 219
    Pnone call. 219
    Public servant. 219
    Restoring the wood. 219
    Tne resurrection. 219
    Roadside flowers. 219
    Rock collection. 219
    658.386/B 972.   219
    Tape recorder. 219
    Waitingroom. 219
    War games in the bath. 219
The bus. John F. Barker. 201
Buses
    The bus. John F. Barker. 201
    "I collapse my." Madison
        Morrison. 327
    Trans-American express. Steve
        Kowit. 299

Bush. Phillips Kloss. 294
Business and Businessmen
    "The entrepreneur chicken shed
        his tail feathers, surplus."
        Josephine Miles. 319
    Mr. Belknap's use of deep
        imagery in business. Bradford
        Morrow. 329
    The record. Charles Olson. 337
Business as usual. Mark Vinz. 387
Bust lust on the bus or horny on
    muni. Kirk Lumpkin. 306
"Busy little sandpipers." Sally
    Love Saunders. 358
But never the spirit. Iefke
    Goldberger. 262
But once upon a very young time.
    Thomas McGrath. 315
But rabbits. Aileen Fisher. 244
The butchering. Robert Peters.
    343
Butchers and Butchering
    Tne butchering. Robert Peters.
        343
    Michael's. Albert Goldbarth. 261
Butterflies
    "The butterfly." Sally Love
        Saunders. 358
    Games. Sandra McPherson. 317
    Lady butterfly. Rachel A. Hazen.
        271
    Little butterfly. Jacques
        Sollov. 371
The butterfly and the scorpion:
    James McNeill Whistler. James
    Schevill. 360
Butterfly sheets. Charles Edward
    Eaton. 236
"The butterfly.". Sally Love
    Saunders. 358
Buttons
    Looking for buttons. Carolyn
        Stoloff. 376
Buying the Brooklyn Bridge. James
    Magorian. 308
The buzzard. Roy Marz. 312
By antique vogues. John Godfrey.
    260
By any other name. Josephine B.
    Moretti. 324
By degrees. Josephine B. Moretti.
    324
By La Push. Marc Hudson. 277
By rote. Rod McKuen. 316
By sea stone, sels. Edwin Honig.
    275
By starlight. David Wagoner. 390
By the gate at York. Paul Davis.
    228
By Wm MacKinnon, in memory. Paul

Davis. 228

By your leaf. Marie Daerr
    Boehringer. 210

By-gone seniors 1982. Rachel A.
    Hazen. 271

'Bye, Baby Bun-ting! Harlan
    Usher. 386

Cabbage
    The red cabbages. Sandra
        Gilbert. 255
Cabin opening. Robert Pawlowski.
    341
A cabinet of few affections.
    James A. Emanuel. 239
Cable to Florence. Roy Marz. 312
Cabo verde. Michael Gizzi. 259
Caddy and Annie and these and
    thee. Gene Detro. 230
Cadenza. Phillips Kloss. 294
Cafeteria. Miriam Goodman. 264
Cage. Josephine Miles. 319
The cage. Sam Fishman. 246
Caged. Norman Andrew Kirk. 293
The caisson passes. May Miller.
    320
Cakes and Cookies
    Chocolate cake. Charles Edward
        Eaton. 236
    Grandma's chocolate cake. Alice
        Spohn Newton. 333
    My special cake. Jack Prelutsky.
        348
Calculation. Josephine Miles. 319
Calcutta, India
    In a gradually moving car
        somewhere in Calcutta. Miller
        Williams. 399
Calendar days, yellow page
    nights. Laura Boss. 213
Calendars
    The Chinese lunar calendar
        horoscope. Robin Becker. 202
Calico caribes. Margaret Key
    Biggs. 205
California. John Reed. 350
California
    "Apart from branches in
        courtyards and small stones."
        Josephine Miles. 319
    California. John Reed. 350
    If Osiris were to die in New
        York. Mitchell Howard. 276
    Sebastopol. William Oandasan.
        335
    "We came across the desert."
        Michael Robert Pick. 345

"Yesterday evening as the sun
    set late." Josephine Miles.
    319
The California crack. Wanda
    Coleman. 225
Call it fear. Joy Harjo. 269
Call it hope. Rochelle DuBois.
    234
Call of the Ozarks. James
    Magorian. 309
Callahan Park Field, Bradford,
    Pennsylvania. Richard
    Blessing. 208
Calling the bears. Jeanne
    Lohmann. 305
Calling them back. Eileen
    Silver-Lillywite. 364
Calms between. Alice Spohn
    Newton. 332
Calvary. Patsie Black. 206
Cambodia
    Bronzed by frost. Mary
        Gilliland. 257
Cambria. Robert A. Sears. 362
Cambridge. Michael Gizzi. 259
Camels
    A dromedary standing still. Jack
        Prelutsky. 349
A cameo of your mother. William
    Stafford. 373
Camomile. Robert Gibb. 253
Camouflage. Amy Clampitt. 222
Camp field: icicle river. Franz
    Schneider. 361
Camp-songs. Anne Bailie. 199
Campagna picnic. Roy Marz. 312
The campaign. Josephine Miles.
    319
Camping
    Calling the bears. Jeanne
        Lohmann. 305
    An event at Big Eddy. William
        Stafford. 373
    Making camp. David Wagoner. 390
    Mantra for Fred's trailer court.
        James Magorian. 309
    May 8 (1979). Mary Gilliland.
        257
    Their shelter. David Wagoner.
        390
    Tom and Henry, camping out.
        Stephen Sandy. 357
    With Ann on Cape Breton. Paul
        Violi. 388
The campus on the hill. W.D.
    (William De Witt) Snodgrass.
    369
Can. David Wann. 394
"Can one be good." Da Free John.
    284

"Can you remember beginning?"
    Edwin Honig. 275
Can you see us? Ruth Lisa
    Schechter. 359
"Can you walk on tiptoe." Jan
    Ormerod. 338
Can you? Josephine B. Moretti.
    324
Can't beet it. Marie Daerr
    Boehringer. 210
Canada
    I like Canadians. Ernest
        Hemingway. 272
    In Canada. Greg Kuzma. 300
    Toward Calgary. Timothy Steele.
        374
Cancer
    What the heart can bear. Robert
        Gibb. 253
Cancer (disease)
    Mignonette. Donald Revell. 351
    The rose. Steve Kowit. 299
    The scar. Carol Frost. 249
    To Uncle Oscar, dead of lung
        cancer. J.W. Rivers. 354
Candied cash. Norman Andrew Kirk.
    293
"The candle does not know/... and
    yet its flame." Joan Walsh
    Anglund. 197
Candlelight service. Marie Daerr
    Boehringer. 210
Candlemas. Mary Gilliland. 257
Candlemas
    The ghouls of Candlemas. Andrei
        Codrescu. 223
    A procession at Candlemas. Amy
        Clampitt. 222
Candles
    Watching a candle. William
        Stafford. 373
Candy
    Candied cash. Norman Andrew
        Kirk. 293
    "Handy pandy, Jack-a-dandy." Jan
        Ormerod. 338
The candy lady. Laura Boss. 213
Cannibal mantis. Tom Smith. 368
The cannibal. Charles Edward
    Eaton. 236
Canoe beneath the trees. Harry
    Humes. 278
Canoe journey. Robert Peters. 343
Canoes and Canoeing
    Ballade for a canoeist. Harry
        Humes. 278
    Canoe beneath the trees. Harry
        Humes. 278
    Canoe journey. Robert Peters.
        343

It could be. Harry Humes. 278
Canterbury, England
    As at the cathedral, the young
        man. Paul Davis. 228
Canticle for Xmas Eve. David
    Wagoner. 390
Canticle: tightening. Jenne
    Andrews. 196
Canto. Patsie Black. 206
Canto. Marilyn Kallet. 287
Canto ("In this locust summer.")
    Franz Schneider. 361
Canto CVI, sels. Ezra Pound. 235
Canto CXX. Ezra Pound. 235
Canto I, sels. Ezra Pound. 235
Canto IC, sels. Ezra Pound. 235
Canto XCIII, sels. Ezra Pound.
    235
Canto XCV, sels. Ezra Pound. 235
Canto XLVII, sels. Ezra Pound.
    235
Canton. Michael Gizzi. 259
The canyon wren. Phillips Kloss.
    294
Cape Ann, Massachusetts
    Letter 23. Charles Olson. 337
    Motel view. Donald Revell. 351
    Some good news. Charles Olson.
        337
Cape Canaveral. Michael Gizzi.
    259
Capitol. Josephine Miles. 319
A capsized boat. James
    Applewhite. 198
Capt Christopher Levett (of
    York). Charles Olson. 337
The captain's hannele. Roy Marz.
    312
Captive. Marie Daerr Boehringer.
    210
Captives. Ernest Hemingway. 272
Captivities. Robin Becker. 202
Captured. Robert L. Wilson. 401
"Capturing visions relay my mind
    to infinity." Michael Robert
    Pick. 345
"The car appears." Madison
    Morrison. 327
"A car horn." Larry Eigner. 237
"A car in the garage." Madison
    Morrison. 327
Car trip. Robert Peters. 343
Car-shopper's guide. Marie Daerr
    Boehringer. 210
Caravan. James Magorian. 309
Card Games
    Players. Josephine Miles. 319
    Rummy. Greg Kuzma. 300
    Tough decision. Josephine B.
        Moretti. 324

A cardinal. W.D. (William De
    Witt) Snodgrass. 369
Cardinals (birds)
    In charge. Marie Daerr
        Boehringer. 210
Cardona-Hine, Alvaro
    Totems (V). Thomas McGrath. 315
Care. Josephine Miles. 319
The careful bump. Barry
    Wallenstein. 393
"The caretaker takes." Madison
    Morrison. 327
Caring with care. Alice Spohn
    Newton. 332
Carl Perusick. Anthony Petrosky.
    344
Carnal verdict. Colette Inez. 280
Carnival man. Robert Peters. 343
Carnivals
    From the dunked clown at the
        carnival. Betty Adcock. 192
    Two at the fair. James
        Applewhite. 198
    White lake. James Applewhite.
        198
Carol. Tom Smith. 368
Carousel. James Torio. 281
Carousels
    The wheel. Sandra McPherson. 317
Carpenter bees. Robert Gibb. 253
The carpenter is knocking. Maria
    Gillan. 256
The carpenter of Brooklyn. Royal
    Murdoch. 330
Carpentry and Carpenters
    Letter 7. Charles Olson. 337
    Restoring the wood. Christopher
        Bursk. 219
Carrots
    Augusta discusses carrots, their
        meaning and use. Carolyn
        Stoloff. 376
    The carrots. Sandra Gilbert. 255
The carrots. Sandra Gilbert. 255
Carrousels
    Carousel. James Torio. 281
"Cars.". Larry Eigner. 237
Carson, Johnny
    The parable of the pecan tree.
        James Magorian. 309
Cartoons
    Dagwood's day of wrath. Harrison
        Fisher. 245
The carver. Gary Margolis. 311
Cashes. Charles Olson. 337
The casino at Constanta. Keith
    Wilson. 400
Casino royale. Keith Wilson. 400
Cast your vote. Alice Joyce
    Davidson. 227

Casting. Andrei Codrescu. 223
Castle keep. Rod McKuen. 316
Castro, Fidel
    Fidel Castro. Andrei Codrescu.
        223
Casualty. Ernesto Galarza. 252
Casualty report. John F. Barker.
    201
Cat. Josephine Miles. 319
Cat. Tom Smith. 368
Cat and I. Robert L. Wilson. 401
The cat at the last supper. Roy
    Marz. 312
Cat in glass, fr. A pride of four
    small lions. Everett A.
    Gillis. 258
Cat in the bric-a-brac, fr. A
    pride of four small lions.
    Everett A. Gillis. 258
Cat on the corner, fr. A pride of
    four small lions. Everett A.
    Gillis. 258
A cat screams. Carolyn Stoloff.
    376
"A cat/stops.". Larry Eigner. 237
The catalogue. Alice Spohn
    Newton. 333
Catch you catch me not. James R.
    Rhodes. 352
The catch. Iefke Goldberger. 262
Catchism. Tom Smith. 368
A catechism. William Stafford.
    373
The caterpillar. David Wagoner.
    390
Caterpillars
    The caterpillar. David Wagoner.
        390
    Moral of the caterpillar story.
        Phillips Kloss. 294
Catfish. Tom Smith. 368
Catfish
    Feeding. David Wagoner. 390
Catharsis. James R. Rhodes. 352
Cathedral in the pines. Norman
    Andrew Kirk. 293
The cathedral. Jacqueline Frank.
    248
Cats
    Cat. Tom Smith. 368
    Cat and I. Robert L. Wilson. 401
    Cat in glass, fr. A pride of
        four small lions. Everett A.
        Gillis. 258
    Cat in the bric-a-brac, fr. A
        pride of four small lions.
        Everett A. Gillis. 258
    Cat on the corner, fr. A pride
        of four small lions. Everett
        A. Gillis. 258

A cat screams. Carolyn Stoloff. 376

"A cat/stops." Larry Eigner. 237

Catfish. Tom Smith. 368

The cats of time. Cynthia Grenfell. 266

Chester is lake water. Cynthia Grenfell. 266

Coneflower groundcover. Cynthia Grenfell. 266

Death of a cat. James Schevill. 360

Feline favorites. Alice Spohn Newton. 332

The garden. Steve Kowit. 298, 299

Howdy. Andrei Codrescu. 223

"In winter when the sun shone." Edwin Honig. 275

Kitten in the sun, fr. A pride of four small lions. Everett A. Gillis. 258

Magic. Rod McKuen. 316

Me and the cat. Rod McKuen. 316

Mornings with Bingo. Rod McKuen. 316

Murphy. Josephine B. Moretti. 324

Musa, steward, makes amends for losing our cat. Robert A. Sears. 362

My electric cat. Robert L. Wilson. 401

Never more than alien. May Miller. 320

Old cat. Carol Frost. 249

The old woman and the cat. James Schevill. 360

Only because. Ghita Orth. 339

Ounce. X.J. Kennedy. 290

"queen/has new-born cats." Madison Morrison. 327

Stray animals. Cathy Song. 372

Tiger cat. Robert A. Sears. 362

To crazy Christian. Ernest Hemingway. 272

The cats of time. Cynthia Grenfell. 266

Cattle
  Among cattle. Dennis Hinrichsen. 273

Catullus in his book. Royal Murdoch. 330

Cause and effect. Martha Janssen. 283

Caution
  "Hopes racing." Sally Love Saunders. 358

Cavafy, Constantine
  The sign for the sun. Anneliese

Wagner. 389

Cave Art. See Paleolithic Art

Caves
  Geji cave. Robert A. Sears. 362
  Our cave. William Stafford. 373

Cecropia. Thomas Hornsby Ferril. 243

Cedar Trees
  One cedar tree. Joy Harjo. 269
  Red cedar. Marc Hudson. 277

Ceilings
  Walking on the ceiling. David Wagoner. 390

Celebration. Sister Maura. 313

Celebration. Robert L. Wilson. 401

Celebration
  Condensing exaltation mantra. Kirk Lumpkin. 306

Celebration with geraniums. Miriam Goodman. 264

Celery
  The celery bushes. Sandra Gilbert. 255

The celery bushes. Sandra Gilbert. 255

Celestial destiny. Jacques Sollov. 371

Celestial evening, October 1967. Charles Olson. 337

Celestial scenes. Alice Spohn Newton. 332

Celestial timepiece. Joyce Carol Oates. 336

Cell damage. George Eklund. 238

The cell. Louise Gluck. 259A

Cellars
  Intrinsic cellar. James Magorian. 309
  Mining the cellar, fr. Nostalgia. Robert A. Sears. 362

The Celt in me. Keith Wilson. 400

Celts
  The Celt in me. Keith Wilson. 400

Cemeteries
  At the Woodstock cemetery. Carolyn Stoloff. 376
  Black angel. Jim Simmerman. 365
  A bright defiance. Paul Davis. 228
  By Wm MacKinnon, in memory. Paul Davis. 228
  The cemetery is empty. Carol Frost. 249
  Common prayer. Sharon Bryan. 217
  Cover. Marie Daerr Boehringer. 210

Crocus. Greg Kuzma. 300
Digger. Jim Simmerman. 365
A fashioner of stone roses.
  Keith Wilson. 400
The father. Keith Wilson. 400
Gravedigging in August. George
  Eklund. 238
Graves in east Tennessee. Donald
  Revell. 351
Hilltop house. James Torio. 281
It was a happy little grave.
  James A. Emanuel. 239
Looking at old tombstones in a
  New England graveyard. James
  Schevill. 360
A mother's stone. Keith Wilson.
  400
The old cemetery in Cluj. Keith
  Wilson. 400
Old tomb carving: the nameless
  prince. Keith Wilson. 400
On a high hill. John F. Barker.
  201
One rose of stone. Keith Wilson.
  400
Peace, father, where you lie.
  James Schevill. 360
Poet's stone at steepletop. Gary
  Margolis. 311
"The professional man." Madison
  Morrison. 327
Snift. Josephine Miles. 319
St. Paul's Union Church and
  cemetery, Seiberlingsville,
  Pa. Robert Gibb. 253
Stone roses. Keith Wilson. 400
Village cemetery Sunday morning.
  Jeanne Lohmann. 305
Walk by a cemetery wall. Michael
  Akillian. 193
The white grave. Rachel A.
  Hazen. 271
Wife Mary. Paul Davis. 228
The cemetery is empty. Carol
  Frost. 249
The cemetery. Roy Marz. 312
Censored. Ruth Lisa Schechter.
  359
Center. Josephine Miles. 319
Center piece. Andrei Codrescu.
  223
Central Park South. Donald
  Revell. 351
Ceramic. James R. Rhodes. 352
Ceremonial. Robert A. Sears. 362
Ceremonial. Mark Vinz. 387
Ceremony for Minneconjoux. Brenda
  Marie Osbey. 340
Certain months for years. Larry
  Eigner. 237

A certain order of divinity.
  Larry Moffi. 322
Certainties. Alice Joyce
  Davidson. 227
Certification. Clayton Eshleman.
  240
"Chain his body." Michael Robert
  Pick. 345
Chain letter. James Magorian. 308
Chains of fires. Elsa Gidlow. 254
Chair. Carolyn Stoloff. 376
"The chair.". Madison Morrison.
  327
Chairs
  Sixteenth-century Icelandic
    chair. Marc Hudson. 277
Challenge, taken hard. James A.
  Emanuel. 239
Chamber of commerce. Josephine
  Miles. 319
The chameleon. Jack Prelutsky.
  349
Chameleons
  The chameleon. Jack Prelutsky.
    349
Champlain, Samuel de
  The savages, or voyages of
    Samuel de Champlain of
    Brouage. Charles Olson. 337
Champs d'honneur. Ernest
  Hemingway. 272
Chance. Elsa Gidlow. 254
The chances of magic. Keith
  Waldrop. 392
Change. Connie Hunt. 279
Change. Anthony Petrosky. 344
Change. Martha Janssen. 283
Change
  Autumn apology. Carol Frost. 249
  Credo. Steve Kowit. 299
  How we resist the new. Evelyn
    Golden. 263
  "A kaleidoscope you." Sally Love
    Saunders. 358
  Manifold. Josephine Miles. 319
  Musicke of division. Thomas R.
    Sleigh. 366
  Notes from the California House.
    Rod McKuen. 316
  The photograph. Debra Bruce. 216
  Taking off. Barry Wallenstein.
    393
  Teethering. Edwin Honig. 275
Change for three-dollar bill.
  John Godfrey. 260
Change of climate. Marie Daerr
  Boehringer. 210
Change of territory. Melvin
  Dixon. 231
Changeling. Ghita Orth. 339

Changeling. Erin Jolly. 285
Changes on the organ theme. Roy
    Marz. 312
Changes!. Rachel A. Hazen. 271
Changing the guard. Mark Vinz.
    387
Chanukah madonna. Lyn Lifshin.
    303
Chapter. Frances Mayes. 314
Chapter heading. Ernest
    Hemingway. 272
Character. Josephine Miles. 319
Charenton - Jardin de Sade.
    Michael Gizzi. 259
The charge of the political
    brigade. John Reed. 350
Charioteer. Erin Jolly. 285
Charlatan. Erin Jolly. 285
Charles VII, King of France
    To Charles, Duke of Orleans.
        Richmond Lattimore. 301
"Charlie is a giant size." Sally
    Love Saunders. 358
Charlotte to Emily. Roy Marz. 312
Charm for attracting wild money.
    Marge Piercy. 346
Charming child. Martha Janssen.
    283
Charms
    Juju. Robert A. Sears. 362
    The philtre. Charles Edward
        Eaton. 236
Charon. James R. Rhodes. 352
Charter line. Mark Vinz. 387
Chartres - Couvent du Sacre
    Coeur? Michael Gizzi. 259
Cheating on company time. Miriam
    Goodman. 264
Cheatwood, Kiarri T-H
    The flower of our journey (so
        Sonia travels). 220
    The giver of darkness (so Zenzi
        sings). 220
    In the earth's abiding sweetness
        (where Fannie Lou rests). 220
    In the gathering forest (where
        Kimatni lives). 220
    In the Rastaman's agony and
        peace (where Marley
        recreates). 220
Check. Ierke Goldberger. 262
Check-out. Joan Colby. 224
Cheer up! Josephine B. Moretti.
    324
Cheese
    Grandma's cheese. Alice Spohn
        Newton. 333
    The wild cheese. James Tate. 379
Cheeseburger serenade. Paul
    Violi. 388

The cheetah. Jack Prelutsky. 349
Cheetahs
    The cheetah. Jack Prelutsky. 349
Chemical Warfare
    Defoliage - agent orange.
        Jocelyn Hollis. 274
"The chemical, high and low." Da
    Free John. 284
Chemistry
    Heroic discoverer. James
        Applewhite. 198
Cherche - midi. Kenneth Koch. 297
Cherokee Indians
    From the Cherokee. Stephen
        Knauth. 295
Cherries. Lucien Stryk. 377
Cherries
    The pointillist. Charles Edward
        Eaton. 236
The cherry tree in a storm. James
    Schevill. 360
Cherry Trees
    Casualty. Ernesto Galarza. 252
    The cherry tree in a storm.
        James Schevill. 360
Chester is lake water. Cynthia
    Grenfell. 266
Chestnut Hill, N.C. Josephine B.
    Moretti. 324
Chestnut Hill, North Carolina
    Chestnut Hill, N.C. Josephine B.
        Moretti. 324
Chiaro di luna. James Torio. 281
Chiaroscuro. Robert A. Sears. 362
Chiaroscuro. Marge Piercy. 346
Chicago
    The city: a cycle. Lucien Stryk.
        377
    From Burnside to Goldblatt's by
        streetcar. J.W. Rivers. 354
    Hog's elegy to the butchers.
        James Schevill. 360
    O. Madison Morrison. 328
The Chicago notebook, sels. J.W.
    Rivers. 354
The Chicago poetry team going 457
    days without an accident.
    James Magorian. 309
The Chicago train. Louise Gluck.
    259A
Chicanos
    Manuela come out the kitchen.
        Wanda Coleman. 225
    New Mexico territory. Jenne
        Andrews. 196
    The wetbacks. Ernesto Galarza.
        252
The chicken. John Reed. 350
Chickens
    Slaughtering chickens. Anthony

Petrosky. 344
The west main book store
   chickens. Marge Piercy. 346
Wet feathers. Alice Spohn
   Newton. 333
When the sun came, the rooster
   expanded to meet it. Josephine
   Miles. 319
The Chiclets paragraphs. Paul
   Violi. 388
Chief cook and waiter. Josephine
   B. Moretti. 324
Chief Joseph of the Nez Perce.
   Robert Penn Warren. 395
Chifalta. Brenda Marie Osbey. 340
Child Abuse
   It was assumed a God-head.
      Judson Crews. 226
   Young eyes. Rosa Bogar. 211
Child in the evening. William
   Stafford. 373
A child's face in a small town.
   William Stafford. 373
A child's meditation. Alice Joyce
   Davidson. 227
Child's tale. Keith Wilson. 400
Child, Julia
   The great debate. James Torio.
      281
The child-bride. Joyce Carol
   Oates. 336
Childbirth. Judson Crews. 226
Childhood Memories
   Acute memory. Martha Janssen.
      283
   All that autumn. Eileen
      Silver-Lillywite. 364
   "Baying dogs." Michael Robert
      Pick. 345
   Calling them back. Eileen
      Silver-Lillywite. 364
   Chiaroscuro. Robert A. Sears.
      362
   The country fair of childhood.
      James Schevill. 360
   Dayton: non-memories. Jim
      Everhard. 241
   The diamond in shadow. James
      Applewhite. 198
   The eye on the corner. Everett
      A. Gillis. 258
   Flight of steps. Stephen Sandy.
      357
   Gatherings. James L. White. 396
   Gifts. Jim Everhard. 241
   Hazzuzzah! Alice Spohn Newton.
      332
   Herstory. Marilyn Kallet. 287
   Hymn to childhood. Maurice W.
      Britts. 215

I was a child. Evelyn Golden.
   263
The ice house. Eileen
   Silver-Lillywite. 364
Imago. Amy Clampitt. 222
Late morning. Anthony Petrosky.
   344
Letter to Mimi. Eileen
   Silver-Lillywite. 364
"Locust Street revisited."
   Michael Robert Pick. 345
A map of simplicities. James
   Applewhite. 198
No return address. Dave Smith.
   367
The oak tree. Dennis Hinrichsen.
   273
Old thoughts in a zoo room.
   Norman Andrew Kirk. 293
On a mulberry tree branch in
   Jackson Park. J.W. Rivers. 354
Parking lot. Thomas Hornsby
   Ferril. 243
The path that separates. Robert
   L. Wilson. 401
A pocket full of yesterdays.
   Alice Spohn Newton. 333
Pressed flowers. Albert
   Goldbarth. 261
Recollection. Martha Janssen.
   283
Shimmering pediment. John Yau.
   404
The shortcut. Timothy Steele.
   374
Summer was ending. James
   Applewhite. 198
Sweet memories. Alice Joyce
   Davidson. 227
The tree house. Louise Gluck.
   259A
"Walking through old haunts."
   Michael Robert Pick. 345
Wisconsin village. Anne Bailie.
   199
The childling. Stephen Todd
   Booker. 212
Children. Martha Janssen. 283
Children and Childhood
   Afterall, the children. Norman
      Andrew Kirk. 293
   Alley. David Wann. 394
   And you? James R. Rhodes. 352
   The argument. John F. Barker.
      201
   Asthma, 1948. Betty Adcock. 192
   At Eve's house. Margaret Key
      Biggs. 205
   Augusta tells how she chose a
      profession. Carolyn Stoloff.

376

Bronzed baby shoes. James
    Magorian. 309
But once upon a very young time.
    Thomas McGrath. 315
Carol. Tom Smith. 368
Charming child. Martha Janssen.
    283
The childling. Stephen Todd
    Booker. 212
Conception. Rosa Bogar. 211
Condensation. Stephen Sandy. 357
Disney. Debra Bruce. 216
A dream of small children. Cathy
    Song. 372
Elisabeth at seven. Evelyn
    Golden. 263
The fearful child. Carol Frost.
    249
Flesh of the fawn. James
    Schevill. 360
Four years old. Martha Janssen.
    283
Fourth grade. David Wann. 394
Free to love. Connie Hunt. 279
"Gentle children." Michael
    Robert Pick. 345
Glories of the world. Stephen
    Sandy. 357
I play with his son. Anneliese
    Wagner. 389
In knowledge of young boys. Toi
    Derricote. 229
In the dark. Jeanne Lohmann. 305
Legacy. Martha Janssen. 283
Lemonade stand. Marie Daerr
    Boehringer. 210
Lines written for Mrs. Hagood.
    John F. Barker. 201
Manque. Robert A. Sears. 362
My wish. Maurice W. Britts. 215
The night of the censustakers.
    Stephen Todd Booker. 212
"On Bemo Ledge ne fell" Charles
    Olson. 337
One basket. Sharon Bryan. 217
Parent. Josephine Miles. 319
Peaches. John Godfrey. 260
Protection. Martha Janssen. 283
Quicksand. Maurice Kenny. 291
Returning a lost child. Louise
    Gluck. 259A
Revelations. Maria Gillan. 256
Sadface at five. James A.
    Emanuel. 239
Searching the endless. Alice
    Spohn Newton. 333
Silent, soft, forever still.
    Rachel A. Hazen. 271
Someone else's children. Robin

Becker. 202
"Sounded like." Larry Eigner.
    237
Stages of chilhood. Anne Bailie.
    199
The swan story. Betty Adcock.
    192
To a child. Roy Marz. 312
Tribe. Cathy Song. 372
Twilight. Carolyn Stoloff. 376
Under the eaves. Stephen Sandy.
    357
Unique. Iefke Goldberger. 262
The visitor. James Applewhite.
    198
A vote for Harold. Steve Kowit.
    298, 299
"When Jack's a good boy." Jan
    Ormerod. 338
Children's games. Miller
    Williams. 399
Children's Games
    Children's games. Miller
        Williams. 399
    Games. Robert Peters. 343
    "One-ery, two-ery, dickery dan."
        Jan Ormerod. 338
    Pig-family game. Robert Peters.
        343
    Unforgettable games. James
        Torio. 281
Children. See also Adoption

The children. Roy Marz. 312
The children. Wanda Coleman. 225
The children. Eileen
        Silver-Lillywite. 364
Chile
    The dead madonnas of Santiago.
        Jim Simmerman. 365
Chill. Randy Blasing. 207
China
    After the war (I). John Yau. 404
    History of China. Herbert
        Morris. 326
    Li Ho. Steve Kowit. 298, 299
    Lost sister. Cathy Song. 372
    Shanhaikuan. Richmond Lattimore.
        301
China and silver. Miriam Goodman.
    264
Chinatown. Cathy Song. 372
Chincoteague. Dennis Hinrichsen.
    273
Chinese doll. Wanda Coleman. 225
The Chinese lunar calendar
    horoscope. Robin Becker. 202
Chinese villanelle. John Yau. 404
The chipmunk. Jack Prelutsky. 349
Chipmunks

The chipmunk. Jack Prelutsky. 349

Chips. May Miller. 320

Chisholm, Scott
Adirondacks. 221
Apology for a sudden voyage. 221
Axetime autumn. 221
Blood wedding. 221
Island. 221
Nights at the opera. 221
Only the best line holds. 221
Screaming for this event. 221
Signing in tongues of absence. 221
Survivors. 221
Tending the lamp. 221
Throwing the apple. 221
Waiting out November. 221
Weeping for a man in the brown chair legless, with a cane. 221

Chocolate cake. Charles Edward Eaton. 236

Choice. James R. Rhodes. 352

Choir birds of another time. Paul Davis. 228

The chooser and the chosen. Robert Kelly. 289

Choosing a death. Alberta Turner. 384

Chores. Christopher Bursk. 219

Chorus. Andrei Codrescu. 223

Chorus for Neruda #1. Thomas McGrath. 315

Chorus for Neruda #2. Thomas McGrath. 315

Chorus from a play. Thomas McGrath. 315

Chorus from a play (2). Thomas McGrath. 315

The chosen. Maria Gillan. 256

Chrestien (Chretien) de Troyes
Reading Chretien by Hood Canal. Marc Hudson. 277

Christ. Jacques Sollov. 371

Christ just spoke. Alice Spohn Newton. 332

Christ within. Jacques Sollov. 370

The Christ, sels. Tom Smith. 368

Christams day misadventures. Josephine B. Moretti. 324

Christenings
The anointing. Sandra McPherson. 317

Christianity
The bur. Roy Marz. 312
A certain order of divinity. Larry Moffi. 322
Dinner at Mary's. Roy Marz. 312

The door. May Miller. 320
First quartets. Roy Marz. 312
Good Friday. Amy Clampitt. 222
Mark. Josephine Miles. 319

Christmas
A blessing. Jim Simmerman. 365
The blue light. Jacques Sollov. 370
Candlelight service. Marie Daerr Boehringer. 210
Canticle for Xmas Eve. David Wagoner. 390
Christams day misadventures. Josephine B. Moretti. 324
Christmas at the Quaker Center (Paris, 1981). James A. Emanuel. 239
The christmas cactus. Rod McKuen. 316
Christmas Eve carol. Marie Daerr Boehringer. 210
Christmas homecomings. Marie Daerr Boehringer. 210
Christmas section III. Thomas McGrath. 315
Christmas within the walls. Norman Andrew Kirk. 293
Christmas: what is it all about. Evelyn Golden. 263
Heritage. John F. Barker. 201
Hillbilly night before Christmas. Thomas Noel Turner. 385
Letter to an imaginary friend. Part three. Thomas McGrath. 315
"Lovingly I stow the car." Madison Morrison. 327
Pastoral. Cynthia Grenfell. 266
The reason. Sister Maura. 313
Teacher's prayer. Josephine B. Moretti. 324
Two legends: a birthday party. Tom Smith. 368
What is Christmas? Alice Spohn Newton. 332
Winter solstice-Christ mass poem. Kirk Lumpkin. 306

Christmas at the Quaker Center (Paris, 1981). James A. Emanuel. 239

The christmas cactus. Rod McKuen. 316

A Christmas card from Romania. Keith Wilson. 400

Christmas Eve carol. Marie Daerr Boehringer. 210

Christmas Eve, 1980. J.W. Rivers. 354

Christmas homecomings. Marie

Daerr Boehringer. 210
Christmas in a valley of the
    Uwharrie. Stephen Knauth. 295
Christmas in Hawaii. Tefke
    Goldberger. 262
Christmas section III. Thomas
    McGrath. 315
Christmas Trees
    Antique tree ornaments.
        Christopher Bursk. 219
    January. Ghita Orth. 339
Christmas within the walls.
    Norman Andrew Kirk. 293
Christmas: what is it all about.
    Evelyn Golden. 263
Christopher's pond. Phyllis A.
    Tickle. 382
Chrome alba. Bradford Morrow. 329
Chronicles. Charles Olson. 337
Church burning: Mississippi.
    James A. Emanuel. 239
The **church.** Evelyn Golden. 263
"Churchbells/years ago." Larry
    Eigner. 237
Churches
    The cathedral. Jacqueline Frank.
        248
    The church. Evelyn Golden. 263
    If God does not see you. James
        Schevill. 360
    Kirk. Kirk Lumpkin. 306
    The new site of the Calvary
        Temple. Harry Humes. 278
    Tableau in a Lutheran church.
        Robert Peters. 343
Churchill, Winston
    Sir Winston. John F. Barker. 201
Cicada song. Colette Inez. 280
Cid, The (Rodrigo Diaz de Bivar)
    El Cid. Jacques Sollov. 370
Cigarette smoke, afterward. Keith
    Wilson. 400
Cinderella. James Magorian. 308
Circadian. Frances Mayes. 314
Circe. James Torio. 281
Circe
    A crone's tale. Irving Feldman.
        242
Circle without end. Mitchell
    Howard. 276
"The circle/has no beginning."
    Joan Walsh Anglund. 197
Circles
    "Bucking and rolling,the ship
        bent." Josephine Miles. 319
    "Circles crowd the sky." Michael
        Robert Pick. 345
"Circling around." Michael Robert
    Pick. 345
The **circuit** of despair. James A.

Emanuel. 239
Circuit of the intruder. Cathryn
    Hankla. 268
The **circular** staircase. Charles
    Edward Eaton. 236
Circus. Josephine Miles. 319
Circus
    Billboard. Erin Jolly. 285
    Home life of the circus dancers.
        James Schevill. 360
    The moral circus. Edwin Honig.
        275
    A Yugoslav circus. Keith Wilson.
        400
Cities
    "At night I lay with you."
        Ernest Hemingway. 272
    At the up-town window. George
        Eklund. 238
    Autobiography. Dennis
        Hinrichsen. 273
    Brief item. John Yau. 404
    By antique vogues. John Godfrey.
        260
    City eyes. Barry Wallenstein.
        393
    The city in the sea (The doomed
        city) Edgar Allan Poe. 347
    City people. Maria Gillan. 256
    The city planner. James
        Schevill. 360
    Coming to town. Barry
        Wallenstein. 393
    "Dogtown the dog town." Charles
        Olson. 337
    Dressed to the last. Barry
        Wallenstein. 393
    "The earth with a city in her
        hair." Charles Olson. 337
    El Toro. George Eklund. 238
    Eleventh Avenue racket. John
        Reed. 350
    Entry. Josephine Miles. 319
    Fair city. Greg Kuzma. 300
    1st Avenue basics f. Andrei
        Codrescu. 223
    Flat roofs. Ernest Hemingway.
        272
    "History is something to take
        shelter in." Robert Kelly. 289
    Journey. James Torio. 281
    June in the city. John Reed. 350
    "Large city life." Madison
        Morrison. 327
    Los Ninos. George Eklund. 238
    Nature visits the city. Mitchell
        Howard. 276
    Old cities. Andrei Codrescu. 223
    Pussywillows: a city poem.
        Jeanne Lohmann. 305

Recurrent city. Marieve Rugo.
  356
Return. Marilyn Kallet. 287
A road and clouds. Donald
  Revell. 351
The secular city. Franz
  Schneider. 361
A snort response to Robert
  Frost. Ernesto Galarza. 252
Skyscraper. Anne Bailie. 199
"The sleeping city." Sally Love
  Saunders. 358
"Sounds/quiet." Garry Bigner.
  237
Subdivision. Josephine Miles.
  319
"Tantrist." Charles Olson. 337
Winter. George Eklund. 238
City. Josephine Miles. 319
City eyes. Barry Wallenstein. 393
The city in the sea (The doomed
  city) Edgar Allan Poe. 347
The city in the sea (The doomed
  city). Edgar Allan Poe. 347
The city is a battery. Barry
  Wallenstein. 393
City lilac. Marie Daerr
  Boehringer. 210
City love. John Godfrey. 260
City people. Maria Gillan. 256
The city planner. James Schevill.
  360
The city rat. Barry Wallenstein.
  393
The city that is set upon a hill.
  Mitchell Howard. 276
The city: a cycle. Lucien Stryk.
  377
Civic diasters. Charles Olson.
  337
Civic pride. Josephine Miles. 319
Civil liberty. John F. Barker.
  201
Civil Rights Movement
  Bakke's law, or lateral
    movement. Ray Fleming. 247
  Church burning: Mississippi.
    James A. Emanuel. 239
  Jerry 1964. Wanda Coleman. 225
  "We shall overcome" : a smile
    for the 1960's. James A.
    Emanuel. 239
Civil War, American
  The black cottage. Robert Frost.
    250
  High water mark. Paul Davis. 228
Civil Wars. See also specific
  names

Civilian. Josephine Miles. 319

A civilian defender, port of Vera
  Cruz. J.W. Rivers. 354
Civitavecchia, Italy
  Coastal stuff. Richmond
    Lattimore. 301
Clampitt, Amy
  Amaranth and Moly. 222
  The anniversary. 222
  Balms. 222
  Beach glass. 222
  Beethoven, Opus 111. 222
  Berceuse. 222
  Botanical nomenclature. 222
  The burning child. 222
  Camouflage. 222
  The cormorant in its element.
    222
  The cove. 222
  The Dahlia Gardens. 222
  The Dakota. 222
  Dancers exercising. 222
  Easter morning. 222
  The edge of the hurricane. 222
  Exmoor. 222
  Fog. 222
  Good Friday. 222
  Gradual clearing. 222
  A hairline fracture. 222
  Imago. 222
  The kingfisher. 222
  Letters from Jerusalem. 222
  Lidenbloom. 222
  The local genius. 222
  Marginal employment. 222
  Marine surface, low overcast.
    222
  Meridan. 222
  On the disadvantages of central
    heating. 222
  Or consider Prometheus. 222
  The outer bar. 222
  Palm Sunday. 222
  A procession at Candlemas. 222
  The quarry. 222
  Rain at Bellagio. 222
  Remembering Greece. 222
  The reservoirs of Mount Helicon.
    222
  A resumption, or possibly a
    remission. 222
  Salvage. 222
  Sea mouse. 222
  Slow motion. 222
  The smaller orchid. 222
  Stacking the straw. 222
  The sun underfoot among the
    sundews. 222
  Sunday music. 222
  Tepoztlan. 222
  Times Square water music. 222

Trasimene. 222
The woodlot. 222
"Clap hands, Daddy comes." Jan
    Ormerod. 338
Clarities. Maria Gillan. 256
Class reunion. William Stafford.
    373
Class struggle in music (1).
    Amiri Baraka (LeRoi Jones).
    200
Class struggle in music (2) Amiri
    Baraka (LeRoi Jones). 200
Classroom. Lucien Stryk. 377
The clay dancer. James L. White.
    396
Cleaning up. Ernesto Galarza. 252
Cleanliness
    Black soap. Sandra McPherson.
        317
    "Dan, Dan/Dirty old man." Jan
        Ormerod. 338
    Sarah at the sink. James A.
        Emanuel. 239
Clenching. Alberta Turner. 384
Cleopatra. Jacques Sollov. 370
Cleopatra
    Cleopatra. Jacques Sollov. 370
Clergy
    Bandages. James A. Emanuel. 239
    Ecumenicity. James R. Rhodes.
        352
    His hat was on straight. Judson
        Crews. 226
    "I served to priest the
        pharaohs." Da Free John. 284
    Rev. Joseph Krubsack. Robert
        Peters. 343
    Winter combat. Paul Davis. 228
Clerks
    The treason of the clerks takes
        many forms. Herbert Morris.
        326
"Cleveland is a city." Madison
    Morrison. 327
Cleveland summer of nickel tips.
    Colette Inez. 280
Cleveland, Ohio
    "Cleveland is a city." Madison
        Morrison. 327
Cliches
    So what else is new? Harlan
        Usher. 386
Clickstone. Rokwaho. 355
The climate of your plans. Miriam
    Goodman. 264
Climbing. Judson Crews. 226
Climbing Montmartre. Melvin
    Dixon. 231
"Climbing stairs so low." Michael
    Robert Pick. 345

Climbing the stairs. Mark Vinz.
    387
Climbing the walls. Steve Kowit.
    299
"Climbing to the second/floor..."
    Madison Morrison. 327
Climbing together. Marc Hudson.
    277
Clinical jungle. James Magorian.
    309
The clock of moss. Judson Crews.
    226
The clock outran the mouse.
    Norman Andrew Kirk. 293
Clockmaker with bad eyes. C.D.
    Wright. 402
Clocks
    "The key to/making the alarm
        clock." Madison Morrison. 327
Clockwatcher series, sels.
    Rochelle DuBois. 234
"Close/-up.". Larry Eigner. 237
The closet. Bill Knott. 296
Closing song. Marie Daerr
    Boehringer. 210
A closing. May Miller. 320
Cloth. Alberta Turner. 384
Clothing and Dress
    "The assistant offers." Madison
        Morrison. 327
    Chores. Christopher Bursk. 219
    The disrobing. Royal Murdoch.
        330
    Dress dilemma. Josephine B.
        Moretti. 324
    The love of a coat. Andrei
        Codrescu. 223
    Revolutionary. Mark Vinz. 387
    The T-shirt phenomenon in
        Minnesota on the Fourth of
        July. James Schevill. 360
    "Undo buttons." Jan Ormerod. 338
    The undressing. Carol Frost. 249
    Wear. Alberta Turner. 384
Cloud. Josephine Miles. 319
Cloud of unknowing. Elsa Gidlow.
    254
The cloud of unknowing. David
    James. 282
Cloud Valley. Rod McKuen. 316
The clouded leopards of Cambodia
    and Viet Nam. Betty Adcock.
    192
Clouds. Sally Love Saunders. 358
Clouds
    Clouds. Sally Love Saunders. 358
    "Clouds like mountains." Sally
        Love Saunders. 358
    Clouds over the sea. Haig
        Khatchadourian. 292

"A hole in the clouds moves."
   Larry Eigner. 237
"Now/here." Larry Eigner. 237
Two in June. Ralph J., Jr.
   Mills. 321
"Clouds like mountains." Sally
   Love Saunders. 358
Clouds over the sea. Haig
   Khatchadourian. 292
Cloudy day in Alaska. Sally Love
   Saunders. 358
Cloudy night, new moon. Mary
   Gilliland. 257
Clover rain. Aileen Fisher. 244
Clown. James R. Rhodes. 352
Clowns
   Clown. James R. Rhodes. 352
   White clown. Charles Edward
      Eaton. 236
Club for elders. Anneliese
   Wagner. 389
Co-hereing. Kirk Lumpkin. 306
"Co-op.". Larry Eigner. 237
"The coast goes from Hurrian
   Hazzi to Tyre." Charles Olson.
   337
Coastal stuff. Richmond
   Lattimore. 301
Coaxing. Martha Janssen. 283
Cobras
   Snake charmer. James Magorian.
      309
Cobwebs. Evelyn Golden. 263
"The cock does crow." Jan
   Ormerod. 338
Cocks
   The day's cock of morning.
      Judson Crews. 226
Cocktail-party puzzler. Marie
   Daerr Boehringer. 210
Cocoon. Erin Jolly. 285
Coda. Robert Anbian. 194
Coda: "bringing up baby" Gerard
   Malanga. 310
The code. Robert Frost. 250
Codicil. Steve Kowit. 298, 299
Codrescu, Andrei
   About photography. 223
   Against meaning. 223
   Alberta. 223
   Alice's brilliance. 223
   All wars are noly. 223
   &.a. 223
   Architecture. 223
   Arthur Bremer blues. 223
   At home. 223
   Attempt to spell, incantate and
      annoy. 223
   Au bout du temps. 223
   Ballad of the typist. 223

Beach in Sebastopol, California.
   223
The best side of me. 223
Bi-lingual. 223
Blues are American haikus. 223
Body blues. 223
Books. 223
Casting. 223
Center piece. 223
Chorus. 223
A cook in hell. 223
Crimes. 223
Dawn. 223
De rerum natura. 223
Designs. 223
The differences. 223
Don't wait for me. 223
Dream. 223
Dream dogs. 223
Drowning another peasant
   inquisition. 223
Drums and believers. 223
Epitaph. 223
Eugenio Montale in California.
   223
Evening particular. 223
Execution. 223
Face portrait. 223
A face. 223
Faith relearned. 223
Fascination. 223
Fear. 223
Fidel Castro. 223
The first icon with gun. 223
1st Avenue basics f. 223
For Marg so she could... 223
For Max Jacob, sels. 223
A Francis Ponge. 223
From a trilogy of birds. 223
The ghouls of Candlemas. 223
Gist. 223
The goldrush. 223
The good spirit. 223
A good thing when I see one. 223
Grammar & money, sels. 223
A grammar. 223
Guillotine. 223
The,here, what, where, sels. 223
The history of the growth of
   heaven. 223
The Holy Grail. 223
Howdy. 223
The imagination of necessity.
   223
Irony as nursery. 223
Junk dawn, NYC. 223
Junk mail. 223
The lady painter, sels. 223
Les fleurs du cinema. 223
The License to carry a gun. 223

The life on film of St. Theresa. 223
Looks from money. 223
The love of a coat. 223
Love poem (for Alice). 223
Love simmers the stew of the dead. 223
Love things. 223
Mail. 223
"'Man' and 'woman', these are horrid words..." 223
Manifesto. 223
The marriage of insult and injury, sels. 223
The masses are constantly on the telephone. 223
Model work. 223
The monk. 223
More about monks. 223
More about poems. 223
Muffled by a belt across the mouth. 223
My next book. 223
Near sonnet. 223
Necrocorrida, sels. 223
New York. 223
Ode to curiosity. 223
Ode to laryngitis. 223
Ode to Mexico. 223
Old cities. 223
On organization. 223
Opium for Archie Anderson. 223
Opium for Britt Wilkie. 223
Paper on humor. 223
The park. 223
The penal cavalry. 223
Poem. 223
Poem for Kyra. 223
Poems from the river Aurelia (sels.) 223
The police. 223
Politics. 223
Port of call. 223
Power. 223
The question of personnel. 223
Rain. 223
Remembrance of my forgotten skinniness. 223
Reverse. 223
Revolution. 223
Sadness unhinged. 223
Saturnian dilemma. 223
Sea sickness. 223
Secret training, sels. 223
Selavie. 223
A serious morning, sels. 223
a serious morning. 223
Silence. 223
Silence at the top. 223
The sin of wanting a new

refrigerator. 223
Souls looking for bodies. 223
Space souffle. 223
Stanley the Archer. 223
The status of the monk. 223
A still. 223
Stock report. 223
Sunday sermon. 223
Symmetry. 223
Talismanic ceremony for Lucian, March 9, 1971... 223
Testing. testing. 223
Tete-a-tete. 223
A textual recording. 223
"There is an orange rotting on the table." 223
The threat. 223
To my heart. 223
To the virgin as she now stands to the monk after a... 223
Toward the end of 1969. 223
Trains. 223
The urges. 223
Us. 223
The west is the best and the future is near. 223
Why write. 223
Winter in Istanbul. 223
Womb and city. 223
Work. 223
The worst poems make the best "poems" 223
The yes log. 223
Your fantastic outlines. 223
Zzzzzzzzzzzzz. 223
Coffins
"Over a forest of coffins morning rings." Carolyn Stoloff. 376
"Cogito ergo sum." Patsie Black. 206
"Coiled.". Charles Olson. 337
Colby, Joan
Bird, flower, child. 224
Check-out. 224
A comparison of charts. 224
Detecting love. 224
Diagnostician. 224
The disaster plan. 224
Disparities. 224
Divorce. 224
During a fight I tear up my wedding picture. 224
Endangered species. 224
Epidemics. 224
Festering. 224
Fever in August. 224
Flights. 224
Glossies. 224
The guilt formula. 224

Hawk like an anchor. 224
House of shadows. 224
How the sky begins to fall. 224
In the lake. 224
Inflammable abodes. 224
Jewelry. 224
Last supper. 224
Let's. 224
Looking at posters. 224
Marriage. 224
Mica flaking from my eyelashes.
  224
Monopoly. 224
Poem for the letters of my name.
  224
Poem for the letters of your
  name. 224
The postures of sleep. 224
Prairie path. 224
Recidivists. 224
Red Lake. 224
Rockhounds. 224
The sea-changes. 224
Skin. 224
Space. 224
Spell against weather. 224
Stopping places. 224
Strange tongues, other
  languages. 224
Surgery. 224
Under the patronage of the moon.
  224
Unroofed. 224
What I want. 224
What it takes. 224
What you remember of me. 224
Working on our masters in
  communications. 224
Cold
    On the disadvantages of central
      heating. Amy Clampitt. 222
Cold frame. Carol Frost. 249
Cold water creek. Stephen Knauth.
  295
Cole's Island. Charles Olson. 337
Coleman, Wanda
    About God & things. 225
    After the poem. 225
    After the poem (2). 225
    After work. 225
    Angel baby. 225
    Anticipating murder. 225
    April in Hollywood. 225
    At the jazz club he comes on a
      ghost. 225
    At the record hop. 225
    At vital statistics. 225
    Bad. 225
    The big empty. 225
    Blue. 225

Blue song sung in room of torrid
  goodbyes. 225
Broke up. 225
Burglars. 225
The California crack. 225
The children. 225
Chinese doll. 225
Daddyboy. 225
Day. 225
Dear mama (2). 225
Death 424. 225
Death 577. 225
Diagnosis...with complications.
  225
Dinner with a friend. 225
Doctor's report. 225
Dream 13. 225
Eviction. 225
Felon. 225
First affair. 225
Flight of the California condor.
  225
Fly boy. 225
Giving birth. 225
Good mama. 225
Ground zero. 225
History. 225
I am everything. 225
I arrive home to the funeral.
  225
I carry the moon. 225
I have watched them come back to
  the village. 225
I live for my car. 225
I love the dark. 225
I sweat I mop I stink. 225
I've written this poem before.
  225
Imagoes. 225
In search of the mythology of do
  wah wah. 225
In this waking. 225
The ISM. 225
Jerry 1964. 225
Jerry 1966. 225
Jerry 1967. 225
Junk. 225
Kate. 225
The lady with bougainvillea in
  her eyes. 225
Lessons. 225
Love the letters. 225
M'sai. 225
Mama's man. 225
Manuela come out the kitchen.
  225
Men lips. 225
Moot. 225
Murder. 225
My love brings flowers. 225

Night owl. 225
Office politics. 225
On green money street. 225
On speed. 225
The one who can. 225
Pam. 225
Parked. 225
Pigging out. 225
Pretty face. 225
Prisoner of Los Angeles (2). 225
Rape. 225
The reading. 225
Reasons why. 225
Recorder. 225
Rehabilitation. 225
The rider. 225
Rose. 225
Saint Theresa. 225
The saturday afternoon blues.
    225
Shop of signs. 225
Shopping bag lady. 225
Silly bitches institute. 225
6:50 PM. The phone rings. It's
    him.   225
Snakes. 225
Stephen's monkey. 225
Storm clouds. 225
Swan. 225
Sweet Mama Wanda tells fortunes
    for a price (2). 225
Television story. 225
'Tis morning makes mother a
    killer. 225
Under arrest. 225
Under arrest (2). 225
The wait. 225
Wanda and Steve. 225
What he is. 225
When my times comes. 225
Where he is. 225
Worker. 225
"Yes/there must have been." 225
Collection. Mark Vinz. 387
Collection agency. James
    Magorian. 308
Collector's item. Josephine B.
    Moretti. 324
Colleges and Universities
    At the university: to William
        Blackburn. James Applewhite.
        198
    Attending chapel. James
        Applewhite. 198
    The campus on the hill. W.D.
        (William De Witt) Snodgrass.
        369
    Cheer up! Josephine B. Moretti.
        324
    Collitch bread. Harlan Usher.

    386
    Flower studies: tigerlily. Tom
        Smith. 368
    Institutions. Josephine Miles.
        319
    Letter to Dean Picker. Steve
        Kowit. 299
    Prick song at Compline. Tom
        Smith. 368
    Thank you. Steve Kowit. 299
Collitch bread. Harlan Usher. 386
Color
    Coloring book. James Magorian.
        308
    Grandfather. Josephine Miles.
        319
Color blind. Aileen Fisher. 244
'The color of evening.' Rochelle
    DuBois. 234
The color rake of time. Clayton
    Eshleman. 240
The color that really is. William
    Stafford. 373
Colorado. Robert Kelly. 289
Colorado (state)
    Stories of three summers. Thomas
        Hornsby Ferril. 243
a colored girl. James L. White.
    396
Coloring book. James Magorian.
    308
Colors
    Black/white. Cynthia Grenfell.
        266
    Explaining the rainbow. Rochelle
        DuBois. 234
    The reading of an ever-changing
        tale. John Yau. 404
    Watercolors. Martha Janssen. 283
"Columbian Glacier." Sally Love
    Saunders. 358
Columbus, Christopher
    The first one. Rose Basile
        Green. 265
    Voyage. Josephine Miles. 319
The columnist listening to "you
    know" in the park. James
    Schevill. 360
Comas
    Where you have been. Gary
        Margolis. 311
The comb. Charles Edward Eaton.
    236
Come. Edwin Honig. 275
Come. Marilyn Kallet. 287
Come a daisy. Jacqueline Frank.
    248
Come and lie with me. Elsa
    Gidlow. 254
Come April. John Godfrey. 260

Come back. Larry Moffi. 322
Come back home. Jacques Sollov. 371
Come closer. Jacques Sollov. 371
Come, look quietly. James Wright. 403
Comeback. Richard Blessing. 208
"Comets clash." Michael Robert Pick. 345
Comic Books
    Motor matter. Marie Daerr Boenringer. 210
Coming. Jim Everhard. 241
Coming again upon Mensch's mill by accident... Robert Gibb. 253
Coming alive. Maria Gillan. 256
Coming into different country. Jeanne Lohmann. 305
Coming now. Timothy Steele. 374
The coming of snow. Haig Khatchadourian. 292
Coming to town. Barry Wallenstein. 393
The coming. Roy Marz. 312
Commencement Day
    After the high school graduation, 1944. David Wagoner. 390
    Graduation. Connie Hunt. 279
    Peter's graduation. Norman Andrew Kirk. 293
    A son's commencement day. Rose Basile Green. 265
    The term's end. Anne Bailie. 199
    Upon graduation. Rachel A. Hazen. 271
Commentary text commentary text commentary text. David Shapiro. 363
Committal day. James R. Rhodes. 352
Committee decision on pecans for asylum. Josephine Miles. 319
Committee report on smoke abatement in residential area. Josephine Miles. 319
The common living dirt. Marge Piercy. 346
Common prayer. Sharon Bryan. 217
Commoners. Robert L. Wilson. 401
Communication
    A cardinal. W.D. (William De Witt) Snodgrass. 369
    "Deepest thoughts we spoke in silence." Robert A. Sears. 362
    "Misunderstandings." Theta Burke. 218
    Say it again,Sam. Josephine B. Moretti. 324

Talk to me. Rachel A. Hazen. 271
10 A.M t. Rochelle DuBois. 234
What I should have said. Joy Harjo. 269
When you don't speak to me. John Hawkes. 270
Communion. Rose Basile Green. 265
Communion. William Oandasan. 335
Communion with the dead. Robert L. Wilson. 401
Communique on cork. Gary Margolis. 311
Commute. Dave Smith. 367
The commuter in the car tunnels. James Schevill. 360
The commuter's dream. Bill Knott. 296
Commuters
    Bouncing vision of the commuter. James Schevill. 360
    The commuter in the car tunnels. James Schevill. 360
    The commuter's dream. Bill Knott. 296
A comparison of charts. Joan Colby. 224
Compassion. Alice Joyce Davidson. 227
Compassion
    Night call. Sister Maura. 313
    Song of whales. Gerard Malanga. 310
    Tarantulas on the lifebuoy. Thomas Lux. 307
    Were you there? James R. Rhodes. 352
    "Who shall we raise up, who glorify-our wounded." Josephine Miles. 319
Compensatory. Ghita Orth. 339
Competition
    "As a four-year-old." Sally Love Saunders. 358
Complaint. Cynthia Grenfell. 266
Complaint against time. Cornel Lengyel. 302
Complete freedom. Greg Kuzma. 300
Composed. Ernesto Galarza. 252
Composition. Stephen Todd Booker. 212
Computer lab. Miriam Goodman. 264
Computers
    Computer lab. Miriam Goodman. 264
    Computers ▬ those "in" things. Harlan Usher. 386
    Printout. James Torio. 281
Computers ▬ those "in" things. Harlan Usher. 386
Computing God. Norman Andrew

Kirk. 293
Comrade. Royal Murdoch. 330
Conant, James Bryant
    Letter 10. Charles Olson. 337
Concealed words II. David
    Shapiro. 363
Conceit
    "In the town where every man is
    king." Josephine Miles. 319
Concentration Camps
    Dachau. Paul Davis. 228
    Remembering the children of
    Auschwitz. Thomas McGrath. 315
    When I read of the rose of
    Dachau. James A. Emanuel. 239
Conception. Josephine Miles. 319
Conception. Rosa Bogar. 211
Conception (embryology)
    Birthmarks. Cathy Song. 372
    "Publish my own soul..." Charles
    Olson. 337
    Seed. Cathy Song. 372
Concerning Belinda. Harrison
    Fisher. 245
Concerning the idea of vase.
    Carolyn Stoloff. 376
Concerning Tsiganes. Keith
    Wilson. 400
Concomitants. Bradford Morrow.
    329
Concordance. Paul Violi. 388
"Concrete actions." Theta Burke.
    218
Condensation. Stephen Sandy. 357
Condensing exaltation mantra.
    Kirk Lumpkin. 306
"The condition of the light from
    the sun." Charles Olson. 337
Conduct. Josephine Miles. 319
Conduct of Life. See Life, Conduct

"The conductor arrives with."
    Madison Morrison. 327
"The conductor does/a repeat
    performance." Madison
    Morrison. 327
"The conductor is/a figure..."
    Madison Morrison. 327
Coneflower groundcover. Cynthia
    Grenfell. 266
Coney Island
    Ideal disorders, fr. Fresh air.
    Irving Feldman. 242
Conference room: the golden
    years. Miriam Goodman. 264
Confession. Marie Daerr
    Boehringer. 210
Confession
    Holy orders. Robert Pawlowski.

341
Confessions. Martha Janssen. 283
Confessions of a stardreamer.
    Harrison Fisher. 245
Confessions of an American
    visitor of the large screen.
    James Schevill. 360
Confessor. William Stafford. 373
Confidence. Josephine Miles. 319
Confidence
    To Alice Notely. Marilyn Kallet.
    287
Confidential data on the loyalty
    investigation... James
    Schevill. 360
Configuration. Robin Becker. 202
Configurations of a dead
    language. Maria Gillan. 256
Confirmation. Robert Pawlowski.
    341
The Congress creed (the
    Eucharistic Congress...) Rose
    Basile Green. 265
Conjure. Josephine Miles. 319
Connection. Joy Harjo. 269
Connie's song. S. Bradford
    Williams (Jr.). 398
The connoisseur's history of the
    bathroom. James Schevill. 360
The conqueror worm. Edgar Allan
    Poe. 347
Conquistador. Steve Kowit. 299
"Conrad saw behind the wheel."
    Edwin Honig. 275
Conrad, Joseph
    "Conrad saw behind the wheel."
    Edwin Honig. 275
Conscience
    Witness. Josephine Miles. 319
Consecration. Susan Tichy. 381

Consent. Erin Jolly. 285
Conservancies. Josephine Miles.
    319
Conservation
    Recycle. Kirk Lumpkin. 306
Consider the lilies. Cornel
    Lengyel. 302
The consolations of sociobiology.
    Bill Knott. 296
Constancy. Elsa Gidlow. 254
Constancy. Phillips Kloss. 294
Constant defender. James Tate.
    379
Constant tenderness. Ray Fleming.
    247
Constantinople. Michael Gizzi.
    259
Constellation. Carol Frost. 249
"Constellations collapse." James
    Torio. 281

Consummation. Norman Andrew Kirk. 293

Contained. Josephine Miles. 319

Contented. Rosa Bogar. 211

Contentment
    The birds. Greg Kuzma. 300
    "Grievances:the warm fogs of summer." Josephine Miles. 319
    Porch steps. Ralph J., Jr. Mills. 321
    The rain gone. Ralph J., Jr. Mills. 321
    Tonight I feel content. Evelyn Golden. 263
    Woman on a park bench. James R. Rhodes. 352

Continents
    "Between Cruiser & Plato..." Charles Olson. 337

Contingency plan. Mark Vinz. 387

Continuing. Ghita Orth. 339

Contorted light. Kirk Lumpkin. 306

Contraband. James Torio. 281

Contraband s.o.s. Stephen Todd Booker. 212

Contrast. Marie Daerr Boehringer. 210

Contrasts
    A comparison of charts. Joan Colby. 224

Contrition. Ernesto Galarza. 252

Controversy
    Double exposure. Marieve Rugo. 356
    Long distance bickering (day rate) Jim Simmerman. 365
    "When burly men." Madison Morrison. 327

Conversation. Josephine Miles. 319

Conversation
    "Along these sidewalks." Madison Morrison. 327
    Configuration. Robin Becker. 202
    Festival of light. Mark Vinz. 387
    Imperative. Josephine Miles. 319
    Slack. Josephine Miles. 319
    We will walk by the trail. Carolyn Stoloff. 376
    You don't understand me. Marge Piercy. 346

Conversation on a yam. Irving Feldman. 242

Conversation with the giver of names. Harry Humes. 278

"Conversation.". Madison Morrison. 327

Conversion. Marc Kaminsky. 288

The conversion of the Jews. Robin Becker. 202

The convict and his radio. Robert Bly. 209

Convinced. Marie Daerr Boehringer. 210

A cook in hell. Andrei Codrescu. 223

Cook's voyage. James Tate. 379

Cooks and Cooking
    Grandma's starter. Alice Spohn Newton. 333
    "Hokey, pokey, winky, wum." Jan Ormerod. 338
    Hollandaise. Sharon Bryan. 217
    "Mix a pancake, stir a pancake." Jan Ormerod. 338
    The summer kitchen. Sandra Gilbert. 255

Cool Hand Kelly pleads extenuating circumstances. Thomas McGrath. 315

Coping with the news. Jeanne Lohmann. 305

Coproatavism. Clayton Eshleman. 240

"Cops keep metropole." Madison Morrison. 327

Copy from an old master. Ernesto Galarza. 252

Corey, Mabelle Gilman
    At the Chateau de Villegenis that summer. Herbert Morris. 326

The cork-lined room. Charles Edward Eaton. 236

The cormorant in its element. Amy Clampitt. 222

"The cormorant.". Charles Olson. 337

Cormorants
    The cormorant in its element. Amy Clampitt. 222
    For a fisherman who dynamited a cormorant rookery. David Wagoner. 390

Corn
    An easy way to roast corn. James Magorian. 309
    Indian corn. Mark Vinz. 387

Corn-planter. Maurice Kenny. 291

"Cornely.". Charles Olson. 337

Corner drugstore, fr. Nostalgia poems. Robert A. Sears. 362

The corner is turned. Cynthia Grenfell. 266

Corner lot. Sharon Bryan. 217

"The corner of the block's in." Madison Morrison. 327

Corners

In a corner. William Stafford.
373

Cornwall, Vermont
Passions of the flowering apple.
Gary Margolis. 311

Corporations and Corporate Life
Cafeteria. Miriam Goodman. 264
Conference room: the golden
years. Miriam Goodman. 264
Elizabethan fool applies for a
corporate execeutive position.
James Schevill. 360
Going concern. Miriam Goodman.
264
Happy endings. Miriam Goodman.
264
The office suite sequence, 1965.
J.W. Rivers. 354

Corpse and mirror (I). John Yau.
404

Corpse and mirror (II). John Yau.
404

Corpse and mirror (III). John
Yau. 404

Cosmetics
On the face of it. Marie Daerr
Boehringer. 210
Song of Aeterna 27 over Los
Angeles. James Schevill. 360

Cosmic dust. Erin Jolly. 285

Cosmos (universe)
Intuition - metaphysical mosaic.
R. Buckminster Fuller. 251
Just this once. James Torio. 281
Startalk in the Greek
luncheonette. Colette Inez.
280

The cost. Rod McKuen. 316

Costly treasure. Alice Joyce
Davidson. 227

Cotton tails. Aileen Fisher. 244

Cottonmouth country. Louise
Gluck. 259A

Could be. Ernesto Galarza. 252

Counseling. Martha Janssen. 283

The count and the rose. Roy Marz.
312

Count to ten. Anneliese Wagner.
389

The counter-example. David
Shapiro. 363

Counting backward. Richard
Blessing. 208

Counting lessons. Rochelle
DuBois. 234

Counting the days. Gary Margolis.
311

Counting-Out Rhymes
Counting lessons. Rochelle
DuBois. 234

"One I love." Jan Ormerod. 338

Countless blessings. Alice Joyce
Davidson. 227

The country fair of childhood.
James Schevill. 360

Country girls. Rod McKuen. 316

Country Life
A hundred collars. Robert Frost.
250
In country light. Maurice Kenny.
291
Love theme from 'The mummy's
kiss meets Dracula.' Mitchell
Howard. 276

Country marriage. Carol Frost.
249

Country poem with little country.
Ernest Hemingway. 272

The couple. Margaret Key Biggs.
205

Couplet for Prus. Gene Detro. 230

Coupons. Josephine B. Moretti.
324

Courage. James R. Rhodes. 352

Courage. Martha Janssen. 283

Courage
Courage. James R. Rhodes. 352
Courage. Martha Janssen. 283
How to get back. William
Stafford. 373
"One courage is the way." Robert
A. Sears. 362

A course in creative writing.
William Stafford. 373

"The court repairs to." Madison
Morrison. 327

Courtship
Goodby madonna. Lyn Lifshin. 303
The man who brought the emerald
mandarins. Lyn Lifshin. 303
No sitting duck. Carolyn
Stoloff. 376
Not letting you see what you
don't want to. Lyn Lifshin.
303
Push pussy madonna. Lyn Lifshin.
303
The stable. Gary Margolis. 311

The courtship. Charles Edward
Eaton. 236

Cousin: snapshot 1. Robert
Peters. 343

Cousins. Robert Peters. 343

Couvet. Michael Gizzi. 259

The cove. Amy Clampitt. 222

Covenant beyond sorrow. Anneliese
Wagner. 389

Cover. Marie Daerr Boehringer.
210

Cow. Robert Peters. 343

The cow of Dogtown. Charles
    Olson. 337
The cow. Jack Prelutsky. 349
Cowardice court. Harrison Fisher.
    245
Cowboys
    Gone with the cowboys. Rod
        McKuen. 316
    The last cowboy. Stephen Knauth.
        295
Cowboys. See also Ranch Life

Cowley, Malcolm (about)
    Survivor, walking. Stephen
        Sandy. 357
Cows
    Bossie. Alice Spohn Newton. 332
    The cow. Jack Prelutsky. 349
    In place. Gary Margolis. 311
Coy glen. Mary Gilliland. 257
Coy glen again. Mary Gilliland.
    257
Coyote bone. Gene Anderson. 195
The coyote in the orchard. Harry
        Humes. 278
Coyote lovesong. Gene Anderson.
    195
Coyote song. John Reed. 350
Coyotes
    Breaking up. Gene Anderson. 195
    The coyote in the orchard. Harry
        Humes. 278
    Coyote song. John Reed. 350
Crabs and Crabbing
    Drudge crabber. Dave Smith. 367
    Ode to the horseshoe crab. Carol
        Frost. 249
    Snapshot of a crab-picker among
        barrels spilling over... Dave
        Smith. 367
    Xiphosuran. X.J. Kennedy. 290
Cradle song. Cornel Lengyel. 302
The craftsman. Ruth Lisa
        Schechter. 359
Cram session. Stephen Todd
        Booker. 212
Crane. Robert Peters. 343
Crane, Hart (about)
    1934. A sailor's letter to Hart
        Crane N. Stephen Knauth. 295
Cranes (birds)
    Crane. Robert Peters. 343
    The cranes. Phyllis A. Tickle.
        382
The cranes. Phyllis A. Tickle.
    382
Crash course. Bill Knott. 296
Crayfish. Anthony Petrosky. 344
Crazy. Martha Janssen. 283
Crazy Carlson's meadow. Robert

    Bly. 209
Crazy wife. Anthony Petrosky. 344
Creation. Alice Joyce Davidson.
    227
Creation
    Abrak. Robert Kelly. 289
    Affirmation. Alice Joyce
        Davidson. 227
    Anything. James R. Rhodes. 352
    Creation. Alice Joyce Davidson.
        227
    Generation. Josephine Miles. 319
    The museum of the second
        creation. Sandra McPherson.
        317
    None. Josephine Miles. 319
Creative writing. Robin Becker.
    202
"The creator has a master plan."
    David James. 282
Credit Cards
    Killer credit card still at
        large. David Wann. 394
The creditor. May Miller. 320
Credo. Steve Kowit. 299
A creed for a free woman. Elsa
        Gidlow. 254
Creek Indians
    New Orleans. Joy Harjo. 269
Creeks. See Brooks and Streams

Creep. Alberta Turner. 384
The creep. Steve Kowit. 299
Cremation. James A. Emanuel. 239
The creosote bush. Gene Anderson.
    195
Crescendo. C.D. Wright. 402
Crete, Nebraska
    Death in Crete. Greg Kuzma. 300
Creusa (mythology)
    Creusa, the wife. May Miller.
        320
Creusa, the wife. May Miller. 320
Crews, Judson
    Among the craggy rocks. 226
    The bones of my ribs. 226
    Brighter places. 226
    Childbirth. 226
    Climbing. 226
    The clock of moss. 226
    The day's cock of morning. 226
    Friend of forty years. 226
    God, the idiotic plaints. 226
    He was drunk. 226
    He was walking sideways. 226
    His hat was on straight. 226
    How bright the morning. 226
    How clearly we entered. 226
    How many crushed skulls. 226
    I am still as stone. 226

If I had gone quietly. 226
If I had sorted out. 226
If it is an objective. 226
If she had spoken. 226
If the beginning were clear. 226
In Texas we got persimmons. 226
It is not Golgotha. 226
It was assumed a God-head. 226
It's not that she led me on. 226
It's the sly-wolf-fart. 226
It's waking. 226
A kind of knowledge. 226
Returning to Taos. 226
She came out in black. 226
She found her heights. 226
She hated rattlers. 226
Sleeping. 226
So it happened. 226
A storm of sand. 226
Then the children came. 226
There were other places. 226
They drove them out. 226
This view of things. 226
Those spines. 226
Through all the San Joaquin
    area. 226
We ate green apples. 226
What goes on inside. 226
White water. 226
A widowhood. 226
You clasped your hands. 226
Cricket on the hearth. Sister
    Maura. 313
Crickets. Rod McKuen. 316
Crickets
    Crickets. Rod McKuen. 316
    "In these cold October woods."
    James Torio. 281
Crime and Criminals
    Birthday party. Robert Peters.
    343
    Felon. Wanda Coleman. 225
    In the booking room. David
    Wagoner. 390
    Mary Lams. Harlan Usher. 386
Crime and Criminals = Humor
    Poeme noir. Bill Knott. 296
Crime and Criminals
    Poet, seeking credentials...
    Mark Vinz. 387
    The raid. Robert Peters. 343
    Summer litany. Robert Peters.
    343
    "A tremendous night-/time
    robbery..." Madison Morrison.
    327
    Under arrest (2). Wanda Coleman.
    225
    The watchdogs. Robert Peters.
    343

Crimes. Andrei Codrescu. 223
A criminology. Jenne Andrews. 196
The cripple in the subway. Louise
    Gluck. 259A
A crippled girl's clothes. Norman
    Andrew Kirk. 293
Critic's bliss. Mitchell Howard.
    276
Criticism and Critics
    Asphalt paving contractor taking
    a dead parakeet to... James
    Magorian. 309
    Critic's bliss. Mitchell Howard.
    276
    Hate mail. Steve Kowit. 299
    Lycanthropy in South Pasadena.
    Steve Kowit. 299
    On a malicious critic. Cornel
    Lengyel. 302
    A pastoral. Norman Andrew Kirk.
    293
    Valentine. Ernest Hemingway. 272
Crocheted table cloth. James
    Magorian. 309
Crocodile. X.J. Kennedy. 290
The crocodile. Jack Prelutsky.
    349
Crocodiles
    Crocodile. X.J. Kennedy. 290
    The crocodile. Jack Prelutsky.
    349
Crocodiles don't cry. May Miller.
    320
Crocus. Greg Kuzma. 300
"'Cromlech' of course..." Charles
    Olson. 337
A crone's tale. Irving Feldman.
    242
Cross pollination. Sally Love
    Saunders. 358
Cross, The
    The garnet cross. Phillips
    Kloss. 294
    Rescuing something. Jeanne
    Lohmann. 305
Cross-country, & motif appears.
    Albert Goldbarth. 261
Crossing. Deborah Tall. 378
Crossing over. James Applewhite.
    198
Crossing the lawn. Debra Bruce.
    216
Crossing the river. Steve Kowit.
    299
Crossing the square,
    Montparnasse. James A.
    Emanuel. 239
Crow love. George Eklund. 238
The crown. Jacques Sollov. 371
Crows

Concerning Belinda. Harrison
Fisher. 245
Crow love. George Eklund. 238
Crucifixion
Calvary. Patsie Black. 206
The crucifixion. John F. Barker.
201
Domingo de Ramos. Mitchell
Howard. 276
Gabbatha. Patsie Black. 206
If I had gone quietly. Judson
Crews. 226
A night to remember. Patsie
Black. 206
Two legends: nails. Tom Smith.
368
The crucifixion. John F. Barker.
201
Cruelty
Battery. Robin Morgan. 325
"I find it hard to believe."
Madison Morrison. 327
Is true that you get born dumb
and bald. Thomas Lux. 307
Minestrone madonna. Lyn Lifsnin.
303
The probation. Roy Marz. 312
Cruelty. See also Inhumanity

Cruising. Jim Everhard. 241
The crusted earth. John F.
Barker. 201
Cry, ethnics? Rose Basile Green.
265
Cry-bones. James R. Rhodes. 352
Crying
Crocodiles don't cry. May
Miller. 320
Tears of white jade. Kirk
Lumpkin. 306
Cuchillo. Joy Harjo. 269
Cudgels
"In a magazine." Ernest
Hemingway. 272
Cuitlacoche. Clayton Eshleman.
240
Culpepper and the public health
physician. J.W. Rivers. 354
Culpepper goes bass fishing. J.W.
Rivers. 354
Culpepper is politicized. J.W.
Rivers. 354
Culpepper of the low country,
sels. J.W. Rivers. 354
Culpepper redeemed. J.W. Rivers.
354
The cup. Jacques Sollov. 371
Cure-all. Josephine B. Moretti.
324
Cures

At the counter. Josephine Miles.
319
Curing homosexuality. Jim
Everhard. 241
Curiosity
Ode to curiosity. Andrei
Codrescu. 223
A curious erotic custom. Debra
Bruce. 216
Currents. Mark Vinz. 387
Curriculum. Josephine Miles. 319
Curriculum. Bradford Morrow. 329
Curtains fall, eyes close.
Michael Robert Pick. 345
"Curtains/shades.". Larry Eigner.
237
Curtains:a pasticcio. Frances
Mayes. 314
Curvature of sound. Robert Kelly.
289
"'Cut Creek,' the river is..."
Charles Olson. 337
The cut. Charles Olson. 337
Cute. Jim Everhard. 241
Cutlery
Sharpening scissors and knives
for fun and profit. James
Magorian. 309
Cutting our losses. Steve Kowit.
298, 299
Cyanotype. Stephen Sandy. 357
Cybele: a fragment. Randy
Blasing. 207
Cyclades. Richmond Lattimore. 301
Cycle. Frances Mayes. 314
The cycle. Sam Fishman. 246
Cynicism
Apathy award. James Magorian.
308
The lesson. Cornel Lengyel. 302
New alphabet. May Miller. 320
Pediatricians firing canisters
of tear gas into a group...
James Magorian. 309
Cynthia. Maurice W. Britts. 215
Cypresses
Cybele: a fragment. Randy
Blasing. 207
Cyprus. John F. Barker. 201
Cyprus
Cyprus. John F. Barker. 201
"Cyprus/the
strangled/Aphrodite-Rhodes."
Charles Olson. 337
Cyrano de Bergerac. Ernesto
Galarza. 252

61

D'Annunzio. Ernest Hemingway. 272
D'Annunzio, Gabriele
    D'Annunzio. Ernest Hemingway.
    272
Dabble. John Godfrey. 260
Dachau. Paul Davis. 228
Dad's song. S. Bradford Williams
    (Jr.). 398
Daddyboy. Wanda Coleman. 225
Dagwood's day of wrath. Harrison
    Fisher. 245
The Dahlia Gardens. Amy Clampitt.
    222
Daisies
    Come a daisy. Jacqueline Frank.
    248
Daisies won't tell (and neither
    will I!) Josephine B. Moretti.
    324
Daisy fields, enchanted forests.
    Richmond Lattimore. 301
Dakar, Senegal
    Sandaga market women. Melvin
    Dixon. 231
The Dakota. Amy Clampitt. 222
Dalila. Jacques Sollov. 370
Dams
    Monticello. Michael Gizzi. 259
"Dan, Dan/Dirty old man." Jan
    Ormerod. 338
The dance of Theodore Roethke.
    James Schevill. 360
Dancer. Josephine Miles. 319
The dancer. Jeanne Lohmann. 305
Dancers exercising. Amy Clampitt.
    222
Dancing and Dancers
    At the park dance. W.D. (William
    De Witt) Snodgrass. 369
    The best slow dancer. David
    Wagoner. 390
    The big dance on the hill.
    Ernest Hemingway. 272
    Dancer. Josephine Miles. 319
    Dancers exercising. Amy
    Clampitt. 222
    Dancing fills us with exquisite
    emptiness. Kirk Lumpkin. 306
    The flawless dancer. Mitchell
    Howard. 276
    High school dance. Josephine B.
    Moretti. 324
    Jenny Fish. Thomas R. Sleigh.
    366
    Lines for dancers. Edwin Honig.
    275
    Lines to a young lady on her
    having very nearly won a
    vogel. Ernest Hemingway. 272
    Martinete. Carolyn Stoloff. 376

Modern dance program:American
    document. Josephine Miles. 319
The prom. Robert Peters. 343
Satiesme. Donald Revell. 351
She came out in black. Judson
    Crews. 226
Street dance. Robert Pawlowski.
    341
The Yolorai dance. Stephen
    Knauth. 295
Dancing fills us with exquisite
    emptiness. Kirk Lumpkin. 306
Dancing with the skanks. Gene
    Detro. 230
The dancing women. John Reed. 350
Danger. Martha Janssen. 283
Daniel. Robert Peters. 343
Daniel's ship. Stephen Todd
    Booker. 212
Daniel (Bible)
    Daniel. Robert Peters. 343
"Daniel Boone stepped up to a
    window." Josephine Miles. 319
Daniel in Paris. James A.
    Emanuel. 239
Daniel reviews his critics.
    Cornel Lengyel. 302
Danny. John F. Barker. 201
Danse macabre. David Wagoner. 390
Dante Alighieri
    Francesca da Rimini. Tom Smith.
    368
    Nel mezzo dell'autostrada di
    nostra vita. Mitchell Howard.
    276
Daphne (mythology)
    Laurel tree. May Miller. 320
Dark. Greg Kuzma. 300
Dark body bright. Paul Davis. 228
Dark continent. Robert A. Sears.
    362
"A dark day." Larry Eigner. 237
The dark face of love. Elsa
    Gidlow. 254
Dark latitude. Jenne Andrews. 196
A dark moor bird. James Wright.
    403
Dark seed. Maria Gillan. 256
Dark wind. William Stafford. 373
The dark. Cathryn Hankla. 268
Darkness
    I love the dark. Wanda Coleman.
    225
    "Outer darkness..." Charles
    Olson. 337
The daughter. Carol Frost. 249
Daughters and Sons
    Anchorage. Ghita Orth. 339
    Barbara. Rosa Bogar. 211
    The beautiful and lovely face.

Greg Kuzma. 300
Benediction for my daughters.
    Anneliese Wagner. 389
Brad and Tade's song. S.
    Bradford Williams (Jr.). 398
The coming. Roy Marz. 312
The cycle. Sam Fishman. 246
The daughter. Carol Frost. 249
First aid at 4 a.m. Christopher
    Bursk. 219
football game/The. Maurice W.
    Britts. 215
Heart's needle. W.D. (William De
    Witt) Snodgrass. 369
His daughter. Albert Goldbarth.
    261
"If she went down to the town."
    Robert Kelly. 289
Janet. Sam Fishman. 246
Listening to my son's heart.
    Anthony Petrosky. 344
"Little son." Michael Robert
    Pick. 345
The magic triad. Ghita Orth. 339
A momentary son. Ghita Orth. 339
Mothers and daughters. Maria
    Gillan. 256
My daughter. Maria Gillan. 256
My daughters. Evelyn Golden. 263
No timid sawyer. Harrison
    Fisher. 245
Poem for my daughters. Marieve
    Rugo. 356
Prayer to my son. Carol Frost.
    249
Roadside flowers. Christopher
    Bursk. 219
Second day song. Edwin Honig.
    275
Seconds. Louise Gluck. 259A
Son. James A. Emanuel. 239
Talismanic ceremony for Lucian,
    March 9, 1971... Andrei
    Codrescu. 223
Talking to Fernando. Irving
    Feldman. 242
To a daughter on her wedding
    day. Phyllis A. Tickle. 382
To Sylvia, grown daughter. Betty
    Adcock. 192
We are sisters. Maria Gillan.
    256
What hit me in the newspaper
    article. Laura Boss. 213
David. Roy Marz. 312
David. Josephine Miles. 319
David
    David. Josephine Miles. 319
    In the king's rooms. Timothy
        Steele. 374

Davidson, Alice Joyce
Add your love to my love. 227
Affirmation. 227
Alighting. 227
America. 227
As you think. 227
Autumn ball. 227
The beach of time. 227
Bedtime question. 227
Birthday bouquet. 227
Bright hope. 227
Cast your vote. 227
Certainties. 227
A child's meditation. 227
Compassion. 227
Costly treasure. 227
Countless blessings. 227
Creation. 227
Dawn to dusk. 227
Day of wonder, day of peace. 227
Days of love. 227
Ebb of time. 227
Entreaty. 227
Everlasting candle. 227
Family tree. 227
Fathers. 227
Fellowship. 227
Finding peace. 227
First step. 227
Flower of the field. 227
A forever friend. 227
From my heart to yours. 227
Gift list. 227
Gifts! gifts! gifts! 227
A goal. 227
God believes in You. 227
God is there with you. 227
God lives. 227
The good shepherd. 227
Grandmother's gift. 227
Grief. 227
Growing closer. 227
Growing in grace. 227
Heaven's gate. 227
Holiday prayer. 227
Hugs. 227
I am an American. 227
In plain sight. 227
Insomnia. 227
A leaf of life. 227
Legacy. 227
Let there be light! 227
Link of faith. 227
Little prayer. 227
Love glow. 227
Love power. 227
Love song. 227
Loving gentle, loving strong.
    227
Loving heart. 227

Lull-a-baby. 227
Make me a channel, Lord! 227
A merry heart. 227
Mirror. 227
Morning. 227
Mothers are love. 227
My father's home. 227
My friend. 227
New life. 227
"O give thanks." 227
One song is sung. 227
A pact. 227
Partnership. 227
Perfect love. 227
A poet's prayer. 227
Possibilities. 227
Proposal. 227
A question. 227
Quiet place. 227
Remember me? 227
Resolution. 227
Seasons of love. 227
Showers of blessings. 227
Sing, sing, sing a song. 227
Stepping-stone. 227
Sunbeam. 227
Supreme power. 227
Sweet memories. 227
Thanks giving. 227
This is the day. 227
To mother. 227
To whom our praise is due. 227
Today. 227
A touch of love. 227
Twin circles. 227
Uninvited. 227
Warm snow. 227
The ways of love. 227
Wedding prayer. 227
Well of love. 227
When you find love. 227
When you have faith. 227
Within our choosing. 227
Working for peace. 227
Davis, Paul
Among many to decide. 228
As at the cathedral, the young
  man. 228
At the church of Elijah Lovejoy.
  228
Breakthrough. 228
A bright defiance. 228
By the gate at York. 228
By Wm MacKinnon, in memory. 228
Choir birds of another time. 228
Dachau. 228
Dark body bright. 228
Deaf stones and daisies. 228
Dramas and the drama. 228
English summer. 228

Gaelic trilogy. 228
Handel and the beast. 228
Happy New Year. 228
High water mark. 228
Ice storm remembered. 228
Israel and Rome curbstoned. 228
It looks a war. 228
It was the tender way. 228
Language. 228
Mary Conway. 228
McFadden, McFadden. 228
A momentary change of weather.
  228
More sensuous than these. 228
The mourning. 228
Our names the only known. 228
Reflections at Gettysburg. 228
Right there in Rand McNally. 228
Road construction. 228
Some pure heart saying. 228
Summer marathon. 228
Survivors. 228
Sweat, and reflections at the
  symphony. 228
Thoughts at York Cathedral. 228
Thoughts during Mozart. 228
Time enough for grass. 228
Time to die or fly. 228
To focus somewhere. 228
To pulse a jubilee. 228
To settle awhile. 228
Union Square, San Francisco. 228
Walls. 228
Washington's man. 228
Whether awe or loss. 228
Wife Mary. 228
Winter combat. 228
Dawn. Andrei Codrescu. 223
Dawn. Lucien Stryk. 377
Dawn opens. Elsa Gidlow. 254
"Dawn overcomes the darkness."
  Michael Robert Pick. 345
Dawn serenade. John Reed. 350
Dawn thoughts. Maria Gillan. 256
Dawn to dusk. Alice Joyce
  Davidson. 227
"The dawn woke the hats up in
  Tuscany." Kenneth Koch. 297
Dawn, ruins on Lake Inchiquin.
  Deborah Tall. 378
Dawn. See Morning

Day. Josephine Miles. 319
Day. Wanda Coleman. 225
Day aborning. James R. Rhodes.
  352
The day after Christmas.
  Josephine B. Moretti. 324
"Day by night." Robert A. Sears.
  362

Day in February. Marie Daerr
    Boehringer. 210
A day in the life of a magpie.
    Charles Edward Eaton. 236
Day into night. Rosa Bogar. 211
Day of judgment. Deborah Tall.
    378
The day of the body, sels. Carol
    Frost. 249
Day of wonder, day of peace.
    Alice Joyce Davidson. 227
Day of wrath. Cornel Lengyel. 302
The day the sassafras shed.
    Robert L. Wilson. 401
The day the winds. Josephine
    Miles. 319
The day they came back. Marieve
    Rugo. 356
Day they say. John Godfrey. 260
A day to remember. William
    Stafford. 373
Day trip. Rod McKuen. 316
The day without the dream.
    Cathryn Hankla. 268
The day's beginnings. Charles
    Olson. 337
The day's cock of morning. Judson
    Crews. 226
Daybreak. Patsie Black. 206
Daydreaming in the Bodleian
    Library. Ray Fleming. 247
Days. Debra Bruce. 216
Days
    Love's yin-yang of days. James
        R. Rhodes. 352
    New day. William Oandasan. 335
    This is the day. Alice Joyce
        Davidson. 227
    Trilogy. Michael Akillian. 193
Days and nights. Kenneth Koch.
    297
The days are long. Rachel A.
    Hazen. 271
Days of love. Alice Joyce
    Davidson. 227
Days pass overhead like birds.
    Rod McKuen. 316
"The days the motors burn past."
    Larry Eigner. 237
Daytime nightmares, stretched
    along five blocks of 42nd St.
    Mitchell Howard. 276
Dayton: non-memories. Jim
    Everhard. 241
De chroot. Stephen Todd Booker.
    212
De profundo. John Reed. 350
De rerum natura. Andrei Codrescu.
    223
De Sica? John Godfrey. 260

Dead animals. Harry Humes. 278
The dead madonnas of Santiago.
    Jim Simmerman. 365
The dead magician. Steve Kowit.
    299
Dead Sea. Haig Khatchadourian.
    292
Dead Sea (Middle East)
    Dead Sea. Haig Khatchadourian.
        292
"The dead.". Larry Eigner. 237
The dead. Edwin Honig. 275
"Dealing out lonely games of
    solitaire." Michael Robert
    Pick. 345
Dean of brids. Erin Jolly. 285
Dean, James
    James Dean. Jim Everhard. 241
Dear Broyard whose copy clicks.
    Gene Detro. 230
"Dear Frank, here is a poem."
    Josephine Miles. 319
Dear heart. John Reed. 350
Dear mama (2). Wanda Coleman. 225
Dear Mom. Rosa Bogar. 211
Dearest Florence Maud. Gene
    Detro. 230
Deat stones and daisies. Paul
    Davis. 228
Death. Norman Andrew Kirk. 293
Death
    Acceptance. Evelyn Golden. 263
    After the dying. Ghita Orth. 339
    Always open. Ralph J., Jr.
        Mills. 321
    "And then the old woman."
        Michael Robert Pick. 345
    Annabel Lee. Edgar Allan Poe.
        347
    April parable. May Miller. 320
    Armageddon. Michael Gizzi. 259
    Augusta speaks about the first
        manifestation of the dead...
        Carolyn Stoloff. 376
    Bal des ardents. Donald Revell.
        351
    The blue, the dead one. Donald
        Revell. 351
    Burning. Robert Peters. 343
    Cable to Florence. Roy Marz. 312
    Catharsis. James R. Rhodes. 352
    Charon. James R. Rhodes. 352
    Check. Iefke Goldberger. 262
    Choosing a death. Alberta
        Turner. 384
    Codicil. Steve Kowit. 298, 299
    Cole's Island. Charles Olson.
        337
    Communion with the dead. Robert
        L. Wilson. 401

Conception. Josephine Miles. 319
Corpse and mirror (I). John Yau. 404
Corpse and mirror (II). John Yau. 404
The cost. Rod McKuen. 316
Covenant beyond sorrow. Anneliese Wagner. 389
Danse macabre. David Wagoner. 390
Dark wind. William Stafford. 373
The dead. Edwin Honig. 275
"Dealing out lonely games of solitaire." Michael Robert Pick. 345
Dear Mom. Rosa Bogar. 211
Death. Norman Andrew Kirk. 293
Death benefits. Robin Morgan. 325
"Death is the eternal mystery of life." Michael Robert Pick. 345
Death is the mother binding us to our end. Charles Olson. 337
The death of such a one. James A. Emanuel. 239
Death with its cup of hopefulness. Edwin Honig. 275
"The desperate/situation..." Madison Morrison. 327
For Dickie MacGregor. Roy Marz. 312
Die. Alberta Turner. 384
The door of question of the narrowing choice. Mitchell Howard. 276
Dying. Martha Janssen. 283
The dying man's shame. Robert Anbian. 194
Eileen. Brenda Marie Osbey. 340
Elegy. Robin Morgan. 325
Elegy. Marc Kaminsky. 288
Elegy. Haig Khatchadourian. 292
Elegy in fifths. Jim Simmerman. 365
En route. Ernesto Galarza. 252
The ending. Rachel A. Hazen. 271
Entombment. Robert L. Wilson. 401
Epitaph for the bomb. Jocelyn Hollis. 274
Extreme unction. Robert Pawlowski. 341
The fate of waking. Cathryn Hankla. 268
Feet at the end of their path. Terke Goldberger. 262
First death, 1950. Joyce Carol Oates. 336
Flash. Stephen Todd Booker. 212

"Flat sky/going down." Larry Eigner. 237
For Avraham. Susan Tichy. 381
For Bill. Ernest Tedlock. 380
For Louise. Jeanne Lohmann. 305
For one who could not stay. Everett A. Gillis. 258
Forest floor North America. Colette Inez. 280
The four o'clocks. Eve Triem. 383
Frailties. Maria Gillan. 256
Friends, farewell. William Stafford. 373
Funeral. Josephine Miles. 319
The garden. Carol Frost. 249
Genealogical chart. James Magorian. 308
Genevieve dying. Donald Revell. 351
Gloom. Sam Fishman. 246
Go ask the dead. Thomas McGrath. 315
Grief. Alice Joyce Davidson. 227
Grim, dark morning. Robert L. Wilson. 401
"Haggard, torn and beat." Michael Robert Pick. 345
"The hand still curves." Robert A. Sears. 362
"Have you ever held a man's hand." Michael Robert Pick. 345
"He died/shoveling snow." Theta Burke. 218
He's young except for death. Frances Mayes. 314
Heaven's going away party. Alice Spohn Newton. 332
Her hand. Edwin Honig. 275
Hide and seek. Jocelyn Hollis. 274
Homage. Greg Kuzma. 300
Home. Jenne Andrews. 196
"The Hook, a name of a man." Michael Robert Pick. 345
Horace - Book IV Ode 7. John Reed. 350
How many crushed skulls. Judson Crews. 226
Huck Finn at ninety, dying in a Chicago boarding house room. James Schevill. 360
I become a dream. Rachel A. Hazen. 271
I hear you cry, my friends. Michael Robert Pick. 345
"I remember times I spent." Michael Robert Pick. 345
"I seemed to die." Da Free John.

284

If she had spoken. Judson Crews. 226

If the deaths do not stop... Charles Olson. 337

In Nashville, standing in the wooden circle... Miller Williams. 399

In the Chinese death house. Carolyn Stoloff. 376

The island. Edwin Honig. 275

"It had to be, I thought at first." Robert A. Sears. 362

Karen. Anneliese Wagner. 389

The killing. Rosa Bogar. 211

Last act. Edwin Honig. 275

The last laugh. James R. Rhodes. 352

Last rites. Marc Hudson. 277

Last things. Joyce Carol Oates. 336

Last will. Steve Kowit. 298, 299

Late snow. Louise Gluck. 259A

Lazarus. Anne Bailie. 199

Lenore. Edgar Allan Poe. 347

Letters. Miller Williams. 399

Letting go. Ghita Orth. 339

Like fallen angels. Jocelyn Hollis. 274

The lives of a Bengal lancer. Harrison Fisher. 245

Love death. Tom Smith. 368

Love poem. Haig Khatchadourian. 292

Love's song. S. Bradford Williams (Jr.). 398

The magician. Eileen Silver-Lillywite. 364

Maximus, from Dogtown: 1. Charles Olson. 337

Memorabilia. Deborah Tall. 378

Minefield. James Magorian. 308

A moment of violence. Cathryn Hankla. 268

The morning after midnight. A. Dovichi. 233

Mother. Robert Peters. 343

The mourning II. Joyce Carol Oates. 336

My dead professor. Roy Marz. 312

Near the ocean, Culpepper lies in state. J.W. Rivers. 354

Not a sparrow shall fall. Phillips Kloss. 294

"Not to be listening." Edwin Honig. 275

Notes for a novel to be burned on a cold winter evening. Stephen Knauth. 295

Now, my usefulness over. Edwin Honig. 275

O part of life! Alice Spohn Newton. 333

Obituary. Ernesto Galarza. 252

Odile. Donald Revell. 351

The old man and the morning bus. Rosa Bogar. 211

The old wives. John F. Barker. 201

On a quick-change artist. Cornel Lengyel. 302

On Jan. 17th 1980 Stephen Todd Booker. 212

On seeing a flag-draped casket. Jocelyn Hollis. 274

Opening. Edwin Honig. 275

Ophelia. Marilyn Kallet. 287

Our response to death. Maurice W. Britts. 215

A paean. Edgar Allan Poe. 347

The pleasure principle. Marge Piercy. 346

Poem to a friend. Susan Stock. 375

Practicing for death. Robert L. Wilson. 401

Prediction. Josephine Miles. 319

A pretty box. Thomas Hornsby Ferril. 243

Psalm. Joyce Carol Oates. 336

Rain: the funeral: the woman's voice. Anthony Petrosky. 344

The raven. Edgar Allan Poe. 347

Recorder. Wanda Coleman. 225

Rene. Norman Andrew Kirk. 293

Requiem. Erin Jolly. 285

Requiem for a wife. James Torio. 281

The resurrection. Christopher Bursk. 219

Reviewing the possibilities. Miriam Goodman. 264

The rider. Wanda Coleman. 225

Ridgeline. Dennis Hinrichsen. 273

Rock. Susan Stock. 375

A room ready to erase its darkness. Gary Margolis. 311

Running into things. Miller Williams. 399

Sectarian murder victim. Deborah Tall. 378

A sense of completion. Evelyn Golden. 263

Sestina, fr. Friday night quartet. David Shapiro. 363

"Shadows.../doubt is a shadow." Joan Walsh Anglund. 197

She speaks at graveside. Ghita Orth. 339

The shepherd. Roy Marz. 312
The sirens. David Wann. 394
Six spoons with the initial K.
  Frances Mayes. 314
Sleep. Susan Stock. 375
Sleigh of hand. Eileen
  Silver-Lillywite. 364
Some lines finished just before
  dawn... Miller Williams. 399
Spikenard and roses. Erin Jolly.
  285
Spirits of the dead. Edgar Allan
  Poe. 347
Spring two, sels. Edwin Honig.
  275
SRO. Robert Pawlowski. 341
Stranger in the night. Robert L.
  Wilson. 401
Studying the light. Harry Humes.
  278
The sum of its parts. Miller
  Williams. 399
Sun-truths. Joyce Carol Oates.
  336
A table with people. Marc
  Kaminsky. 288
Tears so long. Rachel A. Hazen.
  271
Tending the lamp. Scott
  Chisholm. 221
The terminal patient to his
  wife. Franz Schneider. 361
Terminal sickness. Anne Bailie.
  199
"There's to be." Madison
  Morrison. 327
Third variation on Corpse and
  mirror. John Yau. 404
"This day/is almost done." A.
  Dovichi. 233
This will kill that. Gerard
  Malanga. 310
Thread. Alberta Turner. 384
"Through his entrance." Madison
  Morrison. 327
To touch a star. Alice Spohn
  Newton. 332
Tourists. Roy Marz. 312
The traveler. John Reed. 350
Trip wire. Miriam Goodman. 264
Under capricorn. Rod McKuen. 316
The varnish of their days.
  Mitchell Howard. 276
Vigil. Marieve Rugo. 356
Viris illustribus. Harrison
  Fisher. 245
"Visiting yesterday/today
  burying." Larry Eigner. 237
Waitingroom. Christopher Bursk.
  219

"We walked out of time." Edwin
  Honig. 275
What is it. Roy Marz. 312
What to say. Sharon Bryan. 217
"When I am lost I like to."
  Michael Robert Pick. 345
When you go. James R. Rhodes.
  352
A white horse. Cathryn Hankla.
  268
"Who are you sir." A. Dovichi.
  233
Who sit watch in daylight. C.D.
  Wright. 402
"Why fear death?" Joan Walsh
  Anglund. 197
Why? Sam Fishman. 246
The wind. Eileen
  Silver-Lillywite. 364
Witness. Betty Adcock. 192
"World is endlessly allowed to
  be." Da Free John. 284
Yellow newspaper and a wooden
  leg. James Tate. 379
A young woman found in the
  woods. David Wagoner. 390
Death 424. Wanda Coleman. 225
Death 577. Wanda Coleman. 225
Death = Children
  "As the light descended." Edwin
    Honig. 275
  Baby picture, circa 1932.
    Stephen Knauth. 295
  The dying child. Robert
    Pawlowski. 341
  For Robert Hollabaugh, M.D.
    Phyllis A. Tickle. 382
  For Wade. Phyllis A. Tickle. 382
  Grief. Lucien Stryk. 377
  Home burial. Robert Frost. 250
  Murder bridge. William Stafford.
    373
  1925.n. Edwin Honig. 275
  To restore a dead child, sels.
    Edwin Honig. 275
  The wake. Phyllis A. Tickle. 382
Death = Prenatal
  "I curse the dying foetus in
    your womb." Robert A. Sears.
    362
  If. Jim Simmerman. 365
  Miscarriage. Phyllis A. Tickle.
    382
  Miscarriage. Robert Peters. 343
Death benefits. Robin Morgan. 325
Death comes to my father.
  Jacqueline Frank. 248
Death in Crete. Greg Kuzma. 300
Death in Pisa. Franz Schneider.
  361

Death in winter. Carol Frost. 249
"Death is the eternal mystery of
    life." Michael Robert Pick.
    345
Death is the mother binding us to
    our end. Charles Olson. 337
Death of a Buick. Larry Moffi.
    322
Death of a cat. James Schevill.
    360
Death of a great man. Everett A.
    Gillis. 258
The death of a small beast.
    Christopher Bursk. 219
The death of a submarine. Jocelyn
    Hollis. 274
Death of a teacher. James
    Schevill. 360
The death of a word. Alice Spohn
    Newton. 333
The death of Bill Evans. Clayton
    Eshleman. 240
The death of Carl Olsen. Charles
    Olson. 337
The death of such a one. James A.
    Emanuel. 239
The death of the hired man.
    Robert Frost. 250
Death of the Hungarian hot pepper
    bush. Marge Piercy. 346
Death of the mirror: midnight,
    fr. Mirror suite. Everett A.
    Gillis. 258
Death of the old orange orchard.
    Gene Anderson. 195
The death of Whitman. Stephen
    Knauth. 295
Death wish. Mark Vinz. 387
Death with its cup of
    hopefulness. Edwin Honig. 275
A debate on posture. Marge
    Piercy. 346
Debauch of the chauvinist.
    Charles Edward Eaton. 236
Debts and Debtors
    Augusta receives a communication
      concerning a bill. Carolyn
      Stoloff. 376
    Collection agency. James
      Magorian. 308
    The parable of the two debtors.
      James Magorian. 309
Debussy, Claude
    Art and society. Kenneth Koch.
      297
Dec. 7, 1941. Josephine Miles.
    319
Decadence
    The wise man. Jacques Sollov.
      371

"Deceived by winter thaw." James
    Torio. 281
December. Franz Schneider. 361
December
    December. Franz Schneider. 361
    Four in December. Ralph J., Jr.
      Mills. 321
December 18th. Charles Olson. 337
December 23nd. Charles Olson. 337
December 31, 1979. Marge Piercy.
    346
December field. Deborah Tall. 378
December, 1960. Charles Olson.
    337
Deception. Barry Wallenstein. 393
Deception
    The last man in all
      Pennsylvania. Larry Moffi. 322
Deception pass, fr. Salt Air.
    Sharon Bryan. 217
Decision. Marie Daerr Boehringer.
    210
Decision. Martha Janssen. 283
The deck that Oouts. Marge
    Piercy. 346
Declension. Stephen Sandy. 357
The decline of the wasp? Rose
    Basile Green. 265
Deconstruction in San Diego. Ray
    Fleming. 247
Decoration Day. Alice Spohn
    Newton. 333
Decoration Day. See Memorial Day
    . .
Dedicated to F.W. Ernest
    Hemingway. 272
Dedication. Harlan Usher. 386
A dedication to Max Eastman. John
    Reed. 350
Deed. Josephine Miles. 319
"Deep currents foam on the
    surface." Michael Robert Pick.
    345
Deep rivers. C.D. Wright. 402
The deep shade. Robert Pawlowski.
    341
Deep-water song. John Reed. 350
"Deepest thoughts we spoke in
    silence." Robert A. Sears. 362
Deer
    A boy, a dog, a deer. Robert A.
      Sears. 362
    The doe. Marge Piercy. 346
    Hope, Arkansas. Phyllis A.
      Tickle. 382
    "There was this deer standing."
      Rochelle DuBois. 234
    Three apparitions. Carol Frost.
      249
    Waiting for the warden. Stephen

Sandy. 357

Deerskin flowage. Robert Peters. 343

Defense of Luxembourg. Ernest Hemingway. 272

Defenses. Susan Ticny. 381

Deference
"I don't expect." Madison Morrison. 327

Define a satellite. Albert Goldbarth. 261

Definition. Josephine Miles. 319

Defoliage - agent orange. Jocelyn Hollis. 274

Deirdre of the sorrows. Deborah Tall. 378

Deja vu. Anne Bailie. 199

Deja vu. Mark Vinz. 387

Delay. Josephine Miles. 319

The delicacy. Sandra McPherson. 317

Delirium in a small room. Jacqueline Frank. 248

Deliverance. Patsie Black. 206

Deliverances. Ghita Orth. 339

Delivery. Toi Derricote. 229

Delivery guaranteed. Marie Daerr Boehringer. 210

Delp, Alfred
Last letter of a condemned priest. Franz Schneider. 361

Delphi. Carolyn Stoloff. 376

Delphi, Greece
Delphi. Carolyn Stoloff. 376

Delusions of grandeur. Jim Simmerman. 365

Demeter (goddess)
The rage of Demeter. Richmond Lattimore. 301

The demon of Elloree. Larry Moffi. 322

Denial. Josephine Miles. 319

The dental assistant. Iefke Goldberger. 262

Dentists
The dental assistant. Iefke Goldberger. 262
Drill skill. Josephine B. Moretti. 324

Departures
Fresco:departure for an imperialist war. Thomas McGrath. 315
What I need to hear. Jeanne Lohmann. 305

The depressed woman. Rochelle DuBois. 234

Depressionism. Bill Knott. 296

Depth perception. Robin Morgan. 325

Derelicts
Shopping bag lady. Wanda Coleman. 225

Derricote, Toi
Delivery. 229
Holy Cross Hospital. 229
In knowledge of young boys. 229
Leaving. 229
Maternity. 229
November. 229
The presentation. 229
10:29.t. 229
Transition. 229
The visiting hour. 229

"Descartes soldier/in a time of religious." Charles Olson. 337

Descendant. Rose Basile Green. 265

Desdemona's throat. Sharon Bryan. 217

Desensitized. Robert L. Wilson. 401

Desert epilog. Thomas Hornsby Ferril. 243

Desert mystery. Phillips Kloss. 294

Desert rose. Gene Anderson. 195

The desert. John Reed. 350

Deserts
Bush. Phillips Kloss. 294
Desert epilog. Thomas Hornsby Ferril. 243
Desert mystery. Phillips Kloss. 294
The desert. John Reed. 350
Homes??!! Norman Andrew Kirk. 293
Living color. Phillips Kloss. 294
The ocean floor as it would look without water, fr. Salt Air. Sharon Bryan. 217

Desideratum. Patsie Black. 206

A design of choice. Maurice W. Britts. 215

Designs. Andrei Codrescu. 223

Desire. George Eklund. 238

Desire
"Bottled up for days..." Charles Olson. 337
De Sica? John Godfrey. 260
Desire. George Eklund. 238
Dreaming of her. Elsa Gidlow. 254
Early December in Croton-on-Hudson. Louise Gluck. 259A
Esterhazy and the cat woman. J.W. Rivers. 354
Esterhazy and the swimmer. J.W.

Rivers. 354
Francoise and the fruit farmer.
    James A. Emanuel. 239
"Just to have her body in my
    mind..." Charles Olson. 337
Looking at posters. Joan Colby.
    224
Memory of the present. David
    Shapiro. 363
Ornaments. Anthony Petrosky. 344
A perfect skyline. Donald
    Revell. 351
Sealed with promise? Rochelle
    DuBois. 234
Sex. Rochelle DuBois. 234
Sleeping. Judson Crews. 226
Sonnet upon three kings' day.
    Mitchell Howard. 276
The stone of all souls. Mitchell
    Howard. 276
Stopped for a beer in
    Charleston, West Virginia.
    George Eklund. 238
A swell idea. Steve Kowit. 299
The telesphere. Charles Olson.
    337
Through all the San Joaquin
    area. Judson Crews. 226
To the unknown goddess. Elsa
    Gidlow. 254
Wonderful moments. Jacques
    Sollov. 370
"Desire and curiosity." Kenneth
    Koch. 297
Desire in Manitoba. Rodney
    Nelson. 331
Desks
    Portrait. Rod McKuen. 316
Despair. Maurice W. Britts. 215
Despair
    Boss of darkness. C.D. Wright.
        402
    The circuit of despair. James A.
        Emanuel. 239
    Coyote bone. Gene Anderson. 195
    Deirdre of the sorrows. Deborah
        Tall. 378
    Desert rose. Gene Anderson. 195
    Empty is. Rod McKuen. 316
    "The eyes/act as dams." A.
        Dovichi. 233
    Futility. Rachel A. Hazen. 271
    Head in hands. Josephine Miles.
        319
    Hope no more. Robert L. Wilson.
        401
    I cannot stay. Rachel A. Hazen.
        271
    Jordan River. Gene Anderson. 195
    The last of the wine. Rod

McKuen. 316
    Lone girl at the bus stop. Susan
        Stock. 375
    Man of courage. Josephine Miles.
        319
    Never. Elsa Gidlow. 254
    Not waving but drowning. Laura
        Boss. 213
    "Raging lonely wave." Michael
        Robert Pick. 345
    River side. John Reed. 350
    Sadness unhinged. Andrei
        Codrescu. 223
    The secret. Jacqueline Frank.
        248
    Sleeve. Josephine Miles. 319
    "Those times when I can feel no
        hope." Theta Burke. 218
    Trapped. Rachel A. Hazen. 271
    Tuneless wand'rings. Rachel A.
        Hazen. 271
    Turning. Marilyn Kallet. 287
    Year of the dog. Gene Anderson.
        195
Desperate solutions. Steve Kowit.
    299
"The desperate/situation...".
    Madison Morrison. 327
Despite astronomical arguments.
    Marilyn Kallet. 287
Destiny
    Celestial destiny. Jacques
        Sollov. 371
    De profundo. John Reed. 350
    Fate. Connie Hunt. 279
    The raven. Edgar Allan Poe. 347
    Whatever our final fate.
        Phillips Kloss. 294
Detecting love. Joan Colby. 224
Detective Shoes. James Tate. 379
Detective story. Robert Kelly.
    289
Detour. Jacqueline Frank. 248
Detro, Gene
    Caddy and Annie and these and
        thee. 230
    Couplet for Prus. 230
    Dancing with the skanks. 230
    Dear Broyard whose copy clicks.
        230
    Dearest Florence Maud. 230
    Discovery under Lenten
        waterstorm. 230
    Franny Glass at forty-seven. 230
    Had been a slow note to Stella
        Grace. 230
    Hot mountain poem. 230
    'Jobs on film'- one more service
        from the hall of records. 230
    Lubbock tune. 230

Mermaid alley: after rain. 230
Nuke burns. 230
Radio man. 230
Writ on the back of an airline part bag. 230
Detroit, Michigan
The good part. Greg Kuzma. 300
Devil. See Satan

The **devil**. Alberta Turner. 384
Devotion. Gerard Malanga. 310
Devotion
Devotion's song. S. Bradford Williams (Jr.). 398
Fanatic. Josephine Miles. 319
Devotion's song. S. Bradford Williams (Jr.). 398
Dewato. Marc Hudson. 277
"The **diadem** of the dog." Charles Olson. 337
Diagnosis...with complications. Wanda Coleman. 225
Diagnostician. Joan Colby. 224
Diagrams. Albert Goldbarth. 261
Dialectic. Josephine Miles. 319
Dialogue. Josephine Miles. 319
Dialogue. Robert Peters. 343
C...:Dialogue among rumbled sheets. Elsa Gidlow. 254
Dialogue at midnight: Elizabeth to John. Sister Maura. 313
Dialogue in the sleeping house. Edwin Honig. 275
Dialogues: Johann Joachim Winckelmann and Joseph Busch. Albert Goldbarth. 261
The **diamond** in shadow. James Applewhite. 198
Diamonion taxi driver. Clayton Eshleman. 240
Diana (goddess)
Entering the temple in Nimes. James Wright. 403
Leaving the temple in Nimes. James Wright. 403
The **diapason**. Charles Edward Eaton. 236
Diary aus Deutschland. Marie Daerr Boehringer. 210
The **diary** is open at two o'clock. Kenneth Koch. 297
Diary May 15, 1980 - twin cities. Sandra McPherson. 317
Diatribe. Erin Jolly. 285
A **diatribe** to Dr. Steele. Charles Gullans. 267
Dichotomy. James R. Rhodes. 352
For Dickie MacGregor. Roy Marz. 312
Dickinson, Emily (about)

Emily Dickinson. James Schevill. 360
Perhapps, Emily. Ruth Lisa Schechter. 359
Dictatorship of myself. Mitchell Howard. 276
Did ye know? Lake Hamilton, day after Easter. Cynthia Grenfell. 266
"**Diddle**, diddle, dumpling." Jan Ormerod. 338
Die. Alberta Turner. 384
Die awake. Rachel A. Hazen. 271
Dieter's due. Marie Daerr Boehringer. 210
Diets and Dieting
Adding padding. Josephine B. Moretti. 324
Dieter's due. Marie Daerr Boehringer. 210
On metal corsets. Marge Piercy. 346
On wishing to avoid the bill. Miriam Goodman. 264
Short commons. Alberta Turner. 384
The **difference**. Rachel A. Hazen. 271
The **differences**. Andrei Codrescu. 223
A **difficult** demand. Carolyn Stoloff. 376
Digger. Jim Simmerman. 365
Digging and Diggers
Digging stick. Phillips Kloss. 294
Press. Alberta Turner. 384
"**Digging** deeps my destiny." Michael Robert Pick. 345
Digging in. Marge Piercy. 346
Digging stick. Phillips Kloss. 294
Dillinger in Wisconsin. Robert Peters. 343
Dillinger, John
Cow. Robert Peters. 343
Dillinger in Wisconsin. Robert Peters. 343
Night visitor. Robert Peters. 343
Now. Robert Peters. 343
Radio report. Robert Peters. 343
Snow image. Robert Peters. 343
Song ("He has gunpowder on his breath.") Robert Peters. 343
Waiting. Robert Peters. 343
What John Dillinger meant to me. Robert Peters. 343
Dingo. X.J. Kennedy. 290
The **dining** room. Charles Edward

Eaton. 236
Dinner at Mary's. Roy Marz. 312
Dinner bell. Josephine Miles. 319
Dinner invitation from a tribe of
cannibals. James Magorian. 308
Dinner party. Jeanne Lohmann. 305
Dinner time. Carolyn Stoloff. 376
Dinner with a friend. Wanda
Coleman. 225
Dip trip. Marie Daerr Boehringer.
210
Diplomatic relations with
America. Ray Fleming. 247
The **direction** of the fence. David
James. 282
Directive. Robert Frost. 250
The **directors**. Josephine Miles.
319
Dirge. Lucien Stryk. 377
Dirty old man. James A. Emanuel.
239
"**Dirty** sheet." Michael Robert
Pick. 345
Dis-ease. Marge Piercy. 346
Disadvantages. Richmond
Lattimore. 301
Disarmed. Josephine Miles. 319
The **disaster** plan. Joan Colby.
224
Disasters
Three stages. Josephine Miles.
319
"What do you think caused the
disaster here." Josephine
Miles. 319
The **discarded**. Marge Piercy. 346
Discernment. Jeanne Lohmann. 305
The **disciple**. Roy Marz. 312
Discipline
Tears. Martha Janssen. 283
Disconnected. Ruth Lisa
Schechter. 359
Discount shopping. Mark Vinz. 387
Discoursing kisses. Mitchell
Howard. 276
Discoveries mid-letter. Sandra
McPherson. 317
Discovering it is too late.
Robert L. Wilson. 401
Discovery under Lenten
waterstorm. Gene Detro. 230
Discussing apples. Elsa Gidlow.
254
Disguises
"To get out of here." Madison
Morrison. 327
Disney. Debra Bruce. 216
Disney Boheme. Kenneth Koch. 297
Disparities. Joan Colby. 224
Displaced persons. Marieve Rugo.

356
The **dispute** over bodies in water.
Cathryn Hankla. 268
The **disrobing**. Royal Murdoch. 330
Dissipation. Norman Andrew Kirk.
293
The **dissolving** coin trick step 25
James Magorian. 309
Distance. Jim Everhard. 241
Distance
Aesthetic distance. Miller
Williams. 399
Distances. Albert Goldbarth. 261
Extension. Josephine Miles. 319
Distances. Albert Goldbarth. 261
"The **distances**.". Charles Olson.
337
Distant sky and sea. Evelyn
Golden. 263
Distant weather. Mitchell Howard.
276
Distorted views. Rochelle DuBois.
234
The **disturbance**. Marge Piercy.
346
The **disturbed**. Josephine Miles.
319
Ditty to his love. Edwin Honig.
275
The **divine** right of kings. Edgar
Allan Poe. 347
Diving and Divers
The catch. Tefke Goldberger. 262
Fantasy after a science report.
Jeanne Lohmann. 305
The jumper. Michael Akillian.
193
Divorce. Joan Colby. 224
Divorce. Evelyn Golden. 263
Divorce. Marge Piercy. 346
Divorce
After the separation papers had
been signed. Laura Boss. 213
After the separation. Edwin
Honig. 275
Brief. Debra Bruce. 216
A broken house. Marc Kaminsky.
288
China and silver. Miriam
Goodman. 264
Divorce. Joan Colby. 224
Divorce. Evelyn Golden. 263
"A divorce is a man." Madison
Morrison. 327
"Divorce." Madison Morrison. 327
A Doll's House revisited. Laura
Boss. 213
Dream caught in a train. Marieve
Rugo. 356
The house. Edwin Honig. 275

"I was/a product of divorce."
    Michael Robert Pick. 345
Inventory. Jacqueline Frank. 248
Last supper. Joan Colby. 224
Matrimony. Robert Pawlowski. 341
Monster talk. Edwin Honig. 275
Mrs. Frankenstein. Marge Piercy.
    346
My analyst told me. Laura Boss.
    213
Pain. Evelyn Golden. 263
Poem for an ex-husband. Rochelle
    DuBois. 234
Separated. Laura Boss. 213
Simplicity. John F. Barker. 201
Strange vision after divorce.
    Gene Anderson. 195
A visit from the ex. Marge
    Piercy. 346
"A divorce is a man." Madison
    Morrison. 327
"Divorce.". Madison Morrison. 327
Divorced men. Debra Bruce. 216
Divorced women. Debra Bruce. 216
Dixon, Melvin
    Angels of ascent. 231
    Bobo Baoule. 231
    Change of territory. 231
    Climbing Montmartre. 231
    Fingering the jagged grains. 231
    Getting directions. 231
    Going to Africa. 231
    Grandmother. 231
    Harlem footage. 231
    Hemispheres. 231
    Hungry travel. 231
    Kin of crossroads. 231
    Richard, Richard: American fuel.
        231
    Richard, Richard: an American
        hunger. 231
    Richmond Barthe: meeting in
        Lyon. 231
    Sandaga market women. 231
    Sightseeing. 231
    Tour guide: La Maison des
        Esclaves. 231
    Voodoo mambo: to the tourists.
        231
    Zora Neale Hurston. 231
"Do not ask/... but listen." Joan
    Walsh Anglund. 197
"Do not desire the way/for the
    way/is yours." Joan Walsh
    Anglund. 197
"Do queens have." Madison
    Morrison. 327
Do rabbits have Christmas? Aileen
    Fisher. 244
'Do you love me?' Edwin Honig.
    275
Doctor. Robert Peters. 343
Doctor Dionysus. Charles Edward
    Eaton. 236
A doctor of the soul. Iefke
    Goldberger. 262
"The doctor who sits at the
    bedside of a rat." Josephine
    Miles. 319
The doctor's quarantine. Gary
    Margolis. 311
Doctor's report. Wanda Coleman.
    225
Documentary. Robin Morgan. 325
Documentary. Robin Becker. 202
Documenting it. Miller Williams.
    399
Dodge, Mary Mapes
    Mary Anne. 232
The doe. Marge Piercy. 346
"Does the world look like a park
    to you?Yes,almost..."
    Josephine Miles. 319
Dogs
    Back country. Joyce Carol Oates.
        336
    "The diadem of the dog." Charles
        Olson. 337
    Dingo. X.J. Kennedy. 290
    Dogs in weather. Ernest Tedlock.
        380
    Dogs of the city. Ernest
        Tedlock. 380
    "Eventually I pass the." Madison
        Morrison. 327
    Golden retriever. David Wagoner.
        390
    "Here's a beastly/fable."
        Madison Morrison. 327
    How it all began. William
        Stafford. 373
    "How to train a dog." Michael
        Robert Pick. 345
    I made my dog a valentine. Jack
        Prelutsky. 348
    "If they're not chained."
        Madison Morrison. 327
    Ishtar, the monastery dog.
        Sister Maura. 313
    Just an old tease. Alice Spohn
        Newton. 332
    La Resolana. Steve Kowit. 298,
        299
    Mad dogs in August. Norman
        Andrew Kirk. 293
    Marijuana ha-ha: a real smart
        dog. James A. Emanuel. 239
    Mealtime moocher. Marie Daerr
        Boehringer. 210
    "My dog and I yesterday." Sally

Love Saunders. 358
"My dog sparkles." Sally Love
  Saunders. 358
My dogs. Jacques Sollov. 370
The new dog:variations on a text
  by Jules Laforgue. Carol
  Frost. 249
"Oliver, our dog, went around
  squirting." Michael Robert
  Pick. 345
Only once. Sandra McPherson. 317
"Out saunter the doggies."
  Madison Morrison. 327
A pair of intuitive dogs.
  Stephen Todd Booker. 212
Police. Greg Kuzma. 300
A question. Alice Joyce
  Davidson. 227
Requiem for a golden retriever.
  Ruth Lisa Schechter. 359
Satisfied. Stephen Todd Booker.
  212
Strange move. Alice Spohn
  Newton. 333
Sue Hilton's dog. Josephine B.
  Moretti. 324
Training the dog to come. Robin
  Becker. 202
The vigil. James Torio. 281
Visionary adventures of a wild
  dog pack. Joyce Carol Oates.
  336
"Words penetrate a poem."
  Kenneth Koch. 297
Dogs in weather. Ernest Tedlock.
  380
Dogs of the city. Ernest Tedlock.
  380
"Dogtown the dog town." Charles
  Olson. 337
Dogtown-Ann. Charles Olson. 337
Doing without. Mitchell Howard.
  276
Doll. Josephine Miles. 319
A Doll's House revisited. Laura
  Boss. 213
Dolls
  Beatrice. Alice Spohn Newton.
    333
  Doll. Josephine Miles. 319
  Mary Anne. Mary Mapes Dodge. 232
  "Miss Polly had a dolly who was
    sick, sick, sick." Jan
    Ormerod. 338
Dolor. Josephine Miles. 319
Domestic miracles. Joyce Carol
  Oates. 336
Domingo de Ramos. Mitchell
  Howard. 276
Don Juan in autumn. Charles

Edward Eaton. 236
Don't ever seize a weasel by the
  tail. Jack Prelutsky. 349
Don't go near the water...
  Josephine B. Moretti. 324
Don't let the dreams die out, my
  friend. Robert L. Wilson. 401
Don't look back. Jim Everhard.
  241
Don't talk, sing! Alice Spohn
  Newton. 332
Don't wait for me. Andrei
  Codrescu. 223
"Don't worry, woman." Michael
  Robert Pick. 345
Donald Duck
  Apparition of the duck. Clayton
    Eshleman. 240
"The door is closed." Madison
  Morrison. 327
The door of question of the
  narrowing choice. Mitchell
  Howard. 276
Door song. Colette Inez. 280
The door: four sonnets for
  married lovers. Everett A.
  Gillis. 258
The door. May Miller. 320
Doors. Robert Kelly. 289
Doors
  Door song. Colette Inez. 280
  Doors. Robert Kelly. 289
Doors and keys. Carolyn Stoloff.
  376
The doorway. Mitchell Howard. 276
Doper's song at Little Ah Sid's.
  Thomas McGrath. 315
The double cherry. Jim Simmerman.
  365
Double exposure. Marieve Rugo.
  356
Double sonnet. John Godfrey. 260
Double trouble. Marie Daerr
  Boehringer. 210
Dove tailed madonna. Lyn Lifshin.
  303
Dover, England
  Approaching Dover. May Miller.
    320
Dovichi, A.
  "All of the joy." 233
  "Alone now/together." 233
  "And/so it ends/quickly." 233
  "And/with the passing/of time."
    233
  "Are you/from this earth?" 233
  "The eyes/act as dams." 233
  "Hope/comes to all." 233
  "How/could the cost." 233
  "I am lost/in the graveyard."

233
"I am man." 233
"I apologize." 233
"I was man." 233
"I would have/om another day." 233
"If it were/that I." 233
Introduction. 233
"Is it possible/that man." 233
"It is difficult/for me." 233
"Let me tread/softly." 233
"Look at him." 233
A lull in battle. 233
Man. 233
The morning after midnight. 233
"Not even/the width of oceans." 233
"Our/sense of values." 233
"Perhaps,/upon another day." 233
The refugees. 233
The soldier. 233
"There was another world." 233
"This day/is almost done." 233
"We/are being devoured." 233
"Who are you sir." 233
"The worlds/likes and dislikes." 233
Down at the bottom of things. Marge Piercy. 346
Down at the plant. David Wann. 394
"Down from another planet they have settled to mend." Josephine Miles. 319
"Down on the bed you." Larry Eigner. 237
Down riverside with Ulysses. Thomas Hornsby Ferril. 243
"Down the rump and out." Madison Morrison. 327
Down under. Rod McKuen. 316
Dr. Martin's day off. Debra Bruce. 216
Dracula
    Legends. Keith Wilson. 400
    The undead. Keith Wilson. 400
Dracula, Blacula. Josephine B. Moretti. 324
Dragons. James Torio. 281
The dragons of Machinato. Stephen Todd Booker. 212
Drama
    Curtains fall, eyes close. Michael Robert Pick. 345
    A drama of significant events. Robert Pawlowski. 341
A drama of significant events. Robert Pawlowski. 341
Dramas and the drama. Paul Davis. 228

Dramas of the rose. James Schevill. 360
"Drawers open and winter escapes." Carolyn Stoloff. 376
Drawings
    To make perspective. May Miller. 320
"Drawn aside." Madison Morrison. 327
Dream. Josephine Miles. 319
Dream. Andrei Codrescu. 223
Dream. Greg Kuzma. 300
Dream 13. Wanda Coleman. 225
The dream and the reality. Maurice W. Britts. 215
Dream caught in a train. Marieve Rugo. 356
Dream dogs. Andrei Codrescu. 223
A dream from Hokusai. Charles Edward Eaton. 236
Dream house. Mark Vinz. 387
Dream I am St. Augustine. Susan Tichy. 381
The dream life of a coffin factory in Lynn, Massachusetts. John Yau. 404
A dream of fair women. Harrison Fisher. 245
Dream of fireworks on Fire Island. Ruth Lisa Schechter. 359
A dream of fish. Mark Vinz. 387
A dream of heaven. Deborah Tall. 378
The dream of life. Maurice W. Britts. 215
The dream of returning to school and facing the oral exam. James Tate. 379
A dream of salt. Jenne Andrews. 196
A dream of small children. Cathy Song. 372
A dream of snow. Mark Vinz. 387
The dream of the guilt bird, or water. Lyn Lifshin. 303
Dream of the long distance swimmer. Ruth Lisa Schechter. 359
Dream-land. Edgar Allan Poe. 347
A dream of spring horses. Harry Humes. 278
Dream on. Connie Hunt. 279
A dream within a dream. Edgar Allan Poe. 347
A dream. Edgar Allan Poe. 347
A dream. Martha Janssen. 283
The dream. Keith Wilson. 400
The dreamer's regiment. Ruth Lisa Schechter. 359

Dreaming. Robin Becker. 202
Dreaming. Eileen
        Silver-Lillywite. 364
Dreaming America. Joyce Carol
        Oates. 336
Dreaming of her. Elsa Gidlow. 254
Dreams. Maurice W. Britts. 215
Dreams. Edgar Allan Poe. 347
Dreams
     The Bowery of dreams. Clayton
        Eshleman. 240
     The burning child. Amy Clampitt.
        222
     Castle keep. Rod McKuen. 316
     The color rake of time. Clayton
        Eshleman. 240
     Dream. Josephine Miles. 319
     Dream. Greg Kuzma. 300
     Dream 13. Wanda Coleman. 225
     The dream of life. Maurice W.
        Britts. 215
     A dream of snow. Mark Vinz. 387
     Dream on. Connie Hunt. 279
     A dream within a dream. Edgar
        Allan Poe. 347
     A dream. Edgar Allan Poe. 347
     A dream. Martha Janssen. 283
     Dreaming. Robin Becker. 202
     Dreaming. Eileen
        Silver-Lillywite. 364
     Dreams. Maurice W. Britts. 215
     Dreams. Edgar Allan Poe. 347
     The guilt formula. Joan Colby.
        224
     Her dream and the awakening.
        David Wagoner. 390
     His dream. David Wagoner. 390
     His dream. Edwin Honig. 275
     Hole in the stream's ice. Harry
        Humes. 278
     How the sky begins to fall. Joan
        Colby. 224
     Images of recall. May Miller.
        320
     In a country of lost bearings.
        Colette Inez. 280
     In a dream. Elsa Gidlow. 254
     In dreams, a violinist. Jenne
        Andrews. 196
     In the illustration of a dream.
        Ruth Lisa Schechter. 359
     Innocence returned. Rokwaho. 355
     Insomniac. Mark Vinz. 387
     Lace covered memories. Rachel A.
        Hazen. 271
     The late-night realities. Rachel
        A. Hazen. 271
     Naked oddments of the night.
        Marieve Rugo. 356
     Night stalker. James Torio. 281

     Nightmares. Martha Janssen. 283
     9 P.M.N. Rochelle DuBois. 234
     101 dreams of briar rose>The O.
        Tom Smith. 368
     Pay me. Norman Andrew Kirk. 293
     The sacred shore. Greg Kuzma.
        300
     Saturday. Lyn Lifshin. 303
     Scattered dreams. Rosa Bogar.
        211
     September night. Franz
        Schneider. 361
     Sleeping in the loft of dreams.
        Cathryn Hankla. 268
     Soldier home. Roy Marz. 312
     A Spanish painting. David
        Shapiro. 363
     That idea of visiting places in
        dreams. Cathryn Hankla. 268
     "Things more or less" Larry
        Eigner. 237
     This dream. Marilyn Kallet. 287
     Tomorrow. James R. Rhodes. 352
     Two kinds of song. John Yau. 404
     The unbeliever dreams. George
        Eklund. 238
     Unsafe. Tefke Goldberger. 262
     Waking in Jordan. Larry Moffi.
        322
Dreams are not in season. Robert
        Pawlowski. 341
Dreams of a man without children.
        Susan Tichy. 381
The dreams of wild horses. Thomas
        McGrath. 315
Dress dilemma. Josephine B.
        Moretti. 324
Dressed to the last. Barry
        Wallenstein. 393
The dried sturgeon. Robert Bly.
        209
Drift. Alberta Turner. 384
Drift. C.D. Wright. 402
Driftwood moments. Maria Gillan.
        256
"Driftwood/the sands." Larry
        Eigner. 237
Drill skill. Josephine B.
        Moretti. 324
Drinks and Drinking
     Above a dry pool. Larry Moffi.
        322
     "Arrested on drunk driving."
        Michael Robert Pick. 345
     Breath test. David Wagoner. 390
     Chinese doll. Wanda Coleman. 225
     Documenting it. Miller Williams.
        399
     Drunkard. William Oandasan. 335
     "Fill with mingled cream and

amber." Edgar Allan Poe. 347
The Friday before the long
    weekend. Joy Harjo. 269
Halfway into a fifth of Irish
    whiskey he sings of the...
    Robert Gibb. 253
Home brew. Josephine B. Moretti.
    324
Mezcal. Robert Gibb. 253
Mixed drinks. Charles Edward
    Eaton. 236
Muscatel. Greg Kuzma. 300
Nautilaus. Joy Harjo. 269
Over drinks. Randy Blasing. 207
The rules. David Wagoner. 390
"Something that I." Madison
    Morrison. 327
Splurge. Paul Violi. 388
The three pilgrims. Roy Marz.
    312
"Twenty days of leave." Michael
    Robert Pick. 345
View of the corporation lady in
    bughouse square, Chicago.
    James Schevill. 360
Drinks and Drinking. See also
    Bars

A **drip** poem for Jackson Pollock.
    James Schevill. 360
Drive-in theatre. James Magorian.
    309
The **drive.** Miriam Goodman. 264
The **drive.** Marilyn Kallet. 287
Driver. Robert Pawlowski. 341
Driver saying. Josephine Miles.
    319
"**Driving** along in my car." Sally
    Love Saunders. 358
Driving her back to Wisconsin.
    George Eklund. 238
Driving the Green Mountains.
    Dennis Hinrichsen. 273
Driving to the 10Am PCC reading.
    Laura Boss. 213
A **dromedary** standing still. Jack
    Prelutsky. 349
Drop-out. James R. Rhodes. 352
Drought
    Dry July. Marge Piercy. 346
    In a drought year. Mark Vinz.
    387
The **drought.** Evelyn Golden. 263
The **drought.** Eileen
    Silver-Lillywite. 364
Drowing horses. Joy Harjo. 269
The **drowned** man. Irving Feldman.
    242
Drowning. Eileen
    Silver-Lillywite. 364

Drowning
    Alberta Abrams fishes for
    mullet. J.W. Rivers. 354
    Family. Josephine Miles. 319
    Lifesaving. David Wagoner. 390
    Second letter on Georges'
    Charles Olson. 337
    Wind is my friend. Tefke
    Goldberger. 262
Drowning another peasant
    inquisition. Andrei Codrescu.
    223
Drudge crabber. Dave Smith. 367
Drug Addiction
    The California crack. Wanda
    Coleman. 225
    Doper's song at Little Ah Sid's.
    Thomas McGrath. 315
    "I am approached." Madison
    Morrison. 327
    Junk. Wanda Coleman. 225
    The lady with bougainvillea in
    her eyes. Wanda Coleman. 225
    Manifesto. Andrei Codrescu. 223
    Opium for Britt Wilkie. Andrei
    Codrescu. 223
    Parked. Wanda Coleman. 225
    Stephen's monkey. Wanda Coleman.
    225
    Television story. Wanda Coleman.
    225
    Wards Island. Ruth Lisa
    Schechter. 359
    The wound. Louise Gluck. 259A
Drugstores
    Corner drugstore, fr. Nostalgia
    poems. Robert A. Sears. 362
Drums and believers. Andrei
    Codrescu. 223
Drunkard. William Oandasan. 335
Dry ice. Dave Smith. 367
Dry July. Marge Piercy. 346
Dry pump. Sally Love Saunders.
    358
Dry spells. Paul Violi. 388
Dublin, Ireland
    River gods, Dublin. Ghita Orth.
    339
DuBois, Rochelle
    Anxiety. 234
    Art. 234
    The astrological houses. 234
    Beyond time, sels. 234
    Call it hope. 234
    Clockwatcher series, sels. 234
    'The color of evening.' 234
    Counting lessons. 234
    The depressed woman. 234
    Distorted views. 234
    Easter moonrise. 234

8 A.M.   234
8 P.M.   234
Elastic romance. 234
11:15 P.M   234
The elusive rose. 234
Escape. 234
Escape to a friend. 234
Explaining the rainbow. 234
Fairfield Harbor at New Bern,
   N.S. August 22, 1982. 234
Family. 234
Fear. 234
Feminist writers. 234
5 P.M.   234
For shells. 234
For the jazzman. 234
Fossils in the sand. 234
4 A.M.   234
4 P.M.   234
The geisha. 234
Good morning, day. 234
Guilt. 234
Hourglass conflicts, sels. 234
"It's that one understood
   barely." 234
"Learning widsom." 234
"Living by fiction." 234
Love. 234
Man. 234
Memory of another time. 234
Money. 234
9 A.M.   234
9 P.M.   234
Noon. 234
Old fashioned & timeworn. 234
Poem for an ex-husband. 234
Prayer No. 2. 234
The pulse of the zodiac puzzle.
   234
Reality. 234
The robot lover. 234
Sealed with promise? 234
September rain. 234
7 P.M.   234
Sex. 234
Snapshots of love. 234
Summertree sketch. 234
10 A.M.   234
"There was this deer standing."
   234
The throwaway woman. 234
A timebomb inside. 234
Timelapse. 234
Timeshare anyone? 234
Trust. 234
12 midnight.   234
2 P.M.   234
Vocation. 234
Duck blind. Charles Edward Eaton.
   236

The duck watcher. James Schevill.
   360
Ducking: after Maupassant. Dave
   Smith. 367
Ducks
   Duck blind. Charles Edward
      Eaton. 236
   The duck watcher. James
      Schevill. 360
   Epithalamion: the ducks at Lake
      Lotawana. Jim Simmerman. 365
   Love belongs to the north.
      Thomas McGrath. 315
   My happy ducks. Alice Spohn
      Newton. 332
Duels and Dueling
   Limitation. Marilyn Kallet. 287
Duet. Patsie Black. 206
Duluth, Minnesota
   Parallax. Mitchell Howard. 276
Dumb love. James Schevill. 360
During a fight I tear up my
   wedding picture. Joan Colby.
   224
"During siesta..." Susan Tichy.
   381
During the war. Gary Margolis.
   311
Dusk in the Cuyamacas. Steve
   Kowit. 299
Dusting the sill. Marc Hudson.
   277
Dusty dragoon, pious Quaker.
   Phillips Kloss. 294
Dying. Martha Janssen. 283
The dying child. Robert
   Pawlowski. 341
The dying man's shame. Robert
   Anbian. 194
Dying of it. Carolyn Stoloff. 376
Dying out. James L. White. 396
"The dynamic silence moving."
   Connie Hunt. 279
The dynamite artist. James
   Schevill. 360
Dynamiter blasting ice jams.
   James Magorian. 309

Each. James R. Rhodes. 352
Each day. Sister Maura. 313
Each midsummer, love. Mary
   Gilliland. 257
"Each moment fills him with a
   desire." Kenneth Koch. 297
Each morning at four. Laura Boss.
   213
Each new dress you've never seen.

Laura Boss. 213

Each night is no loss... Charles
    Olson. 337
Each of us here has fought this
    battle. Haig Knatchadourian.
    292
Each other. James R. Rhodes. 352
Eagle bridge farm. Stephen Sandy.
    357
Eagle River, Wisconsin: 1930.
    Robert Peters. 343
Eagles
    Golden eagle. Gene Anderson. 195
    The golden eagle. Jacques
        Sollov. 370
    There were other places. Judson
        Crews. 226
Early and late. Colette Inez. 280
Early December in
    Croton-on-Hudson. Louise
    Gluck. 259A
An early Egyptian ship. David
    Shapiro. 363
Early morning through the door.
    Susan Stock. 375
"Early needs/unmet," Theta Burke.
    218
Early spring. Aileen Fisner. 244
Early spring green. William
    Oandasan. 335
The earnest liberal's lament.
    Ernest Hemingway. 272
Ears
    Headless. Josephine Miles. 319
Earth & apples. Cathryn Hankla.
    268
"The Earth is not a place for
    me." Da Free John. 284
Earth music. Margaret Key Biggs.
    205
Earth wisdom: two sonnets in an
    early mode. Elsa Gidlow. 254
"The earth with a city in her
    hair." Charles Olson. 337
"The earth you may as well."
    Larry Eigner. 237
Earthbird. David Wagoner. 390
Earthling. Randy Blasing. 207
Earthstars, birthparent's house.
    Sandra McPherson. 317
Earthworks. Robert Gibb. 253
Earthworks. James Tate. 379
Easter. Josephine Miles. 319
Easter. Cathryn Hankla. 268
Easter. Haig Khatchadourian. 292
Easter
    Augusta summons Easter. Carolyn
        Stoloff. 376
    Easter. Josephine Miles. 319
    Easter morning. Amy Clampitt.

222
Easter Sunday. Evelyn Golden.
    263
An Easter apology to my guineas.
    Phyllis A. Tickle. 382
Easter moonrise. Rochelle DuBois.
    234
Easter morning. Amy Clampitt. 222
Easter morning. Aileen Fisher.
    244
Easter season. Louise Gluck. 259A
Easter Sunday. Evelyn Golden. 263
Easter: Wahiawa, 1959. Cathy
    · Song. 372
The Eastern Montana obsolete
    poetry award. James Magorian.
    308
"Eastern Oklahoma." Madison
    Morrison. 327
Eastman, Max
    To John Reed. 350
Eastman, Max (about)
    A dedication to Max Eastman.
        John Reed. 350
Easy to remember. Jeanne Lohmann.
    305
An easy way to roast corn. James
    Magorian. 309
Eating my tail. Marge Piercy. 346
The eating of names. Michael
    Akillian. 193
Eaton, Charles Edward
    An American expressed. 236
    The amputee. 236
    Architectural visions. 236
    Articulation of the ruby
        bracelet. 236
    Artists anonymous. 236
    The avocado connection. 236
    The blood buoy. 236
    The blue pajamas. 236
    Bodies of water. 236
    Bonsai. 236
    Butterfly sheets. 236
    The cannibal. 236
    Chocolate cake. 236
    The circular staircase. 236
    The comb. 236
    The cork-lined room. 236
    The courtship. 236
    A day in the life of a magpie.
        236
    Debauch of the chauvinist. 236
    The diapason. 236
    The dining room. 236
    Doctor Dionysus. 236
    Don Juan in autumn. 236
    A dream from Hokusai. 236
    Duck blind. 236
    El Dorado. 236

Exhibition of blue ladies. 236
Fata morgana. 236
The gargoyle. 236
The gestalt. 236
The hanging gardens. 236
Haruspex of the happy country. 236
The haystack. 236
Idyll of Isolato. 236
In search of the sunbather as a very safe thing. 236
In the garden of the fire plants. 236
The kiosk. 236
The kiss. 236
Lady Charisma. 236
Mackerel. 236
The man from Buena Vista. 236
The man who was not. 236
The manuscript collection. 236
Mixed drinks. 236
The muscle. 236
Needlepoint in Autumn. 236
The non sequiturs of summer. 236
The palm voyeur. 236
The paperweight. 236
Paracelsus in Puerto Rico. 236
The peacock in the bed. 236
The philtre. 236
The pointillist. 236
Portrait of a man rising in his profession. 236
Praying mantis. 236
Purple lilacs, blue water. 236
The raid. 236
Red. 236
Red snapper. 236
Repentimento. 236
Rose-colored glasses. 236
Sentimental education. 236
Sleeping nude. 236
Slides. 236
Steps taken in a debris of day lilies. 236
Suit of lights. 236
Sumptuous siesta. 236
The thing king. 236
View from a balloon. 236
White clown. 236
The winch. 236
The woman in black. 236
World without end: a Japanese screen. 236
Ebb of time. Alice Joyce Davidson. 227
Eberhart, Richard (about)
For Richard Eberhart. Ralph J., Jr. Mills. 321
Eberheim. Irving Feldman. 242
"Echidna is the bite." Charles
Olson. 337
"Echoes careen." Michael Robert Pick. 345
Echoing laughter. Alice Spohn Newton. 332
"Echoing the fierce belief that time." Edwin Honig. 275
The echolaliac. Robin Becker. 202
Eclipses
Saying the word. Gary Margolis. 311
Total eclipse. Gary Margolis. 311
Ecology
"When I telephoned a friend, her husband told me." Josephine Miles. 319
Economics. Dennis Hinrichsen. 273
Ecstasy of boredom at the Berlin Wall. Joyce Carol Oates. 336
Ecstasy of flight. Joyce Carol Oates. 336
Ecstasy of motion. Joyce Carol Oates. 336
Ecstatic moment. Jacques Sollov. 370
Ecumene. James R. Rhodes. 352
Ecumenicity. James R. Rhodes. 352
Eden. Michael Gizzi. 259
The Edgartown heat. Mitchell Howard. 276
The edge of return. May Miller. 320
The edge of the hurricane. Amy Clampitt. 222
The edge. Louise Gluck. 259A
Edibility test. Marie Daerr Boehringer. 210
The editor's reply. Franz Schneider. 361
Editors
The editor's reply. Franz Schneider. 361
Education. Josephine Miles. 319
Education
Curriculum. Josephine Miles. 319
Fields of learning. Josephine Miles. 319
On a slow student. Cornel Lengyel. 302
Paths. Josephine Miles. 319
School. Josephine Miles. 319
Study. Josephine Miles. 319
To a child who shot a robin. Larry Moffi. 322
The education of a mouse. Richard Moore. 323
Edward's birthday. Rod McKuen. 316
Edward's song. Mitchell Howard.

276
Eels
    Electric eel. X.J. Kennedy. 290
    Electric eels. Jack Prelutsky.
    349
Effigy. James A. Emanuel. 239
Effort for distraction. Josephine
    Miles. 319
The egg and I. Ernesto Galarza.
    252
The egg. Louise Gluck. 259A
The egg. Jack Prelutsky. 349
Eggs
    The great egg. Joyce Carol
        Oates. 336
    The housewife laments her
        purchase of floating eggs. Jim
        Simmerman. 365
    The secret. Carol Frost. 249
Ego sum via, veritas et vita.
    Maurice W. Britts. 215
Egrets
    The helper. Stephen Todd Booker.
    212
Egypt
    An early Egyptian ship. David
        Shapiro. 363
    Exodus. Patsie Black. 206
    Luxor. Betty Adcock. 192
    To Fuzzy. James Tate. 379
Eichmann, (Karl) Adolf
    Eichmann, slide no. 6. James A.
        Emanuel. 239
Eichmann, slide no. 6. James A.
    Emanuel. 239
1836. In the Cherokee overhills.
        Stephen Knauth. 295
Eight minutes from the sun.
    Colette Inez. 280
Eight-aught. John Godfrey. 260
8 A.M.   Rochelle DuBois. 234
8 P.M.   Rochelle DuBois. 234
Eighth grade. Martha Janssen. 283
Eigner, Larry
    "Aggre-/gates." 237
    Air. 237
    "All matter/standing." 237
    "Along walls." 237
    "Angelic youth." 237
    "Another plane is/gas..." 237
    "Begin a/mid things." 237
    "A bird/bath a cloud." 237
    "Break the dogfight." 237
    "Broken cement." 237
    "A car horn." 237
    "Cars." 237
    "A cat/stops." 237
    Certain months for years. 237
    "Churchbells/years ago." 237
    "Close/-up." 237

"Co-op." 237
"Curtains/shades." 237
"A dark day." 237
"The days the motors burn past."
    237
"The dead." 237
"Down on the bed you." 237
"Driftwood/the sands." 237
"The earth you may as well." 237
The end of a film. 237
Environs. 237
"Europe a map." 237
"The faces set." 237
"Fall of a leaf." 237
"The far bliss..." 237
"The 5 and 1/2 million."f. 237
"Flat sky/going down." 237
"Flock of birds." 237
"The flock." 237
"The fog holds." 237
"The force." 237
"The/frosted car." 237
"Glad to have." 237
"Good and bad/time goes." 237
"Great multiple." 237
"Grief dry the/council." 237
"Head full/of birds..." 237
"High piled/clouds." 237
"High society." 237
History is for tourist. 237
"A hole in the clouds moves."
    237
Hotrods. 237
Hour minute hands seconds. 237
"How many languages..." 237
"How much could they/flicker."
    237
"How much the moon may be." 237
"How you/stand." 237
"In the shadow." 237
"In the trees." 237
"Insect/leaf." 237
"The intersection." 237
"It is music." 237
"The jets jet." 237
"Last year's pink." 237
"Life/night." 237
"Like stores, banks." 237
"Little finger suddenly/not so
    small." 237
Low. 237
"Microphones." 237
"Mirrors scattered." 237
"The moon." 237
"Motion unperceived..." 237
"Muggy." 237
"Museum or/the endless insides
    of the store." 237
"The music of/the sea." 237
"New/ballgame." 237

"Not the same." 237
"Now/here." 237
"One died by this tremendous
   headache." 237
"Open road." 237
"Out of the wind and leaves."
   237
"Palestrina from/invisible
   source." 237
"Parking lot but." 237
"Perfect/strangers, dining." 237
"Piano and strings." 237
"Pigeons..." 237
Place to place. 237
"A quiet staircase." 237
"Rainy/days." 237
"The reality behind." 237
(Resting or doing something...)
   237
"Reticent." 237
"Shadowy." 237
"Siren/people look." 237
A sleep. 237
Slide. 237
"Snow." 237
"So muggy/in the thread." 237
"The sound." 237
"Sounded like." 237
"Sounds/quiet." 237
"Sparrows gather on the
   chimney." 237
"Strength feels/babies..." 237
"The sun solid." 237
"That's all figures." 237
"There is no community." 237
"There's movies." 237
"There's no such thing
   as/identical!" 237
"Things more or less" 237
3/4 time.   237
"To find/the weight." 237
"To open your ears." 237
"To see the ocean." 237
"Trees." 237
"The two lights in/unison..."
   237
"Visiting yesterday/today
   burying." 237
"Washing between the buildings."
   237
"What damp paper." 237
"What time is/it day." 237
"What/to study with." 237
"White clouds in the sky." 237
"Who's intelligent." 237
"Whoppers whoppers whoppers!"
   237
Winter. 237
"You never know." 237
"You ride for some hours." 237

Eileen. Robert Peters. 343
Eileen. Brenda Marie Osbey. 340
Einstein in the orchard. Harry
   Humes. 278
Eklund, George
   Affirmation. 238
   Again, Van Gogh. 238
   At an open window. 238
   At the up-town window. 238
   Bennet. 238
   The bloody harvest. 238
   Bone breaker. 238
   Cell damage. 238
   Crow love. 238
   Desire. 238
   Driving her back to Wisconsin.
      238
   El Toro. 238
   Fingers. 238
   Fulton Street. 238
   Gravedigging in August. 238
   Headline. 238
   Hubie French needs a letter. 238
   July First. 238
   A little life in a summer room.
      238
   Los Ninos. 238
   Love me. 238
   The medal. 238
   Night of the first frost. 238
   Polly. 238
   The quiet, angry man. 238
   Saturday, dusk. 238
   The silo burns in Brooklyn. 238
   The sleeper. 238
   Starting. 238
   Stopped for a beer in
      Charleston, West Virginia. 238
   Sunday. 238
   Talking with my brother, who
      came to visit. 238
   That boy, in winter or rain. 238
   The ticks. 238
   To market. 238
   Tornado warnings, fourth night.
      238
   The unbeliever dreams. 238
   Vince and Joe. 238
   Winter. 238
   Wintering. 238
El Cid. Jacques Sollov. 370
El Dorado. Charles Edward Eaton.
   236
El Salvador
   Certification. Clayton Eshleman.
      240
   Psalm:El Salvador. Thomas
      McGrath. 315
   Stud-farms of cooked shadows.
      Clayton Eshleman. 240

El Toro. George Eklund. 238
Elaine. Marilyn Kallet. 287
Elastic romance. Rochelle DuBois.
    234
Elba
    Elba unvisited. Robert A. Sears.
    362
Elba unvisited. Robert A. Sears.
    362
Eldorado. Edgar Allan Poe. 347
Electric eel. X.J. Kennedy. 290
Electric eels. Jack Prelutsky.
    349
Electricity
    Like now! Josephine B. Moretti.
    324
The elegance of the slug. Sally
    Love Saunders. 358
Elegy. Robin Morgan. 325
Elegy. Clayton Eshleman. 240
Elegy. Eileen Silver-Lillywite.
    364
Elegy. Keith Waldrop. 392
Elegy. Marc Kaminsky. 288
Elegy. Haig Khatchadourian. 292
Elegy and epitaph, sels. Everett
    A. Gillis. 258
Elegy for America. Eileen
    Silver-Lillywite. 364
Elegy for an soldier in any war,
    fr. Elegy and epitaph. Everett
    A. Gillis. 258
Elegy for cliches. Debra Bruce.
    216
Elegy for Martin Heidegger. Marc
    Hudson. 277
Elegy for my brother. Jacqueline
    Frank. 248
Elegy for my mother. David
    Wagoner. 390
Elegy for soldiers. Anne Bailie.
    199
Elegy for the twenty-four shelves
    of books. David Wagoner. 390
Elegy from a dark country. Anne
    Bailie. 199
Elegy in fifths. Jim Simmerman.
    365
Elegy spoken to a tree. Dennis
    Hinrichsen. 273
Elegy spoken to my grandfather.
    Dennis Hinrichsen. 273
Element of the act. Robert
    Anbian. 194
Elena. Irving Feldman. 242
The elephant graveyard. Roy Marz.
    312
Elephant ride. David Wagoner. 390
Elephants
    The drought. Evelyn Golden. 263

The elephant graveyard. Roy
    Marz. 312
Elephant ride. David Wagoner.
    390
Elephants-a mythology. Ghita
    Orth. 339
Elephants-a mythology. Ghita
    Orth. 339
Elevator shaft. James Magorian.
    309
Eleven o'clock at night. Robert
    Bly. 209
11 o'clock at night..."
    Charles Olson. 337
11/80.   Ralph J., Jr. Mills. 321
11:15 P.M.   Rochelle DuBois. 234
Eleventh Avenue racket. John
    Reed. 350
Eleventh hour. Patsie Black. 206
Eli Lu's rose. Ernesto Galarza.
    252
Eliot, Thomas Stearns (about)
    William Carlos Williams and T.S.
    Eliot dancing... James
    Schevill. 360
Elisabeth at seven. Evelyn
    Golden. 263
The elite. Richmond Lattimore.
    301
Eliza. Brenda Marie Osbey. 340
Elizabeth. Edgar Allan Poe. 347
Elizabeth Bay evening. Rod
    McKuen. 316
The Elizabeth poems. Betty
    Adcock. 192
Elizabethan fool applies for a
    corporate execeutive position.
    James Schevill. 360
Elk poem. James Magorian. 309
Elks
    Elk poem. James Magorian. 309
Elliott, Cass
    Memorial for Cass Elliott.
    Mitchell Howard. 276
Elloree. Larry Moffi. 322
Elm. Lucien Stryk. 377
Elm Trees
    Elm. Lucien Stryk. 377
The elusive rose. Rochelle
    DuBois. 234
Elves. See Fairies

Emancipation from a Bach jig.
    Phillips Kloss. 294
Emanuel, James A.
    Accident, from a Wajda movie.
    239
    All's fair. 239
    Andrew's cyclones. 239
    Antonic Gomic (at Monument Park

in Yugoslavia). 239
Bandages. 239
A bench to bear. 239
Beyond the clearing. 239
Black Muslim boy in a hospital.
  239
Blood's the only secret. 239
The broken bowl. 239
The burlesque queen. 239
A cabinet of few affections. 239
Challenge, taken hard. 239
Christmas at the Quaker Center
  (Paris, 1981). 239
Church burning: Mississippi. 239
The circuit of despair. 239
Cremation. 239
Crossing the square,
  Montparnasse. 239
Daniel in Paris. 239
The death of such a one. 239
Dirty old man. 239
Effigy. 239
Eichmann, slide no. 6. 239
A fable for animals. 239
A fool for evergreen. 239
For a farmer. 239
For Fernand Lagarde (died 13
  April 1982). 239
For Sousa Junior High, 1967. 239
Fourteen. 239
Francoise and the fruit farmer.
  239
Gone. 239
Her diary. 239
In black suburbia. 239
It was a happy little grave. 239
Jimboy's ad. 239
The kitchen phone. 239
Little old black historian. 239
Lovers, do not think of this.
  239
Marijuana ha-ha: a real smart
  dog. 239
A pause for a fine phrase. 239
A poem for Claire of London. 239
A poem for Sarah's tears. 239
A poet does not choose to run.
  239
Prayer for a bigot. 239
Primavera. 239
Racism in France. 239
Sadface at five. 239
Sarah at the sink. 239
Scarecrow: the road to Toulouse.
  239
Sis and the pidgeon man. 239
Ski boots in storage. 239
Snowman. 239
Snowpit in Switzerland. 239
Son. 239

Sonnet for a writer. 239
Sooner or later, a close=up. 239
Taps. 239
The telephone mashers. 239
To a Negro pitcher. 239
Tomorrow. 239
"We shall overcome" : a smile
  for the 1960's. 239
Whatever broken thing you have.
  239
When I read of the rose of
  Dachau. 239
The embrace. Marc Kaminsky. 288
The embroidery. Carol Frost. 249
Emerson, Ralph Waldo (about)
  Ralph Waldo Emerson receives a
    visit from the sane man...
    James Schevill. 360
Emigration. See Immigration

Emily Dickinson. James Schevill.
  360
Employment
  Job hunting. Miriam Goodman. 264
Empty harbor. Rod McKuen. 316
Empty is. Rod McKuen. 316
Empty pitchforks. Thomas Lux. 307
The empty place. Elsa Gidlow. 254
En Gev. Eileen Silver-Lillywite.
  364
En-gai. Ray Fleming. 247
En route. Ernesto Galarza. 252
Enchant. Josephine Miles. 319
Enchanted. Norman Andrew Kirk.
  293
Encore. Marie Daerr Boehringer.
  210
Encounter. Ernesto Galarza. 252
Encounter. James Torio. 281
The encounter of the pet store
  owner with Sarah L. Burkett.
  James Schevill. 360
Encounter with sirens. Anne
  Bailie. 199
Encounters. Ernesto Galarza. 252
Encounters
  "Yes, I will meet him." Madison
    Morrison. 327
The end of a film. Larry Eigner.
  237
The end of a war (Jan.1973).
  Rodney Nelson. 331
End of the picaro. Stephen Sandy.
  357
The end of the season. Eileen
  Silver-Lillywite. 364
The end of winter. Larry Moffi.
  322
Endangered species. Joan Colby.
  224

Endangered species. Mark Vinz. 387
The ending. Rachel A. Hazen. 271
Enemies. Robert Kelly. 289
Enemies
    Bomb, bullet or arrow. Phillips
        Kloss. 294
    The enemy. Bill Knott. 296
    M'sai. Wanda Coleman. 225
The enemies of cold water. Gerard
    Malanga. 310
Enemy. Jim Everhard. 241
The enemy. Bill Knott. 296
England
    Exmoor. Amy Clampitt. 222
    In the Cotswolds. Ray Fleming.
        247
    Semi-detached in Oxford. Ray
        Fleming. 247
    A walk into the Cumner Hills.
        Ray Fleming. 247
English summer. Paul Davis. 228
Enlightenment. Sister Maura. 313
Enlightenment. Josephine Miles.
    319
Ensemble. Rose Basile Green. 265
Ensinanca. Gayl Jones. 286
Enter no exit. Norman Andrew
    Kirk. 293
Entering experience. Kirk
    Lumpkin. 306
Entering the temple in Nimes.
    James Wright. 403
Entombment. Robert L. Wilson. 401
Entreaty. Alice Joyce Davidson.
    227
"The entrepreneur chicken shed
    his tail feathers, surplus."
    Josephine Miles. 319
Entry. Josephine Miles. 319
Environment. Kenneth Koch. 297
Environmentalism
    Coy glen. Mary Gilliland. 257
    The muse is muzak in this age.
        Mary Gilliland. 257
Environs. Larry Eigner. 237
Envoi. Gerard Malanga. 310
Envy
    And now, the others. Rachel A.
        Hazen. 271
    Envy no man. Sam Fishman. 246
    "Seeing you have a woman." W.D.
        (William De Witt) Snodgrass.
        369
Envy no man. Sam Fishman. 246
"Enyalion of/brown earth."
    Charles Olson. 337
The ephebe of Tarsus. Royal
    Murdoch. 330
Epidemics. Joan Colby. 224

Epilogue. Jocelyn Hollis. 274
The epiphanies. Irving Feldman.
    242
Epiphany. Patsie Black. 206
An episode for reflection. John
    F. Barker. 201
Episodes. Miriam Goodman. 264
Epistemology. Debra Bruce. 216
Epitaph. Andrei Codrescu. 223
Epitaph. Sam Fishman. 246
Epitaph for a humble hero, fr.
    Elegy and epitaph. Everett A.
    Gillis. 258
Epitaph for the bomb. Jocelyn
    Hollis. 274
Epithalamion: the ducks at Lake
    Lotawana. Jim Simmerman. 365
Equinox. John Godfrey. 260
Equivocal elegy. Steve Kowit. 299
Eroteschatology. Mitchell Howard.
    276
Erotic Love
    After making love. Robin Becker.
        202
    After the poem. Wanda Coleman.
        225
    Analytic hymn. Robert Kelly. 289
    An aubade. Timothy Steele. 374
    Behavior modification. Martha
        Janssen. 283
    Blood ties: for Jan. James
        Applewhite. 198
    Carnal verdict. Colette Inez.
        280
    The children. Eileen
        Silver-Lillywite. 364
    Climbing together. Marc Hudson.
        277
    Come and lie with me. Elsa
        Gidlow. 254
    Diagnosis...with complications.
        Wanda Coleman. 225
    Eucalyptus. Robert Kelly. 289
    Exultations in late summer.
        Jenne Andrews. 196
    First date. Eileen
        Silver-Lillywite. 364
    Fragment. Rod McKuen. 316
    The guise is all the difference.
        Robert L. Wilson. 401
    The having. Sam Fishman. 246
    "I sing." Madison Morrison. 327
    Independence Day. Rod McKuen.
        316
    Indoor sports. Harlan Usher. 386
    Maithuna. Clayton Eshleman. 240
    Making up. Tefke Goldberger. 262
    Man and the woman, fr. The day
        of the body. Carol Frost. 249
    Marriage. Joan Colby. 224

Maximus, at the harbor. Charles
   Olson. 337
Morning, meadow, wife. Anthony
   Petrosky. 344
My life before dawn. Louise
   Gluck. 259A
The northern lights. Rod McKuen.
   316
"Nothing shall stay me from my
   journey." James Torio. 281
Our night. Carol Frost. 249
Painter. Anneliese Wagner. 389
A private business. Marge
   Piercy. 346
Relays. Rod McKuen. 316
Renewal. Steve Kowit. 299
Screaming for this event. Scott
   Chisholm. 221
So still the dawn. Elsa Gidlow.
   254
Sonnet ("In the sunniness of the
   particular noon.") John
   Godfrey. 260
Techniques. Martha Janssen. 283
Three anecdotes. Deborah Tall.
   378
Too bloated to boogie. Mitchell
   Howard. 276
Under the patronage of the moon.
   Joan Colby. 224
"When she is moved by her
   man..." David James. 282
Why this loving is better. Jenne
   Andrews. 196
Wintering. George Eklund. 238
The errors. Albert Goldbarth. 261
Escape. Rochelle DuBois. 234
Escape. Martha Janssen. 283
Escape
   August islands. Rod McKuen. 316
   Blind Leon's escape. Stephen
      Knauth. 295
   "The car appears." Madison
      Morrison. 327
   "Down the rump and out." Madison
      Morrison. 327
   "An escape attempt transforms."
      Michael Robert Pick. 345
   Everywhere, but nowhere. Robert
      Peters. 343
   "From the steep incline a."
      Madison Morrison. 327
   "In the middle." Madison
      Morrison. 327
   A life of intimate fleeing.
      Robert Kelly. 289
   Paperweight escape. Stephen Todd
      Booker. 212
"An escape attempt transforms."
   Michael Robert Pick. 345

The escape from monkey island.
   David Wagoner. 390
Escape into autumn. Anne Bailie.
   199
Escape of a polar bear from the
   city zoo. James Torio. 281
Escape to a friend. Rochelle
   DuBois. 234
Eshleman, Clayton
   Apparition of the duck. 240
   The arcade's discourse on
      method. 240
   The aut Ignatian summation. 240
   The Bowery of dreams. 240
   Certification. 240
   The color rake of time. 240
   Coproatavism. 240
   Cuitlacoche. 240
   The death of Bill Evans. 240
   Diamonion taxi driver. 240
   Elegy. 240
   Foetus graffiti. 240
   Forty-seven years. 240
   Fracture. 240
   The inn of the empty egg. 240
   Inseminator vortex. 240
   The kill. 240
   A kind of moisture on the wall.
      240
   The language orphan. 240
   The loaded sleeve of Hades. 240
   Magdalenian. 240
   Maithuna. 240
   Manticore vortex. 240
   Millennium. 240
   Notes on a visit to Le Tuc
      D'Audoubert. 240
   Nothing follows. 240
   Rhapsody. 240
   Saturos. 240
   The seeds of narrative. 240
   The severing. 240
   A small cave. 240
   The soul of intercourse. 240
   The spiritual hunt. 240
   The staked woman. 240
   Stud-farms of cooked shadows.
      240
   Tangerine dawn. 240
   Tantrik X-ray. 240
   The tears of Christ pulled
      inside out. 240
   The terrace at Hotel du
      Centenaire. 240
   Terrestrial. 240
   Through Breuil's eyes. 240
   Tiresia's drinking. 240
   Toddler under glass. 240
   Visions of the fathers of
      Lascaux. 240

Eskimos
Hiemal watch. Robert Anbian. 194
Ode to an Eskimo. Sally Love
Saunders. 358
Espionage
Esterhazy's honeymoon. J.W.
Rivers. 354
Essay on Queen Tiy. Charles
Olson. 337
The **essence** of things. Ernesto
Galarza. 252
Esterhazy and the cat woman. J.W.
Rivers. 354
Esterhazy and the swimmer. J.W.
Rivers. 354
The **Esterhazy** family picnic. J.W.
Rivers. 354
Esterhazy in the hospital. J.W.
Rivers. 354
Esterhazy on Mount Everest. J.W.
Rivers. 354
Esterhazy shakes his fist at the
Sunday sky. J.W. Rivers. 354
Esterhazy's honeymoon. J.W.
Rivers. 354
Esterhazy's memoirs. J.W. Rivers.
354
Esterhazy's Vienna stopover,
1973. J.W. Rivers. 354
An **etching**. Patsie Black. 206
"The **eternal** cathedral." Madison
Morrison. 327
Eternal friendship. Jacques
Sollov. 371
Eternal peace. Jacques Sollov.
370
The **eternal** snow. Connie Hunt.
279
Eternity
Could be. Ernesto Galarza. 252
New life. Alice Joyce Davidson.
227
The purest form of eternity.
Rachel A. Hazen. 271
Why. Connie Hunt. 279
Ethan. Ruth Lisa Schechter. 359
An **ethnic-American** crying. Rose
Basile Green. 265
An **ethnic-American** singing. Rose
Basile Green. 265
Ethnic-American woman. Rose
Basile Green. 265
Ethnic-Americans. Rose Basile
Green. 265
Etiquette
Conduct. Josephine Miles. 319
Manners. Larry Moffi. 322
"Manners in the dining room."
Jan Ormerod. 338
Etruscan burial. Roy Marz. 312

Eucalyptus. Robert Kelly. 289
Eugenio Montale in California.
Andrei Codrescu. 223
Eulalie: a song. Edgar Allan Poe.
347
Eulogy for Colonel Sanders. James
Magorian. 309
Europe
"Europe a map." Larry Eigner.
237
Rain waste. John Godfrey. 260
"**Europe** a map." Larry Eigner. 237
Evangel. Josephine Miles. 319
Evans, Bill
The death of Bill Evans. Clayton
Eshleman. 240
Eve. See Adam and Eve

Evelyn. Josephine B. Moretti. 324
"**Even** now lost winds carry silent
memories." Michael Robert
Pick. 345
Even paranoiacs. Bradford Morrow.
329
Evening
Evening song. John Godfrey. 260
Maybe night. Marilyn Kallet. 287
Safety zone. Harry Humes. 278
Water color II. Haig
Khatchadourian. 292
Evening news. Josephine Miles.
319
Evening particular. Andrei
Codrescu. 223
Evening song. John Godfrey. 260
Evening star. Edgar Allan Poe.
347
An **evening** walk. Cornel Lengyel.
302
"**Evening**, wedged in the door like
a grand piano..." Carolyn
Stoloff. 376
Evening: matters. Bradford
Morrow. 329
Evensong. Marie Daerr Boehringer.
210
An **event** at Big Eddy. William
Stafford. 373
"**Eventually** I pass the." Madison
Morrison. 327
"**Ever** catch a butterfly or moth."
Michael Robert Pick. 345
Ever onward. Alice Spohn Newton.
332
Ever since my operation.
Josephine B. Moretti. 324
Ever-beyond. James R. Rhodes. 352
Everhard, Jim
After sleep. 241
Anything but murder. 241

Blondes and brunettes. 241
Coming. 241
Cruising. 241
Curing homosexuality. 241
Cute. 241
Dayton: non-memories. 241
Distance. 241
Don't look back. 241
Enemy. 241
For Marcie. 241
Gifts. 241
The invisible brother. 241
James Dean. 241
Knots. 241
Looking for the lumberjack. 241
Memory of Roanoke. 241
Momma's vision. 241
Monologue for an aging queen.
    241
Mysteries of the heart. 241
Ode to the Duchess La Blah. 241
Poppa's vision. 241
Reasons why I love you. 241
Rosa Luxemburg, drag queen. 241
Sailor. 241
South Yuma River, Summer 1971.
    241
You can't f*** with mother
    nature. 241
"Your hair/is not the most
    beautiful." 241
Everlasting candle. Alice Joyce
    Davidson. 227
Every apartment faces a pentagon.
    Carolyn Stoloff. 376
"Every body is an island." Da
    Free John. 284
"Every day when she came to the
    steps that led." Josephine
    Miles. 319
"Every day." Da Free John. 284
Everyday miracles. Marie Daerr
    Boenringer. 210
Everywhere, but nowhere. Robert
    Peters. 343
Eviction. Wanda Coleman. 225
Evidence. Deborah Tall. 378
Evil
    Absolute zero in the brain.
        Marge Piercy. 346
    The invisible craft of evil.
        James Schevill. 360
    Reading Hannah Arendt's Eichmann
        in Jerusalem. Jacqueline
        Frank. 248
    A vision of Abraxas. Evelyn
        Golden. 263
Evolution
    "Brang that thing out." Charles
        Olson. 337

Contorted light. Kirk Lumpkin.
    306
The ex-seminarian comes home. Ray
    Fleming. 247
Exacta. Paul Violi. 388
An example of work. David
    Shapiro. 363
Excalibur. Robert Kelly. 289
Excavating hardpan. Mary
    Gilliland. 257
Exchange. Laura Boss. 213
The exchange, Margaret Key Biggs.
    205
Exchanging prisoners. Gary
    Margolis. 311
"The excise tax has." Madison
    Morrison. 327
Excretion
    Cuitlacoche. Clayton Eshleman.
        240
    Free fuel. Alice Spohn Newton.
        333
    Night-soil. Robert Peters. 343
Excursion from grief. May Miller.
    320
Execution. Andrei Codrescu. 223
Executions
    Execution. Andrei Codrescu. 223
    Guillotine. Andrei Codrescu. 223
    Hanging at Galgahraun. Marc
        Hudson. 277
    The images of execution. James
        Schevill. 360
    Lynched. Stephen Todd Booker.
        212
    Miguel Pro, S.J., faces a Calles
        firing squad. J.W. Rivers. 354
    On Jan. 10th 1981, the nite.
        Stephen Todd Booker. 212
    "Three times life size." Madison
        Morrison. 327
    To Will Davies. Ernest
        Hemingway. 272
    Whether they feared or whether
        they loved. Roy Marz. 312
The executive at fifty. James
    Schevill. 360
"An executive/wears a
    professional smock." Madison
    Morrison. 327
An exercise in futility. David
    Shapiro. 363
Exercise: to hope to invite to
    continue. Carolyn Stoloff. 376
Exeter, England
    Whether awe or loss. Paul Davis.
        228
Exeter, Pennsylvania
    Photograph. Anthony Petrosky.
        344

Exhibition of blue ladies.
      Charles Edward Eaton. 236
Exiles
   Displaced persons. Marieve Rugo.
      356
   Havana. Herbert Morris. 326
   The pleasures of exile. John
      Yau. 404
   To a young exile. David Shapiro.
      363
"Existed/3000/BC?" Charles
   Olson. 337
Existence
   The careful bump. Barry
      Wallenstein. 393
   Elegy. Keith Waldrop. 392
   Zen. Susan Tichy. 381
The exit. Deborah Tall. 378
Exmoor. Amy Clampitt. 222
Exodus. Patsie Black. 206
Expatriate. Marieve Rugo. 356
Expected guests. Alice Spohn
   Newton. 332
Expecting. Elsa Gidlow. 254
Experience. Anne Bailie. 199
Experience. Elsa Gidlow. 254
Experience
   Entering experience. Kirk
      Lumpkin. 306
   I've been to town. Rod McKuen.
      316
   "Ideal soil/makes for shallow
      roots." Theta Burke. 218
   Initiation. Deborah Tall. 378
Explaining the rainbow. Rochelle
   DuBois. 234
Explanations. Josephine B.
   Moretti. 324
Explanations
   Of it. Norman Andrew Kirk. 293
Exploitation. Martha Janssen. 283
Explorers and Exploring
   Badly-gored explorer reading
      poetry at a debutante party.
      James Magorian. 309
   Caravan. James Magorian. 309
   The Magellan heart. Robert A.
      Sears. 362
   Maximus, to Gloucester : I don't
      mean, just like that. Charles
      Olson. 337
   On first looking out through
      Juan de la Coas'a eyes.
      Charles Olson. 337
   Solo. James Torio. 281
   The song and dance of. Charles
      Olson. 337
   Tarascan names. Robert A. Sears.
      362
Exploring the natural history

      museum. Mark Vinz. 387
Explosion. Joy Harjo. 269
Explosives
   The dynamite artist. James
      Schevill. 360
"Extend the family and." Madison
   Morrison. 327
Extension. Josephine Miles. 319
Exterior. Josephine Miles. 319
Exterminator. Lucien Stryk. 377
The exterminator. James Schevill.
   360
Exterminators
   Exterminator. Lucien Stryk. 377
   The exterminator. James
      Schevill. 360
Extinctions, schedule of. Bill
   Knott. 296
Extreme unction. Robert
   Pawlowski. 341
Extremity. Rose Basile Green. 265
Exultations in late summer. Jenne
   Andrews. 196
The eye on the corner. Everett A.
   Gillis. 258
"Eye winker." Jan Ormerod. 338
Eye witness. Richmond Lattimore.
   301
Eyeless in Corinth. Cornel
   Lengyel. 302
Eyelines. Colette Inez. 280
Eyes. Jacqueline Frank. 248
Eyes. Elsa Gidlow. 254
Eyes
   Eye witness. Richmond Lattimore.
      301
   Eyes. Elsa Gidlow. 254
   "If the globe eye." Madison
      Morrison. 327
   Kyoto. Michael Gizzi. 259
   Muffled, blind, silent. Everett
      A. Gillis. 258
   My similar eyes. Susan Stock.
      375
   The paperweight. Charles Edward
      Eaton. 236
   Two stars in a row. Alice Spohn
      Newton. 332
The eyes of a girl. Jacques
   Sollov. 370
"The eyes/act as dams." A.
   Dovichi. 233
Eyesight. Josephine Miles. 319

F-. Joyce Carol Oates. 336
A fable for animals. James A.
   Emanuel. 239

Fabulous debris. James Schevill. 360

"Face at a window." Robert Kelly. 289

'The face of the precipice is black with lovers' Thomas McGrath. 315

Face portrait. Andrei Codrescu. 223

A face without lines. John Godfrey. 260

(Face) (autumn) (en face). Bill Knott. 296

A face. Andrei Codrescu. 223

Faces. Josephine Miles. 319

Faces
Face portrait. Andrei Codrescu. 223
Made shine. Josephine Miles. 319

"The faces set." Larry Eigner. 237

The fact of the matter is. Robert L. Wilson. 401

Factories
Down at the plant. David Wann. 394
Metamorphosis. Josephine Miles. 319

The factory poem. Brenda Marie Osbey. 340

Faery song. John Reed. 350

The failing sea. Evelyn Golden. 263

Failure
"A car horn." Larry Eigner. 237
Esterhazy's memoirs. J.W. Rivers. 354
Eyes. Jacqueline Frank. 248
Inventory at year's end. James Magorian. 308
Willows. Lucien Stryk. 377
Yr amanuensis. Bradford Morrow. 329

Fair city. Greg Kuzma. 300

Fairfield Harbor at New Bern, N.S. August 22, 1982. Rochelle DuBois. 234

Fairs
Carnival man. Robert Peters. 343
The great county fair. Alice Spohn Newton. 333
"In 1856 she won second prize..." Albert Goldbarth. 261
P.T.A. fair. Josephine B. Moretti. 324

The fairy tale. Carol Frost. 249

Fairy Tales
Bedtime story. James Magorian. 308

Count to ten. Anneliese Wagner. 389
Faery song. John Reed. 350
Jack and the beanstalk. David Wagoner. 390
Sleeping Beauty. David Wagoner. 390

Faith. Evelyn Golden. 263

Faith. Jacques Sollov. 370

Faith
"Because/the sun dips/its bright face/beneath the horizon." Joan Walsh Anglund. 197
Believing. Connie Hunt. 279
"The candle does not know/... and yet its flame." Joan Walsh Anglund. 197
A child's meditation. Alice Joyce Davidson. 227
Confirmation. Robert Pawlowski. 341
Cosmic dust. Erin Jolly. 285
"Do not ask/... but listen." Joan Walsh Anglund. 197
"Do not desire the way/for the way/is yours." Joan Walsh Anglund. 197
Everlasting candle. Alice Joyce Davidson. 227
Faith. Evelyn Golden. 263
Faith. Jacques Sollov. 370
Faith relearned. Andrei Codrescu. 223
The faith. Josephine Miles. 319
The healer. Jacques Sollov. 371
A leaf of life. Alice Joyce Davidson. 227
Lent. Phyllis A. Tickle. 382
Let there be light! Alice Joyce Davidson. 227
Link of faith. Alice Joyce Davidson. 227
Me. Robert L. Wilson. 401
"Only the open gate/can receive." Joan Walsh Anglund. 197
A pact. Alice Joyce Davidson. 227
R.S.V.P. Patsie Black. 206
See, God? James R. Rhodes. 352
"The spirit is still." Joan Walsh Anglund. 197
"The spirit is the unseen circle/within." Joan Walsh Anglund. 197
Stepping-stone. Alice Joyce Davidson. 227
Sunbeam. Alice Joyce Davidson. 227
Twin circles. Alice Joyce

Davidson. 227
When you have faith. Alice Joyce
Davidson. 227
Faith relearned. Andrei Codrescu.
223
The faith. Josephine Miles. 319
A faithful likeness. Colette
Inez. 280
Falcons
Tourists. Josephine Miles. 319
Fall. John F. Barker. 201
Fall. Robert L. Wilson. 401
Fall garden: 1. Gene Anderson.
195
Fall garden: 2. Gene Anderson.
195
Fall guise. Richmond Lattimore.
301
"Fall of a leaf." Larry Eigner.
237
The fall of a sparrow. Robin
Morgan. 325
Fall rituals in America. James
Schevill. 360
Fall song. Cornel Lengyel. 302
A fall song. Ralph J., Jr. Mills.
321
Fall through air. Eileen
Silver-Lillywite. 364
Falling beasts. C.D. Wright. 402
Falling fast, clutching dogma.
David Wann. 394
Falling upwards. David Shapiro.
363
False prophets, false poets.
Norman Andrew Kirk. 293
False spring. Marge Piercy. 346
False spring: late snow. Dave
Smith. 367
A fame for Marilyn Monroe. James
Schevill. 360
Families. See Home and Family
Life

Family. Josephine Miles. 319
Family. Rochelle DuBois. 234
Family. Anneliese Wagner. 389
Family. Martha Janssen. 283
Family album. Robin Becker. 202
Family album. Stephen Sandy. 357
Family snapshot. Iefke
Goldberger. 262
Family tree. Alice Joyce
Davidson. 227
Fanatic. Josephine Miles. 319
Fanny. Edgar Allan Poe. 347
Fantastic. Barry Wallenstein. 393
Fantasy. Martha Janssen. 283
Fantasy
Mirage. James Magorian. 308

Mobile home tires. James
Magorian. 309
Fantasy after a science report.
Jeanne Lohmann. 305
Far beyond distance, fr. Voyages.
Everett A. Gillis. 258
"The far bliss..." Larry Eigner.
237
Fargo fall. Rodney Nelson. 331
The farm. Betty Adcock. 192
A farmer's woman. John Reed. 350
Farming and Farmers
Blueberries. Robert Frost. 250
Cold water creek. Stephen
Knauth. 295
Come. Edwin Honig. 275
The death of the hired man.
Robert Frost. 250
Eagle bridge farm. Stephen
Sandy. 357
The farm. Betty Adcock. 192
Fiction. William Stafford. 373
Fields. C.D. Wright. 402
For a farmer. James A. Emanuel.
239
The forgotten earth. Alice Spohn
Newton. 332
Hardscrabble homestead. Robert
A. Sears. 362
Heaven, circa 1938. Dennis
Hinrichsen. 273
House of sod. Alice Spohn
Newton. 333
The housekeeper. Robert Frost.
250
Limerick. Josephine B. Moretti.
324
Line storm. Mark Vinz. 387
Love on the farm. Jenne Andrews.
196
Map of the world. Dennis
Hinrichsen. 273
North Dakota Gothic. Mark Vinz.
387
The pasture. Robert Frost. 250
Poet in residence. Mary
Gilliland. 257
Probing various facets of hybrid
corn. James Magorian. 309
A prologue to some elegies.
Dennis Hinrichsen. 273
Promise. Edwin Honig. 275
Suprise atonement. James
Magorian. 309
Farmington, NM. William Oandasan.
335
Farolita. Mei-Mei Berssenbrugge.
203
Fascination. Andrei Codrescu. 223
Fascination. C.D. Wright. 402

Fascism = Humor
   Penny wise. Bill Knott. 296
A fashioner of stone roses. Keith
      Wilson. 400
Fasting. Debra Bruce. 216
Fata morgana. Charles Edward
      Eaton. 236
Fate. Connie Hunt. 279
Fate and the goddess never.
      Norman Andrew Kirk. 293
The fate of waking. Cathryn
      Hankla. 268
Fate. See Destiny

Fates, The (mythology)
   For "Moira". Charles Olson. 337
Father. Robert Peters. 343
Father and daughter. Cathy Song.
      372
"Father and Mother and Uncle
      John." Jan Ormerod. 338
Father and son. Sam Fishman. 246
Father sky, mother earth. Charles
      Olson. 337
"The father/pursues...". Madison
      Morrison. 327
Father: as recollection or the
      drug decides. Robert Peters.
      343
The father. Keith Wilson. 400
Fathers. Alice Joyce Davidson.
      227
Fathers and Fatherhood
   Amnesia. Cynthia Grenfell. 266
   "And you, Pa." Michael Robert
      Pick. 345
   Arms. Martha Janssen. 283
   Athena. Debra Bruce. 216
   Bedridden. Christopher Bursk.
      219
   Betrayals. Maria Gillan. 256
   Blue mountain. Debra Bruce. 216
   Canticle: tightening. Jenne
      Andrews. 196
   Changeling. Ghita Orth. 339
   Chartres - Couvent du Sacre
      Coeur? Michael Gizzi. 259
   "Clap hands, Daddy comes." Jan
      Ormerod. 338
   Coaxing. Martha Janssen. 283
   Come back. Larry Moffi. 322
   Dad's song. S. Bradford Williams
      (Jr.). 398
   Daddyboy. Wanda Coleman. 225
   Death comes to my father.
      Jacqueline Frank. 248
   The death of Carl Olsen. Charles
      Olson. 337
   Decision. Martha Janssen. 283
   Drowning. Eileen

   Silver-Lillywite. 364
The ex-seminarian comes home.
      Ray Fleming. 247
Father. Robert Peters. 343
Father and daughter. Cathy Song.
      372
Father and son. Sam Fishman. 246
Father: as recollection or the
      drug decides. Robert Peters.
      343
Fathers. Alice Joyce Davidson.
      227
Fishing upstream with my father.
      Thomas Hornsby Ferril. 243
Fragments. Anthony Petrosky. 344
"Gaunt but conscient." Madison
      Morrison. 327
The gift. Maria Gillan. 256
Going back. Sharon Bryan. 217
Grass. Dennis Hinrichsen. 273
The harvesters' psalm. Cornel
      Lengyel. 302
Heart's needle. W.D. (William De
      Witt) Snodgrass. 369
I am my father's daughter. Laura
      Boss. 213
"I have an ability - a
      machine..." Charles Olson. 337
'I'm nobody's little girl
      anymore since daddy died.'
      Maria Gillan. 256
Ill at fifteen. Christopher
      Bursk. 219
In lieu of an elegy. Jacqueline
      Frank. 248
Journey. Robert Pawlowski. 341
Laps. Martha Janssen. 283
Letter from a son. Rosa Bogar.
      211
Letter to my father. Eileen
      Silver-Lillywite. 364
Lingering melody. Rose Basile
      Green. 265
Love and the father. Ernest
      Tedlock. 380
The magician. Robert Pawlowski.
      341
My father as house-builder.
      Robert Peters. 343
My father deep and late on the
      route south. Herbert Morris.
      326
My father in the basement. David
      Wagoner. 390
My father is. Anthony Petrosky.
      344
My father's valentine. Jack
      Prelutsky. 348
My old man. Jim Simmerman. 365
Mysterious delight. Martha

Janssen. 283

The necessary webs. Thomas R.
Sleigh. 366

The night-father was found
alive. Cathryn Hankla. 268

No better words. Jeanne Lohmann.
305

Nude father in a lake. Robert
Peters. 343

On not attending my father's
funeral. Robert Peters. 343

Other dads. Martha Janssen. 283

Pa. Sam Fishman. 246

Papa. Susan Stock. 375

Philomela's tapestry. Debra
Bruce. 216

Phone call. Christopher Bursk.
219

Plea. Martha Janssen. 283

Poem to my father. Maria Gillan.
256

Poise. Josephine Miles. 319

Poppa's vision. Jim Evernard.
241

Posture. Martha Janssen. 283

Roses in Cleveland. Ray Fleming.
247

Seascape: Santa Monica
Palisades. Everett A. Gillis.
258

Semiotics/the doctor's doll.
Albert Goldbarth. 261

Shadow. Stephen Sandy. 357

Shop of signs. Wanda Coleman.
225

16th Street. Robert Gibb. 253

Son. Josephine Miles. 319

Spring afternoon. Martha
Janssen. 283

St. Barnabas, fr. Friday night
quartet. David Shapiro. 363

This stranger. Tefke Goldberger.
262

Sunday morning: Celia's father.
Dave Smith. 367

Talent. Rosa Bogar. 211

"Tall is the fort." Charles
Olson. 337

Terrestrial. Clayton Eshleman.
240

The test. Roy Marz. 312

Thirty-six. Martha Janssen. 283

"To enter into their bodies."
Charles Olson. 337

To my father, killed in a
hunting accident. Betty
Adcock. 192

The visiting hour. Toi
Derricote. 229

"What happened, Pa." Michael

Robert Pick. 345

You and I. Martha Janssen. 283

Your shroud, papa. Anneliese
Wagner. 389

Fatta l'America. Rose Basile
Green. 265

Faulkner, William (about)
Last words for Count No'count.
James Schevill. 360

FBI kills Martin Luther King.
Bill Knott. 296

Fear. Anne Bailie. 199

Fear. Andrei Codrescu. 223

Fear. Rochelle DuBois. 234

Fear. Martha Janssen. 283

Fear
Aggressor. Josephine Miles. 319

Bad. Wanda Coleman. 225

Call it fear. Joy Harjo. 269

Danger. Martha Janssen. 283

Denial. Josephine Miles. 319

Fear. Andrei Codrescu. 223

Fear. Rochelle DuBois. 234

Fear. Martha Janssen. 283

The fear. Robert Frost. 250

"Fears are chasing." Sally Love
Saunders. 358

Flower studies: bittersweet. Tom
Smith. 368

Four fears. Alberta Turner. 384

"The gunman always rides with
two eyes in the back..." David
James. 282

The howling darkness. Sam
Fishman. 246

I give you back. Joy Harjo. 269

Impatient florist lashing out at
pussyfooting customers. James
Magorian. 309

Intruder. Miriam Goodman. 264

'It is for me to know what I
fear.' Susan Stock. 375

July madonna. Lyn Lifshin. 303

A love poem, of sorts. Gerard
Malanga. 310

Mold madonna. Lyn Lifshin. 303

Night walker. Roy Marz. 312

Off the path. Evelyn Golden. 263

One morning. Lyn Lifshin. 303

Phobophilia. Robin Morgan. 325

The prowler. Mark Vinz. 387

Three A.M. Jacqueline Frank. 248

3 fears in triptych. Anne
Bailie. 199

To one afraid. James R. Rhodes.
352

Warning. Rod McKuen. 316

A warning. Evelyn Golden. 263

Weary. Mitchell Howard. 276

"The windy urban street scene."

Madison Morrison. 327
"Fear is for the multitude."
    James Torio. 281
Fear of love. Debra Bruce. 216
The fear. Robert Frost. 250
The fearful child. Carol Frost.
    249
"Fears are chasing." Sally Love
    Saunders. 358
Feast of all fools. Mark Vinz.
    387
The feast. Unig Khatchadourian.
    292
The feathered bird of the harbor
    of Gloucester. Charles Olson.
    337
February 3rd 1966 High tide...
    Charles Olson. 337
February rain. Evelyn Golden. 263
February woods. Harry Humes. 278
Federal judge rust-proofing an
    ornamental porch railing.
    James Magorian. 309
Feeding. David Wagoner. 390
Feeding the sun. Bill Knott. 296
Feelings
    Black square/white field. David
        James. 282
    Chill. Randy Blasing. 207
    The factory poem. Brenda Marie
        Osbey. 340
    If. Rachel A. Hazen. 271
    The outdoor screen. May Miller.
        320
    People. Miller Williams. 399
    Somewhere. Patsie Black. 206
    Thread. Josephine Miles. 319
    Tokens. Donald Revell. 351
Feet
    A curious erotic custom. Debra
        Bruce. 216
Feet at the end of their path.
    Iefke Goldberger. 262
Feet on familiar ground. Mary
    Gilliland. 257
The fefe women. Brenda Marie
    Osbey. 340
Feldman, Irving
    Albert Feinstein. 242
    The all-stars. 242
    The bathers. 242
    Beauty. 242
    The biographers of solitude. 242
    Conversation on a yam. 242
    A crone's tale. 242
    The drowned man. 242
    Eberheim. 242
    Elena. 242
    The epiphanies. 242
    Flight from the center. 242

Fresh air, sels. 242
The grand magic theater finale.
    242
The gymnasts, fr. Fresh air. 242
Happiness. 242
Ideal disorders, fr. Fresh air.
    242
In old San Juan. 242
Just another smack. 242
The memorable. 242
Millions of strange shadows. 242
A new world, fr. Fresh air. 010
Progress. 242
Read to the animals, or Orpheus
    at the SPCA. 242
The salon of famouse babies. 242
Talking to Fernando. 242
Teach me, dear sister. 242
They. 242
To what's-her-name. 242
The tower, fr. Fresh air. 242
Feline favorites. Alice Spohn
    Newton. 332
Fellowship. Alice Joyce Davidson.
    227
Felon. Wanda Coleman. 225
Feminism. See Women's Rights

Feminist writers. Rochelle
    DuBois. 234
Fences
    The direction of the fence.
        David James. 282
Ferragosto: Viareggio. Robert A.
    Sears. 362
Ferril, Thomas Hornsby
    Absalom. 243
    Anagoge for an island. 243
    Begin again. 243
    Cecropia. 243
    Desert epilog. 243
    Down riverside with Ulysses. 243
    First hour. 243
    Fishing upstream with my father.
        243
    Foreshadowing. 243
    Gnomon. 243
    Invitation. 243
    Jack-knife. 243
    Metamorphoses: 1806. 243
    Night of datura. 243
    Owl. 243
    A parable of prophecy. 243
    Parking lot. 243
    A pretty box. 243
    Silence. 243
    Sleeping longer. 243
    Stories of three summers. 243
    Waterbug. 243
Fertilizing the continent. Joyce

Carol Oates. 336
Festering. Joan Colby. 224
Festival of light. Mark Vinz. 387
Fever in August. Joan Colby. 224
A **few** discretions. Donald Revell. 351
Few of us feel safe anywhere. Robert Peters. 343
Few thing about B-Girl. Harrison Fisher. 245
Fickle. Martha Janssen. 283
Fiction. William Stafford. 373
Fiction study. Gayl Jones. 286
Fidel Castro. Andrei Codrescu. 223
Fidelity
    A broken house. Marc Kaminsky. 288
    Constancy. Elsa Gidlow. 254
    Passage. Carol Frost. 249
    Ricochet off water. Mei-Mei Berssenbrugge. 203
    You say. Elsa Gidlow. 254
"Fidelity to one's soul." Theta Burke. 218
Field Hockey
    Hockey season. Robin Becker. 202
Fields. C.D. Wright. 402
Fields
    The American field. Stephen Knauth. 295
    Another March. Edwin Honig. 275
    Avenal. Ernesto Galarza. 252
    Meadow. Jacqueline Frank. 248
    No return. Marie Daerr Boehringer. 210
    The open field. Jacqueline Frank. 248
    Scything the meadow. Robert Gibb. 253
    Warning. Josephine Miles. 319
    "Wounds sing in the red meadow." Carolyn Stoloff. 376
Fields of learning. Josephine Miles. 319
Fields of vision. Marieve Rugo. 356
Fifteen. Tefke Goldberger. 262
Fifty males sitting together. Robert Bly. 209
Fifty-ninth street. Herbert Morris. 326
Fifty, fifty-one. Maurice Kenny. 291
Fifty/fifty. Rod McKuen. 316
53 slaughtered in Mid-East skirmish. David Wann. 394
Fights and Fighting
    The award for the best argument of the year in Omaha. James

Magorian. 309
    Big-time wrestling. Dennis Hinrichsen. 273
    Cage. Josephine Miles. 319
    Film at eleven. Rod McKuen. 316
    "I hear you, Jacob." Michael Robert Pick. 345
    Reason. Josephine Miles. 319
    The training of a fighter. J.W. Rivers. 354
Figs
    No fig. Stephen Todd Booker. 212
Figure. Josephine Miles. 319
Figure/ground. Miriam Goodman. 264
Filament. Erin Jolly. 285
Filaree. Phillips Kloss. 294
Filarees
    Filaree. Phillips Kloss. 294
"Filipino art and life." Madison Morrison. 327
"Fill with mingled cream and amber." Edgar Allan Poe. 347
Filling two vacancies in the neighborhood car pool. James Magorian. 309
Film at eleven. Rod McKuen. 316
The **final** breath. Rachel A. Hazen. 271
The **final** falling. James R. Rhodes. 352
The **final** virtue. May Miller. 320
Finale - to my country. Rose Basile Green. 265
Finale. Rachel A. Hazen. 271
Find. Josephine Miles. 319
Finding a lake. Tefke Goldberger. 262
Finding an old ant mansion. Robert Bly. 209
Finding out. William Stafford. 373
Finding peace. Alice Joyce Davidson. 227
Finding the one. Rose Basile Green. 265
Finger touching magic. Alice Sponn Newton. 332
Fingering the jagged grains. Melvin Dixon. 231
Fingers. George Eklund. 238
Fingers
    Lady fingers. Norman Andrew Kirk. 293
Finished country. Stephen Sandy. 357
Fire
    Apartment complex manager getting the low-down on... James Magorian. 309

Chains of fires. Elsa Gidlow. 254

The fire-drill. Bradford Morrow. 329

Flowers of fire. John Reed. 350

"He is the one who sees it." Madison Morrison. 327

The lighting of a small fire in the grate. Josephine Miles. 319

The lumber mill fire. James Applewhite. 198

A newspaper picture of spectators at a hotel fire. Miller Williams. 399

The open fire. John F. Barker. 201

Salvaged parts. William Stafford. 373

"Siren/people look." Larry Eigner. 237

Their fire. David Wagoner. 390

The tower, fr. Fresh air. Irving Feldman. 242

"When the fire is low." Theta Burke. 218

Fire agate, fr. Gem show. Everett A. Gillis. 258

"Fire it back into the contintent." Charles Olson. 337

Fire lookout playing with matches. James Magorian. 309

The fire-drill. Bradford Morrow. 329

Fire-eaters
    The firebreathers at the Cafe Deux Magots. Miller Williams. 399

The firebreathers at the Cafe Deux Magots. Miller Williams. 399

Fireflies. Ghita Orth. 339

Firefly. Cathryn Hankla. 268

The firefly. Sandra McPherson. 317

Firing a field. Joyce Carol Oates. 336

First affair. Wanda Coleman. 225

First aid at 4 a.m. Christopher Bursk. 219

First by the sea. James Applewhite. 198

First communion and thereafter. Robert Pawlowski. 341

First dark. Joyce Carol Oates. 336

First date. Eileen Silver-Lillywite. 364

The first day of spring at the

cabin... Anthony Petrosky. 344

First death, 1950. Joyce Carol Oates. 336

The first eviction. Cornel Lengyel. 302

First hour. Thomas Hornsby Ferril. 243

The first icon with gun. Andrei Codrescu. 223

First job. Christopher Bursk. 219

First letter on Georges. Charles Olson. 337

First light. Mark Vinz. 387

First light. David Wagoner. 390

First London conference in the American campaign... James Schevill. 360

First love. Jacques Sollov. 370

The first mate. John Reed. 350

First morning. Edwin Honig. 275

The first night of summer. Eileen Silver-Lillywite. 364

"The first of morning was always over there." Charles Olson. 337

The first one. Rose Basile Green. 265

First poem to Mary in London. Ernest Hemingway. 272

The first prayer of angles. Cathryn Hankla. 268

First quartets. Roy Marz. 312

The first reality. Rachel A. Hazen. 271

First step. Alice Joyce Davidson. 227

First steps. Mary Gilliland. 257

The first subdivider. Cornel Lengyel. 302

First taste. John Godfrey. 260

First ticket. Debra Bruce. 216

The first time. James L. White. 396

1st lot from the Cutt.">"The f. Charles Olson. 337

1st Avenue basics f. Andrei Codrescu. 223

Firstborn. Louise Gluck. 259A

Fish. Josephine Miles. 319

Fish. Jack Prelutsky. 349

Fish
    Aquarium. Ruth Lisa Schechter. 359

    The delicacy. Sandra McPherson. 317

    A dream of fish. Mark Vinz. 387

    Fish. Jack Prelutsky. 349

    I see three fish in the bowl of water. Carolyn Stoloff. 376

    Mackerel. Charles Edward Eaton.

236
The muskellunge. Harry Humes.
  278
Pigfish. Stephen Todd Booker.
  212
Predators from a branch of the
  blackthorned sloe. Susan
  Stock. 375
Red snapper. Charles Edward
  Eaton. 236
To the deepest level. Evelyn
  Golden. 263
Fish kill in January. Harry
  Humes. 278
Fisher, Aileen
  Beneath the snowy trees. 244
  Bulgy eyes. 244
  But rabbits. 244
  Clover rain. 244
  Color blind. 244
  Cotton tails. 244
  Do rabbits have Christmas? 244
  Early spring. 244
  Easter morning. 244
  Hop, skip, and jump. 244
  Jack Rabbit. 244
  Rabbit world. 244
  Ready... set... 244
  Run, rabbit! 244
  Says the rabbit. 244
  Secrets. 244
  Snowshoe hare. 244
  Spring fever. 244
  Thinking. 244
  To a lady cottontail. 244
  Who scans the meadow. 244
Fisher, Harrison
  American beauties. 245
  American belles. 245
  The American girl. 245
  Bachelor belles. 245
  Beauties. 245
  Concerning Belinda. 245
  Confessions of a stardreamer.
    245
  Cowardice court. 245
  Dagwood's day of wrath. 245
  A dream of fair women. 245
  Few thing about B-Girl. 245
  Gangsterism and cooltn. 245
  A garden of girls. 245
  A girl's life & other pictures.
    245
  The Harrison Fisher book. 245
  Harrison Fisher girls. 245
  Harrison Fisher's American girls
    in miniature. 245
  Harry noir. 245
  The lives of a Bengal lancer.
    245

Maidens fair. 245
No timid sawyer. 245
Pictures in color. 245
Primitive chic. 245
Scrabble revisited. 245
Spaghetti westerns and the cult
  of cowboy blood. 245
UFO scenarios. 245
UHFO. 245
Viris illustribus. 245
X wives. 245
Fishing. Betty Adcock. 192
Fishing. Franz Schneider. 361
Fishing Aeneas creek. Franz
  Schneider. 361
Fishing and Fishermen
  "As I stand, he." Madison
    Morrison. 327
  Culpepper goes bass fishing.
    J.W. Rivers. 354
  Fish kill in January. Harry
    Humes. 278
  Fishing. Betty Adcock. 192
  Fishing. Franz Schneider. 361
  Fishing Aeneas creek. Franz
    Schneider. 361
  "George Decker..." Charles
    Olson. 337
  The Gulf of Maine. Charles
    Olson. 337
  History is the memory of time.
    Charles Olson. 337
  The ice fisherman's dream. Harry
    Humes. 278
  Learning to fish fresh water.
    Larry Moffi. 322
  Letter 6. Charles Olson. 337
  A letter, on fishing grounds...
    Charles Olson. 337
  Maximus, to Gloucester, Sunday,
    July 19. Charles Olson. 337
  Moyie River: welcome ranch.
    Franz Schneider. 361
  Night-fishing on Irish Buffalo
    Creek. Stephen Knautn. 295
  O John Josselyn you. Charles
    Olson. 337
  The river fishes. Robert
    Pawlowski. 341
  Small boats. Steve Kowit. 299
  Talking from Inverness. Susan
    Tichy. 381
  3rd letter on Georges, unwritten.
    Charles Olson. 337
  "This town." Charles Olson. 337
  Three anecdotes. Deborah Tall.
    378
  To fish. Carol Frost. 249
  Water we walked on. Larry Moffi.
    322

Fishing License. James Magorian. 308
Fishing upstream with my father. Thomas Hornsby Ferril. 243
Fishman, Sam
  And so on. 246
  Another thought. 246
  At home. 246
  Ballad of Claudine. 246
  The brothers. 246
  The cage. 246
  The cycle. 246
  Envy no man. 246
  Epitaph. 246
  Father and son. 246
  Friends. 246
  The fun. 246
  Gloom. 246
  Harbor night. 246
  The having. 246
  Heil! 246
  Hope. 246
  The howling darkness. 246
  Janet. 246
  Just a thought. 246
  The lesson. 246
  Let reason reign. 246
  The losing. 246
  The loving. 246
  Ma on her ninetieth birthday. 246
  The madness. 246
  Munich. 246
  No more, no more. 246
  No one knows. 246
  The old ones. 246
  Pa. 246
  Paradise lost and found. 246
  The prophet. 246
  Psycho love. 246
  Regret. 246
  Remembering. 246
  The restless mind. 246
  Song of the retired senior citizen. 246
  The stepchild. 246
  A swimmer in the sea. 246
  The telling. 246
  Thinking of her. 246
  To Milly on our thirty-fifth wedding anniversary. 246
  Van Gogh. 246
  The wanting. 246
  When love leaves. 246
  Why man? 246
  Why? 246
  Winter land. 246
Fit. Josephine Miles. 319
Fitzgerald, Scott
  Lines to be read at the casting

of Scott Fitzgerald... Ernest Hemingway. 272
"The 5 and 1/2 million." Larry Eigner. 237
Five potatoes. Sandra Gilbert. 255
Five precious stones. Robert Kelly. 289
Five years old. James Tate. 379
5 P.M. Rochelle DuBois. 234
The fivefold root of insufficient reason. Phillips Kloss. 294
Flags. Jocelyn Hollis. 274
Flags
  Flags. Jocelyn Hollis. 274
Flash. Stephen Todd Booker. 212
Flat roofs. Ernest Hemingway. 272
"Flat sky/going down." Larry Eigner. 237
The flawless dancer. Mitchell Howard. 276
Flea. Norman Andrew Kirk. 293
Fleas
  Flea. Norman Andrew Kirk. 293
Fleming, Ray
  Academic circles. 247
  Alternative lifestyle. 247
  At the land's end. 247
  Bakke's law, or lateral movement. 247
  Constant tenderness. 247
  Daydreaming in the Bodleian Library. 247
  Deconstruction in San Diego. 247
  Diplomatic relations with America. 247
  En-gai. 247
  The ex-seminarian comes home. 247
  For Paul Robeson. 247
  Graveyard in the jungle. 247
  Icicles. 247
  In the Cotswolds. 247
  The La Jolla ladies. 247
  The life expectancy of black American males. 247
  Old men sailing the Baltic. 247
  On the face of my words. 247
  Oxfordshire spring. 247
  The post-modern poem as clean-up hitter. 247
  Pragmatic sanction. 247
  Roses in Cleveland. 247
  San Diego. 247
  Semi-detached in Oxford. 247
  Simultaneous translation. 247
  The split end with average speed. 247
  Sudden death overtime. 247
  Sunset on mission bay. 247

Unlimited timeouts. 247
Vedi Napoli e muori. 247
The Viking's horn at Sogne. 247
A walk into the Cumner Hills.
  247
Werenskiold's portrait of Henrik
  Ibsen. 247
What the king saw. 247
Where are the lovers? 247
The world before it became a
  poem. 247
Young black man teaching Italian
  to middle-class white... 247
Flesh. David Shapiro. 363
Flesh. Marieve Rugo. 356
Flesh. Greg Kuzma. 300
Flesh and bones. Marieve Rugo.
  356
The flesh of discovery. James
  Schevill. 360
Flesh of the fawn. James
  Schevill. 360
Flesh tones. Richmond Lattimore.
  301
Flies
  Bound. John F. Barker. 201
  Fly. X.J. Kennedy. 290
  Mayflies. Colette Inez. 280
Flight. Erin Jolly. 285
Flight from the center. Irving
  Feldman. 242
Flight of steps. Stephen Sandy.
  357
Flight of the California condor.
  Wanda Coleman. 225
Flights. Joan Colby. 224
Flirting
  Hey baby. Debra Bruce. 216
  Riding to work with the
    gastarbeiter. Larry Moffi. 322
"Flock of birds." Larry Eigner.
  237
"The flock.". Larry Eigner. 237
Flocking. Harry Humes. 278
Flood. Robert Pawlowski. 341
Floodlight. Erin Jolly. 285
Floods
  Bridal Veil Falls in Yosemite
    Valley. Evelyn Golden. 263
  Flood. Robert Pawlowski. 341
  "In the mountain meadow."
    Madison Morrison. 327
The floods of spring. Keith
  Wilson. 400
Florence, Italy
  Three Florentines summoned.
    Franz Schneider. 361
Florida
  Palm Beach, 1928. Herbert
    Morris. 326

To Florida. Louise Gluck. 259A
Florida Keys
  The keys. Randy Blasing. 207
Florida Scott-Maxwell helps
  recite my grandmother's life.
  Susan Tichy. 381
Florin. Ernesto Galarza. 252
The flower of our journey (so
  Sonia travels). Kiarri T-H
  Cheatwood. 220
Flower of the field. Alice Joyce
  Davidson. 227
Flower of the underworld. Charles
  Olson. 337
The flower-washer in New York.
  James Schevill. 360
Flower studies, sels. Tom Smith.
  368
Flower studies: bittersweet. Tom
  Smith. 368
Flower studies: brown-eyed Susan.
  Tom Smith. 368
Flower studies: holly. Tom Smith.
  368
Flower studies: tigerlily. Tom
  Smith. 368
A flower. Rachel A. Hazen. 271
The flower. David Wagoner. 390
Flowers
  Anemones. Maurice Kenny. 291
  Expected guests. Alice Spohn
    Newton. 332
  Fit. Josephine Miles. 319
  A flower. Rachel A. Hazen. 271
  Ho hum. Marie Daerr Boehringer.
    210
  "Imbued/with light." Charles
    Olson. 337
  In the language of flowers. Jim
    Simmerman. 365
  Language of flowers. Jacques
    Sollov. 370
  The last five flowers. James R.
    Rhodes. 352
  Lines written for June. John F.
    Barker. 201
  Man with purple beard. Anneliese
    Wagner. 389
  Nature's garden: an aid to
    knowledge of wild flowers.
    Robin Morgan. 325
  North American wildflowers.
    Stephen Knauth. 295
  Peony. Robin Morgan. 325
  The rare flower. Rosa Bogar. 211
  There would be large cuttings of
    flowers. Edwin Honig. 275
  This view of the meadow. Robert
    Gibb. 253
  Valentines. Rod McKuen. 316

Flowers of fire. John Reed. 350
Flowers of shadow. Keith Wilson.
    400
Flowers, James Alma
    The land. Jim Simmerman. 365
Floyd, Pretty Boy (outlaw)
    Strange woman. Alice Spohn
        Newton. 333
Flutes
    Remembering flute house. Gary
        Margolis. 311
Fly. X.J. Kennedy. 290
Fly boy. Wanda Coleman. 225
Flying
    "Ever catch a butterfly or
        moth." Michael Robert Pick.
        345
    "How would you like to grow
        wings with me." Michael Robert
        Pick. 345
    'Neither fish nor fowle.'
        Christopher Bursk. 219
    Soaring. Jeanne Lohmann. 305
    "Swimming through the air..."
        Charles Olson. 337
A flying machine. Alice Spohn
    Newton. 333
The flying people. Stephen
    Knauth. 295
The flying snake. Alice Spohn
    Newton. 333
Flying solo. Brenda Marie Osbey.
    340
Flying up. Gary Margolis. 311
Flying. See also Aviation

Foetus graffiti. Clayton
    Eshleman. 240
Fog. Amy Clampitt. 222
Fog. Sally Love Saunders. 358
Fog. John Reed. 350
Fog
    Captured. Robert L. Wilson. 401
    Fog. Amy Clampitt. 222
    Fog. Sally Love Saunders. 358
    The fog. Everett A. Gillis. 258
    Gradual clearing. Amy Clampitt.
        222
    Hawk Mountain in the fog. Harry
        Humes. 278
"The fog holds." Larry Eigner.
    237
The fog. Everett A. Gillis. 258
Folie. Michael Gizzi. 259
Folk music of Tibet. Robert
    Kelly. 289
"Followed his sow to apples."
    Charles Olson. 337
Fond. Alberta Turner. 384
Food and Eating

Ars poetica. Frances Mayes. 314
Augusta tells the milkman.
    Carolyn Stoloff. 376
The baker. Gary Margolis. 311
Before meat. Alberta Turner. 384
"Being near dinner time."
    Madison Morrison. 327
Bisbane's flower. Bradford
    Morrow. 329
Chief cook and waiter. Josephine
    B. Moretti. 324
Eulogy for Colonel Sanders.
    James Magorian. 309
Fasting. Debra Bruce. 216
Figure/ground. Miriam Goodman.
    264
Firstborn. Louise Gluck. 259A
The gourmet minces his words.
    Gary Margolis. 311
"Here they come." Madison
    Morrison. 327
Kitchen maid. Frances Mayes. 314
Late at night in the kitchen.
    J.W. Rivers. 354
Making cakes and dumplings. J.W.
    Rivers. 354
On being swallowed whole. Alice
    Spohn Newton. 332
Pass the paprika. Josephine B.
    Moretti. 324
Peak activity in boardwalk ham
    concession. Josephine Miles.
    319
"Perfect/strangers, dining."
    Larry Eigner. 237
Pigging out. Wanda Coleman. 225
Poem to a super market.
    Josephine B. Moretti. 324
"A round/table..." Madison
    Morrison. 327
"The sinewy descendant." Madison
    Morrison. 327
Small town grocer. Josephine B.
    Moretti. 324
Smithfield ham. Dave Smith. 367
Spaghetti O's. David Wann. 394
Sterling Mountain. Stephen
    Sandy. 357
"The suitors do the." Madison
    Morrison. 327
Table manners. James Magorian.
    309
Tranquilizers. Josephine B.
    Moretti. 324
Uppsala. Michael Gizzi. 259
Whalefeathers. Paul Violi. 388
When the cook's not hungry.
    Josephine B. Moretti. 324
A fool for evergreen. James A.
    Emanuel. 239

Fool's song. Cornel Lengyel. 302
Fooled dearly. Rachel A. Hazen. 271
Football
 Fall rituals in America. James Schevill. 360
 High school football coach. James Schevill. 360
 The punt, fr. Athletic verse. Ernest Hemingway. 272
 Running back. Dave Smith. 367
 The safety man, fr. Athletic verse. Ernest Hemingway. 272
 The split end with average speed. Ray Fleming. 247
 Sudden death overtime. Ray Fleming. 247
 The suicide runner. James Schevill. 360
 Sunday morning sandlot football. J.W. Rivers. 354
 The tackle, fr. Athletic verse. Ernest Hemingway. 272
football game/The. Maurice W. Britts. 215
Footnote to love. Erin Jolly. 285
Footnote to the classics. Royal Murdoch. 330
Footprints. Joyce Carol Oates. 336
For "Moira". Charles Olson. 337
For a farmer. James A. Emanuel. 239
For a fisherman who dynamited a cormorant rookery. David Wagoner. 390
For a friend-with the gift of a recording. Sister Maura. 313
For a gifted lady, often masked. Elsa Gidlow. 254
For a woman sitting by a creek. David Wagoner. 390
For A.J.: on finding she's on her boat to China. Cathy Song. 372
For Alan Dugan. Greg Kuzma. 300
For Alexander Pope's gardens. John Yau. 404
For all inside. Rachel A. Hazen. 271
For Allan. Susan Tichy. 381
For Alva Benson, and for those who have learned to speak. Joy Harjo. 269
For an electric man. Carolyn Stoloff. 376
For an immigrant grandmother. Edwin Honig. 275
For an infant whose heart stopped for eleven minutes. Carol Frost. 249

For Annie. Edgar Allan Poe. 347
For Avraham. Susan Tichy. 381
For bad grandmother and Betty Bumhead. Debra Bruce. 216
For Bill. Ernest Tedlock. 380
For Bill who passed on with the summer. Mary Gilliland. 257
For Bob Schuler. Ralph J., Jr. Mills. 321
For Bonnie, my swim teacher. Anneliese Wagner. 389
For C. Edwin Honig. 275
For Elizabeth Bishop. Sandra McPherson. 317
"For everyone the call of light." Edwin Honig. 275
For Fernand Lagarde (died 13 April 1982). James A. Emanuel. 239
For futures. Josephine Miles. 319
For Gaby. Susan Tichy. 381
For Heidi. Robert Pawlowski. 341
For him. Royal Murdoch. 330
For his mother flying into her seventy-seventh. Edwin Honig. 275
For lack of you. Bill Knott. 296
For Lael, dead at Nahariya. Ghita Orth. 339
For Louise. Jeanne Lohmann. 305
For luck. Anthony Petrosky. 344
For magistrates. Josephine Miles. 319
For Marcie. Jim Everhard. 241
For Marg so she could... Andrei Codrescu. 223
For Margot. Edwin Honig. 275
For Max Jacob, sels. Andrei Codrescu. 223
For me? James R. Rhodes. 352
For my brother. Cathy Song. 372
For my name's sake. Ghita Orth. 339
For my sister. Debra Bruce. 216
For my son Noah, ten years old. Robert Bly. 209
For now. Laura Boss. 213
For now. Robert Gibb. 253
For one who could not stay. Everett A. Gillis. 258
For Paul Robeson. Ray Fleming. 247
For Rebecca on a Sunday morning in the spring. Phyllis A. Tickle. 382
For Richard Eberhart. Ralph J., Jr. Mills. 321
For Robert Hollabaugh, M.D. Phyllis A. Tickle. 382
For Robt Duncan, who nderstands

what's going on... Charles Olson. 337

For Ron McKernan. Kirk Lumpkin. 306

For Sarah, home after a weekend in the country. Robin Becker. 202

For shells. Rochelle DuBois. 234

"For so long you've." Sally Love Saunders. 358

For Sousa Junior High, 1967. James A. Emanuel. 230

For Stan Getz. Susan Stock. 375

For the boy reading Playboy. Debra Bruce. 216

For the furies. Marge Piercy. 346

For the goddess too well known. Elsa Gidlow. 254

"For the harlot has a hardlot." Ernest Hemingway. 272

For the jazzman. Rochelle DuBois. 234

For the new occupants. Sister Maura. 313

For the saxophonist, Brew Moore. James Schevill. 360

For the wind. James R. Rhodes. 352

For those yet unborn. Maurice W. Britts. 215

For travelers on the sabbath. Cornel Lengyel. 302

For Victor Jara. Miller Williams. 399

For Wade. Phyllis A. Tickle. 382

For Wang Wei. Marc Hudson. 277

For Weldon Kees. Greg Kuzma. 300

For you. John Godfrey. 260

The forbidden. Joyce Carol Oates. 336

"The force.". Larry Eigner. 237

Forced entry. Marieve Rugo. 356

The ford. Jacqueline Frank. 248

Forecast. Josephine Miles. 319

Forecast. Jenne Andrews. 196

Forecast. Marie Daerr Boehringer. 210

"Forehead, breath, and smile." Da Free John. 284

A foreign country. Josephine Miles. 319

Foreign waters. Randy Blasing. 207

Foreman of a hung jury. James Magorian. 308

Foreshadowing. Thomas Hornsby Ferril. 243

Forest children. Colette Inez. 280

Forest floor North America.

Colette Inez. 280

Forest walk. Robert Peters. 343

Forest years. Cornel Lengyel. 302

Forests
For Bob Schuler. Ralph J., Jr. Mills. 321
Forest children. Colette Inez. 280
Forest walk. Robert Peters. 343
Fragrant forest. Ralph J., Jr. Mills. 321
How clearly we entered. Judson Crews. 226
In the wilds. Maurice Kenny. 291
La pineta di Migliarino. Robert A. Sears. 362
The light asks. Carol Frost. 249
Like any great forest. Michael Akillian. 193
Lucky with woods. Robert Gibb. 253
Near Pamet marsh. Stephen Sandy. 357
Rain forest. Jeanne Lohmann. 305
Survival manual. Mark Vinz. 387
Time lapse. David Wann. 394
A walk in the woods. Evelyn Golden. 263
The wood-pile. Robert Frost. 250

Foretold. C.D. Wright. 402

A forever friend. Alice Joyce Davidson. 227

The forgetful life. Stephen Knauth. 295

Forgetfulness
The forgetful life. Stephen Knauth. 295
In the dark. Steve Kowit. 299
Pete. Susan Stock. 375

Forgive. Alberta Turner. 384

Forgive us. Elsa Gidlow. 254

Forgiveness. John F. Barker. 201

Forgiveness. Connie Hunt. 279

Forgiveness. Martha Janssen. 283

Forgiveness
Answering thr past. Cathryn Hankla. 268
Compassion. Alice Joyce Davidson. 227
Escape into autumn. Anne Bailie. 199
First communion and thereafter. Robert Pawlowski. 341
Forgive. Alberta Turner. 384
Forgiveness. John F. Barker. 201
Forgiveness. Connie Hunt. 279
Forgiveness. Martha Janssen. 283
The hallowing of hell: a psalm in nine circles. Robin Morgan. 325

The lattice. Robert Kelly. 289
Soon. Jim Simmerman. 365
The toaster. Greg Kuzma. 300
Forgotten. John Reed. 350
The forgotten earth. Alice Spohn
    Newton. 332
The forgotten wall. James
    Schevill. 360
Forlorn dream song. Richmond
    Lattimore. 301
Form. Roy Marz. 312
Form and actuality. Richmond
    Lattimore. 301
The form and function of the
    novel. Albert Goldbarth. 261
A formal occasion. Thomas R.
    Sleigh. 366
Former bank examiner feigning
    sleep in a monastery in Tibet.
    James Magorian. 309
Former residence. Richmond
    Lattimore. 301
Formulas for non-violence.
    Mitchell Howard. 276
Forseeing the journey. James
    Applewhite. 198
Forspent. Erin Jolly. 285
Forsythia
    Decision. Marie Daerr
    Boehringer. 210
Fortune
    Loser. Josephine Miles. 319
    Stanzas (to F.S.O.). Edgar Allan
    Poe. 347
Fortune cookies. Debra Bruce. 216
Fortune Cookies

    Fortunes. Josephine Miles. 319
Fortune Tellers
    Mind songs. James R. Rhodes. 352
    Seer. Josephine Miles. 319
    Your fortune: a cold reading.
    David Wagoner. 390
Fortunes. Josephine Miles. 319
Forty-seven years. Clayton
    Eshleman. 240
Forum (Rome)
    The vestal in the Forum. James
    Wright. 403
Fossils in the sand. Rochelle
    DuBois. 234
Foster Parents
    In a country of condolences.
    Colette Inez. 280
The foundations of a sky-scraper.
    John Reed. 350
Fountain, fr. Friday night
    quartet. David Shapiro. 363
The fountain. Sister Maura. 313
Four fears. Alberta Turner. 384
405.   Steve Kowit. 298, 299

Four in December. Ralph J., Jr.
    Mills. 321
Four lines. David Shapiro. 363
The four o'clocks. Eve Triem. 383
Four portraits of beans. David
    James. 282
Four quotes that didn't make the
    bible. Michael Akillian. 193
Four songs. Josephine Miles. 319
Four springs, sels. Edwin Honig.
    275
Four unfinished prisoners by
    Michelangelo. Roy Marz. 312
Four ways of knowledge. Robert
    Bly. 209
Four years old. Martha Janssen.
    283
4 A.M.   Rochelle DuBois. 234
4 P.M.   Rochelle DuBois. 234
Fourteen. James A. Emanuel. 239
14 January.   Ralph J., Jr.
    Mills. 321
Fourteen men stage head winter
    1624/5. Charles Olson. 337
Fourteenth Century
    A natural history of the
    fourteenth century. Marc
    Hudson. 277
Fourth commandment. Martha
    Janssen. 283
The fourth confrontation with
    Tina Turner. David James. 282
Fourth dimension. Anne Bailie.
    199
Fourth grade. David Wann. 394
Fourth of July. See Independence
    Day

4-wheeler, with. Stephen Todd
    Booker. 212
Fowl
    An Easter apology to my guineas.
    Phyllis A. Tickle. 382
"A fox and a girl meet among
    stars." Carolyn Stoloff. 376
Fox and bee. Tom Smith. 368
The fox and the geese. James
    Magorian. 308
Foxes
    Sampson and the foxes. Cornel
    Lengyel. 302
Fra Elbertus or the inspector
    general. James Schevill. 360
Fracture. Clayton Eshleman. 240
Fragile ladies. Erin Jolly. 285
Fragment. Rod McKuen. 316
Fragment of ancient skull. Steve
    Kowit. 299
A fragment of relief. David
    Shapiro. 363

Fragments. Anthony Petrosky. 344
Fragrant forest. Ralph J., Jr.
    Mills. 321
Frailties. Maria Gillan. 256
Frameless. Roy Marz. 312
Fran's birthday. Mitchell Howard.
    276
France
    Fraternite. John F. Barker. 201
    The French night. Herbert
        Morris. 326
    Garcon. John F. Barker. 201
    La cite de Carcassonne. John F.
        Barker. 201
    Racism in France. James A.
        Emanuel. 239
    The road to Avallon. Ernest
        Hemingway. 272
    "The two-room/apartment..."
        Madison Morrison. 327
France, Anatole
    The stable. Roy Marz. 312
France, Marie de
    After Marie. Marilyn Kallet. 287
Francesca da Rimini. Tom Smith.
    368
Francis of Assisi, Saint
    A faithful likeness. Colette
        Inez. 280
    Saint Francis. Everett A.
        Gillis. 258
A Francis Ponge. Andrei Codrescu.
    223
Franco, Francisco
    In 1970 in Madrid, President
        Nixon presents General
        Franco.. James Schevill. 360
Francoise and the fruit farmer.
    James A. Emanuel. 239
Frank, Anne
    In season. Debra Bruce. 216
Frank, Jacqueline
    At seventeen. 248
    The cathedral. 248
    Come a daisy. 248
    Death comes to my father. 248
    Delirium in a small room. 248
    Detour. 248
    Elegy for my brother. 248
    Eyes. 248
    The ford. 248
    From the other side of the
        keyhole. 248
    The garden. 248
    Ghettos and gardens. 248
    Homage to the moon. 248
    I put my trust in the river. 248
    In danger of drowning. 248
    In lieu of an elegy. 248
    In the face of anger. 248
    In time of praise. 248
    Inventory. 248
    Love poem. 248
    Mail. 248
    The man from Western Union. 248
    Meadow. 248
    My brother, the bishop. 248
    The new bed. 248
    No one took a country from me.
        248
    Nothing ever happens only once.
        248
    The open field. 248
    Oysters. 248
    Passing through Les Eyzies. 248
    Reading Hannah Arendt's Eichmann
        in Jerusalem. 248
    The relatives. 248
    Rite. 248
    Season. 248
    The secret. 248
    The table. 248
    A thing like stone. 248
    Thirteen lines. 248
    Three A.M. 248
    Translating. 248
    Waiting for you. 248
    When the deer will flee. 248
    Winter. 248
    World War II. 248
Frankfurt '76. James Torio. 281
Franklin, John Hope
    Little old black historian.
        James A. Emanuel. 239
Franklin, Massachusetts. Eileen
    Silver-Lillywite. 364
Franny Glass at forty-seven. Gene
    Detro. 230
Fraternite. John F. Barker. 201
Free. Patsie Black. 206
Free associations on Mother's
    Day. Tefke Goldberger. 262
Free fuel. Alice Spohn Newton.
    333
Free pass. Mitchell Howard. 276
Free to love. Connie Hunt. 279
Freedom
    Alive. Joy Harjo. 269
    Attempted kidnapping. Robert L.
        Wilson. 401
    Beyond limits. May Miller. 320
    The box. Connie Hunt. 279
    "Chain his body." Michael Robert
        Pick. 345
    Change. Martha Janssen. 283
    Complete freedom. Greg Kuzma.
        300
    Drowning another peasant
        inquisition. Andrei Codrescu.
        223

Freedom, freedom,
    freedom-hosiery. Stephen Todd
    Booker. 212
I am free. Connie Hunt. 279
Maturity. Martha Janssen. 283
"A moment of high excitement."
    Theta Burke. 218
Now. Patsie Black. 206
"Oh but rest in the sheltor of
    love." Michael Robert Pick.
    345
The old woman of Patras. James
    Torio. 281
Outside Martins Ferry, Ohio.
    Dave Smith. 367
The price of freedom. Robert L.
    Wilson. 401
A quarrel put to rest. Colette
    Inez. 280
Viva la libertad! Royal Murdoch.
    330
"We cling to/and espouse a
    creed." Theta Burke. 218
Where are you going?, fr. The
    day of the body. Carol Frost.
    249
The white bird. Jacques Sollov.
    371
Freedom of expression. Connie
    Hunt. 279
Freedom, freedom,
    freedom-hosiery. Stephen Todd
    Booker. 212
"Freedom/is the coming of
    one/unto himself." Theta
    Burke. 218
Freefall can be fun. Mitchell
    Howard. 276
Freeway. Stephen Sandy. 357
French and Indian Wars
    "The last man except
    conceivably." Charles Olson.
    337
French club - Kano. Robert A.
    Sears. 362
The French night. Herbert Morris.
    326
Frenzied forecast. Marie Daerr
    Boehringer. 210
Fresco:departure for an
    imperialist war. Thomas
    McGrath. 315
Fresh air, sels. Irving Feldman.
    242
Fresh roses along the path. Sally
    Love Saunders. 358
The Friday before the long
    weekend. Joy Harjo. 269
Friday night quartet, sels. David
    Shapiro. 363

Friday night quartet, fr. Friday
    night quartet. David Shapiro.
    363
Friday's child. John Godfrey. 260
Friday, the day Mariana Penko
    quit cooking... Anthony
    Petrosky. 344
Friend. Josephine Miles. 319
The friend departs. Elsa Gidlow.
    254
Friend me a friend. Patsie Black.
    206
Friend of forty years. Judson
    Crews. 226
A friend starts west on
    Melville's birthday. Robert
    Gibb. 253
A friend?. Evelyn Golden. 263
Friendly persuasion. Josephine B.
    Moretti. 324
"A friendly smile." Connie Hunt.
    279
Friends. Sam Fishman. 246
Friends. Sally Love Saunders. 358
Friends. William Stafford. 373
Friends. Connie Hunt. 279
Friends in a lonely time. Rachel
    A. Hazen. 271
"Friends in our questions, we
    looked together." Josephine
    Miles. 319
Friends, farewell. William
    Stafford. 373
Friends: a recognition. William
    Stafford. 373
Friendship
    Acceptance. Connie Hunt. 279
    All hallow's eve. Gerard
    Malanga. 310
    Alone inside. Rachel A. Hazen.
    271
    And for Jenny. Rachel A. Hazen.
    271
    Baring friendship. Mary
    Gilliland. 257
    Bennet. George Eklund. 238
    '"Blood is thicker than water.'"
    Ernest Hemingway. 272
    Blueberries. Dennis Hinrichsen.
    273
    Buddy - in and not in arms.
    Stephen Todd Booker. 212
    Captivities. Robin Becker. 202
    Carl Perusick. Anthony Petrosky.
    344
    Comrade. Royal Murdoch. 330
    Confidence. Josephine Miles. 319
    Costly treasure. Alice Joyce
    Davidson. 227
    Cynthia. Maurice W. Britts. 215

Dinner with a friend. Wanda
  Coleman. 225
Enchant. Josephine Miles. 319
The first reality. Rachel A.
  Hazen. 271
Fooled dearly. Rachel A. Hazen.
  271
A forever friend. Alice Joyce
  Davidson. 227
Four songs. Josephine Miles. 319
Friend. Josephine Miles. 319
Friend me a friend. Patsie
  Black. 206
A friend? Evelyn Golden. 263
Friends. Sam Fishman. 246
Friends. Sally Love Saunders.
  358
Friends. William Stafford. 373
Friends. Connie Hunt. 279
Friends in a lonely time. Rachel
  A. Hazen. 271
Friends: a recognition. William
  Stafford. 373
Grandpa's friend Pete. Alice
  Spohn Newton. 333
Imagine the dreams we dream
  today. Rachel A. Hazen. 271
Karen. Rachel A. Hazen. 271
Karen. Anneliese Wagner. 389
The last of me. Rachel A. Hazen.
  271
Liana. Rachel A. Hazen. 271
A lost friend. Ernest Tedlock.
  380
My friend. Josephine B. Moretti.
  324
My friend who's afraid of the
  dark. Cathryn Hankla. 268
My friends are a song. Alice
  Spohn Newton. 332
Night-walk, Montrose,
  Pennsylvania. Dave Smith. 367
"Okay, Hawk, where are you when
  I need you." Michael Robert
  Pick. 345
On nameless days. Rachel A.
  Hazen. 271
Pam. Wanda Coleman. 225
Past and fantasy. Rachel A.
  Hazen. 271
A snarl for loose friends. Marge
  Piercy. 346
A sometimes wondering. Rachel A.
  Hazen. 271
Spring lunch. Colette Inez. 280
Table song. Cornel Lengyel. 302
Three moments for George
  Sullivan. Edwin Honig. 275
To Beata. Rachel A. Hazen. 271
To Heather. Rachel A. Hazen. 271
To Monica and Liz. Rachel A.
  Hazen. 271
To Sue. Rachel A. Hazen. 271
The touch of something solid.
  Cathryn Hankla. 268
A valentine for my best friend.
  Jack Prelutsky. 348
Water burning wills away.
  Cathryn Hankla. 268
When dreams are dreams. Rachel
  A. Hazen. 271
When friends leave. Robin
  Becker. 202
While gardens grow their roses.
  Alice Spohn Newton. 332
Your friend. Rosa Bogar. 211
Frogs
An answer for my daughter. Ghita
  Orth. 339
Green frog at Roadstead,
  Wisconsin. James Schevill. 360
The marvelous blue frog. William
  Oandasan. 335
The other house. David Wagoner.
  390
Simply marvelous. Kirk Lumpkin.
  306
"Tree frogs busily singing."
  Sally Love Saunders. 358
From. Robert Kelly. 289
From a conversation in a street.
  Keith Wilson. 400
From a dictionary of common
  terms, sels. Alberta Turner.
  384
From a snapshot of the poet.
  Carolyn Stoloff. 376
From a trilogy of birds. Andrei
  Codrescu. 223
From Burnside to Goldblatt's by
  streetcar. J.W. Rivers. 354
"From centuries your line."
  Robert A. Sears. 362
From Hallmark or somewhere.
  William Stafford. 373
From herewhere? David Wann. 394
From Hindi, sels. Josephine
  Miles. 319
"From inner battle he has come."
  Theta Burke. 218
From Malay. David Shapiro. 363
From my heart to yours. Alice
  Joyce Davidson. 227
"From now on..." Susan Tichy. 381
From our balloon over the
  provinces. William Stafford.
  373
From something, nothing. Marge
  Piercy. 346
From the Cherokee. Stephen

Knauth. 295
From the dunked clown at the carnival. Betty Adcock. 192
From the moving circle. May Miller. 320
From the other side of the keyhole. Jacqueline Frank. 248
From the peak of years. Elsa Gidlow. 254
"From the shadow and." Madison Morrison. 327
From the shore. Jeanne Lohmann. 305
"From the steep incline a." Madison Morrison. 327
"From the turntable's." Madison Morrison. 327
From the white place. Cathy Song. 372
From the womanflower. Margaret Key Biggs. 205
From this ledge. Carolyn Stoloff. 376
From whence comes love? Alice Spohn Newton. 332
"The front lawn." Madison Morrison. 327
The front-yard squirrel. Rod McKuen. 316
Front porch. Betty Adcock. 192
The frontlet. Charles Olson. 337
Frost. Carol Frost. 249
Frost. Mary Gilliland. 257
Frost
    Frost. Mary Gilliland. 257
Frost, Carol
    An adolescent girl. 249
    Aubade of an early homo sapiens. 249
    Autumn apology. 249
    The cemetery is empty. 249
    Cold frame. 249
    Constellation. 249
    Country marriage. 249
    The daughter. 249
    The day of the body, sels. 249
    Death in winter. 249
    The embroidery. 249
    The fairy tale. 249
    The fearful child. 249
    For an infant whose heart stopped for eleven minutes. 249
    Frost. 249
    The garden. 249
    A good cafeteria. 249
    The haircut. 249
    The heron. 249
    His mind ceases. 249
    The homemade piano. 249

If a model, fr. The day of the body. 249
Influenza. 249
The light asks. 249
Man and the woman, fr. The day of the body. 249
The new dog: variations on a text by Jules Laforgue. 249
No batter. 249
Ode to the horseshoe crab. 249
Old cat. 249
Our night. 249
Packing mother's things. 249
Passage. 249
Prayer to my son. 249
A red nightgown. 249
The scar. 249
The secret. 249
She thinks of love, fr. The day of the body. 249
So when he leaves, fr. The day of the body. 249
Sometimes we say it is love. 249
Stags and salmon. 249
Three apparitions. 249
To fish. 249
Two poems/Toward silence. 249
The undressing. 249
Unfinished song. 249
What will become of the fat and slow performing woman? 249
Where are you going?, fr. The day of the body. 249
The winter without snow. 249
Frost, Robert
    After apple-picking. 250
    The ax-helve. 250
    The black cottage. 250
    Blueberries. 250
    The code. 250
    The death of the hired man. 250
    Directive. 250
    The fear. 250
    The generations of men. 250
    Good hours. 250
    The grindstone. 250
    Home burial. 250
    The housekeeper. 250
    A hundred collars. 250
    In the home stretch. 250
    "In winter in the woods." 250
    Mending wall. 250
    The mountain. 250
    An old man's winter night. 250
    'Out, out -.' 250
    The pasture. 250
    Paul's wife. 250
    The self-seeker. 250
    A servant to servants. 250
    Snow. 250

The star-splitter. 250
Two tramps in mud time. 250
West-running brook. 250
The witch of Coos. 250
The wood-pile. 250
Frost, Robert (about)
At Frost's farm in Derry, New
Hampshire. James Schevill. 360
"The/frosted car." Larry Eigner.
237
Fruit
Conservancies. Josephine Miles.
319
Fruit Farming
Orange, California. Gary
Margolis. 311
The **fugitive.** Roy Marz. 312
Fulani girl. Robert A. Sears. 362
Fulfillment. Marie Daerr
Boehringer. 210
Fulfillment. Connie Hunt. 279
Full circle. Marieve Rugo. 356
"The **full** moon." Sally Love
Saunders. 358
"**Full** moon..." Charles Olson. 337
Fuller, R. Buckminster
Brain and mind. 251
Intuition - metaphysical mosaic.
251
Love. 251
Two versions of the Lord's
Prayer, sels. 251
Fulton Street. George Eklund. 238
The **fun.** Sam Fishman. 246
Fund-raising. Josephine Miles.
319
The **fundamentalist.** Phyllis A.
Tickle. 382
Funeral. Josephine Miles. 319
A **funeral** for Hinky Dink. James
Schevill. 360
The **funeral.** Jim Simmerman. 365
The **funeral.** Mark Vinz. 387
Funerals
Air burial. Harry Humes. 278
Boy buried on Sunday. Roy Marz.
312
Burial. Robert Peters. 343
The caisson passes. May Miller.
320
Cremation. James A. Emanuel. 239
Etruscan burial. Roy Marz. 312
A funeral for Hinky Dink. James
Schevill. 360
The funeral. Jim Simmerman. 365
The funeral. Mark Vinz. 387
Grandpop John's funeral. Sally
Love Saunders. 358
Legend stones. May Miller. 320
Muddy bootheels click to

attention. Stephen Todd
Booker. 212
My grandmother's funeral. Eileen
Silver-Lillywite. 364
Sea burial. Robert Pawlowski.
341
Viewing the body. Sharon Bryan.
217
The **furnace.** Edwin Honig. 275
Furnaces
The boilerman. James Schevill.
360
The furnace. Edwin Honig. 275
Further completion of plat.
Charles Olson. 337
The **fury** of a midwestern
thunderstorm. James Schevill.
360
Futility. Rachel A. Hazen. 271
Future
"All of the joy." A. Dovichi.
233
Chair. Carolyn Stoloff. 376
Eight-aught. John Godfrey. 260
For all inside. Rachel A. Hazen.
271
For those yet unborn. Maurice W.
Britts. 215
"From now on..." Susan Tichy.
381
Melodrama. Paul Violi. 388
My hope for the future. Maurice
W. Britts. 215
On not being able to imagine the
future. Robin Becker. 202
Save tomorrow. Rachel A. Hazen.
271
She remembers the future. Joy
Harjo. 269
The Tramontane sonata. Paul
Violi. 388
UHFO. Harrison Fisher. 245
Until... Rod McKuen. 316
The west is the best and the
future is near. Andrei
Codrescu. 223
When my times comes. Wanda
Coleman. 225
The world in the year 2000.
Marge Piercy. 346
A year from now. Rachel A.
Hazen. 271
The **future** now. Gerard Malanga.
310
The **future** of jazz. David Wann.
394
Fydor's invisible mending. Larry
Moffi. 322

G.W.M.. Edwin Honig. 275
Gabbatha. Patsie Black. 206
Gaby at the U.N. observation
    post. Susan Tichy. 381
Gaelic trilogy. Paul Davis. 228
Galarza, Ernesto
    Almaden road. 252
    Among wild oats. 252
    Avenal. 252
    Bayou water. 252
    Bikini man. 252
    Biscayne Bay. 252
    Breathless interlude. 252
    Casualty. 252
    Cleaning up. 252
    Composed. 252
    Contrition. 252
    Copy from an old master. 252
    Could be. 252
    Cyrano de Bergerac. 252
    The egg and I. 252
    Eli Lu's rose. 252
    En route. 252
    Encounter. 252
    Encounters. 252
    The essence of things. 252
    Florin. 252
    The grand banks of Coalinga. 252
    Musical. 252
    My friend Lutner. 252
    No complaints. 252
    Obituary. 252
    Our eyes have seen the glory.
        252
    Pietro Lazzari. 252
    Psalm of success. 252
    Psychoanalysis in one easy
        sonnet. 252
    Rain moods. 252
    Rock creek fall. 252
    Santa Clara spring. 252
    The season of repose. 252
    Sequoia semper virens. 252
    A short response to Robert
        Frost. 252
    Spring dirge. 252
    Variations on a theme by a
        sycamore. 252
    The way it is. 252
    The wetbacks. 252
    The women of Huanuni. 252
    Woodpile whistler. 252
Galileo
    "The life of Galileo as it is
        reset." Josephine Miles. 319
The gallivanting gecko. Jack
    Prelutsky. 349
Gambling

Casino royale. Keith Wilson. 400
Lottery ticket. James Magorian.
    308
Poker game in a ghost town.
    James Magorian. 308
Gambling in Las Vegas. James
    Schevill. 360
The game-master explains the
    rules of the game for
    bombings. James Schevill. 360
A game against age. James
    Schevill. 360
A game of snow. Tom Smith. 368
Game talk. Rose Basile Green. 265
The game. Louise Gluck. 259A
The game. Norman Andrew Kirk. 293
Games. Sandra McPherson. 317
Games. Robert Peters. 343
Games
    Beard-growing contest. James
        Magorian. 309
    Hide and seek. Jeanne Lohmann.
        305
    Monopoly. Joan Colby. 224
Games with some. Iefke
    Goldberger. 262
Games. See also Children's Games

Gangsterism and coolth. Harrison
    Fisher. 245
Garbage
    Collector's item. Josephine B.
        Moretti. 324
    Fabulous debris. James Schevill.
        360
    Shadow royal. Paul Violi. 388
    What are the most unusual things
        you find in garbage cans?
        James Schevill. 360
Garbage. See also Junkyards

"Garbo's knees are gateposts to
    violets and chateaux." Carolyn
    Stoloff. 376
Garbo, Greta
    "Garbo's knees are gateposts to
        violets and chateaux." Carolyn
        Stoloff. 376
Garcon. John F. Barker. 201
The garden at Nemi. Maria Gillan.
    256
The garden in ruins. Harry Humes.
    278
Garden of earthly delights =
    luxuria. Michael Gizzi. 259
A garden of girls. Harrison
    Fisher. 245
Garden of my life. Jacques
    Sollov. 370
Garden song. Rod McKuen. 316

The **garden**. Jacqueline Frank. 248
The **garden**. Carol Frost. 249
The **garden**. William Oandasan. 335
The **garden**. Steve Kowit. 298, 299
Gardener in March. David Wann.
    394
The **gardener's** dream. David
    Wagoner. 390
The **gardener's** letter from
    Stalingrad. Franz Schneider.
    361
Gardens. Jeanne Lohmann. 305
Gardens
    Can't beet it. Marie Daerr
        Boehringer. 210
    Detective Shoes. James Tate. 379
    Edibility test. Marie Daerr
        Boehringer. 210
    For Alexander Pope's gardens.
        John Yau. 404
    The garden. Jacqueline Frank.
        248
    Gardener in March. David Wann.
        394
    The gardener's dream. David
        Wagoner. 390
    The hanging gardens. Charles
        Edward Eaton. 236
    In Mary Frank's garden. Robert
        Kelly. 289
    In search of scenery. Marge
        Piercy. 346
    In the Japanese tea garden in
        San Francisco. James Schevill.
        360
    Late garden. Marc Hudson. 277
    Letter 72. Charles Olson. 337
    Looking west to China. Elsa
        Gidlow. 254
    Missing person. Mark Vinz. 387
    New garden. Marie Daerr
        Boehringer. 210
    Our garden. Deborah Tall. 378
    Out of the hospital Peter. Marge
        Piercy. 346
    The sculpture garden. Cynthia
        Grenfell. 266
    Waking up in a garden. David
        Wagoner. 390
    The Walden Pond caper. James
        Magorian. 309
    Weeds. Robert Gibb. 253
    Wild garden. Marie Daerr
        Boehringer. 210
The **gargoyle**. Charles Edward
    Eaton. 236
Gargoyles
    Love, do not shun the dark
        gargoyle. James Schevill. 360
Garibaldi posthume in Washington

Sq. Bradford Morrow. 329
Garibaldi, Giuseppe
    Garibaldi posthume in Washington
        Sq. Bradford Morrow. 329
Garmisch-Partenkirchen. John F.
    Barker. 201
The **garnet** cross. Phillips Kloss.
    294
Garter snakes. Robert Peters. 343
Gasoline Stations
    The station. James Applewhite.
        198
    "Two attendants." Madison
        Morrison. 327
Gathering fire. Mary Gilliland.
    257
Gatherings. Robert Gibb. 253
Gatherings. James L. White. 396
"**Gaunt** but conscient." Madison
    Morrison. 327
The **gazabos**: forty-one poems,
    sels. Edwin Honig. 275
The **gazabos**. Edwin Honig. 275
The **Ge** poems, sels. Phyllis A.
    Tickle. 382
Geckoes (lizards)
    The gallivanting gecko. Jack
        Prelutsky. 349
"**Gee**, what I call the upper road
    was the way" Charles Olson.
    337
Geese
    The egg. Jack Prelutsky. 349
    Geese overhead. Gary Margolis.
        311
    The giggling gaggling gaggle of
        geese. Jack Prelutsky. 349
    The long geese. Robert
        Pawlowski. 341
    Ringnecks return. Phyllis A.
        Tickle. 382
    Suprised by a flock of Canada
        geese... Robert Gibb. 253
Geese overhead. Gary Margolis.
    311
Gehenna. Richmond Lattimore. 301
The **geisha**. Rochelle DuBois. 234
Geji cave. Robert A. Sears. 362
Gem show, sels. Everett A.
    Gillis. 258
Gems
    Intaglio. Everett A. Gillis. 258
Genealogical chart. James
    Magorian. 308
Generation. Josephine Miles. 319
The **generations** of men. Robert
    Frost. 250
Generic: after reading Plath and
    Sexton. Bill Knott. 296
Genesis. Mark Vinz. 387

Genesis. Connie Hunt. 279
The genesis of the egg. Stephen
    Todd Booker. 212
Genet, Jean
    Fund-raising. Josephine Miles.
    319
Genetics
    Unbiased geneticist visiting a
    wax museum. James Magorian.
    309
Geneva. Michael Gizzi. 259
Genevieve dying. Donald Revell.
    351
Genitals
    C...:Dialogue among rumbled
    sheets. Elsa Gidlow. 254
Genius loci. Michael Gizzi. 259
"Gentle children." Michael Robert
    Pick. 345
Geode. Everett A. Gillis. 258
Geodes
    Geode. Everett A. Gillis. 258
Geology of the Huleh. Susan
    Tichy. 381
Geopolitics. David Wann. 394
"George Decker..." Charles Olson.
    337
George E. Harlan Usher. 386
George Vancouver's death dream.
    Marc Hudson. 277
German cameroun. Michael Gizzi.
    259
A German printmaker. Marc Hudson.
    277
Germany
    Dialogues: Johann Joachim
    Winckelmann and Joseph Busch.
    Albert Goldbarth. 261
    Diary aus Deutschland. Marie
    Daerr Boehringer. 210
    Garmisch-Partenkirchen. John F.
    Barker. 201
    The hat. Anneliese Wagner. 389
    Schwarzwald. Ernest Hemingway.
    272
    Self-exiled. Carolyn Stoloff.
    376
    Skies: a Jew in Germany, 1979.
    Ghita Orth. 339
    A walk in early winter. Rodney
    Nelson. 331
The gestalt. Charles Edward
    Eaton. 236
Gethsemane. Michael Gizzi. 259
Getting away. David Wagoner. 390
Getting directions. Melvin Dixon.
    231
Getting there. Robert Kelly. 289
Gettysburg, Pennsylvania
    Reflections at Gettysburg. Paul

Davis. 228
    Views from Gettysburg. Josephine
    Miles. 319
Getz, Stan
    For Stan Getz. Susan Stock. 375
Ghazal: the impasse. Robin
    Becker. 202
Ghettos and gardens. Jacqueline
    Frank. 248
Ghost talk. Thomas McGrath. 315
Ghosts
    Ghost talk. Thomas McGrath. 315
    The lingering ghost. Erin Jolly.
    285
    The story. Miller Williams. 399
The ghouls of Candlemas. Andrei
    Codrescu. 223
Giacometti, Alberto
    Feet on familiar ground. Mary
    Gilliland. 257
Giants
    In praise of a photograph by
    Diane Arbus... James Schevill.
    360
Gibb, Robert
    The apple tree. 253
    At Sutter's grave: Lititz, PA.
    253
    Aubade. 253
    Camomile. 253
    Carpenter bees. 253
    Coming again upon Mensch's mill
    by accident... 253
    Earthworks. 253
    For now. 253
    A friend starts west on
    Melville's birthday. 253
    Gatherings. 253
    Halfway into a fifth of Irish
    whiskey he sings of the... 253
    Last things. 253
    Lucky with woods. 253
    Menses. 253
    Mezcal. 253
    The minotaur. 253
    Monet. 253
    Scything the meadow. 253
    16th Street. 253
    St. Paul's Union Church and
    cemetery, Seiberlingsville,
    Pa. 253
    Stems. 253
    Suprised by a flock of Canada
    geese... 253
    This view of the meadow. 253
    Vespers. 253
    Weeds. 253
    What the heart can bear. 253
    The white birches. 253
    Widening the road. 253

Wind. 253
The woodchuck. 253
Gibson, Mel
Elizabeth Bay evening. Rod
McKuen. 316
Gidlow, Elsa
All farewells. 254
Anomaly. 254
The artist. 254
As usual. 254
Bewitched visit. 254
The bird flew off. 254
Chains of fires. 254
Chance. 254
Cloud of unknowing. 254
Come and lie with me. 254
Constancy. 254
A creed for a free woman. 254
The dark face of love. 254
Dawn opens. 254
C...:Dialogue among rumbled
sheets. 254
Discussing apples. 254
Dreaming of her. 254
Earth wisdom: two sonnets in an
early mode. 254
The empty place. 254
Expecting. 254
Experience. 254
Eyes. 254
For a gifted lady, often masked.
254
For the goddess too well known.
254
Forgive us. 254
The friend departs. 254
From the peak of years. 254
Grey morning. 254
The grey thread. 254
Heart's laughter. 254
Hymn to a mystery. 254
In a dream. 254
In the lover's arms. 254
Invocation to Sappho. 254
Is she found? 254
The laughter of women. 254
Let the sea speak. 254
Let wisdom wear the crown: hymn
for gaia. 254
Looking west to China. 254
Love a peacock. 254
Love in age. 254
Love song. 254
Love's acolyte. 254
Marriage song. 254
Married. 254
May rain. 254
Never. 254
A new moon rises. 254
Not asking for love. 254

Of forbidden love. 254
Only the old are gay. 254
Out of love's timeless egg. 254
Out on the hills. 254
Outsiders. 254
Philosophy. 254
Region of no birds. 254
Reliquishment. 254
Sappho twined roses. 254
Secret Sapphic. 254
So still the dawn. 254
Sobered. 254
Song for Guenevere. 254
Those I have loved. 254
To an old lover at a distance.
254
To the unknown goddess. 254
Ultimate aloneness. 254
Unpitying Aphrodite. 254
Valley with girls. 254
What if? 254
When love becomes a stranger.
254
When she is absent. 254
Where love is still. 254
Wild swan singing. 254
Women at the lakeside. 254
Would she vanish, kissed? 254
You say. 254
Gift list. Alice Joyce Davidson.
227
The gift of pain. Roy Marz. 312
The gift. Maria Gillan. 256
Gifts. Jim Everhard. 241
Gifts and Giving
Gifts! gifts! gifts! Alice Joyce
Davidson. 227
The golden plate. Jacques
Sollov. 371
The moon. Tom Smith. 368
Mother's chocolate valentine.
Jack Prelutsky. 348
The promised coat. Cathryn
Hankla. 268
The simplest joy. Rachel A.
Hazen. 271
What I have I give. Rachel A.
Hazen. 271
Your Christmas present. Dave
Smith. 367
Gifts! gifts! gifts! Alice Joyce
Davidson. 227
The **giggling** gaggling gaggle of
geese. Jack Prelutsky. 349
Gila Wilderness, New Mexico
Untitled: "walking up/down
mountains" Kirk Lumpkin. 306
Gilbert, Sandra
Autumn song. 255
Beets. 255

The Brussels sprouts. 255
The carrots. 255
The celery bushes. 255
Five potatoes. 255
Ginger root. 255
The leeks. 255
The red cabbages. 255
The summer kitchen. 255
Turnips. 255
The wild grasses. 255
Gilgamesh visits Ephesus. Randy
    Blasing. 207
Gillan, Maria
Affirmations. 256
Another spring. 256
Ash Wednesday. 256
Autumn words. 256
Awakening. 256
Betrayals. 256
The carpenter is knocking. 256
The chosen. 256
City people. 256
Clarities. 256
Coming alive. 256
Configurations of a dead
    language. 256
Dark seed. 256
Dawn thoughts. 256
Driftwood moments. 256
Frailties. 256
The garden at Nemi. 256
The gift. 256
'I'm nobody's little girl
    anymore since daddy died.' 256
Illusions. 256
Inconsistencies. 256
Language is a chain. 256
Leavings. 256
Litanies. 256
Looking sideways. 256
Ma, your voice. 256
Mercies. 256
The moment's psalm. 256
Morning song. 256
Mother. 256
The mother poem. 256
Mothers and daughters. 256
My brother, my stranger. 256
My crooked city. 256
My daughter. 256
The new grace. 256
On seeing the play, "The
    Elephant Man," December, 1979.
    256
Our scales are off-center. 256
Our secret selves. 256
Paterson is glass. 256
Petals of silence. 256
Poem to my father. 256
Raritan reflections. 256

Resurrections. 256
Revelations. 256
Rome, 1978. 256
Santa Fe, New Mexico, 1970. 256
September Monday. 256
Shadow pictures. 256
Signs. 256
Sister Vivian, Caldwell College,
    1978. 256
Song of a dark pine morning. 256
Song of praise. 256
Theseus. 256
Think of it: the river. 256
The tree inside us. 256
We are sisters. 256
Woman song. 256
Gilliland, Mary
About our lips. 257
After running, for Peter. 257
The air clears, after. 257
Bald woman needs no title. 257
Baring friendship. 257
Bitter light. 257
A blue chicken. 257
Bronzed by frost. 257
Candlemas. 257
Cloudy night, new moon. 257
Coy glen. 257
Coy glen again. 257
Each midsummer, love. 257
Excavating hardpan. 257
Feet on familiar ground. 257
First steps. 257
For Bill who passed on with the
    summer. 257
Frost. 257
Gathering fire. 257
It all comes back. 257
Madame Bovary falls on my head.
    257
May 8 (1979). 257
Mayday. 257
The muse is muzak in this age.
    257
Night prayer. 257
Not having a house is not a
    permanent situation. 257
Poem to heal David. 257
Poet in residence. 257
Purple aster. 257
Reassurance: what gets done. 257
Shaking in the autumn wind. 257
Song to hug by. 257
Square hole day. 257
Standing under the mystery. 257
Steubenville: "Home of quality
    flat-rolled products." 257
Strolling on the giant woman.
    257
The third thaw. 257

Threshing in my mother's arms.
257
Water is air to the kingfisher.
257
When rain doesn't fall. 257
When you're away. 257
Wolf. 257

Gillis, Everett A.
The adolescents. 258
Age is not what we are but where
we have been in time. 258
Ars poetica. 258
Cat in glass, fr. A pride of
four small lions. 258
Cat in the bric-a-brac, fr. A
pride of four small lions. 258
Cat on the corner, fr. A pride
of four small lions. 258
Death of a great man. 258
Death of the mirror: midnight,
fr. Mirror suite. 258
The door: four sonnets for
married lovers. 258
Elegy and epitaph, sels. 258
Elegy for an soldier in any war,
fr. Elegy and epitaph. 258
Epitaph for a humble hero, fr.
Elegy and epitaph. 258
The eye on the corner. 258
Far beyond distance, fr.
Voyages. 258
Fire agate, fr. Gem show. 258
The fog. 258
For one who could not stay. 258
Gem show, sels. 258
Geode. 258
Girl at the piano. 258
Halcyon days. 258
Hospital. 258
The house. 258
Intaglio. 258
This jeweled beast: a fable. 258
Kitten in the sun, fr. A pride
of four small lions. 258
Legend, fr. Mirror suite. 258
Love song: winter. 258
Madonna and daughter. 258
The man who grew trees from his
hands. 258
Mask of everyman, fr. Masks. 258
Masks, sels. 258
Memories. 258
Mirror suite, sels. 258
Mirror, mirror, fr. Mirror
suite. 258
Moment before elegy. 258
Muffled, blind, silent. 258
The naked print, fr. Masks. 258
Ohio Yankee. 258
Pioneer. 258

A pride of four small lions,
sels. 258
The quick of roses. 258
Saint. 258
Saint Francis. 258
Scholar. 258
Seascape: Santa Monica
Palisades. 258
The seed. 258
Signature. 258
Spider flight. 258
Strangers in a photograph. 258
Sweet singing blues. 258
Sweet summer of our years. 258
Time beyond time, fr. Mirror
suite. 258
Time's fabled sanctuary. 258
Voyages, sels. 258
The winds blow long, fr.
Voyages. 258
Woman at window. 258
The year. 258

Ginger root. Sandra Gilbert. 255
Ginger Roots
Ginger root. Sandra Gilbert. 255
Giraffes
What a giraffe eats. Albert
Goldbarth. 261
Girdles
Cure-all. Josephine B. Moretti.
324
Girl and baby florist sidewalk
pram nineteen seventy...
Kenneth Koch. 297
Girl at the piano. Everett A.
Gillis. 258
Girl powdering her neck. Cathy
Song. 372
Girl scout cookies. James
Magorian. 309
Girl Scouts
Girl scout cookies. James
Magorian. 309
Girl under streetlight. Margaret
Key Biggs. 205
A girl's life & other pictures.
Harrison Fisher. 245
Girls in ragtime. Norman Andrew
Kirk. 293
Girls on a spring campus. Cornel
Lengyel. 302
"The 'girls' gather." Madison
Morrison. 327
Girls. See Youth

Gist. Andrei Codrescu. 223
The giver of darkness (so Zenzi
sings). Kiarri T-H Cheatwood.
220
Giving birth. Wanda Coleman. 225

Gizzi, Michael
  Aleppo. 259
  Aranjuez. 259
  Arcadia - River Ladon. 259
  Arden. 259
  Armageddon. 259
  Arnold Arboretum. 259
  Babylon. 259
  The backyard. 259
  Baden-baden. 259
  Baghdad. 259
  Barbary Coast. 259
  Braintree. 259
  Brooklyn Botanic Garden. 259
  Cabo verde. 259
  Cambridge. 259
  Canton. 259
  Cape Canaveral. 259
  Charenton - Jardin de Sade. 259
  Chartres - Couvent du Sacre
    Coeur? 259
  Constantinople. 259
  Couvet. 259
  Eden. 259
  Folie. 259
  Garden of earthly delights =
    luxuria. 259
  Geneva. 259
  Genius loci. 259
  German cameroun. 259
  Gethsemane. 259
  Haddam meadow. 259
  Hyde Park. 259
  Jardin des Plantes. 259
  Kew Gardens - the compost. 259
  Kyoto. 259
  Leipzig - das glashaus. 259
  Limousin. 259
  Locus solus. 259
  Malmaison. 259
  Milano - Il Conservatorio. 259
  Monticello. 259
  Mt. Athos. 259
  Paris - Les Tuileries. 259
  Rhinebeck. 259
  Rio Maranon. 259
  Sherwood. 259
  Silicon Valley. 259
  Toulouse - jocs florals. 259
  Trinidad. 259
  Uppsala. 259
  Utrecht. 259
  Versailles - Galerie des Glaces.
    259
  Versailles - le hameau. 259
  White Flower Farm. 259
  Williamsburg. 259
  Zurich - the hidden patient. 259
Glad day. Edwin Honig. 275
"Glad to have." Larry Eigner. 237

Glancing behind. Alice Spohn
    Newton. 333
Glass
  Through you. Edwin Honig. 275
A glass face in the rain. William
    Stafford. 373
Glass. See also Windows

Gleanings from the yacata. Robert
    A. Sears. 362
"Glenn's definition of equality."
    Sally Love Saunders. 358
A glimpse in the crowd. William
    Stafford. 373
Glimpsed. Ralph J., Jr. Mills.
    321
Glimpses. William Stafford. 373
Gloom. Sam Fishman. 246
Glories of the world. Stephen
    Sandy. 357
The glorious devil at the
    dovecot... James Schevill. 360
Glossies. Joan Colby. 224
Gloucester, Massachusetts
  "Above the head of John Day's
    pasture land." Charles Olson.
    337
  April today main street. Charles
    Olson. 337
  'At the boundry of the mighty
    world.' Charles Olson. 337
  The cow of Dogtown. Charles
    Olson. 337
  "'Cromlech' of course..."
    Charles Olson. 337
  "'Cut Creek,' the river is..."
    Charles Olson. 337
  Father sky, mother earth.
    Charles Olson. 337
  "Fire it back into the
    contintent." Charles Olson.
    337
  The frontlet. Charles Olson. 337
  Further completion of plat.
    Charles Olson. 337
  Golden Venetian light... Charles
    Olson. 337
  I, Maximus of Gloucester, to
    you. Charles Olson. 337
  "Into the stream or entrance..."
    Charles Olson. 337
  "The island, the river, the
    shore." Charles Olson. 337
  June 6th, 1963. Charles Olson.
    337
  "Lane's eye-view of Gloucester"
    Charles Olson. 337
  Letter, May 2, 1959. Charles
    Olson. 337
  Maximus of Gloucester. Charles

Olson. 337
Maximus, in Gloucester Sunday,
   LXV. Charles Olson. 337
The new empire. Charles Olson.
   337
"Or Lindsay." Charles Olson. 337
"Out over the land skope."
   Charles Olson. 337
Part of the flower of
   Gloucester. Charles Olson. 337
A plantation a beginning.
   Charles Olson. 337
Proem. Charles Olson. 337
The river map and we're done.
   Charles Olson. 337
"The sky." Charles Olson. 337
"They brawled in the streets..."
   Charles Olson. 337
13 vessels, and David Pearce's
   T. Charles Olson. 337
Thurs Sept 14th 1961. Charles
   Olson. 337
"To my Portuguese..." Charles
   Olson. 337
West Gloucester. Charles Olson.
   337
The glove of silence. Norman
   Andrew Kirk. 293
Gluck, Louise
   Bridal piece. 259A
   The cell. 259A
   The Chicago train. 259A
   Cottonmouth country. 259A
   The cripple in the subway. 259A
   Early December in
      Croton-on-Hudson. 259A
   Easter season. 259A
   The edge. 259A
   The egg. 259A
   Firstborn. 259A
   The game. 259A
   Grandmother in the garden. 259A
   Hesitate to call. 259A
   The inlet. 259A
   The islander. 259A
   La force. 259A
   Labor day. 259A
   The lady in the single. 259A
   Late snow. 259A
   Letter from our man in
      blossomtime. 259A
   Letter from Provence. 259A
   Medidian. 259A
   Memo from the cave. 259A
   My cousin in April. 259A
   My life before dawn. 259A
   My neighbor in the mirror. 259A
   Nurse's song. 259A
   Phenomenal survivals of death in
      Nantucket. 259A

Pictures of the people in the
   war. 259A
Portrait of the queen in tears.
   259A
The racer's widow. 259A
Returning a lost child. 259A
Saturnalia. 259A
Scraps. 259A
Seconds. 259A
Silverpoint. 259A
The slave ship. 259A
Solstice. 259A
Thanksgiving. 259A
To Florida. 259A
The tree house. 259A
The wound. 259A
Gluck, Louise (about)
   Poet. Bill Knott. 296
Gnomic Poetry
   Some gnomic verses. Marc Hudson.
      277
Gnomon. Thomas Hornsby Ferril.
   243
Go ask the dead. Thomas McGrath.
   315
Go away little bee! Josephine B.
   Moretti. 324
Go from regret to the magic
   worlds. Kirk Lumpkin. 306
"Go to bed late." Jan Ormerod.
   338
A goal. Alice Joyce Davidson. 227
Goats
   She-goat at puck fair. Anneliese
      Wagner. 389
God. Martha Janssen. 283
God
   Affirmations. Maria Gillan. 256
   After the Anglican communion.
      Jenne Andrews. 196
   Alpenglow. Patsie Black. 206
   Altar cross. Patsie Black. 206
   Apocaylpse in me. Mitchell
      Howard. 276
   As is. Patsie Black. 206
   "As the soft white." Sally Love
      Saunders. 358
   Ash Wednesday. Maria Gillan. 256
   Be or be not. James R. Rhodes.
      352
   Beyond. Patsie Black. 206
   Brahman. Jacques Sollov. 371
   Bridge of return. Patsie Black.
      206
   Catchism. Tom Smith. 368
   Certainties. Alice Joyce
      Davidson. 227
   "The circle/has no beginning."
      Joan Walsh Anglund. 197
   Computing God. Norman Andrew

Kirk. 293
Countless blessings. Alice Joyce Davidson. 227
The crown. Jacques Sollov. 371
Day of wrath. Cornel Lengyel. 302
Days of love. Alice Joyce Davidson. 227
Death of a great man. Everett A. Gillis. 258
Deliverance. Patsie Black. 206
"Digging deeps my destiny." Michael Robert Pick. 345
Discernment. Jeanne Lohmann. 305
Ego sum via, veritas et vita. Maurice W. Britts. 215
Epiphany. Patsie Black. 206
An etching. Patsie Black. 206
Eternal peace. Jacques Sollov. 370
Ever-beyond. James R. Rhodes. 352
First step. Alice Joyce Davidson. 227
Free. Patsie Black. 206
Gift list. Alice Joyce Davidson. 227
God. Martha Janssen. 283
God is there with you. Alice Joyce Davidson. 227
God lives. Alice Joyce Davidson. 227
God was there. James R. Rhodes. 352
God's song. S. Bradford Williams (Jr.). 398
Going by the pattern. Alice Spohn Newton. 332
The golden lamp. Jacques Sollov. 370
The good shepherd. Alice Joyce Davidson. 227
He's surely blessing you. Rosa Bogar. 211
Hugs. Alice Joyce Davidson. 227
"I am trying to think what it means to be right." Josephine Miles. 319
"I believe in God." Charles Olson. 337
"I sing a song to thee, O God." Michael Robert Pick. 345
In plain sight. Alice Joyce Davidson. 227
Invincible force. Maurice W. Britts. 215
The island-maker. Roy Marz. 312
June garden. Marie Daerr Boehringer. 210
Life's song. S. Bradford

Williams (Jr.). 398
Little giant. Jacques Sollov. 370
Looking sideways. Maria Gillan. 256
Love song. Alice Joyce Davidson. 227
Loving gentle, loving strong. Alice Joyce Davidson. 227
Make me a channel, Lord! Alice Joyce Davidson. 227
Maran'atha. Patsie Black. 206
Mercies. Maria Gillan. 256
Mirror. Alice Joyce Davidson. 227
"Mornings, no." Da Free John. 284
Mother-father God. Evelyn Golden. 263
My father's home. Alice Joyce Davidson. 227
My friend. Alice Joyce Davidson. 227
Naming his call. James R. Rhodes. 352
Neothomist poem. Ernest Hemingway. 272
The new grace. Maria Gillan. 256
"O give thanks." Alice Joyce Davidson. 227
Ode to Trinity. Patsie Black. 206
Pas-de-deux. Patsie Black. 206
Prayer. Evelyn Golden. 263
The proofs of God. Joyce Carol Oates. 336
A quiet truth. Alice Spohn Newton. 332
Rightside up. Patsie Black. 206
The score. Maurice W. Britts. 215
Spaceship earth. Patsie Black. 206
"spirit is not the flesh." Joan Walsh Anglund. 197
Still waters. James R. Rhodes. 352
Stoned by the Lord. Mitchell Howard. 276
Strain. Roy Marz. 312
Supreme power. Alice Joyce Davidson. 227
Thanks giving. Alice Joyce Davidson. 227
The throne. Jacques Sollov. 371
To be. S. Bradford Williams (Jr.). 397
To the last. Robert Pawlowski. 341
To you in particular. Jim

Simmerman. 365

A touch of love. Alice Joyce Davidson. 227

The triangle of love. Jacques Sollov. 370

Uninvited. Alice Joyce Davidson. 227

"We live in the body/... but we are not of the body." Joan Walsh Anglund. 197

Well of love. Alice Joyce Davidson. 227

"When things have left him." Da Free John. 284

Where it all ends. Alice Spohn Newton. 332

Who are we? Evelyn Golden. 263

Who can know God? Evelyn Golden. 263

Who? James R. Rhodes. 352

Windows of the world. Patsie Black. 206

Woman at midnight. Phyllis A. Tickle. 382

The word. Phillips Kloss. 294

God believes in You. Alice Joyce Davidson. 227

"God is away for the summer." Ernest Hemingway. 272

God is there with you. Alice Joyce Davidson. 227

God lives. Alice Joyce Davidson. 227

God was there. James R. Rhodes. 352

God's song. S. Bradford Williams (Jr.). 398

God, the idiotic plaints. Judson Crews. 226

Godfrey, John

As who knows, so goes. 260

Astral roulette. 260

Atlas. 260

Audition. 260

Back in an hour. 260

Blond, carlight. 260

In brittle molds of love. 260

By antique vogues. 260

Change for three-dollar bill. 260

City love. 260

Come April. 260

Dabble. 260

Day they say. 260

De Sica? 260

Double sonnet. 260

Eight-aught. 260

Equinox. 260

Evening song. 260

A face without lines. 260

First taste. 260

For you. 260

Friday's child. 260

Gray blazing pit. 260

Head. 260

Here comes yesterday. 260

Hers. 260

Hotel du Nord. 260

Idiots. 260

In memory of Pablo Picasso. 260

La gloire. 260

Love knife. 260

Love peon. 260

Mirrors at night. 260

Morning poem. 260

Morning star. 260

The music of the curbs. 260

Nativity day. 260

Next case. 260

No embarking at Rockaway. 260

Our knees. 260

Our lady. 260

Passive aspic. 260

Peaches. 260

Playing off. 260

Poem ("At home in the diner, flagman sprints.") 260

Poem ("Mezzanines of nightfall clashing like.") 260

Poem ("Not the beating of wings, not the curled-lip.") 260

Poem ("Seldom to any human is there a gold this pure.") 260

Poem ("The gravity of our situation is matched.") 260

Poem ("Why, even the sun was a vassal on that set.") 260

Poem ("You make me think of sleep, and you're lying.") 260

Poem for saps. 260

Poor John. 260

The prophet. 260

Provolone lane. 260

Radiant dog. 260

Rain waste. 260

Sailing. 260

Saint Augustine. 260

Schnapps sonata. 260

Show me a rose. 260

Slipping standards of light. 260

Sonnet ("An afternoon splashed all grapefruit...") 260

Sonnet ("Eyes to no awesome wind, bred.") 260

Sonnet ("Harbor open your eyes.") 260

Sonnet ("In the sunniness of the particular noon.") 260

Sonnet ("Ragamuffins as all outdoors.") 260

Sonnet ("Snow falls exclusively
   for the voice to mount.") 260
Sonnet ("Where was tnat lazy
   river?...") 260
Sympathetic fallacy. 260
Touch. 260
Two eastern places. 260
Under Virgo. 260
Unnoly spring. 260
Veins. 260
Venus. 260
Whiskers and moon. 260
Wings. 260
Without thirst. 260
Gods. Robert Kelly. 289
"Gods no matter how huge."
   Stephen Todd Booker. 212
Going. Miller Williams. 399
Going back. Sharon Bryan. 217
Going back. Robert L. Wilson. 401
Going blind: the woman's voice.
   Anthony Petrosky. 344
Going by jet. Eve Triem. 383
Going by the pattern. Alice Spohn
   Newton. 332
Going concern. Miriam Goodman.
   264
Going for a newspaper. Stephen
   Knauth. 295
Going right out of the century.
   Charles Olson. 337
Going to Africa. Melvin Dixon.
   231
Going to sleep. Eileen
   Silver-Lillywite. 364
Going to the orchard. Jeanne
   Lohmann. 305
Going to the sea. Cynthia
   Grenfell. 266
Gold. Phillips Kloss. 294
Gold
   Gold. Phillips Kloss. 294
   The goldrush. Andrei Codrescu.
      223
Gold Rush, California
   Eldorado. Edgar Allan Poe. 347
Gold? Chick? Food? Alberta
   Turner. 384
Goldbarth, Albert
   The accountings. 261
   Alkest, property of M. Valerius;
      and Nicolas Flamel. 261
   All-nite donuts. 261
   And. 261
   "And in tne preface..." 261
   "And now Farley is going to
      sing..." 261
   Before. 261
   Bird. 261
   Blue flowers. 261

The British in Africa. 261
Cross-country, & motif appears.
   261
Define a satellite. 261
Diagrams. 261
Dialogues: Johann Joachim
   Winckelmann and Joseph Busch.
   261
Distances. 261
The errors. 261
The form and function of the
   novel. 261
The harem boy. 261
His daughter. 261
A history of civilization. 261
The importance of artists'
   biographies. 261
"In 1856 she won second
   prize..." 261
In pain. 261
M-L/T. 261
Michael's. 261
Mnemonic devices. 261
"On the outskirts of London..."
   261
Pleasures. 261
Praise/complaint. 261
Pressed flowers. 261
Puritania. 261
Remembering the typo. 261
Return to the world. 261
A sanguinary, sels. 261
Semiotics/the doctor's doll. 261
Ssh. 261
Still lives. 261
A theory of wind. 261
"There is a legend about a
   piano..." 261
Trying. 261
Vacation: an extended postcard.
   261
Village wizard. 261
Water pie: tonight, 12/11/72.
   261
The well. 261
What a giraffe eats. 261
What a tribal unit is. 261
Wings. 261
Witch trial, transcript. 261
The world of expectations. 261
Worlds. 261
"Yet leaving here a name..." 261
Goldberger, Tefke
   After the rain. 262
   Amsterdam, student round-up. 262
   An I for an T. 262
   But never the spirit. 262
   The catch. 262
   Check. 262
   Christmas in Hawaii. 262

The dental assistant. 262
A doctor of the soul. 262
Family snapshot. 262
Feet at the end of their path. 262
Fifteen. 262
Finding a lake. 262
Free associations on Mother's Day. 262
Games with some. 262
The Hague, 5 May 1945. 262
Hanging on. 262
Jogging. 262
Luctor et emergo. 262
Making up. 262
A matter of life and dirt. 262
Memories of World War II: The decision. 262
Mother. 262
My fellow at Stanford think tank. 262
A new chance. 262
The other side of marriage. 262
Pajaro dunes. 262
Room for more. 262
A song of rain. 262
This stranger. 262
This morning. 262
Three with a boat on Pine Lake. 262
Unique. 262
Unsafe. 262
View from the hill. 262
Wind is my friend. 262
Woman's dream of man thinking of his woman. 262
Writer's blues. 262
Writing poetry in the woods. 262
Golden eagle. Gene Anderson. 195
The golden eagle. Jacques Sollov. 370
Golden eyelids. Erin Jolly. 285
The golden fish. Jacques Sollov. 370
The golden lamp. Jacques Sollov. 370
The golden plate. Jacques Sollov. 371
Golden retriever. David Wagoner. 390
Golden Venetian light... Charles Olson. 337
Golden, Evelyn
A distant day. 263
Acceptance. 263
Agent orange. 263
Autumn's prophecy. 263
Bridal Veil Falls in Yosemite Valley. 263
Buchenwald: the beginnings. 263
Christmas: what is it all about. 263
The church. 263
Cobwebs. 263
Distant sky and sea. 263
Divorce. 263
The drought. 263
Easter Sunday. 263
Elisabeth at seven. 263
The failing sea. 263
Faith. 263
February rain. 263
A friend? 263
How we resist the new. 263
'I and Thou.' 263
I draw a circle. 263
I flee the night. 263
I was a child. 263
Intimations. 263
Ketchikan Creek. 263
Letting go. 263
Listening to an old man. 263
The Lord's Prayer paraphrased. 263
Love. 263
A mockingbird. 263
Mother-father God. 263
Mother. 263
A mountain stream. 263
My daily walk. 263
My daughters. 263
My father & World War Two. 263
My husband and I. 263
Night in the Sierras. 263
Off the path. 263
On Interstate 5, near San Francisco. 263
Pain. 263
Paradox. 263
Poised for flight. 263
Prayer. 263
Searching. 263
A sense of completion. 263
Solitude. 263
A stone and I. 263
Strange duality. 263
This moment. 263
To my grandchildren. 263
To the deepest level. 263
Tonight I feel content. 263
Untouched moment. 263
Up is down. 263
Vietnam. 263
A vision of Abraxas. 263
A walk in the woods. 263
A warning. 263
The web we spin. 263
Who are we? 263
Who can know God? 263
Goldfish

The two goldfish. Greg Kuzma.
    300
The **goldrush**. Andrei Codrescu.
    223
Gondwanaland
    Letter 41 (broken off). Charles
    Olson. 337
Gone. Ralph J., Jr. Mills. 321
Gone. James A. Emanuel. 239
Gone with the cowboys. Rod
    McKuen. 316
Good. Alberta Turner. 384
"**Good** and bad/time goes." Larry
    Eigner. 237
A **good** cafeteria. Carol Frost.
    249
A **good** education. Robin Becker.
    202
Good Friday. Amy Clampitt. 222
Good hours. Robert Frost. 250
Good intentions. May Miller. 320
Good living. Josephine B.
    Moretti. 324
Good mama. Wanda Coleman. 225
Good morning. Joyce Carol Oates.
    336
Good morning, day. Rochelle
    DuBois. 234
Good morning, Eugene. Norman
    Andrew Kirk. 293
The **good** part. Greg Kuzma. 300
The **good** shepherd. Alice Joyce
    Davidson. 227
The **good** spirit. Andrei Codrescu.
    223
A **good** thing when I see one.
    Andrei Codrescu. 223
The **good-bye-hello** handbook.
    Cathryn Hankla. 268
Goodby madonna. Lyn Lifshin. 303
Goodbye. Josephine Miles. 319
Goodman, Miriam
    Accommodations. 264
    Another chance. 264
    Argument for parting. 264
    Burrow. 264
    Cafeteria. 264
    Celebration with geraniums. 264
    Cheating on company time. 264
    China and silver. 264
    The climate of your plans. 264
    Computer lab. 264
    Conference room: the golden
      years. 264
    The drive. 264
    Episodes. 264
    Figure/ground. 264
    Going concern. 264
    Happy endings. 264
    Home sick. 264

    Industrial park from the air.
      264
    Interior design. 264
    Intruder. 264
    Job hunting. 264
    Longing. 264
    Lunch at the desk with the news.
      264
    The method. 264
    Miami Beach. 264
    Morning, Swan's island. 264
    On the island. 264
    On wishing to avoid the bill.
      264
    Reviewing the possibilities. 264
    Secretary. 264
    Signal-to-noise. 264
    Spring in the industrial park.
      264
    Staircase. 264
    Trespass. 264
    Trip wire. 264
    Vinebrook Plaza demolition. 264
    Waiting. 264
    The women study in workshop
      together. 264
    Xerox. 264
A **gopher** in the garden. Jack
    Prelutsky. 349
Gophers
    A gopher in the garden. Jack
    Prelutsky. 349
Gordu wisdom. Kenneth Koch. 297
Goshawk. X.J. Kennedy. 290
Gospel in the drifts. Colette
    Inez. 280
"The **gospel** that can be written."
    Da Free John. 284
Gossip. Marc Kaminsky. 288
Gossip
    Calico caribes. Margaret Key
    Biggs. 205
    Daisies won't tell (and neither
    will I!) Josephine B. Moretti.
    324
    Girls in ragtime. Norman Andrew
    Kirk. 293
Got me home, the light snow gives
    the air, falling. Charles
    Olson. 337
Gould, Joe
    Listening in a 1920's Greenwich
    Village bar... James Schevill.
    360
The **gourmet** minces his words.
    Gary Margolis. 311
Government
    After a governmental purge. Anne
    Bailie. 199
    Civic pride. Josephine Miles.

319
    Silence at the top. Andrei
      Codrescu. 223
    Sir. Miller Williams. 399
Government injunction restraining
    Harlem Cosmetic Co. Josephine
    Miles. 319
Goya, Francisco Jose de
    Dusting the sill. Marc Hudson.
    277
Grace
    The plastic glass. Josephine
    Miles. 319
    Swift current. Cathryn Hankla.
    268
Gradual clearing. Amy Clampitt.
    222
Graduation. Connie Hunt. 279
Graduation. See Commencement Day

Graffiti
    The graffiti fingers of a
    theology student. James
    Schevill. 360
    The phantom artist. Ruth Lisa
    Schechter. 359
The graffiti fingers of a
    theology student. James
    Schevill. 360
Graham, Martha
    Illuminations: Martha Graham.
    James Schevill. 360
Graham-paige. Josephine Miles.
    319
The grail. John F. Barker. 201
Grain
    Market. Josephine Miles. 319
Grain sale to the Soviet Union.
    James Magorian. 309
Grainne. Deborah Tall. 378
Gramercy Park Hotel. Dave Smith.
    367
Grammar & money, sels. Andrei
    Codrescu. 223
A grammar. Andrei Codrescu. 223
Grammarian thumbing an old text.
    Edwin Honig. 275
The grand banks of Coalinga.
    Ernesto Galarza. 252
Grand Canyon. Robert A. Sears.
    362
Grand Canyon
    Grand Canyon. Robert A. Sears.
    362
    "The Santa Ana turns the air to
    dust." Robert A. Sears. 362
The grand magic theater finale.
    Irving Feldman. 242
Grandchildren
    Ethan. Ruth Lisa Schechter. 359

The grandmother speaks. Sister
    Maura. 313
Shalom. Ruth Lisa Schechter. 359
To my grandchildren. Evelyn
    Golden. 263
Grandfather. Josephine Miles. 319
Grandfather Noah. James
    Applewhite. 198
Grandfather's grove. Phillips
    Kloss. 294
Grandma's cheese. Alice Spohn
    Newton. 333
Grandma's chocolate cake. Alice
    Spohn Newton. 333
Grandma's starter. Alice Spohn
    Newton. 333
Grandmas. Josephine B. Moretti.
    324
Grandmother. Melvin Dixon. 231
Grandmother in the garden. Louise
    Gluck. 259A
The grandmother speaks. Sister
    Maura. 313
Grandmother's gift. Alice Joyce
    Davidson. 227
Grandpa and the Model T Ford.
    Alice Spohn Newton. 333
Grandpa's friend Pete. Alice
    Spohn Newton. 333
Grandparents
    Bequest. Marie Daerr Boehringer.
    210
    Easter: Wahiawa, 1959. Cathy
    Song. 372
    Elegy. Eileen Silver-Lillywite.
    364
    Elegy spoken to my grandfather.
    Dennis Hinrichsen. 273
    The embroidery. Carol Frost. 249
    Florida Scott-Maxwell helps
    recite my grandmother's life.
    Susan Tichy. 381
    For an immigrant grandmother.
    Edwin Honig. 275
    For bad grandmother and Betty
    Bumhead. Debra Bruce. 216
    Grandfather Noah. James
    Applewhite. 198
    Grandfather's grove. Phillips
    Kloss. 294
    Grandmas. Josephine B. Moretti.
    324
    Grandmother's gift. Alice Joyce
    Davidson. 227
    Her kitchen. Michael Akillian.
    193
    Home ground. Randy Blasing. 207
    In memoriam: S.E.G. Rodney
    Nelson. 331
    Oblique. Anneliese Wagner. 389

Obsequies. Thomas R. Sleigh. 366
Old woman. Robert Anbian. 194
Old women and hills. Robin Becker. 202
Past closing time. Carolyn Stoloff. 376
Places. Jim Simmerman. 365
A scene. William Stafford. 373
Scheherezade. Deborah Tall. 378
Sunday lunch at grandpa's. Phyllis A. Tickle. 382
The very end. Thomas R. Sleigh. 366
"What is life for knotted lives." Michael Robert Pick. 345
Grandparents and grandchildren. Gene Anderson. 195
Grandpop John's funeral. Sally Love Saunders. 358
Grant, Ulysses S.
    Down riverside with Ulysses. Thomas Hornsby Ferril. 243
Grapefruits
    Breakfast. David Wann. 394
Grass. Dennis Hinrichsen. 273
Grass
    Affirmation. George Eklund. 238
    "The front lawn." Madison Morrison. 327
    "Grass is plastic with." Madison Morrison. 327
    Time enough for grass. Paul Davis. 228
    The wild grasses. Sandra Gilbert. 255
"Grass is plastic with." Madison Morrison. 327
Grass smooth on the prairies. Ernest Hemingway. 272
Grasshoppers
    Cricket on the hearth. Sister Maura. 313
Gratitude
    Blessings of the day. Rod McKuen. 316
    I kiss your cold silent lips. Maurice W. Britts. 215
    Thank you. Rod McKuen. 316
    Thank you. Jacques Sollov. 371
Grave discovery. Robert L. Wilson. 401
The grave thumps. Edwin Honig. 275
Gravedigging in August. George Eklund. 238
Graves in east Tennessee. Donald Revell. 351
Graves, Robert
    Robert Graves. Ernest Hemingway. 272
Graves. See Cemeteries

Graveyard in the jungle. Ray Fleming. 247
Gravity. Josephine Miles. 319
Gravity (physics)
    Earth & apples. Cathryn Hankla. 268
    "Have you ever held a string." Michael Robert Pick. 345
Gray blazing pit. John Godfrey. 260
The great adventure. Rod McKuen. 316
The great books of the dead. Thomas Lux. 307
The great county fair. Alice Spohn Newton. 333
The great debate. James Torio. 281
The great egg. Joyce Carol Oates. 336
The great exception. Lucien Stryk. 377
Great expectations. Robin Becker. 202
"Great multiple." Larry Eigner. 237
Great Plains (United States)
    The Great Plains states. Dennis Hinrichsen. 273
The Great Plains states. Dennis Hinrichsen. 273
Great rock unchanging. Alice Spohn Newton. 332
Great Salt Lake, Utah
    The back of Antelope Island. Sharon Bryan. 217
    The Great Salt Lake. Sharon Bryan. 217
The Great Salt Lake. Sharon Bryan. 217
"Great Washing Rock..." Charles Olson. 337
The great Winter Park sinkhole. Ruth Lisa Schechter. 359
The greater Peoria perversity contest. James Magorian. 309
The greatest gift. Connie Hunt. 279
Grebanier, Bernard
    Equivocal elegy. Steve Kowit. 299
Greece
    Bearing it. Carolyn Stoloff. 376
    Behind the starched light. Carolyn Stoloff. 376
    Deja vu. Anne Bailie. 199
    Gilgamesh visits Ephesus. Randy

Blasing. 207

How can a child hope along
avenues. Carolyn Stoloff. 376

I will not go to Mikonos.
Carolyn Stoloff. 376

"'A learned man' sd Strabo
(meaning Pytheus)." Charles
Olson. 337

Memory. Gary Margolis. 311

Remembering Greece. Amy
Clampitt. 222

Scheria: ? Charles Olson. 337

Sonnet ("An afternoon splashed
all grapefruit...") John
Godfrey. 260

The waitress. Eve Triem. 383

Greed

"Addicts progress from
saturation." Josephine Miles.
319

The king is in his counting
house. James R. Rhodes. 352

Green April. Marie Daerr
Boehringer. 210

Green April. Robert L. Wilson.
401

Green frog at Roadstead,
Wisconsin. James Schevill. 360

Green morning, full summer.
Marieve Rugo. 356

Green Mountains (New England)

Driving the Green Mountains.
Dennis Hinrichsen. 273

The green step, sels. Kenneth
Koch. 297

The green step. Kenneth Koch. 297

The green tide. Mitchell Howard.
276

Green tomatoes. Anneliese Wagner.
389

Green, Rose Basile

AI nostri. 265

America, all singing. 265

Americadians. 265

Americans to Europeans. 265

Anthem. 265

Arrival. 265

Aspiration. 265

Brother's farewell. 265

Communion. 265

The Congress creed (the
Eucharistic Congress...) 265

Cry, ethnics? 265

The decline of the wasp? 265

Descendant. 265

Ensemble. 265

An ethnic-American crying. 265

An ethnic-American singing. 265

Ethnic-American woman. 265

Ethnic-Americans. 265

Extremity. 265

Fatta l'America. 265

Finale - to my country. 265

Finding the one. 265

The first one. 265

Game talk. 265

I still can hear the singing.
265

Intermezzo at Vendemmia. 265

Invitation. 265

Involvement. 265

Irish love. 265

Italian-American woman. 265

Jenni's love. 265

L'ora. 265

Land rights. 265

Lars Italica. 265

Lingering melody. 265

Mater eterna. 265

Minority. 265

Mother, alone - the way we are.
265

New direction. 265

New marching song. 265

No landing. 265

One ethnic-American. 265

Passing the wand (August 15,
1975). 265

Pioneer. 265

Plurality. 265

Pro patria. 265

Racism. 265

Rediscovery. 265

Remembering. 265

Remembering Nonno. 265

Reprise. 265

Scene revisited. 265

Sempre natale. 265

The singing we. 265

Singing, maker of peace. 265

A son's commencement day. 265

Songport. 265

Soundscape. 265

Struggle at the sanctum. 265

Theme. 265

They will remember. 265

To the media. 265

To the mother republic. 265

A toast to the ancestors. 265

Urban society. 265

Wasp conscious. 265

The way we love. 265

We, ethnics, had the dream. 265

Greenhouses

Winter in Lincoln Park
Conservatory. Robin Becker.
202

Greening song. James R. Rhodes.
352

Greenough, Horatio

Horatio Greenough writes of
    reason. James Schevill. 360
Greenwich Village, New York
    Beneath the friable moon.
        Bradford Morrow. 329
    Garibaldi posthume in Washington
        Sq. Bradford Morrow. 329
Greeting Cards
    From Hallmark or somewhere.
        William Stafford. 373
Grenfell, Cynthia
    Amnesia. 266
    As we sit in the garden, early
        and late. 266
    Black/white. 266
    The cats of time. 266
    Chester is lake water. 266
    Complaint. 266
    Coneflower groundcover. 266
    The corner is turned. 266
    Did ye know? Lake Hamilton, day
        after Easter. 266
    Going to the sea. 266
    Hot night. 266
    In Pan's world. 266
    Junco song. 266
    Lament. 266
    Morning at the ranch I. 266
    Morning at the ranch II:
        Memorial Day. 266
    Morning at the ranch IV: Ridge
        Road above Annie Green Spring.
        266
    Morning at the ranch IV: photo:
        the negative. 266
    Not chaos but. 266
    Not ready. 266
    Pastoral. 266
    Prologue. 266
    The puffing tree. 266
    Reflections on rose quartz. 266
    The sculpture garden. 266
    The shining mountains. 266
    Song: a new poem of war. 266
    Summer song. 266
    The three of them. 266
    Trace. 266
    Trio. 266
    Twilight path. 266
    Two scenes. 266
    Verbatim I. 266
    Verbatim II. 266
    Verbatim III. 266
    Visit on the beach. 266
"The grey man works." Madison
    Morrison. 327
Grey morning. Elsa Gidlow. 254
The grey thread. Elsa Gidlow. 254
"A grey woman has snow-white."
    Madison Morrison. 327

"A grey woman of." Madison
    Morrison. 327
"The grey woman." Madison
    Morrison. 327
Greyed rainbow. James Torio. 281
Grief. Alice Joyce Davidson. 227
Grief. Lucien Stryk. 377
Grief. Martha Janssen. 283
"Grief dry the/council." Larry
    Eigner. 237
The grief of men. Robert Bly. 209
Grief. See Sorrow

"Grievances:the warm fogs of
    summer." Josephine Miles. 319
"The grill is robbed." Madison
    Morrison. 327
Grim, dark morning. Robert L.
    Wilson. 401
Grinding stone. Phillips Kloss.
    294
The grindstone. Robert Frost. 250
Grindstones
    Grinding stone. Phillips Kloss.
        294
    The grindstone. Robert Frost.
        250
"The groaner shakes louder than
    the whistling buoy..." Charles
    Olson. 337
Grocers
    The Jewish grocer and the
        vegetable forest. James
        Schevill. 360
Grosstadtpoesie. Rodney Nelson.
    331
Ground Hogs
    An apology to the groundhog.
        Mitchell Howard. 276
    Wejack. Maurice Kenny. 291
Ground zero. Wanda Coleman. 225
The grounds keeper. James Torio.
    281
Groupings. Stephen Sandy. 357
Growing closer. Alice Joyce
    Davidson. 227
Growing in grace. Alice Joyce
    Davidson. 227
Growing Up
    About the time. Rod McKuen. 316
    At seventeen. Jacqueline Frank.
        248
    Baby. Joyce Carol Oates. 336
    Bridge to eternity. Alice Spohn
        Newton. 333
    Chorus from a play. Thomas
        McGrath. 315
    A day to remember. William
        Stafford. 373
    Eliza. Brenda Marie Osbey. 340

Faces. Josephine Miles. 319

Fifteen. Tefke Goldberger. 262

First job. Christopher Bursk. 219

Fool's song. Cornel Lengyel. 302

Hands. Larry Moffi. 322

Hero's song. Barry Wallenstein. 393

"I can tie my shoelaces." Jan Ormerod. 338

I mature and I grow. S. Bradford Williams (Jr.), 398

In a season of change. Ghita Orth. 339

"In the neighborhood of my childhood, a hundred lungers." Josephine Miles. 319

Junior high. Martha Janssen. 283

Marching from a closet. Rachel A. Hazen. 271

Ode to a friend from the early sixties. Sandra McPherson. 317

The particles. Randy Blasing. 207

Pax vobiscum. John F. Barker. 201

Rites of passage. Robert Peters. 343

Trying to drive away from the past. James Applewhite. 198

A tunnel to the moon. Cathryn Hankla. 268

"When I was a little man." Michael Robert Pick. 345

Wings and seeds. Sandra McPherson. 317

The yum-yum song. Susan Stock. 375

Guanajuato, Mexico
    Two mediations on Guanajuato. John Yau. 404

Guerillas. See Revolution

Guess what was ripped out of the wall today? Mitchell Howard. 276

Guests
    Housecleaning. Roy Marz. 312

Guests of the nation. Steve Kowit. 298, 299

Guevara, Che
    They are looking for Che Guevara. Steve Kowit. 299

Guide. Ghita Orth. 339

A guide to the field. David Wagoner. 390

Guiffre's nightmusic. Thomas McGrath. 315

Guillotine. Andrei Codrescu. 223

Guilt. Rochelle DuBois. 234

Guilt
    Death of the Hungarian hot pepper bush. Marge Piercy. 346
    The dream of the guilt bird, or water. Lyn Lifshin. 303
    Guilt. Rochelle DuBois. 234
    My fault. Bill Knott. 296
    Retrospective. Josephine Miles. 319

The guilt formula. Joan Colby. 224

Guilty creatures at play. Bill Knott. 296

A guilty father to his daughter. James Schevill. 360

Guinevere. John Reed. 350

Guinevere, Queen
    Guinevere. John Reed. 350

The guise is all the difference. Robert L. Wilson. 401

The Gulf of Maine. Charles Olson. 337

Gullans, Charles
    A diatribe to Dr. Steele. 267

Gulls
    Choir birds of another time. Paul Davis. 228
    On the beach watched by a seagull. James Schevill. 360
    The sea-gull. John Reed. 350
    "Shag Rock, bull's eye" Charles Olson. 337
    A woman feeding gulls. David Wagoner. 390

Gum (chewing)
    The Chiclets paragraphs. Paul Violi. 388

"The gunman always rides with two eyes in the back..." David James. 282

Guns
    Sawed-off shotgun. James Magorian. 308

Gylfaginning VI. Charles Olson. 337

"The gym instructor." Madison Morrison. 327

Gym seal madonna. Lyn Lifshin. 303

The gymnasts, fr. Fresh air. Irving Feldman. 242

Gymnasts. See Acrobats

Gymnopedie: the exhibition. Donald Revell. 351

Gypsies
    Concerning Tsiganes. Keith Wilson. 400
    Reg gypsy wagon, with flowers. Keith Wilson. 400

Gypsy. Josephine Miles. 319
Gypsy bears. Keith Wilson. 400

Had been a slow note to Stella
    Grace. Gene Detro. 230
Haddam meadow. Michael Gizzi. 259
"Haggard, torn and beat." Michael
    Robert Pick. 345
Hagiography. Jim Simmerman. 365
The Hague, 5 May 1945. Tefke
    Goldberger. 262
Haiku au surreal. William
    Oandasan. 335
Hair. Lyn Lifshin. 303
Hair
    The comb. Charles Edward Eaton.
    236
    Hair. Lyn Lifshin. 303
    The haircut. Carol Frost. 249
    Odyssey of the hair. Carolyn
        Stoloff. 376
    Weavers. Ghita Orth. 339
    The white porch. Cathy Song. 372
    Woody's wool. Marge Piercy. 346
The haircut. Carol Frost. 249
A hairline fracture. Amy
    Clampitt. 222
Halcyon days. Everett A. Gillis.
    258
Halfway into a fifth of Irish
    whiskey he sings of the...
    Robert Gibb. 253
Halloween
    All hallow. Josephine Miles. 319
    Ask Sindbad. Stephen Todd
        Booker. 212
    Dracula, Blacula. Josephine B.
        Moretti. 324
    Halloween: Thayer Street. Robert
        Kelly. 289
    A witches brew. Alice Spohn
        Newton. 333
Halloween: Thayer Street. Robert
    Kelly. 289
The hallowing of hell: a psalm in
    nine circles. Robin Morgan.
    325
The halt. Josephine Miles. 319
Hamer, Fannie Lou
    In the earth's abiding sweetness
    (where Fannie Lou rests).
    Kiarri T-H Cheatwood. 220
Hamlet. Edwin Honig. 275
Hamlet
    Hamlet. Edwin Honig. 275
    A student of tragedy. Norman
        Andrew Kirk. 293

Hammock reading, fr. Nostalgia
    poems. Robert A. Sears. 362
Hammond Museum, North Salem, N.Y.
    Along the Katsura walk. Ruth
    Lisa Schechter. 359
Hammond, John Hays, Jr.
    One of the bronze plaques...
    Charles Olson. 337
Hampton Hawes in the Alps.
    Bradford Morrow. 329
Hamsa: in memoriam. Gene
    Anderson. 195
Hand made. Betty Adcock. 192
"The hand still curves." Robert
    A. Sears. 362
Hand work. Anneliese Wagner. 389
Handbag assemblers up shit creek
    without a paddle. James
    Magorian. 309
Handel and the beast. Paul Davis.
    228
Handel, George Frederick
    Handel and the beast. Paul
    Davis. 228
Handicapped, The
    The cripple in the subway.
    Louise Gluck. 259A
    The halt. Josephine Miles. 319
    Weeping for a man in the brown
    chair legless, with a cane.
    Scott Chisholm. 221
    "Wheels walk, never talk."
    Michael Robert Pick. 345
Hands. Larry Moffi. 322
Hands
    As the hand goes. Carolyn
    Stoloff. 376
    In praise of hands. Anthony
    Petrosky. 344
    "The leaf is growing." Josephine
    Miles. 319
    Sailmaker's palm. Robin Becker.
    202
    "See what a fine job." David
    Wann. 394
The hands in exile. Susan Tichy.
    381
The hands of time. Robert L.
    Wilson. 401
"Handy pandy, Jack-a-dandy." Jan
    Ormerod. 338
Handymen
    The island handyman. James
    Schevill. 360
Hanging at Galgahraun. Marc
    Hudson. 277
The hanging gardens. Charles
    Edward Eaton. 236
Hanging on. Tefke Goldberger. 262
Hanging tough. William Stafford.

373

Hank Snow, the evangelist, prays for the president. James Schevill. 360

Hankla, Cathryn
Answering the past. 268
Circuit of the intruder. 268
The dark. 268
The day without the dream. 268
The dispute over bodies in water. 268
Earth & apples. 268
Easter. 268
The fate of waking. 268
Firefly. 268
The first prayer of angles. 268
The good-bye-hello handbook. 268
I dream my return. 268
The journey. 268
Last night a light. 268
Mockingbird. 268
A moment of violence. 268
Mothlight. 268
Motions of weather. 268
My friend who's afraid of the dark. 268
The night-father was found alive. 268
The night hunting. 268
Nothing is obvious. 268
Paradox of gravity. 268
Past visions, future events. 268
Phenomena, a photograph. 268
Possessions. 268
The promised coat. 268
Raking with leaves in the wind. 268
Sleeping in the loft of dreams. 268
So lightly she must be air. 268
Some day when it is dark. 268
Swift current. 268
That idea of visiting places in dreams. 268
The touch of something solid. 268
A tunnel to the moon. 268
Volume 13: Jirasek to lighthouses. 268
Walking in the path of the moon. 268
Water burning wills away. 268
The water is the skin of the river. 268
A white horse. 268
White summer, museum piece, Montague Street in winter. 268
A wilderness of light. 268

Happening. Edwin Honig. 275
The happiest day. Edgar Allan Poe. 347

Happiness. Irving Feldman. 242
Happiness
Bliss. Alberta Turner. 384
An ethnic-American singing. Rose Basile Green. 265
"I'm on top of the world." Sally Love Saunders. 358
"I'm so happy." Sally Love Saunders. 358
Idea of joy. Josephine Miles. 319
In Pan's world. Cynthia Grenfell. 266
"It's good to be with you." Sally Love Saunders. 358
Joy. Connie Hunt. 279
Joy: an end song. Edwin Honig. 275
A merry heart. Alice Joyce Davidson. 227
Once in the 40's. William Stafford. 373
Out on the hills. Elsa Gidlow. 254
Sing, sing, sing a song. Alice Joyce Davidson. 227
"So many good things." Sally Love Saunders. 358
Song of praise. Maria Gillan. 256
Subject. Josephine Miles. 319
To make a summer. Josephine Miles. 319
Waiting in paradise for Adam to come back from the city. Jenne Andrews. 196
"Walking along in barefoot shoes." Michael Robert Pick. 345
"The woman who said she went out every Sunday." Charles Olson. 337

Happy birthday and lettuce. James Magorian. 309
Happy birthday b/w Say Hay. Mitchell Howard. 276
Happy endings. Miriam Goodman. 264
Happy New Year. Paul Davis. 228
Happy what, author? Harlan Usner. 386
Harbor. Michael Akillian. 193
Harbor night. Sam Fishman. 246
Harboring some tinny escape plans. Mitchell Howard. 276
Harbors
"Why light, and flowers? Paul Oakley." Charles Olson. 337
Hard travellin'. Thomas McGrath.

315
Hardball. J.W. Rivers. 354
Hardscrabble homestead. Robert A.
    Sears. 362
Hardy, Thomas
    To Thomas Hardy. Ernest Tedlock.
    380
The harem boy. Albert Goldbarth.
    261
Hares. See also Rabbits

Harjo, Joy
    Alive. 269
    Anchorage. 269
    Backwards. 269
    The black room. 269
    Call it fear. 269
    Connection. 269
    Cuchillo. 269
    Drowing horses. 269
    Explosion. 269
    For Alva Benson, and for those
        who have learned to speak. 269
    The Friday before the long
        weekend. 269
    Heartbeat. 269
    I give you back. 269
    Ice horses. 269
    Jemez. 269
    Kansas City. 269
    Late summer leaving. 269
    Leaving. 269
    Moonlight. 269
    Motion. 269
    Nandia. 269
    Nautilaus. 269
    New Orleans. 269
    Night out. 269
    One cedar tree. 269
    The poem I just wrote. 269
    Rain. 269
    Remember. 269
    The returning. 269
    September moon. 269
    She had some horses. 269
    She remembers the future. 269
    Skeleton of winter. 269
    Song for Thantog. 269
    Two horses. 269
    Untitled. 269
    Vision. 269
    What I should have said. 269
    What music. 269
    White bear. 269
    The woman hanging from the
        thirteenth floor window. 269
    Your phone call at 8a.m. 269
Hark! Norman Andrew Kirk. 293
Harlem footage. Melvin Dixon. 231
Harlem, New York

Harlem footage. Melvin Dixon.
    231
Harmony tomorrow. May Miller. 320
A harmony. John F. Barker. 201
Harper's Ferry. Steve Kowit. 298,
    299
The Harrison Fisher book.
    Harrison Fisher. 245
Harrison Fisher girls. Harrison
    Fisher. 245
Harrison Fisher's American girls
    in miniature. Harrison Fisher.
    245
The harrowing of heaven. Robin
    Morgan. 325
Harry noir. Harrison Fisher. 245
Haruspex of the happy country.
    Charles Edward Eaton. 236
Harvest song. Cornel Lengyel. 302
A harvest. Mark Vinz. 387
The harvesters' psalm. Cornel
    Lengyel. 302
Harvests and Harvesting
    In the interleaved Almanacks for
        1646 and 1647 of Danforth.
        Charles Olson. 337
    The season of repose. Ernesto
        Galarza. 252
The hat. Anneliese Wagner. 389
Hate. Martha Janssen. 283
Hate
    Aim. Josephine Miles. 319
    &. Andrei Codrescu. 223
    Bitterness. Martha Janssen. 283
    Care. Josephine Miles. 319
    "Circles crowd the sky." Michael
        Robert Pick. 345
    Dialectic. Josephine Miles. 319
    Hate. Martha Janssen. 283
    Misgiving. Gerard Malanga. 310
    "Pretty hard to face the facts."
        Michael Robert Pick. 345
    Self-hate. Martha Janssen. 283
    The stone orchard. Joyce Carol
        Oates. 336
Hate mail. Steve Kowit. 299
Hathaway, Donny
    In memory of Donny Hathaway.
        Rosa Bogar. 211
Hats and ears for Charles Ives.
    James Schevill. 360
The haunted palace. Edgar Allan
    Poe. 347
Havana. Herbert Morris. 326
Have a cup of bygones. Alice
    Spohn Newton. 333
Have I caught myself? Norman
    Andrew Kirk. 293
"Have I outgrown you?" Josephine
    Miles. 319

Have kids, will travel. Josephine
B. Moretti. 324
"Have you ever held a man's
hand." Michael Robert Pick.
345
"Have you ever held a string."
Michael Robert Pick. 345
"Having descried the nation."
Charles Olson. 337
"Having developed the
differences..." Charles Olson.
337
Having the right name. William
Stafford. 373
The having. Sam Fishman. 246
Hawaii
Christmas in Hawaii. Tefke
Goldberger. 262
Leaving. Cathy Song. 372
Hawes, Hampton
Hampton Hawes in the Alps.
Bradford Morrow. 329
Hawk. Marc Hudson. 277
Hawk like an anchor. Joan Colby.
224
Hawk Mountain in the fog. Harry
Humes. 278
The hawk's backyard. Rod McKuen.
316
Hawk-man. Richard Blessing. 208
The hawk. Franz Schneider. 361
Hawkes, John
The bestowal. 270
He motioned for the words. 270
The little hand. 270
"A poem set down to convince..."
270
Profane desert. 270
When you don't speak to me. 270
Hawkins, Sir John
Maximus to Gloucester: Letter
14. Charles Olson. 337
Hawks
Friend of forty years. Judson
Crews. 226
Goshawk. X.J. Kennedy. 290
Hawk. Marc Hudson. 277
Hawk like an anchor. Joan Colby.
224
The hawk. Franz Schneider. 361
He dreams of a hawk. Harry
Humes. 278
"I see you hawk." Michael Robert
Pick. 345
Red wing hawk. James Applewhite.
198
"Sometimes I wish I was a hawk."
Michael Robert Pick. 345
To a farmer who hung five hawks
on his barbed wire. David

Wagoner. 390
Hay and Haying
The code. Robert Frost. 250
Snow in April. Anneliese Wagner.
389
Hayden, Robert
Angels of ascent. Melvin Dixon.
231
Haysatck needle. James Magorian.
309
The haystack. Charles Edward
Eaton. 236
Hazen, Rachel A.
A-glitter with radiance. 271
Alone inside. 271
And for Jenny. 271
And nobody cries. 271
And now, the others. 271
The beaten one. 271
Beyond the mountain. 271
A bit of me. 271
By-gone seniors 1982. 271
Changes! 271
The days are long. 271
Die awake. 271
The difference. 271
The ending. 271
The final breath. 271
Finale. 271
The first reality. 271
A flower. 271
Fooled dearly. 271
For all inside. 271
Friends in a lonely time. 271
Futility. 271
Horizon. 271
I become a dream. 271
I cannot stay. 271
I follow the snow. 271
I stopped looking. 271
If. 271
Imagine the dreams we dream
today. 271
Implications. 271
In a darkened corridor. 271
It isn't meant to end this way.
271
Karen. 271
Lace covered memories. 271
Lady butterfly. 271
The last of me. 271
The late-night realities. 271
Laughter and pain. 271
Liana. 271
The lonely shadow. 271
The lonely wall. 271
Love's confusing. 271
Marching from a closet. 271
The masquerade. 271
A matter of minutes. 271

May I. 271
Me inside. 271
The modest rainbow. 271
Must there be a reason? 271
My idol. 271
My new house. 271
My only gift. 271
Neither rhythm nor rhyme. 271
A note. 271
Nothing changes. 271
Nothing falls down. 271
Nothing's song. 271
Oasis. 271
An ode to roses. 271
Oft' I ask, what is a show? 271
On nameless days. 271
A one of music. 271
Only a mem'ry. 271
Past and fantasy. 271
The playing. 271
A puppet on a string. 271
The purest form of eternity. 271
Reminders. 271
Rivers filled with tears. 271
The satin star. 271
Save tomorrow. 271
Sessions. 271
Silent, soft, forever still. 271
The simplest joy. 271
The sky-high ballet. 271
The smallest soldier. 271
A sometimes wondering. 271
Somewhere to go? 271
Spotlight. 271
Stillness around me. 271
Talk to me. 271
Tears so long. 271
Those that dance to the music.
   271
To Beata. 271
To Heather. 271
To Monica and Liz. 271
To Sue. 271
Trapped. 271
Tuneless wand'rings. 271
Upon graduation. 271
A variety show. 271
Volar. 271
Washington D.C. too. 271
What I have I give. 271
When dreams are dreams. 271
The whistling woo. 271
The white grave. 271
Words and magic hands. 271
A year from now. 271
Hazzuzzah!. Alice Spohn Newton.
   332
"He came." Charles Olson. 337
"He died/shoveling snow." Theta
   Burke. 218

He dreams of a hawk. Harry Humes.
   278
"He finds himself." Madison
   Morrison. 327
"He has not been burned." Madison
   Morrison. 327
"He is the one who sees it."
   Madison Morrison. 327
He motioned for the words. John
   Hawkes. 270
"He says/remember..." Madison
   Morrison. 327
He was drunk. Judson Crews. 226
He was walking sideways. Judson
   Crews. 226
"He who addresses you." Kenneth
   Koch. 297
"He who had seemed/to seek
   battle." Theta Burke. 218
"He who walks with his house on."
   Charles Olson. 337
He's a nice potato. Alice Spohn
   Newton. 332
"He's about to arrive." Madison
   Morrison. 327
He's packing I hear. Carolyn
   Stoloff. 376
He's surely blessing you. Rosa
   Bogar. 211
He's young except for death.
   Frances Mayes. 314
Head. John Godfrey. 260
"Head full/of birds..." Larry
   Eigner. 237
Head in hands. Josephine Miles.
   319
Head of a smiling priest:
   Limestone, Egypt. Roy Marz.
   312
The head of Orpheus. Robert
   Kelly. 289
Head of the state parks police.
   Lyn Lifshin. 303
Headless. Josephine Miles. 319
Headline. George Eklund. 238
The healer. Jacques Sollov. 371
Health Resorts
   Baden-baden. Michael Gizzi. 259
   The spa of the posthumous :
      Pearl Karsten speaks. Sandra
      McPherson. 317
Hear it out. Norman Andrew Kirk.
   293
Hearing. Jeanne Lohmann. 305
"Hearing it wake, we feel." Edwin
   Honig. 275
Heart (human)
   Blind sight. James R. Rhodes.
      352
   Debauch of the chauvinist.

Charles Edward Eaton. 236
Location. Josephine Miles. 319
Merchant marine. Josephine
Miles. 319
Mysteries of the heart. Jim
Everhard. 241
Nageire. James Torio. 281
Notes for an autobiography.
Sister Maura. 313
A parachute. Sally Love
Saunders. 358
Passion. Josephine Miles. 319
Speaker. Josephine Miles. 319
Tachycardiac seizure. Joyce
Carol Oates. 336
To my heart. Andrei Codrescu.
223
"The heart and soul." Madison
Morrison. 327
Heart's laughter. Elsa Gidlow.
254
Heart's needle. W.D. (William De
Witt) Snodgrass. 369
Heartbeat. Joy Harjo. 269
Heartbreak. Barry Wallenstein.
393
Heat
Heat wave. James Magorian. 308
What to wear. Josephine B.
Moretti. 324
When rain doesn't fall. Mary
Gilliland. 257
The heat bird. Mei-Mei
Berssenbrugge. 203
"Heat unrelieved at midnight."
Robert A. Sears. 362
Heat wave. James Magorian. 308
"Heating up T boil mad." Michael
Robert Pick. 345
Heaven. Josephine Miles. 319
Heaven
The grand magic theater finale.
Irving Feldman. 242
Heaven (fairy-land). Edgar Allan
Poe. 347
Heaven's gate. Alice Joyce
Davidson. 227
The history of the growth of
heaven. Andrei Codrescu. 223
Home. Steve Kowit. 298, 299
"Out of the light of heaven..."
Charles Olson. 337
There is a kingdom. Jacques
Sollov. 370
Trying. Albert Goldbarth. 261
"The vault/of heaven." Charles
Olson. 337
White angel. Jacques Sollov. 371
Heaven (fairy-land). Edgar Allan
Poe. 347

"Heaven as sky is made of
stone..." Charles Olson. 337
Heaven furnished the flowers.
Alice Spohn Newton. 333
Heaven's gate. Alice Joyce
Davidson. 227
Heaven's going away party. Alice
Spohn Newton. 332
Heaven, circa 1938. Dennis
Hinrichsen. 273
Hebrew stones. Keith Wilson. 400
Hecht, Anthony (about)
After the reading. Herbert
Morris. 326
"Hector-body.". Charles Olson.
337
Heidegger, Martin
Elegy for Martin Heidegger. Marc
Hudson. 277
Height. Josephine Miles. 319
Height
Height. Josephine Miles. 319
Heil!. Sam Fishman. 246
Heir. Josephine Miles. 319
Heirloom. Robin Morgan. 325
Heldenleben. Josephine Miles. 319
Helen and me. Debra Bruce. 216
Helen Todd : My birthname. Sandra
McPherson. 317
Hell
A cook in hell. Andrei Codrescu.
223
Gehenna. Richmond Lattimore. 301
Hello, I'm Erica Jong. Kathy
Acker. 191
Helluva big neighborhood.
Mitchell Howard. 276
The helper. Stephen Todd Booker.
212
Helpfulness
"Needed help from someone."
Michael Robert Pick. 345
Hemingway, Ernest
Across the board. 272
Advice to a son. 272
The age demanded. 272
"All armies are the same." 272
Along with youth. 272
"And everything the author
knows." 272
"Arsiero, Asiago." 272
"At night T lay with you." 272
Athletic verse, sels. 272
The battle of Coppenhagen. 272
The big dance on the hill. 272
Bird of night. 272
Black-ass poem after talking to
Pamela Churchill. 272
[Blank verse.]. 272
'"Blood is thicker than water.'"

272
Captives. 272
Champs d'nonneur. 272
Chapter heading. 272
Country poem with little
  country. 272
D'Annunzio. 272
Dedicated to F.W. 272
Defense of Luxembourg. 272
The earnest liberal's lament.
  272
First poem to Mary in London.
  272
Flat roofs. 272
"For the harlot has a hardlot."
  272
"God is away for the summer."
  272
Grass smooth on the prairies.
  272
How ballad writing affects our
  seniors. 272
I like Americans. 272
I like Canadians. 272
"I think that I have never
  trod." 272
I'm off'n wild wimmen. 272
"If my Valentine you won't be."
  272
"In a magazine." 272
The inexpressible. 272
Killed. 272
Kipling. 272
The lady poets with foot notes.
  272
Lines to a girl 5 days after her
  21st birthday. 272
Lines to a young lady on her
  having very nearly won a
  vogel. 272
Lines to be read at the casting
  of Scott Fitsgerald... 272
"Little drops of grain alcohol."
  272
"Little Mr. Wilson." 272
Mitrailliatrice. 272
A modern version of Polonius'
  advice. 272
Montparnasse. 272
Neothomist poem. 272
"Night comes with soft and
  drowsy plumes." 272
Oily weather. 272
Oklahoma. 272
On weddynge gyftes. 272
The opening game. 272
Poem ("The only man I ever
  loved.") 272
The poem is by Maera. 272
Poem to Mary. 272

Poem to Miss Mary. 272
Poem, 1928. 272
Poetry. 272
Portrait of a lady. 272
The punt, fr. Athletic verse.
  272
"The rail ends do not meet." 272
Riparto d'assalto. 272
The road to Avallon. 272
Robert Graves. 272
Roosevelt. 272
The safety man, fr. Athletic
  verse. 272
Schwarzwald. 272
Sequel. 272
The ship (Translated being La
  paquebot). 272
Shock troops. 272
"Some day when you are picked
  up." 272
The soul of Spain with McAlmon
  and Bird the publishers. 272
The sport of kings. 272
Stevenson. 272
The tackle, fr. Athletic verse.
  272
"There was Ike and Tony and
  Jacque and me." 272
They all made peace - what is
  peace? 272
To a tragic poetess. 272
To Chink whose trade is
  soldiering. 272
To crazy Christian. 272
To good guys dead. 272
To Will Davies. 272
Translations from the Esquimaux:
  there are seasons. 272
Travel poem. 272
Ultimately. 272
Valentine. 272
The worker. 272
Hemingway, Ernest (about)
  And: a funeral hymn for Ernest
  Hemingway. James Schevill. 360
Hemispheres. Melvin Dixon. 231
Henry. Jim Simmerman. 365
Hens
  From whence comes love? Alice
  Spohn Newton. 332
Hepit-naga-atosis. Charles Olson.
  337
The hepplewhite madonna. Lyn
  Lifshin. 303
Her chronicle. Carolyn Stoloff.
  376
Her diary. James A. Emanuel. 239
Her dream and the awakening.
  David Wagoner. 390
Her hand. Edwin Honig. 275

"Her headland." Charles Olson. 337

Her kitchen. Michael Akillian. 193

Her mornings and evenings. Carolyn Stoloff. 376

Her room. Gary Margolis. 311

"Her stern like a box..." Charles Olson. 337

"Her vestibule." Madison Morrison. 327

Her yellow roses. Carolyn Stoloff. 376

Herald. Josephine Miles. 319

Herbs
    Gatherings. Robert Gibb. 253

Hercules builds its new corporate headquarters... Jocelyn Hollis. 274

Hercules, Dow, - agent orange. Jocelyn Hollis. 274

"Here by the Pacific shore." Robert A. Sears. 362

Here comes yesterday. John Godfrey. 260

"Here in the Fort my heart doth." Charles Olson. 337

"Here they come." Madison Morrison. 327

Here to there. Donald Revell. 351

"Here's a beastly/fable." Madison Morrison. 327

The,here, what, where, sels. Andrei Codrescu. 223

A hereditary ailment. Cornel Lengyel. 302

Heritage. John F. Barker. 201

Heritage
    Ancestors. Dennis Hinrichsen. 273
    Ancestors. Edwin Honig. 275
    Bird. Albert Goldbarth. 261
    Descendant. Rose Basile Green. 265
    The generations of men. Robert Frost. 250
    Grandmother. Melvin Dixon. 231
    Hand made. Betty Adcock. 192
    Ohio Yankee. Everett A. Gillis. 258
    On my father's side. Laura Boss. 213
    The painting. Michael Akillian. 193
    Pioneer. Rose Basile Green. 265
    Remember. Joy Harjo. 269
    Scion. Robert Kelly. 289
    Singing, maker of peace. Rose Basile Green. 265
    A table with people. Marc Kaminsky. 288
    They will remember. Rose Basile Green. 265
    A toast to the ancestors. Rose Basile Green. 265
    Voodoo mambo: to the tourists. Melvin Dixon. 231

The hermit-woman. Gayl Jones. 286

Hermits
    Monk's song. Keith Wilson. 400

Hero. Josephine Miles. 319

Hero's song. Barry Wallenstein. 393

Heroes and Heroines
    The author says goodbye to his hero. David Wagoner. 390
    Epitaph for a humble hero, fr. Elegy and epitaph. Everett A. Gillis. 258
    Hero. Josephine Miles. 319
    "I am no hero." Michael Robert Pick. 345
    Standing close to greatness. Miller Williams. 399
    "We make heroes of some." Theta Burke. 218
    "Why did the tragic hero." Madison Morrison. 327
    "You and I." Madison Morrison. 327

Heroic discoverer. James Applewhite. 198

Heroic standard. Kenneth Koch. 297

Heroine tied to the railroad tracks. James Magorian. 308

"The heroine/is cross..." Madison Morrison. 327

The heron. Carol Frost. 249

Hers. John Godfrey. 260

Herstory. Marilyn Kallet. 287

Hesitate to call. Louise Gluck. 259A

Hey baby. Debra Bruce. 216

Hey, young folks. Rosa Bogar. 211

Hicks, Edward
    The peaceable kingdom of Edward Hicks. James Schevill. 360
    The well. Albert Goldbarth. 261

Hidden desire. Jacques Sollov. 370

Hide and seek. Jeanne Lohmann. 305

Hide and seek. Jocelyn Hollis. 274

Hiemal watch. Robert Anbian. 194

Hieroglyphs
    The Rosetta Stone. James Magorian. 309

High blood pressure. Gene

Anderson. 195
"High piled/clouds." Larry
    Eigner. 237
High road from Naples. Anne
    Bailie. 199
High school. James Schevill. 360
High school dance. Josephine B.
    Moretti. 324
High school dropout continually
    hoodwinked by knotty... James
    Magorian. 309
High school football coach. James
    Schevill. 360
High school reunion. James
    Magorian. 308
"High society." Larry Eigner. 237
High water mark. Paul Davis. 228
High-wire artist. Joyce Carol
    Oates. 336
Higher criticism. Thomas McGrath.
    315
Highroad. Josephine Miles. 319
Highway patrol roadblock. James
    Magorian. 309
Hillbilly night before Christmas.
    Thomas Noel Turner. 385
The hills at Cambria School.
    Ernest Tedlock. 380
The hills of San Francisco. Sally
    Love Saunders. 358
Hills. See Mountains

Hilltop house. James Torio. 281
Hillwalker. Stephen Knauth. 295
Himalayas
    At night in the high mountains.
    Carolyn Stoloff. 376
Hindus
    Pharisees and Sadducees.
    Phillips Kloss. 294
Hinrichsen, Dennis
    Among cattle. 273
    Ancestors. 273
    At the gravesite. 273
    Autobiography. 273
    Big-time wrestling. 273
    Blueberries. 273
    Chincoteague. 273
    Driving the Green Mountains. 273
    Economics. 273
    Elegy spoken to a tree. 273
    Elegy spoken to my grandfather.
    273
    Grass. 273
    The Great Plains states. 273
    Heaven, circa 1938. 273
    The last perfect moment. 273
    Late leaving train. 273
    Living in the other world. 273
    Love poem after years without

    remorse. 273
    Map of the world. 273
    New York City. 273
    November streets. 273
    The oak tree. 273
    On the attraction of heavenly
    bodies. 273
    Portraits by Matisse. 273
    A prologue to some elegies. 273
    Ridgeline. 273
    To a ghost. 273
    Towards a pure economy. 273
Hippogriff. X.J. Kennedy. 290
Hippopotami
    The hippopotamus. Jack
    Prelutsky. 349
The hippopotamus. Jack Prelutsky.
    349
His chain. Edwin Honig. 275
His daughter. Albert Goldbarth.
    261
His dream. David Wagoner. 390
His dream. Edwin Honig. 275
His hat was on straight. Judson
    Crews. 226
His health, his poetry, and his
    love all in one. Charles
    Olson. 337
His mind ceases. Carol Frost. 249
His neighbor talks of Monet.
    Jeanne Lohmann. 305
The histories of morning. Thomas
    McGrath. 315
History. Thomas McGrath. 315
History. Wanda Coleman. 225
History
    Form. Roy Marz. 312
    A later note on Letter #15.
    Charles Olson. 337
    Museum curator filling display
    cases with trenchant griefs.
    James Magorian. 309
    On a popular historian. Cornel
    Lengyel. 302
    Saturnalia. Louise Gluck. 259A
    So graven. Josephine Miles. 319
    Tales from the father of
    history. Richmond Lattimore.
    301
    "We have the generation which
    carries something new..."
    Josephine Miles. 319
History is for tourist. Larry
    Eigner. 237
"History is something to take
    shelter in." Robert Kelly. 289
History is the memory of time.
    Charles Olson. 337
History lesson. Thomas R. Sleigh.
    366

History of China. Herbert Morris. 326

A history of civilization. Albert Goldbarth. 261

The history of it. Bradford Morrow. 329

A history of rain. Marc Hudson. 277

The history of the growth of heaven. Andrei Codrescu. 223

History's library. James Applewhite. 198

"The history/of earth..." Charles Olson. 337

"Hitchhiking in blinding storm." Michael Robert Pick. 345

Hitler, Adolph
    The madness. Sam Fishman. 246

Ho hum. Marie Daerr Boehringer. 210

Hockey season. Robin Becker. 202

Hog's elegy to the butchers. James Schevill. 360

"Hokey, pokey, winky, wum." Jan Ormerod. 338

Hokusai's 'Wild Horses.' Sharon Bryan. 217

Hokusai, Katsushika
    The lifeline. Carolyn Stoloff. 376

Holan, Vladimir
    Elegy. Clayton Eshleman. 240

"Holding hands/we are a circle/...of the spirit." Joan Walsh Anglund. 197

Holding on. Rod McKuen. 316

Holding on. Robert L. Wilson. 401

Holding on. Colette Inez. 280

"A hole in the clouds moves." Larry Eigner. 237

Hole in the stream's ice. Harry Humes. 278

Holiday. Josephine Miles. 319

Holiday Inn. Mark Vinz. 387

Holiday prayer. Alice Joyce Davidson. 227

Holland
    Amsterdam, student round-up. Iefke Goldberger. 262
    "Washing between the buildings." Larry Eigner. 237

Hollandaise. Sharon Bryan. 217

Hollis, Jocelyn
    The arming of the bomb. 274
    The army. 274
    At Penn's Landing, Philadelphia, Pa. 274
    The death of a submarine. 274
    Defoliage - agent orange. 274
    Epilogue. 274
    Epitaph for the bomb. 274
    Flags. 274
    Hercules builds its new corporate headquarters... 274
    Hercules, Dow, - agent orange. 274
    Hide and seek. 274
    In the jungle in Vietnam. 274
    In the name of the children. 274
    Like fallen angels. 274
    A man of plastic. 274
    Memorial Day in Wilmington, Delaware. 274
    The modern alchemists. 274
    On a loved one going to war. 274
    On seeing a flag-draped casket. 274
    Prayer in Vietnam. 274
    The soldier-poet. 274
    War and evolution. 274
    War zone 1961-1975. 274
    We are not Achilles. 274
    Yet are you wounded, soldier? 274

Hollow. Rod McKuen. 316

Hollywood, California
    April in Hollywood. Wanda Coleman. 225

Holocaust
    A transport fo children. Cornel Lengyel. 302

Holy Cross Hospital. Toi Derricote. 229

Holy grail. James R. Rhodes. 352

The Holy Grail. Andrei Codrescu. 223

Holy orders. Robert Pawlowski. 341

Homage. Donald Revell. 351

Homage. Greg Kuzma. 300

Homage to Plotinus. Eve Triem. 383

Homage to the moon. Jacqueline Frank. 248

Homage to Virginia Woolf. Joyce Carol Oates. 336

Home. Marieve Rugo. 356

Home. Marc Hudson. 277

Home. Steve Kowit. 298, 299

Home. Richmond Lattimore. 301

Home and Family Life
    A distant day. Evelyn Golden. 263
    Afternoon, playing on a bed. Betty Adcock. 192
    Apple, the family love and asshole. James Schevill. 360
    As I live and I feel. S. Bradford Williams (Jr.). 398
    Blueprint to forever. Alice

Spohn Newton. 332

Breaking the ice again. Larry
   Moffi. 322

Building houses. Dave Smith. 367

A burning:a poem in nine parts.
   Frances Mayes. 314

Business as usual. Mark Vinz.
   387

A catechism. William Stafford.
   373

Celebration. Robert L. Wilson.
   401

Child in the evening. William
   Stafford. 373

Chinatown. Cathy Song. 372

Christmas in a valley of the
   Uwharrie. Stephen Knauth. 295

Civil liberty. John F. Barker.
   201

"Climbing to the
   second/floor..." Madison
   Morrison. 327

Contingency plan. Mark Vinz. 387

Corner lot. Sharon Bryan. 217

Crossing the lawn. Debra Bruce.
   216

Cycle. Frances Mayes. 314

Dawn thoughts. Maria Gillan. 256

Domestic miracles. Joyce Carol
   Oates. 336

A dream of heaven. Deborah Tall.
   378

A dream of salt. Jenne Andrews.
   196

Family. Rochelle DuBois. 234

Family. Anneliese Wagner. 389

Family. Martha Janssen. 283

Family album. Robin Becker. 202

Family album. Stephen Sandy. 357

Family snapshot. Tefke
   Goldberger. 262

Family tree. Alice Joyce
   Davidson. 227

"The far bliss..." Larry Eigner.
   237

Fascination. C.D. Wright. 402

Fireflies. Ghita Orth. 339

The first night of summer.
   Eileen Silver-Lillywite. 364

Forced entry. Marieve Rugo. 356

Former residence. Richmond
   Lattimore. 301

Fourth commandment. Martha
   Janssen. 283

The genesis of the egg. Stephen
   Todd Booker. 212

Grandmother in the garden.
   Louise Gluck. 259A

"A grey woman of." Madison
   Morrison. 327

Hanging tough. William Stafford.
   373

Home. Marieve Rugo. 356

Home. Marc Hudson. 277

Home movies. Josephine Miles.
   319

Hometown blues. Mark Vinz. 387

House guests. Alice Spohn
   Newton. 333

Hungry travel. Melvin Dixon. 231

"I live in one room." Madison
   Morrison. 327

Ida Maria. John F. Barker. 201

Image. Martha Janssen. 283

In pursuit of the family. Jenne
   Andrews. 196

In the house of the judge. Dave
   Smith. 367

Island. Scott Chisholm. 221

Knowledge. Martha Janssen. 283

Land of little sticks, 1945.
   James Tate. 379

Leaving. Cathy Song. 372

Letter from our man in
   blossomtime. Louise Gluck.
   259A

A little yard. Stephen Sandy.
   357

"Locust Street, a garage full of
   beer cans." Michael Robert
   Pick. 345

Loudoun. John F. Barker. 201

Mermaid alley: after rain. Gene
   Detro. 230

A mirror. Eileen
   Silver-Lillywite. 364

Missing them. David Wann. 394

Mountains behind us. Alice Spohn
   Newton. 333

Mourning cloak. Anthony
   Petrosky. 344

"My childhood, turbulent
   peaceful years." Michael
   Robert Pick. 345

My father's house. Debra Bruce.
   216

My mother's parlor. Phyllis A.
   Tickle. 382

New tract. Josephine Miles. 319

Notes from a gutted house.
   Colette Inez. 280

Notes on an early room. Carolyn
   Stoloff. 376

Odor. Anneliese Wagner. 389

On a black and photograph of a
   house. Jim Simmerman. 365

Part of the story. Robert
   Pawlowski. 341

Patriarch. Mark Vinz. 387

A Pennsylvania family. Anthony

Petrosky. 344
"Physically, I am home..."
    Charles Olson. 337
Portrait of the queen in tears.
    Louise Gluck. 259A
Quabbin Reservoir. Robin Becker.
    202
Quiet. Martha Janssen. 283
Quiet, so quiet. Eileen
    Silver-Lillywite. 364
Redlands journey. Betty Adcock.
    192
Returning to Eagle Bridge.
    Stephen Sandy. 357
Room filler. Alice Spohn Newton.
    332
Root-bound. Sharon Bryan. 217
Saying the word. Gary Margolis.
    311
Scraps. Louise Gluck. 259A
Signs. Harry Humes. 278
The song. Michael Akillian. 193
"Standing in a hole." Michael
    Robert Pick. 345
The storm. Debra Bruce. 216
Street. Josephine Miles. 319
Surprise! Surprise! Alice Spohn
    Newton. 333
Talking with my brother, who
    came to visit. George Eklund.
    238
Thanksgiving. Louise Gluck. 259A
That boy, in winter or rain.
    George Eklund. 238
To a ghost. Dennis Hinrichsen.
    273
To market. George Eklund. 238
Today and tomorrow. Anthony
    Petrosky. 344
Tours. C.D. Wright. 402
We live in this room. Eileen
    Silver-Lillywite. 364
Windmill valley. Alice Spohn
    Newton. 333
Winter, your father's house. Jim
    Simmerman. 365
Home body. James R. Rhodes. 352
Home brew. Josephine B. Moretti.
    324
Home burial. Robert Frost. 250
Home ground. Rod McKuen. 316
Home life of the circus dancers.
    James Schevill. 360
Home movies. Josephine Miles. 319
Home place: bear creek in autumn.
    Franz Schneider. 361
Home sick. Miriam Goodman. 264
Home town. W.D. (William De Witt)
    Snodgrass. 369
"'Home', to the shore." Charles
Olson. 337
Home-sick. Patsie Black. 206
Home. Jenne Andrews. 196
Home ground. Randy Blasing. 207
Homecoming. Richard Blessing. 208
Homecoming. Marge Piercy. 346
Homecoming. James Torio. 281
Homecoming
    Alien. Ghita Orth. 339
    American genesis. Phyllis A.
        Tickle. 382
    "Angelic youth." Larry Eigner.
        237
    Bibbiena. Robert A. Sears. 362
    Commute. Dave Smith. 367
    Driving her back to Wisconsin.
        George Eklund. 238
    A face without lines. John
        Godfrey. 260
    For A.J.: on finding she's on
        her boat to China. Cathy Song.
        372
    Full circle. Marieve Rugo. 356
    Going back. Robert L. Wilson.
        401
    The good-bye-hello handbook.
        Cathryn Hankla. 268
    Got me home, the light snow
        gives the air, falling.
        Charles Olson. 337
    Grandparents and grandchildren.
        Gene Anderson. 195
    "Hector-body." Charles Olson.
        337
    The hills at Cambria School.
        Ernest Tedlock. 380
    Homage to the moon. Jacqueline
        Frank. 248
    Home ground. Rod McKuen. 316
    Homecoming. Marge Piercy. 346
    Homecoming. James Torio. 281
    I dream my return. Cathryn
        Hankla. 268
    In conversation. Robin Becker.
        202
    Interstate 40. Phyllis A.
        Tickle. 382
    Making it. Robert L. Wilson. 401
    Nobody's business. James Tate.
        379
    North Dakota: 1979. Rodney
        Nelson. 331
    Partita. Edwin Honig. 275
    Passing through Les Eyzies.
        Jacqueline Frank. 248
    Puzzle. Marie Daerr Boehringer.
        210
    Rain. Josephine Miles. 319
    Returned to Frisco, 1946. W.D.
        (William De Witt) Snodgrass.

369
Returning to Taos. Judson Crews. 226
Reunion. J.W. Rivers. 354
Revelation and return. Robert L. Wilson. 401
Revisiting Thrudvang farm. Rodney Nelson. 331
Same thought-2. Charles Olson. 337
Sis and the pidgeon man. James A. Emanuel. 239
Sister Celia. Dave Smith. 367
Sources. Adrienne Rich. 353
Tell them. James Tate. 379
A telling. Jenne Andrews. 196
Ten days leave. W.D. (William De Witt) Snodgrass. 369
They used to have a homecoming day. Richmond Lattimore. 301
Time. Frances Mayes. 314
A vision. Mitchell Howard. 276
Winter bouquet. W.D. (William De Witt) Snodgrass. 369
Winter return. Richmond Lattimore. 301
"You come home to." Madison Morrison. 327

Homeland
Albemarle. Donald Revell. 351
Great rock unchanging. Alice Spohn Newton. 332
"Here by the Pacific shore." Robert A. Sears. 362
Luctor et emergo. Tefke Goldberger. 262

The **homemade** piano. Carol Frost. 249

Homes??!! Norman Andrew Kirk. 293

Homesickness. Maurice W. Britts. 215

Homesickness
Home-sick. Patsie Black. 206
Homesickness. Maurice W. Britts. 215
"I'm a/different person." Madison Morrison. 327

Homesickness. See also Nostalgia

Hometown blues. Mark Vinz. 387
The **homilies** of Bedrock Jones. Thomas McGrath. 315
"**Homo** anthropos." Charles Olson. 337
Homo Sapiens. John F. Barker. 201
Homosexuality
Anything but murder. Jim Everhard. 241
The clay dancer. James L. White.

396
Coming. Jim Everhard. 241
Curing homosexuality. Jim Everhard. 241
Distance. Jim Everhard. 241
The ephebe of Tarsus. Royal Murdoch. 330
The first time. James L. White. 396
For the goddess too well known. Elsa Gidlow. 254
The invitation. Royal Murdoch. 330
Looking for the lumberjack. Jim Everhard. 241
Love in age. Elsa Gidlow. 254
Making love to myself. James L. White. 396
Memory of Roanoke. Jim Everhard. 241
Monologue for an aging queen. Jim Everhard. 241
Mr. Castle's vacation drive. James Schevill. 360
A new moon rises. Elsa Gidlow. 254
Ode to the Duchess La Blah. Jim Everhard. 241
Oshi. James L. White. 396
Pedro Nel Mejia. Royal Murdoch. 330
Prairie. Robin Becker. 202
Reasons why I love you. Jim Everhard. 241
Rosa Luxemburg, drag queen. Jim Everhard. 241
The salt ecstasies. James L. White. 396
Seascape. Royal Murdoch. 330
Secret Sapphic. Elsa Gidlow. 254
Skin movers. James L. White. 396
Soldier. Royal Murdoch. 330
South Yuma River, Summer 1971. Jim Everhard. 241
The spy. Royal Murdoch. 330
Summer news. James L. White. 396
Taken to a room. James L. White. 396
Up, liberation! Royal Murdoch. 330
Who will it be? Rosa Bogar. 211
Women at the lakeside. Elsa Gidlow. 254
Women in love. Robin Becker. 202
Honesty
Lecture on Creeley. Gerard Malanga. 310
Honeymoon. Ghita Orth. 339
Honeymoon. Joyce Carol Oates. 336
Honig, Edwin

The abstract man encounters the adjutant, sels. 275
The affinities of Orpheus, sels. 275
After the letter. 275
After the separation. 275
All the nights the house slept through. 275
Ancestors. 275
Another. 275
Another March. 275
Another Orpheus. 275
An art of summer. 275
As a great prince. 275
"As the light descended." 275
"As we would have it." 275
Being somebody. 275
Birth song: in the wing seat, at night. 275
"Blackening ebbtide." 275
Bodega, goodbye. 275
By sea stone, sels. 275
"Can you remember beginning?" 275
Come. 275
"Conrad saw behind the wheel." 275
The dead. 275
Death with its cup of hopefulness. 275
Dialogue in the sleeping house. 275
Ditty to his love. 275
'Do you love me?' 275
"Echoing the fierce belief that time." 275
First morning. 275
For an immigrant grandmother. 275
For C. 275
"For everyone the call of light." 275
For his mother flying into her seventy-seventh. 275
For Margot. 275
Four springs, sels. 275
The furnace. 275
G.W.M. 275
The gazabos: forty-one poems, sels. 275
The gazabos. 275
Glad day. 275
Grammarian thumbing an old text. 275
The grave thumps. 275
Hamlet. 275
Happening. 275
"Hearing it wake, we feel." 275
Her hand. 275
His chain. 275

His dream. 275
The house. 275
I need you. 275
"In his ordinary world." 275
"In winter when the sun shone." 275
Island storm. 275
The island. 275
The isolated house he sometimes visited. 275
It cannot be it is. 275
Jane Retreat. 275
Joy: an end song. 275
Last act. 275
Last song. 275
Lease and loss. 275
Letter from New Hampshire. 275
Lines for dancers. 275
Listen. 275
The marriage. 275
May 1945. 275
Melting song. 275
Monster talk. 275
The moral circus. 275
My love is asleep. 275
Nativity. 275
Night island. 275
1925.n. 275
"No longer would he have to run." 275
"Not to be listening." 275
"Nothing much left." 275
November through a giant copper beech. 275
Now, before the end, I think. 275
Now, my usefulness over. 275
Opening. 275
Outer drive. 275
Pablo Nerunda. 275
The painter in the montain. 275
Partita. 275
Passes for Nicanor Parra. 275
Passing. 275
Passionflower. 275
Promise. 275
Quest. 275
Race. 275
Rilke's white horse. 275
Second day song. 275
Soldier. 275
Speech. 275
Spring four, sels. 275
Spring journal: poems, sels. 275
Spring one, sels. 275
Spring three, sels. 275
Spring two, sels. 275
Starting the hostilities. 275
Stumbling out of the Prado. 275
"Suddenly out of the hedge." 275

Survivals, sels. 275
Sweeping the room. 275
The tall Toms. 275
Teethering. 275
Tete-a-tete. 275
There would be large cuttings of
    flowers. 275
"These stones if they spoke."
    275
Three moments for George
    Sullivan. 275
Through you. 275
To be alive be bold. 275
To restore a dead child, sels.
    275
Unless love die. 275
Walt Whitman. 275
"Watching the immense self
    scattering ocean." 275
"We walked out of time." 275
The weather's criminal. 275
What changes, my love. 275
Who. 275
Wife. 275
A wind dies. 275
Without love. 275
Honorarium. Erin Jolly. 285
Hood Canal, Washington
    Walking to Dewato. Marc Hudson.
    277
"The **Hook**, a name of a man."
    Michael Robert Pick. 345
Hoolehua. Cathy Song. 372
Hop, skip, and jump. Aileen
    Fisher. 244
Hope. Maurice W. Britts. 215
Hope. Sam Fishman. 246
Hope. Connie Hunt. 279
Hope
    April people. Rod McKuen. 316
    Bright hope. Alice Joyce
        Davidson. 227
    Call it hope. Rochelle DuBois.
        234
    Don't let the dreams die out, my
        friend. Robert L. Wilson. 401
    Encounter. Ernesto Galarza. 252
    "Even now lost winds carry
        silent memories." Michael
        Robert Pick. 345
    Falling beasts. C.D. Wright. 402
    Hope. Maurice W. Britts. 215
    Hope. Sam Fishman. 246
    Hope. Connie Hunt. 279
    "Hope/comes to all." A. Dovichi.
        233
    The new 'ism.' Connie Hunt. 279
    Now, going on eternity. Robert
        L. Wilson. 401
    Passing. Edwin Honig. 275

Pedestrian. Thomas Lux. 307
Proctologist on a sentimental
    journey. James Magorian. 309
Star of life. Maurice W. Britts.
    215
Stone, paper, knife. Marge
    Piercy. 346
Tomorrow. James A. Emanuel. 239
Wishes. Deborah Tall. 378
Yellow cars. William Stafford.
    373
"**Hope** life is good to you."
    Michael Robert Pick. 345
Hope no more. Robert L. Wilson.
    401
Hope, Arkansas. Phyllis A.
    Tickle. 382
"**Hope/comes** to all." A. Dovichi.
    233
"**Hopes** racing." Sally Love
    Saunders. 358
Horace - Book IV Ode 7. John
    Reed. 350
Horatio Greenough writes of
    reason. James Schevill. 360
Horizon. Josephine Miles. 319
Horizon. Rachel A. Hazen. 271
Horizons
    Steadying the lanscape. Jeanne
    Lohmann. 305
Hornets
    "Two hornets feast upon my
    plate." James Torio. 281
Horoscope. James Magorian. 308
A **horse** brought the day. Alice
    Spohn Newton. 333
Horse latitudes. Colette Inez.
    280
A **horse** lost. Ernest Tedlock. 380
Horse Racing
    Exacta. Paul Violi. 388
    The sport of kings. Ernest
    Hemingway. 272
The **horsemen.** David Wagoner. 390
Horses. Maurice Kenny. 291
Horses
    A dream of spring horses. Harry
        Humes. 278
    The dreams of wild horses.
        Thomas McGrath. 315
    Explosion. Joy Harjo. 269
    A horse lost. Ernest Tedlock.
        380
    The horsemen. David Wagoner. 390
    Horses. Maurice Kenny. 291
    Ice horses. Joy Harjo. 269
    Jesse and Jeanie. Alice Spohn
        Newton. 332
    The love of horses. Jenne
        Andrews. 196

Mare. Susan Tichy. 381
Mountain man. Randy Blasing. 207
She had some horses. Joy Harjo.
    269
Tete-a-tete. Edwin Honig. 275
Three horses. Thomas R. Sleigh.
    366
The truth is. Jeanne Lohmann.
    305
The two white horses. Roy Marz.
    312
Vision. Joy Harjo. 269
The horseshoe. James Tate. 379
Hospital. Everett A. Gillis. 258
Hospital notes. John Reed. 350
Hospital sequence. Jeanne
    Lohmann. 305
Hospitals
    Animal cracker box. Eileen
        Silver-Lillywite. 364
    At the Chateau de Villegenis
        that summer. Herbert Morris.
        326
    The burning wards of
        Meadowbrook. Colette Inez. 280
    Esterhazy in the hospital. J.W.
        Rivers. 354
    Ever since my operation.
        Josephine B. Moretti. 324
    Heirloom. Robin Morgan. 325
    Holy Cross Hospital. Toi
        Derricote. 229
    Hospital. Everett A. Gillis. 258
    Hospital notes. John Reed. 350
    Hospital sequence. Jeanne
        Lonmann. 305
    In the hospital. Eileen
        Silver-Lillywite. 364
    Intensives. Josephine Miles. 319
    Leaving. Toi Derricote. 229
    A momentary change of weather.
        Paul Davis. 228
    Orderly. Josephine Miles. 319
    Patient observation. James R.
        Rhodes. 352
    Scott. Richard Blessing. 208
    Semi-private. Richard Blessing.
        208
    Seton Hospital. Eileen
        Silver-Lillywite. 364
    Sundowner. Richard Blessing. 208
    Two rooms. John Reed. 350
    V.A. nospital. Anthony Petrosky.
        344
    Waiting. James R. Rhodes. 352
Hostages
    Counting the days. Gary
        Margolis. 311
Hot and sweaty. Mitchell Howard.
    276

Hot bread. Robert Peters. 343
Hot mountain poem. Gene Detro.
    230
Hot night. Cynthia Grenfell. 266
Hot tubbers. Harlan Usher. 386
Hotel du Nord. John Godfrey. 260
Hotel Geneve. Cathy Song. 372
"The hotel room." Madison
    Morrison. 327
Hotel Steinplatz, Berlin,
    December 25 (1966). Charles
    Olson. 337
Hotels
    Gramercy Park Hotel. Dave Smith.
        367
    Holiday Inn. Mark Vinz. 387
    "In a hotel room." Madison
        Morrison. 327
    Motel discoveries. Josephine B.
        Moretti. 324
    Purchase of lodging for the
        night. Josephine Miles. 319
    Ten dreamers in a motel.
        Josephine Miles. 319
Hotrods. Larry Eigner. 237
Houdini, Harry
    The artist of escape: Houdini.
        James Schevill. 360
Hour minute hands seconds. Larry
    Eigner. 237
"The hour of evening..." Charles
    Olson. 337
Hourglass conflicts, sels.
    Rochelle DuBois. 234
"Hours knock in the wrists of
    gypsies." Carolyn Stoloff. 376
"Hours line gray streaks in a
    warrior's face." Michael
    Robert Pick. 345
The hours. Susan Tichy. 381
House guests. Alice Spohn Newton.
    333
The house mouse. Jack Prelutsky.
    349
The house next door. Robert L.
    Wilson. 401
The house of eternity. James
    Torio. 281
The house of lions. Keith Wilson.
    400
House of shadows. Joan Colby. 224
House of sod. Alice Spohn Newton.
    333
"The house of sturdy." Madison
    Morrison. 327
House-movers. Dave Smith. 367
House. David Shapiro. 363
The house. Everett A. Gillis. 258
The house. Edwin Honig. 275
Housecleaning. Roy Marz. 312

Householder. Mark Vinz. 387
The housekeeper. Robert Frost.
      250
Housekeeping
      Cleaning up. Ernesto Galarza.
      252
Houses
      All the nights the house slept
          through. Edwin Honig. 275
      Curtains:a pasticcio. Frances
          Mayes. 314
      Dialogue in the sleeping house.
          Edwin Honig. 275
      "Down from another planet they
          have settled to mend."
          Josephine Miles. 319
      Dream house. Mark Vinz. 387
      For the new occupants. Sister
          Maura. 313
      Golden eyelids. Erin Jolly. 285
      Happening. Edwin Honig. 275
      "Her vestibule." Madison
          Morrison. 327
      "The house of sturdy." Madison
          Morrison. 327
      The house. Everett A. Gillis.
          258
      "I don't care at all." Madison
          Morrison. 327
      Leavetaking, at dusk. Joyce
          Carol Oates. 336
      Outline. Frances Mayes. 314
      Pattern. Frances Mayes. 314
      A 17th century New England
          house. Sharon Bryan. 217
      $7,500 Josephine Miles.
          319
      "These old houses." Madison
          Morrison. 327
      Turn-of-the-century house. Dave
          Smith. 367
      "When September tells the."
          Madison Morrison. 327
Housewife. Josephine Miles. 319
The housewife laments her
      purchase of floating eggs. Jim
      Simmerman. 365
Housewives. See Women -
      Housewives

Houston's Negroes. Robert
      Pawlowski. 341
How ballad writing affects our
      seniors. Ernest Hemingway. 272
How bright the morning. Judson
      Crews. 226
How can a child hope along
      avenues. Carolyn Stoloff. 376
"How can one/who has always
      heard." Theta Burke. 218

How clearly we entered. Judson
      Crews. 226
"How do old men walk." James
      Torio. 281
"How far can a single mind go."
      Michael Robert Pick. 345
"How far does the heart travel."
      Michael Robert Pick. 345
How gentle. Joyce Carol Oates.
      336
"How goes a crowd where it goes?"
      Josephine Miles. 319
How I caught up in my reading.
      Josephine Miles. 319
How it all began. William
      Stafford. 373
How it is. William Stafford. 373
How many crushed skulls. Judson
      Crews. 226
"How many languages..." Larry
      Eigner. 237
"How many things we are attentive
      to!" Kenneth Koch. 297
"How much could they/flicker."
      Larry Eigner. 237
"How much the moon may be." Larry
      Eigner. 237
How old are you? Josephine B.
      Moretti. 324
"How peaceful to ride in the
      arms." Sally Love Saunders.
      358
"How quickly/the fire of joy."
      Theta Burke. 218
How the sky begins to fall. Joan
      Colby. 224
How to create music by William
      Billings. James Schevill. 360
How to get back. William
      Stafford. 373
How to improve your personality.
      Herbert Morris. 326
"How to train a dog." Michael
      Robert Pick. 345
How we resist the new. Evelyn
      Golden. 263
"How would you like to grow wings
      with me." Michael Robert Pick.
      345
"How you/stand." Larry Eigner.
      237
"How/could the cost." A. Dovichi.
      233
Howard, Mitchell
      The abuses of New York. 276
      An ambassador from the future.
          276
      American baroque. 276
      Anthropological sonnet. 276
      Apocaylpse in me. 276

An apology to the groundhog. 276
The back-door ghost. 276
Bloomsday sermon. 276
Circle without end. 276
The city that is set upon a
    hill. 276
Critic's bliss. 276
Daytime nightmares, stretched
    along five blocks of 42nd St.
    276
Dictatorship of myself. 276
Discoursing kisses. 276
Distant weather. 276
Doing without. 276
Domingo de Ramos. 276
The door of question of the
    narrowing choice. 276
The doorway. 276
The Edgartown heat. 276
Edward's song. 276
Eroteschatology. 276
The flawless dancer. 276
Formulas for non-violence. 276
Fran's birthday. 276
Free pass. 276
Freefall can be fun. 276
The green tide. 276
Guess what was ripped out of the
    wall today? 276
Happy birthday b/w Say Hay. 276
Harboring some tinny escape
    plans. 276
Helluva big neighborhood. 276
Hot and sweaty. 276
I haven't seen my grandmother
    since she died. 276
If Osiris were to die in New
    York. 276
Invasion of the huge spirits.
    276
John Lennon murdered on wild
    west side walk. 276
The kiss. 276
Lockdance. 276
Lonely without reason. 276
Losses. 276
Love theme from 'The mummy's
    kiss meets Dracula.' 276
Memorial for Cass Elliott. 276
Morning tide. 276
The myth of Cancer. 276
Nature visits the city. 276
Nel mezzo dell'autostrada di
    nostra vita. 276
Next year in Jerusalem, this
    year in Philadelphia. 276
Nut-brown bird. 276
On the midway. 276
Orbital bunnes, inc. 276
Pantry secrets. 276

Parallax. 276
Passing through. 276
The perfect fool. 276
Planting H-bombs on the moon.
    276
Playbill. 276
Polarity. 276
Psych ward. 276
The railroad still runs to
    Connecticut... 276
Rama holds an orgy. 276
Recipe for the anxious one. 276
Resolving. 276
Ritornello. 276
Rock & roll snowstorm. 276
Rosary portraits of improbable
    saints. 276
Shutout. 276
Snow patterns. 276
Some nasty business. 276
Sonnet upon three kings' day.
    276
The stone of all souls. 276
Stoned by the Lord. 276
The story of what happens. 276
Suburban rebellions. 276
Surprise party. 276
Terror hiding in glossy sexy
    magazines. 276
Third day of the baseball
    playoffs. 276
Time-line. 276
Tiresias. 276
Too bloated to boogie. 276
The uses of New York. 276
The varnish of their days. 276
Very late thoughts. 276
A vision. 276
Warm, friendly creatures. 276
Weary. 276
What happens when it rains. 276
Words to persons who find
    themselves feeling small. 276
Yea and nay. 276
Howdy. Andrei Codrescu. 223
The **howling** darkness. Sam
    Fishman. 246
Hubbard, Elbert
Fra Elbertus or the inspector
    general. James Schevill. 360
Hubie French needs a letter.
    George Eklund. 238
Huck Finn at ninety, dying in a
    Chicago boarding house room.
    James Schevill. 360
Huckleberries
Huckleberrying. Maurice Kenny.
    291
Huckleberrying. Maurice Kenny.
    291

Hudson River
    Along the Hudson. Maurice Kenny.
    291
Hudson, Marc
    Above Moraine Park. 277
    Afterlight. 277
    At Berkeley Park. 277
    At Keflavik. 277
    At Suthurstrond. 277
    By La Push. 277
    Climbing together. 277
    Dewato. 277
    Dusting the sill. 277
    Elegy for Martin Heidegger. 277
    For Wang Wei. 277
    George Vancouver's death dream.
    277
    A German printmaker. 277
    Hanging at Galgahraun. 277
    Hawk. 277
    A history of rain. 277
    Home. 277
    Island. 277
    Last rites. 277
    Late garden. 277
    Late winter sky. 277
    Letter to Scardanelli. 277
    A natural history of the
    fourteenth century. 277
    Okanogan sleep. 277
    Painter at dusk. 277
    Reading Chretien by Hood Canal.
    277
    Red cedar. 277
    A road in the Willapa Hills. 277
    Sixteenth-century Icelandic
    chair. 277
    Soley. 277
    Some gnomic verses. 277
    Summer, Aeneas Valley. 277
    Under Snaefellsjokull. 277
    Voices overheard on a night of
    the Perseid shower. 277
    Walking to Dewato. 277
    Winter, Aeneas Valley. 277
Huerta, Victoriano
    Victoriano Huerta. J.W. Rivers.
    354
Hugo, Richard
    Totems (IV). Thomas McGrath. 315
Hugs. Alice Joyce Davidson. 227
Huleh Valley, Israel
    Geology of the Huleh. Susan
    Tichy. 381
Human. James R. Rhodes. 352
Human logic. James R. Rhodes. 352
Humes, Harry
    Air burial. 278
    Ballade for a canoeist. 278
    Bird feeder. 278

Canoe beneath the trees. 278
Conversation with the giver of
    names. 278
The coyote in the orchard. 278
Dead animals. 278
A dream of spring horses. 278
Einstein in the orchard. 278
February woods. 278
Fish kill in January. 278
Flocking. 278
The garden in ruins. 278
Hawk Mountain in the fog. 278
He dreams of a hawk. 278
Hole in the stream's ice. 278
Hunters keep out. 278
Hunting for north in the fog.
    278
The ice fisherman's dream. 278
It could be. 278
The man who carves whales. 278
The man who often turned to
    stone. 278
The muskellunge. 278
The new site of the Calvary
    Temple. 278
The owl in the refrigerator. 278
The rain walkers. 278
Reading late by a simple light.
    278
Safety zone. 278
Savage remembers a horse. 278
Signs. 278
Something more. 278
The spheres of October. 278
Stalling for time. 278
Studying the light. 278
Targets. 278
Through the ice tree. 278
Whales. 278
Winter stream. 278
Winter weeds. 278
The woman who loved wool. 278
Hummingbird. Marge Piercy. 346
"The hummingbird is a docile
    woodpecker." Stephen Todd
    Booker. 212
The hummingbird. Jack Prelutsky.
    349
Hummingbirds
    Hummingbird. Marge Piercy. 346
    The hummingbird. Jack Prelutsky.
    349
The humor of Helen. Roy Marz. 312
Humorous Verse
    The fun. Sam Fishman. 246
    Spring dirge. Ernesto Galarza.
    252
Humpty Dumpty
    Humpty Dumpty traveling in
    Montana. James Magorian. 309

"Humpty Dumpty sat on a wall."
    Jan Ormerod. 338
Humpty Dumpty traveling in
    Montana. James Magorian. 309
Humpty who? Harlan Usher. 386
A hundred collars. Robert Frost.
    250
A hundred years ago. John F.
    Barker. 201
Hunger
    "The personality of the feeding
    bin." Kenneth Koch. 297
Hungry travel. Melvin Dixon. 231
Hunt, Connie
    Acceptance. 279
    All is one. 279
    Another me. 279
    Author's acknowledgment. 279
    Being. 279
    Believing. 279
    The box. 279
    Change. 279
    Dream on. 279
    "The dynamic silence moving."
        279
    The eternal snow. 279
    Fate. 279
    Forgiveness. 279
    Free to love. 279
    Freedom of expression. 279
    "A friendly smile." 279
    Friends. 279
    Fulfillment. 279
    Genesis. 279
    Graduation. 279
    The greatest gift. 279
    Hope. 279
    I am. 279
    I am free. 279
    Incredible day. 279
    Joy. 279
    The joy of light. 279
    Life's work. 279
    Maturity. 279
    Memories. 279
    More or less. 279
    The new 'ism.' 279
    "Oh spirit locked within." 279
    Peace. 279
    Potential. 279
    Reality. 279
    Refraction. 279
    Reunions. 279
    Saying no. 279
    Saying yes. 279
    The search. 279
    Solitude. 279
    Someday. 279
    Stillness. 279
    Symbiosis. 279

    "Take the stillness with you."
        279
    Transition. 279
    The tree of life. 279
    "Truth does not change." 279
    Upward mobility. 279
    Voice of truth. 279
    "We are all made of star stuff."
        279
    Who will listen. 279
    Why. 279
    You've touched me. 279
Hunter. Mark Vinz. 387
The hunter's game wife. Colette
    Inez. 280
Hunter's moon. Erin Jolly. 285
Hunter's point. Rod McKuen. 316
Hunters keep out. Harry Humes.
    278
Hunting and Hunters
    Balance. Stephen Sandy. 357
    Boyhood country creek. Maurice
        Kenny. 291
    The cemetery. Roy Marz. 312
    Hunter. Mark Vinz. 387
    Hunters keep out. Harry Humes.
        278
    Hunting for north in the fog.
        Harry Humes. 278
    Hunting interlude. Franz
        Schneider. 361
    Hunting season. Franz Schneider.
        361
    Innovative game warden. James
        Magorian. 309
    Natural law. William Oandasan.
        335
    The night hunting. Cathryn
        Hankla. 268
    Snapshots with buck, Model-A
        Ford, and kitchen. Robert
        Peters. 343
    Something in the hunter. James
        R. Rhodes. 352
    Trio. Cynthia Grenfell. 266
    Vince and Joe. George Eklund.
        238
Hunting for north in the fog.
    Harry Humes. 278
Hunting interlude. Franz
    Schneider. 361
Hunting season. Franz Schneider.
    361
Hurricanes
    The edge of the hurricane. Amy
        Clampitt. 222
Hurtling ahead to nowhere. Eileen
    Silver-Lillywite. 364
Husbands. See Marriage

Huxley,Aldous
    Noon. Josephine Miles. 319
Hyde Park. Michael Gizzi. 259
Hydra, Greece
    View of Hydra, Greece. Carolyn
        Stoloff. 376
The hyena. Jack Prelutsky. 349
Hyenas
    The hyena. Jack Prelutsky. 349
Hymn to a mystery. Elsa Gidlow.
    254
Hymn to childhood. Maurice W.
    Britts. 215
A hymn to Manhattan. John Reed.
    350
"Hymns to me." Da Free John. 284
Hypnotist and Bird. Gary
    Margolis. 311
Hypocrisy
    Exterior. Josephine Miles. 319
    On everybody's friend. Cornel
        Lengyel. 302
Hysteria. Lyn Lifshin. 303

I am. Connie Hunt. 279
"I am a deep still lake." Sally
    Love Saunders. 358
"I am a little boy sometimes."
    Michael Robert Pick. 345
I am an American. Alice Joyce
    Davidson. 227
"I am approached." Madison
    Morrison. 327
"I am as one." Da Free John. 284
"I am born to purify myself of
    the world." Da Free John. 284
I am everything. Wanda Coleman.
    225
I am free. Connie Hunt. 279
"I am living life full and long."
    Michael Robert Pick. 345
"I am lost/in the graveyard." A.
    Dovichi. 233
"I am man." A. Dovichi. 233
"I am mindless in this world." Da
    Free John. 284
I am my father's daughter. Laura
    Boss. 213
"I am no hero." Michael Robert
    Pick. 345
I am ordered to go and say so
    long. Gary Margolis. 311
I am still as stone. Judson
    Crews. 226
"I am the bright." Da Free John.
    284
"I am the gold machine..."

Charles Olson. 337
"I am together with you in my
    mind." Sally Love Saunders.
    358
"I am truly vulnerable." Theta
    Burke. 218
"I am trying to think what it
    means to be right." Josephine
    Miles. 319
"I am W.B., and." Madison
    Morrison. 327
"I am/(not because I do)." Theta
    Burke. 218
'I and Thou.' Evelyn Golden. 263
"I apologize." A. Dovichi. 233
I appraise the probability of
    improving. Gary Margolis. 311
I arrive home to the funeral.
    Wanda Coleman. 225
I become a dream. Rachel A.
    Hazen. 271
"I believe in God." Charles
    Olson. 337
 "I believe in religion..."
    Charles Olson. 337
 "I can sing." Michael Robert
    Pick. 345
"I can support myself." Madison
    Morrison. 327
"I can tie my shoelaces." Jan
    Ormerod. 338
I cannot hold nor let you go.
    David Shapiro. 363
I cannot stay. Rachel A. Hazen.
    271
I care. Rosa Bogar. 211
I carry the moon. Wanda Coleman.
    225
"I charge again." Michael Robert
    Pick. 345
"I collapse my." Madison
    Morrison. 327
"I cry with no tears." Michael
    Robert Pick. 345
"I curse the dying foetus in your
    womb." Robert A. Sears. 362
"I don't care anymore." Da Free
    John. 284
"I don't care at all." Madison
    Morrison. 327
"I don't expect." Madison
    Morrison. 327
"I don't like." Sally Love
    Saunders. 358
I draw a circle. Evelyn Golden.
    263
I dream. Jacques Sollov. 370
I dream my return. Cathryn
    Hankla. 268
I elevate my mind. Rosa Bogar.

211
"I fear to take a step;along the
     edge." Josephine Miles. 319
"I feel your presence." Michael
     Robert Pick. 345
"I find it hard to believe."
     Madison Morrison. 327
"I find myself now." Madison
     Morrison. 327
I flee the night. Evelyn Golden.
     263
I follow the snow. Rachel A.
     Hazen. 271
I give you back. Joy Harjo. 269
"I have an ability - a
     machine..." Charles Olson. 337
"I have been lost in karmas of
     rejection." Da Free John. 284
"I have come/to tell you/of the
     way." Joan Walsh Anglund. 197
"I have fallen short a time or
     two." Michael Robert Pick. 345
"I have heard and seen enough.
     You cannot imagine." Da Free
     John. 284
"I have two ways." Da Free John.
     284
I have watched them come back to
     the village. Wanda Coleman.
     225
I haven't been able to get
     anything done since I met you.
     Debra Bruce. 216
I haven't seen my grandmother
     since she died. Mitchell
     Howard. 276
I hear you cry, my friends.
     Michael Robert Pick. 345
"I hear you, Jacob." Michael
     Robert Pick. 345
I held my little sisters. Michael
     Robert Pick. 345
"I hunger for you." Michael
     Robert Pick. 345
I kiss your cold silent lips.
     Maurice W. Britts. 215
"I lap the poem." Madison
     Morrison. 327
"I leave this room." Madison
     Morrison. 327
I like Americans. Ernest
     Hemingway. 272
I like Canadians. Ernest
     Hemingway. 272
"I like running gentle streams."
     Michael Robert Pick. 345
I live for my car. Wanda Coleman.
     225
"I live in a human file cabinet."
     Sally Love Saunders. 358

"I live in one room." Madison
     Morrison. 327
I live my life by three minute
     phone calls. Laura Boss. 213
"I live underneath." Charles
     Olson. 337
"I looked up and saw." Charles
     Olson. 337
"I looked up." Charles Olson. 337
I love the dark. Wanda Coleman.
     225
I love you more than applesauce.
     Jack Prelutsky. 348
I made a giant valentine. Jack
     Prelutsky. 348
I made my dog a valentine. Jack
     Prelutsky. 348
I marvel at this comic creature.
     Stephen Todd Booker. 212
I mature and I grow. S. Bradford
     Williams (Jr.). 398
"I need to be." Sally Love
     Saunders. 358
I need you. Edwin Honig. 275
I never was a wary one. Jeanne
     Lohmann. 305
"I often think of buying a cane."
     Da Free John. 284
I only got one valentine. Jack
     Prelutsky. 348
"I opened a box of memories."
     Michael Robert Pick. 345
I packed my trunk for Albany.
     David Shapiro. 363
I painted a picture. Rosa Bogar.
     211
"I pass between." Charles Olson.
     337
I play with his son. Anneliese
     Wagner. 389
I pray. Norman Andrew Kirk. 293
I put my trust in the river.
     Jacqueline Frank. 248
"I remember times I spent."
     Michael Robert Pick. 345
"I saw you dance with Don
     Carlos." Robert A. Sears. 362
I see me. Rosa Bogar. 211
I see the ending in our eyes.
     Norman Andrew Kirk. 293
I see three fish in the bowl of
     water. Carolyn Stoloff. 376
"I see you hawk." Michael Robert
     Pick. 345
"I seemed to die." Da Free John.
     284
"I served to priest the
     pharaohs." Da Free John. 284
"I set out now." Charles Olson.
     337

"I sing a song to thee, O God."
    Michael Robert Pick. 345
"I sing." Madison Morrison. 327
"I sit here." Sally Love
    Saunders. 358
"I smell you on your pillow."
    Michael Robert Pick. 345
"I stand before you in all my
    forms." Da Free John. 284
"I stand upon you, Fort Place."
    Charles Olson. 337
"I stare hard into the wind."
    Michael Robert Pick. 345
I still can hear the singing.
    Rose Basile Green. 265
I stopped looking. Rachel A.
    Hazen. 271
I sweat I mop I stink. Wanda
    Coleman. 225
"I swung out, at 8 or 10."
    Charles Olson. 337
"I think now of all the wars."
    Michael Robert Pick. 345
"I think that I have never trod."
    Ernest Hemingway. 272
"I told the woman." Charles
    Olson. 337
"I turn directly West." Madison
    Morrison. 327
"I walk the sidewalk." Madison
    Morrison. 327
"I walk." Madison Morrison. 327
"I want my dressing/room..."
    Madison Morrison. 327
I want to be your everything.
    Jacques Sollov. 371
I want to know you. Rosa Bogar.
    211
"I want to tell you why husbands
    stop loving wives." Robert
    Kelly. 289
"I want to tell you." Robert
    Kelly. 289
"I want to write down." Sally
    Love Saunders. 358
I want you. Kirk Lumpkin. 306
I was a child. Evelyn Golden. 263
"I was bold, I had courage, the
    tide tonight." Charles Olson.
    337
"I was man." A. Dovichi. 233
"I was/a product of divorce."
    Michael Robert Pick. 345
"I weep for you brothers of war."
    Michael Robert Pick. 345
"I will be thirty one years."
    Michael Robert Pick. 345
I will not go to Mikonos. Carolyn
    Stoloff. 376
"I will set out from." Madison
    Morrison. 327
I will survive. Maurice W.
    Britts. 215
"I would have/om another day." A.
    Dovichi. 233
I'd trade these words. James L.
    White. 396
"I'll never know you." Sally Love
    Saunders. 358
I'll read you my current poems.
    Sally Love Saunders. 358
"I'll wear a wig." Da Free John.
    284
"I'm a little teapot." Jan
    Ormerod. 338
"I'm a sunny side up egg." Sally
    Love Saunders. 358
"I'm a/different person." Madison
    Morrison. 327
"I'm captured in a brown bag."
    Sally Love Saunders. 358
"I'm going to hate to leave this
    earthly paradise." Charles
    Olson. 337
I'm no vet, pet! Josephine B.
    Moretti. 324
'I'm nobody's little girl anymore
    since daddy died.' Maria
    Gillan. 256
I'm off'n wild wimmen. Ernest
    Hemingway. 272
"I'm on top of the world." Sally
    Love Saunders. 358
"I'm sitting here at Grieg's
    home." Sally Love Saunders.
    358
"I'm so happy." Sally Love
    Saunders. 358
I'm squeezed somewhere in his
    appointment book. Laura Boss.
    213
I'm trading in my car today.
    Laura Boss. 213
"I've been going around
    everywhere without any skin."
    Josephine Miles. 319
I've been to town. Rod McKuen.
    316
"I've been with annoying people
    so long." Sally Love Saunders.
    358
"I've grown used to miracles." Da
    Free John. 284
"I've seen the halyards of the
    sun." Michael Robert Pick. 345
"I've taken a balder walk..."
    Madison Morrison. 327
I've written this poem before.
    Wanda Coleman. 225
I, Maximus of Gloucester, to you.

Charles Olson. 337

I.M. Eugenio Montale. Lucien
    Stryk. 377

Ibsen, Henrik
    Werenskiold's portrait of Henrik
    Ibsen. Ray Fleming. 247

Ice
    At the edge of the glacier.
        Thomas McGrath. 315
    Ice carnival. Roy Marz. 312
Ice age. Joyce Carol Oates. 336
Ice carnival. Roy Marz. 312
The ice fisherman's dream. Harry
    Humes. 278
Ice fishing. James Magorian. 309
Ice horses. Joy Harjo. 269
The ice house. Eileen
    Silver-Lillywite. 364
Ice show. James Magorian. 309
Ice skating. Greg Kuzma. 300
Ice storm remembered. Paul Davis.
    228
Icicles. Ray Fleming. 247
Ida Maria. John F. Barker. 201
Idea of joy. Josephine Miles. 319
Ideal disorders, fr. Fresh air.
    Irving Feldman. 242
The ideal photo. Barry
    Wallenstein. 393
"Ideal soil/makes for shallow
    roots." Theta Burke. 218

Ideas
    Nutmeet rose bud. David Wann.
        394

Identity. Josephine Miles. 319
Identity. Marie Daerr Boehringer.
    210

Identity
    Abraham, without papers. Norman
        Andrew Kirk. 293
    Closing song. Marie Daerr
        Boehringer. 210
    Depth perception. Robin Morgan.
        325
    I want you. Kirk Lumpkin. 306
    Identity. Josephine Miles. 319
    Invisible woman. Joyce Carol
        Oates. 336
    Masks in 1980 for age 60 James
        Schevill. 360
    Maximus, at Tyre and at Boston.
        Charles Olson. 337
    "My name is Felicity." Brenda
        Marie Osbey. 340
    Norman. Norman Andrew Kirk. 293
    The question of identity.
        Timothy Steele. 374
    Rover. William Stafford. 373
    Whose was it. Carolyn Stoloff.
        376

The woman and the man, fr. The
    green step. Kenneth Koch. 297
Identity card. Susan Tichy. 381
Idiots. John Godfrey. 260
Idyll of Tsolato. Charles Edward
    Eaton. 236
If. Rosa Bogar. 211
If. Rachel A. Hazen. 271
If. Jim Simmerman. 365
If a model, fr. The day of the
    body. Carol Frost. 249
"If connections are." Madison
    Morrison. 327
"If dawn would only quiet me the
    host." Robert Kelly. 289
If God does not see you. James
    Schevill. 360
If he bucks. Carolyn Stoloff. 376
"If I ask of you/what I would
    give." Theta Burke. 218
If I could be like Wallace
    Stevens. William Stafford. 373
If I had a crown. Jacques Sollov.
    370
If I had gone quietly. Judson
    Crews. 226
If I had sorted out. Judson
    Crews. 226
If it is an objective. Judson
    Crews. 226
"If it were/that I." A. Dovichi.
    233
If it would all please hurry.
    James Tate. 379
If love could sing. Alice Spohn
    Newton. 332
"If my Valentine you won't be."
    Ernest Hemingway. 272
"If only time was a fantasy."
    Michael Robert Pick. 345
If only you could see. Rosa
    Bogar. 211
If Osiris were to die in New
    York. Mitchell Howard. 276
If she had spoken. Judson Crews.
    226
"If she went down to the town."
    Robert Kelly. 289
If the beginning were clear.
    Judson Crews. 226
If the cardinals were like us.
    Sandra McPherson. 317
If the deaths do not stop...
    Charles Olson. 337
"If the globe eye." Madison
    Morrison. 327
"If the wall of your anger."
    Theta Burke. 218
"If the war is over." Michael
    Robert Pick. 345

"If the weather vane." Sally Love
    Saunders. 358
If there were only this music.
    Jenne Andrews. 196
"If they're not chained." Madison
    Morrison. 327
If you go away. Rod McKuen. 316
If you go poking around in my
    journal you deserve the worst.
    Lyn Lifshin. 303
If you must go. Jacques Sollov.
    371
If you will. Josephine Miles. 319
If you're here now, you win.
    David Wann. 394
Ignatow, David
    Totems (VI). Thomas McGrath. 315
Ignorance
    Benediction. Susan Tichy. 381
    The cloud of unknowing. David
        James. 282
    Eyesight. Josephine Miles. 319
    Mysteries. Steve Kowit. 299
"An ignorant one who read
    nothing." Da Free John. 284
The ignorant set. Norman Andrew
    Kirk. 293
Iguana. X.J. Kennedy. 290
Iguanas
    Iguana. X.J. Kennedy. 290
Ikebana. Cathy Song. 372
Il salto mortale. Marieve Rugo.
    356
Il Vecchio. Robert A. Sears. 362
Ile des monts deserts, fr. Salt
    Air. Sharon Bryan. 217
Ill at fifteen. Christopher
    Bursk. 219
Illinois winter. Robin Becker.
    202
Illness
    Appointment in doctor's office.
        Josephine Miles. 319
    Concomitants. Bradford Morrow.
        329
    The cork-lined room. Charles
        Edward Eaton. 236
    The doctor's quarantine. Gary
        Margolis. 311
    For Alan Dugan. Greg Kuzma. 300
    "The gym instructor." Madison
        Morrison. 327
    Hawk-man. Richard Blessing. 208
    Heldenleben. Josephine Miles.
        319
    Home sick. Miriam Goodman. 264
    In the hospital for tests.
        Thomas R. Sleigh. 366
    Influenza. Carol Frost. 249
    It weeps away. Marge Piercy. 346

King Kong flu. Josephine B.
    Moretti. 324
Metal and stone. Anne Bailie.
    199
Misnomer. Marie Daerr
    Boehringer. 210
Motive. Josephine Miles. 319
Poem for saps. John Godfrey. 260
Purely psychological. Robert L.
    Wilson. 401
Question. Josephine B. Moretti.
    324
Resistance. Josephine Miles. 319
Rheumatic fever. James
    Applewhite. 198
Storm clouds. Wanda Coleman. 225
Those who must stay indoors, fr.
    Friday night quartet. David
    Shapiro. 363
Illumination. Josephine Miles.
    319
Illuminations: Martha Graham.
    James Schevill. 360
The illusionist. David Wagoner.
    390
Illusions. Maria Gillan. 256
Illusions. Anthony Petrosky. 344
Illusions
    Fresh roses along the path.
        Sally Love Saunders. 358
    Illusions. Maria Gillan. 256
    Secret agent. Keith Wilson. 400
Im-poet-ent. Harlan Usher. 386
Image. Martha Janssen. 283
The image. James R. Rhodes. 352
The images of execution. James
    Schevill. 360
Images of recall. May Miller. 320
Imagination
    Aubade. Robert Pawlowski. 341
    Evening particular. Andrei
        Codrescu. 223
    I haven't seen my grandmother
        since she died. Mitchell
        Howard. 276
    I painted a picture. Rosa Bogar.
        211
    Science fiction. James
        Applewhite. 198
    Sentimental education. Charles
        Edward Eaton. 236
    Twelfth Street. Roy Marz. 312
    Walking. Barry Wallenstein. 393
    Why we need fantasy. William
        Stafford. 373
The imagination of necessity.
    Andrei Codrescu. 223
Imagine the dreams we dream
    today. Rachel A. Hazen. 271
Imago. Amy Clampitt. 222

Imagoes. Wanda Coleman. 225
"Imbued/with light." Charles
    Olson. 337
Imitation. Edgar Allan Poe. 347
The immigrant's story. Robin
    Becker. 202
Immigration and Emigration
    America. Eileen
        Silver-Lillywite. 364
    Americadians. Rose Basile Green.
        265
    Americans to Europeans. Rose
        Basile Green. 265
    Cry, ethnics? Rose Basile Green.
        265
    Fertilizing the continent. Joyce
        Carol Oates. 336
    "Having developed the
        differences..." Charles Olson.
        337
    The immigrant's story. Robin
        Becker. 202
    Italian-American woman. Rose
        Basile Green. 265
    Land rights. Rose Basile Green.
        265
    Letter 3. Charles Olson. 337
    New York City. Dennis
        Hinrichsen. 273
    No one took a country from me.
        Jacqueline Frank. 248
    Our stories. Anneliese Wagner.
        389
    Plurality. Rose Basile Green.
        265
    Refugee, 1940. Anneliese Wagner.
        389
    The singing we. Rose Basile
        Green. 265
    These people sat right out my
        window too. Charles Olson. 337
    To the media. Rose Basile Green.
        265
    Trinity. Randy Blasing. 207
    Two kinds of language. John Yau.
        404
    The usefulness. Charles Olson.
        337
    War bride. Robert A. Sears. 362
    We, ethnics, had the dream. Rose
        Basile Green. 265
Immolation. Erin Jolly. 285
Immortality
    "All parts/are necessary/to the
        circle." Joan Walsh Anglund.
        197
    Horizon. Josephine Miles. 319
    The mother. Sister Maura. 313
    The star of my destiny. Jacques
        Sollov. 371

"We all have to die..." Michael
    Robert Pick. 345
Impatient florist lashing out at
    pussyfooting customers. James
    Magorian. 309
Imperative. Josephine Miles. 319
Imperfections
    Ecumene. James R. Rhodes. 352
    Remedial. James Schevill. 360
    "So often/she seemed to speak
        too quickly." Theta Burke. 218
    You bastard. Norman Andrew Kirk.
        293
    "Your hair/is not the most
        beautiful." Jim Everhard. 241
Impermanence
    Brief is beautiful. Cornel
        Lengyel. 302
    Moving. Jeanne Lohmann. 305
    Rustic song. Cornel Lengyel. 302
Implications. Rachel A. Hazen.
    271
The importance of artists'
    biographies. Albert Goldbarth.
    261
Impotence
    The toast. Royal Murdoch. 330
"In 1856 she won second prize..."
    Albert Goldbarth. 261
In 1970 in Madrid, President
    Nixon presents General
    Franco.. James Schevill. 360
In ▬ between. Ralph J., Jr.
    Mills. 321
In a 3-way mirror. Ruth Lisa
    Schechter. 359
"In a central/chamber..." Madison
    Morrison. 327
In a corner. William Stafford.
    373
In a country of condolences.
    Colette Inez. 280
In a country of lost bearings.
    Colette Inez. 280
In a darkened corridor. Rachel A.
    Hazen. 271
In a daze. Rosa Bogar. 211
In a dream. Elsa Gidlow. 254
In a drought year. Mark Vinz. 387
In a gradually moving car
    somewhere in Calcutta. Miller
    Williams. 399
"In a hotel room." Madison
    Morrison. 327
"In a magazine." Ernest
    Hemingway. 272
In a minor key. Haig
    Khatchadourian. 292
"In a palm tree, drowsy." Madison
    Morrison. 327

In a pueblo in Chiapas. J.W. Rivers. 354

In a season of change. Ghita Orth. 339

In a station oof the Metro. Ezra Pound. 235

"In a step upward he." Madison Morrison. 327

In air. Josephine Miles. 319

"In alternate stripes." Madison Morrison. 327

In an Arab town. Susan Tichy. 381

In and out. Gerard Malanga. 310

In another town. Miller Williams. 399

In bed. Kenneth Koch. 297

In black suburbia. James A. Emanuel. 239

In Canada. Greg Kuzma. 300

In charge. Marie Daerr Boehringer. 210

In childhood education. David James. 282

In conversation. Robin Becker. 202

In country light. Maurice Kenny. 291

In danger of drowning. Jacqueline Frank. 248

In defense of uncertainty and disarray. Miller Williams. 399

In dreams, a violinist. Jenne Andrews. 196

In early September. Ralph J., Jr. Mills. 321

"In his ordinary world." Edwin Honig. 275

In hot pursuit. Robert L. Wilson. 401

In Ireland. Colette Inez. 280

"In Jamaica." Sally Love Saunders. 358

In Kiryat Shmona. Susan Tichy. 381

In knowledge of young boys. Toi Derricote. 229

In lieu of a love poem for America. Steve Kowit. 298, 299

In lieu of an elegy. Jacqueline Frank. 248

In Lombardy. Donald Revell. 351

In love. David Wagoner. 390

In love with wholes. Alberta Turner. 384

In Mary Frank's garden. Robert Kelly. 289

In memoriam. James Torio. 281

In memoriam: S.E.G. Rodney Nelson. 331

In memoriam: Santayana. Cornel Lengyel. 302

In memory of a man. John F. Barker. 201

In memory of Donny Hathaway. Rosa Bogar. 211

In memory of Dr. Martin Luther King. Haig Khatchadourian. 292

In memory of Mahalia Jackson. Rosa Bogar. 211

In memory of Minnie Ripperton. Rosa Bogar. 211

In memory of my mother. Haig Khatchadourian. 292

In memory of Pablo Picasso. John Godfrey. 260

In Michigan. Ralph J., Jr. Mills. 321

In my own curved bones, sels. Ghita Orth. 339

In Nashville, standing in the wooden circle... Miller Williams. 399

In nervous moment: Charles Wilson Peale. James Schevill. 360

In old San Juan. Irving Feldman. 242

In our time. Lucien Stryk. 377

In pain. Albert Goldbarth. 261

In Pan's world. Cynthia Grenfell. 266

"In passageways." Madison Morrison. 327

In place. Gary Margolis. 311

In plain sight. Alice Joyce Davidson. 227

In praise of a photograph by Diane Arbus... James Schevill. 360

In praise of difference. Rod McKuen. 316

In praise of hands. Anthony Petrosky. 344

In pursuit of the family. Jenne Andrews. 196

In remembrance. Haig Khatchadourian. 292

In Rome. Jenne Andrews. 196

In search of a second dawn. Margaret Key Biggs. 205

In search of scenery. Marge Piercy. 346

In search of the mythology of do wah wah. Wanda Coleman. 225

In search of the sunbather as a very safe thing. Charles Edward Eaton. 236

In search of yesterday. Robert L. Wilson. 401

In season. Debra Bruce. 216

In tapestry, the pattern. Ghita

Orth. 339
In Texas we got persimmons.
    Judson Crews. 226
In the Apennines. Franz
    Schneider. 361
In the blind. Carolyn Stoloff.
    376
In the booking room. David
    Wagoner. 390
"In the cafe the salesman."
    Madison Morrison. 327
In the Chinese death house.
    Carolyn Stoloff. 376
In the Cotswolds. Ray Fleming.
    247
In the Dakotas. Stephen Sandy.
    357
In the dark. Jeanne Lohmann. 305
In the dark. Steve Kowit. 299
"In the darkness of." Madison
    Morrison. 327
In the dreams of exiles. Frances
    Mayes. 314
In the earth's abiding sweetness
    (where Fannie Lou rests).
    Kiarri T-H Cheatwood. 220
In the face of a Chinese view of
    the city. Charles Olson. 337
In the face of anger. Jacqueline
    Frank. 248
In the face of solitude. Marilyn
    Kallet. 287
In the gallery. Robert A. Sears.
    362
In the garden of the fire plants.
    Charles Edward Eaton. 236
In the gathering forest (where
    Kimathi lives). Kiarri T-H
    Cheatwood. 220
In the great night. Marilyn
    Kallet. 287
"In the half light summits rise."
    Carolyn Stoloff. 376
"In the harbor." Charles Olson.
    337
In the home stretch. Robert
    Frost. 250
In the hospital. Eileen
    Silver-Lillywite. 364
In the hospital for tests. Thomas
    R. Sleigh. 366
In the house of the judge. Dave
    Smith. 367
In the illustration of a dream.
    Ruth Lisa Schechter. 359
In the interleaved Almanacks for
    1646 and 1647 of Danforth.
    Charles Olson. 337
In the Japanese tea garden in San
    Francisco. James Schevill. 360

In the jungle in Vietnam. Jocelyn
    Hollis. 274
In the king's rooms. Timothy
    Steele. 374
In the lake. Joan Colby. 224
In the language of flowers. Jim
    Simmerman. 365
In the lover's arms. Elsa Gidlow.
    254
In the marshes of the blood
    river, sels. Marge Piercy. 346
In the Medici Chapels. Jeanne
    Lohmann. 305
"In the middle." Madison
    Morrison. 327
"In the morning of clarity and
    distinction." Josephine Miles.
    319
"In the mountain meadow." Madison
    Morrison. 327
In the name of the children.
    Jocelyn Hollis. 274
"In the neighborhood of my
    childhood, a hundred lungers."
    Josephine Miles. 319
"In the outdoor." Madison
    Morrison. 327
In the Piastsa of Matei Corvin.
    Keith Wilson. 400
In the Plaza de Toros. David
    Wagoner. 390
In the present we take refuge
    from the past. Haig
    Khatchadourian. 292
"In the public/bath..." Madison
    Morrison. 327
"In the purple and." Madison
    Morrison. 327
In the Rastaman's agony and peace
    (where Marley recreates).
    Kiarri T-H Cheatwood. 220
In the red meadow, sels. Carolyn
    Stoloff. 376
"In the shadow." Larry Eigner.
    237
In the sleep of reason. Thomas
    McGrath. 315
In the sonata/I wear a surgeon's
    mask. Ruth Lisa Schechter. 359
In the theater of the absurd.
    James Schevill. 360
"In the town where every man is
    king." Josephine Miles. 319
"In the trees." Larry Eigner. 237
In the wilds. Maurice Kenny. 291
In the wind before a storm.
    Stephen Knauth. 295
"In these cold October woods."
    James Torio. 281
In this city. Marc Kaminsky. 288

In this story. Jeanne Lohmann.
    305
In this waking. Wanda Coleman.
    225
In time of praise. Jacqueline
    Frank. 248
In transit. Carolyn Stoloff. 376
In which she begs (like everybody
    else) that love may last.
    Marge Piercy. 346
In winter. Michael Akillian. 193
"In winter in the woods." Robert
    Frost. 250
"In winter when the sun shone."
    Edwin Honig. 275
"In you arms." Sally Love
    Saunders. 358
In your house, the museum. Debra
    Bruce. 216
Incarnation, The
    Heaven. Josephine Miles. 319
Incest
    Children. Martha Janssen. 283
    Confessions. Martha Janssen. 283
    Crazy. Martha Janssen. 283
    Eighth grade. Martha Janssen.
        283
    Fantasy. Martha Janssen. 283
    Point of view. Martha Janssen.
        283
    Remembering youth. Martha
        Janssen. 283
    Therapist. Martha Janssen. 283
    Twelve. Martha Janssen. 283
Incident. William Stafford. 373
Incidental gift catalog love song
    poem. Colette Inez. 280
Inconsistencies. Maria Gillan.
    256
Incredible day. Connie Hunt. 279
Increment. Josephine Miles. 319
Indecision
    The little official of maybe.
        James Schevill. 360
Independence Day. Rod McKuen. 316
Independence Day
    Blazes in the night. Alice Spohn
        Newton. 333
Index. Paul Violi. 388
The index of first lines. David
    Shapiro. 363
India
    "India is the mountain end." Da
        Free John. 284
"India is the mountain end." Da
    Free John. 284
Indian corn. Mark Vinz. 387
Indian summer. James Schevill.
    360
Indian Summer

Halcyon days. Everett A. Gillis.
    258
Indian summer. James Schevill.
    360
The quick of roses. Everett A.
    Gillis. 258
Indians of America
    Acoma. William Oandasan. 335
    Chief Joseph of the Nez Perce.
        Robert Penn Warren. 395
    Communion. William Oandasan. 335
    Connection. Joy Harjo. 269
    Corn-planter. Maurice Kenny. 291
    1836. In the Cherokee overhills.
        Stephen Knauth. 295
    Farmington, NM. William
        Oandasan. 335
    He was drunk. Judson Crews. 226
    Hepit-naga-atosis. Charles
        Olson. 337
    Las cuatro ijadas de una
        palabra. Colette Inez. 280
    Little Spokane river: Indian
        paintings. Franz Schneider.
        361
    Maximus, to Gloucester, Letter
        157. Charles Olson. 337
    Night out. Joy Harjo. 269
    Ninet'1984.' James R. Rhodes.
        352
    Origo. John Reed. 350
    The savages. Josephine Miles.
        319
    The sungod Huitzilopochtli.
        Phillips Kloss. 294
    Tee-Pee living. Larry Moffi. 322
    "That there was a woman in
        Gloucester..." Charles Olson.
        337
    Twoborn. Rokwaho. 355
    Where you first saw the eyes of
        coyote. Linda Noel. 334
    "While on/Obadiah Bruen's
        Island, the Algonquins"
        Charles Olson. 337
    Yadkin Valley sketchbook.
        Stephen Knauth. 295
Indians of America=Women. See
    Women...

Individuality
    Untic...ov tic. W.D. (William De
        Witt) Snodgrass. 369
Indoor sports. Harlan Usher. 386
Industrial park from the air.
    Miriam Goodman. 264
The inexpressible. Ernest
    Hemingway. 272
Inez, Colette
    All things are one, said

Empodocles... 280
Along the Garonne. 280
Balloon sleeves and velvet, the century turned. 280
Blizzard. 280
The bone walkers, post world war three underground dream. 280
The burning wards of Meadowbrook. 280
Carnal verdict. 280
Cicada song. 280
Cleveland summer of nickel tips. 280
Door song. 280
Early and late. 280
Eight minutes from the sun. 280
Eyelines. 280
A faithful likeness. 280
Forest children. 280
Forest floor North America. 280
Gospel in the drifts. 280
Holding on. 280
Horse latitudes. 280
The hunter's game wife. 280
In a country of condolences. 280
In a country of lost bearings. 280
In Ireland. 280
Incidental gift catalog love song poem. 280
Lake song. 280
Las cuatro ijadas de una palabra. 280
Letters not answered. 280
The letters of a name. 280
Mayflies. 280
Notes from a gutted house. 280
Out of the frame. 280
Prison songs. 280
A quarrel put to rest. 280
Roads of quicksand time. 280
Rosecap. 280
School's out. 280
Skokie river cadenzas. 280
Spring lunch. 280
Startalk in the Greek luncheonette. 280
Sunsong. 280
Travel songs. 280
Triptych. 280
Twindream. 280
Warrior daughters. 280
Weight of days. 280
Word songs. 280
Inference. Miller Williams. 399
Infidelity
All's fair. James A. Emanuel. 239
The arrangement. Debra Bruce. 216
Each new dress you've never seen. Laura Boss. 213
First affair. Wanda Coleman. 225
Long distance. Laura Boss. 213
The night my son packed for college. Laura Boss. 213
The other woman. Debra Bruce. 216
Protector. Laura Boss. 213
"She who met the serpent..." Charles Olson. 337
Sitting in the doctor's office the next day. Laura Boss. 213
Soul in distress. Jacques Sollov. 371
The stone, fr. The green step. Kenneth Koch. 297
A tangential death. Marge Piercy. 346
Weird terminations. David James. 282
Infinitude. James R. Rhodes. 352
Inflammable abodes. Joan Colby. 224
Influenza. Carol Frost. 249
Information booth. James Magorian. 308
Inheritance. Marieve Rugo. 356
Inhumanity
Agent orange. Evelyn Golden. 263
A criminology. Jenne Andrews. 196
Someone ought to cry. Patsie Black. 206
Initiation. Deborah Tall. 378
Initimations of spring. Robert L. Wilson. 401
The inlet. Louise Gluck. 259A
The inn of the empty egg. Clayton Eshleman. 240
Innocence
Lurid confessions. Steve Kowit. 298, 299
"My heart hastens." Susan Stock. 375
Nuns at a retreat. Lyn Lifshin. 303
"The innocence of youth." Michael Robert Pick. 345
Innocence returned. Rokwaho. 355
Innovative game warden. James Magorian. 309
Insanity
The analyst's report on his convalescent patient. Franz Schneider. 361
In a daze. Rosa Bogar. 211
Psych ward. Mitchell Howard. 276
Psychiatric referral. James Magorian. 308

Senile information officer at a plumbing supply company. James Magorian. 309

A servant to servants. Robert Frost. 250

Visiting hour. Josephine Miles. 319

"Insect/leaf.". Larry Eigner. 237

Insects

Cicada song. Colette Inez. 280

"In a central/chamber..." Madison Morrison. 327

My garden insects. Robert Pawlowski. 341

Potato bugs. Robert Peters. 343

Rose lice. Roy Marz. 312

Verbatim III. Cynthia Grenfell. 266

Waterbug. Thomas Hornsby Ferril. 243

Inseminator vortex. Clayton Eshleman. 240

Inside silence. Rod McKuen. 316

Insight. Randy Blasing. 207

Insomnia. Debra Bruce. 216

Insomnia. Alice Joyce Davidson. 227

Insomnia

Changing the guard. Mark Vinz. 387

Insomnia. Debra Bruce. 216

Insomnia. Alice Joyce Davidson. 227

O Wendy, Arthur. Maurice Kenny. 291

Resilience. Anthony Petrosky. 344

Roses. Jim Simmerman. 365

Summer insomnia. Franz Schneider. 361

Tally. Josephine Miles. 319

The insomnia of Oscar Keinemann. Stephen Todd Booker. 212

Insomniac. Mark Vinz. 387

Inspiration

My friend Luther. Ernesto Galarza. 252

Institutions. Josephine Miles. 319

Instructions. Rod McKuen. 316

Insurance. Rod McKuen. 316

Insurance

Training session for insurance adjusters. James Magorian. 309

Intaglio. Everett A. Gillis. 258

Intellect

"Because things inside/felt so tenuous and uncertain." Theta Burke. 218

Brain and mind. R. Buckminster Fuller. 251

Devotion. Gerard Malanga. 310

I elevate my mind. Rosa Bogar. 211

In and out. Gerard Malanga. 310

Intuition - metaphysical mosaic. R. Buckminster Fuller. 251

The magician. Jacques Sollov. 371

Man of letters. Josephine Miles. 319

Night in the old house. Sister Maura. 313

Physiologus. Josephine Miles. 319

The shape. David Wagoner. 390

Views to see Clayton from. Josephine Miles. 319

"Who's intelligent." Larry Eigner. 237

Intensives. Josephine Miles. 319

Interception. David Wann. 394

Interior. Frances Mayes. 314

Interior design. Miriam Goodman. 264

Interlude. Josephine Miles. 319

Intermezzo at Vendemmia. Rose Basile Green. 265

Interruptions. James Tate. 379

Intersection. Carolyn Stoloff. 376

"The intersection.". Larry Eigner. 237

Interstate 40. Phyllis A. Tickle. 382

Intimations. Evelyn Golden. 263

Into the dark. Mark Vinz. 387

"Into the hill..." Charles Olson. 337

"Into the stream or entrance..." Charles Olson. 337

Intrinsic cellar. James Magorian. 309

Introduction. A. Dovichi. 233

Intruder. Miriam Goodman. 264

Intuition - metaphysical mosaic. R. Buckminster Fuller. 251

The invalid. Thomas R. Sleigh. 366

Invasion of the huge spirits. Mitchell Howard. 276

Inventory. Jacqueline Frank. 248

Inventory at year's end. James Magorian. 308

Inverted sunday. Robert Anbian. 194

Invincible force. Maurice W. Britts. 215

The invisible brother. Jim Everhard. 241

The **invisible** craft of evil.
    James Schevill. 360
Invisible splendor. Alice Spohn
    Newton. 332
Invisible woman. Joyce Carol
    Oates. 336
Invitation. Thomas Hornsby
    Ferril. 243
Invitation. Rose Basile Green.
    265
The **invitation**. Royal Murdoch.
    330
Invocation. Patsie Black. 206
Invocation to Sappho. Elsa
    Gidlow. 254
Involvement. Rose Basile Green.
    265
Ions. Josephine Miles. 319
Iorio, James
    Abstraction no. 1. 281
    Afternoon of the faun. 281
    Carousel. 281
    Chiaro di luna. 281
    Circe. 281
    "Constellations collapse." 281
    Contraband. 281
    "Deceived by winter thaw." 281
    Dragons. 281
    Encounter. 281
    Escape of a polar bear from the
        city zoo. 281
    "Fear is for the multitude." 281
    Frankfurt '76. 281
    The great debate. 281
    Greyed rainbow. 281
    The grounds keeper. 281
    Hilltop house. 281
    Homecoming. 281
    The house of eternity. 281
    "How do old men walk." 281
    In memoriam. 281
    "In these cold October woods."
        281
    Jet lag. 281
    Journey. 281
    Just this once. 281
    A lament for Willie Wyler. 281
    Landscape. 281
    The last look. 281
    "Leaves not yet fallen." 281
    A letter from Mama San. 281
    Magus. 281
    Meditations on an old waiter of
        some distinction. 281
    Metamorphosis. 281
    Morskie Oko. 281
    The mummy. 281
    "My beautiful crab tree." 281
    Nageire. 281
    Night call. 281

    Night stalker. 281
    Nightclub. 281
    "No one should die mute." 281
    Nostalgia in yellow. 281
    "Nothing shall stay me from my
        journey." 281
    The old woman of Patras. 281
    On contemplating the speed of a
        tiny red spider. 281
    Opera buffa. 281
    The oracle. 281
    Pastoral '17. 281
    Printout. 281
    Proof mark. 281
    Rediscovery. 281
    Requiem for a wife. 281
    Schizophrenic. 281
    Self portrait. 281
    "She peers at me." 281
    Sleep little poems, rest
        tonight. 281
    Solo. 281
    Spring storm. 281
    The steamer trunk. 281
    Sunday afternoon. 281
    The thirty-six master poets. 281
    "This morning." 281
    Triptych. 281
    "Two hornets feast upon my
        plate." 281
    Unforgettable games. 281
    The vigil. 281
    Weekend. 281
    "Will she be aware." 281
    Winterset. 281
Iran
    Nomads. Lucien Stryk. 377
Irascible numismatist regaining
    consiousness in an... James
    Magorian. 309
Ireland
    Belfast. Donald Revell. 351
    Bishop's rock. Deborah Tall. 378
    Dawn, ruins on Lake Inchiquin.
        Deborah Tall. 378
    Gaelic trilogy. Paul Davis. 228
    In Ireland. Colette Inez. 280
    McFadden, McFadden. Paul Davis.
        228
    To pulse a jubilee. Paul Davis.
        228
Irene (the sleeper). Edgar Allan
    Poe. 347
Irish love. Rose Basile Green.
    265
Irish violin. James R. Rhodes.
    352
Iron age flying. James
    Applewhite. 198
Irony

Irony as nursery. Andrei
    Codrescu. 223
Irony as nursery. Andrei
    Codrescu. 223
Irreciprocate. Royal Murdoch. 330
Irrigation. Susan Tichy. 381
"Is it possible/for one to come
    unto." Theta Burke. 218
"Is it possible/that man." A.
    Dovichi. 233
Is she found? Elsa Gidlow. 254
Is this my love? Robert
    Pawlowski. 341
Is this the place? Carolyn
    Stoloff. 376
Is true that you get born dumb
    and bald. Thomas Lux. 307
Isabel. Richmond Lattimore. 301
Ishtar, the monastery dog. Sister
    Maura. 313
Islam
    Near East Aubade. Randy Blasing.
        207
    Ramazan at New Phocaea. Randy
        Blasing. 207
Island. Scott Chisholm. 221
Island. Marc Hudson. 277
The island handyman. James
    Schevill. 360
Island storm. Edwin Honig. 275
"The island, the river, the
    shore." Charles Olson. 337
The island-maker. Roy Marz. 312
Island. Josephine Miles. 319
The island. Edwin Honig. 275
The islander. Louise Gluck. 259A
Islands
    Andros. John F. Barker. 201
    At Peaks Island. Stephen Sandy.
        357
    Brace. Alberta Turner. 384
    Crossing. Deborah Tall. 378
    Island. Marc Hudson. 277
    The islands. Richmond Lattimore.
        301
    The lost colony. John Yau. 404
    Missing pages. John Yau. 404
    Night island. Edwin Honig. 275
    The outer bar. Amy Clampitt. 222
    Sonnet - to Zante. Edgar Allan
        Poe. 347
    "That island/floating in the
        sea." Charles Olson. 337
    Thunderbolt island. Phyllis A.
        Tickle. 382
The islands. Richmond Lattimore.
    301
Isle unforgotten. Alice Spohn
    Newton. 332
The ISM. Wanda Coleman. 225

The isolated house he sometimes
    visited. Edwin Honig. 275
Israel
    Artillery. Susan Tichy. 381
    Defenses. Susan Tichy. 381
    En Gev. Eileen Silver-Lillywite.
        364
    For Gaby. Susan Tichy. 381
    The hours. Susan Tichy. 381
    Identity card. Susan Tichy. 381
    Irrigation. Susan Tichy. 381
    Letters from Jerusalem. Amy
        Clampitt. 222
    Staying. Susan Tichy. 381
    To an Irgun soldier. Susan
        Tichy. 381
    Volunteers. Susan Tichy. 381
    "When I stop work..." Susan
        Tichy. 381
    Why we don't sleep. Susan Tichy.
        381
Israel and Rome curbstoned. Paul
    Davis. 228
Israfel. Edgar Allan Poe. 347
Istanbul
    Winter in Istanbul. Andrei
        Codrescu. 223
It all comes back. Mary
    Gilliland. 257
It breaks. Marge Piercy. 346
"It came in a hole." Michael
    Robert Pick. 345
It cannot be it is. Edwin Honig.
    275
"It cools the booth." Madison
    Morrison. 327
It could be. Harry Humes. 278
It goes like this. Susan Stock.
    375
"It had to be, I thought at
    first." Robert A. Sears. 362
It happened that my uncle liked
    to take my hand in his. Thomas
    Lux. 307
"It is an ashtray of dead
    cigarettes." Gerard Malanga.
    310
"It is difficult/for me." A.
    Dovichi. 233
'It is for me to know what I
    fear.' Susan Stock. 375
"It is more compact." Madison
    Morrison. 327
"It is music." Larry Eigner. 237
It is new to you too. Norman
    Andrew Kirk. 293
It is not Golgotha. Judson Crews.
    226
It isn't meant to end this way.
    Rachel A. Hazen. 271

"It lifts my spirits." Sally Love
  Saunders. 358
It looks a war. Paul Davis. 228
"It says the Amitie sailed."
  Charles Olson. 337
"It takes the young to
  understand." Robert A. Sears.
  362
"It takes/a special man." Madison
  Morrison. 327
It thinks. Thomas Lux. 307
It was a happy little grave.
  James A. Emanuel. 239
It was assumed a God-head. Judson
  Crews. 226
It was the tender way. Paul
  Davis. 228
It was your song. Steve Kowit.
  299
It wasn't me. James Tate. 379
"It wasn't that." Robert A.
  Sears. 362
It weeps away. Marge Piercy. 346
It's a snap. Marie Daerr
  Boehringer. 210
"It's good to be with you." Sally
  Love Saunders. 358
It's not that she led me on.
  Judson Crews. 226
It's snow fun. Marie Daerr
  Boehringer. 210
"It's so nice to be with you."
  Sally Love Saunders. 358
"It's that one understood
  barely." Rochelle DuBois. 234
It's the Passaic poetry reading
  tonight. Laura Boss. 213
It's the sly-wolf-fart. Judson
  Crews. 226
It's Valentine's Day. Jack
  Prelutsky. 348
It's waking. Judson Crews. 226
"The Italian counts." Madison
  Morrison. 327
The Italian lesson. Roy Marz. 312
Italian-American woman. Rose
  Basile Green. 265
Italy
  High road from Naples. Anne
    Bailie. 199
  Il Vecchio. Robert A. Sears. 362
  L'ora. Rose Basile Green. 265
  Le Torri. Robert A. Sears. 362
  Lost in Ladispoli. Miller
    Williams. 399
  Luni. Robert A. Sears. 362
  Marina di Carrara. Robert A.
    Sears. 362
  Night travel. Richmond
    Lattimore. 301

  Rain at Bellagio. Amy Clampitt.
    222
  Scene revisited. Rose Basile
    Green. 265
  Summer storm: Alpe di San
    Benedetto. Franz Schneider.
    361
  Tartiglia. Robert A. Sears. 362
  Tourists in Italy. Robin Becker.
    202
  Trento. Robert A. Sears. 362
  Umbrian plain. Roy Marz. 312
  Valdarno. Franz Schneider. 361
  Vallombrosa. Franz Schneider.
    361
Itinerant. Ghita Orth. 339
Its edges audible. Thomas Lux.
  307
Iuatzio waters. Robert A. Sears.
  362
Ives, Charles
  Hats and ears for Charles Ives.
    James Schevill. 360

Jack & Jill. Harlan Usher. 386
Jack and the beanstalk. David
  Wagoner. 390
Jack-knife. Thomas Hornsby
  Ferril. 243
Jack Rabbit. Aileen Fisher. 244
Jackson, Mahalia
  In memory of Mahalia Jackson.
    Rosa Bogar. 211
Jailbreak. James Magorian. 308
Jamaica, West Indies
  "In Jamaica." Sally Love
    Saunders. 358
James Dean. Jim Everhard. 241
James Gates Percival pleads for a
  unity of vision. James
  Schevill. 360
For James Wright from a dream,
  1978 Ralph J., Jr. Mills. 321
James, David
  After the revolution. 282
  Anthropology. 282
  Baja trip. 282
  Black square/white field. 282
  The burning of bridges. 282
  The cloud of unknowing. 282
  "The creator has a master plan."
    282
  The direction of the fence. 282
  Four portraits of beans. 282
  The fourth confrontation with
    Tina Turner. 282
  "The gunman always rides with

two eyes in the back..." 282
In childhood education. 282
Kyle Canyon, Thanksgiving 1978.
  282
"Of words in their material
  form." 282
The picture of Wittgenstein. 282
Say what? 282
The second confrontation with
  Tina Turner. 282
Shining star. 282
Weird terminations. 282
"When she is moved by her
  man..." 282
When the world was steady. 282
Yi, yi, the sky. 282
The zigzag means lightning. 282
Jane. Jim Simmerman. 365
Jane Retreat. Edwin Honig. 275
Janet. Sam Fishman. 246
A **jangling** yarn. James Tate. 379
Janssen, Martha
  Acute memory. 283
  Adolescence. 283
  Alone. 283
  Aloof. 283
  Anger. 283
  Arms. 283
  Bath time. 283
  Behavior modification. 283
  Bitterness. 283
  Cause and effect. 283
  Change. 283
  Charming child. 283
  Children. 283
  Coaxing. 283
  Confessions. 283
  Counseling. 283
  Courage. 283
  Crazy. 283
  Danger. 283
  Decision. 283
  A dream. 283
  Dying. 283
  Eighth grade. 283
  Escape. 283
  Exploitation. 283
  Family. 283
  Fantasy. 283
  Fear. 283
  Fickle. 283
  Forgiveness. 283
  Four years old. 283
  Fourth commandment. 283
  God. 283
  Grief. 283
  Hate. 283
  Image. 283
  Junior high. 283
  Knowledge. 283

Laps. 283
Legacy. 283
Maturity. 283
Mother. 283
Music. 283
My body. 283
Mysterious delight. 283
Nightmares. 283
Obedience. 283
Older men. 283
Other dads. 283
A patsy. 283
Plea. 283
Point of view. 283
Posture. 283
Powerful words. 283
Princess. 283
Protection. 283
Quiet. 283
Recollection. 283
Redemption. 283
Relief. 283
Remembering youth. 283
Rules. 283
Secrets. 283
Self-hate. 283
Sex education. 283
Shame. 283
Sixteen. 283
Spring afternoon. 283
Struggle. 283
Survival. 283
Tears. 283
Techniques. 283
Therapist. 283
Third-grade teacher. 283
Thirteen. 283
Thirty-six. 283
Twelve. 283
Uncle Louie. 283
Victim. 283
Vocation. 283
Volcano. 283
Watercolors. 283
Well-meaning. 283
You and I. 283
January. Cathy Song. 372
January. Ghita Orth. 339
January
  14 January.   Ralph J., Jr.
    Mills. 321
January 18, 1979. John Yau. 404
January morning. J.W. Rivers. 354
Japan
  At dawn. Susan Tichy. 381
  A letter from Mama San. James
    Torio. 281
Jara, Victor
  For Victor Jara. Miller
    Williams. 399

Jardin des Plantes. Michael
    Gizzi. 259
Jay. Susan Stock. 375
Jazz at the intergalactic
    nightclub. Thomas McGrath. 315
Jazz impressions in the garden.
    C.D. Wright. 402
Jazz Music
    For the jazzman. Rochelle
        DuBois. 234
    Jazz-drift. James Schevill. 360
    Playin' jazz. Kirk Lumpkin. 306
Jazz Music. See also Blues (Jazz
    Music)

Jazz-drift. James Schevill. 360
Je suis un orange. David Wann.
    394
Jealous madonna. Lyn Lifshin. 303
Jealousy. Lyn Lifshin. 303
Jealousy
    "Daniel Boone stepped up to a
        window." Josephine Miles. 319
    Documentary. Robin Becker. 202
    "Each moment fills him with a
        desire." Kenneth Koch. 297
    Jealous madonna. Lyn Lifshin.
        303
    Letters to Michael. Robin
        Becker. 202
    Thirst. Marilyn Kallet. 287
Jean, my Jean. Alice Spohn
    Newton. 332
Jefferson dreaming. James
    Schevill. 360
Jefferson, Thomas
    Jefferson dreaming. James
        Schevill. 360
Jelka. James Tate. 379
Jelly Jill loves Weasel Will.
    Jack Prelutsky. 348
Jelly madonna. Lyn Lifshin. 303
Jemez. Joy Harjo. 269
Jemez Mountains
    Jemez. Joy Harjo. 269
Jenni's love. Rose Basile Green.
    265
Jenny Fish. Thomas R. Sleigh. 366
Jerboa. X.J. Kennedy. 290
Jerboa
    Jerboa. X.J. Kennedy. 290
Jerome Avenue. Donald Revell. 351
Jerry 1964. Wanda Coleman. 225
Jerry 1966. Wanda Coleman. 225
Jerry 1967. Wanda Coleman. 225
Jerusalem. Haig Khatchadourian.
    292
Jerusalem
    At the Western Wall. Ghita Orth.
        339

Bargaining. Susan Tichy. 381
    Jerusalem. Haig Khatchadourian.
        292
    "The rich don't have children."
        Susan Tichy. 381
Jerusalem, Pittsburgh. Anthony
    Petrosky. 344
Jesse and Jeanie. Alice Spohn
    Newton. 332
Jesus Christ
    Advent. John F. Barker. 201
    The captain's hannele. Roy Marz.
        312
    Christ. Jacques Sollov. 371
    Christ within. Jacques Sollov.
        370
    Daniel reviews his critics.
        Cornel Lengyel. 302
    Jesus, heal me. Joyce Carol
        Oates. 336
    The last forgotten lover. Royal
        Murdoch. 330
    Love thought. Jacques Sollov.
        370
    Rejoice. Patsie Black. 206
    The sawdust trail. Patsie Black.
        206
    Seven salvations: a mixed bag.
        Tom Smith. 368
    Thursday. Patsie Black. 206
    Veronica's veil. Sister Maura.
        313
Jesus, heal me. Joyce Carol
    Oates. 336
The jet engine. Sandra McPherson.
    317
Jet lag. James Torio. 281
"The jets jet." Larry Eigner. 237
This jeweled beast: a fable.
    Everett A. Gillis. 258
Jewelry. Joan Colby. 224
Jewelry
    Jewelry. Joan Colby. 224
    Opal. Josephine Miles. 319
The Jewish grocer and the
    vegetable forest. James
    Schevill. 360
Jews
    The angel passes over. Larry
        Moffi. 322
    The conversion of the Jews.
        Robin Becker. 202
    Finding the one. Rose Basile
        Green. 265
    Ghettos and gardens. Jacqueline
        Frank. 248
    Hebrew stones. Keith Wilson. 400
    Heil! Sam Fishman. 246
    Konoutek. Phyllis A. Tickle. 382
    Letter from my grandmother

interned in France. Anneliese
    Wagner. 389
The maggid speaks of a dog in
    the night. Ghita Orth. 339
The magic triad. Ghita Orth. 339
Off the sea into the merchant's
    life... James Schevill. 360
Report from the Jewish Museum.
    Anneliese Wagner. 389
Skies: a Jew in Germany, 1979.
    Ghita Orth. 339
Songs of transmutation. Ghita
    Orth. 339
Sources. Adrienne Rich. 353
A table with people. Marc
    Kaminsky. 288
Teshuvah. Jeanne Lohmann. 305
Translation. Ghita Orth. 339
What they say about us. Susan
    Tichy. 381
Jill in the box. Marge Piercy.
    346
Jimboy's ad. James A. Emanuel.
    239
Jirasek, Alois
    Volume 13: Jirasek to
        lighthouses. Cathryn Hankla.
        268
Jl 17 1961. Charles Olson. 337
Jo poised. Robert A. Sears. 362
Job hunting. Miriam Goodman. 264
'Jobs on film'- one more service
    from the hall of records. Gene
    Detro. 230
Jogging. Tefke Goldberger. 262
Jogging in the parlor,
    remembering a summer moment...
    Dave Smith. 367
Jogging. See Runnings and Runners

John Burke. Charles Olson. 337
John Lennon murdered on wild west
    side walk. Mitchell Howard.
    276
John Milton. John Reed. 350
"John Watts took." Charles Olson.
    337
John, Da Free
    "All the names are already
        written." 284
    "Alone is the consitions of
        bliss." 284
    "Blue meal." 284
    "The blues and lights." 284
    "Can one be good." 284
    "The chemical, high and low."
        284
    "The Earth is not a place for
        me." 284
    "Every body is an island." 284

"Every day." 284
"Forehead, breath, and smile."
    284
"The gospel that can be
    written." 284
"Hymns to me." 284
"I am as one." 284
"I am born to purify myself of
    the world." 284
"I am mindless in this world."
    284
"I am the bright." 284
"I don't care anymore." 284
"I have been lost in karmas of
    rejection." 284
"I have heard and seen enough.
    You cannot imagine." 284
"I have two ways." 284
"I often think of buying a
    cane." 284
"I seemed to die." 284
"I served to priest the
    pharaohs." 284
"I stand before you in all my
    forms." 284
"I'll wear a wig." 284
"I've grown used to miracles."
    284
"An ignorant one who read
    nothing." 284
"India is the mountain end." 284
"Mornings, no." 284
"My dear ones, my own." 284
"My loved one sits upon my
    knee." 284
"My room is slanted." 284
"My worth is on the eye." 284
"Narcissus is the pig who sleeps
    in my navel. He rests." 284
"No one like me has appeared in
    this place." 284
"No path." 284
"The One who crawled me off His
    knee." 284
"Servicing space." 284
"There are two ways." 284
"There is a force of loneliness
    around my heart." 284
"Those who despise me love me in
    secret." 284
"We are waiting for something to
    happen to this." 284
"When I am heard." 284
"When I know the Truth and the
    world becomes." 284
"When things have left him." 284
"Who is my inheritor?" 284
"World is endlessly allowed to
    be." 284
"Worlds are an exclamation of my

names." 284
"The worlds fall out of my right
hand." 284
The joker is wild. Cornel
Lengyel. 302
Jolly sane. Susan Stock. 375
Jolly, Erin
Ballade. 285
Billboard. 285
The boa-constrictor. 285
Changeling. 285
Charioteer. 285
Charlatan. 285
Cocoon. 285
Consent. 285
Cosmic dust. 285
Dean of brids. 285
Diatribe. 285
Filament. 285
Flight. 285
Floodlight. 285
Footnote to love. 285
Forspent. 285
Fragile ladies. 285
Golden eyelids. 285
Honorarium. 285
Hunter's moon. 285
Immolation. 285
The lingering ghost. 285
Lion on the frieze of time. 285
Lorn. 285
Memorial. 285
Name me a stranger. 285
Octagon. 285
Pen point. 285
Pomegranate. 285
Protocol. 285
Repeal. 285
Requiem. 285
Rudiment. 285
Song of the infidel. 285
Spikenard and roses. 285
The storm. 285
The street cleaner. 285
The swinging door. 285
Token. 285
Two poems on the New Year. 285
Walpurgis. 285
Wave of unreason. 285
The wayfarer. 285
What must be. 285
Woman at the mirror. 285
Jonah
Jonah's house. Anneliese Wagner.
389
A question for Jonah. Cornel
Lengyel. 302
Jonah's house. Anneliese Wagner.
389
Jones, Gayl

Ensinanca. 286
Fiction study. 286
The hermit-woman. 286
The machete woman. 286
Stranger. 286
Wild figs and secret places. 286
Jong, Erica
Hello, I'm Erica Jong. Kathy
Acker. 191
Jordan River. Gene Anderson. 195
Jose, age 8. J.W. Rivers. 354
Joseph, Chief of the Nez Perce
Indians
Chief Joseph of the Nez Perce.
Robert Penn Warren. 395
Joshua. Josephine Miles. 319
Joshua
Joshua. Josephine Miles. 319
Journey. William Stafford. 373
Journey. Mark Vinz. 387
Journey. Robert Pawlowski. 341
Journey. James Torio. 281
The journey. Cathryn Hankla. 268
The jovial mortician. James
Schevill. 360
Joy. Connie Hunt. 279
The joy of light. Connie Hunt.
279
Joy to the fishes. Steve Kowit.
299
Joy's song. S. Bradford Williams
(Jr.). 398
Joy: an end song. Edwin Honig.
275
Joyce, James
Bloomsday sermon. Mitchell
Howard. 276
Joyrider. James Schevill. 360
Joysome apples. Alice Spohn
Newton. 332
Judas Iscariot
Judas waking. Thomas R. Sleigh.
366
Judas waking. Thomas R. Sleigh.
366
Judges and Juries
Afterglow. May Miller. 320
Federal judge rust-proofing an
ornamental porch railing.
James Magorian. 309
For magistrates. Josephine
Miles. 319
Foreman of a hung jury. James
Magorian. 308
"Public eyes perceive." Robert
A. Sears. 362
Verdict. Josephine Miles. 319
Juggler. Lucien Stryk. 377
Jugglers and Juggling
Juggler. Lucien Stryk. 377

Juju. Robert A. Sears. 362
July
    Very late July. Marge Piercy.
    346
July First. George Eklund. 238
July madonna. Lyn Lifshin. 303
The jumper. Michael Akillian. 193
Junco song. Cynthia Grenfell. 266
Juncos
    Junco song. Cynthia Grenfell.
    266
Juncos feeding. Marie Daerr
    Boehringer. 210
June 6th, 1963. Charles Olson.
    337
June garden. Marie Daerr
    Boehringer. 210
June in the city. John Reed. 350
June miracle. Marie Daerr
    Boehringer. 210
A June walk. Greg Kuzma. 300
Jungles
    Clinical jungle. James Magorian.
    309
    Surviving the jungle. Marieve
    Rugo. 356
Junior executive making a good
    impression on his boss. James
    Magorian. 309
Junior high. Martha Janssen. 283
Junk. Wanda Coleman. 225
Junk dawn, NYC. Andrei Codrescu.
    223
Junk mail. Andrei Codrescu. 223
Junkyards
    Salvage. Amy Clampitt. 222
Junkyards. See also Garbage

Junta. Mark Vinz. 387
Jurgis Petraskas, the workers'
    angel... Anthony Petrosky. 344
Just a thought. Sam Fishman. 246
Just an old tease. Alice Spohn
    Newton. 332
Just another evening esse.
    Bradford Morrow. 329
Just another smack. Irving
    Feldman. 242
Just as morning twilight...
    Charles Olson. 337
Just lord. Donald Revell. 351
Just me. Rosa Bogar. 211
"Just running as fast as I can."
    Michael Robert Pick. 345
Just this once. James Torio. 281
"Just to have her body in my
    mind..." Charles Olson. 337
Juvenile Delinquents
    Portrait of a juvenile
    delinquent. Susan Stock. 375

"JW (from the Danelaw) says."
    Charles Olson. 337

"A kaleidoscope you." Sally Love
    Saunders. 358
Kallet, Marilyn
    After Marie. 287
    Against the weather. 287
    The aliens. 287
    All literature. 287
    As if. 287
    Borges sang. 287
    Briar rose. 287
    Canto. 287
    Come. 287
    Despite astronomical arguments.
    287
    The drive. 287
    Elaine. 287
    Herstory. 287
    In the face of solitude. 287
    In the great night. 287
    Limitation. 287
    Love. 287
    Love tears the rind. 287
    Maybe night. 287
    Night enters. 287
    Not just poetry. 287
    On eliminating the astronomer
    from photographs of gases. 287
    Ophelia. 287
    Out. 287
    Return. 287
    Setting limits. 287
    Spleen. 287
    Spleen: Geneva, New York. 287
    Thirst. 287
    This dream. 287
    This side of the window. 287
    To Alice Notely. 287
    To break the hold. 287
    Turning. 287
    Weaver star. 287
    What the sky holds. 287
    The whitewashed wall. 287
    Who do you accuse? 287
    Without. 287
    The woman chained to the shore
    unchains herself. 287
Kaminsky, Marc
    American men. 288
    A broken house. 288
    Conversion. 288
    Elegy. 288
    The embrace. 288
    Gossip. 288
    In this city. 288

Milk. 288
Surrender. 288
A table with people. 288
Kansas City. Joy Harjo. 269
Kar. Gerard Malanga. 310
Karen. Rachel A. Hazen. 271
Karen. Anneliese Wagner. 389
Kate. Wanda Coleman. 225
Keeping. Alberta Turner. 384
Keeping in touch. Mark Vinz. 387
Kees, Weldon (about)
For Weldon Kees. Greg Kuzma. 300
Keller, Helen
Helen and me. Debra Bruce. 216
Kelly, Robert
Abrak. 289
Analytic hymn. 289
The angel of the dialectic. 289
The archer. 289
Auguries. 289
"Between two birches." 289
Binding by striking. 289
The chooser and the chosen. 289
Colorado. 289
Curvature of sound. 289
Detective story. 289
Doors. 289
Enemies. 289
Eucalyptus. 289
Excalibur. 289
"Face at a window." 289
Five precious stones. 289
Folk music of Tibet. 289
From. 289
Getting there. 289
Gods. 289
Halloween: Thayer Street. 289
The head of Orpheus. 289
"History is something to take
shelter in." 289
"I want to tell you why husbands
stop loving wives." 289
"I want to tell you." 289
"If dawn would only quiet me the
host." 289
"If she went down to the town."
289
In Mary Frank's garden. 289
The lattice. 289
A life of intimate fleeing. 289
Limits. 289
Looking. 289
"A mark on paper." 289
Mounted policemen. 289
The mouth of the blue dog is
bound beforehand. 289
"My boyhood was a raft of
poems." 289
The nature of metaphor. 289
"Needing quiet the men of old."

289
"Notices darker form move." 289
Ode to language. 289
Original women. 289
Orphee. 289
Postcards from the underworld.
289
Riverboat. 289
"Saying/is elegy." 289
Scion. 289
The secret agent. 289
"Seek out the far capillaries."
289
Size. 289
Some prince of the Trojans here.
289
Stanzas. 289
A stone wall in Providence. 289
The story. 289
Then. 289
"Those who are beautiful." 289
"To my friends when I am
eighty-five." 289
Tune. 289
Twenty. 289
Ubiquist. 289
Une semaine de silence. 289
Variations on a poem of Stefan
George. 289
Variations on some stirrings of
Mallarme. 289
What she found in the river. 289
"When the brokers were raining
on Wall Street." 289
Kelp
Research chemist stomping on a
colleague's sack lunch. James
Magorian. 309
Kennedy's inauguration. Robert
Bly. 209
Kennedy, John Fitzgerald
Assassination. John F. Barker.
201
The back-door ghost. Mitchell
Howard. 276
11/22/63. John F. Barker. 201
November. Greg Kuzma. 300
A November afternoon. John F.
Barker. 201
Soapbox speech for Kennedy.
Thomas McGrath. 315
Kennedy, X.J.
Archeopteryx. 290
Bee. 290
Crocodile. 290
Dingo. 290
Electric eel. 290
Fly. 290
Goshawk. 290
Hippogriff. 290

Iguana. 290
Jerboa. 290
Kraken. 290
Lion. 290
Minotaur. 290
Narwhal. 290
Ounce. 290
Pangolin. 290
Quetzal. 290
Roc. 290
Snail. 290
Tyrannosaur. 290
Vinegarroon. 290
Xipnosuran. 290
Zzzzz. 290

Kenny, Maurice
Along the Hudson. 291
Anemones. 291
At that time. 291
Beaded turtle. 291
Boyhood country creek. 291
Corn=planter. 291
Fifty, fifty-one. 291
Horses. 291
Huckleberrying. 291
In country light. 291
In the wilds. 291
Mole. 291
North summer. 291
O Wendy, Arthur. 291
Pokeweed. 291
Quicksand. 291
Sacrifice. 291
Steps. 291
They tell me I am lost. 291
Wejack. 291
Wildies of Burnett Lane. 291
Woodcock. 291

Kent Circle song. Charles Olson. 337

Kentucky
Right there in Rand McNally. Paul Davis. 228
Roots among these rocks. Robert L. Wilson. 401

Ketchikan Creek. Evelyn Golden. 263

Kew Gardens - the compost. Michael Gizzi. 259

A **key** to common lethal fungi. Marge Piercy. 346

"The **key** to/making the alarm clock." Madison Morrison. 327

Keynote address. James Magorian. 309

The **keys**. Randy Blasing. 207

Khatchadourian, Haig
Angelus. 292
Clouds over the sea. 292
The coming of snow. 292
Dead Sea. 292
Each of us here has fought this battle. 292
Easter. 292
Elegy. 292
The feast. 292
In a minor key. 292
In memory of Dr. Martin Luther King. 292
In memory of my mother. 292
In remembrance. 292
In the present we take refuge from the past. 292
Jerusalem. 292
The long waiting. 292
Love poem. 292
Nocturn for a winter night. 292
A poem is an organic thing. 292
Proem. 292
Rain on the pond. 292
Seascape: woman on the beach. 292
Shy eyes shy looks. 292
Silence. 292
Suffering does not ennoble. 292
Traffic with time is a terrible thing. 292
Water color. 292
Water color II. 292
We live alone. 292
You seemed so poised and tender tonight. 292

Kibbutzim
Consecration. Susan Tichy. 381
For Allan. Susan Tichy. 381
Kovah Tembel. Susan Tichy. 381
Lying on my coat. Susan Tichy. 381
Painting the fence. Susan Tichy. 381
Shabbat morning. Susan Tichy. 381
Shabbat, matah. Susan Tichy. 381
Work. Susan Tichy. 381

The **kill**. Clayton Eshleman. 240

Killed iave-July 8-1918. Ernest Hemingway. 272

Killer credit card still at large. David Wann. 394

"**Killing**, taking a man's life..." Michael Robert Pick. 345

The **killing**. Rosa Bogar. 211

Kilmer, Joyce - Satire
"I think that I have never trod." Ernest Hemingway. 272

Kimathi, Dedan
In the gathering forest (where Kimathi lives). Kiarri T-H Cheatwood. 220

Kin of crossroads. Melvin Dixon.

231
Kind. Josephine Miles. 319
Kind of a love poem. Steve Kowit.
    298, 299
A kind of knowledge. Judson
    Crews. 226
A kind of magic. Marie Daerr
    Boehringer. 210
A kind of moisture on the wall.
    Clayton Eshleman. 240
A kind of victory. Mark Vinz. 387
Kindness
    "Bodily kindness is
    common;though some" Josephine
    Miles. 319
    "Climbing stairs so low."
    Michael Robert Pick. 345
    Jay. Susan Stock. 375
    On the attraction of heavenly
    bodies. Dennis Hinrichsen. 273
    A toast. James R. Rhodes. 352
The king is in his counting
    house. James R. Rhodes. 352
King Kong flu. Josephine B.
    Moretti. 324
King, Martin Luther, Jr.
    Blessed Martin. Maurice W.
    Britts. 215
    FBI kills Martin Luther King.
    Bill Knott. 296
    In memory of Dr. Martin Luther
    King. Haig Khatchadourian. 292
The kingdom shore. Jacques
    Sollov. 370
Kingfisher. David Wagoner. 390
The kingfisher. Amy Clampitt. 222
Kingfishers
    Kingfisher. David Wagoner. 390
    Water is air to the kingfisher.
    Mary Gilliland. 257
The kiosk. Charles Edward Eaton.
    236
Kipling. Ernest Hemingway. 272
Kipling, Rudyard
    Kipling. Ernest Hemingway. 272
Kirk. Kirk Lumpkin. 306
Kirk, Norman Andrew
    Abraham, without papers. 293
    Afterall, the children. 293
    The assassination. 293
    Burningly cold. 293
    Caged. 293
    Candied cash. 293
    Cathedral in the pines. 293
    Christmas within the walls. 293
    The clock outran the mouse. 293
    Computing God. 293
    Consummation. 293
    A crippled girl's clothes. 293
    Death. 293

Dissipation. 293
Enchanted. 293
Enter no exit. 293
False prophets, false poets. 293
Fate and the goddess never. 293
Flea. 293
The game. 293
Girls in ragtime. 293
The glove of silence. 293
Good morning, Eugene. 293
Hark! 293
Have I caught myself? 293
Hear it out. 293
Homes??!! 293
I pray. 293
I see the ending in our eyes.
    293
The ignorant set. 293
It is new to you too. 293
Lady fingers. 293
The last trance. 293
Life. 293
Lost conquest. 293
Mad dogs in August. 293
March on. 293
Moon-sun one. 293
Museum of poetry. 293
'My home town, stranger -
    N.Y.C.' 293
Norman. 293
Nostalgia. 293
Not forever. 293
Of it. 293
Old thoughts in a zoo room. 293
On the street after hours. 293
P.S. 293
Panda zoo. 293
Panda zoo review. 293
A pastoral. 293
Pay me. 293
Peter's graduation. 293
Pianissimo. 293
Planetarium. 293
Power to me people. 293
Reborn. 293
Rene. 293
Retreat. 293
A room, loneliness. 293
Sanctuary. 293
Sea venture. 293
Smart set. 293
Snow warning. 293
A solo for Charles Munch. 293
Sometime something. 293
Soundifferously. 293
Stage sounds. 293
The starting point of we. 293
Stompin'. 293
Storyville, the painted, the
    pure. 293

A student of tragedy. 293
There is an orange happening.
    293
Tiger sparrow. 293
To the sea=side girls passing
    by. 293
Today, no hour. 293
Togetner. 293
Transpose. 293
Virgins at one time. 293
The walk. 293
The web. 293
Wes Turley. 293
What chance ignorance. 293
White lady. 293
You bastard. 293
Kiryat Shmona, Israel
    In Kiryat Shmona. Susan Tichy.
        381
The **kiss**. Charles Edward Eaton.
    236
The **kiss**. Mitchell Howard. 276
Kisses
    "The corner of the block's in."
        Madison Morrison. 327
    Discoursing kisses. Mitchell
        Howard. 276
    In the lover's arms. Elsa
        Gidlow. 254
    The kiss. Charles Edward Eaton.
        236
    The kiss. Mitchell Howard. 276
    Native language. Debra Bruce.
        216
    Oh no! Jack Prelutsky. 348
Kitchen. Josephine Miles. 319
Kitchen maid. Frances Mayes. 314
The **kitchen** phone. James A.
    Emanuel. 239
Kites
    "Just running as fast as I can."
        Michael Robert Pick. 345
    Two poems on definitions of
        bitch. Sandra McPherson. 317
Kitten in the sun, fr. A pride of
    four small lions. Everett A.
    Gillis. 258
Kloss, Phillips
    As a man thinketh. 294
    The atom and the poet. 294
    Bards of the golden west. 294
    Bomb, bullet or arrow. 294
    Brain on the beach. 294
    Bush. 294
    Cadenza. 294
    The canyon wren. 294
    Constancy. 294
    Desert mystery. 294
    Digging stick. 294
    Dusty dragoon, pious Quaker. 294

Emancipation from a Bach jig.
    294
Filaree. 294
The fivefold root of
    insufficient reason. 294
The garnet cross. 294
Gold. 294
Grandfather's grove. 294
Grinding stone. 294
Living color. 294
Machines. 294
Mirage. 294
The moaning of the buoy. 294
Moral of the caterpillar story.
    294
The most dangerous desire. 294
Not a sparrow shall fall. 294
Ocotillo. 294
Otter slide. 294
The oyster catcher's cry. 294
Pharisees and Sadducees. 294
Platitudes of want. 294
Retrospect. 294
The sonata in D minor. 294
A static population, dynamic
    civilization. 294
Sun watcher. 294
The sungod Huitzilopochtli. 294
Taos lightning. 294
That's Karl, my husband. 294
Whatever our final fate. 294
Winter sonnet. 294
Witch of the sea. 294
With this to come back to. 294
The woman in the woods. 294
The word. 294
Yucca moth. 294
Knauth, Stephen
    Ambrose Remy. 295
    The American field. 295
    Amnesia. 295
    An audiovisual glimpse of
        Cabarrus County, North
        Carolina. 295
    August nocturne. 295
    Baby picture, circa 1932. 295
    Beast. 295
    Blind Leon's escape. 295
    Christmas in a valley of the
        Uwharrie. 295
    Cold water creek. 295
    The death of Whitman. 295
    1836. In the Cherokee overhills.
        295
    The flying people. 295
    The forgetful life. 295
    From the Cherokee. 295
    Going for a newspaper. 295
    Hillwalker. 295
    In the wind before a storm. 295

The last cowboy. 295
Mama lamenting. 295
Mark Twain's torch song. 295
Midwest patio behavior. 295
The midwinter death of Olivia
    Stroud. 295
The new science. 295
Night-fishing on Irish Buffalo
    Creek. 295
1934. A sailor's letter to Hart
    Crane N. 295
North American wildflowers. 295
North Carolina life cycle. 295
Notes for a novel to be burned
    on a cold winter evening. 295
On the midway. 295
The pier dwellers. 295
Pisgan. 295
Six forty-five. 295
Someday. 295
Uncle Aubrey. 295
Viper Sunday. 295
The visceral arts. 295
Yadkin Valley sketchbook. 295
The Yolorai dance. 295
Kneeling down to look into a
    culvert. Robert Bly. 209
Knees. Alberta Turner. 384
Knees
    May. Tom Smith. 368
The knife sharpener. Anthony
    Petrosky. 344
Knitting
    The woman who loved wool. Harry
    Humes. 278
Knives
    Jack-knife. Thomas Hornsby
        Ferril. 243
    The knife sharpener. Anthony
        Petrosky. 344
Knots. Jim Everhard. 241
Knott, Bill
    Assorted short poems. 296
    At the museum this week. 296
    The closet. 296
    The commuter's dream. 296
    The consolations of
        sociobiology. 296
    Crash course. 296
    Depressionism. 296
    The enemy. 296
    Extinctions, schedule of. 296
    (Face) (autumn) (en face). 296
    FBI kills Martin Luther King.
        296
    Feeding the sun. 296
    For lack of you. 296
    Generic: after reading Plath and
        Sexton. 296
    Guilty creatures at play. 296

Lesson. 296
Lourdes. 296
The misunderstanding. 296
Mitts and gloves. 296
More guilt. 296
My fault. 296
Obsolescent. 296
October. 296
The oldest story. 296
The panther. 296
Penny wise. 296
Per request. 296
The permission. 296
Poeme noir. 296
Poet. 296
Problem. 296
The question. 296
Reader. 296
Reading the gaps. 296
The signs of the stopsign. 296
Sudden departure. 296
(Sun, sea, rain)(rain
    season)(Port Townsend,
    Washington). 296
Vacancies, occupancies. 296
The vigilances of evening. 296
"Knotted guts inside." Michael
    Robert Pick. 345
Knowing. William Stafford. 373
Knowing. Alberta Turner. 384
Knowledge. Martha Janssen. 283
Knowledge
    Dry ice. Dave Smith. 367
    Enlightenment. Sister Maura. 313
    For a friend-with the gift of a
        recording. Sister Maura. 313
    "An ignorant one who read
        nothing." Da Free John. 284
    Its edges audible. Thomas Lux.
        307
    Knowing. William Stafford. 373
    Lost. Jeanne Lohmann. 305
    Metamorphosis. Josephine Miles.
        319
    On the edge of knowledge. Anne
        Bailie. 199
    Recognition. Josephine Miles.
        319
    Seasoned. Margaret Key Biggs.
        205
    Supreme knowledge. Jacques
        Sollov. 370
    Them capybaras of alabac.
        Stephen Todd Booker. 212
    Things you should know. Paul
        Violi. 388
    The unseen. Larry Moffi. 322
    Verse/re-verse mantra. Kirk
        Lumpkin. 306
Koch, Kenneth

After some verses by Morvaen Le
  Gaelique & Paul Verlaine. 297
Art and society. 297
At night. 297
"At the fish market we walked
  back and forth." 297
The book, fr. The green step.
  297
The brook, fr. The green step.
  297
Cherche - midi. 297
"The dawn woke the hats up in
  Tuscany." 297
Days and nights. 297
"Desire and curiosity." 297
The diary is open at two
  o'clock. 297
Disney Boheme. 297
"Each moment fills him with a
  desire." 297
Environment. 297
Girl and baby florist sidewalk
  pram nineteen seventy... 297
Gordu wisdom. 297
The green step, sels. 297
The green step. 297
"He who addresses you." 297
Heroic standard. 297
"How many things we are
  attentive to!" 297
In bed. 297
The music, fr. The green step.
  297
1958.   297
"Notices are sent up into the
  music." 297
"The personality of the feeding
  bin." 297
The silencers. 297
The stone, fr. The green step.
  297
This story, fr. The green step.
  297
The train, fr. The green step.
  297
Twenty poems, sels. 297
With Janice. 297
The woman and the man, fr. The
  green step. 297
"Words penetrate a poem." 297
The world. 297
Kohoutek. Phyllis A. Tickle. 382
Kovah Tembel. Susan Tichy. 381
Kowit. Steve Kowit. 299
Kowit, Steve
  Amabo, mea dulcis ipsithilla.
    299
  Blue movies. 299
  Climbing the walls. 299
  Codicil. 298, 299

Conquistador. 299
Credo. 299
The creep. 299
Crossing the river. 299
Cutting our losses. 298, 299
The dead magician. 299
Desperate solutions. 299
Dusk in the Cuyamacas. 299
Equivocal elegy. 299
405.   298, 299
Fragment of ancient skull. 299
The garden. 298, 299
Guests of the nation. 298, 299
Harper's Ferry. 298, 299
Hate mail. 299
Home. 298, 299
In lieu of a love poem for
  America. 298, 299
In the dark. 299
It was your song. 299
Joy to the fishes. 299
Kind of a love poem. 298, 299
Kowit. 299
La Mujer. 299
La Resolana. 298, 299
Last will. 298, 299
Letter to Dean Picker. 299
Li Ho. 298, 299
Lullaby ("Sweet love,
  everything"). 299
Lurid confessions. 298, 299
Lycanthropy in South Pasadena.
  299
Millie. 299
Mysteries. 299
'Neruda's remains were expelled
  this week...' 298, 299
The novios. 299
Out of McHenry. 298, 299
Poem for my parents. 299
The poetry reading was a
  disaster. 299
The prize. 299
The queue. 299
Raking in. 299
Renewal. 299
The rose. 299
Small boats. 299
A swell idea. 299
Thank you. 299
They are looking for Che
  Guevara. 299
Trans-American express. 299
A vote for Harold. 298, 299
Wanted - sensuous woman who can
  handle 12 inches of man. 299
Xochicalco. 299
Kraken. X.J. Kennedy. 290
Kristallnecht. James Schevill.
  360

Kuzma, Greg
Archibald MacLeish. 300
The beautiful and lovely face.
  300
The bird. 300
The birds. 300
Complete freedom. 300
Crocus. 300
Dark. 300
Death in Crete. 300
Dream. 300
Fair city. 300
Flesh. 300
For Alan Dugan. 300
For Weldon Kees. 300
The good part. 300
Homage. 300
Ice skating. 300
In Canada. 300
A June walk. 300
The lawn mowing. 300
Love poem. 300
The lovers. 300
May. 300
Morning. 300
The moth. 300
Muscatel. 300
The music. 300
My son skating on Doane's Lake.
  300
November. 300
The owls. 300
The poets. 300
Police. 300
Remembering the fifties. 300
Rhyme. 300
Robert Lowell is dead. 300
Rummy. 300
The sacred shore. 300
The sexual would eat up all
  attention. 300
The snowfall. 300
Sunday. 300
Ten thousand years. 300
The toaster. 300
Travel. 300
The truck. 300
The two goldfish. 300
Who was killed in the car. 300
Kyle Canyon, Thanksgiving 1978.
  David James. 282
Kyoto. Michael Gizzi. 259

L'envoi. John F. Barker. 201
L'ora. Rose Basile Green. 265
La bufadora. Thomas R. Sleigh.
  366

La cite de Carcassonne. John F.
  Barker. 201
La force. Louise Gluck. 259A
La gloire. John Godfrey. 260
The La Jolla ladies. Ray Fleming.
  247
La Mujer. Steve Kowit. 299
La pineta di Migliarino. Robert
  A. Sears. 362
La Resolana. Steve Kowit. 298,
  299
La ronde. Rod McKuen. 316
Labor and Laborers
The baron of bulk. James
  Schevill. 360
Bloom. Josephine Miles. 319
Chorus from a play (2). Thomas
  McGrath. 315
Dynamiter blasting ice jams.
  James Magorian. 309
Good living. Josephine B.
  Moretti. 324
Handbag assemblers up shit creek
  without a paddle. James
  Magorian. 309
Office machine blues. Josephine
  B. Moretti. 324
Sunday morning:migrant labor
  camp. Sister Maura. 313
"Throwing watermelons." Michael
  Robert Pick. 345
Working woman. Josephine B.
  Moretti. 324
Young secretaries. Josephine B.
  Moretti. 324
Labor day. Louise Gluck. 259A
Labor Unions
Jurgis Petraskas, the workers'
  angel... Anthony Petrosky. 344
Lace covered memories. Rachel A.
  Hazen. 271
The lacquer box. John F. Barker.
  201
Lacul Gilaului. Keith Wilson. 400
The ladie's locker room at the
  Concord. Laura Boss. 213
"Lady artist does her." Madison
  Morrison. 327
Lady asleep. Tom Smith. 368
Lady butterfly. Rachel A. Hazen.
  271
Lady Charisma. Charles Edward
    Eaton. 236
Lady fingers. Norman Andrew Kirk.
  293
The lady in the single. Louise
  Gluck. 259A
"The lady of desserts." Madison
  Morrison. 327
Lady on a bus. Jeanne Lohmann.

305

The lady painter, sels. Andrei
    Codrescu. 223
The lady poets with foot notes.
    Ernest Hemingway. 272
The lady who drove me to the
    airport. Diane Wakoski. 391
The lady with bougainvillea in
    her eyes. Wanda Coleman. 225
Lagarde, Fernand
    For Fernand Lagarde (died 13
    April 1982). James A. Emanuel.
    239
Laguna by moonlight. Robert A.
    Sears. 362
Laguna landscape. William
    Oandasan. 335
Laguna, California
    Laguna landscape. William
    Oandasan. 335
Lake George, 1970. Eileen
    Silver-Lillywite. 364
Lake George, New York
    Lake George, 1970. Eileen
    Silver-Lillywite. 364
Lake song. Colette Inez. 280
The lake. Edgar Allan Poe. 347
The lake. Robert Peters. 343
Lakemont. Frances Mayes. 314
Lakes
    Bear gulch: home place. Franz
    Schneider. 361
    Did ye know? Lake Hamilton, day
    after Easter. Cynthia
    Grenfell. 266
    Finding a lake. Tefke
    Goldberger. 262
    I am still as stone. Judson
    Crews. 226
    In the lake. Joan Colby. 224
    The lake. Edgar Allan Poe. 347
    The lake. Robert Peters. 343
    Lizard Pond. Robert A. Sears.
    362
    Returns. Ralph J., Jr. Mills.
    321
    There are northern lakes...
    Joyce Carol Oates. 336
Lambs
    Death in winter. Carol Frost.
    249
    Three Easters. Alberta Turner.
    384
Lament. Cynthia Grenfell. 266
A lament for Willie Wyler. James
    Torio. 281
Laments
    The earnest liberal's lament.
    Ernest Hemingway. 272
Land

Further completion of plat.
    Charles Olson. 337
The land as haitubu. Charles
    Olson. 337
The land behind the wind, sels.
    David Wagoner. 390
Land of little sticks, 1945.
    James Tate. 379
The land of Michoacan. Robert A.
    Sears. 362
Land rights. Rose Basile Green.
    265
Land song at the Exeter mines.
    Anthony Petrosky. 344
Land speculation. Franz
    Schneider. 361
Land's end dialectic. Thomas R.
    Sleigh. 366
"Land's End-." Charles Olson. 337
The land. Jim Simmerman. 365
Landlocked, fallen, unsung. C.D.
    Wright. 402
Landlords
    Apartment. Josephine Miles. 319
    Augusta's confrontation with her
    landlady. Carolyn Stoloff. 376
Landscape. James Torio. 281
Landscape with ascet ic. Deborah
    Tall. 378
"Lane's eye-view of Gloucester"
    Charles Olson. 337
Language. Paul Davis. 228
Language
    Bi-lingual. Andrei Codrescu. 223
    Configurations of a dead
    language. Maria Gillan. 256
    "Echoing the fierce belief that
    time." Edwin Honig. 275
    Expatriate. Marieve Rugo. 356
    Good morning. Joyce Carol Oates.
    336
    "How many languages..." Larry
    Eigner. 237
    My wife's dream. James Schevill.
    360
    "Needing quiet the men of old."
    Robert Kelly. 289
    "Notices darker form move."
    Robert Kelly. 289
    Ode to language. Robert Kelly.
    289
    Say what? David James. 282
    Translation. Marieve Rugo. 356
    Two kinds of language. John Yau.
    404
Language is a chain. Maria
    Gillan. 256
Language of flowers. Jacques
    Sollov. 370
The language orphan. Clayton

Eshleman. 240
Languages. Keith Wilson. 400
Laocoon is the name of the
    figure. Marge Piercy. 346
"The **lap**.". Charles Olson. 337
Laps. Martha Janssen. 283
"**Large** city life." Madison
    Morrison. 327
Lark. Josephine Miles. 319
Larks
    Lark. Josephine Miles. 319
Lars Italica. Rose Basile Green.
    265
Laryngitis
    Ode to laryngitis. Andrei
    Codrescu. 223
Las cuatro ijadas de una palabra.
    Colette Inez. 280
Las Vegas
    Gambling in Las Vegas. James
    Schevill. 360
Lascaux, Cave of
    Visions of the fathers of
    Lascaux. Clayton Eshleman. 240
Last act. Edwin Honig. 275
Last blast. Robert L. Wilson. 401
The **last** chapter. Robert L.
    Wilson. 401
The **last** cowboy. Stephen Knauth.
    295
Last day in Istanbul. Randy
    Blasing. 207
The **last** five flowers. James R.
    Rhodes. 352
The **last** forgotten lover. Royal
    Murdoch. 330
The **last** laugh. James R. Rhodes.
    352
Last letter of a condemned
    priest. Franz Schneider. 361
The **last** look. James Torio. 281
"The **last** man except
    conceivably." Charles Olson.
    337
The **last** man in all Pennsylvania.
    Larry Moffi. 322
The **last** New England
    transcendentalist. James
    Schevill. 360
Last night a light. Cathryn
    Hankla. 268
The **last** night and morning. Kirk
    Lumpkin. 306
The **last** of me. Rachel A. Hazen.
    271
The **last** of the Wallendas.
    Stephen Sandy. 357
The **last** of the wine. Rod McKuen.
    316
The **last** perfect moment. Dennis

Hinrichsen. 273
A **last** poem. Gerard Malanga. 310
Last rites. Marc Hudson. 277
Last song. Edwin Honig. 275
Last summer's bones. Carolyn
    Stoloff. 376
Last supper. Joan Colby. 224
Last things. Robert Gibb. 253
Last things. Joyce Carol Oates.
    336
The **last** tie. Jacques Sollov. 371
The **last** trance. Norman Andrew
    Kirk. 293
Last week of winter. Sandra
    McPherson. 317
Last will. Steve Kowit. 298, 299
Last words for Count No'count.
    James Schevill. 360
"**Last** year's pink." Larry Eigner.
    237
Late at night in the kitchen.
    J.W. Rivers. 354
Late garden. Marc Hudson. 277
Late harvest. Joyce Carol Oates.
    336
Late leaving train. Dennis
    Hinrichsen. 273
Late morning. Anthony Petrosky.
    344
Late news. Richard Blessing. 208
Late night movies. John Yau. 404
Late snow. Louise Gluck. 259A
Late song. Cornel Lengyel. 302
Late to school. J.W. Rivers. 354
Late verbs. Marieve Rugo. 356
Late winter sky. Marc Hudson. 277
The **late-night** realities. Rachel
    A. Hazen. 271
The **late** flight. William
    Stafford. 373
A **late** guest. William Stafford.
    373
Late summer leaving. Joy Harjo.
    269
Later. William Stafford. 373
A **later** note on Letter #15.
    Charles Olson. 337
Later Tyrian business. Charles
    Olson. 337
The **lattice**. Robert Kelly. 289
Lattimore, Richmond
    Aspects of time. 301
    Blood relations. 301
    Bone structure. 301
    Coastal stuff. 301
    Cyclades. 301
    Daisy fields, enchanted forests.
    301
    Disadvantages. 301
    The elite. 301

Eye witness. 301
Fall guise. 301
Flesh tones. 301
Forlorn dream song. 301
Form and actuality. 301
Former residence. 301
Gehenna. 301
Home. 301
Isabel. 301
The islands. 301
Lesefruchte. 301
A marriage. 301
Monadology. 301
Night travel. 301
Of truth and fact. 301
Painter. 301
The pearl. 301
Protoprimavera. 301
The rage of Demeter. 301
Return to the light. 301
Riviera railway. 301
Shanhaikuan. 301
Sliding scales. 301
Spanish succession. 301
Tales from the father of
    history. 301
Tales of Hoffmann. 301
They used to have a homecoming
    day. 301
To Charles, Duke of Orleans. 301
A votive offering. 301
Waves. 301
Western ways. 301
Winter return. 301
Laughter
    Echoing laughter. Alice Spohn
        Newton. 332
    Heart's laughter. Elsa Gidlow.
        254
Laughter and pain. Rachel A.
    Hazen. 271
The laughter of women. Elsa
    Gidlow. 254
Launched. Herbert Morris. 326
Laundry and Laundering
    The ignorant set. Norman Andrew
        Kirk. 293
    Lost patterns. Alice Spohn
        Newton. 333
    The sheets. Timothy Steele. 374
Laurel tree. May Miller. 320
Lavatories
    The connoisseur's history of the
        bathroom. James Schevill. 360
    Path oft' trod. Alice Spohn
        Newton. 333
Law and Lawyers
    Amicus Curiae. Jeanne Lohmann.
        305
    No man's land. Alice Spohn

Newton. 333
The lawn mowing. Greg Kuzma. 300
Lawrence Welk's musical salute to
    pawnshops. James Magorian. 308
Lax alba at Quinnipiac. Bradford
    Morrow. 329
Lazaro Cardenas. J.W. Rivers. 354
Lazarus. Anne Bailie. 199
Le Torri. Robert A. Sears. 362
"The leaf is growing." Josephine
    Miles. 319
A leaf of life. Alice Joyce
    Davidson. 227
Leaning. Carolyn Stoloff. 376
The learned lady. Roy Marz. 312
"'A learned man' sd Strabo
    (meaning Pytheus." Charles
    Olson. 337
Learning. Miller Williams. 399
Learning - Satire
    Things I learned last week.
        William Stafford. 373
Learning the elements. Sharon
    Bryan. 217
Learning to bake bread. Gene
    Anderson. 195
Learning to fish fresh water.
    Larry Moffi. 322
Learning to like the new school.
    William Stafford. 373
Learning to read. Miller
    Williams. 399
"Learning widsom." Rochelle
    DuBois. 234
Lease and loss. Edwin Honig. 275
Leaves. Sally Love Saunders. 358
Leaves
    Autumn leaves. Josephine B.
        Moretti. 324
    By your leaf. Marie Daerr
        Boehringer. 210
    Commoners. Robert L. Wilson. 401
    The final breath. Rachel A.
        Hazen. 271
    Leaves. Sally Love Saunders. 358
    November leaves. Robert L.
        Wilson. 401
    Raking in. Steve Kowit. 299
"Leaves not yet fallen." James
    Torio. 281
"Leaves sail in the shadow of a
    pond." Carolyn Stoloff. 376
Leavetaking, at dusk. Joyce Carol
    Oates. 336
Leaving. Michael Akillian. 193
Leaving. Toi Derricote. 229
Leaving. Joy Harjo. 269
Leaving. Jim Simmerman. 365
Leaving. Cathy Song. 372
Leaving him. Anneliese Wagner.

389
Leaving New England. Gary
     Margolis. 311
Leaving Queensland. Rod McKuen.
     316
Leaving the temple in Nimes.
     James Wright. 403
Leaving town. Dave Smith. 367
Leavings. Maria Gillan. 256
Lebanon
     Ode to the trees of Lebanon.
          Maurice W. Britts. 215
Lecture on Creeley. Gerard
     Malanga. 310
Leda (mythology)
     The humor of Helen. Roy Marz.
          312
Leeks
     The leeks. Sandra Gilbert. 255
The leeks. Sandra Gilbert. 255
"The left hand is the clayx of
     the flower." Charles Olson.
     337
Left hand view. John F. Barker.
     201
Legacy. Alice Joyce Davidson. 227
Legacy. Martha Janssen. 283
Legacy. Cornel Lengyel. 302
Legend stones. May Miller. 320
Legend, fr. Mirror suite. Everett
     A. Gillis. 258
Legends. Keith Wilson. 400
Legs
     Before. Josephine Miles. 319
     11:15 P.M.   Rochelle DuBois.
          234
     Garden of earthly delights ▬
          luxuria. Michael Gizzi. 259
Leipzig - das glashaus. Michael
     Gizzi. 259
Lemonade stand. Marie Daerr
     Boehringer. 210
The length of your absence. Anne
     Bailie. 199
Lengyel, Cornel
     Academic fowl. 302
     Adam's fault. 302
     Advice to the lovelorn. 302
     Boy in a pit. 302
     Brief is beautiful. 302
     Complaint against time. 302
     Consider the lilies. 302
     Cradle song. 302
     Daniel reviews his critics. 302
     Day of wrath. 302
     An evening walk. 302
     Eyeless in Corinth. 302
     Fall song. 302
     The first eviction. 302
     The first subdivider. 302

Fool's song. 302
For travelers on the sabbath.
     302
Forest years. 302
Girls on a spring campus. 302
Harvest song. 302
The harvesters' psalm. 302
A hereditary ailment. 302
In memoriam: Santayana. 302
The joker is wild. 302
Late song. 302
Legacy. 302
The lesson. 302
The lookout's report. 302
The lost garden. 302
Man in orbit. 302
A meeting. 302
Memento. 302
Noon song. 302
Nota bene. 302
An old feud. 302
On a malicious critic. 302
On a marginal bore. 302
On a popular historian. 302
On a quick-change artist. 302
On a slow student. 302
On an unpublished author. 302
On astronauts who lost their
     lives when their rocket... 302
On everybody's friend. 302
On players unknown. 302
On the newcomers. 302
Petition. 302
The proverbs of clowns. 302
Psalm-maker to his son. 302
Public notice. 302
A question for Jonah. 302
Runes with variations. 302
Rustic song. 302
Sampson and the foxes. 302
The sparrows that fell. 302
Spring song. 302
Table song. 302
Teresa's garden. 302
A transport fo children. 302
A truth-teller's complaint. 302
Wedding dance. 302
Young Yorick's confession. 302
Lennon, John
     The Dakota. Amy Clampitt. 222
     John Lennon murdered on wild
          west side walk. Mitchell
          Howard. 276
     A tangential death. Marge
          Piercy. 346
Lenore. Edgar Allan Poe. 347
Lent. Phyllis A. Tickle. 382
Leopards
     The clouded leopards of Cambodia
          and Viet Nam. Betty Adcock.

192

Leosan. Alberta Turner. 384
Les fleurs du cinema. Andrei
    Codrescu. 223
Lesbianism. See Homosexuality

Lesefruchte. Richmond Lattimore.
    301
Lesley. Josephine B. Moretti. 324
Lesson. Bill Knott. 296
The lesson. Sam Fishman. 246
The lesson. Cornel Lengyel. 302
Lessons. Wanda Coleman. 225
"Let me tread/softly." A.
    Dovichi. 233
Let reason reign. Sam Fishman.
    246
Let the sea speak. Elsa Gidlow.
    254
Let there be light! Alice Joyce
    Davidson. 227
Let us gather at the river. Marge
    Piercy. 346
Let wisdom wear the crown: hymn
    for gaia. Elsa Gidlow. 254
Let's. Joan Colby. 224
Let's smash. Carolyn Stoloff. 376
Letter 10. Charles Olson. 337
Letter 16. Charles Olson. 337
Letter 20: not a pastoral letter.
    Charles Olson. 337
Letter 22. Charles Olson. 337
Letter 23. Charles Olson. 337
Letter 3. Charles Olson. 337
Letter 41 (broken off). Charles
    Olson. 337
Letter 5. Charles Olson. 337
Letter 6. Charles Olson. 337
Letter 7. Charles Olson. 337
Letter 72. Charles Olson. 337
Letter 9. Charles Olson. 337
Letter from a shipwrecked sailor.
    Kirk Lumpkin. 306
Letter from a son. Rosa Bogar.
    211
Letter from Cremona. Jeanne
    Lohmann. 305
A letter from Mama San. James
    Torio. 281
Letter from my grandmother
    interned in France. Anneliese
    Wagner. 389
Letter from New Hampshire. Edwin
    Honig. 275
Letter from our man in
    blossomtime. Louise Gluck.
    259A
Letter from Provence. Louise
    Gluck. 259A
Letter from Santa Cruz. Sister

Maura. 313
A letter not to deliver. William
    Stafford. 373
Letter to an imaginary friend.
    Part three. Thomas McGrath.
    315
Letter to Dean Picker. Steve
    Kowit. 299
A letter to Louise. John Reed.
    350
Letter to Mimi. Eileen
    Silver-Lillywite. 364
Letter to my father. Eileen
    Silver-Lillywite. 364
Letter to Scardanelli. Marc
    Hudson. 277
Letter to the outside. Mark Vinz.
    387
Letter, May 2, 1959. Charles
    Olson. 337
A letter, on fishing grounds...
    Charles Olson. 337
The letter. Alice Spohn Newton.
    332
Letters. Miller Williams. 399
Letters and Letter Writing
    Chain letter. James Magorian.
        308
    Hubie French needs a letter.
        George Eklund. 238
    Keeping in touch. Mark Vinz. 387
    Liebe mutter. Anneliese Wagner.
        389
    Listen. Edwin Honig. 275
    Love the letters. Wanda Coleman.
        225
    Mail. Jacqueline Frank. 248
    The morning's mail. Christopher
        Bursk. 219
    Old letters. Timothy Steele. 374
    "A thump on/the porch..."
        Madison Morrison. 327
    Wallpaper hanger squashing an
        ant with his thumb. James
        Magorian. 309
    Why you don't hear from me.
        Thomas McGrath. 315
Letters from Jerusalem. Amy
    Clampitt. 222
Letters not answered. Colette
    Inez. 280
The letters of a name. Colette
    Inez. 280
Letters to Brasil. Brenda Marie
    Osbey. 340
Letters to Michael. Robin Becker.
    202
Letting go. Evelyn Golden. 263
Letting go. Ghita Orth. 339
Letting you go. William Stafford.

373
Levine, Philip
    Read to the animals, or Orpheus
    at the SPCA. Irving Feldman.
    242
Li Ho. Steve Kowit. 298, 299
Liana. Rachel A. Hazen. 271
Liberty Avenue. Anthony Petrosky.
    344
Libraries and Librarians
    Daydreaming in the Bodleian
    Library. Ray Fleming. 247
Libretto. C.D. Wright. 402
License. Stephen Todd Booker. 212
The **License** to carry a gun.
    Andrei Codrescu. 223
"**Licked** man (as such) out of the
    ice." Charles Olson. 337
Lidenbloom. Amy Clampitt. 222
The **lie.** James R. Rhodes. 352
Liebe mutter. Anneliese Wagner.
    389
Lies. Christopher Bursk. 219
Lies and Lying
    "Circling around." Michael
    Robert Pick. 345
    I never was a wary one. Jeanne
    Lohmann. 305
    The lie. James R. Rhodes. 352
    The light in the refrigerator.
    James Magorian. 309
    Prevarications. Robert A. Sears.
    362
    Promise. Josephine Miles. 319
    So I lie. Carolyn Stoloff. 376
    The storyteller. David Wagoner.
    390
    The word for it. May Miller. 320
    You fed me well. Rosa Bogar. 211
Life. Norman Andrew Kirk. 293
Life
    Aesthete's complaint. Donald
    Revell. 351
    And so on. Sam Fishman. 246
    Another chance. Miriam Goodman.
    264
    Barricade. Josephine Miles. 319
    The beach of time. Alice Joyce
    Davidson. 227
    Begin again. Thomas Hornsby
    Ferril. 243
    Beginning again. Rod McKuen. 316
    Being. Connie Hunt. 279
    Blue movies. Steve Kowit. 299
    Bonsai. Charles Edward Eaton.
    236
    "Boxes of old tattered photos."
    Michael Robert Pick. 345
    Buddhist meditation while
    fertilizing. Gene Anderson.

195
The cage. Sam Fishman. 246
The carpenter is knocking. Maria
    Gillan. 256
Center. Josephine Miles. 319
Change. Connie Hunt. 279
Changes! Rachel A. Hazen. 271
Cherche - midi. Kenneth Koch.
    297
A child's face in a small town.
    William Stafford. 373
Circus. Josephine Miles. 319
Co-hereing. Kirk Lumpkin. 306
Coming alive. Maria Gillan. 256
The creditor. May Miller. 320
The dining room. Charles Edward
    Eaton. 236
The drowned man. Irving Feldman.
    242
Dusk in the Cuyamacas. Steve
    Kowit. 299
Easter. Haig Khatchadourian. 292
The edge of return. May Miller.
    320
Eleventh hour. Patsie Black. 206
Empty pitchforks. Thomas Lux.
    307
Enemies. Robert Kelly. 289
Fall garden: 1. Gene Anderson.
    195
The fate of waking. Cathryn
    Hankla. 268
Fields of vision. Marieve Rugo.
    356
Fish. Josephine Miles. 319
The forbidden. Joyce Carol
    Oates. 336
Foretold. C.D. Wright. 402
4 A.M F. Rochelle DuBois. 234
Girl under streetlight. Margaret
    Key Biggs. 205
Hand work. Anneliese Wagner. 389
Harbor night. Sam Fishman. 246
Harry noir. Harrison Fisher. 245
A history of civilization.
    Albert Goldbarth. 261
Housewife. Josephine Miles. 319
"I have come/to tell you/of the
    way." Joan Walsh Anglund. 197
If you're here now, you win.
    David Wann. 394
Inconsistencies. Maria Gillan.
    256
Invitation. Thomas Hornsby
    Ferril. 243
"It is an ashtray of dead
    ciarettes." Gerard Malanga.
    310
Jo poised. Robert A. Sears. 362
Ketchikan Creek. Evelyn Golden.

263
Lease and loss. Edwin Honig. 275
Legacy. Cornel Lengyel. 302
"Life is free you know." Michael
  Robert Pick. 345
Life's a funny song. Alice Spohn
  Newton. 332
"Living by fiction." Rochelle
  DuBois. 234
Living in the other world.
  Dennis Hinrichsen. 273
"Long roads shorten time."
  Michael Robert Pick. 345
The lost garden. Cornel Lengyel.
  302
A miniature passion. Joyce Carol
  Oates. 336
Murder. Wanda Coleman. 225
My another road. Eve Triem. 383
"My beautiful crab tree." James
  Torio. 281
Mystery. James R. Rhodes. 352
No complaints. Ernesto Galarza.
  252
No one knows. Sam Fishman. 246
Not having a house is not a
  permanent situation. Mary
  Gilliland. 257
On the newcomers. Cornel
  Lengyel. 302
An ordinary composure. James L.
  White. 396
"Our/sense of values." A.
  Dovichi. 233
Photographs of architecture.
  Gerard Malanga. 310
'Promiscuity.' Joyce Carol
  Oates. 336
A puppet on a string. Rachel A.
  Hazen. 271
Refraction. Connie Hunt. 279
Retrospect. Phillips Kloss. 294
Rivers filled with tears. Rachel
  A. Hazen. 271
Rudiment. Erin Jolly. 285
"Scattered bits." Theta Burke.
  218
Seizure. Richard Blessing. 208
Siege. Josephine Miles. 319
Sleep. Josephine Miles. 319
Slowing down on a trampoline.
  James Magorian. 309
Song ("Observe the cautious
  toadstools.") W.D. (William De
  Witt) Snodgrass. 369
South woods in October, with the
  spiders of memory. Betty
  Adcock. 192
The sparrows that fell. Cornel
  Lengyel. 302

The splash of being. David Wann.
  394
Standing under the mystery. Mary
  Gilliland. 257
Steps. Maurice Kenny. 291
Subtraction. Richard Blessing.
  208
Sunday. Greg Kuzma. 300
Swearing. Kirk Lumpkin. 306
Sweeping the room. Edwin Honig.
  275
"There's a certain button."
  Sally Love Saunders. 358
These are lives. Herbert Morris.
  326
"Throwing his liofe away."
  Josephine Miles. 319
Time to die or fly. Paul Davis.
  228
To live. S. Bradford Williams
  (Jr.). 397
A touch on your sleeve. William
  Stafford. 373
"Touched by my ignorance of
  victory." Michael Robert Pick.
  345
View from a tower. James
  Applewhite. 198
"Watching the immense self
  scattering ocean." Edwin
  Honig. 275
Ways and means. Gerard Malanga.
  310
We both know. James R. Rhodes.
  352
White Sound. Robin Morgan. 325
Why the question of
  reincarnation doesn't concern
  me. Carolyn Stoloff. 376
The life course. Michael
  Akillian. 193
Life cycle of the Pacific
  mermaid. Susan Tichy. 381
The life expectancy of black
  American males. Ray Fleming.
  247
"Life has no meaning without
  you." Michael Robert Pick. 345
The life in common. Jenne
  Andrews. 196
"Life is free you know." Michael
  Robert Pick. 345
Life is what we make of it.
  Robert L. Wilson. 401
"The life of Galileo as it is
  reset." Josephine Miles. 319
A life of intimate fleeing.
  Robert Kelly. 289
Life of the party. Mark Vinz. 387
Life of the Virgin. Roy Marz. 312

The life on film of St. Theresa.
  Andrei Codrescu. 223
Life styles. Marie Daerr
  Boehringer. 210
Life's a funny song. Alice Spohn
  Newton. 332
Life's song. S. Bradford Williams
  (Jr.). 398
Life's work. Connie Hunt. 279
Life, Brevity of
  The broken-field runner through
    age. James Schevill. 360
  So little time. James R. Rhodes.
    352
  "These bricks, moss-covered
    now." Robert A. Sears. 362
  Tragedy's greatest hits. James
    Tate. 379
Life, Conduct of
  Advice to a son. Ernest
    Hemingway. 272
  At home. Sam Fishman. 246
  Bedtime question. Alice Joyce
    Davidson. 227
  Belief. Josephine Miles. 319
  Cast your vote. Alice Joyce
    Davidson. 227
  Ceremonial. Mark Vinz. 387
  Chapter heading. Ernest
    Hemingway. 272
  Charioteer. Erin Jolly. 285
  Coyote lovesong. Gene Anderson.
    195
  Detour. Jacqueline Frank. 248
  Directive. Robert Frost. 250
  Each of us here has fought this
    battle. Haig Khatchadourian.
    292
  El Dorado. Charles Edward Eaton.
    236
  From herewhere? David Wann. 394
  Growing closer. Alice Joyce
    Davidson. 227
  Human. James R. Rhodes. 352
  "I saw you dance with Don
    Carlos." Robert A. Sears. 362
  Involvement. Rose Basile Green.
    265
  A jangling yarn. James Tate. 379
  Landscape with ascet ic. Deborah
    Tall. 378
  Let's. Joan Colby. 224
  Living on the surface. Miller
    Williams. 399
  Madonna of the demolition derby.
    Lyn Lifshin. 303
  Pegleg lookout. William
    Stafford. 373
  Place. James Schevill. 360
  The pool that swims in us. Marge

    Piercy. 346
  Postposterous. Jim Simmerman.
    365
  Puddles on ice. Paul Violi. 388
  Questions. Gerard Malanga. 310
  Reckoning. Anneliese Wagner. 389
  Ritornello. Mitchell Howard. 276
  Sequence toward a beginning.
    Marieve Rugo. 356
  Smoke signals. William Stafford.
    373
  "Someone would say/we are
    responsible." Theta Burke. 218
  Summer lullaby. Robert L.
    Wilson. 401
  Surprise party. Mitchell Howard.
    276
  To be alive be bold. Edwin
    Honig. 275
  To settle awhile. Paul Davis.
    228
  Today, no hour. Norman Andrew
    Kirk. 293
  The tree of life. Connie Hunt.
    279
  View from a balloon. Charles
    Edward Eaton. 236
  What am I to do? Rosa Bogar. 211
  Within our choosing. Alice Joyce
    Davidson. 227
  "Wrote my first poems." Charles
    Olson. 337
  Yea and nay. Mitchell Howard.
    276
  You must change your life.
    Lucien Stryk. 377
"Life/night.". Larry Eigner. 237
Lifeguard longing to ride
  roughshod over subordinates.
  James Magorian. 308
The lifeline. Carolyn Stoloff.
  376
Lifesaving. Sandra McPherson. 317
Lifesaving. David Wagoner. 390
Lifshin, Lyn
  Alone on a blanket. 303
  Another backward stripper
    madonna. 303
  Backwards stripping madonna. 303
  Blood red nail polish madonna.
    303
  Chanukah madonna. 303
  Dove tailed madonna. 303
  The dream of the guilt bird, or
    water. 303
  Goodby madonna. 303
  Gym seal madonna. 303
  Hair. 303
  Head of the state parks police.
    303

The hepplewhite madonna. 303
Hysteria. 303
If you go poking around in my
   journal you deserve the worst.
   303
Jealous madonna. 303
Jealousy. 303
Jelly madonna. 303
July madonna. 303
Madonna anorexia nervosa. 303
Madonna nymphomania. 303
Madonna of the demolition derby.
   303
Madonna who writes ten poems a
   day. 303
Madonna's finger on him. 303
The man who brought the emerald
   mandarins. 303
Men and publishers. 303
The midwest is full of
   vibrators. 303
Minestrone madonna. 303
Mold madonna. 303
Monongahela madonna. 303
Non returnable bottle madonna.
   303
Not letting you see what you
   don't want to. 303
Nuns at a retreat. 303
One morning. 303
Parachute madonna. 303
Pedestal madonna. 303
Poet as a stripper. 303
Push pussy madonna. 303
Pussy madonna. 303
Radiator madonna. 303
Roomates. 303
Saturday. 303
The secret eater. 303
Sheet rock madonna. 303
Shifting for herself madonna.
   303
Slug nmadonna. 303
Soil pipe madonna. 303
Stamp madonna. 303
Stripper madonna. 303
Tin can madonna. 303
With you. 303
The woman who buries. 303
The woman who collects boxes.
   303
Light
   For futures. Josephine Miles.
      319
   "How much could they/flicker."
      Larry Eigner. 237
   The joy of light. Connie Hunt.
      279
   The lighting of the
      streetlights. Josephine Miles.

   319
   Premiere. Josephine Miles. 319
   "Scattered lights." Sally Love
      Saunders. 358
   Spleen: Geneva, New York.
      Marilyn Kallet. 287
The light asks. Carol Frost. 249
The light bearer. Jacques Sollov.
   371
The light in the refrigerator.
   James Magorian. 309
"Light pecks the lilacs..."
   Carolyn Stoloff. 376
"Light signals & mass points."
   Charles Olson. 337
Light year. Josephine Miles. 319
Lighted windows. Robert
   Pawlowski. 341
The lighting of a small fire in
   the grate. Josephine Miles.
   319
The lighting of the streetlights.
   Josephine Miles. 319
Lightning
   Taos lightning. Phillips Kloss.
      294
Like abortion haikus. Stephen
   Todd Booker. 212
Like any great forest. Michael
   Akillian. 193
Like Ester. Stephen Todd Booker.
   212
Like fallen angels. Jocelyn
   Hollis. 274
Like girder haikus. Stephen Todd
   Booker. 212
"Like Mr. Pester acknowledges his
   sinfulness in being" Charles
   Olson. 337
Like now! Josephine B. Moretti.
   324
"Like stores, banks." Larry
   Eigner. 237
Likes and Dislikes
   A priori. David Wann. 394
   Cheeseburger serenade. Paul
      Violi. 388
   Fond. Alberta Turner. 384
   "I don't like." Sally Love
      Saunders. 358
   One for the monk of Montaudon.
      Paul Violi. 388
   Rite for the beautification of
      all beings. John Brandi. 214
   The road. Herbert Morris. 326
   There's someone I know. Jack
      Prelutsky. 348
   What I want. Joan Colby. 224
   "The worlds/likes and dislikes."
      A. Dovichi. 233

Lilacs
  City lilac. Marie Daerr
    Boehringer. 210
Lilacs on Mother's Day. Maurice
  W. Britts. 215
Lilies
  Bounty. Ghita Orth. 339
  Consider the lilies. Cornel
    Lengyel. 302
  Steps taken in a debris of day
    lilies. Charles Edward Eaton.
    236
Limbo. Marieve Rugo. 356
Limerick. Josephine B. Moretti.
  324
Limerick hagiograph. Tom Smith.
  368
Limericks
  Limerick hagiograph. Tom Smith.
    368
  "There was a cold pig from North
    Stowe." Arnold Lobel.
  "There was a fair pig from
    Cohoes" Arnold Lobel. 304
  "There was a fast pig from East
    Flushing." Arnold Lobel. 304
  "There was a fat pig from
    Savannah." Arnold Lobel. 304
  "There was a light pig from
    Montclair." Arnold Lobel. 304
  There was a loud pig. Arnold
    Lobel. 304
  "There was a pale pig from
    Spokane." Arnold Lobel. 304
  "There was a plain pig, far from
    pretty," Arnold Lobel. 304
  There was a poor pig. Arnold
    Lobel. 304
  There was a rich pig. Arnold
    Lobel. 304
  "There was a rude pig from
    Duluth." Arnold Lobel. 304
  "There was a sad pig with a
    tail." Arnold Lobel. 304
  "There was a shy pig by a wall."
    Arnold Lobel. 304
  "There was a sick pig with a
    cold." Arnold Lobel. 304
  "There was a slow pig from
    Decatur." Arnold Lobel. 304
  "There was a small pig who wept
    tears." Arnold Lobel. 304
  "There was a small pig from
    Woonsocket." Arnold Lobel. 304
  "There was a smart pig who was
    able." Arnold Lobel. 304
  "There was a stout pig from Oak
    Ridge." Arnold Lobel. 304
  "There was a strange pig in the
    park." Arnold Lobel. 304

  "There was a tough pig from Pine
    Bluff." Arnold Lobel. 304
  "There was a warm pig from Key
    West." Arnold Lobel. 304
  "There was a wet pig from Fort
    Wayne." Arnold Lobel. 304
  "There was a young pig from
    Schenectady." Arnold Lobel.
    304
  "There was a young pig from
    Chanute." Arnold Lobel. 304
  "There was a young pig who, in
    bed," Arnold Lobel. 304
  "There was a young pig by a
    cradle." Arnold Lobel. 304
  "There was a young pig from
    Moline." Arnold Lobel. 304
  "There was a young pig from
    Nantucket." Arnold Lobel. 304
  "There was an old pig from West
    Wheeling." Arnold Lobel. 304
  "There was an old pig with a
    clock." Arnold Lobel. 304
  "There was an old pig from New
    York." Arnold Lobel. 304
  "There was an old pig in a
    chair." Arnold Lobel. 304
  "There was an old pig with a
    pen." Arnold Lobel. 304
  There was an old pig. Arnold
    Lobel.
Limitation. Marilyn Kallet. 287
Limited service in World War II.
  James Schevill. 360
Limits. Robert Kelly. 289
Limousin. Michael Gizzi. 259
Lincoln, Abraham
  Going for a newspaper. Stephen
    Knauth. 295
Linden Trees
  Lidenbloom. Amy Clampitt. 222
Line storm. Mark Vinz. 387
The **lineaments** of unsatisfied
  desire. Thomas McGrath. 315
Lines for dancers. Edwin Honig.
  275
The **lines** of living. Laura Boss.
  213
Lines on a poet's face. Betty
  Adcock. 192
Lines to a girl 5 days after her
  21st birthday. Ernest
  Hemingway. 272
Lines to a young lady on her
  having very nearly won a
  vogel. Ernest Hemingway. 272
Lines to be read at the casting
  of Scott Fitzgerald... Ernest
  Hemingway. 272
Lines written for June. John F.

183   Lobel, Arnold

Barker. 201
Lines written for Mrs. Hagood.
    John F. Barker. 201
The lingering ghost. Erin Jolly.
    285
Lingering melody. Rose Basile
    Green. 265
Link of faith. Alice Joyce
    Davidson. 227
Lion. X.J. Kennedy. 290
Lion on the frieze of time. Erin
    Jolly. 285
Lion's loss. Rod McKuen. 316
The lion. Jack Prelutsky. 349
Lions
    Lion. X.J. Kennedy. 290
    The lion. Jack Prelutsky. 349
Lips
    Men lips. Wanda Coleman. 225
List. Carolyn Stoloff. 376
Listen. Edwin Honig. 275
Listen to me. Jacques Sollov. 370
The listener to noise and
    silence. James Schevill. 360
Listening in a 1920's Greenwich
    Village bar... James Schevill.
    360
Listening to a brown-eyed man
    play it for somebody else.
    C.D. Wright. 402
Listening to an old man. Evelyn
    Golden. 263
Listening to my son's heart.
    Anthony Petrosky. 344
Litanies. Maria Gillan. 256
Literacy
    My own name. Jeanne Lohmann. 305
(Literary result). Charles Olson.
    337
Littering
    Roadside reflection. Marie Daerr
    Boehringer. 210
Little angel. Jacques Sollov. 371
Little boots. Josephine B.
    Moretti. 324
Little butterfly. Jacques Sollov.
    371
Little Compton. Randy Blasing.
    207
"Little drops of grain alcohol."
    Ernest Hemingway. 272
"Little finger suddenly/not so
    small." Larry Eigner. 237
Little giant. Jacques Sollov. 370
The little hand. John Hawkes. 270
Little Italy. Gerard Malanga. 310
Little Jack. Harlan Usher. 386
A little life in a summer room.
    George Eklund. 238
"Little man in a coal pit." Jan

Ormerod. 338
"The little man, who." Madison
    Morrison. 327
The little mermaid. Deborah Tall.
    378
"Little Mr. Wilson." Ernest
    Hemingway. 272
Little night stories. William
    Stafford. 373
The little official of maybe.
    James Schevill. 360
Little old black historian. James
    A. Emanuel. 239
Little old red schoolhouse.
    Robert L. Wilson. 401
Little one. Jacques Sollov. 370
Little Orphan Annie in black
    nylons. James Magorian. 309
Little Orphan Annie
    Little Orphan Annie in black
    nylons. James Magorian. 309
Little Pend Oreille river. Franz
    Schneider. 361
"Little pig." Jan Ormerod. 338
Little prayer. Alice Joyce
    Davidson. 227
Little Red Riding Hood
    Near grandmother's house. James
    Magorian. 308
"Little son." Michael Robert
    Pick. 345
Little Spokane river: Indian
    paintings. Franz Schneider.
    361
A little yard. Stephen Sandy. 357
Livelihoods of freaks and poets
    of the western world, sels.
    C.D. Wright. 402
The lives of a Bengal lancer.
    Harrison Fisher. 245
Livestock auction. James
    Magorian. 309
"Living by fiction." Rochelle
    DuBois. 234
Living color. Phillips Kloss. 294
Living glass. Sandra McPherson.
    317
Living in a boxcar in San
    Francisco. James Schevill. 360
Living in the other world. Dennis
    Hinrichsen. 273
Living in the tan house. Brenda
    Marie Osbey. 340
Living on the surface. Miller
    Williams. 399
Lizard Pond. Robert A. Sears. 362
The loaded sleeve of Hades.
    Clayton Eshleman. 240
Lobel, Arnold
    "There was a cold pig from North

Stowe."
"There was a fair pig from Cohoes" 304
"There was a fast pig from East Flushing." 304
"There was a fat pig from Savannah." 304
"There was a light pig from Montclair." 304
There was a loud pig. 304
"There was a pale pig from Spokane." 304
"There was a plain pig, far from pretty," 304
There was a poor pig. 304
There was a rich pig. 304
"There was a rude pig from Duluth." 304
"There was a sad pig with a tail." 304
"There was a shy pig by a wall." 304
"There was a sick pig with a cold." 304
"There was a slow pig from Decatur." 304
"There was a small pig who wept tears." 304
"There was a small pig from Woonsocket." 304
"There was a smart pig who was able." 304
"There was a stout pig from Oak Ridge." 304
"There was a strange pig in the park." 304
"There was a tough pig from Pine Bluff." 304
"There was a warm pig from Key West." 304
"There was a wet pig from Fort Wayne." 304
"There was a young pig from Schenectady." 304
"There was a young pig from Chanute." 304
"There was a young pig who, in bed," 304
"There was a young pig by a cradle." 304
"There was a young pig from Moline." 304
"There was a young pig whose delight." 304
"There was a young pig from Nantucket." 304
"There was an old pig from West Wheeling." 304
"There was an old pig with a clock." 304
"There was an old pig from New York." 304
"There was an old pig in a chair." 304
"There was an old pig with a pen." 304
There was an old pig.
"Local boy shines in relief." Larry Moffi. 322
The local genius. Amy Clampitt. 222
Locale. Robert Peters. 343
Location. Josephine Miles. 319
Lockdance. Mitchell Howard. 276
Locus solus. Michael Gizzi. 259
"Locust Street revisited." Michael Robert Pick. 345
"Locust Street, a garage full of beer cans." Michael Robert Pick. 345
Locusts
"Locusts older than alphabets." Carolyn Stoloff. 376
"Locusts older than alphabets." Carolyn Stoloff. 376
Log-rolling contest. James Magorian. 309
Logos. Thomas R. Sleigh. 366
Logos. Miller Williams. 399
Lohmann, Jeanne
The abortion: words for a young woman. 305
After a southern visit. 305
After all these years. 305
All that is necessary. 305
Amicus Curiae. 305
At the museum. 305
Beginning over. 305
Bluejays. 305
Breaking the spell. 305
Calling the bears. 305
Coming into different country. 305
Coping with the news. 305
The dancer. 305
Dinner party. 305
Discernment. 305
Easy to remember. 305
Fantasy after a science report. 305
For Louise. 305
From the shore. 305
Gardens. 305
Going to the orchard. 305
Hearing. 305
Hide and seek. 305
His neighbor talks of Monet. 305
Hospital sequence. 305
I never was a wary one. 305
In the dark. 305

In the Medici Chapels. 305
In this story. 305
Lady on a bus. 305
Letter from Cremona. 305
Looking for alligators. 305
Lost. 305
Making angels in Chicago. 305
The man who throws knives at the
  trees. 305
Moving. 305
My own name. 305
Natural history museum. 305
No better words. 305
Nothing so wise. 305
Old country. 305
The old men visit. 305
Patterns in the sky. 305
Picking plums. 305
Pussywillows: a city poem. 305
Rain forest. 305
Rescuing something. 305
Shell beach. 305
Snorth poem, long story. 305
Sidewalk cafe. 305
Single in our double bed. 305
Soaring. 305
A song for the queen. 305
Steadying the lanscape. 305
Teshuvah. 305
This morning. 305
Travel plan. 305
The truth is. 305
Variations. 305
Village cemetery Sunday morning.
  305
Watercolor. 305
What I need to hear. 305
Lollipop. Sally Love Saunders.
  358
Lone. Josephine Miles. 319
Lone girl at the bus stop. Susan
  Stock. 375
Loneliness
  After leaving you. Eileen
    Silver-Lillywite. 364
  Alone. Martha Janssen. 283
  Alone (to-). Edgar Allan Poe.
    347
  Another poem about colored
    leaves. Michael Akillian. 193
  Autumn words. Maria Gillan. 256
  Awakening. Maria Gillan. 256
  The bird flew off. Elsa Gidlow.
    254
  Charlatan. Erin Jolly. 285
  Conjure. Josephine Miles. 319
  The days are long. Rachel A.
    Hazen. 271
  Dying out. James L. White. 396
  Elloree. Larry Moffi. 322

The feast. Haig Khatchadourian.
  292
Floodlight. Erin Jolly. 285
The flying people. Stephen
  Knauth. 295
Fog. John Reed. 350
Gym seal madonna. Lyn Lifshin.
  303
The hawk's backyard. Rod McKuen.
  316
In a darkened corridor. Rachel
  A. Hazen. 271
The language orphan. Clayton
  Eshleman. 240
The life in common. Jenne
  Andrews. 196
Lonely heart and heavy. Robert
  L. Wilson. 401
The lonely wall. Rachel A.
  Hazen. 271
Lonely without reason. Mitchell
  Howard. 276
Looking across the river.
  William Stafford. 373
Lost conquest. Norman Andrew
  Kirk. 293
Love, let me not hunger. Rod
  McKuen. 316
Many summers ago. Rod McKuen.
  316
Marcus Nathaniel Simpson: his
  voice. Anthony Petrosky. 344
Mirrors at night. John Godfrey.
  260
Narcissus. James R. Rhodes. 352
Night enters. Marilyn Kallet.
  287
No return address. Dave Smith.
  367
Nowhere is a lonely, lonely
  place. Maurice W. Britts. 215
The Olive Mountain coyote pack.
  Gene Anderson. 195
Overweight. James L. White. 396
A room, loneliness. Norman
  Andrew Kirk. 293
Saturday night. May Miller. 320
Single in our double bed. Jeanne
  Lohmann. 305
Sky coyote loses the year's
  gambling game for rain. Gene
  Anderson. 195
Song ("Sweet beast, I have gone
  prowling.") W.D. (William De
  Witt) Snodgrass. 369
Spleen. Marilyn Kallet. 287
Spotlight. Rachel A. Hazen. 271
Survival. Ernest Tedlock. 380
"There is a force of loneliness
  around my heart." Da Free

John. 284

To reach me. Gary Margolis. 311

Transition. Connie Hunt. 279

Ultimate aloneness. Elsa Gidlow. 254

Urban Ode. Sandra McPherson. 317

Variations. Jeanne Lohmann. 305

The voyeur directs an ending. Larry Moffi. 322

When lonely. Carolyn Stoloff. 376

When the bars close. Rod McKuen. 318

Why in Toronto? Marge Piercy. 346

Woman untouched. Margaret Key Biggs. 205

You said. Debra Bruce. 216

Lonely heart and heavy. Robert L. Wilson. 401

The lonely shadow. Rachel A. Hazen. 271

The lonely wall. Rachel A. Hazen. 271

Lonely without reason. Mitchell Howard. 276

Long distance. Laura Boss. 213

Long distance bickering (day rate) Jim Simmerman. 365

A long distance. Robin Becker. 202

The long geese. Robert Pawlowski. 341

Long gone. Jack Prelutsky. 349

"Long roads shorten time." Michael Robert Pick. 345

The long waiting. Haig Khatchadourian. 292

"Long years ago." Theta Burke. 218

Longing. Miriam Goodman. 264

Longing

After waking from my nap. Christopher Bursk. 219

Come. Marilyn Kallet. 287

Drums and believers. Andrei Codrescu. 223

Eternal friendship. Jacques Sollov. 371

If I had a crown. Jacques Sollov. 370

In the Dakotas. Stephen Sandy. 357

Interruptions. James Tate. 379

Letter from New Hampshire. Edwin Honig. 275

Longing. Miriam Goodman. 264

Luminous jewel. Jacques Sollov. 370

Papageno. W.D. (William De Witt)

Snodgrass. 369

"So many times." Robert A. Sears. 362

Song like a thin wire. Marge Piercy. 346

"Today I started lunching in the cheater's corner." Robert A. Sears. 362

A variety show. Rachel A. Hazen. 271

The world that lives in me. Jacques Sollov. 370

Yearning. Deborah Tall. 378

"Look at him." A. Dovichi. 233

Look at us. Ruth Lisa Schechter. 359

Look away/look away. Stephen Todd Booker. 212

Look through my window. James R. Rhodes. 352

Lookin' for gas at the youth guidance center. James Schevill. 360

Looking. Robert Kelly. 289

Looking across the river. William Stafford. 373

Looking at old tombstones in a New England graveyard. James Schevill. 360

Looking at posters. Joan Colby. 224

Looking at wealth in Newport. James Schevill. 360

Looking for alligators. Jeanne Lohmann. 305

Looking for buttons. Carolyn Stoloff. 376

Looking for the lumberjack. Jim Everhard. 241

Looking on. Stephen Sandy. 357

"Looking over toward Tamalpais." Josephine Miles. 319

Looking sideways. Maria Gillan. 256

Looking through trees into holes. Carolyn Stoloff. 376

Looking up and beyond. William Oandasan. 335

Looking west to China. Elsa Gidlow. 254

The lookout's report. Cornel Lengyel. 302

Looks from money. Andrei Codrescu. 223

Loons

Loons mating. David Wagoner. 390

A remarkable exhibition. David Wagoner. 390

Twoborn (...prelude). Rokwaho. 355

Loons mating. David Wagoner. 390
"Lord I believe. Help me in my
    unbelief." Christopher Bursk.
    219
'The Lord is My Shepherd' James
    R. Rhodes. 352
Lord thank you. Jacques Sollov.
    371
The Lord's Prayer paraphrased.
    Evelyn Golden. 263
For Lorine Niedecker in heaven.
    Ralph J., Jr. Mills. 321
Lorn. Erin Jolly. 285
Los Angeles
    Angel baby. Wanda Coleman. 225
    Angels. Anthony Petrosky. 344
    Near Olympic. Timothy Steele.
    374
    Prisoner of Los Angeles (2).
    Wanda Coleman. 225
Los Ninos. George Eklund. 238
Loser. Josephine Miles. 319
Losing tickets underfoot. Stephen
    Todd Booker. 212
The losing. Sam Fishman. 246
Loss
    Absence. Anneliese Wagner. 389
    Cutting our losses. Steve Kowit.
    298, 299
    "Fear is for the multitude."
    James Torio. 281
    The happiest day. Edgar Allan
    Poe. 347
    The house next door. Robert L.
    Wilson. 401
    Lion's loss. Rod McKuen. 316
    The loss. Joyce Carol Oates. 336
    Losses. Mitchell Howard. 276
    The marsh. W.D. (William De
    Witt) Snodgrass. 369
    Mrs. Simmons to Astolfo. Roy
    Marz. 312
    Three loser's poems. Marge
    Piercy. 346
    To-- ("Should me early life
    seem"). Edgar Allan Poe. 347
    Victim. Martha Janssen. 283
The loss. Joyce Carol Oates. 336
Losses. Mitchell Howard. 276
Lost. Jeanne Lohmann. 305
The lost advent. Royal Murdoch.
    330
The lost colony. John Yau. 404
Lost conquest. Norman Andrew
    Kirk. 293
A lost friend. Ernest Tedlock.
    380
"Lost from the loss of her dagger
    heisted." Charles Olson. 337
The lost garden. Cornel Lengyel.

302
Lost in Ladispoli. Miller
    Williams. 399
Lost patterns. Alice Spohn
    Newton. 333
Lost sister. Cathy Song. 372
Lot (Bible)
    Salt. James R. Rhodes. 352
Lottery ticket. James Magorian.
    308
Loudoun. John F. Barker. 201
Lourdes. Bill Knott. 296
Lousy in center field. James
    Tate. 379
Love. Rochelle DuBois. 234
Love. R. Buckminster Fuller. 251
Love. Evelyn Golden. 263
Love. Marilyn Kallet. 287
Love
    After the letter. Edwin Honig.
    275
    Alighting. Alice Joyce Davidson.
    227
    All-the heart's song. Kirk
    Lumpkin. 306
    Anniversary song. Phyllis A.
    Tickle. 382
    Anticipating murder. Wanda
    Coleman. 225
    "As I love you." Michael Robert
    Pick. 345
    "As I study at." Madison
    Morrison. 327
    As usual. Elsa Gidlow. 254
    As we sit in the garden, early
    and late. Cynthia Grenfell.
    266
    At Mergellina. Anne Bailie. 199
    At night. Barry Wallenstein. 393
    Attempting to make lyrics of my
    lovers. Carolyn Stoloff. 376
    Aureole. James R. Rhodes. 352
    Bachelor belles. Harrison
    Fisher. 245
    The back pockets of love. Marge
    Piercy. 346
    Beauties. Harrison Fisher. 245
    Beautiful stranger. Jacques
    Sollov. 370
    Bewitched visit. Elsa Gidlow.
    254
    The bird is God. Roy Marz. 312
    A blue chicken. Mary Gilliland.
    257
    "The boats' lights in the
    dawn..." Charles Olson. 337
    Bridge builder. Marie Daerr
    Boehringer. 210
    In brittle molds of love. John
    Godfrey. 260

By starlight. David Wagoner. 390
The cannibal. Charles Edward
   Eaton. 236
Catch you catch me not. James R.
   Rhodes. 352
Celebration with geraniums.
   Miriam Goodman. 264
Chance. Elsa Gidlow. 254
Changeling. Erin Jolly. 285
Chinese villanelle. John Yau.
   404
Chips. May Miller. 320
Chorus for Neruda #1. Thomas
   McGrath. 315
Colorado. Robert Kelly. 289
Composed. Ernesto Galarza. 252
Constant tenderness. Ray
   Fleming. 247
Contented. Rosa Bogar. 211
The dark face of love. Elsa
   Gidlow. 254
Detecting love. Joan Colby. 224
The diary is open at two
   o'clock. Kenneth Koch. 297
Digging in. Marge Piercy. 346
Disarmed. Josephine Miles. 319
The disciple. Roy Marz. 312
Disparities. Joan Colby. 224
The divine right of kings. Edgar
   Allan Poe. 347
Don Juan in autumn. Charles
   Edward Eaton. 236
"Don't worry, woman." Michael
   Robert Pick. 345
Driftwood moments. Maria Gillan.
   256
During the war. Gary Margolis.
   311
Each. James R. Rhodes. 352
Each midsummer, love. Mary
   Gilliland. 257
Eden. Michael Gizzi. 259
Elastic romance. Rochelle
   DuBois. 234
Endangered species. Joan Colby.
   224
Ensinanca. Gayl Jones. 286
Ever onward. Alice Spohn Newton.
   332
Eyelines. Colette Inez. 280
(Face) (autumn) (en face). Bill
   Knott. 296
The fall of a sparrow. Robin
   Morgan. 325
Finger touching magic. Alice
   Spohn Newton. 332
Fingers. George Eklund. 238
First love. Jacques Sollov. 370
For a woman sitting by a creek.
   David Wagoner. 390

For C. Edwin Honig. 275
For him. Royal Murdoch. 330
For Margot. Edwin Honig. 275
Forest years. Cornel Lengyel.
   302
The fountain. Sister Maura. 313
Garden of my life. Jacques
   Sollov. 370
Getting away. David Wagoner. 390
Great expectations. Robin
   Becker. 202
A guide to the field. David
   Wagoner. 390
The harrowing of heaven. Robin
   Morgan. 325
Her diary. James A. Emanuel. 239
Hers. John Godfrey. 260
Hidden desire. Jacques Sollov.
   370
Honorarium. Erin Jolly. 285
"How can one/who has always
   heard." Theta Burke. 218
How gentle. Joyce Carol Oates.
   336
I care. Rosa Bogar. 211
I dream. Jacques Sollov. 370
"I feel your presence." Michael
   Robert Pick. 345
I haven't been able to get
   anything done since I met you.
   Debra Bruce. 216
"I hunger for you." Michael
   Robert Pick. 345
I love you more than applesauce.
   Jack Prelutsky. 348
I need you. Edwin Honig. 275
I want to be your everything.
   Jacques Sollov. 371
I want to know you. Rosa Bogar.
   211
I'm off'n wild wimmen. Ernest
   Hemingway. 272
If. Rosa Bogar. 211
If there were only this music.
   Jenne Andrews. 196
In love. David Wagoner. 390
In which she begs (like
   everybody else) that love may
   last. Marge Piercy. 346
Instructions. Rod McKuen. 316
Invisible splendor. Alice Spohn
   Newton. 332
Irish love. Rose Basile Green.
   265
Is she found? Elsa Gidlow. 254
The islander. Louise Gluck. 259A
"It's that one understood
   barely." Rochelle DuBois. 234
The Italian lesson. Roy Marz.
   312

Jelly Jill loves Weasel Will.
  Jack Prelutsky. 348
A key to common lethal fungi.
  Marge Piercy. 346
Languages. Keith Wilson. 400
Lesson. Bill Knott. 296
Limousin. Michael Gizzi. 259
Little angel. Jacques Sollov.
  371
Love. Marilyn Kallet. 287
Love me or not. Carolyn Stoloff.
  376
Love poem (for Alice). Andrei
  Codrescu. 223
Love poem after years without
  remorse. Dennis Hinrichsen.
  273
Love power. Alice Joyce
  Davidson. 227
"Love sees." Theta Burke. 218
Love song. Elsa Gidlow. 254
Love things. Andrei Codrescu.
  223
Love's acolyte. Elsa Gidlow. 254
Lover will you come? Rosa Bogar.
  211
Lovers, do not think of this.
  James A. Emanuel. 239
The lovers. Marieve Rugo. 356
The lovers. Greg Kuzma. 300
The loving. Sam Fishman. 246
Making hay. Deborah Tall. 378
The man who often turned to
  stone. Harry Humes. 278
Matter of Fact. Josephine Miles.
  319
Memo from the cave. Louise
  Gluck. 259A
Midsummer rites. Eve Triem. 383
More or less. Connie Hunt. 279
More sensuous than these. Paul
  Davis. 228
Morning poem. Robin Becker. 202
Musical. Ernesto Galarza. 252
My love brings flowers. Wanda
  Coleman. 225
My love is asleep. Edwin Honig.
  275
"My loved one sits upon my
  knee." Da Free John. 284
The name I call you. Marge
  Piercy. 346
Natural selection. Deborah Tall.
  378
The net. Anneliese Wagner. 389
Nightingale. Jacques Sollov. 370
Noon. Rochelle DuBois. 234
Not asking for love. Elsa
  Gidlow. 254
Not forever. Norman Andrew Kirk.

293
Not the darkness. Barry
  Wallenstein. 393
Of forbidden love. Elsa Gidlow.
  254
"Oh I love you, woman." Michael
  Robert Pick. 345
On the island. Miriam Goodman.
  264
On the warm side. Ernest
  Tedlock. 380
Our blindness. David Wagoner.
  390
Our eyes have seen the glory.
  Ernesto Galarza. 252
Pass me not. Rosa Bogar. 211
Perfect love. Alice Joyce
  Davidson. 227
The permission. Bill Knott. 296
Philosophy. Elsa Gidlow. 254
Planting H-bombs on the moon.
  Mitchell Howard. 276
A plea. Maurice W. Britts. 215
Poem ("Mezzanines of nightfall
  clashing like.") John Godfrey.
  260
Pomegranate. Erin Jolly. 285
Praying mantis. Charles Edward
  Eaton. 236
Prologue. Cynthia Grenfell. 266
The raid. Charles Edward Eaton.
  236
Real love. Jacques Sollov. 370
Reasons why. Wanda Coleman. 225
Red rose. Jacques Sollov. 371
Region of no birds. Elsa Gidlow.
  254
Repeal. Erin Jolly. 285
Reunion. Jenne Andrews. 196
The ruining of the work. Robin
  Morgan. 325
Sailing. John Godfrey. 260
Seasons of love. Alice Joyce
  Davidson. 227
Secrets. Martha Janssen. 283
Serenade ("So sweet the hour -
  so calm the hour"). Edgar
  Allan Poe. 347
Setting the pace. Maurice W.
  Britts. 215
Shadow pictures. Maria Gillan.
  256
Sharon. Maurice W. Britts. 215
She thinks of love, fr. The day
  of the body. Carol Frost. 249
6:50 PM. The phone rings. It's
  him S. Wanda Coleman. 225
Sleeping alone. David Wagoner.
  390
Sleeping nude. Charles Edward

Eaton. 236
Snapshots of love. Rochelle
    DuBois. 234
Sobered. Elsa Gidlow. 254
Sometimes we say it is love.
    Carol Frost. 249
"Somewhere/in some yesterday."
    Theta Burke. 218
Song for Guenevere. Elsa Gidlow.
    254
The song. David Wagoner. 390
Space. Joan Colby. 224
Strange lady. Maurice W. Britts.
    215
Studies from life. Robin Becker.
    202
Surrender. Marc Kaminsky. 288
Targets. Roy Marz. 312
That moment. David Wagoner. 390
These many loves. Alice Spohn
    Newton. 332
Thinking of her. Sam Fishman.
    246
Those I have loved. Elsa Gidlow.
    254
"Those who despise me love me in
    secret." Da Free John. 284
To begin. Donald Revell. 351
To Celia, beyond the yachts.
    Dave Smith. 367
To love. S. Bradford Williams
    (Jr.). 397
To--("I would not lord it o'er
    thy heart"). Edgar Allan Poe.
    347
To Elizabeth (To F-s O-d). Edgar
    Allan Poe. 347
Today. Alice Joyce Davidson. 227
Together again. Rosa Bogar. 211
Token. Erin Jolly. 285
Toulouse - jocs florals. Michael
    Gizzi. 259
Tracing. James R. Rhodes. 352
Ulalume - a ballad. Edgar Allan
    Poe. 347
Unless love die. Edwin Honig.
    275
Upon cutting a flower for my
    mistress. Robert Pawlowski.
    341
Vermont/January. Robin Becker.
    202
Walking together, ducking
    branches. Anneliese Wagner.
    389
Walking with the Lord. Jacques
    Sollov. 371
The wanderer to his heart's
    desire. John Reed. 350
Wave of unreason. Erin Jolly.

285
The way we love. Rose Basile
    Green. 265
The ways of love. Alice Joyce
    Davidson. 227
"We've weathered many storms."
    Michael Robert Pick. 345
What changes, my love. Edwin
    Honig. 275
"When I was lost and needed
    growth for life." Michael
    Robert Pick. 345
"When I'm lost and alone." Theta
    Burke. 218
When you find love. Alice Joyce
    Davidson. 227
Where are the lovers? Ray
    Fleming. 247
Where love is still. Elsa
    Gidlow. 254
White dove. Jacques Sollov. 370
Who will listen. Connie Hunt.
    279
Why do I love you? Maurice W.
    Britts. 215
The winch. Charles Edward Eaton.
    236
"With a heavy heart." Theta
    Burke. 218
"With no love to feel." Theta
    Burke. 218
Without love. Edwin Honig. 275
The woman in the woods. Phillips
    Kloss. 294
Woman's dream of man thinking of
    his woman. Tefke Goldberger.
    262
World without end: a Japanese
    screen. Charles Edward Eaton.
    236
Your fantastic outlines. Andrei
    Codrescu. 223
"Your love." Theta Burke. 218
Love - Plaints and Protests
    "Once upon a time." Sally Love
        Saunders. 358
Love
    "And did you know." Robert A.
        Sears. 362
    "At our best we did outrageous
        things." Robert A. Sears. 362
    The bestowal. John Hawkes. 270
    The drought. Eileen
        Silver-Lillywite. 364
    Implications. Rachel A. Hazen.
        271
    "It wasn't that." Robert A.
        Sears. 362
    My idol. Rachel A. Hazen. 271
    My new house. Rachel A. Hazen.

271
"Of course there was something
    impious." Robert A. Sears. 362
"Our love began skin-deep."
    Robert A. Sears. 362
The playing. Rachel A. Hazen.
    271
Profane desert. John Hawkes. 270
Rain. Joy Harjo. 269
Runaways. Eileen
    Silver-Lillywite. 364
A song ("When a man loves a
    woman.") David Shapiro. 363
Swarming into autumn. Eileen
    Silver-Lillywite. 364
"A swift current." Sally Love
    Saunders. 358
Those that dance to the music.
    Rachel A. Hazen. 271
Two horses. Joy Harjo. 269
The whistling woo. Rachel A.
    Hazen. 271
"You're a large wooden treasure
    chest." Sally Love Saunders.
    358
"Your love." Sally Love
    Saunders. 358

Love = Nature (of)
Advice to the lovelorn. Cornel
    Lengyel. 302
After-hours acrobatics. Rod
    McKuen. 316
Aim. Josephine Miles. 319
Anomaly. Elsa Gidlow. 254
At the same time. James R.
    Rhodes. 352
City. Josephine Miles. 319
"Concrete actions." Theta Burke.
    218
Earth wisdom: two sonnets in an
    early mode. Elsa Gidlow. 254
The final falling. James R.
    Rhodes. 352
For Louise. Jeanne Lohmann. 305
From the moving circle. May
    Miller. 320
The geisha. Rochelle DuBois. 234
"Learning widsom." Rochelle
    DuBois. 234
Letter from a shipwrecked
    sailor. Kirk Lumpkin. 306
Lifesaving. Sandra McPherson.
    317
Love. Rochelle DuBois. 234
Love. R. Buckminster Fuller. 251
Love. Evelyn Golden. 263
"Love at a distance can mean."
    Josephine Miles. 319
Love is laziness. Roy Marz. 312
Love is never silent. Ruth Lisa

Schechter. 359
Love on the Cape. May Miller.
    320
Love's confusing. Rachel A.
    Hazen. 271
"Love/once felt." Theta Burke.
    218
Magic secret. Jacques Sollov.
    370
Old fashioned & timeworn.
    Rochelle DuBois. 234
On players unknown. Cornel
    Lengyel. 302
The robot lover. Rochelle
    DuBois. 234
The salon of famouse babies.
    Irving Feldman. 242
Sometimes. Thomas McGrath. 315
What is love? Maurice W. Britts.
    215
When. Gary Margolis. 311
A white dress. Gerard Malanga.
    310

Love = Plaints and Protests
After work. Wanda Coleman. 225
"All of the fine mist from our
    soles." Sally Love Saunders.
    358
"An almost empty tube." Sally
    Love Saunders. 358
Altitude. Susan Tichy. 381
Anatomy of a mirror. Anne
    Bailie. 199
The archer. Robert Kelly. 289
The artist. Elsa Gidlow. 254
Betrayal. Joyce Carol Oates. 336
Black-ass poem after talking to
    Pamela Churchill. Ernest
    Hemingway. 272
Blue song sung in room of torrid
    goodbyes. Wanda Coleman. 225
Burglars. Wanda Coleman. 225
Burglary. Phyllis A. Tickle. 382
Check-out. Joan Colby. 224
Diatribe. Erin Jolly. 285
'Do you love me?' Edwin Honig.
    275
Dry pump. Sally Love Saunders.
    358
Dumb love. James Schevill. 360
Dying of it. Carolyn Stoloff.
    376
Enemy. Jim Everhard. 241
Fanny. Edgar Allan Poe. 347
Fear. Anne Bailie. 199
Fear of love. Debra Bruce. 216
For now. Laura Boss. 213
Fossils in the sand. Rochelle
    DuBois. 234
Heartbreak. Barry Wallenstein.

393
Hesitate to call. Louise Gluck.
259A
High blood pressure. Gene
Anderson. 195
I'm squeezed somewhere in his
appointment book. Laura Boss.
213
If you go away. Rod McKuen. 316
Irreciprocate. Royal Murdoch.
330
It breaks. Marge Piercy. 346
Knots. Jim Everhard. 241
Labor day. Louise Gluck. 259A
The last tie. Jacques Sollov.
371
A letter not to deliver. William
Stafford. 373
Limits. Robert Kelly. 289
The lost advent. Royal Murdoch.
330
Love peon. John Godfrey. 260
Love tears the rind. Marilyn
Kallet. 287
Man. Rochelle DuBois. 234
Memorandum. Rod McKuen. 316
Mirage. Jacques Sollov. 371
Moot. Wanda Coleman. 225
More guilt. Bill Knott. 296
"Most of you you keep." Sally
Love Saunders. 358
Motion. Joy Harjo. 269
My heart is bleeding. Jacques
Sollov. 371
"My love has deep hurts." Sally
Love Saunders. 358
"My love soars." Sally Love
Saunders. 358
"My love the golden moon." Sally
Love Saunders. 358
Nothing's song. Rachel A. Hazen.
271
Older men. Martha Janssen. 283
Ophelia's last soliloquy. Anne
Bailie. 199
"Our relationship is." Sally
Love Saunders. 358
Phone call at 1 am. Robin
Becker. 202
Police woman. Jacques Sollov.
370
Princess. Martha Janssen. 283
Protocol. Erin Jolly. 285
Sauna. Susan Tichy. 381
Smitten. Kirk Lumpkin. 306
So many others. Rod McKuen. 316
Such sweet sorrow. Royal
Murdoch. 330
"The sweetness of breath."
Michael Robert Pick. 345

This and that. James Wright. 403
The thrall. Royal Murdoch. 330
Tonight is the coldest night of
the year. Laura Boss. 213
Turn on. Laura Boss. 213
Unpitying Aphrodite. Elsa
Gidlow. 254
We are so far apart. Rosa Bogar.
211
Weight of days. Colette Inez.
280
When love becomes a stranger.
Elsa Gidlow. 254
When love leaves. Sam Fishman.
246
Where nothing grows. Marge
Piercy. 346
Worshipping Kali in the San
Bernardino Mountains. Gene
Anderson. 195
Your phone call at 8a.m. Joy
Harjo. 269
Love = Wedded. See Marriage

Love a peacock. Elsa Gidlow. 254
Love Affairs
After all these years. Jeanne
Lohmann. 305
Be my muse. Kirk Lumpkin. 306
Black is the color. Roy Marz.
312
By rote. Rod McKuen. 316
"Dear Frank, here is a poem."
Josephine Miles. 319
Dove tailed madonna. Lyn
Lifshin. 303
If the cardinals were like us.
Sandra McPherson. 317
The kingfisher. Amy Clampitt.
222
The last night and morning. Kirk
Lumpkin. 306
Love poem (tentative title).
Gerard Malanga. 310
Midweek Sunday. Rod McKuen. 316
Nikki. Rod McKuen. 316
Riddle. Josephine Miles. 319
Shell beach. Jeanne Lohmann. 305
So clear the flight. May Miller.
320
Two come to mind. Gary Margolis.
311
The undead: a pentacle of
seasons. Robin Morgan. 325
Voyage to last August. Roy Marz.
312
Love and the father. Ernest
Tedlock. 380
"Love at a distance can mean."
Josephine Miles. 319

Love at sea. John Reed. 350
Love belongs to the north. Thomas McGrath. 315
Love blows in the spring. Dave Smith. 367
Love death. Tom Smith. 368
Love glow. Alice Joyce Davidson. 227
Love in age. Elsa Gidlow. 254
Love is laziness. Roy Marz. 312
Love is never silent. Ruth Lisa Schechter. 359
Love knife. John Godfrey. 260
Love letter. Eileen Silver-Lillywite. 364
Love me. George Eklund. 238
Love me or not. Carolyn Stoloff. 376
Love motiff: a girl's song. Keith Wilson. 400
The love of a coat. Andrei Codrescu. 223
The love of horses. Jenne Andrews. 196
Love on the Cape. May Miller. 320
Love on the farm. Jenne Andrews. 196
Love peon. John Godfrey. 260
Love poem. Jacqueline Frank. 248
Love poem. Haig Khatchadourian. 292
Love poem. Greg Kuzma. 300
Love poem (for Alice). Andrei Codrescu. 223
Love poem (tentative title) Gerard Malanga. 310
Love poem after years without remorse. Dennis Hinrichsen. 273
A love poem, of sorts. Gerard Malanga. 310
Love power. Alice Joyce Davidson. 227
"Love sees." Theta Burke. 218
Love simmers the stew of the dead. Andrei Codrescu. 223
Love song. Alice Joyce Davidson. 227
Love song. Elsa Gidlow. 254
Love song: winter. Everett A. Gillis. 258
Love tears the rind. Marilyn Kallet. 287
Love the letters. Wanda Coleman. 225
Love theme from 'The mummy's kiss meets Dracula.' Mitchell Howard. 276
Love things. Andrei Codrescu. 223
Love thought. Jacques Sollov. 370

Love's acolyte. Elsa Gidlow. 254
Love's confusing. Rachel A. Hazen. 271
Love's song. S. Bradford Williams (Jr.). 398
Love's yin-yang of days. James R. Rhodes. 352
Love, do not shun the dark gargoyle. James Schevill. 360
Love, let me not hunger. Rod McKuen. 316
"Love/once felt." Theta Burke. 218
Lovedeath, sels. Tom Smith. 368
Lovejoy, Elijah Parish
    At the church of Elijah Lovejoy. Paul Davis. 228
Lover will you come? Rosa Bogar. 211
"Lovers should take time from the misery." Michael Robert Pick. 345
Lovers, do not think of this. James A. Emanuel. 239
The lovers. Marieve Rugo. 356
The lovers. Greg Kuzma. 300
Loving gentle, loving strong. Alice Joyce Davidson. 227
Loving heart. Alice Joyce Davidson. 227
The loving. Sam Fishman. 246
"Lovingly I stow the car." Madison Morrison. 327
Low. Larry Eigner. 237
Lowell, Robert (about)
    Robert Lowell is dead. Greg Kuzma. 300
Lowenfels, Walter
    Other snapshots. Ruth Lisa Schechter. 359
Lubbock tune. Gene Detro. 230
Lucifer alone. Josephine Miles. 319
Lucifer. See Satan

Luck. Eileen Silver-Lillywite. 364
Luck
    For luck. Anthony Petrosky. 344
    Luck. Eileen Silver-Lillywite. 364
    The prudence of Nan Corbett. Alberta Turner. 384
Lucky with woods. Robert Gibb. 253
Luctor et emergo. Tefke Goldberger. 262
Lucy at dusk. Phyllis A. Tickle. 382
The Lucy poems, sels. Phyllis A.

Tickle. 382
Lucy Robinson. Robert Peters. 343
Lucy, Tennessee
  All Hallows in Lucy. Phyllis A.
    Tickle. 382
  Lucy at dusk. Phyllis A. Tickle.
    382
  Michaelmas in Lucy, TN. Phyllis
    A. Tickle. 382
A lull in battle. A. Dovichi. 233
Lull-a-baby. Alice Joyce
  Davidson. 227
Lulla - "Buy!"...'Bye!' Harlan
  Usher. 386
Lullabies
  Circadian. Frances Mayes. 314
  Cradle song. Cornel Lengyel. 302
  Lull-a-baby. Alice Joyce
    Davidson. 227
  Lullaby of the wind. Alice Spohn
    Newton. 332
  Now sings the prairie. Alice
    Spohn Newton. 332
  A part of forever. Alice Spohn
    Newton. 332
Lullaby ("Bellying out in the
  full sail of dream.") Thomas
  R. Sleigh. 366
Lullaby ("Sweet love,
  everything"). Steve Kowit. 299
Lullaby of the wind. Alice Spohn
  Newton. 332
The **lumber** mill fire. James
  Applewhite. 198
Lumbering and Lumbermen
  The ax-helve. Robert Frost. 250
  Axetime autumn. Scott Chisholm.
    221
  'Out, out -.' Robert Frost. 250
Luminous jewel. Jacques Sollov.
  370
Lumpkin, Kirk
  All-the heart's song. 306
  Be my muse. 306
  Bust lust on the bus or horny on
    muni. 306
  Co-hereing. 306
  Condensing exaltation mantra.
    306
  Contorted light. 306
  Dancing fills us with exquisite
    emptiness. 306
  Entering experience. 306
  For Ron McKernan. 306
  Go from regret to the magic
    worlds. 306
  I want you. 306
  Kirk. 306
  The last night and morning. 306
  Letter from a shipwrecked

    sailor. 306
  Marriage song. 306
  Monoculture. 306
  Playin' jazz. 306
  The pledge of a human animal, of
    a bloody smiling fool. 306
  Recycle. 306
  The seven lakes of Band-I-Amir.
    306
  Simply marvelous. 306
  Smitten. 306
  Swearing. 306
  Tears of white jade. 306
  Untitled: "Our behavior is
    redundant nonadaptive" 306
  Untitled: "walking up/down
    mountains" 306
  Untitled:"In the place that is
    my self" 306
  Untitled:"Is it my art" 306
  Untitled:"Love the questions"
    306
  Vernal equinox. 306
  Verse/re-verse mantra. 306
  The voice. 306
  War is a wonderful thing. 306
  We, the churches. 306
  The wild creatures of my
    childhood. 306
  Winter solstice-Christ mass
    poem. 306
Lunch
  Interlude. Josephine Miles. 319
Lunch at the desk with the news.
  Miriam Goodman. 264
Luncheon. Josephine Miles. 319
Luncheon 2 Josephine Miles. 319
"The **lunching/art** world." Madison
  Morrison. 327
Luni. Robert A. Sears. 362
The **lure** and the call, sels.
  Robert A. Sears. 362
Lurid confessions. Steve Kowit.
  298, 299
Lust. David Wann. 394
Lust
  Cloud of unknowing. Elsa Gidlow.
    254
  From Malay. David Shapiro. 363
  "In the purple and." Madison
    Morrison. 327
  Lust. David Wann. 394
  Orphee. Robert Kelly. 289
  The reading. Wanda Coleman. 225
  Stage sounds. Norman Andrew
    Kirk. 293
  Terror hiding in glossy sexy
    magazines. Mitchell Howard.
    276
  The wanting. Sam Fishman. 246

Womb and city. Andrei Codrescu. 223

"Women aren't supposed." Sally Love Saunders. 358

Lux, Thomas
Empty pitchforks. 307
The great books of the dead. 307
Is true that you get born dumb and bald. 307
It happened that my uncle liked to take my hand in his. 307
It thinks. 307
Its edges audible. 307
On resumption of the military draft. 307
Pedestrian. 307
Tarantulas on the lifebuoy. 307

Luxemburg, Rosa
Reverse. Andrei Codrescu. 223

Luxor. Betty Adcock. 192

Lycanthropy in South Pasadena. Steve Kowit. 299

Lying in sadness. James L. White. 396

Lying on my coat. Susan Tichy. 381

Lynched. Stephen Todd Booker. 212

Lynn, Massachusetts
The dream life of a coffin factory in Lynn, Massachusetts. John Yau. 404

Lyons, France
Philopolis. Royal Murdoch. 330

Lyric. Josephine Miles. 319

M'sai. Wanda Coleman. 225

M-L/T. Albert Goldbarth. 261

Ma on her ninetieth birthday. Sam Fishman. 246

Ma, your voice. Maria Gillan. 256

The machete woman. Gayl Jones. 286

Machetes. J.W. Rivers. 354

Machettes, sels. J.W. Rivers. 354

The machine stop. Susan Stock. 375

Machines. Lucien Stryk. 377

Machines. Phillips Kloss. 294

Machines
Brake-down. Josephine B. Moretti. 324
The shocking machine. David Wagoner. 390

Mackerel. Charles Edward Eaton. 236

Mackey. Anthony Petrosky. 344

MacLeish, Archibald (about)

Archibald MacLeish. Greg Kuzma. 300

Mad Agnes scrubs the parapet... Anneliese Wagner. 389

Mad dogs in August. Norman Andrew Kirk. 293

The mad waterskier on the cold edge of spring. James Schevill. 360

Madame Bovary falls on my head. Mary Gilliland. 257

Made shine. Josephine Miles. 319

Madeira
Madeira napkins. May Miller. 320

Madeira napkins. May Miller. 320

Madhouses. Brenda Marie Osbey. 340

The madness. Sam Fishman. 246

Madonna. James R. Rhodes. 352

Madonna and daughter. Everett A. Gillis. 258

Madonna anorexia nervosa. Lyn Lifshin. 303

Madonna nymphomania. Lyn Lifshin. 303

Madonna of the demolition derby. Lyn Lifshin. 303

Madonna who writes ten poems a day. Lyn Lifshin. 303

Madonna's finger on him. Lyn Lifshin. 303

Magazines
Letter 5. Charles Olson. 337

Magdalenian. Clayton Eshleman. 240

The Magellan heart. Robert A. Sears. 362

The maggid speaks of a dog in the night. Ghita Orth. 339

Magic. Rod McKuen. 316

Magic
The dead magician. Steve Kowit. 299
The dissolving coin trick step 25 James Magorian. 309
"I want my dressing/room..." Madison Morrison. 327
The illusionist. David Wagoner. 390
Magus. James Torio. 281
Nothing is obvious. Cathryn Hankla. 268
Village wizard. Albert Goldbarth. 261

Magic secret. Jacques Sollov. 370

The magic triad. Ghita Orth. 339

The magician. Eileen Silver-Lillywite. 364

The magician. Jacques Sollov. 371

The magician. Robert Pawlowski.

341
Magorian, James
Apartment complex manager
    getting the low-down on... 309
Apathy award. 308
Asphalt paving contractor taking
    a dead parakeet to... 309
Assistant professor of
    juxtapositions granted
    tenure... 309
The award for the best argument
    of the year in Omaha. 309
Badly-gored explorer reading
    poetry at a debutante party.
    309
Band of essayists trapped in a
    box canyon by bitter... 309
Beard-growing contest. 309
Bedtime story. 308
The best fullback in
    Transylvania. 309
The blind men and the
    disillusioned elephant. 308
A bribed referee. 309
Bronzed baby shoes. 309
Building a snowperson. 308
Buying the Brooklyn Bridge. 308
Call of the Ozarks. 309
Caravan. 309
Chain letter. 308
The Chicago poetry team going
    457 days without an accident.
    309
Cinderella. 308
Clinical jungle. 309
Collection agency. 308
Coloring book. 308
Crocheted table cloth. 309
Dinner invitation from a tribe
    of cannibals. 308
The dissolving coin trick step
    25 309
Drive-in theatre. 309
Dynamiter blasting ice jams. 309
The Eastern Montana obsolete
    poetry award. 308
An easy way to roast corn. 309
Elevator shaft. 309
Elk poem. 309
Eulogy for Colonel Sanders. 309
Federal judge rust-proofing an
    ornamental porch railing. 309
Filling two vacancies in the
    neighborhood car pool. 309
Fire lookout playing with
    matches. 309
Fishing License. 308
Foreman of a hung jury. 308
Former bank examiner feigning
    sleep in a monastery in Tibet.

309
The fox and the geese. 308
Genealogical chart. 308
Girl scout cookies. 309
Grain sale to the Soviet Union.
    309
The greater Peoria perversity
    contest. 309
Handbag assemblers up shit creek
    without a paddle. 309
Happy birthday and lettuce. 309
Haysatck needle, 309
Heat wave. 308
Heroine tied to the railroad
    tracks. 308
High school dropout continually
    hoodwinked by knotty... 309
High school reunion. 308
Highway patrol roadblock. 309
Horoscope. 308
Humpty Dumpty traveling in
    Montana. 309
Ice fishing. 309
Ice show. 309
Impatient florist lashing out at
    pussyfooting customers. 309
Information booth. 308
Innovative game warden. 309
Intrinsic cellar. 309
Inventory at year's end. 308
Irascible numismatist regaining
    consiousness in an... 309
Jailbreak. 308
Junior executive making a good
    impression on his boss. 309
Keynote address. 309
Lawrence Welk's musical salute
    to pawnshops. 308
Lifeguard longing to ride
    roughshod over subordinates.
    308
The light in the refrigerator.
    309
Little Orphan Annie in black
    nylons. 309
Livestock auction. 309
Log-rolling contest. 309
Lottery ticket. 308
Maiden aunt. 308
Mantra for Fred's trailer court.
    309
Method XII. 309
Middle-aged poet charged with
    fraud in Cincinnati. 309
Minefield. 308
Minor league batting champion.
    309
Mirage. 308
Mobile home tires. 309
Montana syndrome not far from

where General Custer perished.
308
Motorcycle gang. 308
Mountain climbing. 308
Muscle collecting. 308
Museum curator filling display
cases with trenchant griefs.
309
Near grandmother's house. 308
The night shift at the poetry
factory. 309
The   1910 street car. 309
Opening day of the world series.
309
Papier-mache cat. 309
The parable of the burnt=out
porch light. 309
The parable of the pecan tree.
309
The parable of the rain-soaked
macrame. 309
The parable of the ten virgins.
309
The parable of the two debtors.
309
The parable of the unpublished
poem. 309
Park filled with statues of
famous airline ticket agents.
309
Pediatricians firing canisters
of tear gas into a group...
309
Playing pinball in Denver. 309
Poem dune. 309
Poemgatherers following a giant
roller from one highway... 309
Poemwreck. 309
Poker game in a ghost town. 308
Polar expedition. 309
Polygraph test. 309
Probing various facets of hybrid
corn. 309
Proctologist on a sentimental
journey. 309
Professor emeritus. 308
Prominent astronomer playing
musical chairs in an... 309
Psychiatric referral. 308
Psychodrama. 308
A quiet day at the vatican. 309
Radio dispatched poetry truck.
309
The reincarnation of Spirow T.
Agnew. 309
Research chemist stomping on a
colleague's sack lunch. 309
Reverie for a nuclear reactor.
308
The Rosetta Stone. 309

Sawed-off shotgun. 308
Second-floor piano. 308
Senile information officer at a
plumbing supply company. 309
Senior prom. 309
Sharpening scissors and knives
for fun and profit. 309
Shelling oysters. 308
Skydive. 309
Slowing down on a trampoline.
309
Small college athletic director.
309
Small dictionary. 309
Snake charmer. 309
Suprise atonement. 309
Switchboard operator fond of
using analogies to make... 309
Table manners. 309
The tomb of the unknown poet.
308
Training session for insurance
adjusters. 309
Traveling art exhibit. 308
Unbiased geneticist visiting a
wax museum. 309
Underground literature. 308
VD-stricken college presidents.
309
Volunteer English department.
309
The Walden Pond caper. 309
Wallpaper hanger squashing an
ant with his thumb. 309
Writing poems on graph paper.
309
Magus. James Torio. 281
Maiden aunt. James Magorian. 308
Maidens fair. Harrison Fisher.
245
Mail. Andrei Codrescu. 223
Mail. Jacqueline Frank. 248
Mail Order Catalogues
The catalogue. Alice Spohn
Newton. 333
The **mailman** and das ewig
weibliche. James Schevill. 360
"The **mailman** is coming from the
next block down." Josephine
Miles. 319
Mailman's lament. Josephine B.
Moretti. 324
"**Main** Street." Charles Olson. 337
Maine (state)
The rain in Maine. Robert A.
Sears. 362
State of Maine. Robert A. Sears.
362
Maithuna. Clayton Eshleman. 240
Make me a channel, Lord! Alice

Joyce Davidson. 227
Makeba, Zensi (Miriam)
The giver of darkness (so Zenzi sings). Kiarri T-H Cheatwood. 220
Makers. Josephine Miles. 319
Making angels in Chicago. Jeanne Lohmann. 305
Making cakes and dumplings. J.W. Rivers. 354
Making camp. David Wagoner. 390
Making hay. Deborah Tall. 378
Making it. Robert L. Wilson. 401
Making it up. Stephen Sandy. 357
Making love to myself. James L. White. 396
Making old bones. Alberta Turner. 384
Making up. Tefke Goldberger. 262
Malanga, Gerard
All hallow's eve. 310
Ananke. 310
Auto-portrait at 1/5th. 310
Briefe an Maxwell Perkins. 310
Coda: "bringing up baby" 310
Devotion. 310
The enemies of cold water. 310
Envoi. 310
The future now. 310
In and out. 310
"It is an ashtray of dead cigarettes." 310
Kar. 310
A last poem. 310
Lecture on Creeley. 310
Little Italy. 310
Love poem (tentative title) 310
A love poem, of sorts. 310
Misgiving. 310
Photographs of architecture. 310
Private moments only. 310
Q:What are you feeling? A:Guilty. 310
Questions. 310
Sentiment/ality. 310
Song of whales. 310
Things to know. 310
This will kill that. 310
Tie dye. 310
To the future. 310
Tracking. 310
Twenty 26:vii:79 nyc. 310
Violence. 310
Wainscott. 310
Ways and means. 310
A white dress. 310
You speak. 310
Mallarme to Zola. David Shapiro. 363
Mallarme, Stephane

Mallarme to Zola. David Shapiro. 363
Malmaison. Michael Gizzi. 259
Mama lamenting. Stephen Knauth. 295
Mama's man. Wanda Coleman. 225
Mama's piano. Alice Spohn Newton. 333
Man. A. Dovichi. 233
Man. Rochelle DuBois. 234
Man
"After the storm was over." Charles Olson. 337
Flower of the field. Alice Joyce Davidson. 227
La gloire. John Godfrey. 260
Man in orbit. Cornel Lengyel. 302
"My memory is" Charles Olson. 337
Poem at the winter solstice. Thomas McGrath. 315
Man and the woman, fr. The day of the body. Carol Frost. 249
"Man comes to roof." Madison Morrison. 327
The **man** from Buena Vista. Charles Edward Eaton. 236
"A man from the South." Madison Morrison. 327
The **man** from Western Union. Jacqueline Frank. 248
Man in an old myth. Sandra McPherson. 317
Man in orbit. Cornel Lengyel. 302
Man in progress. May Miller. 320
Man is part music. Alice Spohn Newton. 332
Man of courage. Josephine Miles. 319
Man of letters. Josephine Miles. 319
The **man** who believes in five. Miller Williams. 399
The **man** who brought the emerald mandarins. Lyn Lifshin. 303
The **man** who grew trees from his hands. Everett A. Gillis. 258
The **man** who throws knives at the trees. Jeanne Lohmann. 305
The **man** who was not. Charles Edward Eaton. 236
Man with purple beard. Anneliese Wagner. 389
"'Man' and 'woman', these are horrid words..." Andrei Codrescu. 223
"The man-with-the-house...". Charles Olson. 337
A **man** of plastic. Jocelyn Hollis.

274
The man who carves whales. Harry
     Humes. 278
The man who is leaving. Marge
     Piercy. 346
The man who often turned to
     stone. Harry Humes. 278
Manhunt. Deborah Tall. 378
Manic Depression
     Parachute madonna. Lyn Lifshin.
          303
Manifest Destiny
     Dusty dragoon, pious Quaker.
          Phillips Kloss. 294
Manifesto. Andrei Codrescu. 223
Manifold. Josephine Miles. 319
Mankind
     "And/with the passing/of time."
          A. Dovichi. 233
     Another thought. Sam Fishman.
          246
     Anthropological sonnet. Mitchell
          Howard. 276
     "As we human beings search for
          life in clues." Michael Robert
          Pick. 345
     The beginning of the end. Randy
          Blasing. 207
     Caged. Norman Andrew Kirk. 293
     Coda. Robert Anbian. 194
     'The color of evening.' Rochelle
          DuBois. 234
     Each other. James R. Rhodes. 352
     Forgotten. John Reed. 350
     From. Robert Kelly. 289
     Gods. Robert Kelly. 289
     Hot and sweaty. Mitchell Howard.
          276
     "The hour of evening..." Charles
          Olson. 337
     "I am man." A. Dovichi. 233
     "I was man." A. Dovichi. 233
     "Is it possible/that man." A.
          Dovichi. 233
     Israfel. Edgar Allan Poe. 347
     Kind. Josephine Miles. 319
     Letter 22. Charles Olson. 337
     Machines. Phillips Kloss. 294
     Man. A. Dovichi. 233
     Monkey. Josephine Miles. 319
     The mortal heroes. James
          Applewhite. 198
     On seeing the play, "The
          Elephant Man," December, 1979.
          Maria Gillan. 256
     Out of Eden. James R. Rhodes.
          352
     A person. James R. Rhodes. 352
     Petty, my love. Alice Spohn
          Newton. 332

The railroad still runs to
     Connecticut... Mitchell
     Howard. 276
Rediscovery. James Torio. 281
Saturos. Clayton Eshleman. 240
The severing. Clayton Eshleman.
     240
Skyscape. Joyce Carol Oates. 336
The stepchild. Sam Fishman. 246
Use capricious in a sentence.
     Sharon Bryan. 217
"We are as a closed eye/...that
     will not see." Joan Walsh
     Anglund. 197
"We are each/a piece of a great
     puzzle." Theta Burke. 218
"We/are being devoured." A.
     Dovichi. 233
What chance ignorance. Norman
     Andrew Kirk. 293
Why man? Sam Fishman. 246
Mannerly memo. Marie Daerr
     Boehringer. 210
Manners. Larry Moffi. 322
"Manners in the dining room." Jan
     Ormerod. 338
Manners. See Etiquette

Manque. Robert A. Sears. 362
Manticore vortex. Clayton
     Eshleman. 240
Mantra for Fred's trailer court.
     James Magorian. 309
Manuela come out the kitchen.
     Wanda Coleman. 225
The manuscript collection.
     Charles Edward Eaton. 236
Many summers ago. Rod McKuen. 316
A map of simplicities. James
     Applewhite. 198
Map-making. Marieve Rugo. 356
Map of the world. Dennis
     Hinrichsen. 273
Maple sugaring. Robin Becker. 202
Maps
     Map-making. Marieve Rugo. 356
Maran'atha. Patsie Black. 206
March
     False spring. Marge Piercy. 346
     In ━ between. Ralph J., Jr.
          Mills. 321
     March light. Ralph J., Jr.
          Mills. 321
     Song for a march. May Miller.
          320
     This time of year. Marie Daerr
          Boehringer. 210
     The winds of March. Maurice W.
          Britts. 215
March for a one-man band. David

Wagoner. 390
March light. Ralph J., Jr. Mills. 321
March on. Norman Andrew Kirk. 293
Marching from a closet. Rachel A. Hazen. 271
Marcus Nathaniel Simpson: his voice. Anthony Petrosky. 344
Mare. Susan Ticny. 381
Mareoceanum. Charles Olson. 337
Marginal employment. Amy Clampitt. 222
Margolis, Gary
Anna, I am here to leave you. 311
Annanda's talk with Buddha. 311
August. 311
Autumn month. 311
Back. 311
The baker. 311
Beethoven's Polish birthday. 311
The carver. 311
Communique on cork. 311
Counting the days. 311
The doctor's quarantine. 311
During the war. 311
Exchanging prisoners. 311
Flying up. 311
Geese overhead. 311
The gourmet minces his words. 311
Her room. 311
Hypnotist and Bird. 311
I am ordered to go and say so long. 311
I appraise the probability of improving. 311
In place. 311
Leaving New England. 311
Memory. 311
Mine is the other. 311
Mother visits her mother. 311
November. 311
On the eve of our anniversary. 311
Orange, California. 311
Passions of the flowering apple. 311
Poet's stone at steepletop. 311
Remembering flute house. 311
A room ready to erase its darkness. 311
Saying the word. 311
The sitter moves. 311
The stable. 311
Stateside. 311
Surfacing. 311
To reach me. 311
Total eclipse. 311
Town meeting. 311
Two come to mind. 311
The visit. 311
Waiting their turn. 311
When. 311
Where you have been. 311
The wind in the orchard. 311
Marijuana ha-ha: a real smart dog. James A. Emanuel. 239
Marina di Carrara. Robert A. Sears. 362
Marine surface, low overcast. Amy Clampitt. 222
Marital dilemma. Maurice W. Britts. 215
Mark. Josephine Miles. 319
"A **mark** on paper." Robert Kelly. 289
Mark Twain's torch song. Stephen Knauth. 295
Market. Josephine Miles. 319
Market report on cotton gray goods. Josephine Miles. 319
Marking time. William Oandasan. 335
Marley, Bob
In the Rastaman's agony and peace (where Marley recreates). Kiarri T-H Cheatwood. 220
Marriage. Joan Colby. 224
Marriage
Advice to older marrieds. Josephine B. Moretti. 324
All things are one, said Empodocles... Colette Inez. 280
Among the maybes, sels. Robert A. Sears. 362
"Among the maybes." Robert A. Sears. 362
Any letters today? Josephine B. Moretti. 324
Bridal ballad. Edgar Allan Poe. 347
Bridal piece. Louise Gluck. 259A
Burning leaves: the groom. Tom Smith. 368
The child-bride. Joyce Carol Oates. 336
Cinderella. James Magorian. 308
Connie's song. S. Bradford Williams (Jr.). 398
Country marriage. Carol Frost. 249
The craftsman. Ruth Lisa Schechter. 359
Crazy wife. Anthony Petrosky. 344
The day without the dream. Cathryn Hankla. 268

The door: four sonnets for
    married lovers. Everett A.
    Gillis. 258
During a fight I tear up my
    wedding picture. Joan Colby.
    224
Early and late. Colette Inez.
    280
The edge. Louise Gluck. 259A
Enter no exit. Norman Andrew
    Kirk. 293
Eulalie: a song. Edgar Allan
    Poe. 347
The form and function of the
    novel. Albert Goldbarth. 261
Fox and bee. Tom Smith. 368
Friday, the day Mariana Penko
    quit cooking... Anthony
    Petrosky. 344
Heaven furnished the flowers.
    Alice Spohn Newton. 333
"The heroine/is cross..."
    Madison Morrison. 327
The hunter's game wife. Colette
    Inez. 280
"I want to tell you why husbands
    stop loving wives." Robert
    Kelly. 289
It's waking. Judson Crews. 226
"Life has no meaning without
    you." Michael Robert Pick. 345
Living in the tan house. Brenda
    Marie Osbey. 340
Marital dilemma. Maurice W.
    Britts. 215
Marriage song. Kirk Lumpkin. 306
A marriage. Richmond Lattimore.
    301
The marriage. Edwin Honig. 275
Married. Elsa Gidlow. 254
"The married man." Madison
    Morrison. 327
Matched set. Robert A. Sears.
    362
The matrimonial bed. Marge
    Piercy. 346
Men and publishers. Lyn Lifshin.
    303
My husband and I. Evelyn Golden.
    263
Nothing changes. Ruth Lisa
    Schechter. 359
Nuptial calendar. May Miller.
    320
On the eve of our anniversary.
    Gary Margolis. 311
Only the best line holds. Scott
    Chisholm. 221
The other side of marriage.
    Tefke Goldberger. 262

Paul's wife. Robert Frost. 250
Peasant song. Keith Wilson. 400
Poem jubilant in place of
    mourning. Joyce Carol Oates.
    336
Race. Edwin Honig. 275
Recidivists. Joan Colby. 224
September Monday. Maria Gillan.
    256
Seven7,22,66 Sandra McPherson.
    317
Silver anniversary. Josephine B.
    Moretti. 324
Song: to--. Edgar Allan Poe. 347
A story as wet as tears. Marge
    Piercy. 346
The story-maker and her husband.
    Carolyn Stoloff. 376
Summer marriage. Keith Wilson.
    400
The table. Jacqueline Frank. 248
Tales of Hoffmann. Richmond
    Lattimore. 301
Then the children came. Judson
    Crews. 226
Those spines. Judson Crews. 226
To Milly on our thirty-fifth
    wedding anniversary. Sam
    Fishman. 246
To my birthday girl. Maurice W.
    Britts. 215
To my married friends. Sally
    Love Saunders. 358
Tromp l'oeil. Marieve Rugo. 356
Trying. Miller Williams. 399
Twentieth anniversary. Betty
    Adcock. 192
Two by two. Robin Morgan. 325
Wedding dance. Cornel Lengyel.
    302
The wedding garment. Jacques
    Sollov. 371
Wedding portrait. Keith Wilson.
    400
Wedding prayer. Alice Joyce
    Davidson. 227
The weight. Marge Piercy. 346
What she found in the river.
    Robert Kelly. 289
"Why do white/women..." Madison
    Morrison. 327
Wife. Edwin Honig. 275
Winter stream. Harry Humes. 278
"Yes/there must have been."
    Wanda Coleman. 225
"You beat them all." Robert A.
    Sears. 362

Marriage = Satire
    Old King Cool. Harlan Usher. 386
    On weddynge gyftes. Ernest

Hemingway. 272
The **marriage** of insult and
    injury, sels. Andrei Codrescu.
    223
Marriage song. Kirk Lumpkin. 306
Marriage song. Elsa Gidlow. 254
A **marriage**. Richmond Lattimore.
    301
The **marriage**. Edwin Honig. 275
Married. Elsa Gidlow. 254
Married cousin. Robert Peters.
    343
"The **married** man." Madison
    Morrison. 327
The **marsh**. W.D. (William De Witt)
    Snodgrass. 369
Martial Arts
    The man who throws knives at the
    trees. Jeanne Lohmann. 305
Martinete. Carolyn Stoloff. 376
Martins Ferry, Ohio
    The sumac in Ohio. James Wright.
    403
Martyrs. Roy Marz. 312
The **marvelous** blue frog. William
    Oandasan. 335
Marx. Harlan Usher. 386
Mary. Susan Stock. 375
Mary Anne. Mary Mapes Dodge. 232
Mary Conway. Paul Davis. 228
Mary Lams. Harlan Usher. 386
Mary, Virgin
    The first icon with gun. Andrei
    Codrescu. 223
    Life of the Virgin. Roy Marz.
    312
    A son. May Miller. 320
Marz, Roy
    The abstract nude. 312
    All men are Gemini. 312
    The amateurs. 312
    The annunciations. 312
    The Belfast swallows. 312
    The bird is God. 312
    Black is the color. 312
    The blind man. 312
    The blue tablecloth. 312
    Boy buried on Sunday. 312
    Buonarotti to his public and
    God. 312
    Buonarotti to Vittoria Colonna.
    312
    The bur. 312
    The buzzard. 312
    Cable to Florence. 312
    Campagna picnic. 312
    The captain's hannele. 312
    The cat at the last supper. 312
    The cemetery. 312
    Changes on the organ theme. 312

Charlotte to Emily. 312
The children. 312
The coming. 312
The count and the rose. 312
David. 312
For Dickie MacGregor. 312
Dinner at Mary's. 312
The disciple. 312
The elephant graveyard. 312
Etruscan burial. 312
First quartets. 312
Form. 312
Four unfinished prisoners by
    Michelangelo. 312
Frameless. 312
The fugitive. 312
The gift of pain. 312
Head of a smiling priest:
    Limestone, Egypt. 312
Housecleaning. 312
The humor of Helen. 312
Ice carnival. 312
The island-maker. 312
The Italian lesson. 312
The learned lady. 312
Life of the Virgin. 312
Love is laziness. 312
Martyrs. 312
Mrs. Simmons to Astolfo. 312
Music lovers. 312
My dead professor. 312
Night walker. 312
Orpheus. 312
Our two birds. 312
The Paulownia tree. 312
Pieta. 312
The poem's words. 312
The probation. 312
Rose lice. 312
Salome. 312
Santa Lucia bar. 312
Savonarola. 312
The shepherd. 312
The sisters. 312
Soldier home. 312
The son's lullaby for the
    mother. 312
Spring. 312
The stable. 312
Strain. 312
Targets. 312
The test. 312
The three pilgrims. 312
To a child. 312
Tourists. 312
Twelfth Street. 312
The two white horses. 312
Umbrian plain. 312
Under. 312
Valentine and the birds. 312

Venus. 312
Voyage to last August. 312
What is it. 312
Whether they feared or whether
  they loved. 312
Winter moon. 312

Masada
  Deliverances. Ghita Orth. 339
Mask of everyman, fr. Masks.
  Everett A. Gillis. 258
The **mask**. John F. Barker. 201
Masks
  The carver. Gary Margolis. 311
Masks in 1980 for age 60 James
  Schevill. 360
Masks in 1980 for age 60. James
  Schevill. 360
Masks, sels. Everett A. Gillis.
  258
The **masquerade**. Rachel A. Hazen.
  271
Massaccio (Tommaso Guidi)
  Two mediations on Guanajuato.
  John Yau. 404
Massacciucoli. Robert A. Sears.
  362
Massachusetts
  Franklin, Massachusetts. Eileen
  Silver-Lillywite. 364
The **masses** are constantly on the
  telephone. Andrei Codrescu.
  223
Matched set. Robert A. Sears. 362
Mater eterna. Rose Basile Green.
  265
Materialism
  Adam's fault. Cornel Lengyel.
  302
  Gypsy. Josephine Miles. 319
Maternity. Toi Derricote. 229
Matisse, Henri
  Portraits by Matisse. Dennis
  Hinrichsen. 273
The **matrimonial** bed. Marge
  Piercy. 346
Matrimony. Robert Pawlowski. 341
Matrix. Stephen Todd Booker. 212
A **matter** of angels. Mark Vinz.
  387
Matter of Fact. Josephine Miles.
  319
A **matter** of life and dirt. Iefke
  Goldberger. 262
A **matter** of minutes. Rachel A.
  Hazen. 271
Maturity. Connie Hunt. 279
Maturity. Martha Janssen. 283
Maturity
  Maturity. Connie Hunt. 279
  On maturity. James R. Rhodes.

352
Maupassant, Guy de
  Ducking: after Maupassant. Dave
  Smith. 367
Maura, Sister
  After gossip. 313
  The aging poet writes of the
  continuing evidence of his...
  313
  The beginning. 313
  Brief lives. 313
  Celebration. 313
  Cricket on the hearth. 313
  Dialogue at midnight: Elizabeth
  to John. 313
  Each day. 313
  Enlightenment. 313
  For a friend-with the gift of a
  recording. 313
  For the new occupants. 313
  The fountain. 313
  The grandmother speaks. 313
  Ishtar, the monastery dog. 313
  Letter from Santa Cruz. 313
  Morning song of hope. 313
  The mother. 313
  Night call. 313
  Night in the old house. 313
  Notes for an autobiography. 313
  The reason. 313
  Roots. 313
  A short history of the teaching
  profession. 313
  Sunday morning:migrant labor
  camp. 313
  Tornado watch. 313
  Try it on. 313
  Veronica's veil. 313
  Woman's liberation. 313
Maxim. Josephine Miles. 319
Maximus further on (December 28th
  1959). Charles Olson. 337
Maximus letter # whatever.
  Charles Olson. 337
Maximus of Gloucester. Charles
  Olson. 337
A **Maximus** song. Charles Olson.
  337
Maximus to Gloucester: Letter 14.
  Charles Olson. 337
Maximus to Gloucester: Letter 15.
  Charles Olson. 337
Maximus to Gloucester, Letter 27
  [withheld]. Charles Olson. 337
Maximus to Gloucester : Letter 2.
  Charles Olson. 337
Maximus to himself June 1964.
  Charles Olson. 337
Maximus, at the harbor. Charles
  Olson. 337

Maximus, at Tyre and at Boston.
    Charles Olson. 337
Maximus, from Dogtown: 1. Charles
    Olson. 337
Maximus, from Dogtown: II.
    Charles Olson. 337
[Maximus, from Dogtown-IV].
    Charles Olson. 337
Maximus, in Gloucester Sunday,
    LXV. Charles Olson. 337
Maximus, March 1961 : I. Charles
    Olson. 337
Maximus, March 1961 : II. Charles
    Olson. 337
Maximus, to Gloucester, letter
    11. Charles Olson. 337
Maximus, to Gloucester : Letter
    19 (A pastoral letter).
    Charles Olson. 337
Maximus, to Gloucester : I don't
    mean, just like that. Charles
    Olson. 337
Maximus, to Gloucester, Sunday,
    July 19. Charles Olson. 337
Maximus, to Gloucester, Letter
    157. Charles Olson. 337
Maximus, to himself. Charles
    Olson. 337
Maximus, to himself, as of
    "Phoenicians." Charles Olson.
    337
A Maximus. Charles Olson. 337
May. Tom Smith. 368
May. Greg Kuzma. 300
May
    May madness. John F. Barker. 201
    A song for May. John Reed. 350
May 1945. Edwin Honig. 275
May 8 (1979). Mary Gilliland. 257
May I. Rachel A. Hazen. 271
May madness. John F. Barker. 201
May rain. Elsa Gidlow. 254
Maybe. William Stafford. 373
Maybe night. Marilyn Kallet. 287
Mayday. Mary Gilliland. 257
Mayes, Frances
    Abattoir. 314
    Ars poetica. 314
    At the light I saw Pam. 314
    A burning:a poem in nine parts.
        314
    Chapter. 314
    Circadian. 314
    Curtains:a pasticcio. 314
    Cycle. 314
    He's young except for death. 314
    In the dreams of exiles. 314
    Interior. 314
    Kitchen maid. 314
    Lakemont. 314

    Outline. 314
    Pattern. 314
    The poem with no end. 314
    Restoration. 314
    Sestina for the owl. 314
    She's behind the curtain playing
        the prepared piano. 314
    Six spoons with the initial K.
        314
    Time. 314
    Tucson, Arizona. 314
    Visit. 314
    Volcano. 314
Mayflies. Colette Inez. 280
Mays, Willie
    Happy birthday b/w Say Hay.
        Mitchell Howard. 276
McFadden, McFadden. Paul Davis.
    228
McGrath, Thomas
    Another day. 315
    Any day of the week:a Sunday
        text. 315
    At the edge of the glacier. 315
    Beyond the red river. 315
    But once upon a very young time.
        315
    Chorus for Neruda #1. 315
    Chorus for Neruda #2. 315
    Chorus from a play. 315
    Chorus from a play (2). 315
    Christmas section III. 315
    Cool Hand Kelly pleads
        extenuating circumstances. 315
    Doper's song at Little Ah Sid's.
        315
    The dreams of wild horses. 315
    'The face of the precipice is
        black with lovers' 315
    Fresco:departure for an
        imperialist war. 315
    Gnost talk. 315
    Go ask the dead. 315
    Guiffre's nightmusic. 315
    Hard travellin'. 315
    Higher criticism. 315
    The histories of morning. 315
    History. 315
    The homilies of Bedrock Jones.
        315
    In the sleep of reason. 315
    Jazz at the intergalactic
        nightclub. 315
    Letter to an imaginary friend.
        Part three. 315
    The lineaments of unsatisfied
        desire. 315
    Love belongs to the north. 315
    News of your death. 315
    No Caribbean cruise. 315

The old McGrath place. 315
Passages. 315
Poem at the winter solstice. 315
The poet of the prison
   Isle:Ritsos against the
   colonels. 315
Psalm:El Salvador. 315
Remembering the children of
   Auschwitz. 315
Residencies. 315
Revolutionary frescoes - the
   ascension. 315
Revolutionary song. 315
Salute. 315
A sirvente for Augusto Trujillo
   Figueroa. 315
Soapbox speech for Kennedy. 315
Sometimes. 315
Song. 315
Song:Miss Penelope Burgess,
   balling the jack. 315
Spiritual exercises. 315
Tantara! Tantara! 315
Time zones. 315
Totems (I). 315
Totems (II). 315
Totems (III). 315
Totems (IV). 315
Totems (V). 315
Totems (VI). 315
Toward paradise. 315
The trembling of the veil. 315
Trinc. 315
Uses of the lost poets. 315
Visions of the city. 315
Weather report. 315
Why you don't hear from me. 315
Winter roads. 315
McKernan, Ron
   For Ron McKernan. Kirk Lumpkin.
   306
McKuen, Rod
   About the time. 316
   Absolution. 316
   After-hours acrobatics. 316
   April people. 316
   August islands. 316
   Australian gold. 316
   Beginning again. 316
   Blessings of the day. 316
   By rote. 316
   Castle keep. 316
   The christmas cactus. 316
   Cloud Valley. 316
   The cost. 316
   Country girls. 316
   Crickets. 316
   Day trip. 316
   Days pass overhead like birds.
   316

Down under. 316
Edward's birthday. 316
Elizabeth Bay evening. 316
Empty harbor. 316
Empty is. 316
Fifty/fifty. 316
Film at eleven. 316
Fragment. 316
The front-yard squirrel. 316
Garden song. 316
Gone with the cowboys. 316
The great adventure. 316
The hawk's backyard. 316
Holding on. 316
Hollow. 316
Home ground. 316
Hunter's point. 316
I've been to town. 316
If you go away. 316
In praise of difference. 316
Independence Day. 316
Inside silence. 316
Instructions. 316
Insurance. 316
La ronde. 316
The last of the wine. 316
Leaving Queensland. 316
Lion's loss. 316
Love, let me not hunger. 316
Magic. 316
Many summers ago. 316
Me and the cat. 316
Memorandum. 316
Midweek Sunday. 316
Mind shifts. 316
Mornings with Bingo. 316
Music room. 316
My brother Edward. 316
New Year's Eve. 316
Night watch. 316
Nikki. 316
The northern lights. 316
Notes from the California House.
   316
Other people's music. 316
The outer reaches of the heart.
   316
Portrait. 316
Relays. 316
The road to Yaramalong. 316
The sense of solitude. 316
Slow dance on the mating ground.
   316
So many others. 316
Solitude's my home. 316
Sommerset. 316
Sonata. 316
Spencer's mountains. 316
Starting up. 316
Summer games. 316

Summer sequence. 316
Thank you. 316
Times gone by. 316
Under capricorn. 316
Until... 316
Valentines. 316
Warning. 316
When the bars close. 316
McPherson, Sandra
Alleys. 317
The anointing. 317
Black soap. 317
The delicacy. 317
Diary May 15, 1980 - twin
    cities. 317
Discoveries mid-letter. 317
Earthstars, birthparent's house.
    317
The firefly. 317
For Elizabeth Bishop. 317
Games. 317
Helen Todd : My birthname. 317
If the cardinals were like us.
    317
The jet engine. 317
Last week of winter. 317
Lifesaving. 317
Living glass. 317
Man in an old myth. 317
The museum of the second
    creation. 317
Night vision : a fragment for
    Lucretius and others. 317
Ode near the Aspen Music School.
    317
Ode to a friend from the early
    sixties. 317
Only once. 317
A poem for my teacher. 317
Pornography, Nebraska. 317
Preparing the will, three
    generations. 317
7,22,66 317
The spa of the posthumous :
    Pearl Karsten speaks. 317
The steps : mother once in the
    '40's. 317
Two poems on definitions of
    pitch. 317
Unexplained absences. 317
Unitarian Easter. 317
Urban Ode. 317
The wheel. 317
Wings and seeds. 317
Writing to a prisoner. 317
Me. Josephine B. Moretti. 324
Me. Robert L. Wilson. 401
Me and the cat. Rod McKuen. 316
Me inside. Rachel A. Hazen. 271
Meadow. Jacqueline Frank. 248

The meadowlark. Gene Anderson.
    195
Meals
    Dinner time. Carolyn Stoloff.
        376
Mealtime moocher. Marie Daerr
    Boehringer. 210
Meaning motion. Josephine Miles.
    319
"Meanwhile, the purser's."
    Madison Morrison. 327
"The mechanic/with dirty hands."
    Madison Morrison. 327
The medal. George Eklund. 238
Media
    Mixed media. James Schevill. 360
Medici Family (Florence)
    In the Medici Chapels. Jeanne
        Lohmann. 305
Medicine
    Pill problem. Marie Daerr
        Boehringer. 210
Medicine Men
    The shaman. Carolyn Stoloff. 376
    Twoborn shaman star dancer.
        Rokwaho. 355
Medicine. See also Remedies

Medidian. Louise Gluck. 259A
A meditation in Perthshire,
    Scotland. Susan Tichy. 381
A meditation on philosophy.
    Robert Bly. 209
Meditations on an old waiter of
    some distinction. James Torio.
    281
Mediterranean Sea
    "The coast goes from Hurrian
        Hazzi to Tyre." Charles Olson.
        337
    "Cyprus/the
        strangled/Aphrodite-Rhodes."
        Charles Olson. 337
Medusa. Debra Bruce. 216
Medusa (mythology)
    Medusa's love. David Wagoner.
        390
Medusa's love. David Wagoner. 390
Meeting. Josephine Miles. 319
A meeting. Cornel Lengyel. 302
Meetings and separations. James
    Schevill. 360
Meetings in October. Gene
    Anderson. 195
Meiklejohn, Alexander
    "So you are thinking of
        principles to go on."
        Josephine Miles. 319
Melancholy
    Dream-land. Edgar Allan Poe. 347

High school dropout continually hoodwinked by knotty... James Magorian. 309
Melisande. John Reed. 350
"Melkarth of Tyre." Charles Olson. 337
Melodrama. Paul Violi. 388
Melting song. Edwin Honig. 275
Melville, Herman (about)
    Mr. and Mrs. Herman Melville, at home... James Schevill. 360
    Small dictionary. James Magorian. 309
Memento. Cornel Lengyel. 302
Memo from the cave. Louise Gluck. 259A
Memo to the dark angel. James Tate. 379
Memoir din Cluj. Keith Wilson. 400
Memoir for a year. Keith Wilson. 400
Memorabilla. Deborah Tall. 378
The memorable. Irving Feldman. 242
Memorandum. Rod McKuen. 316
Memorial. Erin Jolly. 285
Memorial Day. Josephine Miles. 319
Memorial Day
    Decoration Day. Alice Spohn Newton. 333
Memorial Day 1933. Robert Peters. 343
Memorial Day in Wilmington, Delaware. Jocelyn Hollis. 274
Memorial for Cass Elliott. Mitchell Howard. 276
Memories. Everett A. Gillis. 258
Memories. Connie Hunt. 279
Memories
    The accountings. Albert Goldbarth. 261
    Ananke. Gerard Malanga. 310
    At the jazz club he comes on a ghost. Wanda Coleman. 225
    August assignment. Marie Daerr Boehringer. 210
    Beyond the mountain. Rachel A. Hazen. 271
    Blood-remembering. Ghita Orth. 339
    Celestial scenes. Alice Spohn Newton. 332
    Coming again upon Mensch's mill by accident... Robert Gibb. 253
    Coming into different country. Jeanne Lohmann. 305
    "Descartes soldier/in a time of religious." Charles Olson. 337
Diary May 15, 1980 - twin cities. Sandra McPherson. 317
The Edgartown heat. Mitchell Howard. 276
Escape to a friend. Rochelle DuBois. 234
Fall garden: 2. Gene Anderson. 195
For Sarah, home after a weekend in the country. Robin Becker. 202
A glass face in the rain. William Stafford. 373
A glimpse in the crowd. William Stafford. 373
Gravity. Josephine Miles. 319
"He says/remember..." Madison Morrison. 327
Here to there. Donald Revell. 351
Homage. Donald Revell. 351
"I opened a box of memories." Michael Robert Pick. 345
"I pass between." Charles Olson. 337
I still can hear the singing. Rose Basile Green. 265
In memory of a man. John F. Barker. 201
Interior. Frances Mayes. 314
It all comes back. Mary Gilliland. 257
Jogging in the parlor, remembering a summer moment... Dave Smith. 367
A kind of magic. Marie Daerr Boehringer. 210
Lakemont. Frances Mayes. 314
Last song. Edwin Honig. 275
Maximus to Gloucester, Letter 27 [withheld]. Charles Olson. 337
Memories. Everett A. Gillis. 258
Memories. Connie Hunt. 279
Mosquito biting. Dave Smith. 367
Nandia. Joy Harjo. 269
The old McGrath place. Thomas McGrath. 315
One year. Betty Adcock. 192
Only a mem'ry. Rachel A. Hazen. 271
The other life. Anthony Petrosky. 344
Past visions, future events. Cathryn Hankla. 268
Pisgah. Stephen Knauth. 295
The poem with no end. Frances Mayes. 314
Provolone lane. John Godfrey. 260

Raking with leaves in the wind.
   Cathryn Hankla. 268
Remembering. Sam Fishman. 246
Remembering. Rose Basile Green.
   265
Remembering. William Stafford.
   373
Remembering Nonno. Rose Basile
   Green. 265
Remembrance of summers past.
   Anne Bailie. 199
Restoration. Frances Mayes. 314
A resumption, or possibly a
   remission. Amy Clampitt. 222
Ricky Ricardo drinks alone. Jim
   Simmerman. 365
Sideshow. Robin Becker. 202
Silence broken. Robert L.
   Wilson. 401
Skydive. James Magorian. 309
Souvenir. Ghita Orth. 339
Stranded. Marieve Rugo. 356
Survivor. William Stafford. 373
Times gone by. Rod McKuen. 316
To part of myself. Susan Tichy.
   381
Traveling, 1950. Betty Adcock.
   192
Two poems on the New Year. Erin
   Jolly. 285
Two weeks ago today. Robert L.
   Wilson. 401
Vanish. C.D. Wright. 402
The vase. Franz Schneider. 361
The vigilances of evening. Bill
   Knott. 296
Visit. Frances Mayes. 314
Voice. Paul Violi. 388
What must be. Erin Jolly. 285
What you remember of me. Joan
   Colby. 224
The wind in the orchard. Gary
   Margolis. 311
Woman at the mirror. Erin Jolly.
   285
Memories of World War II: The
   decision. Iefke Goldberger.
   262

Memories. See also Childhood
   Memories

Memory. Gary Margolis. 311
Memory
   Counting backward. Richard
      Blessing. 208
   The ford. Jacqueline Frank. 248
   Mnemonic devices. Albert
      Goldbarth. 261
   A story of a memory and his man.
      Miller Williams. 399

Voices overheard on a night of
   the Perseid shower. Marc
   Hudson. 277
"Whoppers whoppers whoppers!"
   Larry Eigner. 237
Memory of another time. Rochelle
   DuBois. 234
Memory of Roanoke. Jim Everhard.
   241
Memory of the present. David
   Shapiro. 363
Men
   Absolute man. Josephine Miles.
      319
   All men are Gemini. Roy Marz.
      312
   Arden. Michael Gizzi. 259
   The beautiful urinals of Paris.
      C.D. Wright. 402
   Blondes and brunettes. Jim
      Everhard. 241
   Buffalo man. James Schevill. 360
   Casting. Andrei Codrescu. 223
   Cute. Jim Everhard. 241
   Divorced men. Debra Bruce. 216
   For an electric man. Carolyn
      Stoloff. 376
   Henry. Jim Simmerman. 365
   The Holy Grail. Andrei Codrescu.
      223
   Homo Sapiens. John F. Barker.
      201
   Jimboy's ad. James A. Emanuel.
      239
   The kiosk. Charles Edward Eaton.
      236
   Love a peacock. Elsa Gidlow. 254
   Mask of everyman, fr. Masks.
      Everett A. Gillis. 258
   "Men living." Michael Robert
      Pick. 345
   The naked print, fr. Masks.
      Everett A. Gillis. 258
   Night of the first frost. George
      Eklund. 238
   Old Bud. James Wright. 403
   The secret. Robert Peters. 343
   Sherwood. Michael Gizzi. 259
   To kick an epic tail. Stephen
      Todd Booker. 212
   What he is. Wanda Coleman. 225
   Where are the wise. Alice Spohn
      Newton. 332
   Where he is. Wanda Coleman. 225
Men = Black
   About God & things. Wanda
      Coleman. 225
   Academic circles. Ray Fleming.
      247
   Bone breaker. George Eklund. 238

Despair. Maurice W. Britts. 215
Fly boy. Wanda Coleman. 225
The life expectancy of black American males. Ray Fleming. 247
Mama's man. Wanda Coleman. 225
Men and publishers. Lyn Lifshin. 303
"The men approach." Madison Morrison. 327
Men friday. Josephine Miles. 319
Men lips. Wanda Coleman. 225
"Men living." Michael Robert Pick. 345
Mending wall. Robert Frost. 250
Menses. Robert Gibb. 253
Menstruation
    Woman's liberation. Sister Maura. 313
Merchant marine. Josephine Miles. 319
Mercies. Maria Gillan. 256
Mercury. Josephine Miles. 319
Mercy
    "As difference blends into identity." Josephine Miles. 319
    Mercury. Josephine Miles. 319
Meridan. Amy Clampitt. 222
Mermaid alley: after rain. Gene Detro. 230
Mermaids and Mermen
    Life cycle of the Pacific mermaid. Susan Tichy. 381
    The little mermaid. Deborah Tall. 378
Merrill, James
    Santorini: stopping the leak. 318
A merry heart. Alice Joyce Davidson. 227
Merry Xmas, author! Harlan Usher. 386
Mertensia (wild flowers)
    Botanical nomenclature. Amy Clampitt. 222
Merwin, William Stanley
    Totems (III). Thomas McGrath. 315
A message from space. William Stafford. 373
Messages in the wind. Rosa Bogar. 211
Metal and stone. Anne Bailie. 199
Metamorphoses: 1806. Thomas Hornsby Ferril. 243
Metamorphosis. Josephine Miles. 319
Metamorphosis. Patsie Black. 206
Metamorphosis. James Torio. 281

Metaphors and Similes
    The nature of metaphor. Robert Kelly. 289
Meteors
    "Ta meteura/meteor things" Charles Olson. 337
Method XII. James Magorian. 309
The method. Miriam Goodman. 264
Mexican Revolution
    Andrea Mendoza is aboard the train from Durango. J.W. Rivers. 354
    A civilian defender, port of Vera Cruz. J.W. Rivers. 354
    In a pueblo in Chiapas. J.W. Rivers. 354
    Jose, age 8. J.W. Rivers. 354
    Lazaro Cardenas. J.W. Rivers. 354
    Machetes. J.W. Rivers. 354
    Ramon F. Iturbe. J.W. Rivers. 354
    Twenty-five panchos. J.W. Rivers. 354
Mexico
    Anenecuilco: the Pueblo speaks. J.W. Rivers. 354
    Gleanings from the yacata. Robert A. Sears. 362
    La Mujer. Steve Kowit. 299
    The municipal president of Tequistalpa to Felix Diaz. J.W. Rivers. 354
    Ode to Mexico. Andrei Codrescu. 223
    Pascual Orozco. J.W. Rivers. 354
    Progress. Irving Feldman. 242
    Xochicalco. Steve Kowit. 299
Mexico City
    Hotel Geneve. Cathy Song. 372
Mezcal. Robert Gibb. 253
Miami Beach. Miriam Goodman. 264
Miami, Florida
    Postmark Miami. Anneliese Wagner. 389
Mica flaking from my eyelashes. Joan Colby. 224
Mice
    The education of a mouse. Richard Moore. 323
    The house mouse. Jack Prelutsky. 349
    "The squeeking noise replaced the awful." Michael Robert Pick. 345
Michael's. Albert Goldbarth. 261
Michaelmas in Lucy, TN. Phyllis A. Tickle. 382
Michelangelo
    Buonarotti to his public and

God. Roy Marz. 312
Buonarotti to Vittoria Colonna.
    Roy Marz. 312
Michigan
    In Michigan. Ralph J., Jr.
        Mills. 321
Michoacan (state), Mexico
    The land of Michoacan. Robert A.
        Sears. 362
"Microphones.". Larry Eigner. 237
Mid stream. Robert Pawlowski. 341
Midcontinent. Mark Vinz. 387
Middle Age
    April inventory. W.D. (William
        De Witt) Snodgrass. 369
    At thirty-nine. Robert
        Pawlowski. 341
    Canto ("In this locust summer.")
        Franz Schneider. 361
    The executive at fifty. James
        Schevill. 360
    Forty-seven years. Clayton
        Eshleman. 240
    Franny Glass at forty-seven.
        Gene Detro. 230
    Home town. W.D. (William De
        Witt) Snodgrass. 369
    Journey. William Stafford. 373
    Just as morning twilight...
        Charles Olson. 337
    On the rocks at forty. Randy
        Blasing. 207
    Such an alliance. Robin Becker.
        202
    Timeshare anyone? Rochelle
        DuBois. 234
    "The tragic hero." Madison
        Morrison. 327
    A woman at middle age. Marieve
        Rugo. 356
Middle East War
    For Lael, dead at Nahariya.
        Gnita Orth. 339
Middle-aged poet charged with
    fraud in Cincinnati. James
    Magorian. 309
Middle aged wife. Josephine B.
    Moretti. 324
Midsummer rites. Eve Triem. 383
Midweek. Josephine Miles. 319
Midweek Sunday. Rod McKuen. 316
Midwest (United States)
    Midcontinent. Mark Vinz. 387
The midwest is full of vibrators.
    Lyn Lifshin. 303
Midwest patio behavior. Stephen
    Knauth. 295
The midwinter death of Olivia
    Stroud. Stephen Knauth. 295
Mignonette. Donald Revell. 351

"Migration in fact..." Charles
    Olson. 337
Migration. See Immingration,
    Moving

Miguel Pro, S.J., faces a Calles
    firing squad. J.W. Rivers. 354
Milano - Il Conservatorio.
    Michael Gizzi. 259
Miles, Josephine
    Absolute man. 319
    Act V. 319
    "Addicts progress from
        saturation." 319
    "After I come home from the
        meeting with friends." 319
    "After noon I lie down." 319
    After this, sea. 319
    Afternoon walk. 319
    Aggressor. 319
    Aim. 319
    Album. 319
    All hallow. 319
    "Along the street where we used
        to stop for bread." 319
    And after. 319
    "Apart from branches in
        courtyards and small stones."
        319
    Apartment. 319
    Appointment in doctor's office.
        319
    Approach. 319
    Art gallery closing time. 319
    "As difference blends into
        identity." 319
    At the counter. 319
    Autumnal. 319
    Away. 319
    Barge. 319
    Barricade. 319
    Beach party given by T.
        Shaughnessy for the sisters.
        319
    Before. 319
    Belief. 319
    Bell. 319
    Bibliographer. 319
    Blocks. 319
    Bloom. 319
    "Bodily kindness is
        common;though some" 319
    Bombay. 319
    Botany. 319
    Breakfast. 319
    Brim. 319
    Brooklyn, Iowa, and west. 319
    "Bucking and rolling,the ship
        bent." 319
    Bureau. 319

Bureau 2. 319
Cage. 319
Calculation. 319
The campaign. 319
Capitol. 319
Care. 319
Cat. 319
Center. 319
Chamber of commerce. 319
Character. 319
Circus. 319
City. 319
Civic pride. 319
Civilian. 319
Cloud. 319
Committee decision on pecans for
  asylum. 319
Committee report on smoke
  abatement in residential area.
  319
Conception. 319
Conduct. 319
Confidence. 319
Conjure. 319
Conservancies. 319
Contained. 319
Conversation. 319
Curriculum. 319
Dancer. 319
"Daniel Boone stepped up to a
  window." 319
David. 319
Day. 319
The day the winds. 319
"Dear Frank, here is a poem."
  319
Dec. 7, 1941. 319
Deed. 319
Definition. 319
Delay. 319
Denial. 319
Dialectic. 319
Dialogue. 319
Dinner bell. 319
The directors. 319
Disarmed. 319
The disturbed. 319
"The doctor who sits at the
  bedside of a rat." 319
"Does the world look like a park
  to you?Yes,almost..." 319
Doll. 319
Dolor. 319
"Down from another planet they
  have settled to mend." 319
Dream. 319
Driver saying. 319
Easter. 319
Education. 319
Effort for distraction. 319

Enchant. 319
Enlightenment. 319
"The entrepreneur chicken shed
  his tail feathers, surplus."
  319
Entry. 319
Evangel. 319
Evening news. 319
"Every day when she came to the
  steps that led." 319
Extension. 319
Exterior. 319
Eyesight. 319
Faces. 319
The faith. 319
Family. 319
Fanatic. 319
Fields of learning. 319
Figure. 319
Find. 319
Fish. 319
Fit. 319
For futures. 319
For magistrates. 319
Forecast. 319
A foreign country. 319
Fortunes. 319
Four songs. 319
Friend. 319
"Friends in our questions, we
  looked together." 319
From Hindi, sels. 319
Fund-raising. 319
Funeral. 319
Generation. 319
Goodbye. 319
Government injunction
  restraining Harlem Cosmetic
  Co. 319
Graham-paige. 319
Grandfather. 319
Gravity. 319
"Grievances:the warm fogs of
  summer." 319
Gypsy. 319
The halt. 319
"Have I outgrown you?" 319
Head in hands. 319
Headless. 319
Heaven. 319
Height. 319
Heir. 319
Heldenleben. 319
Herald. 319
Hero. 319
Highroad. 319
Holiday. 319
Home movies. 319
Horizon. 319
Housewife. 319

"How goes a crowd where it goes?" 319
How I caught up in my reading. 319
"I am trying to think what it means to be right." 319
"I fear to take a step;along the edge." 319
"I've been going around everywhere without any skin." 319
Idea of joy. 319
Identity. 319
If you will. 319
Illumination. 319
Imperative. 319
In air. 319
"In the morning of clarity and distinction." 319
"In the neighborhood of my childhood,a hundred lungers." 319
"In the town where every man is king." 319
Increment. 319
Institutions. 319
Intensives. 319
Interlude. 319
Ions. 319
Island. 319
Joshua. 319
Kind. 319
Kitchen. 319
Lark. 319
"The leaf is growing." 319
"The life of Galileo as it is reset." 319
Light year. 319
The lighting of a small fire in the grate. 319
The lighting of the streetlights. 319
Location. 319
Lone. 319
"Looking over toward Tamalpais." 319
Loser. 319
"Love at a distance can mean." 319
Lucifer alone. 319
Luncheon. 319
Luncheon 2 319
Lyric. 319
Made shine. 319
"The mailman is coming from the next block down." 319
Makers. 319
Man of courage. 319
Man of letters. 319
Manifold. 319

Mark. 319
Market. 319
Market report on cotton gray goods. 319
Matter of Fact. 319
Maxim. 319
Meaning motion. 319
Meeting. 319
Memorial Day. 319
Men friday. 319
Merchant marine. 319
Mercury. 319
Metamorphosis. 319
Midweek. 319
Mines, explosions. 319
Modern dance program:American document. 319
Monkey. 319
Morning in branches. 319
Motive. 319
Moving in. 319
My fear in the crowd. 319
Nadirs. 319
Name. 319
Natural world. 319
New tract. 319
None. 319
Noon. 319
Now that April's here. 319
Numerology. 319
Officers. 319
On inhabiting an orange. 319
Opal. 319
Orderly. 319
Outside. 319
Paint. 319
Parent. 319
Passion. 319
Paths. 319
Peak activity in boardwalk ham concession. 319
Pearl. 319
Pelleas and Melisande. 319
Personal appearance. 319
Personification. 319
Photographer. 319
Physics. 319
Physiologus. 319
The plastic glass. 319
Players. 319
Poise. 319
Polo match. Sunday, 2 PM. 319
Prediction. 319
Preliminary to classroom lecture. 319
Premiere. 319
Pride. 319
Program. 319
Promise. 319
Purchase of a blue, green, or

orange ode. 319
Purchase of hat to wear in the
   sun. 319
Purchase of lodging for the
   night. 319
Questions. 319
Rain. 319
Readers. 319
Reason. 319
Reception. 319
Recognition. 319
Redemption. 319
Resistance. 319
Retrospective. 319
Riddle. 319
Ride. 319
Riot. 319
Romantic letter. 319
Roofs. 319
Rooter. 319
Sale. 319
Salesman. 319
The same. 319
The savages. 319
School. 319
Sea:wind. 319
Seer. 319
Seven $7,500 319
Sheep. 319
Shift. 319
Siege. 319
Sisyphus. 319
Slack. 319
Sleep. 319
Sleeve. 319
So graven. 319
"So you are thinking of
   principles to go on." 319
Solo. 319
"Someone, an engineer, told a
   confab of wires." 319
Son. 319
Sorrow. 319
Speaker. 319
Speed. 319
Speed limit. 319
Spring '44. 319
Statute. 319
"Still early morning,the wind's
   edge." 319
Street. 319
Stroke. 319
Student. 319
Study. 319
Subdivision. 319
Subject. 319
Summer. 319
The sympathizers. 319
Tally. 319
Teacher. 319

Tehachapi south. 319
Ten dreamers in a motel. 319
The thoroughgoing. 319
Thread. 319
Three stages. 319
"Throwing his liofe away." 319
Tide. 319
To a metaphysical amazon. 319
To make a summer. 319
Tourists. 319
Toward I. 319
Toward II. 319
Tract. 319
Trade center. 319
Travelers. 319
Trip. 319
Two kinds of trouble. 319
Upon twelve. 319
Vacuum. 319
Verdict. 319
Views from Gettysburg. 319
Views to see Clayton from. 319
Vigils. 319
Violets. 319
Visit. 319
Visiting hour. 319
Vote. 319
Voter. 319
Voyage. 319
Warden. 319
Warning. 319
"We have the generation which
   carries something new..." 319
Weed. 319
West from Ithaca. 319
"What do you think caused the
   disaster here." 319
What followed. 319
"When I telephoned a friend, her
   husband told me." 319
"When I was eight,I put in the
   left-hand drawer." 319
"When Sanders brings feed to his
   chickens,some sparrows." 319
When the sun came, the rooster
   expanded to meet it. 319
"Who called brought to my mind
   the name of power." 319
"Who shall we raise up, who
   glorify-our wounded." 319
Why we are late. 319
Witness. 319
"A woman with a basket was
   walking." 319
World. 319
Wreck. 319
"Yesterday evening as the sun
   set late." 319
Milhaud, Darius
   Posthumes. Bradford Morrow. 329

Milk. Marc Kaminsky. 288
Milk and Milking
   A broken arm. Alice Spohn
     Newton. 333
Milkmen
   A horse brought the day. Alice
     Spohn Newton. 333
Millennium. Clayton Eshleman. 240
Miller, May
   Afterglow. 320
   Alain LeRoy Locke. 320
   Approaching Dover. 320
   April parable. 320
   Beyond limits. 320
   Blazing accusation. 320
   Bridges. 320
   The caisson passes. 320
   Chips. 320
   A closing. 320
   The creditor. 320
   Creusa, the wife. 320
   Crocodiles don't cry. 320
   The door. 320
   The edge of return. 320
   Excursion from grief. 320
   The final virtue. 320
   From the moving circle. 320
   Good intentions. 320
   Harmony tomorrow. 320
   Images of recall. 320
   Laurel tree. 320
   Legend stones. 320
   Love on the Cape. 320
   Madeira napkins. 320
   Man in progress. 320
   The missing. 320
   Never more than alien. 320
   New alphabet. 320
   Not eye to eye. 320
   Now October. 320
   Nowhere. 320
   Nuptial calendar. 320
   October rain. 320
   Only child. 320
   The outdoor screen. 320
   Perishables. 320
   Red shoes in the rain. 320
   Saturday night. 320
   So born. 320
   So clear the flight. 320
   A son. 320
   Song for a march. 320
   Summit meeting in the spring.
     320
   To make perspective. 320
   Untitled. 320
   With the tide. 320
   The word for it. 320
Millie. Steve Kowit. 299
Millions of strange shadows.

   Irving Feldman. 242
Mills and Millers
   The self-seeker. Robert Frost.
     250
Mills, Ralph J., Jr.
   Always open. 321
   Amherst songs. 321
   April. 321
   Beeches. 321
   Brief thaw. 321
   11/80. 321
   A fall song. 321
   For Bob Schuler. 321
   For Richard Eberhart. 321
   Four in December. 321
   14 January. 321
   Fragrant forest. 321
   Glimpsed. 321
   Gone. 321
   In = between. 321
   In early September. 321
   In Michigan. 321
   For James Wright rom a dream,
     1978 321
   For Lorine Niedecker in heaven.
     321
   March light. 321
   Near four. 321
   Night song. 321
   No moon. 321
   On a birthday. 321
   On a wind. 321
   Poplars. 321
   Porch steps. 321
   The rain gone. 321
   Returns. 321
   7/6. 321
   Song. 321
   Song/for Franklin Brainard. 321
   A stalled spring. 321
   Summer nights. 321
   Three pieces. 321
   Two in June. 321
   Two poems. 321
   Winters. 321
   Woken. 321
   Yellow. 321
Milton, John
   John Milton. John Reed. 350
The **minaret** at Constanta. Keith
    Wilson. 400
Mind shifts. Rod McKuen. 316
Mind songs. James R. Rhodes. 352
Mind. See Intellect

Mindy. Susan Stock. 375
Mine is the other. Gary Margolis.
   311
Minefield. James Magorian. 308
Mineral. Betty Adcock. 192

Mines, explosions. Josephine
      Miles. 319
Minestrone madonna. Lyn Lifshin.
      303
Mingus, Charles
      On the burning of Mingus's bass.
         James Schevill. 360
A miniature passion. Joyce Carol
      Oates. 336
Mining and Miners
      "Little man in a coal pit." Jan
         Ormerod. 338
Mining the cellar, fr. Nostalgia.
      Robert A. Sears. 362
The mink cemetry. James Tate. 379
Minneapolis. Rodney Nelson. 331
Minneapolis
      Minneapolis. Rodney Nelson. 331
Minnows
      The grand banks of Coalinga.
         Ernesto Galarza. 252
      Joy to the fishes. Steve Kowit.
         299
Minor league batting champion.
      James Magorian. 309
Minority. Rose Basile Green. 265
Minotaur. X.J. Kennedy. 290
Minotaur
      Minotaur. X.J. Kennedy. 290
The minotaur. Robert Gibb. 253
Minstrels
      Mireille. John Reed. 350
Miracles
      Everyday miracles. Marie Daerr
         Boehringer. 210
      Holy grail. James R. Rhodes. 352
      "I've grown used to miracles."
         Da Free John. 284
      Lourdes. Bill Knott. 296
      Reading the gaps. Bill Knott.
         296
Mirage. James Magorian. 308
Mirage. Jacques Sollov. 371
Mirage. Phillips Kloss. 294
Mirages
      Mirage. Phillips Kloss. 294
Mireille. John Reed. 350
Mirror. Alice Joyce Davidson. 227
Mirror suite, sels. Everett A.
      Gillis. 258
Mirror, mirror, fr. Mirror suite.
      Everett A. Gillis. 258
A mirror. Eileen
      Silver-Lillywite. 364
Mirrors
      Death of the mirror: midnight,
         fr. Mirror suite. Everett A.
         Gillis. 258
      My neighbor in the mirror.
         Louise Gluck. 259A

      Time beyond time, fr. Mirror
         suite. Everett A. Gillis. 258
      The truth of mirrors. Marieve
         Rugo. 356
Mirrors at night. John Godfrey.
      260
"Mirrors scattered." Larry
      Eigner. 237
Miscarriage. Phyllis A. Tickle.
      382
Miscarriage. Robert Peters. 343
Miscegenation
      Jerry 1966. Wanda Coleman. 225
      Jerry 1967. Wanda Coleman. 225
      Wanda and Steve. Wanda Coleman.
         225
Misfortunes
      A debate on posture. Marge
         Piercy. 346
Misfortunes: uncreated lifetimes.
      David Wann. 394
Misgiving. Gerard Malanga. 310
Misnomer. Marie Daerr Boehringer.
      210
"Miss Polly had a dolly who was
      sick, sick, sick." Jan
      Ormerod. 338
Missing pages. John Yau. 404
Missing person. Mark Vinz. 387
Missing persons. Robert
      Pawlowski. 341
Missing them. David Wann. 394
The missing. May Miller. 320
Missionaries
      Letter from Santa Cruz. Sister
         Maura. 313
Mississippi sheriff at the Klan
      initiation. James Schevill.
      360
"Mist hovering over the
      mountains." Sally Love
      Saunders. 358
The misunderstanding. Bill Knott.
      296
"Misunderstandings.". Theta
      Burke. 218
Mithuna. Stephen Sandy. 357
Mitrailliatrice. Ernest
      Hemingway. 272
Mitts and gloves. Bill Knott. 296
"Mix a pancake, stir a pancake."
      Jan Ormerod. 338
Mixed drinks. Charles Edward
      Eaton. 236
Mixed media. James Schevill. 360
Mnemonic devices. Albert
      Goldbarth. 261
The moaning of the buoy. Phillips
      Kloss. 294
Mobile home tires. James

Magorian. 309
Mockingbird. Cathryn Hankla. 268
A mockingbird. Evelyn Golden. 263
Mockingbirds
    Mockingbird. Cathryn Hankla. 268
    A mockingbird. Evelyn Golden.
        263
    Variations on a theme by a
        sycamore. Ernesto Galarza. 252
Model work. Andrei Codrescu. 223
Moderation
    Extremity. Rose Basile Green.
        265
The modern alchemists. Jocelyn
    Hollis. 274
Modern dance program: American
    document. Josephine Miles. 319
A modern version of Polonius'
    advice. Ernest Hemingway. 272
The modest rainbow. Rachel A.
    Hazen. 271
Moffi, Larry
    Above a dry pool. 322
    After "after apple-picking." 322
    The angel passes over. 322
    Barbeque. 322
    Because radio is a relic. 322
    Breaking the ice again. 322
    A certain order of divinity. 322
    Come back. 322
    Death of a Buick. 322
    The demon of Elloree. 322
    Elloree. 322
    The end of winter. 322
    Fydor's invisible mending. 322
    Hands. 322
    The last man in all
        Pennsylvania. 322
    Learning to fish fresh water.
        322
    "Local boy shines in relief."
        322
    Manners. 322
    No consolation. 322
    Notes for a lecture. 322
    The one indigenous bird. 322
    Putting an end to the war
        stories. 322
    Riding to work with the
        gastarbeiter. 322
    Simple progression. 322
    Tee-Pee living. 322
    To a child who shot a robin. 322
    To the preacher's son paddled
        for dropping his pants... 322
    Toast. 322
    The unseen. 322
    The voyeur directs an ending.
        322
    Waking in Jordan. 322

Water we walked on. 322
The word man. 322
Mohawk Indians
    Twoborn Atataho. Rokwaho. 355
Mold madonna. Lyn Lifshin. 303
Mole. Maurice Kenny. 291
The mole. Jack Prelutsky. 349
Moles (animals)
    Few of us feel safe anywhere.
        Robert Peters. 343
    Mole. Maurice Kenny. 291
    The mole. Jack Prelutsky. 349
Mom's September song. Marie Daerr
    Boehringer. 210
Moment before elegy. Everett A.
    Gillis. 258
A moment in time at Culpepper
    plantation. J.W. Rivers. 354
"A moment of high excitement."
    Theta Burke. 218
A moment of violence. Cathryn
    Hankla. 268
The moment's psalm. Maria Gillan.
    256
A momentary change of weather.
    Paul Davis. 228
The momentary glimpses of women
    through the windows. James
    Schevill. 360
A momentary son. Ghita Orth. 339
"Moments stop my sight." Michael
    Robert Pick. 345
Momma's vision. Jim Everhard. 241
Momoyama. Anne Bailie. 199
Mon oncle. Bradford Morrow. 329
Mona Lisa
    In Lombardy. Donald Revell. 351
Monadology. Richmond Lattimore.
    301
The monastery. Royal Murdoch. 330
Monday morning. Anneliese Wagner.
    389
Monday, November 26th, 1962.
    Charles Olson. 337
Monet. Robert Gibb. 253
Monet, Claude
    Monet. Robert Gibb. 253
Money. Rochelle DuBois. 234
Money
    The account book of B Ellery.
        Charles Olson. 337
    Charm for attracting wild money.
        Marge Piercy. 346
    In search of the sunbather as a
        very safe thing. Charles
        Edward Eaton. 236
    Irascible numismatist regaining
        consiousness in an... James
        Magorian. 309
    Looks from money. Andrei

Codrescu. 223
Money. Rochelle DuBois. 234
The money man. James Schevill.
    360
Money = Satire
    Six pence, and more! Harlan
    Usher. 386
The money man. James Schevill.
    360
Monk's song. Keith Wilson. 400
The monk. Andrei Codrescu. 223
Monkey. Josephine Miles. 319
Monkeys
    The escape from monkey island.
    David Wagoner. 390
    Graveyard in the jungle. Ray
    Fleming. 247
Monks
    The monastery. Royal Murdoch.
    330
    The monk. Andrei Codrescu. 223
Monoculture. Kirk Lumpkin. 306
Monologue for an aging queen. Jim
    Evernard. 241
Monongahela madonna. Lyn Lifshin.
    303
Monopoly. Joan Colby. 224
Monroe, Marilyn
    A broken house. Marc Kaminsky.
    288
    A fame for Marilyn Monroe. James
    Schevill. 360
Monster talk. Edwin Honig. 275
Monsters = Sea
    Kraken. X.J. Kennedy. 290
Montale, Eugenio
    I.M. Eugenio Montale. Lucien
    Stryk. 377
Montana syndrome not far from
    where General Custer perished.
    James Magorian. 308
Montauk. Paul Violi. 388
Montauk, Long Island
    Montauk. Paul Violi. 388
Montessori, Maria
    Blocks. Josephine Miles. 319
Monticello. Michael Gizzi. 259
Montparnasse. Ernest Hemingway.
    272
Montparnasse, Paris
    Montparnasse. Ernest Hemingway.
    272
Moon
    Augusta berates a wayward moon.
    Carolyn Stoloff. 376
    Chiaro di luna. James Torio. 281
    "Driving along in my car." Sally
    Love Saunders. 358
    Easter moonrise. Rochelle
    DuBois. 234

"The full moon." Sally Love
    Saunders. 358
Moon maiden. James R. Rhodes.
    352
"The moon, your toy." Sally Love
    Saunders. 358
"The moon." Larry Eigner. 237
Moonlight. Joy Harjo. 269
Repetition. Betty Adcock. 192
September moon. Joy Harjo. 269
"She peers at me." James Torio.
    281
Silver sliver. James R. Rhodes.
    352
Slides. Charles Edward Eaton.
    236
"Stone tears loosen, they gallop
    into the canyon." Carolyn
    Stoloff. 376
Vacuum. Josephine Miles. 319
"Will she be aware." James
    Torio. 281
Winter moon. Roy Marz. 312
The worth of being less. Robert
    L. Wilson. 401
The moon and the beautiful woman.
    James Schevill. 360
"The moon is the measure..."
    Charles Olson. 337
Moon maiden. James R. Rhodes. 352
Moon rock. Robert A. Sears. 362
"The moon, your toy." Sally Love
    Saunders. 358
Moon-sun one. Norman Andrew Kirk.
    293
"The moon.". Larry Eigner. 237
The moon. Tom Smith. 368
Moonlight. Joy Harjo. 269
Moore, Brew
    For the saxophonist, Brew Moore.
    James Schevill. 360
Moore, Richard
    The education of a mouse. 323
Mooring. Deborah Tall. 378
Moose
    Waiting for an Alaskan moose.
    Sally Love Saunders. 358
Moot. Wanda Coleman. 225
The moral circus. Edwin Honig.
    275
Moral of the caterpillar story.
    Phillips Kloss. 294
More about monks. Andrei
    Codrescu. 223
More about poems. Andrei
    Codrescu. 223
More guilt. Bill Knott. 296
"The more I row away." Sally Love
    Saunders. 358
More or less. Connie Hunt. 279

More sensuous than these. Paul Davis. 228
More than a season. Marie Daerr Boehringer. 210
More that winter ends than spring begins. Marge Piercy. 346
Moretti, Josephine B.
  Adding padding. 324
  Advice to older marrieds. 324
  Another question. 324
  Any letters today? 324
  Armchair traveler. 324
  Autumn leaves. 324
  Autumn picnic. 324
  Beach boy. 324
  Beach story. 324
  Brake-down. 324
  By any other name. 324
  By degrees. 324
  Can you? 324
  Cheer up! 324
  Chestnut Hill, N.C. 324
  Chief cook and waiter. 324
  Christams day misadventures. 324
  Collector's item. 324
  Coupons. 324
  Cure-all. 324
  Daisies won't tell (and neither will I!) 324
  The day after Christmas. 324
  Don't go near the water... 324
  Dracula, Blacula. 324
  Dress dilemma. 324
  Drill skill. 324
  Evelyn. 324
  Ever since my operation. 324
  Explanations. 324
  Friendly persuasion. 324
  Go away little bee! 324
  Good living. 324
  Grandmas. 324
  Have kids, will travel. 324
  High school dance. 324
  Home brew. 324
  How old are you? 324
  I'm no vet, pet! 324
  King Kong flu. 324
  Lesley. 324
  Like now! 324
  Limerick. 324
  Little boots. 324
  Mailman's lament. 324
  Me. 324
  Middle aged wife. 324
  Motel discoveries. 324
  Mother of teen agers. 324
  Murphy. 324
  My friend. 324
  Night train to Gastonia, N.C. 324

No sound of music. 324
Obeservation. 324
Office machine blues. 324
Onion snow (March) 324
P.T.A. fair. 324
Pass the paprika. 324
Poem to a super market. 324
Question. 324
Quiet office. 324
Reflections. 324
Say it again, Sam. 324
Short memory. 324
Short order cook. 324
Silver anniversary. 324
Small town grocer. 324
Sound of summer. 324
Sue Hilton's dog. 324
Teacher's prayer. 324
A tisket, a tasket. 324
Tough decision. 324
Train wheels. 324
Tranquilizers. 324
What to wear. 324
Wheel zeal. 324
When the cook's not hungry. 324
Who has the chair. 324
Window dressing. 324
Working woman. 324
Young secretaries. 324
Morgan, Robin
  Ariel view. 325
  Battery. 325
  Death benefits. 325
  Depth perception. 325
  Documentary. 325
  Elegy. 325
  The fall of a sparrow. 325
  The hallowing of hell: a psalm in nine circles. 325
  The harrowing of heaven. 325
  Heirloom. 325
  Nature's garden: an aid to knowledge of wild flowers. 325
  Peony. 325
  Phobophilia. 325
  Piecing. 325
  The ruining of the work. 325
  Three definitions of poetry. 325
  Three salt sonnets to an incidental lover. 325
  Two by two. 325
  The undead: a pentacle of seasons. 325
  White Sound. 325
Mormons
  An ode to Salt Lake City. Dave Smith. 367
Morning. Alice Joyce Davidson. 227
Morning. Greg Kuzma. 300

Morning
  Act V. Josephine Miles. 319
  Another day. Thomas McGrath. 315
  Aubade of an early homo sapiens.
    Carol Frost. 249
  Aurore. John Reed. 350
  Chrome alba. Bradford Morrow.
    329
  "The cock does crow." Jan
    Ormerod. 338
  Contained. Josephine Miles. 319
  Contrast. Marie Daerr
    Boehringer. 210
  Dawn. Andrei Codrescu. 223
  Dawn opens. Elsa Gidlow. 254
  Dawn serenade. John Reed. 350
  "The dawn woke the hats up in
    Tuscany." Kenneth Koch. 297
  Day aborning. James R. Rhodes.
    352
  The day's beginnings. Charles
    Olson. 337
  Daybreak. Patsie Black. 206
  Early morning through the door.
    Susan Stock. 375
  8 A.M.   Rochelle DuBois. 234
  First light. Mark Vinz. 387
  First light. David Wagoner. 390
  "The first of morning was always
    over there." Charles Olson.
    337
  Good morning, day. Rochelle
    DuBois. 234
  The histories of morning. Thomas
    McGrath. 315
  How bright the morning. Judson
    Crews. 226
  "In the morning of clarity and
    distinction." Josephine Miles.
    319
  "Insect/leaf." Larry Eigner. 237
  Man in an old myth. Sandra
    McPherson. 317
  Meaning motion. Josephine Miles.
    319
  The moment's psalm. Maria
    Gillan. 256
  Monday morning. Anneliese
    Wagner. 389
  Morning. Alice Joyce Davidson.
    227
  Morning song. James R. Rhodes.
    352
  Morning tide. Mitchell Howard.
    276
  Mornings in various years. Marge
    Piercy. 346
  Night whispers. Robert L.
    Wilson. 401
  Nothing changes. Rachel A.

  Hazen. 271
  Oak against bleak sky. Michael
    Akillian. 193
  Rosetree at dawn. Tom Smith. 368
  The screen. Stephen Sandy. 357
  Sitting on the porch at dawn.
    James Schevill. 360
  Six forty-five. Stephen Knauth.
    295
  Starting up. Rod McKuen. 316
  "Still early morning,the wind's
    edge." Josephine Miles. 319
  Sun and amiable air. Eve Triem.
    383
  "Up the steps, along the porch"
    Charles Olson. 337
The **morning** after midnight. A.
    Dovichi. 233
Morning at the ranch I. Cynthia
    Grenfell. 266
Morning at the ranch II: Memorial
    Day. Cynthia Grenfell. 266
Morning at the ranch IV: Ridge
    Road above Annie Green Spring.
    Cynthia Grenfell. 266
Morning at the ranch IV: photo:
    the negative. Cynthia
    Grenfell. 266
Morning come. Carolyn Stoloff.
    376
Morning in branches. Josephine
    Miles. 319
Morning Pablo Neruda. Robert Bly.
    209
Morning poem. Robin Becker. 202
Morning poem. John Godfrey. 260
Morning song. Maria Gillan. 256
Morning song. James R. Rhodes.
    352
Morning song of hope. Sister
    Maura. 313
Morning star. John Godfrey. 260
Morning tide. Mitchell Howard.
    276
The **morning's** mail. Christopher
    Bursk. 219
Morning, meadow, wife. Anthony
    Petrosky. 344
Morning, Swan's island. Miriam
    Goodman. 264
Mornings in fall. Randy Blasing.
    207
Mornings in various years. Marge
    Piercy. 346
Mornings with Bingo. Rod McKuen.
    316
"**Mornings**, no." Da Free John. 284
Moro, Aldo
  An atrocity, a sunset. Jenne
    Andrews. 196

Morris, Herbert
    After the reading. 326
    At the border. 326
    At the Chateau de Villegenis
        that summer. 326
    At the hotel where the long dark
        begins. 326
    Being a soldier. 326
    Fifty-ninth street. 326
    The French night. 326
    Havana. 326
    History of China. 326
    How to improve your personality.
        326
    Launched. 326
    My double in a drama filmed in
        France. 326
    My father deep and late on the
        route south. 326
    Newport, 1930. 326
    Palm Beach, 1928. 326
    River road. 326
    The road. 326
    Scriabin. 326
    These are lives. 326
    Thinking of Darwin. 326
    The treason of the clerks takes
        many forms. 326
    Waiting for Marguerite. 326
    When the silence becomes too
        much to bear. 326
Morrison, Madison
    "An adolescent room." 327
    "After violence the." 327
    "Along these sidewalks." 327
    "Antagonist and/agonist..." 327
    "The apron off the." 327
    "The arch is." 327
    "The art world." 327
    "As I leave him." 327
    "As I stand, he." 327
    "As I study at." 327
    "The assistant offers." 327
    "At dusk I pull in." 327
    "At ten of six I plead." 327
    "At that price." 327
    An auburn girl has. 327
    "The avatar's done." 327
    "Basketball players." 327
    "Being near dinner time." 327
    "The blond dresser." 327
    "The book says 'Record.'" 327
    "The brute man." 327
    "The car appears." 327
    "A car in the garage." 327
    "The caretaker takes." 327
    "The chair." 327
    "Cleveland is a city." 327
    "Climbing to the
        second/floor..." 327

    "The conductor arrives with."
        327
    "The conductor does/a repeat
        performance." 327
    "The conductor is/a figure..."
        327
    "Conversation." 327
    "Cops keep metropole." 327
    "The corner of the block's in."
        327
    "The court repairs to." 327
    "The desperate/situation..." 327
    "A divorce is a man." 327
    "Divorce." 327
    "Do queens have." 327
    "The door is closed." 327
    "Down the rump and out." 327
    "Drawn aside." 327
    "Eastern Oklahoma." 327
    "The eternal cathedral." 327
    "Eventually I pass the." 327
    "The excise tax has." 327
    "An executive/wears a
        professional smock." 327
    "Extend the family and." 327
    "The father/pursues..." 327
    "Filipino art and life." 327
    "From the shadow and." 327
    "From the steep incline a." 327
    "From the turntable's." 327
    "The front lawn." 327
    "Gaunt but conscient." 327
    "The'girls' gather." 327
    "Grass is plastic with." 327
    "The grey man works." 327
    "A grey woman has snow-white."
        327
    "A grey woman of." 327
    "The grey woman." 327
    "The grill is robbed." 327
    "The gym instructor." 327
    "He finds himself." 327
    "He has not been burned." 327
    "He is the one who sees it." 327
    "He says/remember..." 327
    "He's about to arrive." 327
    "The heart and soul." 327
    "Her vestibule." 327
    "Here they come." 327
    "Here's a beastly/fable." 327
    "The heroine/is cross..." 327
    "The hotel room." 327
    "The house of sturdy." 327
    "I am approached." 327
    "I am W.B., and." 327
    "I can support myself." 327
    "I collapse my." 327
    "I don't care at all." 327
    "I don't expect." 327
    "I find it hard to believe." 327

"I find myself now." 327
"I lap the poem." 327
"I leave this room." 327
"I live in one room." 327
"I sing." 327
"I turn directly West." 327
"I walk the sidewalk." 327
"I walk." 327
"I want my dressing/room..." 327
"I will set out from." 327
"I'm a/different person." 327
"I've taken a balder walk..." 327
"If connections are." 327
"If the globe eye." 327
"If they're not chained." 327
"In a central/chamber..." 327
"In a hotel room." 327
"In a palm tree, drowsy." 327
"In a step upward he." 327
"In alternate stripes." 327
"In passageways." 327
"In the cafe the salesman." 327
"In the darkness of." 327
"In the middle." 327
"In the mountain meadow." 327
"In the outdoor." 327
"In the public/bath..." 327
"In the purple and." 327
"It cools the booth." 327
"It is more compact." 327
"It takes/a special man." 327
"The Italian counts." 327
"The key to/making the alarm
  clock." 327
"Lady artist does her." 327
"The lady of desserts." 327
"Large city life." 327
"The little man, who." 327
"Lovingly I stow the car." 327
"The lunching/art world." 327
"Man comes to roof." 327
"A man from the South." 327
"The married man." 327
"Meanwhile, the purser's." 327
"The mechanic/with dirty hands."
  327
"The men approach." 327
"My vote." 327
"My wallet has been." 327
"A natural guess is." 327
"No street hands." 327
"A non-/roofing roofer brings."
  327
"Non-existent globes are." 327
"Now this/is bombardment." 327
O. 328
"An older man." 327
"On a rich sofa." 327
"On the same fall." 327

"An ordinary white sedan." 327
"Our tourist group." 327
"Out saunter the doggies." 327
"The page is damp." 327
"The party host." 327
"People have been gathering."
  327
"The performance of the/little
  girl..." 327
"Play/above the waist." 327
"A political is." 327
"The previous painter." 327
"The professional man." 327
"queen/has new-born cats." 327
"The religious retreat." 327
"A round/table..." 327
"Scratched and peel." 327
"Seated on the grass." 327
"Seated on the right." 327
"Shots fired at once." 327
"The silkworm." 327
"The sinewy descendant." 327
"Someone's in touch." 327
"Something that I." 327
"A southern/morning light." 327
"A square poetess." 327
"Stamping/considered..." 327
"A story of success and." 327
"The suitors do the." 327
"A team is a machine." 327
10:30.   327
"There are twice as." 327
"There's to be." 327
"These are alternating." 327
"These are not." 327
"These old houses." 327
"These public halls." 327
"These stairways." 327
"This is the dark." 327
"This is the toughest." 327
"Though you and I." 327
"Three in the afternoon." 327
"Three tall unicycle rides." 327
"Three times life size." 327
"Through his entrance." 327
"Through the intersection." 327
"A thump on/the porch..." 327
"To get out of here." 327
"The tragic hero." 327
"A tremendous night-/time
  robbery..." 327
"Tremendous rains." 327
"The two-room/apartment..." 327
"Two attendants." 327
"An unemployment office." 327
"A visit to the dead." 327
"The visitors/walk..." 327
"Walk North on the/rock..." 327
"The warehouse." 327
"We drive to the." 327

"We have/nearly finished..." 327
"We open the lid." 327
"We sit about." 327
"We sit on the curb and." 327
"We'll be off to Europe." 327
"When a teenager." 327
"When burly men." 327
"When September tells the." 327
"The white ticket." 327
"Why did the tragic hero." 327
"Why do white/women..." 327
"The windy urban street scene."
  327
"With the bill of a cap." 327
"Without asylum they." 327
"Yes, I will meet him." 327
"Yet the closing episode." 327
"You and I make." 327
"You and I." 327
"You are the sort of." 327
"You come home to." 327
"You went/with me..." 327
"The younger man." 327
Morrow, Bradford
Another posthuem. 329
Artini's kitchen. 329
Beneath the friable moon. 329
Bisbane's flower. 329
Burlesquer's song. 329
Chrome alba. 329
Concomitants. 329
Curriculum. 329
Even paranoiacs. 329
Evening: matters. 329
The fire-drill. 329
Garibaldi posthume in Washington
  Sq. 329
Hampton Hawes in the Alps. 329
The history of it. 329
Just another evening esse. 329
Lax alba at Quinnipiac. 329
Mon oncle. 329
Mr. Belknap's use of deep
  imagery in business. 329
Nett: nil. 329
On Boscovich's law that bodies
  can never actually...contact.
  329
Passing from the provinces. 329
Posthumes. 329
To a friend in wake of a
  ballyhoo. 329
The unfitted passage. 329
Upon looking into Ethel Waters'
  'La vie en blues.' 329
Yr amanuensis. 329
Morskie Oko. James Torio. 281
The mortal heroes. James
  Applewhite. 198
Mortality

The conqueror worm. Edgar Allan
  Poe. 347
"Desire and curiosity." Kenneth
  Koch. 297
Isabel. Richmond Lattimore. 301
Nota bene. Cornel Lengyel. 302
Reformation. James R. Rhodes.
  352
Morticians
The jovial mortician. James
  Schevill. 360
Morton, Thomas
The picture. Charles Olson. 337
Moslems. See Islam

Mosquito biting. Dave Smith. 367
Mosquitoes
Smudge-pot. Robert Peters. 343
Moss
The clock of moss. Judson Crews.
  226
Moss Campion
Moss campion at the snow line.
  David Wagoner. 390
Moss campion at the snow line.
  David Wagoner. 390
The most dangerous desire.
  Phillips Kloss. 294
"Most of you you keep." Sally
  Love Saunders. 358
Motel discoveries. Josephine B.
  Moretti. 324
Motel view. Donald Revell. 351
The moth. Greg Kuzma. 300
Mother. Maria Gillan. 256
Mother. Iefke Goldberger. 262
Mother. Martha Janssen. 283
Mother Goose = Humor
Biographical note on Ms Goose.
  Harlan Usher. 386
Jack & Jill. Harlan Usher. 386
Ms Hubbard. Harlan Usher. 386
Old woman. Tom Smith. 368
Where is she now? Tom Smith. 368
Why it's here. Harlan Usher. 386
Mother of teen agers. Josephine
  B. Moretti. 324
The mother poem. Maria Gillan.
  256
Mother visits her mother. Gary
  Margolis. 311
Mother's chocolate valentine.
  Jack Prelutsky. 348
Mother's Day
Lilacs on Mother's Day. Maurice
  W. Britts. 215
A mother's stone. Keith Wilson.
  400
Mother-father God. Evelyn Golden.
  263

Mother. Evelyn Golden. 263
Mother. Jacques Sollov. 371
Mother, alone - the way we are.
    Rose Basile Green. 265
"Mother-spirit...". Charles
    Olson. 337
Mother. Robert Peters. 343
"Mother of the tides..." Charles
    Olson. 337
The mother. Sister Maura. 313
Mothering. Ghita Orth. 339
Mothers and daughters. Maria
    Gillan. 256
Mothers and Motherhood
    Accommodations. Miriam Goodman.
        264
    After reading parts of Mother
        Goose to a friend's children.
        Jenne Andrews. 196
    After/words. Ruth Lisa
        Schechter. 359
    Breaking the spell. Jeanne
        Lohmann. 305
    By degrees. Josephine B.
        Moretti. 324
    A cameo of your mother. William
        Stafford. 373
    Circe. James Torio. 281
    The closet. Bill Knott. 296
    Dear mama (2). Wanda Coleman.
        225
    Dialogue at midnight: Elizabeth
        to John. Sister Maura. 313
    Diamonion taxi driver. Clayton
        Eshleman. 240
    Disconnected. Ruth Lisa
        Schechter. 359
    Elegy for my mother. David
        Wagoner. 390
    Elegy from a dark country. Anne
        Bailie. 199
    Fountain, fr. Friday night
        quartet. David Shapiro. 363
    Fran's birthday. Mitchell
        Howard. 276
    Free associations on Mother's
        Day. Tefke Goldberger. 262
    Going. Miller Williams. 399
    Good mama. Wanda Coleman. 225
    The heron. Carol Frost. 249
    In memory of my mother. Haig
        Khatchadourian. 292
    Inheritance. Marieve Rugo. 356
    Israel and Rome curbstoned. Paul
        Davis. 228
    Jane. Jim Simmerman. 365
    Jean, my Jean. Alice Spohn
        Newton. 332
    La bufadora. Thomas R. Sleigh.
        366

Last week of winter. Sandra
    McPherson. 317
The letter. Alice Spohn Newton.
    332
Ma on her ninetieth birthday.
    Sam Fishman. 246
Ma, your voice. Maria Gillan.
    256
Madonna and daughter. Everett A.
    Gillis. 258
Mama lamenting. Stephen Knauth.
    295
The man from Western Union.
    Jacqueline Frank. 248
Mineral. Betty Adcock. 192
Mom's September song. Marie
    Daerr Boehringer. 210
Momma's vision. Jim Everhard.
    241
Mother. Maria Gillan. 256
Mother. Tefke Goldberger. 262
Mother. Evelyn Golden. 263
Mother. Jacques Sollov. 371
Mother. Robert Peters. 343
Mother. Martha Janssen. 283
Mother of teen agers. Josephine
    B. Moretti. 324
The mother poem. Maria Gillan.
    256
Mother visits her mother. Gary
    Margolis. 311
Mother, alone - the way we are.
    Rose Basile Green. 265
Mothers are love. Alice Joyce
    Davidson. 227
My favorite place. Alice Spohn
    Newton. 332
My mother. Carolyn Stoloff. 376
"My mother is an old sweater."
    Sally Love Saunders. 358
My mother was a soldier. William
    Stafford. 373
My mother's gloves. Marieve
    Rugo. 356
Naming. James L. White. 396
Night into day. Rosa Bogar. 211
Now I know why. Rosa Bogar. 211
One memory of Rose. Eve Triem.
    383
Only child. May Miller. 320
Our kind. William Stafford. 373
Packing mother's things. Carol
    Frost. 249
A pale arrangement of hands.
    Cathy Song. 372
Rain. Eileen Silver-Lillywite.
    364
Ruby was her name. William
    Stafford. 373
Setting limits. Marilyn Kallet.

287

Short order cook. Josephine B. Moretti. 324

The son's lullaby for the mother. Roy Marz. 312

Spring cleaning. Debra Bruce. 216

The steamer trunk. James Torio. 281

The steps : mother once in the '40's. Sandra McPherson. 317

Till time gives out. Alice Spohn Newton. 332

'Tis morning makes mother a killer. Wanda Coleman. 225

To her daughters. Phyllis A. Tickle. 382

To mother. Alice Joyce Davidson. 227

Upon receiving, after her death, my mother's earrings... Phyllis A. Tickle. 382

Visit. Josephine Miles. 319

The youngest daughter. Cathy Song. 372

For his mother flying into her seventy-seventh. Edwin Honig. 275

Mothering. Ghita Orth. 339

Spring three, sels. Edwin Honig. 275

Mothers are love. Alice Joyce Davidson. 227

Mothers=in=Law
American genesis. Phyllis A. Tickle. 382

To my mother. Edgar Allan Poe. 347

Mothlight. Cathryn Hankla. 268
Moths
Cecropia. Thomas Hornsby Ferril. 243

The moth. Greg Kuzma. 300

Mothlight. Cathryn Hankla. 268

Not very loud. William Stafford. 373

"There was a young pig whose delight." Arnold Lobel. 304

Yucca moth. Phillips Kloss. 294

Motion. Joy Harjo. 269
Motion Pictures
At the drive-in. Debra Bruce. 216

Character. Josephine Miles. 319

Corpse and mirror (III). John Yau. 404

The directors. Josephine Miles. 319

The end of a film. Larry Eigner. 237

A kind of victory. Mark Vinz. 387

Late night movies. John Yau. 404

Les fleurs du cinema. Andrei Codrescu. 223

No sound of music. Josephine B. Moretti. 324

Passing the marquee in Maysville. James Applewhite. 198

Personal appearance. Josephine Miles. 319

"There's movies." Larry Eigner. 237

Warm, friendly creatures. Mitchell Howard. 276

"Motion unperceived..." Larry Eigner. 237

Motions of weather. Cathryn Hankla. 268

Motive. Josephine Miles. 319
Motor matter. Marie Daerr Boehringer. 210
Motorcycle gang. James Magorian. 308
The motorcyclists. James Tate. 379
Motorcyles
1974-the motercycle gang honors the newsboy's...   James Schevill. 360

Mount Everest. John F. Barker. 201
Mount Everest
Esterhazy on Mount Everest. J.W. Rivers. 354

Mount Greylock, Massachusetts
Riding to Greylock. Stephen Sandy. 357

Mount Helicon, Greece
The reservoirs of Mount Helicon. Amy Clampitt. 222

Mountain climbing. James Magorian. 308
Mountain Climbing
After arguing against the contention that art... William Stafford. 373

Ascension. Ghita Orth. 339

Mountain climbing. James Magorian. 308

Mt. Stuart: north wall in October. Franz Schneider. 361

Rescue. Robert Pawlowski. 341

The mountain in you. Rosa Bogar. 211
Mountain man. Randy Blasing. 207
"The mountain of no

difference..." Charles Olson.
337
Mountain ranges. Sally Love
Saunders. 358
A mountain stream. Evelyn Golden.
263
The mountain. Robert Frost. 250
Mountains
Alp. Thomas R. Sleigh. 366
Among dark hills. Robert L.
Wilson. 401
Bridal veil. Sally Love
Saunders. 358
First hour. Thomas Hornsby
Ferril. 243
"Into the hill..." Charles
Olson. 337
"Mist hovering over the
mountains." Sally Love
Saunders. 358
Mountain ranges. Sally Love
Saunders. 358
The mountain. Robert Frost. 250
Mt. Athos. Michael Gizzi. 259
Night in the Sierras. Evelyn
Golden. 263
A road in the Willapa Hills.
Marc Hudson. 277
The shining mountains. Cynthia
Grenfell. 266
This hill. Marie Daerr
Boehringer. 210
To remove mountains. Alice Spohn
Newton. 332
Mountains behind us. Alice Spohn
Newton. 333
Mounted policemen. Robert Kelly.
289
Mourning cloak. Anthony Petrosky.
344
The mourning II. Joyce Carol
Oates. 336
The mourning. Paul Davis. 228
The mourning. Joyce Carol Oates.
336
The mouth of the blue dog is
bound beforehand. Robert
Kelly. 289
Mouths
Muffled by a belt across the
mouth. Andrei Codrescu. 223
Movie Theatres
Drive-in theatre. James
Magorian. 309
Moving. Jeanne Lohmann. 305
Moving
The backyard. Michael Gizzi. 259
I held my little sisters.
Michael Robert Pick. 345
"Migration in fact..." Charles

Olson. 337
Moving in. Josephine Miles. 319
Report to the moving company.
James Schevill. 360
Viper Sunday. Stephen Knauth.
295
Moving in. Josephine Miles. 319
Moving inland, sels. William
Oandasan. 335
Mowing and Mowers
The lawn mowing. Greg Kuzma. 300
Mayday. Mary Gilliland. 257
Sound of summer. Josephine B.
Moretti. 324
Moyie River. Franz Schneider. 361
Moyie River: welcome ranch. Franz
Schneider. 361
Mr. and Mrs. Herman Melville, at
home... James Schevill. 360
Mr. Belknap's use of deep imagery
in business. Bradford Morrow.
329
Mr. Castle's vacation drive.
James Schevill. 360
Mr. Martin in the advertising
agency. James Schevill. 360
Mr. President. Alice Spohn
Newton. 332
Mrs. Frankenstein. Marge Piercy.
346
Mrs. Frankenstein's diary, sels.
Marge Piercy. 346
Mrs. Simmons to Astolfo. Roy
Marz. 312
Ms Hubbard. Harlan Usher. 386
Ms Mary. Harlan Usher. 386
Ms Muffet. Harlan Usher. 386
Ms. Livvy's boy. Brenda Marie
Osbey. 340
Mt. Athos. Michael Gizzi. 259
Mt. Stuart: north wall in
October. Franz Schneider. 361
Much I have traveled. William
Stafford. 373
Mud
Barefoot realiization. David
Wann. 394
Muddy bootheels click to
attention. Stephen Todd
Booker. 212
Muffled by a belt across the
mouth. Andrei Codrescu. 223
Muffled, blind, silent. Everett
A. Gillis. 258
"Muggy.". Larry Eigner. 237
Mulberry Trees
The puffing tree. Cynthia
Grenfell. 266
The multilingual mynah bird. Jack
Prelutsky. 349

Mummies
    The mummy. James Torio. 281
The **mummy**. James Torio. 281
Munch, Charles
    A solo for Charles Munch. Norman
    Andrew Kirk. 293
Munich. Sam Fishman. 246
The **municipal** president of
    Tequistalpa to Felix Diaz.
    J.W. Rivers. 354
Munitions Makers
    Hercules builds its new
    corporate headquarters...
    Jocelyn Hollis. 274
    Hercules, Dow, - agent orange.
    Jocelyn Hollis. 274
    Memorial Day in Wilmington,
    Delaware. Jocelyn Hollis. 274
    The modern alchemists. Jocelyn
    Hollis. 274
Murder. Wanda Coleman. 225
Murder
    Foetus graffiti. Clayton
    Eshleman. 240
    Manhunt. Deborah Tall. 378
    Rubaiyat for Sue Ella Tucker.
    Miller Williams. 399
    Saint Theresa. Wanda Coleman.
    225
Murder bridge. William Stafford.
    373
Murdoch, Royal
    Afterwards. 330
    Burlesque. 330
    The carpenter of Brooklyn. 330
    Catullus in his book. 330
    Comrade. 330
    The disrobing. 330
    The ephebe of Tarsus. 330
    Footnote to the classics. 330
    For him. 330
    The invitation. 330
    Irreciprocate. 330
    The last forgotten lover. 330
    The lost advent. 330
    The monastery. 330
    Of myself. 330
    Pedro Nel Mejia. 330
    Philopolis. 330
    Seascape. 330
    Soldier. 330
    Spring storm over gotham. 330
    The spy. 330
    Such sweet sorrow. 330
    The thrall. 330
    Three times. 330
    The toast. 330
    Up, liberation! 330
    Viva la libertad! 330
Murphy. Josephine B. Moretti. 324

Musa, steward, makes amends for
    losing our cat. Robert A.
    Sears. 362
Muscatel. Greg Kuzma. 300
Muscle collecting. James
    Magorian. 308
The **muscle**. Charles Edward Eaton.
    236
The **muse** is muzak in this age.
    Mary Gilliland. 257
The **muse**. Miller Williams. 399
Museum. Ghita Orth. 339
Museum curator filling display
    cases with trenchant griefs.
    James Magorian. 309
Museum of poetry. Norman Andrew
    Kirk. 293
The **museum** of the second
    creation. Sandra McPherson.
    317
"**Museum** or/the endless insides of
    the store." Larry Eigner. 237
Museums
    "And now Farley is going to
    sing..." Albert Goldbarth. 261
    At the museum. Jeanne Lohmann.
    305
    Exploring the natural history
    museum. Mark Vinz. 387
    In your house, the museum. Debra
    Bruce. 216
    Museum. Ghita Orth. 339
    Natural history museum. Jeanne
    Lohmann. 305
    Stumbling out of the Prado.
    Edwin Honig. 275
Mushrooming. Robert A. Sears. 362
Mushrooms
    It's the sly-wolf-fart. Judson
    Crews. 226
Music. Joseph Penzi. 342
Music. Martha Janssen. 283
Music and Musicians
    After the reading. Herbert
    Morris. 326
    Alla breve loving. C.D. Wright.
    402
    Alyce Bianco. Sally Love
    Saunders. 358
    Class struggle in music (1).
    Amiri Baraka (LeRoi Jones).
    200
    De chroof. Stephen Todd Booker.
    212
    Dramas and the drama. Paul
    Davis. 228
    Emancipation from a Bach jig.
    Phillips Kloss. 294
    "The faces set." Larry Eigner.
    237

Falling upwards. David Shapiro. 363

Friday night quartet, fr. Friday night quartet. David Shapiro. 363

Girl at the piano. Everett A. Gillis. 258

Haysatck needle. James Magorian. 309

The homemade piano. Carol Frost. 249

If love could sing. Alice Spohn Newton. 332

"It is music." Larry Eigner. 237

Lawrence Welk's musical salute to pawnshops. James Magorian. 308

Leipzig - das glashaus. Michael Gizzi. 259

Listening to a brown-eyed man play it for somebody else. C.D. Wright. 402

Man is part music. Alice Spohn Newton. 332

March for a one-man band. David Wagoner. 390

Meetings and separations. James Schevill. 360

Milano - Il Conservatorio. Michael Gizzi. 259

Morning poem. John Godfrey. 260

Music lesson. Mark Vinz. 387

Music lovers. Roy Marz. 312

The music, fr. The green step. Kenneth Koch. 297

Non-poem for my son. Ghita Orth. 339

Note worthy. James R. Rhodes. 352

"Notices are sent up into the music." Kenneth Koch. 297

Ode near the Aspen Music School. Sandra McPherson. 317

A one of music. Rachel A. Hazen. 271

Orange-colored sky, fr. Friday night quartet. David Shapiro. 363

Other people's music. Rod McKuen. 316

Program. Josephine Miles. 319

Run for the roses. C.D. Wright. 402

The secret life of musical instruments. C.D. Wright. 402

She's behind the curtain playing the prepared piano. Frances Mayes. 314

Solo. Josephine Miles. 319

The sonata in D minor. Phillips Kloss. 294

The substitute bassist. C.D. Wright. 402

Sunday music. Amy Clampitt. 222

Sweat, and reflections at the symphony. Paul Davis. 228

"There is a legend about a piano..." Albert Goldbarth. 261

They say. William Stafford. 373

Thoughts during Mozart. Paul Davis. 228

The tingles. Alice Spohn Newton. 333

The Tramontane sonata. Paul Violi. 388

Tune. Robert Kelly. 289

The violin teacher. Cathy Song. 372

"A visit to the dead." Madison Morrison. 327

We. Miller Williams. 399

"We sit about." Madison Morrison. 327

Words to a former musician. Thomas R. Sleigh. 366

The world's greatest two-piece band. Mark Vinz. 387

Zora Neale Hurston. Melvin Dixon. 231

Music lesson. Mark Vinz. 387

Music lovers. Roy Marz. 312

The music of the curbs. John Godfrey. 260

"The music of/the sea." Larry Eigner. 237

Music room. Rod McKuen. 316

The music, fr. The green step. Kenneth Koch. 297

The music. Greg Kuzma. 300

Musical. Ernesto Galarza. 252

Musicke of division. Thomas R. Sleigh. 366

The muskellunge. Harry Humes. 278

Must there be a reason? Rachel A. Hazen. 271

Mutual chord of wonder. Alice Spohn Newton. 332

My analyst told me. Laura Boss. 213

My another road. Eve Triem. 383

"My beautiful crab tree." James Torio. 281

My body. Martha Janssen. 283

"My boyhood was a raft of poems." Robert Kelly. 289

My brother Edward. Rod McKuen. 316

My brother's hands. Jim Simmerman. 365

My brother, my stranger. Maria
    Gillan. 256
My brother, the bishop.
    Jacqueline Frank. 248
"My brothers, two." Michael
    Robert Pick. 345
My carpenter's son's son's will,
    Lt William Stevens, 1701...
    Charles Olson. 337
"My childhood, turbulent peaceful
    years." Michael Robert Pick.
    345
My cousin in April. Louise Gluck.
    259A
My crooked city. Maria Gillan.
    256
My daily walk. Evelyn Golden. 263
My daughter. Maria Gillan. 256
My daughters. Evelyn Golden. 263
My dead professor. Roy Marz. 312
"My dear ones, my own." Da Free
    Jonn. 284
"My dog and I yesterday." Sally
    Love Saunders. 358
"My dog sparkles." Sally Love
    Saunders. 358
My dogs. Jacques Sollov. 370
My double in a drama filmed in
    France. Herbert Morris. 326
My electric cat. Robert L.
    Wilson. 401
My father & World War Two. Evelyn
    Golden. 263
My father as house-builder.
    Robert Peters. 343
My father deep and late on the
    route south. Herbert Morris.
    326
My father in the basement. David
    Wagoner. 390
My father is. Anthony Petrosky.
    344
My father's home. Alice Joyce
    Davidson. 227
My father's house. Debra Bruce.
    216
My father's valentine. Jack
    Prelutsky. 348
My father's wedding 1924. Robert
    Bly. 209
My fault. Bill Knott. 296
My favorite place. Alice Spohn
    Newton. 332
My fear in the crowd. Josephine
    Miles. 319
My fellow at Stanford think tank.
    Iefke Goldberger. 262
My friend. Josephine B. Moretti.
    324
My friend. Alice Joyce Davidson.

227
My friend Luther. Ernesto
    Galarza. 252
My friend who's afraid of the
    dark. Cathryn Hankla. 268
My friends are a song. Alice
    Spohn Newton. 332
My garden insects. Robert
    Pawlowski. 341
"My grandest symphony." Sally
    Love Saunders. 358
My grandmother's funeral. Eileen
    Silver-Lillywite. 364
My happy ducks. Alice Spohn
    Newton. 332
"My heart hastens." Susan Stock.
    375
My heart is bleeding. Jacques
    Sollov. 371
'My home town, stranger - N.Y.C.'
    Norman Andrew Kirk. 293
My hope for the future. Maurice
    W. Britts. 215
My husband and I. Evelyn Golden.
    263
My idol. Rachel A. Hazen. 271
My life. William Stafford. 373
My life before dawn. Louise
    Gluck. 259A
My love brings flowers. Wanda
    Coleman. 225
"My love has deep hurts." Sally
    Love Saunders. 358
My love is asleep. Edwin Honig.
    275
"My love soars." Sally Love
    Saunders. 358
"My love the golden moon." Sally
    Love Saunders. 358
"My loved one sits upon my knee."
    Da Free John. 284
My Maggie machine. Robert
    Pawlowski. 341
"My memory is" Charles Olson. 337
"My mind unravels." Michael
    Robert Pick. 345
My mother. Carolyn Stoloff. 376
"My mother is an old sweater."
    Sally Love Saunders. 358
"My mother swimming." Sally Love
    Saunders. 358
My mother was a soldier. William
    Stafford. 373
My mother's gloves. Marieve Rugo.
    356
My mother's parlor. Phyllis A.
    Tickle. 382
"My name is Felicity." Brenda
    Marie Osbey. 340
My neighbor in the mirror. Louise

Gluck. 259A

My new house. Rachel A. Hazen.
    271
My next book. Andrei Codrescu.
    223
My old man. Jim Simmerman. 365
My only gift. Rachel A. Hazen.
    271
My own name. Jeanne Lohmann. 305
My parents send a ring from tne
    Bahammas. Jim Simmerman. 365
My people. Rosa Bogar. 211
My pole. Carolyn Stoloff. 376
My ringless fingers on the
    steering wheel tell the story.
    Laura Boss. 213
"My room is slanted." Da Free
    Jonn. 284
My shell. Sally Love Saunders.
    358
My similar eyes. Susan Stock. 375
My son skating on Doane's Lake.
    Greg Kuzma. 300
"My son." Michael Robert Pick.
    345
My special cake. Jack Prelutsky.
    348
"My vote." Madison Morrison. 327
"My wallet has been." Madison
    Morrison. 327
My wife's dream. James Schevill.
    360
"My wife, my car, my color and
    myself." Charles Olson. 337
My wish. Maurice W. Britts. 215
"My worth is on the eye." Da Free
    John. 284
Mynah Birds
    The multilingual mynah bird.
    Jack Prelutsky. 349
Mysteries. Steve Kowit. 299
Mysteries of the heart. Jim
    Everhard. 241
Mysterious delight. Martha
    Janssen. 283
Mysterious star! Edgar Allan Poe.
    347
Mystery. James R. Rhodes. 352
Mystic moment. James Tate. 379
Mysticism
    The great books of the dead.
    Thomas Lux. 307
The myth of Cancer. Mitchell
    Howard. 276
Mythology=African
    En-gai. Ray Fleming. 247
Mythology=Greek
    Chronicles. Charles Olson. 337

Nadirs. Josephine Miles. 319
Nageire. James Torio. 281
Nail Polish
    Blood red nail polish madonna.
    Lyn Lifshin. 303
Naked. James Schevill. 360
Naked oddments of the night.
    Marieve Rugo. 356
The naked print, fr. Masks.
    Everett A. Gillis. 258
Name. Josephine Miles. 319
Name. David Shapiro. 363
Name and addresses. David
    Shapiro. 363
The name I call you. Marge
    Piercy. 346
Name me a stranger. Erin Jolly.
    285
Names
    "All the names are already
    written." Da Free John. 284
    By any other name. Josephine B.
    Moretti. 324
    The eating of names. Michael
    Akillian. 193
    Having the right name. William
    Stafford. 373
    The isolated house he sometimes
    visited. Edwin Honig. 275
    Lake song. Colette Inez. 280
    The letters of a name. Colette
    Inez. 280
    A plea for alias. James
    Schevill. 360
    To break the hold. Marilyn
    Kallet. 287
Naming. James L. White. 396
Naming. Ghita Orth. 339
Naming his call. James R. Rhodes.
    352
Nandia. Joy Harjo. 269
Nantucket. John Yau. 404
Nantucket, Massachusetts
    Nantucket. John Yau. 404
    Phenomenal survivals of death in
    Nantucket. Louise Gluck. 259A
Nap time. Marie Daerr Boehringer.
    210
Naples, Italy
    Walking through Naples. Carolyn
    Stoloff. 376
Naploeon I
    Bonaparte. Jacques Sollov. 370
Narcissus. James R. Rhodes. 352
Narcissus
    "Narcissus is the pig who sleeps
    in my navel. He rests." Da
    Free John. 284

"Narcissus is the pig who sleeps
        in my navel. He rests." Da
        Free John. 284
Narragansett snow dance. Randy
        Blasing. 207
Narwhal. X.J. Kennedy. 290
Narwhals
    Narwhal. X.J. Kennedy. 290
The Natalie Bartlum poems, sels.
        Phyllis A. Tickle. 382
Native language. Debra Bruce. 216
Nativity. Stephen Sandy. 357
Nativity. James R. Rhodes. 352
Nativity. Edwin Honig. 275
Nativity day. John Godfrey. 260
Nativity, The. See Christmas

"A natural guess is." Madison
        Morrison. 327
Natural history museum. Jeanne
        Lohmann. 305
A natural history of the
        fourteenth century. Marc
        Hudson. 277
Natural law. William Oandasan.
        335
Natural selection. Deborah Tall.
        378
Natural world. Josephine Miles.
        319
Naturalization
    A new chance. Iefke Goldberger.
        262
Nature
    Earthstars, birthparent's house.
        Sandra McPherson. 317
    Morning song of hope. Sister
        Maura. 313
    Natural world. Josephine Miles.
        319
    Rhapsody. Clayton Eshleman. 240
    Song. Ralph J., Jr. Mills. 321
    Stanzas. Edgar Allan Poe. 347
    Therapeutic. Robert L. Wilson.
        401
    Thirteen lines. Jacqueline
        Frank. 248
    Untouched moment. Evelyn Golden.
        263
    The wrench of love. Barry
        Wallenstein. 393
The nature of metaphor. Robert
        Kelly. 289
Nature visits the city. Mitchell
        Howard. 276
Nature's garden: an aid to
        knowledge of wild flowers.
        Robin Morgan. 325
Nausea, coincidence. James Tate.
        379

Nautilaus. Joy Harjo. 269
Navaho Indians
    For Alva Benson, and for those
        who have learned to speak. Joy
        Harjo. 269
    Wandering Navajo weavers. James
        Schevill. 360
    White woman with the Navajos.
        James Schevill. 360
The naval trainees learn how to
        jump overboard. David Wagoner.
        390
Nazis
    Kristallnecht. James Schevill.
        360
Near East Aubade. Randy Blasing.
        207
Near four. Ralph J., Jr. Mills.
        321
Near grandmother's house. James
        Magorian. 308
Near life. Donald Revell. 351
Near Olympic. Timothy Steele. 374
Near Pamet marsh. Stephen Sandy.
        357
Near Rhinebeck. Donald Revell.
        351
Near sonnet. Andrei Codrescu. 223
Near the ocean, Culpepper lies in
        state. J.W. Rivers. 354
Near the underground railroad.
        Dave Smith. 367
Neat lady. Robert A. Sears. 362
Neatness
    Neat lady. Robert A. Sears. 362
Nebkhebprura (pharoah)
    The house of eternity. James
        Torio. 281
The necessary webs. Thomas R.
        Sleigh. 366
Necrocorrida, sels. Andrei
        Codrescu. 223
"Needed help from someone."
        Michael Robert Pick. 345
"Needing quiet the men of old."
        Robert Kelly. 289
Needlepoint in Autumn. Charles
        Edward Eaton. 236
Needs
    Flesh and bones. Marieve Rugo.
        356
    Just lord. Donald Revell. 351
    Off with the lid. Alice Spohn
        Newton. 332
    Platitudes of want. Phillips
        Kloss. 294
    Speaking to myself. Anthony
        Petrosky. 344
    Trying to attract your attention
        without being too obvious.

Marge Piercy. 346
Nefertiti. Jacques Sollov. 370
Nefertiti, Queen
Nefertiti. Jacques Sollov. 370
Negroes
Andrew's cyclones. James A.
Emanuel. 239
A bench to bear. James A.
Emanuel. 239
Black. Rosa Bogar. 211
Black Muslim boy in a hospital.
James A. Emanuel. 239
Bobo Baoule. Melvin Dixon. 231
Class struggle in music (2)
Amiri Baraka (LeRoi Jones).
200
Hemispheres. Melvin Dixon. 231
History. Wanda Coleman. 225
Houston's Negroes. Robert
Pawlowski. 341
I am everything. Wanda Coleman.
225
In black suburbia. James A.
Emanuel. 239
In search of the mythology of do
wah wah. Wanda Coleman. 225
Jazz impressions in the garden.
C.D. Wright. 402
Kin of crossroads. Melvin Dixon.
231
Libretto. C.D. Wright. 402
My people. Rosa Bogar. 211
Part of America's pride. Maurice
W. Britts. 215
Reggae or not! Amiri Baraka
(LeRoi Jones). 200
To a Negro pitcher. James A.
Emanuel. 239
Vedi Napoli e muori. Ray
Fleming. 247
Young black man teaching Italian
to middle-class white... Ray
Fleming. 247
Negroes. See also Men-Black,
Women-Black

Negroes. See also Racial
Prejudice

Neigbors. James Schevill. 360
Neighborhoods
Tract. Josephine Miles. 319
Neighbors
The boy next door. Eileen
Silver-Lillywite. 364
G.W.M. Edwin Honig. 275
Increment. Josephine Miles. 319
July First. George Eklund. 238
Millie. Steve Kowit. 299
Neigbors. James Schevill. 360

Rose. Wanda Coleman. 225
Subdivision. Josephine Miles.
319
'Neither fish nor fowle.'
Christopher Bursk. 219
Neither rhythm nor rhyme. Rachel
A. Hazen. 271
Nel mezzo dell'autostrada di
nostra vita. Mitchell Howard.
276
Nelson, Baby Face (criminal)
Saturday at Little Bohemia.
Robert Peters. 343
Nelson, Rodney
Desire in Manitoba. 331
The end of a war (Jan.1973). 331
Fargo fall. 331
Grosstadtpoesie. 331
In memoriam: S.E.G. 331
Minneapolis. 331
North Dakota: 1979. 331
Orphan leaves. 331
Prospect park. 331
Revisiting Thrudvang farm. 331
Thor's home. 331
A walk in early winter. 331
Neothomist poem. Ernest
Hemingway. 272
'Neruda's remains were expelled
this week...' Steve Kowit.
298, 299
Neruda, Pablo
The bureau. Carolyn Stoloff. 376
The dreamer's regiment. Ruth
Lisa Schechter. 359
'Neruda's remains were expelled
this week...' Steve Kowit.
298, 299
Pablo Nerunda. Edwin Honig. 275
Widow's poem. Anthony Petrosky.
344
The **net.** Anneliese Wagner. 389
Nett: nil. Bradford Morrow. 329
Never. Elsa Gidlow. 254
Never more than alien. May
Miller. 320
"**Never** quit searching." S.
Bradford Williams (Jr.). 397
Never to wait again. Robert L.
Wilson. 401
The **new** 'ism.' Connie Hunt. 279
New alphabet. May Miller. 320
The **new** bed. Jacqueline Frank.
248
A **new** chance. Iefke Goldberger.
262
New day. William Oandasan. 335
New direction. Rose Basile Green.
265
The **new** dog:variations on a text

by Jules Laforgue. Carol
Frost. 249
The new empire. Charles Olson.
337
New England
The beginnings (facts). Charles
Olson. 337
Leaving New England. Gary
Margolis. 311
"shape of Weymouth..." Charles
Olson. 337
Signature to petition... Charles
Olson. 337
Two eastern places. John
Godfrey. 260
New garden. Marie Daerr
Boehringer. 210
The new grace. Maria Gillan. 256
A new kind of man. Rosa Bogar.
211
New kitchen. Sharon Bryan. 217
New life. Alice Joyce Davidson.
227
New marching song. Rose Basile
Green. 265
New Mexico territory. Jenne
Andrews. 196
A new moon rises. Elsa Gidlow.
254
New Orleans. Joy Harjo. 269
New Orleans
Letters to Brasil. Brenda Marie
Osbey. 340
New passage, sels. Robert A.
Sears. 362
The new science. Stephen Knauth.
295
The new site of the Calvary
Temple. Harry Humes. 278
New tract. Josephine Miles. 319
A new world, fr. Fresh Air.
Irving Feldman. 242
New Year
But never the spirit. Iefke
Goldberger. 262
Happy New Year. Paul Davis. 228
New Year's Day walk. David Wann.
394
Old year's farewell. Marie Daerr
Boehringer. 210
On New Year's Day. Marge Piercy.
346
Resolution. Alice Joyce
Davidson. 227
New Year's Day walk. David Wann.
394
New Year's Eve. Rod McKuen. 316
New York. Stephen Todd Booker.
212
New York. Andrei Codrescu. 223

New York (city)
The abuses of New York. Mitchell
Howard. 276
Central Park South. Donald
Revell. 351
Change for three-dollar bill.
John Godfrey. 260
Come April. John Godfrey. 260
Daytime nightmares, stretched
along five blocks of 42nd St.
Mitchell Howard. 276
Fifty-ninth street. Herbert
Morris. 326
The flower-washer in New York.
James Schevill. 360
Gray blazing pit. John Godfrey.
260
"He finds himself." Madison
Morrison. 327
Hotel du Nord. John Godfrey. 260
A hymn to Manhattan. John Reed.
350
In this city. Marc Kaminsky. 288
Jerome Avenue. Donald Revell.
351
Junk dawn, NYC. Andrei Codrescu.
223
Little Italy. Gerard Malanga.
310
'My home town, stranger –
N.Y.C.' Norman Andrew Kirk.
293
New York. Stephen Todd Booker.
212
New York. Andrei Codrescu. 223
No embarking at Rockaway. John
Godfrey. 260
O. Madison Morrison. 328
On guard in New York. James
Schevill. 360
On returning to the city. John
Reed. 350
Over Manhattan. Donald Revell.
351
Proud New York. John Reed. 350
Recalling the names. Donald
Revell. 351
Spring storm over gotham. Royal
Murdoch. 330
Twenty 26:vii:79 nyc. Gerard
Malanga. 310
The uses of New York. Mitchell
Howard. 276
Visions of the city. Thomas
McGrath. 315
New York City. Dennis Hinrichsen.
273

New York subway rush hour. James
Schevill. 360

"New/ballgame.". Larry Eigner. 237

Newport, 1930. Herbert Morris. 326

Newport, Rhode Island
Looking at wealth in Newport. James Schevill. 360

News
Evening news. Josephine Miles. 319

Herald. Josephine Miles. 319

Report on the times. Carolyn Stoloff. 376

News of your death. Thomas McGrath. 315

The **newsboy** enters the bar. James Schevill. 360

A **newspaper** picture of spectators at a hotel fire. Miller Williams. 399

Newspapers
Smart set. Norman Andrew Kirk. 293

This morning. Jeanne Lohmann. 305

Newton, Alice Spohn
As comes the day. 332
As gentle rain. 332
At last, the secret. 332
Be nice to Bonny. 332
Beatrice. 333
Beaver's first car. 333
Beaver, my love. 332
Blazes in the night. 333
Blueprint to forever. 332
Bossie. 332
Boxed to go. 333
Bridge to eternity. 333
A broken arm. 333
Calms between. 332
Caring with care. 332
The catalogue. 333
Celestial scenes. 332
Christ just spoke. 332
The death of a word. 333
Decoration Day. 333
Don't talk, sing! 332
Echoing laughter. 332
Ever onward. 332
Expected guests. 332
Feline favorites. 332
Finger touching magic. 332
A flying machine. 333
The flying snake. 333
The forgotten earth. 332
Free fuel. 333
From whence comes love? 332
Glancing behind. 333
Going by the pattern. 332
Grandma's cheese. 333

Grandma's chocolate cake. 333
Grandma's starter. 333
Grandpa and the Model T Ford. 333
Grandpa's friend Pete. 333
The great county fair. 333
Great rock unchanging. 332
Have a cup of bygones. 333
Hazzuzzah! 332
He's a nice potato. 332
Heaven furnished the flowers. 333
Heaven's going away party. 332
A horse brought the day. 333
House guests. 333
House of sod. 333
If love could sing. 332
Invisible splendor. 332
Isle unforgotten. 332
Jean, my Jean. 332
Jesse and Jeanie. 332
Joysome apples. 332
Just an old tease. 332
The letter. 332
Life's a funny song. 332
Lost patterns. 333
Lullaby of the wind. 332
Mama's piano. 333
Man is part music. 332
Mountains behind us. 333
Mr. President. 332
Mutual chord of wonder. 332
My favorite place. 332
My friends are a song. 332
My happy ducks. 332
No man's land. 333
Now sings the prairie. 332
O lifting wings of laughter. 332
O part of life! 333
O see, torn heart. 332
Off with the lid. 332
On being swallowed whole. 332
Other me's. 332
A part of forever. 332
Path oft' trod. 333
Petty, my love. 332
A pocket full of yesterdays. 333
Prairie miracle. 333
Primping the windmill pump. 333
A quiet truth. 332
Rock hunting. 332
Room filler. 332
Saturday night bath. 333
Searching the endless. 333
A shade-lending tree. 332
Star storm. 333
Still I hear the silence. 332
Strange move. 333
Strange woman. 333
Surprise! Surprise! 333

The surrender of a skunk. 333
Taking the train to grandpa's. 333
These many loves. 332
Till time gives out. 332
The tingles. 333
To remove mountains. 332
To touch a star. 332
The top of Pike's Peak. 333
Tough hide. 332
A trail of sparkle. 332
Two stars in a row. 332
A walk to school. 333
Wet feathers. 333
What is Christmas? 332
Where are the wise. 332
Where it all ends. 332
While gardens grow their roses. 332
Windmill valley. 333
Windows to scenes divine. 332
A witches brew. 333
Next case. John Godfrey. 260
Next year in Jerusalem, this year in Philadelphia. Mitchell Howard. 276
Nez Perce (Indians)
Chief Joseph of the Nez Perce. Robert Penn Warren. 395
"Niddledy, noddledy, to and fro." Jan Ormerod. 338
Niedecker, Lorine
For Lorine Niedecker in heaven. Ralph J., Jr. Mills. 321
Night
A-glitter with radiance. Rachel A. Hazen. 271
After Tijuana: the pool. Randy Blasing. 207
"Another plane is/gas..." Larry Eigner. 237
Arkansas night. Robert L. Wilson. 401
Bird of night. Ernest Hemingway. 272
Candlemas. Mary Gilliland. 257
Clickstone. Rokwaho. 355
Cloudy night, new moon. Mary Gilliland. 257
The dark. Cathryn Hankla. 268
Deja vu. Mark Vinz. 387
Each night is no loss... Charles Olson. 337
11 o'clock at night... Charles Olson. 337
The firefly. Sandra McPherson. 317
First dark. Joyce Carol Oates. 336
Footprints. Joyce Carol Oates. 336
"A fox and a girl meet among stars." Carolyn Stoloff. 376
"Full moon..." Charles Olson. 337
Hot night. Cynthia Grenfell. 266
I flee the night. Evelyn Golden. 263
"In the darkness of." Madison Morrison. 327
Interception. David Wann. 394
L'envoi. John F. Barker. 201
Last night a light. Cathryn Hankla. 268
Nett: nil. Bradford Morrow. 329
Night. John Reed. 350
"Night comes with soft and drowsy plumes." Ernest Hemingway. 272
Night of datura. Thomas Hornsby Ferril. 243
Nightless nights. Joyce Carol Oates. 336
No moon. Ralph J., Jr. Mills. 321
Nocturn for a winter night. Haig Khatchadourian. 292
Orange blossom trail. Randy Blasing. 207
Outside Baby Moon's. Paul Violi. 388
The pleasures of sleep. Eileen Silver-Lillywite. 364
Pre-morning moment. Marie Daerr Boehringer. 210
Short possible poem... Charles Olson. 337
"So muggy/in the thread." Larry Eigner. 237
This side of the window. Marilyn Kallet. 287
12 midnight. Rochelle DuBois. 234
Village night. Anneliese Wagner. 389
Waking in the endless mountains. Dave Smith. 367
Water pie: tonight, 12/11/72. Albert Goldbarth. 261
White night. David Shapiro. 363
The **night** before the sentence is carried out. C.D. Wright. 402
Night call. Sister Maura. 313
"**Night** comes with soft and drowsy plumes." Ernest Hemingway. 272
The **night** I read my poetry at the Paterson Library. Laura Boss. 213
Night in the nursing home. Marieve Rugo. 356

Night in the old house. Sister
     Maura. 313
Night into day. Rosa Bogar. 211
The night my son packed for
     college. Laura Boss. 213
Night of datura. Thomas Hornsby
     Ferril. 243
The night of the censustakers.
     Stephen Todd Booker. 212
Night of the first frost. George
     Eklund. 238
Night owl. Wanda Coleman. 225
Night prayer. Mary Gilliland. 257
The night shift at the poetry
     factory. James Magorian. 309
Night song. Ralph J., Jr. Mills.
     321
A night to remember. Patsie
     Black. 206
Night train to Gastonia, N.C.
     Josephine B. Moretti. 324
Night travel. Richmond Lattimore.
     301
Night vision : a fragment for
     Lucretius and others. Sandra
     McPherson. 317
Night walker. Roy Marz. 312
Night watch. Rod McKuen. 316
Night whispers. Robert L. Wilson.
     401
Night's beard. Robert Anbian. 194
The night-father was found alive.
     Cathryn Hankla. 268
Night-fishing on Irish Buffalo
     Creek. Stephen Knauth. 295
Night. John Reed. 350
Night call. James Torio. 281
Night enters. Marilyn Kallet. 287
Night stalker. James Torio. 281
Night-soil. Robert Peters. 343
Night accident. Robert Peters.
     343
Night driving, New Year's Eve.
     Joyce Carol Oates. 336
Night island. Edwin Honig. 275
Night swim. Robert Peters. 343
Night visitor. Robert Peters. 343
Night-walk, Montrose,
     Pennsylvania. Dave Smith. 367
The night hunting. Cathryn
     Hankla. 268
Night in the Sierras. Evelyn
     Golden. 263
Night journey. Thomas R. Sleigh.
     366
Night out. Joy Harjo. 269
The night sky and to Walter
     Benjamin. David Shapiro. 363
Nightclub. James Torio. 281
Nightingale. Jacques Sollov. 370

Nightless nights. Joyce Carol
     Oates. 336
Nightmares. Martha Janssen. 283
Nightmares. See Dreams

Nights at the opera. Scott
     Chisholm. 221
Nikki. Rod McKuen. 316
Nimes, France
     Entering the temple in Nimes.
     James Wright. 403
The 1910 street car. James
     Magorian. 309
9 A.M.   Rochelle DuBois. 234
9 P.M.   Rochelle DuBois. 234
'1984.'. James R. Rhodes.
     352
1974-the motercycle gang honors the
     newsboy's...   James
     Schevill. 360
1925..   Edwin Honig. 275
1934. A sailor's letter to Hart
     Crane.   Stephen Knauth. 295
1958.   Kenneth Koch. 297
Ninety-year-old. Marie Daerr
     Boehringer. 210
Nixon, Richard Milhous
     At the White House, Washington,
     D.C., 1973 James Schevill. 360
No batter. Carol Frost. 249
No better words. Jeanne Lohmann.
     305
No Caribbean cruise. Thomas
     McGrath. 315
No complaints. Ernesto Galarza.
     252
No consolation. Larry Moffi. 322
No embarking at Rockaway. John
     Godfrey. 260
No fig. Stephen Todd Booker. 212
"No longer would he have to run."
     Edwin Honig. 275
No man's land. Alice Spohn
     Newton. 333
No matter. Susan Tichy. 381
No moment. Donald Revell. 351
No moon. Ralph J., Jr. Mills. 321
No more, no more. Sam Fishman.
     246
No name. Gene Anderson. 195
No one knows. Sam Fishman. 246
"No one like me has appeared in
     this place." Da Free John. 284
"No one should die mute." James
     Torio. 281
No one took a country from me.
     Jacqueline Frank. 248
"No path." Da Free John. 284
No return. Marie Daerr
     Boehringer. 210

No sitting duck. Carolyn Stoloff. 376

No sound of music. Josephine B. Moretti. 324

"No street hands." Madison Morrison. 327

No timid sawyer. Harrison Fisher. 245

No two hands the same. Robert L. Wilson. 401

The no-name woman in San Francisco. James Schevill. 360

No landing. Rose Basile Green. 265

No return address. Dave Smith. 367

No trespassing in southern Florida. Ruth Lisa Schechter. 359

Nobody cares. Maurice W. Britts. 215

Nobody's business. James Tate. 379

Nocturn for a winter night. Haig Khatchadourian. 292

Noel, Linda
    Where you first saw the eyes of coyote. 334

Nomads. Lucien Stryk. 377

Nome, Alaska
    "Nome, Alaska." Sally Love Saunders. 358

"Nome, Alaska." Sally Love Saunders. 358

Non returnable bottle madonna. Lyn Lifshin. 303

The non sequiturs of summer. Charles Edward Eaton. 236

"A non-/roofing roofer brings." Madison Morrison. 327

"Non-existent globes are." Madison Morrison. 327

Non-poem for my son. Ghita Orth. 339

The non-swimmer advises his nephew about the beach. J.W. Rivers. 354

None. Josephine Miles. 319

Nonomura Sotatsu
    Dragons. James Torio. 281

Nonsense
    Prominent astronomer playing musical chairs in an... James Magorian. 309

Noon. Josephine Miles. 319

Noon. Rochelle DuBois. 234

Noon. John Reed. 350

Noon
    Meridan. Amy Clampitt. 222
    Upon twelve. Josephine Miles. 319

Noon song. Cornel Lengyel. 302

Norfolk, Virginia
    Winter in Norfolk, Virginia. Debra Bruce. 216

Norman. Norman Andrew Kirk. 293

Normandy beach. Miller Williams. 399

North. Robin Becker. 202

North American wildflowers. Stephen Knauth. 295

North Carolina
    An audiovisual glimpse of Cabarrus County, North Carolina. Stephen Knauth. 295

North Carolina life cycle. Stephen Knauth. 295

North Dakota
    Beyond the red river. Thomas McGrath. 315

North Dakota Gothic. Mark Vinz. 387

North Dakota: 1979. Rodney Nelson. 331

North Pole
    Polar expedition. James Magorian. 309

North summer. Maurice Kenny. 291

"North/in the ice..." Charles Olson. 337

The northern lights. Rod McKuen. 316

Northway tanka. Stephen Sandy. 357

"The/northwest course of shifting man..." Charles Olson. 337

Noses
    Augusta's little nose song. Carolyn Stoloff. 376
    "Said Mrs Tarantino." Charles Olson. 337

Nostalgia. Norman Andrew Kirk. 293

Nostalgia
    Across the board. Ernest Hemingway. 272
    Country girls. Rod McKuen. 316
    Have a cup of bygones. Alice Spohn Newton. 333
    Nostalgia. Norman Andrew Kirk. 293
    Nostalgia in yellow. James Torio. 281
    Nostalgia poems, sels. Robert A. Sears. 362
    Reunions. Connie Hunt. 279
    Third day of the baseball playoffs. Mitchell Howard. 276
    The thoroughgoing. Josephine Miles. 319

Nostalgia in yellow. James Torio. 281

Nostalgia poems, sels. Robert A. Sears. 362

Nostalgia. See also Homesickness

Not a sparrow shall fall. Phillips Kloss. 294

Not asking for love. Elsa Gidlow. 254

Not chaos but. Cynthia Grenfell. 266

"Not even/the width of oceans." A. Dovichi. 233

Not eye to eye. May Miller. 320

Not forever. Norman Andrew Kirk. 293

Not having a house is not a permanent situation. Mary Gilliland. 257

Not just poetry. Marilyn Kallet. 287

Not letting you see what you don't want to. Lyn Lifshin. 303

Not ready. Cynthia Grenfell. 266

Not the darkness. Barry Wallenstein. 393

"Not the intaglio method or skating." Charles Olson. 337

"Not the same." Larry Eigner. 237

"Not to be listening." Edwin Honig. 275

Not very loud. William Stafford. 373

Not waving but drowning. Laura Boss. 213

Nota bene. Cornel Lengyel. 302

Note for the birdwatchers of the sublime. Betty Adcock. 192

A note on the above. Charles Olson. 337

Note worthy. James R. Rhodes. 352

A note. Rachel A. Hazen. 271

Notes for a lecture. Larry Moffi. 322

Notes for a novel to be burned on a cold winter evening. Stephen Knauth. 295

Notes for an autobiography. Sister Maura. 313

Notes from a gutted house. Colette Inez. 280

Notes from a journal by the river. James Applewhite. 198

Notes from the California House. Rod McKuen. 316

Notes of a pastoralist. James Wright. 403

Notes on a visit to Le Tuc D'Audoubert. Clayton Eshleman. 240

Notes on an early room. Carolyn Stoloff. 376

Notes on Venice. Anne Bailie. 199

Nothing changes. Rachel A. Hazen. 271

Nothing changes. Ruth Lisa Schechter. 359

Nothing ever happens only once. Jacqueline Frank. 248

Nothing falls down. Rachel A. Hazen. 271

Nothing follows. Clayton Eshleman. 240

Nothing is obvious. Cathryn Hankla. 268

Nothing like a razor. Carolyn Stoloff. 376

"Nothing much left." Edwin Honig. 275

"Nothing shall stay me from my journey." James Torio. 281

Nothing so wise. Jeanne Lohmann. 305

Nothing's song. Rachel A. Hazen. 271

Nothing, nothing at all. Stephen Sandy. 357

"Notices are sent up into the music." Kenneth Koch. 297

"Notices darker form move." Robert Kelly. 289

11/22/63.. John F. Barker. 201

November. Gary Margolis. 311

November. Toi Derricote. 229

November. Lucien Stryk. 377

November. Greg Kuzma. 300

November
    November. Lucien Stryk. 377
    Waiting out November. Scott Chisholm. 221

A November afternoon. John F. Barker. 201

November leaves. Robert L. Wilson. 401

November streets. Dennis Hinrichsen. 273

November through a giant copper beech. Edwin Honig. 275

November twenty seventh. David Shapiro. 363

The novios. Steve Kowit. 299

Now. Patsie Black. 206

Now. Marieve Rugo. 356

Now. Robert Peters. 343

Now I know why. Rosa Bogar. 211

Now let us examine the almond. David Wann. 394

Now October. May Miller. 320

Now sings the prairie. Alice
    Sponn Newton. 332
Now that April's here. Josephine
    Miles. 319
"Now this/is bombardment."
    Madison Morrison. 327
Now wait-. William Stafford. 373
Now, before the end, I think.
    Edwin Honig. 275
Now, going on eternity. Robert L.
    Wilson. 401
Now, my usefulness over. Edwin
    Honig. 275
"Now/here.". Larry Eigner. 237
Nowhere. May Miller. 320
Nowhere is a lonely, lonely
    place. Maurice W. Britts. 215
Nuclear Power
    Cloud. Josephine Miles. 319
    Reverie for a nuclear reactor.
        James Magorian. 308
    Six miles from Indian Point.
        Ruth Lisa Schechter. 359

Nuclear War. See War - Nuclear

Nude father in a lake. Robert
    Peters. 343
Nuisances
    "I've been with annoying people
        so long." Sally Love Saunders.
        358
Nuke burns. Gene Detro. 230
Numbers
    The man who believes in five.
        Miller Williams. 399
    Numerology. Josephine Miles. 319
Numerology. Josephine Miles. 319
Nuns
    Absolution. Rod McKuen. 316
    Beach party given by T.
        Shaughnessy for the sisters.
        Josephine Miles. 319
    The cell. Louise Gluck. 259A
    Sister Vivian, Caldwell College,
        1978. Maria Gillan. 256
Nuns at a retreat. Lyn Lifshin.
    303
Nuptial calendar. May Miller. 320
Nurse's song. Louise Gluck. 259A
Nursery Rhymes
    "Humpty Dumpty sat on a wall."
        Jan Ormerod. 338
    "One, two/Buckle my shoe." Jan
        Ormerod. 338
    "Rain, rain, go away." Jan
        Ormerod. 338
Nurses

I appraise the probability of
    improving. Gary Margolis. 311
Nurse's song. Louise Gluck. 259A
Nursing (suckling)
    Milk. Marc Kaminsky. 288
    Wet nurse. Ghita Orth. 339
Nursing Homes
    Night in the nursing home.
        Marieve Rugo. 356
Nut-brown bird. Mitchell Howard.
    276
Nutmeet rose bud. David Wann. 394
Nuts and Nutting
    Committee decision on pecans for
        asylum. Josephine Miles. 319

O. Madison Morrison. 328
O buffalo, buffalo. Stephen Todd
    Booker. 212
"O give thanks." Alice Joyce
    Davidson. 227
O John Josselyn you. Charles
    Olson. 337
O lifting wings of laughter.
    Alice Spohn Newton. 332
O part of life! Alice Spohn
    Newton. 333
"O Quadriga." Charles Olson. 337
O see, torn heart. Alice Spohn
    Newton. 332
O Wendy, Arthur. Maurice Kenny.
    291
O'Connor, Flannery
    Firing a field. Joyce Carol
        Oates. 336
O'Hara, Frank
    Dream of fireworks on Fire
        Island. Ruth Lisa Schechter.
        359
O'Keefe, Georgia
    Blue and white lines after
        O'Keefe. Cathy Song. 372
    From the white place. Cathy
        Song. 372
O'Neill, Eugene
    Good morning, Eugene. Norman
        Andrew Kirk. 293
Oak against bleak sky. Michael
    Akillian. 193
The oak tree. Dennis Hinrichsen.
    273
Oak Trees
    The watch of the live oaks.
        James Schevill. 360
    "When crumbs from light's black
        bread sink in the water."
        Carolyn Stoloff. 376

Oandasan, William
  Acoma. 335
  Along the street. 335
  Communion. 335
  Drunkard. 335
  Early spring green. 335
  Farmington, NM. 335
  The garden. 335
  Haiku au surreal. 335
  Laguna landscape. 335
  Looking up and beyond. 335
  Marking time. 335
  The marvelous blue frog. 335
  Moving inland, sels. 335
  Natural law. 335
  New day. 335
  Round valley songs. 335
  Sebastopol. 335
  Starlight. 335
  Syrenyu, sels. 335
  Taking off. 335
  Two postcard poems. 335
  Winter rose. 335
Oasis. Rachel A. Hazen. 271
Oates, Joyce Carol
  Abandoned airfield, 1977. 336
  After terror... 336
  Another. 336
  Appetite and terror on the wide
    white sands of...Florida. 336
  Autistic child, no longer child.
    336
  Baby. 336
  Back country. 336
  Betrayal. 336
  Boredom. 336
  Celestial timepiece. 336
  The child-bride. 336
  Domestic miracles. 336
  Dreaming America. 336
  Ecstasy of boredom at the Berlin
    Wall. 336
  Ecstasy of flight. 336
  Ecstasy of motion. 336
  F-. 336
  Fertilizing the continent. 336
  Firing a field. 336
  First dark. 336
  First death, 1950. 336
  Footprints. 336
  The forbidden. 336
  Good morning. 336
  The great egg. 336
  High-wire artist. 336
  Homage to Virginia Woolf. 336
  Honeymoon. 336
  How gentle. 336
  Ice age. 336
  Invisible woman. 336
  Jesus, heal me. 336

  Last things. 336
  Late harvest. 336
  Leavetaking, at dusk. 336
  The loss. 336
  A miniature passion. 336
  The mourning II. 336
  The mourning. 336
  Night driving, New Year's Eve.
    336
  Nightless nights. 336
  Poem jubilant in place of
    mourning. 336
  The present tense. 336
  'Promiscuity.' 336
  The proofs of God. 336
  Psalm. 336
  Query, not to be answered. 336
  A report to an academy. 336
  Season of peril. 336
  Shelley at Viareggio. 336
  Skyscape. 336
  Snow-dunk in Ontario. 336
  Snowfall. 336
  The stone orchard. 336
  The suicide. 336
  Sun-truths. 336
  Tachycardiac seizure. 336
  There are northern lakes... 336
  Visionary adventures of a wild
    dog pack. 336
  The wasp. 336
The **oath.** Stephen Todd Booker.
  212
Obedience. Martha Janssen. 283
Obedience
  Obedience. Martha Janssen. 283
  Rules. Martha Janssen. 283
  "She tried to do/just as they'd
    say." Theta Burke. 218
Obedience of the corpse. C.D.
  Wright. 402
Obeservation. Josephine B.
  Moretti. 324
Obesity
  "I lap the poem." Madison
    Morrison. 327
  What will become of the fat and
    slow performing woman? Carol
    Frost. 249
Obituary. Ernesto Galarza. 252
Oblique. Anneliese Wagner. 389
Obscenity
  The greater Peoria perversity
    contest. James Magorian. 309
  Head of the state parks police.
    Lyn Lifshin. 303
  A tisket, a tasket. Josephine B.
    Moretti. 324
Obsequies. Thomas R. Sleigh. 366
Obsessive American sight. James

Schevill. 360
Obsolescent. Bill Knott. 296
The **ocean** floor as it would look
    without water, fr. Salt Air.
    Sharon Bryan. 217
Ocean. See Sea

"The **ocean**.". Sally Love
    Saunders. 358
The **ocean**. Charles Olson. 337
Oceania. Charles Olson. 337
Oceanology, Robert Anbian. 194
Ocotillo. Phillips Kloss. 294
Octagon. Erin Jolly. 285
October. Susan Tichy. 381
October. John Reed. 350
October. Bill Knott. 296
October
    Deception. Barry Wallenstein.
    393
    Something more. Harry Humes. 278
    The spheres of October. Harry
    Humes. 278
October rain. May Miller. 320
Octopus. David Wagoner. 390
Octopuses
    Octopus. David Wagoner. 390
Ode near the Aspen Music School.
    Sandra McPherson. 317
Ode to a friend from the early
    sixties. Sandra McPherson. 317
Ode to an Eskimo. Sally Love
    Saunders. 358
Ode to curiosity. Andrei
    Codrescu. 223
Ode to language. Robert Kelly.
    289
Ode to laryngitis. Andrei
    Codrescu. 223
Ode to Mexico. Andrei Codrescu.
    223
An **ode** to roses. Rachel A. Hazen.
    271
An **ode** to Salt Lake City. Dave
    Smith. 367
Ode to the Duchess La Blah. Jim
    Everhard. 241
Ode to the horseshoe crab. Carol
    Frost. 249
Ode to the trees of Lebanon.
    Maurice W. Britts. 215
Ode to Trinity. Patsie Black. 206
Odile. Donald Revell. 351
Odium to the dark angel. James
    Tate. 379
Odor. Anneliese Wagner. 389
Odyssey of the hair. Carolyn
    Stoloff. 376
Oedipus
    Eyeless in Corinth. Cornel

Lengyel. 302
Of course it is. David Wann. 394
"**Of** course there was something
    impious." Robert A. Sears. 362
Of forbidden love. Elsa Gidlow.
    254
Of hidden taxes. Marge Piercy.
    346
Of it. Norman Andrew Kirk. 293
Of myself. Royal Murdoch. 330
"**Of** old times, there was a very
    beautiful" Charles Olson. 337
Of oystermen, workboats. Dave
    Smith. 367
Of the parsonses. Charles Olson.
    337
Of truth and fact. Richmond
    Lattimore. 301
"**Of** words in their material
    form." David James. 282
Off the path. Evelyn Golden. 263
Off the sea into the merchant's
    life... James Schevill. 360
Off to the side. John Yau. 404
Off with the lid. Alice Spohn
    Newton. 332
"**Off**-upland.". Charles Olson. 337
Office machine blues. Josephine
    B. Moretti. 324
Office politics. Wanda Coleman.
    225
The **office** suite sequence, 1965.
    J.W. Rivers. 354
Officers. Josephine Miles. 319
Oft' I ask, what is a show?
    Rachel A. Hazen. 271
"**Oh** but rest in the sheltor of
    love." Michael Robert Pick.
    345
"**Oh** I love you, woman." Michael
    Robert Pick. 345
Oh no! Jack Prelutsky. 348
"**Oh** spirit locked within." Connie
    Hunt. 279
Oh, Africa. Rosa Bogar. 211
Ohio Yankee. Everett A. Gillis.
    258
Oil
    Lyric. Josephine Miles. 319
Oily weather. Ernest Hemingway.
    272
Okanogan sleep. Marc Hudson. 277
"**Okay**, Hawk, where are you when I
    need you." Michael Robert
    Pick. 345
Oklahoma. Ernest Hemingway. 272
Oklahoma
    "Eastern Oklahoma." Madison
    Morrison. 327
    Oklahoma. Ernest Hemingway. 272

Old Age

Afternoon walk. Josephine Miles. 319

Ambrose Remy. Stephen Knauth. 295

Aubade. Phyllis A. Tickle. 382

Boy watching a light-bulb death in a country town. James Schevill. 360

Club for elders. Anneliese Wagner. 389

The couple. Margaret Key Biggs. 205

Dirty old man. James A. Emanuel. 239

Earth music. Margaret Key Biggs. 205

Evelyn. Josephine B. Moretti. 324

Fragile ladies. Erin Jolly. 285

Frankfurt '76. James Torio. 281

From the peak of years. Elsa Gidlow. 254

A game against age. James Schevill. 360

"How do old men walk." James Torio. 281

In childhood education. David James. 282

"It takes the young to understand." Robert A. Sears. 362

The last chapter. Robert L. Wilson. 401

Late song. Cornel Lengyel. 302

Listening to an old man. Evelyn Golden. 263

Ninety-year-old. Marie Daerr Boehringer. 210

Old Carlson. Robert Peters. 343

Old folks home. Lucien Stryk. 377

"Old Man Flowers chewed wood." Michael Robert Pick. 345

An old man's winter night. Robert Frost. 250

The old men visit. Jeanne Lohmann. 305

The old ones. Sam Fishman. 246

One street. Betty Adcock. 192

Only the old are gay. Elsa Gidlow. 254

Paint. Josephine Miles. 319

Poised for flight. Evelyn Golden. 263

A table with people. Marc Kaminsky. 288

"To my friends when I am eighty-five." Robert Kelly. 289

A trail of sparkle. Alice Spohn Newton. 332

Visiting hours. Ruth Lisa Schechter. 359

Voter. Josephine Miles. 319

Woman from Sacramento in Westchester. Ruth Lisa Schechter. 359

Old Age. See also Youth and Age

Old Barry, the balloon seller. James Schevill. 360

Old Bud. James Wright. 403

Old Carlson. Robert Peters. 343

Old cat. Carol Frost. 249

The old cemetery in Cluj. Keith Wilson. 400

Old cities. Andrei Codrescu. 223

Old country. Jeanne Lohmann. 305

Old fashioned & timeworn. Rochelle DuBois. 234

An old feud. Cornel Lengyel. 302

Old folks home. Lucien Stryk. 377

Old King Cool. Harlan Usher. 386

Old letters. Timothy Steele. 374

The old man and the morning bus. Rosa Bogar. 211

"Old Man Flowers chewed wood." Michael Robert Pick. 345

An old man's winter night. Robert Frost. 250

The old McGrath place. Thomas McGrath. 315

Old men sailing the Baltic. Ray Fleming. 247

The old men visit. Jeanne Lohmann. 305

The old ones. Sam Fishman. 246

Old photographs of the author. James Tate. 379

An old pickerel in Walden Pond. William Stafford. 373

Old salesman planning the fit of his death. James Schevill. 360

The old things. Maurice W. Britts. 215

Old thoughts in a zoo room. Norman Andrew Kirk. 293

Old tomb carving: the nameless prince. Keith Wilson. 400

Old trees. Robert A. Sears. 362

The old wives. John F. Barker. 201

Old woman. Robert Anbian. 194

Old woman. Tom Smith. 368

Old woman. Phyllis A. Tickle. 382

The old woman and the cat. James Schevill. 360

The old woman of Patras. James Torio. 281

Old women and hills. Robin
  Becker. 202
Old year's farewell. Marie Daerr
  Boehringer. 210
"An older man." Madison Morrison.
  327
Older men. Martha Janssen. 283
"Older than Byblos" Charles
  Olson. 337
The oldest story. Bill Knott. 296
The Olive Mountain coyote pack.
  Gene Anderson. 195
"Oliver, our dog, went around
  squirting." Michael Robert
  Pick. 345
Olson, Charles
  "Above the head of John Day's
    pasture land." 337
  The account book of B Ellery.
    337
  *Added to/making a republic. 337
  "After the storm was over." 337
  All my life I've heard about
    many. 337
  "All night long." 337
  "The alligator." 337
  And melancholy. 337
  "And now let all the ships come
    in." 337
  April today main street. 337
  "Aristotle & Augustine." 337
  An art called gothonic. 337
  "As Cabeza de Vaca..." 337
  As of Parsonses or Fishermans
    Field... 337
  "Astride/the Chabot/fault." 337
  'At the boundry of the mighty
    world.' 337
  "The authority of Cape Ann." 337
  "B. Ellery" 337
  "Bailyn shows sharp rise." 337
  "Barbara Ellis, ramp." 337
  The beginnings (facts). 337
  "Between Cruiser & Plato..." 337
  Bk ii chapter 37. 337
  "The blow is creation." 337
  "The boats' lights in the
    dawn..." 337
  Bohlin 1. 337
  Bohlin 2. 337
  "Bona Dea..." 337
  "Bottled up for days..." 337
  "The bottom/backward." 337
  "Brang that thing out." 337
  Capt Christopher Levett (of
    York). 337
  Cashes. 337
  Celestial evening, October 1967.
    337
  Chronicles. 337
  Civic diasters. 337
  "The coast goes from Hurrian
    Hazzi to Tyre." 337
  "Coiled." 337
  Cole's Island. 337
  "The condition of the light from
    the sun." 337
  "The cormorant." 337
  "Cornely." 337
  The cow of Dogtown. 337
  "'Cromlech' of course..." 337
  "'Cut Creek,' the river is..."
    337
  The cut. 337
  "Cyprus/the
    strangled/Aphrodite-Rhodes."
    337
  The day's beginnings. 337
  Death is the mother binding us
    to our end. 337
  The death of Carl Olsen. 337
  December 18th. 337
  December 23nd. 337
  December, 1960. 337
  "Descartes soldier/in a time of
    religious." 337
  "The diadem of the dog." 337
  "The distances." 337
  "Dogtown the dog town." 337
  Dogtown-Ann. 337
  Each night is no loss... 337
  "The earth with a city in her
    hair." 337
  "Echidna is the bite." 337
  11 o'clock at night...   337
  "Enyalion of/brown earth." 337
  Essay on Queen Tiy. 337
  "Existed/3000/BC?" 337
  Father sky, mother earth. 337
  The feathered bird of the harbor
    of Gloucester. 337
  February 3rd 1966 High tide...
    337
  "Fire it back into the
    contintent." 337
  First letter on Georges. 337
  "The first of morning was always
    over there." 337
  1st lot from the Cutt.
    337
  Flower of the underworld. 337
  "Followed his sow to apples."
    337
  For "Moira". 337
  For Robt Duncan, who. 337
  Fourteen men stage head winter
    1624/5. 337
  The frontlet. 337
  "Full moon..." 337
  Further completion of plat. 337

"Gee, what I call the upper road
   was the way" 337
"George Decker..." 337
Going right out of the century.
   337
Golden Venetian light... 337
Got me home, the light snow
   gives the air, falling. 337
"Great Washing Rock..." 337
"The groaner shakes louder than
   the whistling buoy..." 337
The Gulf of Maine. 337
Gylfaginning VI. 337
"Having descried the nation."
   337
"Having developed the
   differences..." 337
"He came." 337
"He who walks with his house
   on." 337
"Heaven as sky is made of
   stone..." 337
"Hector-body." 337
Hepit-naga-atosis. 337
"Her headland." 337
"Her stern like a box..." 337
"Here in the Fort my heart
   doth." 337
His health, his poetry, and his
   love all in one. 337
History is the memory of time.
   337
"The history/of earth..." 337
"'Home', to the shore." 337
"Homo anthropos." 337
Hotel Steinplatz, Berlin,
   December 25 (1966). 337
"The hour of evening..." 337
"I am the gold machine..." 337
"I believe in God." 337
"I believe in religion..." 337
"I have an ability - a
   machine..." 337
"I live underneath." 337
"I looked up and saw." 337
"I looked up." 337
"I pass between." 337
"I set out now." 337
"I stand upon you, Fort Place."
   337
"I swung out, at 8 or 10." 337
"I told the woman." 337
"I was bold, I had courage, the
   tide tonight." 337
"I'm going to hate to leave this
   earthly paradise." 337
I, Maximus of Gloucester, to
   you. 337
If the deaths do not stop... 337
"Imbued/with light." 337

In the face of a Chinese view of
   the city. 337
"In the harbor." 337
In the interleaved Almanacks for
   1646 and 1647 of Danforth. 337
"Into the hill..." 337
"Into the stream or entrance..."
   337
"The island, the river, the
   shore." 337
"It says the Amitie sailed." 337
Jl 17 1961. 337
John Burke. 337
"John Watts took." 337
June 6th, 1963. 337
Just as morning twilight... 337
"Just to have her body in my
   mind..." 337
"JW (from the Danelaw) says."
   337
Kent Circle song. 337
The land as haitubu. 337
"Land's End-." 337
"Lane's eye-view of Gloucester"
   337
"The lap." 337
"The last man except
   conceivably." 337
A later note on Letter #15. 337
Later Tyrian business. 337
"'A learned man' sd Strabo
   (meaning Pytheus." 337
"The left hand is the clayx of
   the flower." 337
Letter 10. 337
Letter 16. 337
Letter 20: not a pastoral
   letter. 337
Letter 22. 337
Letter 23. 337
Letter 3. 337
Letter 41 (broken off). 337
Letter 5. 337
Letter 6. 337
Letter 7. 337
Letter 72. 337
Letter 9. 337
Letter, May 2, 1959. 337
A letter, on fishing grounds...
   337
"Licked man (as such) out of the
   ice." 337
"Light signals & mass points."
   337
"Like Mr. Pester acknowledges
   his sinfulness in being" 337
(Literary result) 337
"Lost from the loss of her
   dagger heisted." 337
"Main Street." 337

"The man-with-the-house..." 337
Mareoceanum. 337
Maximus further on (December
    28th 1959). 337
Maximus letter # whatever. 337
Maximus of Gloucester. 337
A Maximus song. 337
Maximus to Gloucester: Letter
    14. 337
Maximus to Gloucester: Letter
    15. 337
Maximus to Gloucester, Letter 27
    [withheld]. 337
Maximus to Gloucester : Letter
    2. 337
Maximus to himself June 1964.
    337
Maximus, at the harbor. 337
Maximus, at Tyre and at Boston.
    337
Maximus, from Dogtown: 1. 337
Maximus, from Dogtown: II. 337
[Maximus, from Dogtown-IV]. 337
Maximus, in Gloucester Sunday,
    LXV. 337
Maximus, March 1961 : I. 337
Maximus, March 1961 : II. 337
Maximus, to Gloucester, letter
    11. 337
Maximus, to Gloucester : Letter
    19 (A pastoral letter). 337
Maximus, to Gloucester : I don't
    mean, just like that. 337
Maximus, to Gloucester, Sunday,
    July 19. 337
Maximus, to Gloucester, Letter
    157. 337
Maximus, to himself. 337
Maximus, to himself, as of
    "Phoenicians." 337
A Maximus. 337
"Melkarth of Tyre." 337
"Migration in fact..." 337
Monday, November 26th, 1962. 337
"The moon is the measure..." 337
"Mother of the tides..." 337
"Mother-spirit..." 337
"The mountain of no
    difference..." 337
My carpenter's son's son's will,
    Lt William Stevens, 1701...
    337
"My memory is" 337
"My wife, my car, my color and
    myself." 337
The new empire. 337
"North/in the ice..." 337
"The/northwest course of
    shifting man..." 337
"Not the intaglio method or

skating." 337
A note on the above. 337
O John Josselyn you. 337
"O Quadriga." 337
The ocean. 337
Oceania. 337
"Of old times, there was a very
    beautiful" 337
Of the parsonses. 337
"Off-upland." 337
"Older than Byblos" 337
"On Bemo Ledge he fell" 337
On first looking out through
    Juan de la Coas'a eyes. 337
"On the earth's edge..." 337
"128 a mole."   337
One of the bronze plaques... 337
"Or Lindsay." 337
"Out of the light of heaven..."
    337
"Out over the land skope." 337
"Outer darkness..." 337
Part of the flower of
    Gloucester. 337
"Patriotism/is the preserved
    park" 337
"Peloria the dog's upper lip
    curling" 337
"People want delivery" 337
"Phalaropes." 337
"Physically, I am home..." 337
The picture. 337
A plantation a beginning. 337
Poem 143. The festival aspect.
    337
"A prayer, to the Lord, cast
    down like a good old Catholic"
    337
Proem. 337
"Publish my own soul..." 337
"Rages/strain." 337
The record. 337
"The return to the mail-bag..."
    337
"Right at the cut." 337
The river map and we're done.
    337
The river: I. 337
The river: II. 337
"The rocks in Settlement Cove."
    337
"Rotundum..." 337
"Said Mrs Tarantino." 337
"The salmon of/wisdom." 337
"The salt, & minerals, of the
    earth return..." 337
Same day, later. 337
Same thought-2. 337
The savages, or voyages of
    Samuel de Champlain of

Brouage. 337
Scheria: ? 337
"The sea's/boiling..." 337
Second letter on Georges' 337
Sequentior. 337
"7 years..."S. 337
"Shag Rock, bull's eye" 337
"shape of Weymouth..." 337
"She who met the serpent..." 337
"Ships for the West Indies..."
  337
Short possible poem... 337
Signature to petition... 337
"The sky." 337
"Slownesses/which are
  an/amount." 337
Snow at evening. 337
So sassafras. 337
Some good news. 337
The song and dance of. 337
The songs of Maximus. 337
"Space and time..." 337
Stage Fort Park. 337
Stevens song. 337
Stiffening, in the Master
  Founders' wills. 337
"Strod the water's edge..." 337
"Sun/right in my eye." 337
"Sun/upside down." 337
Sunday, January 16, 1966. 337
"Sweet salmon." 337
"Swimming through the air..."
  337
"Ta meteura/meteor things" 337
"Take the earth in under a
  single review." 337
"Tall is the fort." 337
"Tantrist." 337
The telesphere. 337
Tessarae. 337
"Thank God." 337
"That island/floating in the
  sea." 337
"That there was a woman in
  Gloucester..." 337
"That's/the combination of the
  ocean." 337
There was a salt-works at Stage
  Fort. 337
These people sat right out my
  window too. 337
"They brawled in the streets..."
  337
3rd letter on Georges, unwritten
  T. 337
13 vessels, and David Pearce's
  T. 337
"This living hand..." 337
"This town." 337
Thurs Sept 14th 1961. 337

"To enter into their bodies."
  337
["To get the rituals
  straight..." 337
"To have the bright body of sex
  and love." 337
"To make those silent vessels
  go..." 337
"To my Portuguese..." 337
"To travel Typhon" 337
"Turn out your." 337
"23 School and 16 Columbia.".T.
  337
The twist. 337
Tyrian businesses. 337
"Up the steps, along the porch"
  337
The usefulness. 337
"Valorem is." 337
"The vault/of heaven." 337
"Veda upanishad edda than." 337
The view - July 29, 1961. 337
"View" : fr tge Orontes. 337
"Watch-house." 337
West Gloucester. 337
"When do poppies bloom..." 337
"While on/Obadiah Bruen's
  Island, the Algonquins" 337
"Wholly absorbed." 337
"Why light, and flowers? Paul
  Oakley." 337
"William Stevens." 337
The winning thing. 337
The winter the Gen. Starks was
  stuck. 337
"The wolf/slinks off." 337
"The woman who said she went out
  every Sunday." 337
"Wonis kvam." 337
"Wrote my first poems." 337
"You drew the space in." 337
"The young ladies." 337

Omens
The two rings' lesson. Ghita
  Orth. 339
On a birthday. Ralph J., Jr.
  Mills. 321
On a black and photograph of a
  house. Jim Simmerman. 365
On a high hill. John F. Barker.
  201
"On a holy night, I ask you God."
  Michael Robert Pick. 345
On a loved one going to war.
  Jocelyn Hollis. 274
On a malicious critic. Cornel
  Lengyel. 302
On a marginal bore. Cornel
  Lengyel. 302
On a mulberry tree branch in

Jackson Park. J.W. Rivers. 354
On a popular historian. Cornel
    Lengyel. 302
On a quick-change artist. Cornel
    Lengyel. 302
"On a rich sofa." Madison
    Morrison. 327
On a slow student. Cornel
    Lengyel. 302
On a wind. Ralph J., Jr. Mills.
    321
On an unconceived painting by
    Lautrec. Jim Simmerman. 365
On an unpublished author. Cornel
    Lengyel. 302
On April 24th 1981. Stephen Todd
    Booker. 212
On astronauts who lost their
    lives when their rocket...
    Cornel Lengyel. 302
On being literal-minded. Robin
    Becker. 202
On being swallowed whole. Alice
    Spohn Newton. 332
"On Bemo Ledge he fell" Charles
    Olson. 337
On board the QE2 Laura Boss. 213
On Boscovich's law that bodies
    can never actually...contact.
    Bradford Morrow. 329
On camera. Ghita Orth. 339
On contemplating the speed of a
    tiny red spider. James Torio.
    281
On eliminating the astronomer
    from photographs of gases.
    Marilyn Kallet. 287
On everybody's friend. Cornel
    Lengyel. 302
On first looking into Norton's
    Anthology of Poetry (Revised)
    Richard Blessing. 208
On first looking out through Juan
    de la Coas'a eyes. Charles
    Olson. 337
On green money street. Wanda
    Coleman. 225
On guard in New York. James
    Schevill. 360
On inhabiting an orange.
    Josephine Miles. 319
On Intersate 5, near San
    Francisco. Evelyn Golden. 263
On Jan. 10th 1981, the nite.
    Stephen Todd Booker. 212
On Jan. 17th 1980 Stephen Todd
    Booker. 212
On Jan. 4th 1981 Stephen Todd
    Booker. 212
On March 30th 1981. Stephen Todd
    Booker. 212
On maturity. James R. Rhodes. 352
On metal corsets. Marge Piercy.
    346
On my father's side. Laura Boss.
    213
On nameless days. Rachel A.
    Hazen. 271
On New Year's Day. Marge Piercy.
    346
On not attending my father's
    funeral. Robert Peters. 343
On not being able to imagine the
    future. Robin Becker. 202
On not being the youngest wife at
    the Shop-Rite. Laura Boss. 213
On organization. Andrei Codrescu.
    223
On players unknown. Cornel
    Lengyel. 302
On resumption of the military
    draft. Thomas Lux. 307
On returning to the city. John
    Reed. 350
On seeing a flag-draped casket.
    Jocelyn Hollis. 274
On seeing a page of Virginia's
    Woolf's diary. Anneliese
    Wagner. 389
On seeing the play, "The Elephant
    Man," December, 1979. Maria
    Gillan. 256
On speed. Wanda Coleman. 225
On the attraction of heavenly
    bodies. Dennis Hinrichsen. 273
On the beach watched by a
    seagull. James Schevill. 360
On the burning of Mingus's bass.
    James Schevill. 360
On the disadvantages of central
    heating. Amy Clampitt. 222
"On the earth's edge..." Charles
    Olson. 337
On the edge of knowledge. Anne
    Bailie. 199
On the election of a president.
    Anne Bailie. 199
On the eve of our anniversary.
    Gary Margolis. 311
On the face of it. Marie Daerr
    Boehringer. 210
On the face of my words. Ray
    Fleming. 247
On the great wheel. Anne Bailie.
    199
On the island. Miriam Goodman.
    264
On the midway. Mitchell Howard.
    276
On the midway. Stephen Knauth.

295
On the newcomers. Cornel Lengyel.
    302
"On the outskirts of London..."
    Albert Goldbarth. 261
On the road last night. William
    Stafford. 373
On the rocks at forty. Randy
    Blasing. 207
"On the same fall." Madison
    Morrison. 327
On the street after hours. Norman
    Andrew Kirk. 293
On the train. Carolyn Stoloff.
    376
On the warm side. Ernest Tedlock.
    380
On the world's birthday. James
    Tate. 379
On weddynge gyftes. Ernest
    Hemingway. 272
On wishing to avoid the bill.
    Miriam Goodman. 264
Once in a dream. William
    Stafford. 373
Once in the 40's. William
    Stafford. 373
"Once upon a time." Sally Love
    Saunders. 358
Once when I was walking up the
    stairs. Anthony Petrosky. 344
"One attuned to the spirit."
    Theta Burke. 218
One basket. Sharon Bryan. 217
"One died by this tremendous
    headache." Larry Eigner. 237
One for the monk of Montaudon.
    Paul Violi. 388
"128 a mole."   Charles Olson.
    337
The one indigenous bird. Larry
    Moffi. 322
One March. Randy Blasing. 207
One memory of Rose. Eve Triem.
    383
One morning. Lyn Lifshin. 303
"One never intends/to be
    selfish." Theta Burke. 218
"One reached out/in her need."
    Theta Burke. 218
One rose of stone. Keith Wilson.
    400
One song is sung. Alice Joyce
    Davidson. 227
One street. Betty Adcock. 192
"One tree/holds/a hundred birds."
    Joan Walsh Anglund. 197
The one who can. Wanda Coleman.
    225
"The One who crawled me off His

knee." Da Free John. 284
One year. Betty Adcock. 192
"One-ery, two-ery, dickery dan."
    Jan Ormerod. 338
One-eye and the German prisoners
    of war in Colorado. James
    Schevill. 360
One cedar tree. Joy Harjo. 269
"One courage is the way." Robert
    A. Sears. 362
One ethnic-American. Rose Basile
    Green. 265
101 dreams of briar rose
    Tom Smith. 368
A one of music. Rachel A. Hazen.
    271
One time. William Stafford. 373
"One-eyed Jack, the pirate
    chief." Jan Ormerod. 338
"One hour." Michael Robert Pick.
    345
"One I love." Jan Ormerod. 338
One of the bronze plaques...
    Charles Olson. 337
"One, two/Buckle my shoe." Jan
    Ormerod. 338
Onion snow (March) Josephine B.
    Moretti. 324
Only a mem'ry. Rachel A. Hazen.
    271
Only because. Ghita Orth. 339
Only child. May Miller. 320
"Only in my fantasies." Sally
    Love Saunders. 358
Only once. Sandra McPherson. 317
Only the best line holds. Scott
    Chisholm. 221
Only the old are gay. Elsa
    Gidlow. 254
"Only the open gate/can receive."
    Joan Walsh Anglund. 197
Ontario, Canada
    Snow-dunk in Ontario. Joyce
    Carol Oates. 336
Opal. Josephine Miles. 319
The open field. Jacqueline Frank.
    248
The open fire. John F. Barker.
    201
"Open road." Larry Eigner. 237
The open staircase. David
    Wagoner. 390
Opening. Edwin Honig. 275
Opening day of the world series.
    James Magorian. 309
The opening game. Ernest
    Hemingway. 272
Opera. Jacques Sollov. 371
Opera
    Nights at the opera. Scott

Chisholm. 221
Opera. Jacques Sollov. 371
Opera buffa. James Torio. 281
Opera buffa. James Torio. 281
The operation. W.D. (William De Witt) Snodgrass. 369
Ophelia. Marilyn Kallet. 287
Ophelia's last soliloquy. Anne Bailie. 199
Opium for Archie Anderson. Andrei Codrescu. 223
Opium for Britt Wilkie. Andrei Codrescu. 223
Opposites. Carolyn Stoloff. 376
Optimism
The prize. Steve Kowit. 299
Or consider Prometheus. Amy Clampitt. 222
"Or follow ants to their hill." Michael Robert Pick. 345
"Or Lindsay." Charles Olson. 337
The oracle. James Torio. 281
Oracles
The oracle. James Torio. 281
Orange blossom trail. Randy Blasing. 207
Orange freeway. Randy Blasing. 207
Orange, California. Gary Margolis. 311
Orange-colored sky, fr. Friday night quartet. David Shapiro. 363
Oranges
Je suis un orange. David Wann. 394
There is an orange happening. Norman Andrew Kirk. 293
Orbital bunnes, inc. Mitchell Howard. 276
Orchards
Perishables. May Miller. 320
Orchids
The smaller orchid. Amy Clampitt. 222
Order of battle. Marieve Rugo. 356
Orderly. Josephine Miles. 319
An ordinary composure. James L. White. 396
An ordinary man. Christopher Bursk. 219
Ordinary song. Phyllis A. Tickle. 382
"An ordinary white sedan." Madison Morrison. 327
Original women. Robert Kelly. 289
Origo. John Reed. 350
Ormerod, Jan
"Can you walk on tiptoe." 338
"Clap hands, Daddy comes." 338
"The cock does crow." 338
"Dan, Dan/Dirty old man." 338
"Diddle, diddle, dumpling." 338
"Eye winker." 338
"Father and Mother and Uncle John." 338
"Go to bed late." 338
"Handy pandy, Jack-a-dandy." 338
"Hokey, pokey, winky, wum." 338
"Humpty Dumpty sat on a wall." 338
"I can tie my shoelaces." 338
"I'm a little teapot." 338
"Little man in a coal pit." 338
"Little pig." 338
"Manners in the dining room." 338
"Miss Polly had a dolly who was sick, sick, sick." 338
"Mix a pancake, stir a pancake." 338
"Niddledy, noddledy, to and fro." 338
"One-ery, two-ery, dickery dan." 338
"One-eyed Jack, the pirate chief." 338
"One I love." 338
"One, two/Buckle my shoe." 338
"Rain, rain, go away." 338
"Rigadoon, rigadoon." 338
"Smiling girls, rosy boys." 338
"Star light, star bright." 338
"Stepping over steppuing stones, one, two, three." 338
"To market, to market." 338
"A trot, a canter." 338
"Undo buttons." 338
"Up to the wooden hill." 338
"When Jack's a good boy." 338
Ornaments. Anthony Petrosky. 344
Orphan leaves. Rodney Nelson. 331
Orphans
Tending the sheep at big baas flip. James Tate. 379
Orphee. Robert Kelly. 289
Orpheus. Roy Marz. 312
Orpheus. W.D. (William De Witt) Snodgrass. 369
Orpheus
The affinities of Orpheus, sels. Edwin Honig. 275
Another Orpheus. Edwin Honig. 275
The head of Orpheus. Robert Kelly. 289
His chain. Edwin Honig. 275
Orpheus. Roy Marz. 312
Orpheus. W.D. (William De Witt)

Snodgrass. 369
Orth, Ghita
Acrophobia. 339
After the dying. 339
Alien. 339
Anchorage. 339
An answer for my daughter. 339
Ascension. 339
At the Western Wall. 339
Blood-remembering. 339
Bounty. 339
Breakage. 339
Changeling. 339
Compensatory. 339
Continuing. 339
Deliverances. 339
Elephants-a mythology. 339
Fireflies. 339
For Lael, dead at Nahariya. 339
For my name's sake. 339
Guide. 339
Honeymoon. 339
In a season of change. 339
In my own curved bones, sels.
    339
In tapestry, the pattern. 339
Itinerant. 339
January. 339
Letting go. 339
The maggid speaks of a dog in
    the night. 339
The magic triad. 339
A momentary son. 339
Mothering. 339
Museum. 339
Naming. 339
Non-poem for my son. 339
On camera. 339
Only because. 339
Relinquishing. 339
River gods, Dublin. 339
She speaks at graveside. 339
Skies: a Jew in Germany, 1979.
    339
Songs of the only child. 339
Songs of transmutation. 339
Souvenir. 339
Translation. 339
The two rings' lesson. 339
Weavers. 339
Wet nurse. 339
Osbey, Brenda Marie
Ceremony for Minneconjoux. 340
Chifalta. 340
Eileen. 340
Eliza. 340
The factory poem. 340
The fete women. 340
Flying solo. 340
Letters to Brasil. 340

Living in the tan house. 340
Madhouses. 340
Ms. Livvy's boy. 340
"My name is Felicity." 340
Ramona Veagis. 340
Token stones. 340
Writing the words. 340
Osgood, Francis Sargent
To Francis S. Osgood. Edgar
    Allan Poe. 347
Oshi. James L. White. 396
Osiris
Head of a smiling priest:
    Limestone, Egypt. Roy Marz.
    312
The **ostrich.** Jack Prelutsky. 349
Ostriches
The ostrich. Jack Prelutsky. 349
The **other** and the others. David
    Shapiro. 363
Other dads. Martha Janssen. 283
The **other** house. David Wagoner.
    390
The **other** life. Anthony Petrosky.
    344
Other me's. Alice Spohn Newton.
    332
Other people's music. Rod McKuen.
    316
The **other** side of marriage. Tefke
    Goldberger. 262
Other snapshots. Ruth Lisa
    Schechter. 359
The **other** woman. Debra Bruce. 216
Otilia Colunga on her knees in
    line... J.W. Rivers. 354
Otter slide. Phillips Kloss. 294
Otters
Otter slide. Phillips Kloss. 294
Ounce. X.J. Kennedy. 290
"**Our** answers/are a part of our
    questions." Theta Burke. 218
Our blindness. David Wagoner. 390
"**Our** bombs can now kill all."
    Michael Robert Pick. 345
Our cave. William Stafford. 373
Our classroom has a mailbox. Jack
    Prelutsky. 348
Our eyes have seen the glory.
    Ernesto Galarza. 252
Our garden. Deborah Tall. 378
Our kind. William Stafford. 373
Our knees. John Godfrey. 260
Our lady. John Godfrey. 260
Our Lady of Angel's sight saving
    class. Debra Bruce. 216
Our lady of pain. John Reed. 350
"**Our** love began skin-deep."
    Robert A. Sears. 362
Our names the only known. Paul

Davis. 228
Our night. Carol Frost. 249
"Our relationship is." Sally Love
    Saunders. 358
Our response to death. Maurice W.
    Britts. 215
Our scales are off-center. Maria
    Gillan. 256
Our secret selves. Maria Gillan.
    256
Our stories. Anneliese Wagner.
    389
"Our tourist group." Madison
    Morrison. 327
Our two birds. Roy Marz. 312
"Our vulnerability." Theta Burke.
    218
"Our/sense of values." A.
    Dovichi. 233
Out. Marilyn Kallet. 287
Out of Africa. Robert A. Sears.
    362
Out of Eden. James R. Rhodes. 352
Out of love's timeless egg. Elsa
    Gidlow. 254
Out of McHenry. Steve Kowit. 298,
    299
Out of the frame. Colette Inez.
    280
Out of the hospital Peter. Marge
    Piercy. 346
"Out of the light of heaven..."
    Charles Olson. 337
"Out of the wind and leaves."
    Larry Eigner. 237
Out on the hills. Elsa Gidlow.
    254
"Out over the land skope."
    Charles Olson. 337
"Out saunter the doggies."
    Madison Morrison. 327
'Out, out -.' Robert Frost. 250
The outdoor screen. May Miller.
    320
The outer bar. Amy Clampitt. 222
"Outer darkness..." Charles
    Olson. 337
Outer drive. Edwin Honig. 275
The outer reaches of the heart.
    Rod McKuen. 316
An outing on Pawley's Island.
    J.W. Rivers. 354
Outline. Frances Mayes. 314
Outside. Josephine Miles. 319
Outside Avila's walls. Carolyn
    Stoloff. 376
Outside Baby Moon's. Paul Violi.
    388
Outside Martins Ferry, Ohio. Dave
    Smith. 367

Outsiders. Elsa Gidlow. 254
"Over a forest of coffins morning
    rings." Carolyn Stoloff. 376
Over drinks. Randy Blasing. 207
Over Manhattan. Donald Revell.
    351
Overweight. James L. White. 396
Owen, Wilfrid
    The soldier-poet. Jocelyn
        Hollis. 274
Owl. Thomas Hornsby Ferril. 243
Owl. Rokwaho. 355
The owl in the refrigerator.
    Harry Humes. 278
The owl. Jack Prelutsky. 349
Owling. Gene Anderson. 195
Owls
    Dean of brids. Erin Jolly. 285
    Owl. Thomas Hornsby Ferril. 243
    Owl. Rokwaho. 355
    The owl in the refrigerator.
        Harry Humes. 278
    The owl. Jack Prelutsky. 349
    Owling. Gene Anderson. 195
    Sea owl. Dave Smith. 367
    Sestina for the owl. Frances
        Mayes. 314
    Snow owl. Dave Smith. 367
The owls. Greg Kuzma. 300
Oxfordshire spring. Ray Fleming.
    247
The oyster catcher's cry.
    Phillips Kloss. 294
Oyster cove. Stephen Sandy. 357
Oysters. Jacqueline Frank. 248
Oysters. Jack Prelutsky. 349
Oysters
    Of oystermen, workboats. Dave
        Smith. 367
    Oysters. Jacqueline Frank. 248
    Oysters. Jack Prelutsky. 349
    Shelling oysters. James
        Magorian. 308
Ozark Mountains
    Call of the Ozarks. James
        Magorian. 309

P.S. Norman Andrew Kirk. 293
P.T.A. fair. Josephine B.
    Moretti. 324
Pa. Sam Fishman. 246
Pablo Nerunda. Edwin Honig. 275
Pacific Ocean
    By La Push. Marc Hudson. 277
Pacifism
    Formulas for non-violence.
        Mitchell Howard. 276

Fragment of ancient skull. Steve
    Kowit. 299
Pack rat sieve. Mei-Mei
    Berssenbrugge. 203, 204
The **pack** rat. Jack Prelutsky. 349
Packing mother's things. Carol
    Frost. 249
A **pact**. Alice Joyce Davidson. 227
A **paean**. Edgar Allan Poe. 347
"The **page** is damp." Madison
    Morrison. 327
Pain. Maurice W. Britts. 215
Pain. Evelyn Golden. 263
Pain
    Benumbed. Robert L. Wilson. 401
    Blood wedding. Scott Chisholm.
        221
    Cowardice court. Harrison
        Fisher. 245
    Crayfish. Anthony Petrosky. 344
    Dis-ease. Marge Piercy. 346
    "Early needs/unmet," Theta
        Burke. 218
    "I can sing." Michael Robert
        Pick. 345
    In pain. Albert Goldbarth. 261
    Inverted sunday. Robert Anbian.
        194
    It cannot be it is. Edwin Honig.
        275
    The medal. George Eklund. 238
    Nuke burns. Gene Deetro. 230
    Our lady of pain. John Reed. 350
    Pain. Maurice W. Britts. 215
    The painter in the montain.
        Edwin Honig. 275
    Return to the loss. Ernest
        Tedlock. 380
    A screamer discusses methods of
        screaming. James Scnevill. 360
    Ssh. Albert Goldbarth. 261
    Suffering does not ennoble. Haig
        Khatchadourian. 292
    The sympathizers. Josephine
        Miles. 319
    "There's a lonely part," Theta
        Burke. 218
    Under the mushroom. Margaret Key
        Biggs. 205
    The way I feel. Rosa Bogar. 211
    "You get a cold." Theta Burke.
        218
"The **pain** of a mistake goes by so
    slow." Michael Robert Pick.
    345
"**Pain/phsyical** or emotional."
    Theta Burke. 218
"The **pains** of life and love."
    Theta Burke. 218
Paint. Josephine Miles. 319

Paint 'til you faint. James Tate.
    379
Painter. Anneliese Wagner. 389
Painter. Richmond Lattimore. 301
Painter at dusk. Marc Hudson. 277
The **painter** in the montain. Edwin
    Honig. 275
The **painter** studying trees
    without leaves. James
    Schevill. 360
The **painter**. Stephen Sandy. 357
The **painter**. Thomas R. Sleigh.
    366
Painting the fence. Susan Tichy.
    381
The **painting**. Michael Akillian.
    193
Paintings and Painters
    The angel track. James Schevill.
        360
    The annunciations. Roy Marz. 312
    The cat at the last supper. Roy
        Marz. 312
    "During siesta..." Susan Tichy.
        381
    Four unfinished prisoners by
        Michelangelo. Roy Marz. 312
    Frameless. Roy Marz. 312
    Ghazal: the impasse. Robin
        Becker. 202
    His neighbor talks of Monet.
        Jeanne Lohmann. 305
    Hokusai's 'Wild Horses.' Sharon
        Bryan. 217
    If a model, fr. The day of the
        body. Carol Frost. 249
    January 18, 1979. John Yau. 404
    Momoyama. Anne Bailie. 199
    Paint 'til you faint. James
        Tate. 379
    Painter. Richmond Lattimore. 301
    Painter at dusk. Marc Hudson.
        277
    The painter. Stephen Sandy. 357
    The painter. Thomas R. Sleigh.
        366
    Passionflower. Edwin Honig. 275
    Promises. Stephen Todd Booker.
        212
    Still lives. Albert Goldbarth.
        261
    Traveling art exhibit. James
        Magorian. 308
    Watercolor. Jeanne Lohmann. 305
A **pair** of intuitive dogs. Stephen
    Todd Booker. 212
Pajamas
    The blue pajamas. Charles Edward
        Eaton. 236
Pajaro dunes. Tefke Goldberger.

262

Pakistan
Bashir was my name. James
Schevill. 360
A pale arrangement of hands.
Cathy Song. 372
Paleolithic Art
Coproatavism. Clayton Eshleman.
240
A kind of moisture on the wall.
Clayton Eshleman. 240
The loaded sleeve of Hades.
Clayton Eshleman. 240
Magdalenian. Clayton Eshleman.
240
Notes on a visit to Le Tuc
D'Audoubert. Clayton Eshleman.
240
The seeds of narrative. Clayton
Eshleman. 240
A small cave. Clayton Eshleman.
240
Stags and salmon. Carol Frost.
249
The staked woman. Clayton
Eshleman. 240
Visions of the fathers of
Lascaux. Clayton Eshleman. 240
Palestinian Arabs
In an Arab town. Susan Tichy.
381
Two cities, three loves. Susan
Tichy. 381
"**Palestrina** from/invisible
source." Larry Eigner. 237
Palm Beach, 1928. Herbert Morris.
326
Palm Sunday. Amy Clampitt. 222
Palm Sunday
Palm Sunday. Amy Clampitt. 222
Palm Sunday at Salishan. Franz
Schneider. 361
Palm Sunday debriefing. Jenne
Andrews. 196
Palm Trees
Biscayne Bay. Ernesto Galarza.
252
The palm voyeur. Charles Edward
Eaton. 236
The **palm** voyeur. Charles Edward
Eaton. 236
Palm wine. Robert A. Sears. 362
Pam. Wanda Coleman. 225
Panda zoo. Norman Andrew Kirk.
293
Panda zoo review. Norman Andrew
Kirk. 293
Pandas
Panda zoo. Norman Andrew Kirk.
293

Panda zoo review. Norman Andrew
Kirk. 293
Pandora
Pandora's dream. David Wagoner.
390
Pandora's dream. David Wagoner.
390
Pangolin. X.J. Kennedy. 290
Pangolins
Pangolin. X.J. Kennedy. 290
The **panther.** Bill Knott. 296
Pantry secrets. Mitchell Howard.
276
Papa. Susan Stock. 375
Papageno. W.D. (William De Witt)
Snodgrass. 369
Paper on humor. Andrei Codrescu.
223
Paperweight escape. Stephen Todd
Booker. 212
The **paperweight.** Charles Edward
Eaton. 236
Papier-mache cat. James Magorian.
309
A **parable** of prophecy. Thomas
Hornsby Ferril. 243
The **parable** of the burnt=out
porch light. James Magorian.
309
The **parable** of the pecan tree.
James Magorian. 309
The **parable** of the rain-soaked
macrame. James Magorian. 309
The **parable** of the ten virgins.
James Magorian. 309
The **parable** of the two debtors.
James Magorian. 309
The **parable** of the unpublished
poem. James Magorian. 309
Parables
The blind men and the
disillusioned elephant. James
Magorian. 308
Maximus letter # whatever.
Charles Olson. 337
The parable of the burnt=out
porch light. James Magorian.
309
The parable of the ten virgins.
James Magorian. 309
The parable of the unpublished
poem. James Magorian. 309
Paracelsus in Puerto Rico.
Charles Edward Eaton. 236
Parachute madonna. Lyn Lifshin.
303
A **parachute.** Sally Love Saunders.
358
Parade at the live stock show.
James Schevill. 360

Parades
Parade at the live stock show.
James Schevill. 360
The real parader. James
Schevill. 360
Paradise. Alberta Turner. 384
Paradise lost and found. Sam
Fishman. 246
Paradise. See Heaven

Paradox. Evelyn Golden. 263
Paradox of gravity. Cathryn
Hankla. 268
Parakeets
The encounter of the pet store
owner with Sarah L. Burkett.
James Schevill. 360
Parallax. Mitchell Howard. 276
Parallel lives. John Yau. 404
Paranoia
Even paranoiacs. Bradford
Morrow. 329
Parent. Josephine Miles. 319
Parental puzzlement. Marie Daerr
Boenringer. 210
Parents and Parenthood
Along the Garonne. Colette Inez.
280
Beginning over. Jeanne Lohmann.
305
The children. Wanda Coleman. 225
Firefly. Cathryn Hankla. 268
Friendly persuasion. Josephine
B. Moretti. 324
A guilty father to his daughter.
James Schevill. 360
Learning to bake bread. Gene
Anderson. 195
Poem for my parents. Steve
Kowit. 299
Reflections. Josephine B.
Moretti. 324
"A special spirit in your
birth." Robert A. Sears. 362
Streetlight: the wedding
photograph. Anthony Petrosky.
344
That's Karl, my husband.
Phillips Kloss. 294
A walk with my children. Gene
Anderson. 195
When love is gone. Rosa Bogar.
211
Wings. Albert Goldbarth. 261
Paris - Les Tuileries. Michael
Gizzi. 259
Paris, France
Climbing Montmartre. Melvin
Dixon. 231
Come, look quietly. James

Wright. 403
Crossing the square,
Montparnasse. James A.
Emanuel. 239
Daniel in Paris. James A.
Emanuel. 239
The garden. William Oandasan.
335
Getting directions. Melvin
Dixon. 231
The **park** at Cluj. Keith Wilson.
400
The **park** beckons. Barry
Wallenstein. 393
Park filled with statues of
famous airline ticket agents.
James Magorian. 309
The **park.** Andrei Codrescu. 223
Parked. Wanda Coleman. 225
Parker, Dorothy
To a tragic poetess. Ernest
Hemingway. 272
Parking lot. Thomas Hornsby
Ferril. 243
"Parking lot but." Larry Eigner.
237
Parks
The park beckons. Barry
Wallenstein. 393
Prospect park. Rodney Nelson.
331
Part of America's pride. Maurice
W. Britts. 215
A **part** of forever. Alice Spohn
Newton. 332
Part of the flower of Gloucester.
Charles Olson. 337
Part of the story. Robert
Pawlowski. 341
The **particles.** Randy Blasing. 207
Parties
Afternoon social. Phyllis A.
Tickle. 382
Cocktail-party puzzler. Marie
Daerr Boehringer. 210
Dinner invitation from a tribe
of cannibals. James Magorian.
308
Dinner party. Jeanne Lohmann.
305
Dip trip. Marie Daerr
Boehringer. 210
A formal occasion. Thomas R.
Sleigh. 366
A late guest. William Stafford.
373
Life of the party. Mark Vinz.
387
Smoke rings. C.D. Wright. 402
Toast. Larry Moffi. 322

Twenty. Robert Kelly. 289
Parting. See Separation

Partita. Edwin Honig. 275
Partnership. Alice Joyce
      Davidson. 227
Parts of the body. Christopher
      Bursk. 219
"The **party** host." Madison
      Morrison. 327
Pas-de-deux. Patsie Black. 206
Pascual Orozco. J.W. Rivers. 354
~~Pass me not. Rose Rose. 211~~
Pass the paprika. Josephine B.
      Moretti. 324
Passage. Carol Frost. 249
Passages. Thomas McGrath. 315
Passenger pigeon poem. Rokwaho.
      355
Passes for Nicanor Parra. Edwin
      Honig. 275
Passing. Edwin Honig. 275
Passing a pile of stones. William
      Stafford. 373
Passing from the provinces.
      Bradford Morrow. 329
Passing the marquee in Maysville.
      James Applewhite. 198
Passing the wand (August 15,
      1975). Rose Basile Green. 265
Passing through. Mitchell Howard.
      276
Passing through Les Eyzies.
      Jacqueline Frank. 248
Passion. Josephine Miles. 319
Passion
      As a great prince. Edwin Honig.
         275
      Come closer. Jacques Sollov. 371
      Epidemics. Joan Colby. 224
      "The winds of my passion." Sally
         Love Saunders. 358
Passionflower. Edwin Honig. 275
Passions of the flowering apple.
      Gary Margolis. 311
Passive aspic. John Godfrey. 260
Passports
      When you go anywhere. William
         Stafford. 373
Past
      The aurignacian summation.
         Clayton Esnleman. 240
      Before. Albert Goldbarth. 261
      Earthworks. James Tate. 379
      Eating my tail. Marge Piercy.
         346
      Escape. Martha Janssen. 283
      Essay on Queen Tiy. Charles
         Olson. 337
      A hundred years ago. John F.

Barker. 201
      Memory of another time. Rochelle
         DuBois. 234
      Nap time. Marie Daerr
         Boehringer. 210
      1958.   Kenneth Koch. 297
      Pajaro dunes. Tefke Goldberger.
         262
      The ravine. James Applewhite.
         198
      Remembering the fifties. Greg
         Kuzma. 300
      The Viking's horn at Joyne. Ray
         Fleming. 247
Past and fantasy. Rachel A.
      Hazen. 271
Past closing time. Carolyn
      Stoloff. 376
Past visions, future events.
      Cathryn Hankla. 268
Pastoral. Cynthia Grenfell. 266
Pastoral '17. James Torio. 281
A **pastoral.** Norman Andrew Kirk.
      293
The **pasture.** Robert Frost. 250
Paternoster
      The Lord's Prayer paraphrased.
         Evelyn Golden. 263
      Two versions of the Lord's
         Prayer, sels. R. Buckminster
         Fuller. 251
Paterson is glass. Maria Gillan.
      256
Paterson, New Jersey
      Paterson is glass. Maria Gillan.
         256
Path oft' trod. Alice Spohn
      Newton. 333
The **path** that separates. Robert
      L. Wilson. 401
Paths. Josephine Miles. 319
Paths. See Roads and Trails

Patience
      Bell. Josephine Miles. 319
      Holding on. Rod McKuen. 316
      "Pain/phsyical or emotional."
         Theta Burke. 218
      "When moons peek through
         clouds." Michael Robert Pick.
         345
Patient observation. James R.
      Rhodes. 352
Patriarch. Mark Vinz. 387
"Patriotism/is the preserved
      park" Charles Olson. 337
A **patsy.** Martha Janssen. 283
Pattern. Frances Mayes. 314
Patterns in the sky. Jeanne
      Lohmann. 305

Paul's wife. Robert Frost. 250
The **Paulownia** tree. Roy Marz. 312
A **pause** for a fine phrase. James
   A. Emanuel. 239
Pavlovna, Anna
   The Paulownia tree. Roy Marz.
   312
Pawlowski, Robert
   At the tomb of the unknown
     soldier. 341
   At thirty-nine. 341
   Aubade. 341
   Baptism. 341
   Cabin opening. 341
   Confirmation. 341
   The deep shade. 341
   A drama of significant events.
     341
   Dreams are not in season. 341
   Driver. 341
   The dying child. 341
   Extreme unction. 341
   First communion and thereafter.
     341
   Flood. 341
   For Heidi. 341
   Holy orders. 341
   Houston's Negroes. 341
   Is this my love? 341
   Journey. 341
   Lighted windows. 341
   The long geese. 341
   The magician. 341
   Matrimony. 341
   Mid stream. 341
   Missing persons. 341
   My garden insects. 341
   My Maggie machine. 341
   Part of the story. 341
   Penance. 341
   Rescue. 341
   The river fishes. 341
   Sea burial. 341
   Second-growth trees. 341
   The soldier's poem. 341
   SRO. 341
   Storm. 341
   Street dance. 341
   Suicide. 341
   To the last. 341
   Upon cutting a flower for my
     mistress. 341
   Visit. 341
Pax vobiscum. John F. Barker. 201
Pay me. Norman Andrew Kirk. 293
Paying some slight attention to
   his birthday... Miller
   Williams. 399
Payment. Christopher Bursk. 219
Peace. Connie Hunt. 279

Peace
   "The angels came... and there
     was loveliness." Joan Walsh
     Anglund. 197
   Anniversary sonnet. Stephen
     Sandy. 357
   "Are you/from this earth?" A.
     Dovichi. 233
   "Capturing visions relay my mind
     to infinity." Michael Robert
     Pick. 345
   Cathedral in the pines. Norman
     Andrew Kirk. 293
   Christ just spoke. Alice Spohn
     Newton. 332
   Dinner bell. Josephine Miles.
     319
   Finding peace. Alice Joyce
     Davidson. 227
   Harmony tomorrow. May Miller.
     320
   Marriage song. Elsa Gidlow. 254
   "On a holy night, I ask you
     God." Michael Robert Pick. 345
   Real peace. Rosa Bogar. 211
   Salome. Roy Marz. 312
   Sanctuary. Norman Andrew Kirk.
     293
   They all made peace - what is
     peace? Ernest Hemingway. 272
   Working for peace. Alice Joyce
     Davidson. 227
   Zzzzzzzzzzzzz. Andrei Codrescu.
     223
Peace, father, where you lie.
   James Schevill. 360
"Peace, infinity's plot." Michael
   Robert Pick. 345
The **peaceable** kingdom of Edward
   Hicks. James Schevill. 360
Peach Trees
   Two peach trees. Marge Piercy.
     346
Peaches. John Godfrey. 260
Peacock display. David Wagoner.
   390
Peacock feathers. Patsie Black.
   206
The **peacock** in the bed. Charles
   Edward Eaton. 236
Peacocks
   Peacock display. David Wagoner.
     390
Peak activity in boardwalk ham
   concession. Josephine Miles.
   319
Peale, Charles Wilson
   In nervous moment: Charles
     Wilson Peale. James Schevill.
     360

Pearl. Josephine Miles. 319
The pearl. Richmond Lattimore.
    301
Pears
    Sound arithmetic. Carolyn
        Stoloff. 376
Peasant song. Keith Wilson. 400
Peasants
    Sketch of a peasant man. Keith
        Wilson. 400
Pedestal madonna. Lyn Lifshin.
    303
Pedestrian. Thomas Lux. 307
Pedestrian viewpoint. Marie Daerr
    Boehringer. 210
Pediatricians firing canisters of
    tear gas into a group... James
    Magorian. 309
Pedro Nel Mejia. Royal Murdoch.
    330
Pegleg lookout. William Stafford.
    373
Pelleas and Melisande. Josephine
    Miles. 319
"Peloria the dog's upper lip
    curling" Charles Olson. 337
Pen point. Erin Jolly. 285
The penal cavalry. Andrei
    Codrescu. 223
Penance. Robert Pawlowski. 341
Pennington, Lee
    Recollection. Robert L. Wilson.
        401
A Pennsylvania family. Anthony
    Petrosky. 344
Penny wise. Bill Knott. 296
Penzi, Joseph
    Alchemy. 342
    The bird. 342
    Music. 342
    River. 342
    Scene. 342
    Seascape. 342
    Space. 342
    Spring. 342
    White. 342
    Winter. 342
    You your voice departing. 342
Peonies
    Peony. Robin Morgan. 325
Peons
    No trespassing in southern
        Florida. Ruth Lisa Schechter.
        359
Peony. Robin Morgan. 325
People. Miller Williams. 399
People
    "How goes a crowd where it
        goes?" Josephine Miles. 319
    My fear in the crowd. Josephine

    Miles. 319
    Rosary portraits of improbable
        saints. Mitchell Howard. 276
    Self-righteous wound. James R.
        Rhodes. 352
    Self-same differences. James R.
        Rhodes. 352
    The young lt. col. Miller
        Williams. 399
"People have been gathering."
    Madison Morrison. 327
"People want delivery" Charles
    Olson. 337
The people, us. James R. Rhodes.
    352
Per request. Bill Knott. 296
Perceptions
    Not eye to eye. May Miller. 320
Percival, James Gates
    James Gates Percival pleads for
        a unity of vision. James
        Schevill. 360
Perennial necessity. Marie Daerr
    Boehringer. 210
Perfect. Stephen Sandy. 357
The perfect fool. Mitchell
    Howard. 276
Perfect love. Alice Joyce
    Davidson. 227
A perfect skyline. Donald Revell.
    351
"Perfect/strangers, dining."
    Larry Eigner. 237
"The performance of the/little
    girl..." Madison Morrison. 327
Perhapps, Emily. Ruth Lisa
    Schechter. 359
Perhaps a prayer. James Schevill.
    360
"Perhaps,/upon another day." A.
    Dovichi. 233
Perishables. May Miller. 320
Perkin's cove. Michael Akillian.
    193
Perkins, Maxwell
    Briefe an Maxwell Perkins.
        Gerard Malanga. 310
The permission. Bill Knott. 296
Persephone
    Persephone's descent. Randy
        Blasing. 207
    Spring. Roy Marz. 312
    The tears of Christ pulled
        inside out. Clayton Eshleman.
        240
Persephone's descent. Randy
    Blasing. 207
Perseverance
    "I have fallen short a time or
        two." Michael Robert Pick. 345

The one who can. Wanda Coleman.
    225
Rosa. Rosa Bogar. 211
"There'll be times in life."
    Michael Robert Pick. 345
Tough hide. Alice Spohn Newton.
    332
What do you do with a wasted
    life? Maurice W. Britts. 215
Worker. Wanda Coleman. 225
A person. James R. Rhodes. 352
Personal appearance. Josephine
    Miles. 319
Personal history. Robert Peters.
    343
"The **personality** of the feeding
    pin." Kenneth Koch. 297
Personification. Josephine Miles.
    319
Persons in the presence of a
    metamorphosis. John Yau. 404
Perspective. Debra Bruce. 216
Peru
    At the border. Herbert Morris.
    326
Petals of silence. Maria Gillan.
    256
Pete. Susan Stock. 375
Peter's graduation. Norman Andrew
    Kirk. 293
Peters, Robert
    Albert. 343
    Aunt. 343
    Biology lesson. 343
    Birthday party. 343
    Bridge climbing. 343
    Burial. 343
    Burning. 343
    The butchering. 343
    Canoe journey. 343
    Car trip. 343
    Carnival man. 343
    Cousin: snapshot 1. 343
    Cousins. 343
    Cow. 343
    Crane. 343
    Daniel. 343
    Deerskin flowage. 343
    Dialogue. 343
    Dillinger in Wisconsin. 343
    Doctor. 343
    Eagle River, Wisconsin: 1930.
    343
    Eileen. 343
    Everywhere, but nowhere. 343
    Father. 343
    Father: as recollection or the
    drug decides. 343
    Few of us feel safe anywhere.
    343

Forest walk. 343
Games. 343
Garter snakes. 343
Hot bread. 343
The lake. 343
Locale. 343
Lucy Robinson. 343
Married cousin. 343
Memorial Day 1933. 343
Miscarriage. 343
Mother. 343
My father as house-builder. 343
Night-soil. 343
Night accident. 343
Night swim. 343
Night visitor. 343
Now. 343
Nude father in a lake. 343
Old Carlson. 343
On not attending my father's
    funeral. 343
Personal history. 343
Pig-family game. 343
Potato bugs. 343
The prom. 343
Purvis. 343
Radio report. 343
The raid. 343
Rat. 343
Rev. Joseph Krubsack. 343
Rites of passage. 343
Saturday at Little Bohemia. 343
The secret. 343
Skunks. 343
Smudge-pot. 343
Snapshots with buck, Model-A
    Ford, and kitchen. 343
Snow image. 343
Song ("He has gunpowder on his
    breath.") 343
The sow's head. 343
Summer litany. 343
Tableau in a Lutheran church.
    343
That family. 343
Tommy McQuaker. 343
Uncles. 343
Waiting. 343
The watchdogs. 343
What John Dillinger meant to me.
    343
Woods. 343
Young man on a Sunday. 343
Petition. Marie Daerr Boehringer.
    210
Petition. Cornel Lengyel. 302
Petrosky, Anthony
    Angels. 344
    Carl Perusick. 344
    Change. 344

Crayfish. 344
Crazy wife. 344
The first day of spring at the
    cabin... 344
For luck. 344
Fragments. 344
Friday, the day Mariana Penko
    quit cooking... 344
Going blind: the woman's voice.
    344
Illusions. 344
In praise of hands. 344
Jerusalem, Pittsburgh. 344
Jurgis Petraskas, the workers'
    angel... 344
The knife sharpener. 344
Land song at the Exeter mines.
    344
Late morning. 344
Liberty Avenue. 344
Listening to my son's heart. 344
Mackey. 344
Marcus Nathaniel Simpson: his
    voice. 344
Morning, meadow, wife. 344
Mourning cloak. 344
My father is. 344
Once when I was walking up the
    stairs. 344
Ornaments. 344
The other life. 344
A Pennsylvania family. 344
Photograph. 344
Rain: the funeral: the woman's
    voice. 344
Resilience. 344
Return to the woods. 344
Slaughtering chickens. 344
Speaking to myself. 344
Streetlight: the wedding
    photograph. 344
Talking with my wife. 344
Today and tomorrow. 344
V.A. hospital. 344
What keeps us. 344
Widow's poem. 344
Pets
    Attachments. Ruth Lisa
        Schechter. 359
    The death of a small beast.
        Christopher Bursk. 219
    I'm no vet, pet! Josephine B.
        Moretti. 324
    A matter of life and dirt. Iefke
        Goldberger. 262
Petty, my love. Alice Spohn
    Newton. 332
Phalaropes
    "Phalaropes." Charles Olson. 337
"Phalaropes.". Charles Olson. 337

The phantom artist. Ruth Lisa
    Schechter. 359
Pharisees and Sadducees. Phillips
    Kloss. 294
Phenakistes urges his crew
    onward. Paul Violi. 388
Phenomena
    Something. Jim Simmerman. 365
Phenomena, a photograph. Cathryn
    Hankla. 268
Phenomenal survivals of death in
    Nantucket. Louise Gluck. 259A
Phenomenon. Marie Daerr
    Boehringer. 210
Philadelphia
    Next year in Jerusalem, this
        year in Philadelphia. Mitchell
        Howard. 276
    Urban society. Rose Basile
        Green. 265
Philobiblian. Sharon Bryan. 217
Philodendra
    The secret life of plants. David
        Wann. 394
Philomela (mythology)
    Our two birds. Roy Marz. 312
Philomela's tapestry. Debra
    Bruce. 216
Philopolis. Royal Murdoch. 330
Philosophy. Elsa Gidlow. 254
The philtre. Charles Edward
    Eaton. 236
Phobophilia. Robin Morgan. 325
Phoenix. Tom Smith. 368
Phone call. Christopher Bursk.
    219
Phone call at 1 am. Robin Becker.
    202
Photocopiers
    Xerox. Miriam Goodman. 264
Photograph. Anthony Petrosky. 344
The photograph. Debra Bruce. 216
Photographer. Josephine Miles.
    319
Photographic plate, partly
    spidered, Hampton Roads...
    Dave Smith. 367
Photographs and Photographers
    About photography. Andrei
        Codrescu. 223
    Glossies. Joan Colby. 224
    In old San Juan. Irving Feldman.
        242
    It's a snap. Marie Daerr
        Boehringer. 210
    Love simmers the stew of the
        dead. Andrei Codrescu. 223
    On camera. Ghita Orth. 339
    Photographer. Josephine Miles.
        319

Pictures. Carolyn Stoloff. 376
Posing for the photographer.
    Robin Becker. 202
Strangers in a photograph.
    Everett A. Gillis. 258
Two kinds of trouble. Josephine
    Miles. 319
Untouched photograph of
    passenger. Cathy Song. 372
The water lily. David Wagoner.
    390
Wedding photograph with clock.
    Jim Simmerman. 365
Photographs of architecture.
    Gerard Malanga. 310
Phryne
    A Maximus song. Charles Olson.
    337
"Physically, I am home..."
    Charles Olson. 337
Physicians
    Culpepper and the public health
        physician. J.W. Rivers. 354
    "The doctor who sits at the
        bedside of a rat." Josephine
        Miles. 319
    Dr. Martin's day off. Debra
        Bruce. 216
    Exchange. Laura Boss. 213
    Their bodies. David Wagoner. 390
Physics. Josephine Miles. 319
Physics
    Physics. Josephine Miles. 319
Physiologus. Josephine Miles. 319
Pianissimo. Norman Andrew Kirk.
    293
"Piano and strings." Larry
    Eigner. 237
Pianos
    Mama's piano. Alice Spohn
        Newton. 333
    Second-floor piano. James
        Magorian. 308
Pick, Michael Robert
    "Among a hundred mirrors." 345
    "And then the old woman." 345
    "And you, Pa." 345
    "Arrested on drunk driving." 345
    "As I love you." 345
    "As we human beings search for
        life in clues." 345
    "Baying dogs." 345
    "Bleak dismal stark glazed
        eyes." 345
    "Boxes of old tattered photos."
        345
    "Breaking down my own being."
        345
    "Breaking through trees." 345
    "Brilliance/shooting stars
        erupt." 345
    "Buds unfurl the grace of life."
        345
    "Capturing visions relay my mind
        to infinity." 345
    "Chain his body." 345
    "Circles crowd the sky." 345
    "Circling around." 345
    "Climbing stairs so low." 345
    "Comets clash." 345
    Curtains fall, eyes close. 345
    "Dawn overcomes the darkness."
        345
    "Dealing out lonely games of
        solitaire." 345
    "Death is the eternal mystery of
        life." 345
    "Deep currents foam on the
        surface." 345
    "Digging deeps my destiny." 345
    "Dirty sheet." 345
    "Don't worry, woman." 345
    "Echoes careen." 345
    "An escape attempt transforms."
        345
    "Even now lost winds carry
        silent memories." 345
    "Ever catch a butterfly or
        moth." 345
    "Gentle children." 345
    "Haggard, torn and beat." 345
    "Have you ever held a man's
        hand." 345
    "Have you ever held a string."
        345
    "Heating up T boil mad." 345
    "Hitchhiking in blinding storm."
        345
    "The Hook, a name of a man." 345
    "Hope life is good to you." 345
    "Hours line gray streaks in a
        warrior's face." 345
    "How far can a single mind go."
        345
    "How far does the heart travel."
        345
    "How to train a dog." 345
    "How would you like to grow
        wings with me." 345
    "I am a little boy sometimes."
        345
    "I am living life full and
        long." 345
    "I am no hero." 345
    "I can sing." 345
    "I charge again." 345
    "I cry with no tears." 345
    "I feel your presence." 345
    "I have fallen short a time or
        two." 345

I hear you cry, my friends. 345
"I hear you, Jacob." 345
I held my little sisters. 345
"I hunger for you." 345
"I like running gentle streams."
  345
"I opened a box of memories."
  345
"I remember times I spent." 345
"I see you hawk." 345
"I sing a song to thee, O God."
  345
"I smell you on your pillow."
  345
"I stare hard into the wind."
  345
"I think now of all the wars."
  345
"I was/a product of divorce."
  345
"I weep for you brothers of
  war." 345
"I will be thirty one years."
  345
"I've seen the halyards of the
  sun." 345
"If only time was a fantasy."
  345
"If the war is over." 345
"The innocence of youth." 345
"It came in a hole." 345
"Just running as fast as I can."
  345
"Killing, taking a man's
  life..." 345
"Knotted guts inside." 345
"Life has no meaning without
  you." 345
"Life is free you know." 345
"Little son." 345
"Locust Street revisited." 345
"Locust Street, a garage full of
  beer cans." 345
"Long roads shorten time." 345
"Lovers should take time from
  the misery." 345
"Men living." 345
"Moments stop my sight." 345
"My brothers, two." 345
"My childhood, turbulent
  peaceful years." 345
"My mind unravels." 345
"My son." 345
"Needed help from someone." 345
"Oh but rest in the sheltor of
  love." 345
"Oh I love you, woman." 345
"Okay, Hawk, where are you when
  I need you." 345
"Old Man Flowers chewed wood."

  345
"Oliver, our dog, went around
  squirting." 345
"On a holy night, I ask you
  God." 345
"One hour." 345
"Or follow ants to their hill."
  345
"Our bombs can now kill all."
  345
"The pain of a mistake goes by
  so slow." 345
"Peace, infinity's plot." 345
"Pretty hard to face the facts."
  345
"Raging lonely wave." 345
"Readied in tradition." 345
"Refuge sought on a/moments
  thought." 345
"Sad man returns from war." 345
"Silent memories trickle down a
  stream." 345
"Sinking further through my
  tunnel." 345
"Sometimes I feel like a caged
  animal." 345
"Sometimes I get lost." 345
"Sometimes I wish I was a hawk."
  345
"Spring." 345
"The squeeking noise replaced
  the awful." 345
"Standing in a hole." 345
"The sweetness of breath." 345
"There'll be times in life." 345
"Throwing watermelons." 345
"Time is slow for the hungry."
  345
"Together in our lives." 345
"Touched by my ignorance of
  victory." 345
"Twenty days of leave." 345
"Walking along in barefoot
  shoes." 345
"Walking through old haunts."
  345
"We all have to die..." 345
"We are as a rose." 345
"We are liken to animals." 345
"We came across the desert." 345
"We died." 345
"We're caught in an ambush." 345
"We've weathered many storms."
  345
"What deceptive means do
  politicians weave." 345
What does war do to men? 345
"What happened, Pa." 345
"What is life for knotted
  lives." 345

"Wheels walk, never talk." 345
"When I am lost I like to." 345
"When I was a little man." 345
"When I was just a boy." 345
"When I was lost and needed
   growth for life." 345
"When I was young." 345
"When is the year when I was
   ten." 345
"When moons peek through
   clouds." 345
"When you don't know it." 345
"When you win, they are." 345
"Where can a man go." 345
"Where the hell is my life?" 345
"Winter's melting snow." 345
"You cry for me in your love for
   life." 345
"You must be hurting inside."
   345
"You poor helpless creature of
   power." 345
"Your smile erases all my pain."
   345
"Your sweetness was in my hand."
   345
Picking plums. Jeanne Lohmann.
   305
Picnics
   The Esterhazy family picnic.
   J.W. Rivers. 354
Picture bride. Cathy Song. 372
The picture of Wittgenstein.
   David James. 282
The picture. Charles Olson. 337
Pictures. Carolyn Stoloff. 376
Pictures in color. Harrison
   Fisher. 245
Pictures of the people in the
   war. Louise Gluck. 259A
Piecing. Robin Morgan. 325
The pier dwellers. Stephen
   Knauth. 295
Piercy, Marge
   Absolute zero in the brain. 346
   The annealing. 346
   Ascending scale. 346
   Ashes, ashes, all fall down. 346
   The back pockets of love. 346
   Being left. 346
   Charm for attracting wild money.
      346
   Chiaroscuro. 346
   The common living dirt. 346
   Death of the Hungarian hot
      pepper bush. 346
   A debate on posture. 346
   December 31, 1979. 346
   The deck that douts. 346
   Digging in. 346

Dis-ease. 346
The discarded. 346
The disturbance. 346
Divorce. 346
The doe. 346
Down at the bottom of things.
   346
Dry July. 346
Eating my tail. 346
False spring. 346
For the furies. 346
From something, nothing. 346
Homecoming. 346
Hummingbird. 346
In search of scenery. 346
In the marshes of the blood
   river, sels. 346
In which she begs (like
   everybody else) that love may
   last. 346
It breaks. 346
It weeps away. 346
Jill in the box. 346
A key to common lethal fungi.
   346
Laocoon is the name of the
   figure. 346
Let us gather at the river. 346
The man who is leaving. 346
The matrimonial bed. 346
More that winter ends than
   spring begins. 346
Mornings in various years. 346
Mrs. Frankenstein. 346
Mrs. Frankenstein's diary, sels.
   346
The name I call you. 346
Of hidden taxes. 346
On metal corsets. 346
On New Year's Day. 346
Out of the hospital Peter. 346
The pleasure principle. 346
The pool that swims in us. 346
A private bestiary. 346
Ragged ending. 346
Right wing mag: a found poem.
   346
A snarl for loose friends. 346
Snow, snow. 346
Song like a thin wire. 346
Still waters. 346
Stone, paper, knife. 346
A story as wet as tears. 346
The surf of joy pounding. 346
A tangential death. 346
Three loser's poems. 346
Toad dreams. 346
Touch. 346
Trying to attract your attention
   without being too obvious. 346

Two peach trees. 346
Very late July. 346
A visit from the ex. 346
The watch. 346
The weight. 346
The west main book store
    chickens. 346
What goes us. 346
What's that smell in the
    kitchen? 346
Where nothing grows. 346
Why in Toronto? 346
Wind is the wall of the year.
    346
Woody's wool. 346
The working writer. 346
The world comes back like an old
    cat. 346
The world in the year 2000. 346
You don't understand me. 346
Pieta. Roy Marz. 312
Pietro Lazzari. Ernesto Galarza.
    252
Pig-family game. Robert Peters.
    343
Pigeons
    Passenger pigeon poem. Rokwaho.
        355
    Today, the pigeons fly. Robert
        L. Wilson. 401
"Pigeons...". Larry Eigner. 237
Pigfish. Stephen Todd Booker. 212
Pigging out. Wanda Coleman. 225
Pigs
    "Little pig." Jan Ormerod. 338
    The sow's head. Robert Peters.
        343
Pike's Peak (mountain), Colorado
    The top of Pike's Peak. Alice
        Spohn Newton. 333
Pike, Zebulon Montgomery
    Metamorphoses: 1806. Thomas
        Hornsby Ferril. 243
Pilgrim Fathers
    So sassafras. Charles Olson. 337
Pill problem. Marie Daerr
    Boehringer. 210
Pioneer. Everett A. Gillis. 258
Pioneer. Rose Basile Green. 265
Pioneer Life and Pioneers
    Pioneer. Everett A. Gillis. 258
    Trace. Cynthia Grenfell. 266
    Wes Turley. Norman Andrew Kirk.
        293
Pipers
    You can't ignore a bagpipe.
        Robert A. Sears. 362
Pirates
    "One-eyed Jack, the pirate
        chief." Jan Ormerod. 338

Pisa
    Death in Pisa. Franz Schneider.
        361
Pisgah. Stephen Knauth. 295
Pittsburgh
    Aubade. Robert Gibb. 253
    Jerusalem, Pittsburgh. Anthony
        Petrosky. 344
Pity
    Tis pity. Alberta Turner. 384
Place. James Schevill. 360
Place to place. Larry Eigner. 237
Places. Jim Simmerman. 365
Places are not where we are.
    Marieve Rugo. 356
Places with meaning. William
    Stafford. 373
Planetarium. Norman Andrew Kirk.
    293
Planetary childhood. David Wann.
    394
The plant on my table had seven
    leaves. Carolyn Stoloff. 376
A plantation a beginning. Charles
    Olson. 337
Planting H-bombs on the moon.
    Mitchell Howard. 276
Plants and Planting
    After a southern visit. Jeanne
        Lohmann. 305
    Botany. Josephine Miles. 319
    Camomile. Robert Gibb. 253
    The creosote bush. Gene
        Anderson. 195
    The demon of Elloree. Larry
        Moffi. 322
    "Drawn aside." Madison Morrison.
        327
    The fundamentalist. Phyllis A.
        Tickle. 382
    German cameroun. Michael Gizzi.
        259
    Illumination. Josephine Miles.
        319
    Jardin des Plantes. Michael
        Gizzi. 259
    Ocotillo. Phillips Kloss. 294
    On a wind. Ralph J., Jr. Mills.
        321
    Petition. Marie Daerr
        Boehringer. 210
    The plant on my table had seven
        leaves. Carolyn Stoloff. 376
    Pokeweed. Maurice Kenny. 291
    Replanting a garden. David
        Wagoner. 390
    7/6.   Ralph J., Jr. Mills. 321
    Soley. Marc Hudson. 277
    Song of the shrubs. Anne Bailie.
        199

Trinidad. Michael Gizzi. 259
Visit. Robert Pawlowski. 341
Weed. Josephine Miles. 319
The plastic glass. Josephine
      Miles. 319
Platitudes of want. Phillips
      Kloss. 294
"The play of minds." Robert A.
      Sears. 362
"Play/above the waist." Madison
      Morrison. 327
Playbill. Mitchell Howard. 276
Players. Josephine Miles. 319
Playin' jazz. Kirk Lumpkin. 306
Playing off. John Godfrey. 260
Playing pinball in Denver. James
      Magorian. 309
The playing. Rachel A. Hazen. 271
Plays and Playwrights
      "A woman with a basket was
      walking." Josephine Miles. 319
Plea. Martha Janssen. 283
A plea for alias. James Schevill.
      360
A plea. Maurice W. Britts. 215
Pleasure
      Love knife. John Godfrey. 260
      Pleasures. Albert Goldbarth. 261
The pleasure principle. Marge
      Piercy. 346
Pleasures. Albert Goldbarth. 261
The pleasures of exile. John Yau.
      404
The pleasures of sleep. Eileen
      Silver-Lillywite. 364
The pledge of a human animal, or
      a bloody smiling fool. Kirk
      Lumpkin. 306
Plotinus
      Homage to Plotinus. Eve Triem.
      383
Plowing and Plowmen
      A farmer's woman. John Reed. 350
Plums
      Picking plums. Jeanne Lohmann.
      305
Plurality. Rose Basile Green. 265
Pluto (mythology)
      Spring. Roy Marz. 312
Plymouth Rock, Massachusetts
      At Plymouth Rock. James
      Schevill. 360
A pocket full of yesterdays.
      Alice Spohn Newton. 333
Poe, Edgar Allan
      An acrostic. 347
      Al Aaraaf. 347
      Alone. 347
      Alone (to-). 347
      Annabel Lee. 347

The bells. 347
Bridal ballad. 347
The city in the sea (The doomed
      city) 347
The city in the sea (The doomed
      city). 347
The conqueror worm. 347
The divine right of kings. 347
Dream-land. 347
A dream within a dream. 347
A dream. 347
Dreams. 347
Eldorado. 347
Elizabeth. 347
Eulalie: a song. 347
Evening star. 347
Fanny. 347
"Fill with mingled cream and
      amber." 347
For Annie. 347
The happiest day. 347
The haunted palace. 347
Heaven (fairy-land). 347
Imitation. 347
Irene (the sleeper). 347
Israfel. 347
The lake. 347
Lenore. 347
Mysterious star! 347
A paean. 347
The raven. 347
Romance, sels. 347
Serenade ("So sweet the hour -
      so calm the hour"). 347
Silence, a sonnet. 347
Song: to--. 347
Sonnet - to Zante. 347
Sonnet ("Seldom we find...").
      347
Sonnet: to science. 347
Spirits of the dead. 347
Stanzas. 347
Stanzas (to F.S.O.). 347
Tamerlane. 347
To-- ("Should me early life
      seem"). 347
To-- ("The bowers whereat, in
      dreams, I see"). 347
To--("I would not lord it o'er
      thy heart"). 347
To -- ("Sleep on, sleep on...").
      347
To Elizabeth (To F-s O-d). 347
To Francis S. Osgood. 347
To Helen ("Thy beauty is to
      me"). 347
To Helen (I saw thee once...).
      347
To her whose name is written
      below. 347

To Marie Louise. 347
To Mrs. M.L.S.--. 347
To my mother. 347
To the river. 347
Ulalume - a ballad. 347
The valley Nis (the valley of
    unrest). 347
Poe, Edgar Allan (about)
The glorious devil at the
    dovecot... James Schevill. 360
Poe, Edgar Allen = Parody
The chicken. John Reed. 350
Poem. Andrei Codrescu. 223
Poem ("At home in the diner,
    flagman sprints.") John
    Godfrey. 260
Poem ("Mezzanines of nightfall
    clashing like.") John Godfrey.
    260
Poem ("Not the beating of wings,
    not the curled-lip.") John
    Godfrey. 260
Poem ("Seldom to any human is
    there a gold this pure.") John
    Godfrey. 260
Poem ("The gravity of our
    situation is matched.") John
    Godfrey. 260
Poem ("The only man I ever
    loved.") Ernest Hemingway. 272
Poem ("Why, even the sun was a
    vassal on that set.") John
    Godfrey. 260
Poem ("You make me think of
    sleep, and you're lying.")
    John Godfrey. 260
Poem 143. The festival aspect.
    Charles Olson. 337
Poem about breath. David Wagoner.
    390
Poem at the winter solstice.
    Thomas McGrath. 315
Poem dune. James Magorian. 309
Poem for an ex-husband. Rochelle
    DuBois. 234
Poem for an ex-schoolgirl. Robert
    Anbian. 194
A poem for Claire of London.
    James A. Emanuel. 239
Poem for Kyra. Andrei Codrescu.
    223
Poem for my daughters. Marieve
    Rugo. 356
Poem for my parents. Steve Kowit.
    299
A poem for my teacher. Sandra
    McPherson. 317
Poem for saps. John Godfrey. 260
A poem for Sarah's tears. James
    A. Emanuel. 239

Poem for the letters of my name.
    Joan Colby. 224
Poem for the letters of your
    name. Joan Colby. 224
Poem for the sandman. James Tate.
    379
Poem from memory. Keith Waldrop.
    392
The poem I just wrote. Joy Harjo.
    269
A poem is an organic thing. Haig
    Khatchadourian. 292
The poem is by Maera. Ernest
    Hemingway. 272
Poem jubilant in place of
    mourning. Joyce Carol Oates.
    336
The poem not recorded. Robert L.
    Wilson. 401
"A poem set down to convince..."
    John Hawkes. 270
Poem to a friend. Susan Stock.
    375
Poem to a super market. Josephine
    B. Moretti. 324
Poem to heal David. Mary
    Gilliland. 257
Poem to Mary. Ernest Hemingway.
    272
Poem to Miss Mary. Ernest
    Hemingway. 272
Poem to my father. Maria Gillan.
    256
Poem to some of my recent poems.
    James Tate. 379
The poem with no end. Frances
    Mayes. 314
The poem's words. Roy Marz. 312
Poem, 1928. Ernest Hemingway. 272
A poem. Stephen Todd Booker. 212
Poeme noir. Bill Knott. 296
Poemgatherers following a giant
    roller from one highway...
    James Magorian. 309
Poems from the river Aurelia
    (sels.) Andrei Codrescu. 223
"Poems have been scurrying."
    Sally Love Saunders. 358
Poems of submission. James L.
    White. 396
Poemwreck. James Magorian. 309
Poet. Bill Knott. 296
Poet as a stripper. Lyn Lifshin.
    303
A poet does not choose to run.
    James A. Emanuel. 239
Poet in residence. Mary
    Gilliland. 257
Poet in town. Carolyn Stoloff.
    376

The poet of love. Jacques Sollov.
    371
The poet of the prison
    Isle:Ritsos against the
    colonels. Thomas McGrath. 315
A poet's prayer. Alice Joyce
    Davidson. 227
Poet's stone at steepletop. Gary
    Margolis. 311
Poet, seeking credentials... Mark
    Vinz. 387
The poet. Jacques Sollov. 371
Poetry. Ernest Hemingway. 272
Poetry and Poets
    After an illness. Phyllis A.
        Tickle. 382
    After gossip. Sister Maura. 313
    After some verses by Morvaen Le
        Gaelique & Paul Verlaine.
        Kenneth Koch. 297
    The aging poet writes of the
        continuing evidence of his...
        Sister Maura. 313
    All that is necessary. Jeanne
        Lohmann. 305
    "And in the preface..." Albert
        Goldbarth. 261
    The angel of the dialectic.
        Robert Kelly. 289
    Another question. Josephine B.
        Moretti. 324
    The arcade's discourse on
        method. Clayton Eshleman. 240
    Attempt to spell, incantate and
        annoy. Andrei Codrescu. 223
    Author's acknowledgment. Connie
        Hunt. 279
    Auto-portrait at 1/5th. Gerard
        Malanga. 310
    Bards of the golden west.
        Phillips Kloss. 294
    Birth of the blues. Miller
        Williams. 399
    Bluejays. Jeanne Lohmann. 305
    Boy in a pit. Cornel Lengyel.
        302
    A brief introduction. Jim
        Simmerman. 365
    A broken house. Marc Kaminsky.
        288
    A cardinal. W.D. (William De
        Witt) Snodgrass. 369
    Catullus in his book. Royal
        Murdoch. 330
    Censored. Ruth Lisa Schechter.
        359
    The Chicago poetry team going
        457 days without an accident.
        James Magorian. 309
    The city that is set upon a

    hill. Mitchell Howard. 276
    Classroom. Lucien Stryk. 377
    Collection agency. James
        Magorian. 308
    "The creator has a master plan."
        David James. 282
    Cross pollination. Sally Love
        Saunders. 358
    Dawn. Lucien Stryk. 377
    Days and nights. Kenneth Koch.
        297
    De rerum natura. Andrei
        Codrescu. 223
    Dear Broyard whose copy clicks.
        Gene Detro. 230
    Dedication. Harlan Usher. 386
    Desperate solutions. Steve
        Kowit. 299
    A diatribe to Dr. Steele.
        Charles Gullans. 267
    Driving to the 10Am PCC reading.
        Laura Boss. 213
    Each morning at four. Laura
        Boss. 213
    The Eastern Montana obsolete
        poetry award. James Magorian.
        308
    Elevator shaft. James Magorian.
        309
    The elite. Richmond Lattimore.
        301
    Elizabeth. Edgar Allan Poe. 347
    Encounter. James Torio. 281
    Envoi. Gerard Malanga. 310
    A few discretions. Donald
        Revell. 351
    Forgive us. Elsa Gidlow. 254
    Four lines. David Shapiro. 363
    From a snapshot of the poet.
        Carolyn Stoloff. 376
    The gazabos. Edwin Honig. 275
    Generic: after reading Plath and
        Sexton. Bill Knott. 296
    Genesis. Mark Vinz. 387
    Grosstadtpoesie. Rodney Nelson.
        331
    The hands in exile. Susan Tichy.
        381
    Hark! Norman Andrew Kirk. 293
    Highway patrol roadblock. James
        Magorian. 309
    "I sit here." Sally Love
        Saunders. 358
    "I walk the sidewalk." Madison
        Morrison. 327
    "I want to write down." Sally
        Love Saunders. 358
    I'll read you my current poems.
        Sally Love Saunders. 358
    In our time. Lucien Stryk. 377

In the sonata/I wear a surgeon's mask. Ruth Lisa Schechter. 359

The index of first lines. David Shapiro. 363

The inexpressible. Ernest Hemingway. 272

The inn of the empty egg. Clayton Eshleman. 240

It's the Passaic poetry reading tonight. Laura Boss. 213

The joker is wild. Cornel Lengyel. 302

The lady poets with foot notes. Ernest Hemingway. 272

Letter to Scardanelli. Marc Hudson. 277

(Literary result). Charles Olson. 337

Log-rolling contest. James Magorian. 309

Luncheon. Josephine Miles. 319

Madonna who writes ten poems a day. Lyn Lifshin. 303

Maiden aunt. James Magorian. 308

Manticore vortex. Clayton Eshleman. 240

Marx. Harlan Usher. 386

The masquerade. Rachel A. Hazen. 271

The memorable. Irving Feldman. 242

Memorial. Erin Jolly. 285

Middle-aged poet charged with fraud in Cincinnati. James Magorian. 309

More about poems. Andrei Codrescu. 223

Morning. Greg Kuzma. 300

Motorcycle gang. James Magorian. 308

The muse. Miller Williams. 399

Museum of poetry. Norman Andrew Kirk. 293

"My boyhood was a raft of poems." Robert Kelly. 289

"My grandest symphony." Sally Love Saunders. 358

My next book. Andrei Codrescu. 223

Neither rhythm nor rhyme. Rachel A. Hazen. 271

The night I read my poetry at the Paterson Library. Laura Boss. 213

The night shift at the poetry factory. James Magorian. 309

"No one should die mute." James Torio. 281

Not just poetry. Marilyn Kallet. 287

The novios. Steve Kowit. 299

On April 24th 1981. Stephen Todd Booker. 212

On first looking into Norton's Anthology of Poetry (Revised) Richard Blessing. 208

Pantry secrets. Mitchell Howard. 276

Paper on humor. Andrei Codrescu. 223

The parable of the rain-soaked macrame. James Magorian. 309

Playing pinball in Denver. James Magorian. 309

Poem. Andrei Codrescu. 223

A poem is an organic thing. Haig Khatchadourian. 292

The poem not recorded. Robert L. Wilson. 401

"A poem set down to convince..." John Hawkes. 270

Poem to some of my recent poems. James Tate. 379

The poem's words. Roy Marz. 312

"Poems have been scurrying." Sally Love Saunders. 358

Poemwreck. James Magorian. 309

Poet as a stripper. Lyn Lifshin. 303

A poet does not choose to run. James A. Emanuel. 239

Poet in town. Carolyn Stoloff. 376

A poet's prayer. Alice Joyce Davidson. 227

The poetry reading was a disaster. Steve Kowit. 299

The poets. Greg Kuzma. 300

Polygraph test. James Magorian. 309

The post-modern poem as clean-up hitter. Ray Fleming. 247

Pragmatic sanction. Ray Fleming. 247

Primitive chic. Harrison Fisher. 245

Proposition. Mark Vinz. 387

Purchase of a blue, green, or orange ode. Josephine Miles. 319

Radio dispatched poetry truck. James Magorian. 309

Reader. Bill Knott. 296

A realistic bar and grill. David Shapiro. 363

Reminders. Rachel A. Hazen. 271

Round valley songs. William Oandasan. 335

Scattered remains. Paul Violi. 388

Sending these messages. William
  Stafford. 373
Sessions. Rachel A. Hazen. 271
Sleep little poems, rest
  tonight. James Torio. 281
Sleepwalking. Mark Vinz. 387
Sonnet ("Seldom we find...").
  Edgar Allan Poe. 347
"A square poetess." Madison
  Morrison. 327
Taking off. William Oandasan.
  335
Thin snow. David Shapiro. 363
Things that come. William
  Stafford. 373
The thirty-six master poets.
  James Torio. 281
Three definitions of poetry.
  Robin Morgan. 325
To an idea. David Shapiro. 363
["To get the rituals
  straight..." Charles Olson.
  337
To her whose name is written
  below. Edgar Allan Poe. 347
To industry. David Shapiro. 363
The tomb of the unknown poet.
  James Magorian. 308
Toward the end of 1969. Andrei
  Codrescu. 223
Trade center. Josephine Miles.
  319
Untitled:"Is it my art" Kirk
  Lumpkin. 306
Us. Andrei Codrescu. 223
Uses of the lost poets. Thomas
  McGrath. 315
Vinegar. James L. White. 396
Waking up in Streator. Lucien
  Stryk. 377
The washing machine cycle. James
  Schevill. 360
Weaver star. Marilyn Kallet. 287
Why a poem? Barry Wallenstein.
  393
"Why do I keep on writing love
  songs?" Robert A. Sears. 362
"Will the poems take off their
  garments." Carolyn Stoloff.
  376
The worst poems make the best
  "poems" Andrei Codrescu. 223
Writing an elegy in my sleep.
  David Wagoner. 390
"Writing on scraps..." Susan
  Tichy. 381
Writing poems on graph paper.
  James Magorian. 309
Writing poetry in the woods.
  Iefke Goldberger. 262

"Yet leaving here a name..."
  Albert Goldbarth. 261
Poetry and Poets = Satire
  [Blank verse.]. Ernest
    Hemingway. 272
  Dedicated to F.W. Ernest
    Hemingway. 272
  How ballad writing affects our
    seniors. Ernest Hemingway. 272
  Im-poet-ent. Harlan Usher. 386
The poetry reading was a
  disaster. Steve Kowit. 299
Poetry workshop in a maximum
  security reform school. Betty
  Adcock. 192
The poets. Greg Kuzma. 300
Point of view. Martha Janssen.
  283
The pointillist. Charles Edward
  Eaton. 236
Poise. Josephine Miles. 319
Poised for flight. Evelyn Golden.
  263
Poker game in a ghost town. James
  Magorian. 308
Pokeweed. Maurice Kenny. 291
Poland
  At the museum this week. Bill
    Knott. 296
  Beethoven's Polish birthday.
    Gary Margolis. 311
  In the dreams of exiles. Frances
    Mayes. 314
  Penance. Robert Pawlowski. 341
The polar bear. Jack Prelutsky.
  349
Polar expedition. James Magorian.
  309
Polarity. Mitchell Howard. 276
Police. Greg Kuzma. 300
Police
  First ticket. Debra Bruce. 216
  Officers. Josephine Miles. 319
  The police. Andrei Codrescu. 223
  Purvis. Robert Peters. 343
  Under arrest. Wanda Coleman. 225
  "Without asylum they." Madison
    Morrison. 327
Police woman. Jacques Sollov. 370
The police. Andrei Codrescu. 223
"A political is." Madison
  Morrison. 327
Politics. Andrei Codrescu. 223
Politics and Politicians
  After the war (III). John Yau.
    404
  The campaign. Josephine Miles.
    319
  Culpepper is politicized. J.W.
    Rivers. 354

Hot tubbers. Harlan Usher. 386

Humpty who? Harlan Usher. 386

In the face of a Chinese view of the city. Charles Olson. 337

Jl 17 1961. Charles Olson. 337

John Burke. Charles Olson. 337

The lineaments of unsatisfied desire. Thomas McGrath. 315

New direction. Rose Basile Green. 265

Reception. Josephine Miles. 319

"What deceptive means do politicians weave." Michael Robert Pick. 345

"You poor helpless creature of power." Michael Robert Pick. 345

Pollock, Jackson

A drip poem for Jackson Pollock. James Schevill. 360

Greyed rainbow. James Torio. 281

Pollution

Saturday, dusk. George Eklund. 238

Polly. George Eklund. 238

Polo

Polo match. Sunday, 2 PM. Josephine Miles. 319

Polo match. Sunday, 2 PM. Josephine Miles. 319

Polygamy

Al Haji Nuhu takes a fourth wife. Robert A. Sears. 362

Polygraph test. James Magorian. 309

Pomegranate. Erin Jolly. 285

Pompeii, Italy

Alkest, property of M. Valerius; and Nicolas Flamel. Albert Goldbarth. 261

Ponds. See Lakes

Ponte a Poppi. Robert A. Sears. 362

Pontoons. C.D. Wright. 402

The pool that swims in us. Marge Piercy. 346

Pools. See Lakes

Poor Bill. Maurice W. Britts. 215

Poor John. John Godfrey. 260

Pope, Alexander

Parallel lives. John Yau. 404

Poplars. Ralph J., Jr. Mills. 321

Poppa's vision. Jim Everhard. 241

Poppies

Florin. Ernesto Galarza. 252

"When do poppies bloom..." Charles Olson. 337

Popular Art

Rodeo aesthetique. Donald Revell. 351

Porch steps. Ralph J., Jr. Mills. 321

The porcupine. Jack Prelutsky. 349

Porcupines

The porcupine. Jack Prelutsky. 349

Pornography, Nebraska. Sandra McPherson. 317

Port of call. Andrei Codrescu. 223

Portrait. Rod McKuen. 316

Portrait of a juvenile delinquent. Susan Stock. 375

Portrait of a lady. Ernest Hemingway. 272

Portrait of a man rising in his profession. Charles Edward Eaton. 236

Portrait of the queen in tears. Louise Gluck. 259A

Portraits by Matisse. Dennis Hinrichsen. 273

Posing for the photographer. Robin Becker. 202

Positivism

As you think. Alice Joyce Davidson. 227

Possessions. Cathryn Hankla. 268

Possessions. See Property, see Wealth

Possibilities. Alice Joyce Davidson. 227

The post-modern poem as clean-up hitter. Ray Fleming. 247

Postal protest. Marie Daerr Boehringer. 210

Postal Service

Junk mail. Andrei Codrescu. 223

The mailman and das ewig weibliche. James Schevill. 360

Mailman's lament. Josephine B. Moretti. 324

"People want delivery" Charles Olson. 337

Postal protest. Marie Daerr Boehringer. 210

Purchasing new bicentennial stamps, 1975 James Schevill. 360

"The return to the mail-bag..." Charles Olson. 337

Sympathetic fallacy. John Godfrey. 260

Postcard from a voyage. Robert Anbian. 194

Postcard from Provence. Anne

Bailie. 199
Postcards. Mark Vinz. 387
Postcards from the underworld.
    Robert Kelly. 289
Posthumes. Bradford Morrow. 329
Postmark Miami. Anneliese Wagner.
    389
Postpartum blue. Stephen Sandy.
    357
Postposterous. Jim Simmerman. 365
Posture. Martha Janssen. 283
The postures of sleep. Joan
    Colby. 224
Potato bugs. Robert Peters. 343
Potatoes
    Five potatoes. Sandra Gilbert.
        255
    He's a nice potato. Alice Spohn
        Newton. 332
Potential. Connie Hunt. 279
Potomac River,The
    With the tide. May Miller. 320
The potter. Carolyn Stoloff. 376
Pottery
    Ceramic. James R. Rhodes. 352
Pound, Ezra
    Canto CVI, sels. 235
    Canto CXX. 235
    Canto I, sels. 235
    Canto IC, sels. 235
    Canto XCIII, sels. 235
    Canto XCV, sels. 235
    Canto XLVII, sels. 235
    In a station of the Metro. 235
    The tree. 235
Poverty
    Dialogue. Robert Peters. 343
    Economics. Dennis Hinrichsen.
        273
    Eviction. Wanda Coleman. 225
    The songs of Maximus. Charles
        Olson. 337
Power. Andrei Codrescu. 223
Power
    Shifting for herself madonna.
        Lyn Lifshin. 303
    "Who called brougnt to my mind
        the name of power." Josephine
        Miles. 319
The power of redderrick. Stephen
    Todd Booker. 212
Power to me people. Norman Andrew
    Kirk. 293
Powerful words. Martha Janssen.
    283
Practicing for death. Robert L.
    Wilson. 401
Pragmatic sanction. Ray Fleming.
    247
Prairie. Robin Becker. 202

Prairie miracle. Alice Spohn
    Newton. 333
Prairie path. Joan Colby. 224
Praise/complaint. Albert
    Goldbarth. 261
Prayer. Patsie Black. 206
Prayer. Evelyn Golden. 263
Prayer for a bigot. James A.
    Emanuel. 239
A prayer for a share. Maurice W.
    Britts. 215
A prayer for rivers. Keith
    Wilson. 400
Prayer in Vietnam. Jocelyn
    Hollis. 274
A prayer in winter. Franz
    Schneider. 361
Prayer No. 2. Rochelle DuBois.
    234
Prayer to my son. Carol Frost.
    249
The prayer wheel. John F. Barker.
    201
"A prayer, to the Lord, cast down
    like a good old Catholic"
    Charles Olson. 337
Prayers
    Add your love to my love. Alice
        Joyce Davidson. 227
    As gentle rain. Alice Spohn
        Newton. 332
    Entreaty. Alice Joyce Davidson.
        227
    Holiday prayer. Alice Joyce
        Davidson. 227
    Home body. James R. Rhodes. 352
    I pray. Norman Andrew Kirk. 293
    Listen to me. Jacques Sollov.
        370
    Little prayer. Alice Joyce
        Davidson. 227
    "Lord I believe. Help me in my
        unbelief." Christopher Bursk.
        219
    'The Lord is My Shepherd' James
        R. Rhodes. 352
    Lord thank you. Jacques Sollov.
        371
    "Mother-spirit..." Charles
        Olson. 337
    Night prayer. Mary Gilliland.
        257
    Nothing so wise. Jeanne Lohmann.
        305
    Otilia Colunga on her knees in
        line... J.W. Rivers. 354
    Prayer. Patsie Black. 206
    The prayer wheel. John F.
        Barker. 201
    "A prayer, to the Lord, cast

down like a good old Catholic"
Charles Olson. 337
Song for Thantog. Joy Harjo. 269
Spiritual sun. Jacques Sollov.
371
A thought. Maurice W. Britts.
215
Two versions of the Lord's
Prayer, sels. R. Buckminster
Fuller. 251
White Flower Farm. Michael
Gizzi. 259
Praying mantis. Charles Edward
Eaton. 236
Pre-morning moment. Marie Daerr
Boehringer. 210
Predators from a branch of the
blackthorned sloe. Susan
Stock. 375
Prediction. Josephine Miles. 319
Pregnancy
The beginning. Sister Maura. 313
Bird, flower, child. Joan Colby.
224
The blue tablecloth. Roy Marz.
312
I carry the moon. Wanda Coleman.
225
November. Toi Derricote. 229
Roomates. Lyn Lifshin. 303
Souls looking for bodies. Andrei
Codrescu. 223
With child. Rosa Bogar. 211
Pregnancy. See also Conception

Prehistoric coffins in Provence.
Anneliese Wagner. 389
Preliminary to classroom lecture.
Josephine Miles. 319
Prelude to autumn. Robert L.
Wilson. 401
Prelutsky, Jack
The aardvark. 349
The armadillo. 349
The beaver. 349
Bees. 349
The Bengal tiger. 349
The black bear. 349
The chameleon. 349
The cheetah. 349
The chipmunk. 349
The cow. 349
The crocodile. 349
Don't ever seize a weasel by the
tail. 349
A dromedary standing still. 349
The egg. 349
Electric eels. 349
Fish. 349
The gallivanting gecko. 349

The giggling gaggling gaggle of
geese. 349
A gopher in the garden. 349
The hippopotamus. 349
The house mouse. 349
The hummingbird. 349
The hyena. 349
I love you more than applesauce.
348
I made a giant valentine. 348
I made my dog a valentine. 348
I only got one valentine. 348
It's Valentine's Day. 348
Jelly Jill loves Weasel Will.
348
The lion. 349
Long gone. 349
The mole. 349
Mother's chocolate valentine.
348
The multilingual mynah bird. 349
My father's valentine. 348
My special cake. 348
Oh no! 348
The ostrich. 349
Our classroom has a mailbox. 348
The owl. 349
Oysters. 349
The pack rat. 349
The polar bear. 349
The porcupine. 349
The rabbit. 349
Sheep. 349
The snail. 349
The snake. 349
There's someone I know. 348
The three-toed sloth. 349
Toucans too. 349
The turtle. 349
The two-horned black rhinoceros.
349
A valentine for my best friend.
348
A valentine for my teacher. 348
The wallaby. 349
The walrus. 349
The yak. 349
The zebra. 349
Zoo doings. 349
Premiere. Josephine Miles. 319
Preparing the will, three
generations. Sandra McPherson.
317
The present tense. Joyce Carol
Oates. 336
The presentation. Toi Derricote.
229
Presidents - United States
Hank Snow, the evangelist, prays
for the president. James

Schevill. 360
Mr. President. Alice Spohn
Newton. 332

On the election of a president.
Anne Bailie. 199
Press. Alberta Turner. 384
Pressed flowers. Albert
Goldbarth. 261
A **pretty** box. Thomas Hornsby
Ferril. 243
Pretty face. Wanda Coleman. 225
"Pretty hard to face the facts."
Michael Robert Pick. 345
Prevarications. Robert A. Sears.
362
Preventive medicine. Marie Daerr
Boehringer. 210
"The **previous** painter." Madison
Morrison. 327
The **price** of freedom. Robert L.
Wilson. 401
Prick song at Compline. Tom
Smith. 368
Pride. Josephine Miles. 319
Pride and Vanity
"The court repairs to." Madison
Morrison. 327
Pride. Josephine Miles. 319
A **pride** of four small lions,
sels. Everett A. Gillis. 258
Pride's corner. Robert A. Sears.
362
Primary colors. Cathy Song. 372
Primavera. James A. Emanuel. 239
Primitive chic. Harrison Fisher.
245
Primping the windmill pump. Alice
Spohn Newton. 333
Prince Williams Sound. Sally Love
Saunders. 358
Princess. Martha Janssen. 283
Printout. James Torio. 281
Prints and Printers
A German printmaker. Marc
Hudson. 277
Maple sugaring. Robin Becker.
202
Prison songs. Colette Inez. 280
Prisoner of Los Angeles (2).
Wanda Coleman. 225
Prisoners of War
Captives. Ernest Hemingway. 272
One-eye and the German prisoners
of war in Colorado. James
Schevill. 360
Wiedersehen. Miller Williams.
399
Prisons and Prisoners
Amaranth and Moly. Amy Clampitt.

222
Cool Hand Kelly pleads
extenuating circumstances.
Thomas McGrath. 315
Cram session. Stephen Todd
Booker. 212
Forspent. Erin Jolly. 285
Jailbreak. James Magorian. 308
The License to carry a gun.
Andrei Codrescu. 223
On March 30th 1981. Stephen Todd
Booker. 212
Prison songs. Colette Inez. 280
Rain. Andrei Codrescu. 223
Romantic letter. Josephine
Miles. 319
The service. Michael Akillian.
193
Silly bitches institute. Wanda
Coleman. 225
"This is the dark." Madison
Morrison. 327
Privacy
If you go poking around in my
journal you deserve the worst.
Lyn Lifshin. 303
A **private** bestiary. Marge Piercy.
346
Private moments only. Gerard
Malanga. 310
Privates. Robert A. Sears. 362
The **prize.** Steve Kowit. 299
Pro patria. Rose Basile Green.
265
The **probation.** Roy Marz. 312
Probe and brood. Paul Violi. 388
Probing various facets of hybrid
corn. James Magorian. 309
Problem. Bill Knott. 296
A **procession** at Candlemas. Amy
Clampitt. 222
Proctologist on a sentimental
journey. James Magorian. 309
The **prodigal** son. Robert Bly. 209
Proem. Charles Olson. 337
Proem. Haig Khatchadourian. 292
Profane desert. John Hawkes. 270
"The **professional** man." Madison
Morrison. 327
Professor emeritus. James
Magorian. 308
Program. Josephine Miles. 319
Progress. Irving Feldman. 242
Progress
Late news. Richard Blessing. 208
Meeting. Josephine Miles. 319
Statute. Josephine Miles. 319
Progressive dinner. Michael
Akillian. 193
Prologue. Cynthia Grenfell. 266

A **prologue** to some elegies.
Dennis Hinrichsen. 273
The **prom**. Robert Peters. 343
Prominent astronomer playing
musical chairs in an... James
Magorian. 309
'**Promiscuity.**'. Joyce Carol
Oates. 336
Promise. Josephine Miles. 319
Promise. Marie Daerr Boehringer.
210
Promise. Edwin Honig. 275
The **promised** coat. Cathryn
Hankla. 268
Promises. Stephen Todd Booker.
212
Proof mark. James Torio. 281
The **proofs** of God. Joyce Carol
Oates. 336
Property
Complaint. Cynthia Grenfell. 266
Land speculation. Franz
Schneider. 361
Missing persons. Robert
Pawlowski. 341
Possessions. Cathryn Hankla. 268
Property. See also Wealth

The **prophet**. Sam Fishman. 246
The **prophet**. John Godfrey. 260
Prophets and Prophecy
False prophets, false poets.
Norman Andrew Kirk. 293
A parable of prophecy. Thomas
Hornsby Ferril. 243
The prophet. Sam Fishman. 246
The prophet. John Godfrey. 260
Tiresia's drinking. Clayton
Eshleman. 240
Proposal. Alice Joyce Davidson.
227
Proposition. Mark Vinz. 387
Props. Robert A. Sears. 362
Proserpine. See Persephone

Prospect park. Rodney Nelson. 331
The **prospector**. Jacques Sollov.
371
Prostitution and Prostitutes
All-nite donuts. Albert
Goldbarth. 261
a colored girl. James L. White.
396
"For the harlot has a hardlot."
Ernest Hemingway. 272
Head. John Godfrey. 260
Hunter's point. Rod McKuen. 316
I've written this poem before.
Wanda Coleman. 225
Swan. Wanda Coleman. 225

Vocation. Martha Janssen. 283
Protection. Martha Janssen. 283
Protection
"I've been going around
everywhere without any skin."
Josephine Miles. 319
If you will. Josephine Miles.
319
The woman who collects boxes.
Lyn Lifshin. 303
Protector. Laura Boss. 213
Protocol. Erin Jolly. 285
Protoprimavera. Richmond
Lattimore. 301
Proud New York. John Reed. 350
Provence, France
Letter from Provence. Louise
Gluck. 259A
Postcard from Provence. Anne
Bailie. 199
The **proverbs** of clowns. Cornel
Lengyel. 302
Providence, Rhode Island
A stone wall in Providence.
Robert Kelly. 289
Provolone lane. John Godfrey. 260
The **prowler**. Mark Vinz. 387
The **prudence** of Nan Corbett.
Alberta Turner. 384
Prunes
"When I was eight,I put in the
left-hand drawer." Josephine
Miles. 319
Psalm. Joyce Carol Oates. 336
Psalm of success. Ernesto
Galarza. 252
Psalm-maker to his son. Cornel
Lengyel. 302
Psalm:El Salvador. Thomas
McGrath. 315
Psych ward. Mitchell Howard. 276
Psychiatric referral. James
Magorian. 308
Psychiatry
History's library. James
Applewhite. 198
Psycho love. Sam Fishman. 246
Psychoanalysis in one easy
sonnet. Ernesto Galarza. 252
Psychodrama. James Magorian. 308
"**Public** eyes perceive." Robert A.
Sears. 362
Public notice. Cornel Lengyel.
302
Public servant. Christopher
Bursk. 219
"**Publish** my own soul..." Charles
Olson. 337
Pud and I. Robert L. Wilson. 401
Puddles on ice. Paul Violi. 388

Pueblo Indians
Sun watcher. Phillips Kloss. 294
Puerto Rico
Retrospective. Ruth Lisa
Schechter. 359
The **puffing** tree. Cynthia
Grenfell. 266
The **pulse** of the zodiac puzzle.
Rochelle DuBois. 234
Punishment
For the furies. Marge Piercy.
346
To the preacher's son paddled
for dropping his pants...
Larry Moffi. 322
The **punt**, fr. Athletic verse.
Ernest Hemingway. 272
A **puppet** on a string. Rachel A.
Hazen. 271
Purchase of a blue, green, or
orange ode. Josephine Miles.
319
Purchase of hat to wear in the
sun. Josephine Miles. 319
Purchase of lodging for the
night. Josephine Miles. 319
Purchasing new bicentennial
stamps, 1975 James Schevill.
360
The **pure** light. Jacques Sollov.
371
Purely psychological. Robert L.
Wilson. 401
The **purest** form of eternity.
Rachel A. Hazen. 271
Purification rite. Robert L.
Wilson. 401
Puritania. Albert Goldbarth. 261
Purple aster. Debra Bruce. 216
Purple aster. Mary Gilliland. 257
Purple lilacs, blue water.
Charles Edward Eaton. 236
The **purple** sun. Jacques Sollov.
371
Pursuit of happiness. Robert L.
Wilson. 401
Purvis. Robert Peters. 343
Push pussy madonna. Lyn Lifshin.
303
Pussy madonna. Lyn Lifshin. 303
Pussywillows: a city poem. Jeanne
Lohmann. 305
Putting an end to the war
stories. Larry Moffi. 322
Puzzle. Marie Daerr Boehringer.
210
Pygmalion. Robert A. Sears. 362
Pygmalion. John Reed. 350
Pygmalion (mythology)
Pygmalion. John Reed. 350

Q:What are you feeling? A:Guilty.
Gerard Malanga. 310
Quabbin Reservoir. Robin Becker.
202
Quakers
At a Quaker meeting a man arose
and spoke of love. James
Schevill. 360
A **quarrel** put to rest. Colette
Inez. 280
Quarries
The quarry. Amy Clampitt. 222
San Ceccardo. Robert A. Sears.
362
The **quarry.** Amy Clampitt. 222
Quatrains. Randy Blasing. 207
"queen/has new-born cats."
Madison Morrison. 327
Queensland, Australia
Leaving Queensland. Rod McKuen.
316
Query, not to be answered. Joyce
Carol Oates. 336
Quest. Edwin Honig. 275
Question. Josephine B. Moretti.
324
A **question** for Jonah. Cornel
Lengyel. 302
The **question** of identity. Timothy
Steele. 374
The **question** of personnel. Andrei
Codrescu. 223
A **question.** Alice Joyce Davidson.
227
The **question.** Bill Knott. 296
Questions. Gerard Malanga. 310
Questions. Josephine Miles. 319
Questions
"Friends in our questions, we
looked together." Josephine
Miles. 319
Information booth. James
Magorian. 308
"The mailman is coming from the
next block down." Josephine
Miles. 319
Query, not to be answered. Joyce
Carol Oates. 336
Questions. Josephine Miles. 319
Untitled:"Love the questions"
Kirk Lumpkin. 306
Quetzal. X.J. Kennedy. 290
The **queue.** Steve Kowit. 299
The **quick** of roses. Everett A.
Gillis. 258
Quicksand. Maurice Kenny. 291

Quiet. Martha Janssen. 283
A quiet day at the vatican. James
    Magorian. 309
The quiet man of simplicity.
    James Schevill. 360
Quiet office. Josephine B.
    Moretti. 324
Quiet place. Alice Joyce
    Davidson. 227
"A quiet staircase." Larry
    Eigner. 237
A quiet truth. Alice Spohn
    Newton. 332
The quiet, angry man. George
    Eklund. 238
Quiet, so quiet. Eileen
    Silver-Lillywite. 364
Quilt song. Mark Vinz. 387
The quilt. John F. Barker. 201
Quilts
    Quilt song. Mark Vinz. 387
Quinnipiac (lake)
    Lax alba at Quinnipiac. Bradford
        Morrow. 329
Quotations. James R. Rhodes. 352

R.S.V.P. Patsie Black. 206
Rabbit world. Aileen Fisher. 244
The rabbit. Jack Prelutsky. 349
Rabbits
    At that time. Maurice Kenny. 291
    Beneath the snowy trees. Aileen
        Fisher. 244
    Bulgy eyes. Aileen Fisher. 244
    But rabbits. Aileen Fisher. 244
    Color blind. Aileen Fisher. 244
    Cotton tails. Aileen Fisher. 244
    Do rabbits have Christmas?
        Aileen Fisher. 244
    Early spring. Aileen Fisher. 244
    Easter morning. Aileen Fisher.
        244
    Hop, skip, and jump. Aileen
        Fisher. 244
    Jack Rabbit. Aileen Fisher. 244
    Orbital bunnes, inc. Mitchell
        Howard. 276
    Rabbit world. Aileen Fisher. 244
    The rabbit. Jack Prelutsky. 349
    Ready... set... Aileen Fisher.
        244
    Run, rabbit! Aileen Fisher. 244
    Says the rabbit. Aileen Fisher.
        244
    Secrets. Aileen Fisher. 244
    Snowshoe hare. Aileen Fisher.
        244

Thinking. Aileen Fisher. 244
This morning. Tefke Goldberger.
    262
To a lady cottontail. Aileen
    Fisher. 244
Who scans the meadow. Aileen
    Fisher. 244
Race. Edwin Honig. 275
The racer's widow. Louise Gluck.
    259A
The races at murderloin downs.
    Stephen Todd Booker. 212
Racial Prejudice
    Blazing accusation. May Miller.
        320
    Buchenwald: the beginnings.
        Evelyn Golden. 263
    Government injunction
        restraining Harlem Cosmetic
        Co. Josephine Miles. 319
    Mississippi sheriff at the Klan
        initiation. James Schevill.
        360
    Office politics. Wanda Coleman.
        225
    Prayer for a bigot. James A.
        Emanuel. 239
    Racism. Rose Basile Green. 265
    Simultaneous translation. Ray
        Fleming. 247
    Us. Stephen Todd Booker. 212
Racism. Rose Basile Green. 265
Racism in France. James A.
    Emanuel. 239
Radiant dog. John Godfrey. 260
Radiator madonna. Lyn Lifshin.
    303
Radio
    Radio man. Gene Detro. 230
Radio dispatched poetry truck.
    James Magorian. 309
Radio man. Gene Detro. 230
Radio report. Robert Peters. 343
Raffles
    Midweek. Josephine Miles. 319
The rage of Demeter. Richmond
    Lattimore. 301
"Rages/strain.". Charles Olson.
    337
Ragged ending. Marge Piercy. 346
"Raging lonely wave." Michael
    Robert Pick. 345
The raid. Charles Edward Eaton.
    236
The raid. Robert Peters. 343
"The rail ends do not meet."
    Ernest Hemingway. 272
Railroad road. Randy Blasing. 207
The railroad still runs to
    Connecticut... Mitchell

Howard. 276

Railroads
Another view. Deborah Tall. 378
The Chicago train. Louise Gluck. 259A
The day they came back. Marieve Rugo. 356
Late leaving train. Dennis Hinrichsen. 273
Living in a boxcar in San Francisco. James Schevill. 360
Mystic moment. James Tate. 379
Night train to Gastonia, N.C. Josephine B. Moretti. 324
On the train. Carolyn Stoloff. 376
Riviera railway. Richmond Lattimore. 301
Steel blurs. Sally Love Saunders. 358
Taking the train to grandpa's. Alice Spohn Newton. 333
Toy trains in the landlord's house. Dave Smith. 367
Train wheels. Josephine B. Moretti. 324
The train, fr. The green step. Kenneth Koch. 297
Trains. Andrei Codrescu. 223
When the silence becomes too much to bear. Herbert Morris. 326
Wreck. Josephine Miles. 319

Rain. Josephine Miles. 319
Rain. Andrei Codrescu. 223
Rain. Joy Harjo. 269
Rain. Eileen Silver-Lillywite. 364

Rain
After the rain. Tefke Goldberger. 262
Afternoon. David Wann. 394
The air clears, after. Mary Gilliland. 257
Around you, your house. William Stafford. 373
Benediction. James R. Rhodes. 352
Clover rain. Aileen Fisher. 244
"A dark day." Larry Eigner. 237
Double sonnet. John Godfrey. 260
February rain. Evelyn Golden. 263
The floods of spring. Keith Wilson. 400
Haiku au surreal. William Oandasan. 335
A history of rain. Marc Hudson. 277
May rain. Elsa Gidlow. 254

Mind shifts. Rod McKuen. 316
October rain. May Miller. 320
"Out of the wind and leaves." Larry Eigner. 237
"Pigeons..." Larry Eigner. 237
"A quiet staircase." Larry Eigner. 237
Rain moods. Ernesto Galarza. 252
Rain on the pond. Haig Khatchadourian. 292
September rain. Rochelle DuBois. 234
A song of rain. Tefke Goldberger. 262
Spring storm. James Torio. 281
Summer shower. Sally Love Saunders. 358
Threshing in my mother's arms. Mary Gilliland. 257
"Tremendous rains." Madison Morrison. 327
Weather-wise. Marie Daerr Boehringer. 210
What happens when it rains. Mitchell Howard. 276
Whispering harps. James R. Rhodes. 352
Woken. Ralph J., Jr. Mills. 321

Rain at Bellagio. Amy Clampitt. 222
Rain forest. Jeanne Lohmann. 305
The **rain** gone. Ralph J., Jr. Mills. 321
The **rain** in Maine. Robert A. Sears. 362
Rain moods. Ernesto Galarza. 252
Rain on the pond. Haig Khatchadourian. 292
The **rain** walkers. Harry Humes. 278
Rain waste. John Godfrey. 260
"**Rain**, rain, go away." Jan Ormerod. 338
Rain: the funeral: the woman's voice. Anthony Petrosky. 344
Rainy day: last run. Dave Smith. 367
"**Rainy**/days.". Larry Eigner. 237
Raking in. Steve Kowit. 299
Raking leaves. Debra Bruce. 216
Raking with leaves in the wind. Cathryn Hankla. 268
Ralph Waldo Emerson receives a visit from the sane man... James Schevill. 360
Rama holds an orgy. Mitchell Howard. 276
Ramazan at New Phocaea. Randy Blasing. 207
Rameses TT, King

Ramses II. Jacques Sollov. 370
Ramon F. Iturbe. J.W. Rivers. 354
Ramona Veagis. Brenda Marie
    Osbey. 340
Ramses II. Jacques Sollov. 370
Ranch Life
    The bull shooter. Phyllis A.
        Tickle. 382
    Morning at the ranch I. Cynthia
        Grenfell. 266
    Morning at the ranch II:
        Memorial Day. Cynthia
        Grenfell. 266
    Morning at the ranch IV: Ridge
        Road above Annie Green Spring.
        Cynthia Grenfell. 266
    Morning at the ranch IV: photo:
        the negative. Cynthia
        Grenfell. 266
Ranch Life. See also Cowboys

Rape. Wanda Coleman. 225
Rape
    Headline. George Eklund. 238
    Hysteria. Lyn Lifshin. 303
    Rape. Wanda Coleman. 225
    Wrong suspect raped in
        Sacramento rape case. David
        Wann. 394
The rare flower. Rosa Bogar. 211
Raritan reflections. Maria
    Gillan. 256
Raritan, New Jersey
    Raritan reflections. Maria
        Gillan. 256
Rat. Robert Peters. 343
Rats
    The city rat. Barry Wallenstein.
        393
    The pack rat. Jack Prelutsky.
        349
    Rat. Robert Peters. 343
The raven. Edgar Allan Poe. 347
Ravens
    Under the raven's nest. David
        Wagoner. 390
The ravine. James Applewhite. 198
Razors
    Nothing like a razor. Carolyn
        Stoloff. 376
Read to the animals, or Orpheus
    at the SPCA. Irving Feldman.
    242
Reader. Bill Knott. 296
Readers. Josephine Miles. 319
"Readied in tradition." Michael
    Robert Pick. 345
Reading
    How I caught up in my reading.
        Josephine Miles. 319

Reading Chretien by Hood Canal.
    Marc Hudson. 277
Reading Hannah Arendt's Eichmann
    in Jerusalem. Jacqueline
    Frank. 248
Reading late by a simple light.
    Harry Humes. 278
The reading of an ever-changing
    tale. John Yau. 404
Reading the gaps. Bill Knott. 296
The reading. Wanda Coleman. 225
The reading. Carolyn Stoloff. 376
Ready... set... Aileen Fisher.
    244
Real. James R. Rhodes. 352
Real estate. Robert Anbian. 194
Real love. Jacques Sollov. 370
The real parader. James Schevill.
    360
Real peace. Rosa Bogar. 211
A realistic bar and grill. David
    Shapiro. 363
Reality. Rochelle DuBois. 234
Reality. James R. Rhodes. 352
Reality. Connie Hunt. 279
Reality
    Autograph. Randy Blasing. 207
    The chances of magic. Keith
        Waldrop. 392
    The color that really is.
        William Stafford. 373
    December field. Deborah Tall.
        378
    The difference. Rachel A. Hazen.
        271
    The dream and the reality.
        Maurice W. Britts. 215
    A good thing when I see one.
        Andrei Codrescu. 223
    Grave discovery. Robert L.
        Wilson. 401
    Kind of a love poem. Steve
        Kowit. 298, 299
    The last trance. Norman Andrew
        Kirk. 293
    A lull in battle. A. Dovichi.
        233
    Naked. James Schevill. 360
    Name and addresses. David
        Shapiro. 363
    The penal cavalry. Andrei
        Codrescu. 223
    The poem I just wrote. Joy
        Harjo. 269
    Real. James R. Rhodes. 352
    Reality. Rochelle DuBois. 234
    Reality. James R. Rhodes. 352
    Reality. Connie Hunt. 279
    "The reality behind." Larry
        Eigner. 237

A swimmer in the sea. Sam
    Fishman. 246
That which is. James Applewhite.
    198
Transpose. Norman Andrew Kirk.
    293
Triptych. James Torio. 281
Where the dying live and the
    living die. Robert L. Wilson.
    401
"The reality behind." Larry
    Eigner. 237
Reason. Josephine Miles. 319
Reason
    "Along the street where we used
    to stop for bread." Josephine
    Miles. 319
    The fivefold root of
    insufficient reason. Phillips
    Kloss. 294
    Let reason reign. Sam Fishman.
    246
    With this to come back to.
    Phillips Kloss. 294
The reason. Sister Maura. 313
Reasons for living. Debra Bruce.
    216
Reasons why. Wanda Coleman. 225
Reasons why I love you. Jim
    Everhard. 241
Reassurance: what gets done. Mary
    Gilliland. 257
Rebecca at play. Miller Williams.
    399
Rebellion
    The great exception. Lucien
    Stryk. 377
Reborn. Norman Andrew Kirk. 293
Recalling the names. Donald
    Revell. 351
Receiver. William Stafford. 373
Reception. Josephine Miles. 319
Recess. Dave Smith. 367
Recidivists. Joan Colby. 224
Recipe. Tom Smith. 368
Recipe for the anxious one.
    Mitchell Howard. 276
Reckoning. Anneliese Wagner. 389
Recluse. Mark Vinz. 387
Recognition. Josephine Miles. 319
Recognition of the tigers. Ruth
    Lisa Schechter. 359
Recollection. Robert L. Wilson.
    401
Recollection. Martha Janssen. 283
Reconstruction. Deborah Tall. 378
The record. Charles Olson. 337
Recorder. Wanda Coleman. 225
Recordings and Recorders
    Tape recorder. Christopher

Bursk. 219
Recuperation
    Comeback. Richard Blessing. 208
    Homecoming. Richard Blessing.
    208
Recurrent city. Marieve Rugo. 356
Recycle. Kirk Lumpkin. 306
Red. Charles Edward Eaton. 236
Red (color)
    Red. Charles Edward Eaton. 236
    Winter rose. William Oandasan.
    335
Red bird in a white tree. Marieve
    Rugo. 356
Red bricks and camphor trees.
    James Tate. 379
The red cabbages. Sandra Gilbert.
    255
Red cedar. Marc Hudson. 277
Red Lake. Joan Colby. 224
A red nightgown. Carol Frost. 249
Red rose. Jacques Sollov. 371
Red shoes in the rain. May
    Miller. 320
Red snapper. Charles Edward
    Eaton. 236
Red wing hawk. James Applewhite.
    198
Redemption. Josephine Miles. 319
Redemption. Martha Janssen. 283
Rediscovery. Rose Basile Green.
    265
Rediscovery. James Torio. 281
Redlands journey. Betty Adcock.
    192
Redwood Trees. See Sequoias

Reed, John
    America 1918. 350
    And yet-. 350
    April. 350
    Aurore. 350
    California. 350
    The charge of the political
    brigade. 350
    The chicken. 350
    Coyote song. 350
    The dancing women. 350
    Dawn serenade. 350
    De profundo. 350
    Dear heart. 350
    A dedication to Max Eastman. 350
    Deep-water song. 350
    The desert. 350
    Eleventh Avenue racket. 350
    Faery song. 350
    A farmer's woman. 350
    The first mate. 350
    Flowers of fire. 350
    Fog. 350

Forgotten. 350
The foundations of a
    sky-scraper. 350
Guinevere. 350
Horace - Book IV Ode 7. 350
Hospital notes. 350
A hymn to Manhattan. 350
John Milton. 350
June in the city. 350
A letter to Louise. 350
Love at sea. 350
Melisande. 350
Mireille. 350
Night. 350
Noon. 350
October. 350
On returning to the city. 350
Origo. 350
Our lady of pain. 350
Proud New York. 350
Pygmalion. 350
River side. 350
Sangar. 350
The sea-gull. 350
The slave. 350
A song for May. 350
The sword dance. 350
Tamburlaine. 350
The tempest. 350
'This magazine of ours.' 350
The traveler. 350
Tschaikowsky. 350
Two rooms. 350
Valkyrs. 350
The wanderer to his heart's
    desire. 350
Wanderlust. 350
The wedding ring. 350
Welsh song. 350
The west. 350
Williamette. 350
Winter night. 350
A winter run. 350
Reed, John (about)
    To John Reed. Max Eastman. 350
Reflections. Josephine B.
    Moretti. 324
Reflections at Gettysburg. Paul
    Davis. 228
Reflections on rose quartz.
    Cynthia Grenfell. 266
Reformation. James R. Rhodes. 352
Reformatories
    Poetry workshop in a maximum
        security reform school. Betty
        Adcock. 192
Refraction. Connie Hunt. 279
Refrigerators
    The sin of wanting a new
        refrigerator. Andrei Codrescu.
        223
Refuge. Thomas R. Sleigh. 366
"Refuge sought on a/moments
    thought." Michael Robert Pick.
    345
The refugee and his library.
    James Schevill. 360
Refugee, 1940. Anneliese Wagner.
    389
The refugees. A. Dovichi. 233
Refusals
    Saying no. Connie Hunt. 279
Reg gypsy wagon, with flowers.
    Keith Wilson. 400
Reggae or not! Amiri Baraka
    (LeRoi Jones). 200
Region of no birds. Elsa Gidlow.
    254
A registry of graves. Keith
    Wilson. 400
Regret. Sam Fishman. 246
Regret
    The music. Greg Kuzma. 300
    Yonder. James Tate. 379
Rehabilitation. Wanda Coleman.
    225
Rehabilitation. Ruth Lisa
    Schechter. 359
Reincarnation
    Heir. Josephine Miles. 319
The reincarnation of Spirow T.
    Agnew. James Magorian. 309
Rejoice. Patsie Black. 206
The relatives. Jacqueline Frank.
    248
Relays. Rod McKuen. 316
"Release/...and you will
    receive." Joan Walsh Anglund.
    197
Relief. Martha Janssen. 283
Religion
    Because radio is a relic. Larry
        Moffi. 322
    Biz. James R. Rhodes. 352
    "I believe in religion..."
        Charles Olson. 337
    Jazz at the intergalactic
        nightclub. Thomas McGrath. 315
    Lucifer alone. Josephine Miles.
        319
    M-L/T. Albert Goldbarth. 261
    Maximus, to Gloucester : Letter
        19 (A pastoral letter).
        Charles Olson. 337
    A truth-teller's complaint.
        Cornel Lengyel. 302
Religious observance. Tom Smith.
    368
"The religious retreat." Madison
    Morrison. 327

Relinquishing. Ghita Orth. 339
Reliquishment. Elsa Gidlow. 254
A remarkable exhibition. David
    Wagoner. 390
Rembrandt, Harmenszoon van Rijn
    More about monks. Andrei
    Codrescu. 223
Remedial. James Schevill. 360
Remedies
    Aleppo. Michael Gizzi. 259
    Constantinople. Michael Gizzi.
    259
Remember. Joy Harjo. 269
Remember. Jacques Sollov. 371
Remember me? Alice Joyce
    Davidson. 227
Remembering. Sam Fishman. 246
Remembering. Rose Basile Green.
    265
Remembering. William Stafford.
    373
Remembering brother Bob. William
    Stafford. 373
Remembering flute house. Gary
    Margolis. 311
Remembering Greece. Amy Clampitt.
    222
Remembering Nonno. Rose Basile
    Green. 265
Remembering the children of
    Auschwitz. Thomas McGrath. 315
Remembering the fifties. Greg
    Kuzma. 300
Remembering the man. Miller
    Williams. 399
Remembering the typo. Albert
    Goldbarth. 261
Remembering youth. Martha
    Janssen. 283
Remembrance of my forgotten
    skinniness. Andrei Codrescu.
    223
Remembrance of summers past. Anne
    Bailie. 199
Reminders. Rachel A. Hazen. 271
Rene. Norman Andrew Kirk. 293
Renewal. Marie Daerr Boehringer.
    210
Renewal. Steve Kowit. 299
Rent. See Landlords

Repeal. Erin Jolly. 285
Repentance
    With neighbors one afternoon.
    William Stafford. 373
Repentimento. Charles Edward
    Eaton. 236
Repetition. Betty Adcock. 192
Replanting a garden. David
    Wagoner. 390

Report from the Jewish Museum.
    Anneliese Wagner. 389
Report on the times. Carolyn
    Stoloff. 376
A report to an academy. Joyce
    Carol Oates. 336
Report to the moving company.
    James Schevill. 360
Reprise. Rose Basile Green. 265
Requiem. Erin Jolly. 285
Requiem for a golden retriever.
    Ruth Lisa Schechter. 359
Requiem for a wife. James Torio.
    281
Requiescat. John F. Barker. 201
Required reading. Marie Daerr
    Boehringer. 210
Rescue. Robert Pawlowski. 341
Rescuing something. Jeanne
    Lohmann. 305
Research chemist stomping on a
    colleague's sack lunch. James
    Magorian. 309
The reservoirs of Mount Helicon.
    Amy Clampitt. 222
Residencies. Thomas McGrath. 315
Resilience. Anthony Petrosky. 344
Resistance. Josephine Miles. 319
Resolution. Alice Joyce Davidson.
    227
Resolution. Mark Vinz. 387
Resolving. Mitchell Howard. 276
Resorts. See Health Resorts

Response. Marie Daerr Boehringer.
    210
Responsibilites
    Ride. Josephine Miles. 319
Responsibility occurence. David
    Wann. 394
Responsible. James R. Rhodes. 352
Restaurants
    A good cafeteria. Carol Frost.
    249
    "The grill is robbed." Madison
    Morrison. 327
    "In the outdoor." Madison
    Morrison. 327
    Soda fountain. Mark Vinz. 387
(Resting or doing something...)
    Larry Eigner. 237
The restless mind. Sam Fishman.
    246
Restoration. Frances Mayes. 314
Restoring the wood. Christopher
    Bursk. 219
A resumption, or possibly a
    remission. Amy Clampitt. 222
Resurrection, The. See Easter

The **resurrection**. Christopher
    Bursk. 219
Resurrections. Maria Gillan. 256
"Reticent.". Larry Eigner. 237
Retreat. Norman Andrew Kirk. 293
Retrospect. Phillips Kloss. 294
Retrospective. Josephine Miles.
    319
Retrospective. Ruth Lisa
    Schechter. 359
Return. Marilyn Kallet. 287
Return to center. Robert A.
    Sears. 362
Return to the light. Richmond
    Lattimore. 301
Return to the loss. Ernest
    Tedlock. 380
"The **return** to the mail-bag..."
    Charles Olson. 337
Return to the woods. Anthony
    Petrosky. 344
Return to the world. Albert
    Goldbarth. 261
Returned to Frisco, 1946. W.D.
    (William De Witt) Snodgrass.
    369
Returning. James L. White. 396
Returning a lost child. Louise
    Gluck. 259A
Returning to Eagle Bridge.
    Stephen Sandy. 357
Returning to Taos. Judson Crews.
    226
The **returning**. Joy Harjo. 269
Returns. Ralph J., Jr. Mills. 321
Reunion. Jenne Andrews. 196
Reunion. J.W. Rivers. 354
Reunions. Connie Hunt. 279
Rev. Joseph Krupsack. Robert
    Peters. 343
Revelation. William Stafford. 373
Revelation and return. Robert L.
    Wilson. 401
Revelations. Maria Gillan. 256
Revelations
    Enlightenment. Josephine Miles.
    319
Revell, Donald
    Aesthete's complaint. 351
    Albemarle. 351
    Animaux. 351
    Bal des ardents. 351
    Belfast. 351
    The blue, the dead one. 351
    Central Park South. 351
    A few discretions. 351
    Genevieve dying. 351
    Graves in east Tennessee. 351
    Gymnopedie: the exhibition. 351
    Here to there. 351

    Homage. 351
    In Lombardy. 351
    Jerome Avenue. 351
    Just lord. 351
    Mignonette. 351
    Motel view. 351
    Near life. 351
    Near Rhinebeck. 351
    No moment. 351
    Odile. 351
    Over Manhattan. 351
    A perfect skyline. 351
    Recalling the names. 351
    A road and clouds. 351
    Rodeo aesthetique. 351
    Satiesme. 351
    Stevenson and James at
        Skerryvore. 351
    Theriot cove. 351
    To begin. 351
    Tokens. 351
Revenge
    The fox and the geese. James
        Magorian. 308
    Versailles - Galerie des Glaces.
        Michael Gizzi. 259
Reverie for a nuclear reactor.
    James Magorian. 308
Reverse. Andrei Codrescu. 223
Reviewing the possibilities.
    Miriam Goodman. 264
Revisiting Thrudvang farm. Rodney
    Nelson. 331
Revolution. Andrei Codrescu. 223
Revolution
    After the revolution. David
        James. 282
    Don't look back. Jim Everhard.
        241
    The homilies of Bedrock Jones.
        Thomas McGrath. 315
    No Caribbean cruise. Thomas
        McGrath. 315
    Revolution. Andrei Codrescu. 223
    Revolutionary frescoes - the
        ascension. Thomas McGrath. 315
    Stock report. Andrei Codrescu.
        223
    Sunday sermon. Andrei Codrescu.
        223
Revolutionary. Mark Vinz. 387
Revolutionary frescoes - the
    ascension. Thomas McGrath. 315
Revolutionary song. Thomas
    McGrath. 315
Rewards
    Fifty/fifty. Rod McKuen. 316
Rexroth, Kenneth (about)
    To a friend in wake of a
        ballyhoo. Bradford Morrow. 329

Rhapsody. Clayton Eshleman. 240
Rheumatic fever. James
    Applewhite. 198
Rhinebeck. Michael Gizzi. 259
Rhinoceros
    The two-horned black rhinoceros.
        Jack Prelutsky. 349
    Washing a young rhinoceros.
        David Wagoner. 390
Rhodes, James R.
    All's well. 352
    Aloning. 352
    And you? 352
    Anything. 352
    At the same time. 352
    Atomic detente. 352
    Aureole. 352
    Be or be not. 352
    Belly dancing. 352
    Benediction. 352
    Bittersweet brown. 352
    Biz. 352
    Blind sight. 352
    Building. 352
    Catch you catch me not. 352
    Catharsis. 352
    Ceramic. 352
    Charon. 352
    Choice. 352
    Clown. 352
    Committal day. 352
    Courage. 352
    Cry-bones. 352
    Day aborning. 352
    Dichotomy. 352
    Drop-out. 352
    Each. 352
    Each other. 352
    Ecumene. 352
    Ecumenicity. 352
    Ever-beyond. 352
    The final falling. 352
    For me? 352
    For the wind. 352
    God was there. 352
    Greening song. 352
    Holy grail. 352
    Home body. 352
    Human. 352
    Human logic. 352
    The image. 352
    Infinitude. 352
    Irish violin. 352
    The king is in his counting
        house. 352
    The last five flowers. 352
    The last laugh. 352
    The lie. 352
    Look through my window. 352
    'The Lord is My Shepherd' 352

Love's yin-yang of days. 352
Madonna. 352
Mind songs. 352
Moon maiden. 352
Morning song. 352
Mystery. 352
Naming his call. 352
Narcissus. 352
Nativity. 352
Ninet'1984.' 352
Note worthy. 352
On maturity. 352
Out of Eden. 352
Patient observation. 352
The people, us. 352
A person. 352
Quotations. 352
Real. 352
Reality. 352
Reformation. 352
Responsible. 352
Salt. 352
Sea maiden. 352
See, God? 352
Self-righteous wound. 352
Self-same differences. 352
Silver sliver. 352
So little time. 352
Something in the hunter. 352
Sough and sift. 352
Soul music. 352
Star-eyed boy. 352
Still waters. 352
Success. 352
These faces I see. 352
Thistle down. 352
To be. 352
To become. 352
To one afraid. 352
To the prisoner. 352
A toast. 352
Tomorrow. 352
Tracing. 352
The truth. 352
Up-tight. 352
Waiting. 352
We both know. 352
Were you there? 352
What time is it? 352
When you go. 352
Whispering harps. 352
Who? 352
Wisdom. 352
Woman on a park bench. 352
You are. 352
You're dead! 352
Rhyme. Greg Kuzma. 300
"The rich don't have children."
    Susan Tichy. 381
Rich, Adrienne

Sources. 353

Richard, Richard: American fuel.
    Melvin Dixon. 231

Richard, Richard: an American
    hunger. Melvin Dixon. 231

Richmond Barthe: meeting in Lyon.
    Melvin Dixon. 231

Ricky Ricardo drinks alone. Jim
    Simmerman. 365

Ricochet off water. Mei-Mei
    Berssenbrugge. 203

Riddle. Josephine Miles. 319

Riddle. W.D. (William De Witt)
    Snodgrass. 369

Ride. Josephine Miles. 319

The rider. Wanda Coleman. 225

Rides and Riding - Horses
    Horse latitudes. Colette Inez.
        280
    If he bucks. Carolyn Stoloff.
        376
    The races at murderloin downs.
        Stephen Todd Booker. 212
    Savage remembers a horse. Harry
        Humes. 278
    The Ukian arcade/p.o. box 3838.
        Stephen Todd Booker. 212

Ridgeline. Dennis Hinrichsen. 273

Riding to Greylock. Stephen
    Sandy. 357

Riding to work with the
    gastarbeiter. Larry Moffi. 322

Rifacimento. Paul Violi. 388

"Rigadoon, rigadoon." Jan
    Ormerod. 338

"Right at the cut." Charles
    Olson. 337

Right there in Rand McNally. Paul
    Davis. 228

Right wing mag: a found poem.
    Marge Piercy. 346

Rightside up. Patsie Black. 206

Rilke's white horse. Edwin Honig.
    275

Rilke, Rainer Maria
    Rilke's white horse. Edwin
        Honig. 275

Ringnecks return. Phyllis A.
    Tickle. 382

Rings
    The wedding ring. John Reed. 350

Rings (jewelry)
    My parents send a ring from the
        Bahammas. Jim Simmerman. 365
    My ringless fingers on the
        steering wheel tell the story.
        Laura Boss. 213
    Try it on. Sister Maura. 313

Rio Maranon. Michael Gizzi. 259

Riot. Josephine Miles. 319

Riparto d'assalto. Ernest
    Hemingway. 272

Ripoff artist. Mark Vinz. 387

Ripperton, Minnie
    In memory of Minnie Ripperton.
        Rosa Bogar. 211

Rite. Jacqueline Frank. 248

Rite for the beautification of
    all beings. John Brandi. 214

Rites of passage. Robert Peters.
    343

Ritornello. Mitchell Howard. 276

River. Joseph Penzi. 342

The river fishes. Robert
    Pawlowski. 341

River gods, Dublin. Ghita Orth.
    339

The river map and we're done.
    Charles Olson. 337

River road. Herbert Morris. 326

River side. John Reed. 350

The river: I. Charles Olson. 337

The river: II. Charles Olson. 337

Riverboat. Stephen Sandy. 357

Riverboat. Robert Kelly. 289

Rivers
    Deerskin flowage. Robert Peters.
        343
    Little Pend Oreille river. Franz
        Schneider. 361
    Moyie River. Franz Schneider.
        361
    A prayer for rivers. Keith
        Wilson. 400
    Skokie river cadenzas. Colette
        Inez. 280
    "Stepping over steppuing stones,
        one, two, three." Jan Ormerod.
        338
    Three ways of a river. David
        Wagoner. 390
    To the river. Edgar Allan Poe.
        347

Rivers filled with tears. Rachel
    A. Hazen. 271

Rivers, J.W.
    Alberta Abrams fishes for
        mullet. 354
    Andrea Mendoza is aboard the
        train from Durango. 354
    Anenecuilco: the Pueblo speaks.
        354
    Bloodworms. 354
    The Chicago notebook, sels. 354
    Christmas Eve, 1980. 354
    A civilian defender, port of
        Vera Cruz. 354
    Culpepper and the public health
        physician. 354
    Culpepper goes bass fishing. 354

Culpepper is politicized. 354
Culpepper of the low country,
  sels. 354
Culpepper redeemed. 354
Esterhazy and the cat woman. 354
Esterhazy and the swimmer. 354
The Esterhazy family picnic. 354
Esterhazy in the hospital. 354
Esterhazy on Mount Everest. 354
Esterhazy shakes his fist at the
  Sunday sky. 354
Esterhazy's honeymoon. 354
Esterhazy's memoirs. 354
Esterhazy's Vienna stopover,
  1973. 354
From Burnside to Goldblatt's by
  streetcar. 354
Hardball. 354
In a pueblo in Chiapas. 354
January morning. 354
Jose, age 8. 354
Late at night in the kitchen.
  354
Late to school. 354
Lazaro Cardenas. 354
Macnetes. 354
Machettes, sels. 354
Making cakes and dumplings. 354
Miguel Pro, S.J., faces a Calles
  firing squad. 354
A moment in time at Culpepper
  plantation. 354
The municipal president of
  Tequistalpa to Felix Diaz. 354
Near the ocean, Culpepper lies
  in state. 354
The non-swimmer advises his
  nephew about the beach. 354
The office suite sequence, 1965.
  354
On a mulberry tree branch in
  Jackson Park. 354
Otilia Colunga on her knees in
  line... 354
An outing on Pawley's Island.
  354
Pascual Orozco. 354
Ramon F. Iturbe. 354
Reunion. 354
The scattered poems of
  Esterhazy, sels. 354
Shoveling snow in Chicago. 354
Sir Gander-Puller of the low
  country. 354
The squirrel. 354
Sunday morning sandlot football.
  354
Therapy for Esterhazy in the
  temple of Asklepios. 354
To Uncle Oscar, dead of lung

cancer. 354
Tonsillectomy. 354
The training of a fighter. 354
Twenty-five panchos. 354
Uncle Max leaves for Rumania.
  354
Uncle Max steeps young
  Culpepper... 354
Valentine. 354
Victoriano Huerta. 354
Zapata's sister speaks. 354
Riviera railway. Richmond
  Lattimore. 301
The road ahead. Maurice W.
  Britts. 215
A road and clouds. Donald Revell.
  351
Road construction. Paul Davis.
  228
A road in the Willapa Hills. Marc
  Hudson. 277
The road of kings. Keith Wilson.
  400
The road to Avallon. Ernest
  Hemingway. 272
The road to Yaramalong. Rod
  McKuen. 316
The road. Herbert Morris. 326
Roads and Trails
  Alleys. Sandra McPherson. 317
  Endangered species. Mark Vinz.
    387
  "Gee, what I call the upper road
    was the way" Charles Olson.
    337
  Heroic standard. Kenneth Koch.
    297
  Highroad. Josephine Miles. 319
  Hyde Park. Michael Gizzi. 259
  "In alternate stripes." Madison
    Morrison. 327
  A note on the above. Charles
    Olson. 337
  On inhabiting an orange.
    Josephine Miles. 319
  On the road last night. William
    Stafford. 373
  "Open road." Larry Eigner. 237
  Outside. Josephine Miles. 319
  "The previous painter." Madison
    Morrison. 327
  (Resting or doing something...)
    Larry Eigner. 237
  Road construction. Paul Davis.
    228
  "Roads slide across towers."
    Carolyn Stoloff. 376
  Twilight path. Cynthia Grenfell.
    266
  Verbatim II. Cynthia Grenfell.

266
Widening the road. Robert Gibb. 253
Winter roads. Thomas McGrath. 315
Wrecking for the freeway. James Schevill. 360
Roads of quicksand time. Colette Inez. 280
"Roads slide across towers." Carolyn Stoloff. 376
Roadside flowers. Christopher Bursk. 219
Roadside reflection. Marie Daerr Boehringer. 210
Robert Graves. Ernest Hemingway. 272
Robert Lowell is dead. Greg Kuzma. 300
Robeson, Paul
    For Paul Robeson. Ray Fleming. 247
Robins
    Flower studies: holly. Tom Smith. 368
    Of truth and fact. Richmond Lattimore. 301
The robot lover. Rochelle DuBois. 234
Roc. X.J. Kennedy. 290
Rock. Susan Stock. 375
Rock. Miller Williams. 399
Rock & roll snowstorm. Mitchell Howard. 276
Rock and Roll (music)
    Star? Of what? Harlan Usher. 386
Rock collection. Christopher Bursk. 219
Rock creek fall. Ernesto Galarza. 252
Rock hunting. Alice Spohn Newton. 332
Rockhounds. Joan Colby. 224
Rocks
    Collection. Mark Vinz. 387
    Earthworks. Robert Gibb. 253
    Forecast. Josephine Miles. 319
    'I and Thou.' Evelyn Golden. 263
    Maximus further on (December 28th 1959). Charles Olson. 337
    Moon rock. Robert A. Sears. 362
    An ordinary man. Christopher Bursk. 219
    "Peloria the dog's upper lip curling" Charles Olson. 337
    The river: I. Charles Olson. 337
    Rock collection. Christopher Bursk. 219
    Rock hunting. Alice Spohn Newton. 332

Rockhounds. Joan Colby. 224
A stone and I. Evelyn Golden. 263
"These stones if they spoke." Edwin Honig. 275
"The rocks in Settlement Cove." Charles Olson. 337
Rockwell, Norman
    Wasp conscious. Rose Basile Green. 265
Rodeo aesthetique. Donald Revell. 351
Roethke, Theodore
    The dance of Theodore Roethke. James Schevill. 360
Rokwaho
    Clickstone. 355
    Innocence returned. 355
    Owl. 355
    Passenger pigeon poem. 355
    "Swirling tinsel veils." 355
    Twoborn. 355
    Twoborn (...prelude). 355
    Twoborn Atataho. 355
    Twoborn shaman star dancer. 355
Roller coaster kid. Barry Wallenstein. 393
Roller rink. Betty Adcock. 192
Romance, sels. Edgar Allan Poe. 347
Romanian classroom. Keith Wilson. 400
A Romanian embroidery. Keith Wilson. 400
Romanian song. Keith Wilson. 400
Romanian still life. Keith Wilson. 400
Romanian stones. Keith Wilson. 400
Romanian tale. Keith Wilson. 400
Romanian thoughts. Keith Wilson. 400
Romanian village. Keith Wilson. 400
Romanian village II. Keith Wilson. 400
Romantic letter. Josephine Miles. 319
Rome
    Campagna picnic. Roy Marz. 312
    In Rome. Jenne Andrews. 196
    Is this the place? Carolyn Stoloff. 376
    Mater eterna. Rose Basile Green. 265
    Rome, 1978. Maria Gillan. 256
    To the mother republic. Rose Basile Green. 265
Rome, 1978. Maria Gillan. 256
Romeo and Juliet

Maxim. Josephine Miles. 319
Roofs. Josephine Miles. 319
Roofs
    "The men approach." Madison
        Morrison. 327
    "A non-/roofing roofer brings."
        Madison Morrison. 327
    Roofs. Josephine Miles. 319
    Unroofed. Joan Colby. 224
Room filler. Alice Spohn Newton.
    332
Room for more. Tefke Goldberger.
    262
A room ready to erase its
    darkness. Gary Margolis. 311
A room, loneliness. Norman Andrew
    Kirk. 293
The room. Stephen Todd Booker.
    212
Roomates. Lyn Lifshin. 303
Rooms
    A last poem. Gerard Malanga. 310
    Night watch. Rod McKuen. 316
    The visit. Gary Margolis. 311
Rooms named mercy. James
    Applewhite. 198
Roosevelt. Ernest Hemingway. 272
Roosevelt, Theodore
    Roosevelt. Ernest Hemingway. 272
Root-bound. Sharon Bryan. 217
Rooter. Josephine Miles. 319
Roots. Sister Maura. 313
Roots among these rocks. Robert
    L. Wilson. 401
Rosa. Rosa Bogar. 211
Rosa Luxemburg, drag queen. Jim
    Everhard. 241
Rosary portraits of improbable
    saints. Mitchell Howard. 276
Rose. Wanda Coleman. 225
Rose lice. Roy Marz. 312
Rose's poem. Robin Becker. 202
Rose-colored glasses. Charles
    Edward Eaton. 236
The rose. Steve Kowit. 299
Rosecap. Colette Inez. 280
Roses. Jim Simmerman. 365
Roses
    Along the street. William
        Oandasan. 335
    The count and the rose. Roy
        Marz. 312
    Eli Lu's rose. Ernesto Galarza.
        252
    Identity. Marie Daerr
        Boehringer. 210
    June miracle. Marie Daerr
        Boehringer. 210
    My only gift. Rachel A. Hazen.
        271
    An ode to roses. Rachel A.
        Hazen. 271
    Show me a rose. John Godfrey.
        260
Roses in Cleveland. Ray Fleming.
    247
Rosetree at dawn. Tom Smith. 368
The Rosetta Stone. James
    Magorian. 309
"Rotundum...". Charles Olson. 337
Round valley songs. William
    Oandasan. 335
"A round/table...". Madison
    Morrison. 327
Rover. William Stafford. 373
The rowers. Eileen
    Silver-Lillywite. 364
Rubaiyat for Sue Ella Tucker.
    Miller Williams. 399
Rubberband. Stephen Todd Booker.
    212
Ruby was her name. William
    Stafford. 373
Rudiment. Erin Jolly. 285
Rugo, Marieve
    Borders. 356
    Breakaway. 356
    The day they came back. 356
    Displaced persons. 356
    Double exposure. 356
    Dream caught in a train. 356
    Expatriate. 356
    Fields of vision. 356
    Flesh. 356
    Flesh and bones. 356
    Forced entry. 356
    Full circle. 356
    Green morning, full summer. 356
    Home. 356
    Il salto mortale. 356
    Inheritance. 356
    Late verbs. 356
    Limbo. 356
    The lovers. 356
    Map-making. 356
    My mother's gloves. 356
    Naked oddments of the night. 356
    Night in the nursing home. 356
    Now. 356
    Order of battle. 356
    Places are not where we are. 356
    Poem for my daughters. 356
    Recurrent city. 356
    Red bird in a white tree. 356
    The season of wolves and names.
        356
    Sequence toward a beginning. 356
    Snow as sorrow. 356
    Stranded. 356
    Surviving the jungle. 356

Thrift shop. 356
Translation. 356
Tromp l'oeil. 356
The truth of mirrors. 356
Two sides of a three-sided
    figure. 356
Vigil. 356
What happened. 356
White houses and black roads.
    356
A woman at middle age. 356
The ruining of the work. Robin
    Morgan. 325
Ruins
    Massacciucoli. Robert A. Sears.
        362
Rules. Martha Janssen. 283
The rules. David Wagoner. 390
Rumania
    The American literary
        conference. Keith Wilson. 400
    A Christmas card from Romania.
        Keith Wilson. 400
    From a conversation in a street.
        Keith Wilson. 400
    Lacul Gilaului. Keith Wilson.
        400
    Memoir din Cluj. Keith Wilson.
        400
    The minaret at Constanta. Keith
        Wilson. 400
    The park at Cluj. Keith Wilson.
        400
    A registry of graves. Keith
        Wilson. 400
    The road of kings. Keith Wilson.
        400
    Romanian classroom. Keith
        Wilson. 400
    A Romanian embroidery. Keith
        Wilson. 400
    Romanian song. Keith Wilson. 400
    Romanian still life. Keith
        Wilson. 400
    Romanian tale. Keith Wilson. 400
    Romanian thoughts. Keith Wilson.
        400
    Romanian village. Keith Wilson.
        400
    Romanian village II. Keith
        Wilson. 400
    Seadream. Keith Wilson. 400
    Song. Keith Wilson. 400
    Strada Petru Gorza 45. Keith
        Wilson. 400
    Straw flowers. Keith Wilson. 400
    Transylvania: a heartland. Keith
        Wilson. 400
    Transylvanian set piece. Keith
        Wilson. 400

Rummy. Greg Kuzma. 300
Rumors. John Yau. 404
Run for the roses. C.D. Wright.
    402
Run, rabbit! Aileen Fisher. 244
Runaways. Eileen
    Silver-Lillywite. 364
Runes with variations. Cornel
    Lengyel. 302
The runner who drifted away.
    James Schevill. 360
Running. Stephen Todd Booker. 212
Running and Runners
    Class reunion. William Stafford.
        373
    Jogging. Tefke Goldberger. 262
    Park filled with statues of
        famous airline ticket agents.
        James Magorian. 309
    Rainy day: last run. Dave Smith.
        367
    The runner who drifted away.
        James Schevill. 360
    Running into the old man with
        the fruitstand. James
        Schevill. 360
    Running on Ramsey Hill. Jenne
        Andrews. 196
    Summer games. Rod McKuen. 316
    Summer marathon. Paul Davis. 228
    A winter run. John Reed. 350
Running back. Dave Smith. 367
Running into the old man with the
    fruitstand. James Schevill.
    360
Running into things. Miller
    Williams. 399
Running on Ramsey Hill. Jenne
    Andrews. 196
Rush-hour ramblings. Marie Daerr
    Boehringer. 210
Russia
    A foreign country. Josephine
        Miles. 319
    Grain sale to the Soviet Union.
        James Magorian. 309
    Scriabin. Herbert Morris. 326
Rustic song. Cornel Lengyel. 302
The rustle of the dark. Keith
    Wilson. 400

Sabbath. William Stafford. 373
Sabbath
    Day of wonder, day of peace.
        Alice Joyce Davidson. 227
Saccarappa, Maine
    Why I never left Saccarappa.

Robert A. Sears. 362
The **sacred** shore. Greg Kuzma. 300
Sacrifice. Maurice Kenny. 291
Sacrifice
    Psalm-maker to his son. Cornel
    Lengyel. 302
A **sacrifice** in the orchard.
    Robert Bly. 209
"**Sad** man returns from war."
    Michael Robert Pick. 345
Sadat, Anwar
    Leaving. Michael Akillian. 193
Sade, Comte D.A. Francois de
    Charenton - Jardin de Sade.
    Michael Gizzi. 259
Sadface at five. James A.
    Emanuel. 239
Sadness unhinged. Andrei
    Codrescu. 223
The **safety** man, fr. Athletic
    verse. Ernest Hemingway. 272
Safety zone. Harry Humes. 278
"**Said** Mrs Tarantino." Charles
    Olson. 337
Sailing. John Godfrey. 260
Sailing
    "Older than Byblos" Charles
    Olson. 337
Sailmaker's palm. Robin Becker.
    202
Sailor. Jim Everhard. 241
Sailors. See Seamen

Saint. Everett A. Gillis. 258
Saint Augustine. John Godfrey.
    260
Saint Francis. Everett A. Gillis.
    258
Saint Peter's Church, Rome
    Flying up. Gary Margolis. 311
Saint Sebastian
    Martyrs. Roy Marz. 312
Saint Theresa. Wanda Coleman. 225
Saints
    Valentine and the birds. Roy
    Marz. 312
Salamanders
    Biology lesson. Robert Peters.
    343
Sale. Josephine Miles. 319
Sales and Selling
    Approach. Josephine Miles. 319
    The kitchen phone. James A.
    Emanuel. 239
    Old salesman planning the fit of
    his death. James Schevill. 360
    Salesman. Josephine Miles. 319
Salesman. Josephine Miles. 319
Salmon
    Home place: bear creek in

autumn. Franz Schneider. 361
"**Sweet salmon.**" Charles Olson.
    337
"The **salmon** of/wisdom." Charles
    Olson. 337
Salome. Roy Marz. 312
The **salon** of famouse babies.
    Irving Feldman. 242
Salt. James R. Rhodes. 352
Salt
    Going right out of the century.
    Charles Olson. 337
    There was a salt-works at Stage
    Fort. Charles Olson. 337
    Three salt sonnets to an
    incidental lover. Robin
    Morgan. 325
Salt air. Sharon Bryan. 217
The **salt** ecstasies. James L.
    White. 396
"The **salt**, & minerals, of the
    earth return..." Charles
    Olson. 337
Salute. Thomas McGrath. 315
Salvage. Amy Clampitt. 222
Salvaged parts. William Stafford.
    373
Salvation
    Culpepper redeemed. J.W. Rivers.
    354
Same day, later. Charles Olson.
    337
The **same** river twice. Sharon
    Bryan. 217
Same thought-2. Charles Olson.
    337
The **same.** Josephine Miles. 319
Sampson and the foxes. Cornel
    Lengyel. 302
Samsen at the sin and flesh pond.
    James Schevill. 360
Samson
    Dalila. Jacques Sollov. 370
San Ceccardo. Robert A. Sears.
    362
San Diego. Ray Fleming. 247
San Diego
    Deconstruction in San Diego. Ray
    Fleming. 247
    San Diego. Ray Fleming. 247
San Francisco
    The hills of San Francisco.
    Sally Love Saunders. 358
    "San Francisco doesn't seem as
    hilly." Sally Love Saunders.
    358
"**San Francisco** doesn't seem as
    hilly." Sally Love Saunders.
    358
Sanchez, Sonia

The flower of our journey (so
    Sonia travels). Kiarri T-H
    Cheatwood. 220
Sanctuary. Norman Andrew Kirk.
    293
Sand
    Mail. Andrei Codrescu. 223
Sandaga market women. Melvin
    Dixon. 231
Sandpipers
    "Busy little sandpipers." Sally
    Love Saunders. 358
Sandwich Islands
    The whaler's landfall: Sandwich
    Islands. Franz Schneider. 361
Sandy, Stephen
    After. 357
    Air for air. 357
    Anniversary sonnet. 357
    Arch. 357
    At Peaks Island. 357
    The Austin tower. 357
    Balance. 357
    Bridge of abandonment. 357
    Condensation. 357
    Cyanotype. 357
    Declension. 357
    Eagle bridge farm. 357
    End of the picaro. 357
    Family album. 357
    Finished country. 357
    Flight of steps. 357
    Freeway. 357
    Glories of the world. 357
    Groupings. 357
    In the Dakotas. 357
    The last of the Wallendas. 357
    A little yard. 357
    Looking on. 357
    Making it up. 357
    Mithuna. 357
    Nativity. 357
    Near Pamet marsh. 357
    Northway tanka. 357
    Nothing, nothing at all. 357
    Oyster cove. 357
    The painter. 357
    Perfect. 357
    Postpartum blue. 357
    Returning to Eagle Bridge. 357
    Riding to Greylock. 357
    Riverboat. 357
    The screen. 357
    Shadow. 357
    Shore. 357
    Some flowers. 357
    Sterling Mountain. 357
    Storm-felled tree at Eagle
    Bridge. 357
    Summer mountains. 357

    Survivor, walking. 357
    This chill air. 357
    Tom and Henry, camping out. 357
    Under the eaves. 357
    Waiting for the warden. 357
    When April. 357
    Winter mountain. 357
    Young man with infant. 357
Sangar. John Reed. 350
A sanguinary, sels. Albert
    Goldbarth. 261
"The Santa Ana turns the air to
    dust." Robert A. Sears. 362
Santa Clara spring. Ernesto
    Galarza. 252
Santa Claus
    Hillbilly night before
    Christmas. Thomas Noel Turner.
    385
Santa Fe, New Mexico, 1970. Maria
    Gillan. 256
Santa Lucia bar. Roy Marz. 312
Santayana, George
    In memoriam: Santayana. Cornel
    Lengyel. 302
Santorini: stopping the leak.
    James Merrill. 318
Sappho
    Invocation to Sappho. Elsa
    Gidlow. 254
    Sappho twined roses. Elsa
    Gidlow. 254
Sappho twined roses. Elsa Gidlow.
    254
Sarah at the sink. James A.
    Emanuel. 239
Satan
    The losing. Sam Fishman. 246
The satchel. Stephen Todd Booker.
    212
Satiesme. Donald Revell. 351
The satin star. Rachel A. Hazen.
    271
Satisfied. Stephen Todd Booker.
    212
Saturday. Lyn Lifshin. 303
The saturday afternoon blues.
    Wanda Coleman. 225
Saturday at Little Bohemia.
    Robert Peters. 343
Saturday night. May Miller. 320
Saturday night bath. Alice Spohn
    Newton. 333
Saturday, dusk. George Eklund.
    238
Saturnalia. Louise Gluck. 259A
Saturnian dilemma. Andrei
    Codrescu. 223
Saturos. Clayton Eshleman. 240
Sauna. Susan Tichy. 381

Saunders, Sally Love
    Alaska. 358
    "Alaska, the state of secrets."
      358
    "Alaskan tundra misses." 358
    "All of the fine mist from our
      soles." 358
    "An almost empty tube." 358
    Alyce Bianco. 358
    Anchorage. 358
    "As a four-year-old." 358
    As seen from an airplane. 358
    "As the soft white." 358
    "Black ebony shiny slug." 358
    Bridal veil. 358
    "Busy little sandpipers." 358
    "The butterfly." 358
    "Charlie is a giant size." 358
    Clouds. 358
    "Clouds like mountains." 358
    Cloudy day in Alaska. 358
    "Columbian Glacier." 358
    Cross pollination. 358
    "Driving along in my car." 358
    Dry pump. 358
    The elegance of the slug. 358
    "Fears are chasing." 358
    Fog. 358
    "For so long you've." 358
    Fresh roses along the path. 358
    Friends. 358
    "The full moon." 358
    "Glenn's definition of
      equality." 358
    Grandpop John's funeral. 358
    The hills of San Francisco. 358
    "Hopes racing." 358
    "How peaceful to ride in the
      arms." 358
    "I am a deep still lake." 358
    "I am together with you in my
      mind." 358
    "I don't like." 358
    "I live in a human file
      cabinet." 358
    "I need to be." 358
    "I sit here." 358
    "I want to write down." 358
    "I'll never know you." 358
    I'll read you my current poems.
      358
    "I'm a sunny side up egg." 358
    "I'm captured in a brown bag."
      358
    "I'm on top of the world." 358
    "I'm sitting here at Grieg's
      home." 358
    "I'm so happy." 358
    "I've been with annoying people
      so long." 358
    "If the weather vane." 358
    "In Jamaica." 358
    "In you arms." 358
    "It lifts my spirits." 358
    "It's good to be with you." 358
    "It's so nice to be with you."
      358
    "A kaleidoscope you." 358
    Leaves. 358
    Lollipop. 358
    "Mist hovering over the
      mountains." 358
    "The moon, your toy." 358
    "The more I row away." 358
    Mountain ranges. 358
    "My dog and I yesterday." 358
    "My dog sparkles." 358
    "My grandest symphony." 358
    "My love has deep hurts." 358
    "My love soars." 358
    "My love the golden moon." 358
    "My mother is an old sweater."
      358
    "My mother swimming." 358
    My shell. 358
    "Nome, Alaska." 358
    "The ocean." 358
    Ode to an Eskimo. 358
    "Once upon a time." 358
    "Only in my fantasies." 358
    "Our relationship is." 358
    A parachute. 358
    "Poems have been scurrying." 358
    Prince Williams Sound. 358
    "San Francisco doesn't seem as
      hilly." 358
    "Scattered lights." 358
    Scene from an airplane. 358
    "A single spider web." 358
    "The sleeping city." 358
    "So many good things." 358
    "Sometimes it's creative." 358
    "A spider web." 358
    "The stars." 358
    Steel blurs. 358
    Summer shower. 358
    "The sun spilling everywhere."
      358
    "A swift current." 358
    "There's a certain button." 358
    To my married friends. 358
    "Traveling is fine." 358
    "Tree frogs busily singing." 358
    Two love birds. 358
    Waiting for an Alaskan moose.
      358
    Walking in the redwoods. 358
    Waves hump their backs and then.
      358

"We are looking at each other." 358

"We are two shoes." 358

"Whipped cream." 358

"The winds of my passion." 358

"Women aren't supposed." 358

"You are like the crescent moon-" 358

"You're a large wooden treasure chest." 358

"Your love comes in phases." 358

"Your love." 358

Savage remembers a horse. Harry Humes. 278

The savages, or voyages of Samuel de Champlain of Brouage. Charles Olson. 337

The savages. Josephine Miles. 319

Savants. Lucien Stryk. 377

Save tomorrow. Rachel A. Hazen. 271

Savonarola. Roy Marz. 312

Savonarola, Girolamo
    Savonarola. Roy Marz. 312

The sawdust trail. Patsie Black. 206

Sawed-off shotgun. James Magorian. 308

Say it again,Sam. Josephine B. Moretti. 324

Say what? David James. 282

Saying no. Connie Hunt. 279

Saying the word. Gary Margolis. 311

Saying yes. Connie Hunt. 279

"Saying/is elegy." Robert Kelly. 289

Says the rabbit. Aileen Fisher. 244

The scar. Carol Frost. 249

Scarecrow: the road to Toulouse. James A. Emanuel. 239

"Scattered bits." Theta Burke. 218

Scattered dreams. Rosa Bogar. 211

"Scattered lights." Sally Love Saunders. 358

The scattered poems of Esterhazy, sels. J.W. Rivers. 354

Scattered remains. Paul Violi. 388

Scenario for a species. David Wann. 394

Scene. Joseph Penzi. 342

Scene from an airplane. Sally Love Saunders. 358

Scene revisited. Rose Basile Green. 265

A scene. William Stafford. 373

The scene. James Applewhite. 198

Scenes from the life of Boullee. John Yau. 404

Schechter, Ruth Lisa
    After/words. 359
    Along the Katsura walk. 359
    Aquarium. 359
    Attachments. 359
    Before thunder struck. 359
    Blue tapestry. 359
    Can you see us? 359
    Censored. 359
    The craftsman. 359
    Disconnected. 359
    Dream of fireworks on Fire Island. 359
    Dream of the long distance swimmer. 359
    The dreamer's regiment. 359
    Ethan. 359
    The great Winter Park sinkhole. 359
    In a 3-way mirror. 359
    In the illustration of a dream. 359
    In the sonata/I wear a surgeon's mask. 359
    Look at us. 359
    Love is never silent. 359
    No trespassing in southern Florida. 359
    Nothing changes. 359
    Other snapshots. 359
    Perhapps, Emily. 359
    The phantom artist. 359
    Recognition of the tigers. 359
    Rehabilitation. 359
    Requiem for a golden retriever. 359
    Retrospective. 359
    Shalom. 359
    Six miles from Indian Point. 359
    Speedway. 359
    Sunday picnic: Veteran's anniversary day. 359
    These three. 359
    Toward Senesqua. 359
    Visiting hours. 359
    Wards Island. 359
    Where is Mercy Street? 359
    While I stay. 359
    Who's afraid of Maurice Schwartz? 359
    Woman from Sacramento in Westchester. 359

Scheherazade school screen. David Shapiro. 363

Scheherezade. Deborah Tall. 378

Scheria: ? Charles Olson. 337

Schevill, James
    The age of silence... 360

291   Schevill, James

Always we walk through unknown
  people. 360
American gigantism: Gutzon
  Borglum at Mt. Rushmore. 360
And: a funeral hymn for Ernest
  Hemingway. 360
The angel track. 360
Apple, the family love and
  asshole. 360
The artist of escape: Houdini.
  360
The astonished listener hears
  the radio... 360
At a Quaker meeting a man arose
  and spoke of love. 360
At Frost's farm in Derry, New
  Hampshire. 360
At Plymouth Rock. 360
At the Mexican border. 360
At the White House, Washington,
  D.C., 1973 360
The baron of bulk. 360
Bashir was my name. 360
The boilerman. 360
Bouncing vision of the commuter.
  360
Boy watching a light-bulb death
  in a country town. 360
The broken-field runner through
  age. 360
The Buddhist car. 360
Buffalo man. 360
The butterfly and the scorpion:
  James McNeill Whistler. 360
The cherry tree in a storm. 360
The city planner. 360
The columnist listening to "you
  know" in the park. 360
The commuter in the car tunnels.
  360
Confessions of an American
  visitor of the large screen.
  360
Confidential data on the loyalty
  investigation... 360
The connoisseur's history of the
  bathroom. 360
The country fair of childhood.
  360
The dance of Theodore Roethke.
  360
Death of a cat. 360
Death of a teacher. 360
Dramas of the rose. 360
A drip poem for Jackson Pollock.
  360
The duck watcher. 360
Dumb love. 360
The dynamite artist. 360
Elizabethan fool applies for a

corporate executive position.
  360
Emily Dickinson. 360
The encounter of the pet store
  owner with Sarah L. Burkett.
  360
The executive at fifty. 360
The exterminator. 360
Fabulous debris. 360
Fall rituals in America. 360
A fame for Marilyn Monroe. 360
First London conference in the
  American campaign... 360
The flesh of discovery. 360
Flesh of the fawn. 360
The flower-washer in New York.
  360
For the saxophonist, Brew Moore.
  360
The forgotten wall. 360
Fra Elbertus or the inspector
  general. 360
A funeral for Hinky Dink. 360
The fury of a midwestern
  thunderstorm. 360
Gambling in Las Vegas. 360
The game-master explains the
  rules of the game for
  bombings. 360
A game against age. 360
The glorious devil at the
  dovecot... 360
The graffiti fingers of a
  theology student. 360
Green frog at Roadstead,
  Wisconsin. 360
A guilty father to his daughter.
  360
Hank Snow, the evangelist, prays
  for the president. 360
Hats and ears for Charles Ives.
  360
High school. 360
High school football coach. 360
Hog's elegy to the butchers. 360
Home life of the circus dancers.
  360
Horatio Greenough writes of
  reason. 360
How to create music by William
  Billings. 360
Huck Finn at ninety, dying in a
  Chicago boarding house room.
  360
If God does not see you. 360
Illuminations: Martha Graham.
  360
The images of execution. 360
In 1970 in Madrid, President
  Nixon presents General

Franco.. 360
In nervous moment: Charles Wilson Peale. 360
In praise of a photograph by Diane Arbus... 360
In the Japanese tea garden in San Francisco. 360
In the theater of the absurd. 360
Indian summer. 360
The invisible craft of evil. 360
The island handyman. 360
James Gates Percival pleads for a unity of vision. 360
Jazz-drift. 360
Jefferson dreaming. 360
The Jewish grocer and the vegetable forest. 360
The jovial mortician. 360
Joyrider. 360
Kristallnecht. 360
The last New England transcendentalist. 360
Last words for Count No'count. 360
Limited service in World War II. 360
The listener to noise and silence. 360
Listening in a 1920's Greenwich Village bar... 360
The little official of maybe. 360
Living in a boxcar in San Francisco. 360
Lookin' for gas at the youth guidance center. 360
Looking at old tombstones in a New England graveyard. 360
Looking at wealth in Newport. 360
Love, do not shun the dark gargoyle. 360
The mad waterskier on the cold edge of spring. 360
The mailman and das ewig weibliche. 360
Masks in 1980 for age 60 360
Masks in 1980 for age 60. 360
Meetings and separations. 360
Mississippi sheriff at the Klan initiation. 360
Mixed media. 360
The momentary glimpses of women through the windows. 360
The money man. 360
The moon and the beautiful woman. 360
Mr. and Mrs. Herman Melville, at home... 360

Mr. Castle's vacation drive. 360
Mr. Martin in the advertising agency. 360
My wife's dream. 360
Naked. 360
Neigbors. 360
New York subway rush hour. 360
The newsboy enters the bar. 360
1974-the motercycle gang honors the newsboy's...N. 360
The no-name woman in San Francisco. 360
Obsessive American sight. 360
Off the sea into the merchant's life... 360
Old Barry, the balloon seller. 360
Old salesman planning the fit of his death. 360
The old woman and the cat. 360
On guard in New York. 360
On the beach watched by a seagull. 360
On the burning of Mingus's bass. 360
One-eye and the German prisoners of war in Colorado. 360
The painter studying trees without leaves. 360
Parade at the live stock show. 360
Peace, father, where you lie. 360
The peaceable kingdom of Edward Hicks. 360
Perhaps a prayer. 360
Place. 360
A plea for alias. 360
Purchasing new bicentennial stamps, 1975 360
The quiet man of simplicity. 360
Ralph Waldo Emerson receives a visit from the sane man... 360
The real parader. 360
The refugee and his library. 360
Remedial. 360
Report to the moving company. 360
The runner who drifted away. 360
Running into the old man with the fruitstand. 360
Samsen at the sin and flesh pond. 360
Science fiction: dizzying changes in America. 360
The scientist surveys the protozoa. 360
A screamer discusses methods of screaming. 360
Sculptor in a midwestern town...

360
A seven walk in the Sante Fe
    desert. 360
The shapes our searching arms.
    360
Sitting on the porch at dawn.
    360
Song of Aeterna 27 over Los
    Angeles. 360
Speciality barber in
    beast-heads. 360
Street corner signals. 360
The suicide runner. 360
The T-shirt phenomenon in
    Minnesota on the Fourth of
    July. 360
The terrorist. 360
The tourist on the towers of
    vision. 360
The traveler of lavishness. 360
View of the corporation lady in
    bughouse square, Chicago. 360
The violence and glory of the
    American spirit. 360
Wallace Stevens at ease with
    marble cake. 360
Wandering Navajo weavers. 360
The washing machine cycle. 360
The watch of the live oaks. 360
Watergate dreams of success. 360
What are the most unusual things
    you find in garbage cans? 360
What's wrong? 360
Where we were in the 1960s. 360
White woman with the Navajos.
    360
The white writing of Mark Tobey.
    360
Whitman stock-taking,
    cataloguing. 360
William Carlos Williams and T.S.
    Eliot dancing... 360
A woman staring through a
    telescope at Alcatraz. 360
Wrecking for the freeway. 360
Schizophrenic. James Torio. 281
Schnapps sonata. John Godfrey.
    260
Schneider, Franz
The analyst's report on his
    convalescent patient. 361
Autumn. 361
Beach idyll. 361
Bear gulch: home place. 361
Camp field: icicle river. 361
Canto ("In this locust summer.")
    361
Death in Pisa. 361
December. 361
The editor's reply. 361

Fishing. 361
Fishing Aeneas creek. 361
The gardener's letter from
    Stalingrad. 361
The hawk. 361
Home place: bear creek in
    autumn. 361
Hunting interlude. 361
Hunting season. 361
In the Apennines. 361
Land speculation. 361
Last letter of a condemned
    priest. 361
Little Pend Oreille river. 361
Little Spokane river: Indian
    paintings. 361
Moyie River. 361
Moyie River: welcome ranch. 361
Mt. Stuart: north wall in
    October. 361
Palm Sunday at Salishan. 361
A prayer in winter. 361
The secular city. 361
September night. 361
St. Augustine's prayer to God,
    the Father. 361
Summer idylls. 361
Summer insomnia. 361
Summer storm: Alpe di San
    Benedetto. 361
The terminal patient to his
    wife. 361
Three Florentines summoned. 361
Titian: lady in a mirror. 361
Valdarno. 361
Vallombrosa. 361
The vase. 361
The whaler's landfall: Sandwich
    Islands. 361
Scholar. Everett A. Gillis. 258
Scholars and Scholarship
    Scholar. Everett A. Gillis. 258
School. Josephine Miles. 319
School
By-gone seniors 1982. Rachel A.
    Hazen. 271
The dream of returning to school
    and facing the oral exam.
    James Tate. 379
Education. Josephine Miles. 319
For Sousa Junior High, 1967.
    James A. Emanuel. 239
A good education. Robin Becker.
    202
High school. James Schevill. 360
History lesson. Thomas R.
    Sleigh. 366
Junta. Mark Vinz. 387
Late to school. J.W. Rivers. 354
Learning to like the new school.

William Stafford. 373
Little old red schoolhouse.
    Robert L. Wilson. 401
"An older man." Madison
    Morrison. 327
Our classroom has a mailbox.
    Jack Prelutsky. 348
Our Lady of Angel's sight saving
    class. Debra Bruce. 216
Parental puzzlement. Marie Daerr
    Boehringer. 210
School days. William Stafford.
    373
"Seated on the grass." Madison
    Morrison. 327
"These public halls." Madison
    Morrison. 327
The truant officer's helper.
    David Wagoner. 390
"Walk North on the/rock..."
    Madison Morrison. 327
"We open the lid." Madison
    Morrison. 327
What a tribal unit is. Albert
    Goldbarth. 261
Work? Who, me? Harlan Usher. 386
School days. William Stafford.
    373
School's out. Colette Inez. 280
Schwartz, Barry
    Speedway. Ruth Lisa Schechter.
        359
Schwarzwald. Ernest Hemingway.
    272
Science
    Bikini man. Ernesto Galarza. 252
    Sonnet: to science. Edgar Allan
        Poe. 347
Science fiction. James
    Applewhite. 198
Science fiction: dizzying changes
    in America. James Schevill.
    360
The scientist surveys the
    protozoa. James Schevill. 360
Scion. Robert Kelly. 289
The score. Maurice W. Britts. 215
Scotland
    A meditation in Perthshire,
        Scotland. Susan Tichy. 381
Scott. Richard Blessing. 208
Scott-Maxwell, Florida
    Florida Scott-Maxwell helps
        recite my grandmother's life.
        Susan Tichy. 381
Scrabble
    Scrabble revisited. Harrison
        Fisher. 245
Scrabble revisited. Harrison
    Fisher. 245

Scraps. Louise Gluck. 259A
"Scratched and peel." Madison
    Morrison. 327
A screamer discusses methods of
    screaming. James Schevill. 360
Screaming for this event. Scott
    Chisholm. 221
The screen. Stephen Sandy. 357
Scriabin. Herbert Morris. 326
Sculptor in a midwestern town...
    James Schevill. 360
Sculpture and Sculptors
    The abstract nude. Roy Marz. 312
    David. Roy Marz. 312
    In the gallery. Robert A. Sears.
        362
    The open staircase. David
        Wagoner. 390
    Papier-mache cat. James
        Magorian. 309
    Pygmalion. Robert A. Sears. 362
    Sculptor in a midwestern town...
        James Schevill. 360
    Two kinds of trouble. Josephine
        Miles. 319
The sculpture garden. Cynthia
    Grenfell. 266
Scything the meadow. Robert Gibb.
    253
Sea
    At Suthurstrond. Marc Hudson.
        277
    At the Ballard Locks. Richard
        Blessing. 208
    "Because a sailor's pockets."
        Carolyn Stoloff. 376
    Bk ii chapter 37. Charles Olson.
        337
    "The bottom/backward." Charles
        Olson. 337
    The city in the sea (The doomed
        city). Edgar Allan Poe. 347
    Dark body bright. Paul Davis.
        228
    Day trip. Rod McKuen. 316
    December 23nd. Charles Olson.
        337
    Deep-water song. John Reed. 350
    Dialogue. Josephine Miles. 319
    "The distances." Charles Olson.
        337
    Ditty to his love. Edwin Honig.
        275
    The failing sea. Evelyn Golden.
        263
    Going to the sea. Cynthia
        Grenfell. 266
    "I set out now." Charles Olson.
        337
    Ile des monts deserts, fr. Salt

Air. Sharon Bryan. 217
Intimations. Evelyn Golden. 263
The land as haitubu. Charles
    Olson. 337
Land's end dialectic. Thomas R.
    Sleigh. 366
Let the sea speak. Elsa Gidlow.
    254
Lifeguard longing to ride
    roughshod over subordinates.
    James Magorian. 308
"Lost from the loss of her
    dagger heisted." Charles
    Olson. 337
Love at sea. John Reed. 350
Love poem. Greg Kuzma. 300
Maximus to Gloucester : Letter
    2. Charles Olson. 337
Maximus, from Dogtown: II.
    Charles Olson. 337
Maximus, March 1961 : I. Charles
    Olson. 337
Medidian. Louise Gluck. 259A
Men friday. Josephine Miles. 319
The moaning of the buoy.
    Phillips Kloss. 294
"The music of/the sea." Larry
    Eigner. 237
Name. Josephine Miles. 319
"The ocean." Sally Love
    Saunders. 358
The ocean. Charles Olson. 337
Oceanology. Robert Anbian. 194
Oily weather. Ernest Hemingway.
    272
Or consider Prometheus. Amy
    Clampitt. 222
Probe and brood. Paul Violi. 388
Sea watch. Robert Anbian. 194
"The sound." Larry Eigner. 237
Summer. Josephine Miles. 319
There were estuaries. Jenne
    Andrews. 196
Tide. Josephine Miles. 319
"To see the ocean." Larry
    Eigner. 237
Translations from the Esquimaux:
    there are seasons. Ernest
    Hemingway. 272
Water's edge. Michael Akillian.
    193
"What damp paper." Larry Eigner.
    237
The winds blow long, fr.
    Voyages. Everett A. Gillis.
    258
The winter the Gen. Starks was
    stuck. Charles Olson. 337
Winter voyage. Anne Bailie. 199
Sea burial. Robert Pawlowski. 341

Sea maiden. James R. Rhodes. 352
Sea owl. Dave Smith. 367
Sea Shells. See Shells

Sea Voyages. See Travel

Sea watch. Robert Anbian. 194
"The sea's/boiling...". Charles
    Olson. 337
The sea-changes. Joan Colby. 224
Sea mouse. Amy Clampitt. 222
Sea sickness. Andrei Codrescu.
    223
The sea-gull. John Reed. 350
Sea venture. Norman Andrew Kirk.
    293
Sea:wind. Josephine Miles. 319
Seadream. Keith Wilson. 400
Sealed with promise? Rochelle
    DuBois. 234
Seamen
    All my life I've heard about
        many. Charles Olson. 337
    The first mate. John Reed. 350
    Letter 20: not a pastoral
        letter. Charles Olson. 337
    Maximus to Gloucester: Letter
        15. Charles Olson. 337
    Maximus, to himself. Charles
        Olson. 337
    The naval trainees learn how to
        jump overboard. David Wagoner.
        390
    Phenakistes urges his crew
        onward. Paul Violi. 388
    "The rail ends do not meet."
        Ernest Hemingway. 272
    Sailor. Jim Everhard. 241
    Sequentior. Charles Olson. 337
    "View" : fr tge Orontes. Charles
        Olson. 337
    "William Stevens." Charles
        Olson. 337
    The worker. Ernest Hemingway.
        272
The seamstress. Cathy Song. 372
The search. Connie Hunt. 279
Searches
    Backtracking. David Wagoner. 390
    Can. David Wann. 394
    Cobwebs. Evelyn Golden. 263
    Find. Josephine Miles. 319
    The fugitive. Roy Marz. 312
    I stopped looking. Rachel A.
        Hazen. 271
    Journey. James Torio. 281
    "Never quit searching." S.
        Bradford Williams (Jr.). 397
    An old pickerel in Walden Pond.
        William Stafford. 373

Passages. Thomas McGrath. 315
Theseus. Maria Gillan. 256
Under. Roy Marz. 312
The wayfarer. Erin Jolly. 285
What followed. Josephine Miles. 319
Searching. Evelyn Golden. 263
Searching. Robert L. Wilson. 401
Searching the endless. Alice Spohn Newton. 333
Sears, Robert A.
Al Haji Nuhu takes a fourth wife. 362
Among the maybes, sels. 362
"Among the maybes." 362
"And did you know." 362
Antiquing. 362
"At our best we did outrageous things." 362
Background. 362
Bagnio di Viareggio. 362
Bauchi bird. 362
"Before we could begin our life." 362
Bibbiena. 362
Blackberry weather. 362
A boy, a dog, a deer. 362
Cambria. 362
Ceremonial. 362
Chiaroscuro. 362
Corner drugstore, fr. Nostalgia poems. 362
Dark continent. 362
"Day by night." 362
"Deepest thoughts we spoke in silence." 362
Elba unvisited. 362
Ferragosto: Viareggio. 362
French club - Kano. 362
"From centuries your line." 362
Fulani girl. 362
Geji cave. 362
Gleanings from the yacata. 362
Grand Canyon. 362
Hammock reading, fr. Nostalgia poems. 362
"The hand still curves." 362
Hardscrabble homestead. 362
"Heat unrelieved at midnight." 362
"Here by the Pacific shore." 362
"I curse the dying foetus in your womb." 362
"I saw you dance with Don Carlos." 362
Il Vecchio. 362
In the gallery. 362
"It had to be, I thought at first." 362
"It takes the young to understand." 362
"It wasn't that." 362
Iuatzio waters. 362
Jo poised. 362
Juju. 362
La pineta di Migliarino. 362
Laguna by moonlight. 362
The land of Michoacan. 362
Le Torri. 362
Lizard Pond. 362
Luni. 362
The lure and the call, sels. 362
The Magellan heart. 362
Manque. 362
Marina di Carrara. 362
Massacciucoli. 362
Matched set. 362
Mining the cellar, fr. Nostalgia. 362
Moon rock. 362
Musa, steward, makes amends for losing our cat. 362
Mushrooming. 362
Neat lady. 362
New passage, sels. 362
Nostalgia poems, sels. 362
"Of course there was something impious." 362
Old trees. 362
"One courage is the way." 362
"Our love began skin-deep." 362
Out of Africa. 362
Palm wine. 362
"The play of minds." 362
Ponte a Poppi. 362
Prevarications. 362
Pride's corner. 362
Privates. 362
Props. 362
"Public eyes perceive." 362
Pygmalion. 362
The rain in Maine. 362
Return to center. 362
San Ceccardo. 362
"The Santa Ana turns the air to dust." 362
"Six months without you." 362
"So many times." 362
"A special spirit in your birth." 362
State of Maine. 362
Tarascan names. 362
Tartiglia. 362
Thalassa. 362
"These bricks, moss-covered now." 362
"This morning." 362
Tiger cat. 362
"Today I started lunching in the cheater's corner." 362

Town characters, fr. Noastalgia
    poems. 362
Trento. 362
Tzin-tzun-tzan. 362
Wapa club. 362
War bride. 362
Wheel songs, fr. Nostalgia
    poems. 362
"Why do I keep on writing love
    songs?" 362
Why I never left Saccarappa. 362
"You beat them all." 362
You can't ignore a bagpipe. 362
Seascape. Joseph Penzi. 342
Seascape. Royal Murdoch. 330
Seascape: Santa Monica Palisades.
    Everett A. Gillis. 258
Seascape: woman on the beach.
    Haig Khatchadourian. 292
Seashore
    After this, sea. Josephine
        Miles. 319
    Appetite and terror on the wide
        white sands of...Florida.
        Joyce Carol Oates. 336
    At Keflavik. Marc Hudson. 277
    Augusta at the shore. Carolyn
        Stoloff. 376
    Bagnio di Viareggio. Robert A.
        Sears. 362
    The bathers. Irving Feldman. 242
    Beach glass. Amy Clampitt. 222
    Beach idyll. Franz Schneider.
        361
    Beach story. Josephine B.
        Moretti. 324
    "Blackening ebbtide." Edwin
        Honig. 275
    December, 1960. Charles Olson.
        337
    Don't go near the water...
        Josephine B. Moretti. 324
    The epiphanies. Irving Feldman.
        242
    Ferragosto: Viareggio. Robert A.
        Sears. 362
    First by the sea. James
        Applewhite. 198
    First morning. Edwin Honig. 275
    Freeway. Stephen Sandy. 357
    Groupings. Stephen Sandy. 357
    The gymnasts, fr. Fresh air.
        Irving Feldman. 242
    "Heat unrelieved at midnight."
        Robert A. Sears. 362
    Journey. Mark Vinz. 387
    Living glass. Sandra McPherson.
        317
    Miami Beach. Miriam Goodman. 264
    Perkin's cove. Michael Akillian.

    193
    Poem dune. James Magorian. 309
    "The rocks in Settlement Cove."
        Charles Olson. 337
    Snore. Stephen Sandy. 357
    The view - July 29, 1961.
        Charles Olson. 337
    Waves hump their backs and then.
        Sally Love Saunders. 358
    A woman standing in the surf.
        David Wagoner. 390
    Writing to a prisoner. Sandra
        McPherson. 317
Season. Jacqueline Frank. 248
Season of peril. Joyce Carol
    Oates. 336
The season of repose. Ernesto
    Galarza. 252
The season of wolves and names.
    Marieve Rugo. 356
Seasoned. Margaret Key Biggs. 205
Seasons
    Cadenza. Phillips Kloss. 294
    Flocking. Harry Humes. 278
    Going to the orchard. Jeanne
        Lohmann. 305
    New Year's Eve. Rod McKuen. 316
    Now October. May Miller. 320
    Rhinebeck. Michael Gizzi. 259
    The tree inside us. Maria
        Gillan. 256
Seasons of love. Alice Joyce
    Davidson. 227
"Seated on the grass." Madison
    Morrison. 327
"Seated on the right." Madison
    Morrison. 327
Sebastopol. William Oandasan. 335
Sebastopol, California
    Beach in Sebastopol, California.
        Andrei Codrescu. 223
The second confrontation with
    Tina Turner. David James. 282
Second variation on Corpse and
    mirror. John Yau. 404
Second-floor piano. James
    Magorian. 308
Second letter on Georges' Charles
    Olson. 337
Second-growth trees. Robert
    Pawlowski. 341
Second day song. Edwin Honig. 275
Seconds. Louise Gluck. 259A
Secret agent. Keith Wilson. 400
The secret agent. Robert Kelly.
    289
The secret eater. Lyn Lifshin.
    303
The secret life of musical
    instruments. C.D. Wright. 402

The **secret** life of plants. David
    Wann. 394
Secret Sapphic. Elsa Gidlow. 254
Secret training, sels. Andrei
    Codrescu. 223
The **secret**. Jacqueline Frank. 248
The **secret**. Carol Frost. 249
The **secret**. Robert Peters. 343
Secretaries
    Secretary. Miriam Goodman. 264
Secretary. Miriam Goodman. 264
Secrets. Aileen Fisher. 244
Secrets. Martha Janssen. 283
Secrets
    Alternative lifestyle. Ray
        Fleming. 247
    "I'll never know you." Sally
        Love Saunders. 358
    "You are like the crescent
        moon-" Sally Love Saunders.
        358
Sectarian murder victim. Deborah
    Tall. 378
The **secular** city. Franz
    Schneider. 361
"**See** what a fine job." David
    Wann. 394
See, God? James R. Rhodes. 352
Seed. Cathy Song. 372
Seed
    The seed. Everett A. Gillis. 258
The **seed**. Everett A. Gillis. 258
The **seeds** of narrative. Clayton
    Eshleman. 240
Seeing and perceiving. William
    Stafford. 373
Seeing it. Sharon Bryan. 217
Seeing the wind. David Wagoner.
    390
"**Seeing** you have a woman." W.D.
    (William De Witt) Snodgrass.
    369
"**Seek** out the far capillaries."
    Robert Kelly. 289
Seer. Josephine Miles. 319
Segovia playing. Michael
    Akillian. 193
Segovia, Andres
    Segovia playing. Michael
        Akillian. 193
Seizure. Richard Blessing. 208
Selavie. Andrei Codrescu. 223
A **seldom** wind. John F. Barker.
    201
Self
    The admonitions. Jenne Andrews.
        196
    Alone. Edgar Allan Poe. 347
    Always we walk through unknown
        people. James Schevill. 360

An T for an T. Tefke Goldberger.
    262
And after. Josephine Miles. 319
The angel of - Alberta Turner.
    384
Another me. Connie Hunt. 279
As a man thinketh. Phillips
    Kloss. 294
The astrological houses.
    Rochelle DuBois. 234
Audition. John Godfrey. 260
Author's forward. Stephen Todd
    Booker. 212
The best side of me. Andrei
    Codrescu. 223
"Blue meal." Da Free John. 284
Box-camera snapshot. Betty
    Adcock. 192
"Breaking down my own being."
    Michael Robert Pick. 345
A cabinet of few affections.
    James A. Emanuel. 239
Cause and effect. Martha
    Janssen. 283
Clarities. Maria Gillan. 256
Climbing the walls. Steve Kowit.
    299
"Cogito ergo sum." Patsie Black.
    206
Conversion. Marc Kaminsky. 288
The crusted earth. John F.
    Barker. 201
The deck that Oouts. Marge
    Piercy. 346
Define a satellite. Albert
    Goldbarth. 261
Dictatorship of myself. Mitchell
    Howard. 276
The differences. Andrei
    Codrescu. 223
Dry spells. Paul Violi. 388
The egg and T. Ernesto Galarza.
    252
Enchanted. Norman Andrew Kirk.
    293
Epistemology. Debra Bruce. 216
"Every body is an island." Da
    Free John. 284
"Every day." Da Free John. 284
A face. Andrei Codrescu. 223
Five precious stones. Robert
    Kelly. 289
A fool for evergreen. James A.
    Emanuel. 239
For me? James R. Rhodes. 352
For my name's sake. Ghita Orth.
    339
"Freedom/is the coming of
    one/unto himself." Theta
    Burke. 218

From the other side of the
    keyhole. Jacqueline Frank. 248
Gangsterism and coolth. Harrison
    Fisher. 245
Getting there. Robert Kelly. 289
Girl and baby florist sidewalk
    pram nineteen seventy...
    Kenneth Koch. 297
Good intentions. May Miller. 320
The greatest gift. Connie Hunt.
    279
The grey thread. Elsa Gidlow.
    254
Have I caught myself? Norman
    Andrew Kirk. 293
"He who had seemed/to seek
    battle." Theta Burke. 218
His health, his poetry, and his
    love all in one. Charles
    Olson. 337
"How far can a single mind go."
    Michael Robert Pick. 345
"How quickly/the fire of joy."
    Theta Burke. 218
I am. Connie Hunt. 279
"I am as one." Da Free John. 284
"I am born to purify myself of
    the world." Da Free John. 284
"I am mindless in this world."
    Da Free John. 284
"I am the bright." Da Free John.
    284
"I am truly vulnerable." Theta
    Burke. 218
I draw a circle. Evelyn Golden.
    263
"I live in a human file
    cabinet." Sally Love Saunders.
    358
"I live underneath." Charles
    Olson. 337
"I stand before you in all my
    forms." Da Free John. 284
"I'm a sunny side up egg." Sally
    Love Saunders. 358
Illusions. Anthony Petrosky. 344
The image. James R. Rhodes. 352
Invasion of the huge spirits.
    Mitchell Howard. 276
Island. Josephine Miles. 319
It wasn't me. James Tate. 379
Just me. Rosa Bogar. 211
Kitchen. Josephine Miles. 319
Kowit. Steve Kowit. 299
La force. Louise Gluck. 259A
Learning to read. Miller
    Williams. 399
Letting go. Evelyn Golden. 263
Limbo. Marieve Rugo. 356
Logos. Thomas R. Sleigh. 366

Look through my window. James R.
    Rhodes. 352
Lorn. Erin Jolly. 285
The mask. John F. Barker. 201
Me inside. Rachel A. Hazen. 271
Menses. Robert Gibb. 253
Mica flaking from my eyelashes.
    Joan Colby. 224
Model work. Andrei Codrescu. 223
The modest rainbow. Rachel A.
    Hazen. 271
The most dangerous desire.
    Phillips Kloss. 294
A mountain stream. Evelyn
    Golden. 263
My crooked city. Maria Gillan.
    256
"My dear ones, my own." Da Free
    John. 284
My life. William Stafford. 373
My shell. Sally Love Saunders.
    358
"My wife, my car, my color and
    myself." Charles Olson. 337
Near life. Donald Revell. 351
"No one like me has appeared in
    this place." Da Free John. 284
"No path." Da Free John. 284
Obsolescent. Bill Knott. 296
Of myself. Royal Murdoch. 330
An old feud. Cornel Lengyel. 302
Old photographs of the author.
    James Tate. 379
On Intersate 5, near San
    Francisco. Evelyn Golden. 263
"Or follow ants to their hill."
    Michael Robert Pick. 345
The owls. Greg Kuzma. 300
Personification. Josephine
    Miles. 319
Planetarium. Norman Andrew Kirk.
    293
Poem for the letters of my name.
    Joan Colby. 224
Polarity. Mitchell Howard. 276
Problem. Bill Knott. 296
Psychoanalysis in one easy
    sonnet. Ernesto Galarza. 252
Q:What are you feeling?
    A:Guilty. Gerard Malanga. 310
The reading. Carolyn Stoloff.
    376
Residencies. Thomas McGrath. 315
Resolution. Mark Vinz. 387
Resolving. Mitchell Howard. 276
Rio Maranon. Michael Gizzi. 259
Ripoff artist. Mark Vinz. 387
The room. Stephen Todd Booker.
    212
Saturnian dilemma. Andrei

Codrescu. 223
The search. Connie Hunt. 279
The season of wolves and names. Marieve Rugo. 356
The secret agent. Robert Kelly. 289
Self portrait. Michael Akillian. 193
"She affirmed herself." Theta Burke. 218
Silicon Valley. Michael Gizzi. 259
Sonnet for a writer. James A. Emanuel. 239
Spring one, sels. Edwin Honig. 275
Springtime in David Wann. David Wann. 394
Starting. George Eklund. 238
Stems. Robert Gibb. 253
The story of what happens. Mitchell Howard. 276
Strolling on the giant woman. Mary Gilliland. 257
(Sun, sea, rain)(rain season)(Port Townsend, Washington). Bill Knott. 296
The surf of joy pounding. Marge Piercy. 346
Tete-a-tete. Andrei Codrescu. 223
A textual recording. Andrei Codrescu. 223
"These trees stand very tall under the heavens." W.D. (William De Witt) Snodgrass. 369
They tell me I am lost. Maurice Kenny. 291
A thing like stone. Jacqueline Frank. 248
"This morning." Robert A. Sears. 362
Tiger sparrow. Norman Andrew Kirk. 293
"To resist one's self." Theta Burke. 218
Toward I. Josephine Miles. 319
Toward II. Josephine Miles. 319
Tracking. Gerard Malanga. 310
Twindream. Colette Inez. 280
Two sides of a three-sided figure. Marieve Rugo. 356
Untitled. Joy Harjo. 269
Untitled:"In the place that is my self" Kirk Lumpkin. 306
The web we spin. Evelyn Golden. 263
What is wrong with this picture? Jim Simmerman. 365

"When I fear to speak." Theta Burke. 218
"When the brokers were raining on Wall Street." Robert Kelly. 289
While I stay. Ruth Lisa Schechter. 359
Who am I? Rosa Bogar. 211
"Within/our letting go/is the seed/of our receiving." Joan Walsh Anglund. 197
"Worlds are an exclamation of my names." Da Free John. 284
"The worlds fall out of my right hand." Da Free John. 284
You seemed so poised and tender tonight. Haig Khatchadourian. 292
Self portrait. Michael Akillian. 193
Self portrait. James Torio. 281
Self-righteous wound. James R. Rhodes. 352
Self-same differences. James R. Rhodes. 352
The self-seeker. Robert Frost. 250
Self=Control
"Speak not to others." Theta Burke. 218
Self=exiled. Carolyn Stoloff. 376
Self=hate. Martha Janssen. 283
Self=Hate
Another backward stripper madonna. Lyn Lifshin. 303
Selfishness
Cherries. Lucien Stryk. 377
La ronde. Rod McKuen. 316
On a marginal bore. Cornel Lengyel. 302
"One never intends/to be selfish." Theta Burke. 218
The secret eater. Lyn Lifshin. 303
Semi-detached in Oxford. Ray Fleming. 247
Semi-private. Richard Blessing. 208
Seminary. Stephen Todd Booker. 212
Semiotics/the doctor's doll. Albert Goldbarth. 261
Sempre natale. Rose Basile Green. 265
Sending these messages. William Stafford. 373
Senile information officer at a plumbing supply company. James Magorian. 309
Senior prom. James Magorian. 309

A sense of completion. Evelyn
    Golden. 263
The sense of solitude. Rod
    McKuen. 316
Sentiment/ality. Gerard Malanga.
    310
Sentimental education. Charles
    Edward Eaton. 236
Separated. Laura Boss. 213
Separation
    Absences. William Stafford. 373
    Across a bridge. Anne Bailie.
        199
    After one. Thomas R. Sleigh. 366
    All farewells. Elsa Gidlow. 254
    All literature. Marilyn Kallet.
        287
    And yet-. John Reed. 350
    Anna, I am here to leave you.
        Gary Margolis. 311
    Any day now you will return.
        John Yau. 404
    Apology for a sudden voyage.
        Scott Chisholm. 221
    Argument for parting. Miriam
        Goodman. 264
    As if. Marilyn Kallet. 287
    Autumn month. Gary Margolis. 311
    Away. Josephine Miles. 319
    Back. Gary Margolis. 311
    Being left. Marge Piercy. 346
    A broken house. Marc Kaminsky.
        288
    A closing. May Miller. 320
    Confession. Marie Daerr
        Boehringer. 210
    "Day by night." Robert A. Sears.
        362
    Despite astronomical arguments.
        Marilyn Kallet. 287
    The double cherry. Jim
        Simmerman. 365
    The empty place. Elsa Gidlow.
        254
    The end of the season. Eileen
        Silver-Lillywite. 364
    The end of winter. Larry Moffi.
        322
    Exercise: to hope to invite to
        continue. Carolyn Stoloff. 376
    The exit. Deborah Tall. 378
    Experience. Elsa Gidlow. 254
    Fate and the goddess never.
        Norman Andrew Kirk. 293
    Filament. Erin Jolly. 285
    Footnote to love. Erin Jolly.
        285
    For lack of you. Bill Knott. 296
    The friend departs. Elsa Gidlow.
        254
    Gone. James A. Emanuel. 239
    Hamsa: in memoriam. Gene
        Anderson. 195
    "Have I outgrown you?" Josephine
        Miles. 319
    He's packing I hear. Carolyn
        Stoloff. 376
    Heart's needle. W.D. (William De
        Witt) Snodgrass. 369
    Hollow. Rod McKuen. 316
    "Hope life is good to you."
        Michael Robert Pick. 345
    I arrive home to the funeral.
        Wanda Coleman. 225
    I see the ending in our eyes.
        Norman Andrew Kirk. 293
    If you must go. Jacques Sollov.
        371
    In remembrance. Haig
        Khatchadourian. 292
    In search of yesterday. Robert
        L. Wilson. 401
    In this waking. Wanda Coleman.
        225
    Insurance. Rod McKuen. 316
    It isn't meant to end this way.
        Rachel A. Hazen. 271
    The journey. Cathryn Hankla. 268
    Lament. Cynthia Grenfell. 266
    Last things. Robert Gibb. 253
    Late summer leaving. Joy Harjo.
        269
    Leaving. Jim Simmerman. 365
    Leaving him. Anneliese Wagner.
        389
    Leaving town. Dave Smith. 367
    The length of your absence. Anne
        Bailie. 199
    Letting you go. William
        Stafford. 373
    A long distance. Robin Becker.
        202
    The man who is leaving. Marge
        Piercy. 346
    The man who was not. Charles
        Edward Eaton. 236
    Moment before elegy. Everett A.
        Gillis. 258
    "The more I row away." Sally
        Love Saunders. 358
    Near Rhinebeck. Donald Revell.
        351
    New kitchen. Sharon Bryan. 217
    Night's beard. Robert Anbian.
        194
    No name. Gene Anderson. 195
    Off to the side. John Yau. 404
    Once in a dream. William
        Stafford. 373
    Pack rat sieve. Mei-Mei

Berssenbrugge. 203, 204
Passing from the provinces.
    Bradford Morrow. 329
Pastoral '17. James Torio. 281
Poem ("The gravity of our
    situation is matched.") John
    Godfrey. 260
Pornography, Nebraska. Sandra
    McPherson. 317
Psycho love. Sam Fishman. 246
Red Lake. Joan Colby. 224
Reliquishment. Elsa Gidlow. 254
Remember. Jacques Sollov. 371
Rock & roll snowstorm. Mitchell
    Howard. 276
The same river twice. Sharon
    Bryan. 217
Seventeen years ending. Gene
    Anderson. 195
"Six months without you." Robert
    A. Sears. 362
So far away. Jacques Sollov. 370
So when he leaves, fr. The day
    of the body. Carol Frost. 249
Song of the infidel. Erin Jolly.
    285
Sudden departure. Bill Knott.
    296
Sunrise – moonset. Jacques
    Sollov. 370
Surfacing. Gary Margolis. 311
The swinging door. Erin Jolly.
    285
Take it in your hands. Anneliese
    Wagner. 389
This moment. Anneliese Wagner.
    389
Three anecdotes. Deborah Tall.
    378
Three poems for Li Shang-yin.
    John Yau. 404
Time zones. Thomas McGrath. 315
To the other. Thomas R. Sleigh.
    366
Two poems/Toward silence. Carol
    Frost. 249
The uses of sunday's music.
    Jenne Andrews. 196
Washington D.C. too. Rachel A.
    Hazen. 271
"We are liken to animals."
    Michael Robert Pick. 345
"We are looking at each other."
    Sally Love Saunders. 358
When she is absent. Elsa Gidlow.
    254
When the deer will flee.
    Jacqueline Frank. 248
When you're away. Mary
    Gilliland. 257

"Where the hell is my life?"
    Michael Robert Pick. 345
White shutters. C.D. Wright. 402
Why I say adios. William
    Stafford. 373
Why must I leave you. Jacques
    Sollov. 371
Without. Marilyn Kallet. 287
Years after. Carolyn Stoloff.
    376
"Your sweetness was in my hand."
    Michael Robert Pick. 345
September
    In early September. Ralph J.,
        Jr. Mills. 321
    Prelude to autumn. Robert L.
        Wilson. 401
    Under Virgo. John Godfrey. 260
September afternoon. Marie Daerr
    Boehringer. 210
September in the park. W.D.
    (William De Witt) Snodgrass.
    369
September Monday. Maria Gillan.
    256
September moon. Joy Harjo. 269
September night. Franz Schneider.
    361
September night. Carolyn Stoloff.
    376
September rain. Rochelle DuBois.
    234
Sequel. Ernest Hemingway. 272
Sequence toward a beginning.
    Marieve Rugo. 356
Sequentior. Charles Olson. 337
Sequoia semper virens. Ernesto
    Galarza. 252
Sequoias
    Sequoia semper virens. Ernesto
        Galarza. 252
    Walking in the redwoods. Sally
        Love Saunders. 358
Serenade. Tom Smith. 368
Serenade ("So sweet the hour – so
    calm the hour"). Edgar Allan
    Poe. 347
Serenity. Marie Daerr Boehringer.
    210
A serious morning, sels. Andrei
    Codrescu. 223
a serious morning. Andrei
    Codrescu. 223
Sermons
    Union Square, San Francisco.
        Paul Davis. 228
A servant to servants. Robert
    Frost. 250
The service. Michael Akillian.
    193

"Servicing space." Da Free John.
    284
Sesshu
    Landscape. James Torio. 281
Sessions. Rachel A. Hazen. 271
Sestina for the owl. Frances
    Mayes. 314
Sestina, fr. Friday night
    quartet. David Shapiro. 363
Seton Hospital. Eileen
    Silver-Lillywite. 364
Setting limits. Marilyn Kallet.
    287
Setting the pace. Maurice W.
    Britts. 215
"Settling on tongues, owls close
    their claws." Carolyn Stoloff.
    376
Seurat, George
    Sunday afternoon. James Torio.
    281
A 17th century New England
    house. Sharon Bryan. 217
$7,500 Josephine Miles. 319
Seven (number)
    A seven walk in the Sante Fe
    desert. James Schevill. 360
The seven lakes of Band-I-Amir.
    Kirk Lumpkin. 306
Seven salvations: a mixed bag.
    Tom Smith. 368
A seven walk in the Sante Fe
    desert. James Schevill. 360
"7 years..."   Charles Olson. 337
7,22,66. Sandra McPherson.
    317
7 P.M.   Rochelle DuBois. 234
7/6.   Ralph J., Jr. Mills. 321
Seventeen years ending. Gene
    Anderson. 195
The severing. Clayton Eshleman.
    240
Sewing
    Fydor's invisible mending. Larry
    Moffi. 322
    In tapestry, the pattern. Ghita
    Orth. 339
    Piecing. Robin Morgan. 325
    The seamstress. Cathy Song. 372
Sex. Rochelle DuBois. 234
Sex. Jim Simmerman. 365
Sex
    Breasts in the sun. James
    Applewhite. 198
    Canton. Michael Gizzi. 259
    The children. Roy Marz. 312
    Chincoteague. Dennis Hinrichsen.
    273
    Cousin: snapshot 1. Robert
    Peters. 343

Cousins. Robert Peters. 343
Eileen. Robert Peters. 343
Eroteschatology. Mitchell
    Howard. 276
Fickle. Martha Janssen. 283
For Marcie. Jim Everhard. 241
For the boy reading Playboy.
    Debra Bruce. 216
Girls on a spring campus. Cornel
    Lengyel. 302
Heroine tied to the railroad
    tracks. James Magorian. 308
Madonna nymphomania. Lyn
    Lifshin. 303
Madonna's finger on him. Lyn
    Lifshin. 303
Married cousin. Robert Peters.
    343
The midwest is full of
    vibrators. Lyn Lifshin. 303
Music room. Rod McKuen. 316
Night swim. Robert Peters. 343
Non returnable bottle madonna.
    Lyn Lifshin. 303
"Of old times, there was a very
    beautiful" Charles Olson. 337
"Play/above the waist." Madison
    Morrison. 327
Radiator madonna. Lyn Lifshin.
    303
The river: II. Charles Olson.
    337
Sex. Jim Simmerman. 365
The sexual would eat up all
    attention. Greg Kuzma. 300
Slow dance on the mating ground.
    Rod McKuen. 316
The spiritual hunt. Clayton
    Eshleman. 240
Summer sequence. Rod McKuen. 316
They drove them out. Judson
    Crews. 226
"To have the bright body of sex
    and love." Charles Olson. 337
Untitled. May Miller. 320
Wanted - sensuous woman who can
    handle 12 inches of man. Steve
    Kowit. 299
With you. Lyn Lifshin. 303
The woman who buries. Lyn
    Lifshin. 303
The world of expectations.
    Albert Goldbarth. 261
You can't f*** with mother
    nature. Jim Everhard. 241
Sex education. Martha Janssen.
    283
Sexton, Anne
    Bridge of abandonment. Stephen
    Sandy. 357

Guide. Ghita Orth. 339
Where is Mercy Street? Ruth Lisa
    Schechter. 359
The sexual would eat up all
    attention. Greg Kuzma. 300
Shabbat morning. Susan Tichy. 381
Shabbat, matah. Susan Tichy. 381
A shade-lending tree. Alice Spohn
    Newton. 332
Shadow. Stephen Sandy. 357
Shadow pictures. Maria Gillan.
    256
Shadow royal. Paul Violi. 388
Shadows. Robert L. Wilson. 401
Shadows
    Beast. Stephen Knauth. 295
    "The dead." Larry Eigner. 237
    Flowers of shadow. Keith Wilson.
        400
    House of shadows. Joan Colby.
        224
    "In the shadow." Larry Eigner.
        237
    The lonely shadow. Rachel A.
        Hazen. 271
    Millions of strange shadows.
        Irving Feldman. 242
    Passing a pile of stones.
        William Stafford. 373
    Shadows. Robert L. Wilson. 401
"Shadows.../doubt is a shadow."
    Joan Walsh Anglund. 197
"Shadowy.". Larry Eigner. 237
"Shag Rock, bull's eye" Charles
    Olson. 337
Shaking in the autumn wind. Mary
    Gilliland. 257
Shalom. Ruth Lisa Schechter. 359
The shaman. Carolyn Stoloff. 376
Shame. Martha Janssen. 283
Shame
    "It came in a hole." Michael
        Robert Pick. 345
Shanghai shenanigans. John Yau.
    404
Shanhaikuan. Richmond Lattimore.
    301
"shape of Weymouth..." Charles
    Olson. 337
The shape. David Wagoner. 390
The shapes our searching arms.
    James Schevill. 360
Shapiro, David
    'What does bankruptcy mean to
        you.' 363
    Commentary text commentary text
        commentary text. 363
    Concealed words II. 363
    The counter-example. 363
    An early Egyptian ship. 363

An example of work. 363
An exercise in futility. 363
Falling upwards. 363
Flesh. 363
Fountain, fr. Friday night
    quartet. 363
Four lines. 363
A fragment of relief. 363
Friday night quartet, sels. 363
Friday night quartet, fr. Friday
    night quartet. 363
From Malay. 363
House. 363
I cannot hold nor let you go.
    363
I packed my trunk for Albany.
    363
The index of first lines. 363
Mallarme to Zola. 363
Memory of the present. 363
Name. 363
Name and addresses. 363
The night sky and to Walter
    Benjamin. 363
November twenty seventh. 363
Orange-colored sky, fr. Friday
    night quartet. 363
The other and the others. 363
A realistic bar and grill. 363
Scheherazade school screen. 363
Sestina, fr. Friday night
    quartet. 363
Snow. 363
A song ("When a man loves a
    woman.") 363
Sonnet ("Ice over time.") 363
A Spanish painting. 363
Sphinx skin. 363
St. Barnabas, fr. Friday night
    quartet. 363
Thin snow. 363
Those who must stay indoors, fr.
    Friday night quartet. 363
To a young exile. 363
To an idea. 363
To industry. 363
To painting. 363
To the dead. 363
To the earth. 363
To the page. 363
Unwritten. 363
Valediction cparicen. 363
Venetian blinds. 363
White night. 363
Writing in bed. 363
Sharecroppers
    Landlocked, fallen, unsung. C.D.
        Wright. 402
Sharon. Maurice W. Britts. 215
Sharpening scissors and knives

for fun and profit. James
    Magorian. 309
"She affirmed herself." Theta
    Burke. 218
She came out in black. Judson
    Crews. 226
She found her heights. Judson
    Crews. 226
She had some horses. Joy Harjo.
    269
She hated rattlers. Judson Crews.
    226
"She peers at me." James Torio.
    281
She remembers the future. Joy
    Harjo. 269
She speaks at graveside. Ghita
    Orth. 339
She thinks of love, fr. The day
    of the body. Carol Frost. 249
"She tried to do/just as they'd
    say." Theta Burke. 218
"She who met the serpent..."
    Charles Olson. 337
She who sang the blues. Stephen
    Todd Booker. 212
She's behind the curtain playing
    the prepared piano. Frances
    Mayes. 314
She-goat at puck fair. Anneliese
    Wagner. 389
Sheba. Jacques Sollov. 370
Sheba, Queen of
    Sheba. Jacques Sollov. 370
Sheep. Josephine Miles. 319
Sheep. Jack Prelutsky. 349
Sheep
    Big sheep knocks you about.
        Sharon Bryan. 217
    Sheep. Jack Prelutsky. 349
Sheepherder's song. Keith Wilson.
    400
Sheet rock madonna. Lyn Lifshin.
    303
The sheets. Timothy Steele. 374
Shell beach. Jeanne Lohmann. 305
Shelley at Viareggio. Joyce Carol
    Oates. 336
Shelley, Mary
    No timid sawyer. Harrison
        Fisher. 245
Shelley, Percy Bysshe
    Shelley at Viareggio. Joyce
        Carol Oates. 336
Shelling oysters. James Magorian.
    308
Shells
    For shells. Rochelle DuBois. 234
The shepherd. Roy Marz. 312
Shepherds and Shepherdesses

Morskie Oko. James Torio. 281
Notes of a pastoralist. James
    Wright. 403
Sheepherder's song. Keith
    Wilson. 400
Sherwood. Michael Gizzi. 259
Shetland. Alberta Turner. 384
Shetland Islands
    Shetland. Alberta Turner. 384
Shift. Josephine Miles. 319
Shifting for herself madonna. Lyn
    Lifshin. 303
Shimmering pediment. John Yau.
    404
The shining mountains. Cynthia
    Grenfell. 266
Shining star. David James. 282
The ship (Translated being La
    paquebot). Ernest Hemingway.
    272
The ship's captain looking over
    the rail. Robert Bly. 209
Ships
    "Bailyn shows sharp rise."
        Charles Olson. 337
    Barge. Josephine Miles. 319
    February 3rd 1966 High tide...
        Charles Olson. 337
    "Her stern like a box..."
        Charles Olson. 337
    "It says the Amitie sailed."
        Charles Olson. 337
    "Ships for the West Indies..."
        Charles Olson. 337
    "To make those silent vessels
        go..." Charles Olson. 337
    The winning thing. Charles
        Olson. 337
"Ships for the West Indies..."
    Charles Olson. 337
Shipwrecks
    First letter on Georges. Charles
        Olson. 337
Shock troops. Ernest Hemingway.
    272
The shocking machine. David
    Wagoner. 390
Shoes. See Boots and Shoes

Shop of signs. Wanda Coleman. 225
Shopping bag lady. Wanda Coleman.
    225
Shopping for shoes. Carolyn
    Stoloff. 376
Shops and Shopping
    Boxed to go. Alice Spohn Newton.
        333
    Coupons. Josephine B. Moretti.
        324
    Discount shopping. Mark Vinz.

387
   Thrift shop. Marieve Rugo. 356
   "To market, to market." Jan
    Ormerod. 338
Shore. Stephen Sandy. 357
Short commons. Alberta Turner.
   384
A short history of the teaching
   profession. Sister Maura. 313
Short memory. Josephine B.
   Moretti. 324
Short order cook. Josephine B.
   Moretti. 324
A short play. Miller Williams.
   399
Short possible poem... Charles
   Olson. 337
A short response to Robert Frost.
   Ernesto Galarza. 252
Short subjects. Carolyn Stoloff.
   376
The shortcut. Timothy Steele. 374
Shorth poem, long story. Jeanne
   Lohmann. 305
"Shots fired at once." Madison
   Morrison. 327
Shoveling snow in Chicago. J.W.
   Rivers. 354
Show me a rose. John Godfrey. 260
Showers of blessings. Alice Joyce
   Davidson. 227
Shrikes
   The oyster catcher's cry.
    Phillips Kloss. 294
Shut windows. Maurice W. Britts.
   215
Shutout. Mitchell Howard. 276
Shy eyes shy looks. Haig
   Khatchadourian. 292
Siberia. Lucien Stryk. 377
Siberia
   Siberia. Lucien Stryk. 377
Sideshow. Robin Becker. 202
Sidewalk cafe. Jeanne Lohmann.
   305
Sidewalks. See Roads and Trails

Siege. Josephine Miles. 319
Sighted. Patsie Black. 206
Sightseeing. Melvin Dixon. 231
The sign for the sun. Anneliese
   Wagner. 389
Signal-to-noise. Miriam Goodman.
   264
Signature. Everett A. Gillis. 258
Signature to petition... Charles
   Olson. 337
Signing in tongues of absence.
   Scott Chisholm. 221
Signs. Maria Gillan. 256

Signs. Harry Humes. 278
The signs of the stopsign. Bill
   Knott. 296
Silence. Andrei Codrescu. 223
Silence. Thomas Hornsby Ferril.
   243
Silence. Haig Khatchadourian. 292
Silence
   The arc-welder's blue. James L.
    White. 396
   "As we would have it." Edwin
    Honig. 275
   Cocoon. Erin Jolly. 285
   "The dynamic silence moving."
    Connie Hunt. 279
   The glove of silence. Norman
    Andrew Kirk. 293
   How to improve your personality.
    Herbert Morris. 326
   "I'm sitting here at Grieg's
    home." Sally Love Saunders.
    358
   Kar. Gerard Malanga. 310
   Letters not answered. Colette
    Inez. 280
   The listener to noise and
    silence. James Schevill. 360
   Out. Marilyn Kallet. 287
   Petals of silence. Maria Gillan.
    256
   Silence. Andrei Codrescu. 223
   Silence. Thomas Hornsby Ferril.
    243
   Silence. Haig Khatchadourian.
    292
   Silence, a sonnet. Edgar Allan
    Poe. 347
   So powerfully silent. Robert L.
    Wilson. 401
   Still I hear the silence. Alice
    Spohn Newton. 332
   Stillness. Connie Hunt. 279
   Stillness around me. Rachel A.
    Hazen. 271
   The voice. Kirk Lumpkin. 306
   Walpurgis. Erin Jolly. 285
   The work of the soul. Michael
    Akillian. 193
Silence at the top. Andrei
   Codrescu. 223
Silence broken. Robert L. Wilson.
   401
Silence, a sonnet. Edgar Allan
   Poe. 347
Silencer. Paul Violi. 388
The silencers. Kenneth Koch. 297
Silent grows a loveliness. Patsie
   Black. 206
"Silent memories trickle down a
   stream." Michael Robert Pick.

345

Silent, soft, forever still.
Rachel A. Hazen. 271
Silicon Valley. Michael Gizzi.
259
Silk scroll. Anne Bailie. 199
"The **silkworm**.". Madison
Morrison. 327
Silkworms
Silk scroll. Anne Bailie. 199
Silly bitches institute. Wanda
Coleman. 225
The **silo** burns in Brooklyn.
George Eklund. 238
Silver anniversary. Josephine B.
Moretti. 324
Silver sliver. James R. Rhodes.
352
Silver-Lillywite, Eileen
Adolescence. 364
After leaving you. 364
After the hotwave. 364
All that autumn. 364
America. 364
American beauties. 364
Animal cracker box. 364
Betrayal. 364
The boy next door. 364
Calling them back. 364
The children. 364
Dreaming. 364
The drought. 364
Drowning. 364
Elegy. 364
Elegy for America. 364
En Gev. 364
The end of the season. 364
Fall through air. 364
First date. 364
The first night of summer. 364
Franklin, Massachusetts. 364
Going to sleep. 364
Hurtling ahead to nowhere. 364
The ice house. 364
In the hospital. 364
Lake George, 1970. 364
Letter to Mimi. 364
Letter to my father. 364
Love letter. 364
Luck. 364
The magician. 364
A mirror. 364
My grandmother's funeral. 364
The pleasures of sleep. 364
Quiet, so quiet. 364
Rain. 364
The rowers. 364
Runaways. 364
Seton Hospital. 364
Sleigh of hand. 364

Slow dance. 364
The summer Bruce died. 364
Swarming into autumn. 364
There's a train. 364
Waiting. 364
We live in this room. 364
The wind. 364
Silverpoint. Louise Gluck. 259A
Similes. See Metaphors and
Similes

Simmerman, Jim
Black angel. 365
A blessing. 365
A brief introduction. 365
The dead madonnas of Santiago.
365
Delusions of grandeur. 365
Digger. 365
The double cherry. 365
Elegy in fifths. 365
Epithalamion: the ducks at Lake
Lotawana. 365
The funeral. 365
Hagiography. 365
Henry. 365
The housewife laments her
purchase of floating eggs. 365
If. 365
In the language of flowers. 365
Jane. 365
The land. 365
Leaving. 365
Long distance bickering (day
rate) 365
My brother's hands. 365
My old man. 365
My parents send a ring from the
Bahammas. 365
On a black and photograph of a
house. 365
On an unconceived painting by
Lautrec. 365
Places. 365
Postposterous. 365
Ricky Ricardo drinks alone. 365
Roses. 365
Sex. 365
Something. 365
Soon. 365
Spinner. 365
To you in particular. 365
Wedding photograph with clock.
365
What is wrong with this picture?
365
Winter, your father's house. 365
Simon. Harlan Usher. 386
Simple progression. Larry Moffi.
322

The **simplest** joy. Rachel A.
    Hazen. 271
Simplicity. John F. Barker. 201
Simplicity
    Awareness. Marie Daerr
        Boehringer. 210
    Props. Robert A. Sears. 362
    The quiet man of simplicity.
        James Schevill. 360
    Toad dreams. Marge Piercy. 346
Simply marvelous. Kirk Lumpkin.
    306
Simultaneous translation. Ray
    Fleming. 247
Sin
    The disturbed. Josephine Miles.
        319
    Finding out. William Stafford.
        373
    "Like Mr. Pester acknowledges
        his sinfulness in being"
        Charles Olson. 337
    Purification rite. Robert L.
        Wilson. 401
The **sin** of wanting a new
    refrigerator. Andrei Codrescu.
    223
"The **sinewy** descendant." Madison
    Morrison. 327
Sing, sing, sing a song. Alice
    Joyce Davidson. 227
Singers. Tom Smith. 368
Singing and Singers
    Memento. Cornel Lengyel. 302
    Noon song. Cornel Lengyel. 302
    The same. Josephine Miles. 319
    Simple progression. Larry Moffi.
        322
The **singing** we. Rose Basile
    Green. 265
Singing, maker of peace. Rose
    Basile Green. 265
Single in our double bed. Jeanne
    Lohmann. 305
"A **single** spider web." Sally Love
    Saunders. 358
"**Sinking** further through my
    tunnel." Michael Robert Pick.
    345
Sir. Miller Williams. 399
Sir Gander-Puller of the low
    country. J.W. Rivers. 354
Sir Winston. John F. Barker. 201
"**Siren**/people look." Larry
    Eigner. 237
Sirens (mythology)
    Encounter with sirens. Anne
        Bailie. 199
    Santa Lucia bar. Roy Marz. 312
    Thalassa. Robert A. Sears. 362

The **sirens**. David Wann. 394
A **sirvente** for Augusto Trujillo
    Figueroa. Thomas McGrath. 315
Sis and the pidgeon man. James A.
    Emanuel. 239
Sister Celia. Dave Smith. 367
Sister of the rocks. Carolyn
    Stoloff. 376
Sister Vivian, Caldwell College,
    1978. Maria Gillan. 256
Sisters. Tom Smith. 368
Sisters. See Brothers and Sisters

The **sisters**. Roy Marz. 312
Sisyphus. Josephine Miles. 319
Sisyphus (mythology)
    Sisyphus. Josephine Miles. 319
The **sitter** moves. Gary Margolis.
    311
Sitting in the doctor's office
    the next day. Laura Boss. 213
Sitting on the porch at dawn.
    James Schevill. 360
Six forty-five. Stephen Knauth.
    295
658.386/B 972.   Christopher
    Bursk. 219
Six miles from Indian Point. Ruth
    Lisa Schechter. 359
"**Six** months without you." Robert
    A. Sears. 362
Six pence, and more! Harlan
    Usher. 386
Six spoons with the initial K.
    Frances Mayes. 314
6:50 PM. The phone rings. It's him
    Wanda Coleman. 225
16th Street.   Robert Gibb. 253
Sixteen. Martha Janssen. 283
Sixteenth-century Icelandic
    chair. Marc Hudson. 277
Size. Robert Kelly. 289
Skating and Skaters
    Breakaway. Marieve Rugo. 356
    Ice show. James Magorian. 309
    Ice skating. Greg Kuzma. 300
    My son skating on Doane's Lake.
        Greg Kuzma. 300
    "Not the intaglio method or
        skating." Charles Olson. 337
    Roller rink. Betty Adcock. 192
Skeleton of winter. Joy Harjo.
    269
Sketch of a peasant man. Keith
    Wilson. 400
The **sketchbook**. Robin Becker. 202
Ski boots in storage. James A.
    Emanuel. 239
Skies: a Jew in Germany, 1979.
    Ghita Orth. 339

Skiing

Beyond the parallel lines. Carolyn Stoloff. 376

Of course it is. David Wann. 394

Ski boots in storage. James A. Emanuel. 239

Skin. Joan Colby. 224

Skin movers. James L. White. 396

Skirt. Alberta Turner. 384

Skokie river cadenzas. Colette Inez. 280

Skunks. Robert Peters. 343

Skunks

Skunks. Robert Peters. 343

The surrender of a skunk. Alice Spohn Newton. 333

Sky

Astral roulette. John Godfrey. 260

Day. Josephine Miles. 319

Late winter sky. Marc Hudson. 277

Music. Joseph Penzi. 342

"O Quadriga." Charles Olson. 337

Reflections on rose quartz. Cynthia Grenfell. 266

Scene. Joseph Penzi. 342

Speed limit. Josephine Miles. 319

What goes us. Marge Piercy. 346

Yi, yi, the sky. David James. 282

Sky coyote loses the year's gambling game for rain. Gene Anderson. 195

The **sky-high** ballet. Rachel A. Hazen. 271

"The **sky.**". Charles Olson. 337

Skydive. James Magorian. 309

Skye, Island of

Deat stones and daisies. Paul Davis. 228

Our names the only known. Paul Davis. 228

Skyscape. Joyce Carol Oates. 336

Skyscraper. Anne Bailie. 199

Skyscrapers

The foundations of a sky-scraper. John Reed. 350

Slack. Josephine Miles. 319

Slaughterhouses

The bloody harvest. George Eklund. 238

Yesterday's slaughter. Ernest Tedlock. 380

Slaughtering chickens. Anthony Petrosky. 344

The **slave** ship. Louise Gluck. 259A

The **slave.** John Reed. 350

Slavery

The harem boy. Albert Goldbarth. 261

The machete woman. Gayl Jones. 286

The slave ship. Louise Gluck. 259A

The slave. John Reed. 350

Sleep. Josephine Miles. 319

Sleep. Susan Stock. 375

Sleep. Anneliese Wagner. 389

Sleep

"After I come home from the meeting with friends." Josephine Miles. 319

"After noon I lie down." Josephine Miles. 319

After sleep. Jim Everhard. 241

"All night long." Charles Olson. 337

At night. Kenneth Koch. 297

Berceuse. Amy Clampitt. 222

Bodega, goodbye. Edwin Honig. 275

Butterfly sheets. Charles Edward Eaton. 236

Climbing the stairs. Mark Vinz. 387

Dreams of a man without children. Susan Tichy. 381

The flesh of discovery. James Schevill. 360

For Annie. Edgar Allan Poe. 347

Going to sleep. Eileen Silver-Lillywite. 364

Householder. Mark Vinz. 387

Irene (the sleeper). Edgar Allan Poe. 347

Lady asleep. Tom Smith. 368

Legend, fr. Mirror suite. Everett A. Gillis. 258

Love song: winter. Everett A. Gillis. 258

Lullaby ("Sweet love, everything"). Steve Kowit. 299

"Mirrors scattered." Larry Eigner. 237

Night vision : a fragment for Lucretius and others. Sandra McPherson. 317

Okanogan sleep. Marc Hudson. 277

Poem ("You make me think of sleep, and you're lying.") John Godfrey. 260

The postures of sleep. Joan Colby. 224

The sleeper. George Eklund. 238

Sleeping longer. Thomas Hornsby Ferril. 243

Sleeping with the light on.

Sharon Bryan. 217

Sumptuous siesta. Charles Edward
Eaton. 236

To -- ("Sleep on, sleep on...").
Edgar Allan Poe. 347

Work. Andrei Codrescu. 223

Sleep little poems, rest tonight.
James Torio. 281

A **sleep**. Larry Eigner. 237

The **sleeper**. George Eklund. 238

Sleeping. Judson Crews. 226

Sleeping alone. David Wagoner.
390

Sleeping Beauty. David Wagoner.
390

"The **sleeping** city." Sally Love
Saunders. 358

Sleeping in the loft of dreams.
Cathryn Hankla. 268

Sleeping longer. Thomas Hornsby
Ferril. 243

Sleeping nude. Charles Edward
Eaton. 236

Sleeping with the light on.
Sharon Bryan. 217

Sleepless, reading Machado. Mark
Vinz. 387

Sleepwalking. Mark Vinz. 387

Sleeve. Josephine Miles. 319

Sleigh of hand. Eileen
Silver-Lillywite. 364

Sleigh, Thomas R.
After one. 366
Alp. 366
A formal occasion. 366
History lesson. 366
In the hospital for tests. 366
The invalid. 366
Jenny Fish. 366
Judas waking. 366
La bufadora. 366
Land's end dialectic. 366
Logos. 366
Lullaby ("Bellying out in the
full sail of dream.") 366
Musicke of division. 366
The necessary webs. 366
Night journey. 366
Obsequies. 366
The painter. 366
Refuge. 366
Snakes. 366
Three horses. 366
To the other. 366
Uccello. 366
The utter stranger. 366
The very end. 366
Words to a former musician. 366

Sleighs
Snowpit in Switzerland. James A.

Emanuel. 239

Slide. Larry Eigner. 237

Slides. Charles Edward Eaton. 236

Sliding scales. Richmond
Lattimore. 301

Slipping standards of light. John
Godfrey. 260

Sloths
The three-toed sloth. Jack
Prelutsky. 349

Slow dance. Eileen
Silver-Lillywite. 364

Slow dance on the mating ground.
Rod McKuen. 316

Slow motion. Amy Clampitt. 222

Slowing down on a trampoline.
James Magorian. 309

"**Slownesses/which** are an/amount."
Charles Olson. 337

Slug nmadonna. Lyn Lifshin. 303

Slugs (mollusks)
"Black ebony shiny slug." Sally
Love Saunders. 358
The elegance of the slug. Sally
Love Saunders. 358

Slump. Paul Violi. 388

Slums
And-a-one-2-3-. Stephen Todd
Booker. 212

Small boats. Steve Kowit. 299

A **small** cave. Clayton Eshleman.
240

Small college athletic director.
James Magorian. 309

Small dictionary. James Magorian.
309

Small town grocer. Josephine B.
Moretti. 324

The **smaller** orchid. Amy Clampitt.
222

The **smallest** soldier. Rachel A.
Hazen. 271

Smart set. Norman Andrew Kirk.
293

"A **smell** of gunpowder..." Susan
Tichy. 381

Smiles
"A friendly smile." Connie Hunt.
279

"**Smiling** girls, rosy boys." Jan
Ormerod. 338

Smith, Dave
Bats. 367
Boat building at midnight. 367
Building houses. 367
Commute. 367
Drudge crabber. 367
Dry ice. 367
Ducking: after Maupassant. 367
False spring: late snow. 367

Gramercy Park Hotel. 367
House-movers. 367
In the house of the judge. 367
Jogging in the parlor,
    remembering a summer moment...
    367
Leaving town. 367
Love blows in the spring. 367
Mosquito biting. 367
Near the underground railroad.
    367
Night-walk, Montrose,
    Pennsylvania. 367
No return address. 367
An ode to Salt Lake City. 367
Of oystermen, workboats. 367
Outside Martins Ferry, Ohio. 367
Photographic plate, partly
    spidered, Hampton Roads... 367
Rainy day: last run. 367
Recess. 367
Running back. 367
Sea owl. 367
Sister Celia. 367
Smithfield ham. 367
Snake: a family tale. 367
Snapshot of a crab-picker among
    barrels spilling over... 367
Snow owl. 367
Sunday morning: Celia's father.
    367
To Celia, beyond the yachts. 367
Toy trains in the landlord's
    house. 367
Turn-of-the-century house. 367
Vermont cabin: late summer. 367
Waking in the endless mountains.
    367
Your Christmas present. 367
Smith, John
    Maximus, to Gloucester, letter
    11. Charles Olson. 337
Smith, Stan
    Being a soldier. Herbert Morris.
    326
Smith, Tom
    After Villon: the dead ladies.
    368
    Bestiary, sels. 368
    Burning leaves: the spinster.
    368
    Burning leaves: the groom. 368
    Cannibal mantis. 368
    Carol. 368
    Cat. 368
    Catchism. 368
    Catfish. 368
    The Christ, sels. 368
    Flower studies, sels. 368
    Flower studies: bittersweet. 368

Flower studies: brown-eyed
    Susan. 368
Flower studies: holly. 368
Flower studies: tigerlily. 368
Fox and bee. 368
Francesca da Rimini. 368
A game of snow. 368
Lady asleep. 368
Limerick hagiograph. 368
Love death. 368
Lovedeath, sels. 368
May. 368
The moon. 368
Old woman. 368
101 dreams of briar rose.
    368
Phoenix. 368
Prick song at Compline. 368
Recipe. 368
Religious observance. 368
Rosetree at dawn. 368
Serenade. 368
Seven salvations: a mixed bag.
    368
Singers. 368
Sisters. 368
Two for Mother Goose, sels. 368
Two legends: a birthday party.
    368
Two legends: nails. 368
Where is she now? 368
Why birds sing. 368
Smithfield ham. Dave Smith. 367
Smitten. Kirk Lumpkin. 306
Smog
    The day the winds. Josephine
    Miles. 319
Smoke. Alberta Turner. 384
Smoke
    Committee report on smoke
    abatement in residential area.
    Josephine Miles. 319
    Searching. Robert L. Wilson. 401
Smoke rings. C.D. Wright. 402
Smoke signals. William Stafford.
    373
Smoke valley equinox. Randy
    Blasing. 207
Smudge-pot. Robert Peters. 343
Snail. X.J. Kennedy. 290
The snail. Jack Prelutsky. 349
Snails
    Snail. X.J. Kennedy. 290
    The snail. Jack Prelutsky. 349
Snake charmer. James Magorian.
    309
Snake: a family tale. Dave Smith.
    367
The snake. Jack Prelutsky. 349
Snakes. Wanda Coleman. 225

Snakes. Thomas R. Sleigh. 366
Snakes
    Absalom. Thomas Hornsby Ferril.
      243
    "Conversation." Madison
      Morrison. 327
    The corner is turned. Cynthia
      Grenfell. 266
    The feathered bird of the harbor
      of Gloucester. Charles Olson.
      337
    The flying snake. Alice Spohn
      Newton. 333
    Garter snakes. Robert Peters.
      343
    If it is an objective. Judson
      Crews. 226
    An outing on Pawley's Island.
      J.W. Rivers. 354
    She hated rattlers. Judson
      Crews. 226
    Snake: a family tale. Dave
      Smith. 367
    The snake. Jack Prelutsky. 349
    Snakes. Thomas R. Sleigh. 366
    "Stamping/considered..." Madison
      Morrison. 327
    "Three in the afternoon."
      Madison Morrison. 327
    A walk to school. Alice Spohn
      Newton. 333
Snapshot of a crab-picker among
    barrels spilling over... Dave
    Smith. 367
Snapshots of love. Rochelle
    DuBois. 234
Snapshots with buck, Model-A
    Ford, and kitchen. Robert
    Peters. 343
A **snarl** for loose friends. Marge
    Piercy. 346
Sneakers. See Boots and Shoes

Snodgrass, W.D. (William De Witt)
    April inventory. 369
    At the park dance. 369
    The campus on the hill. 369
    A cardinal. 369
    Heart's needle. 369
    Home town. 369
    The marsh. 369
    The operation. 369
    Orpheus. 369
    Papageno. 369
    Returned to Frisco, 1946. 369
    Riddle. 369
    "Seeing you have a woman." 369
    September in the park. 369
    Song ("Observe the cautious
      toadstools.") 369

    Song ("Sweet beast, I have gone
      prowling.") 369
    Ten days leave. 369
    "These trees stand very tall
      under the heavens." 369
    Untic...ov tic. 369
    Winter bouquet. 369
Snow. Robert Frost. 250
Snow. David Shapiro. 363
Snow
    Beethoven's Polish birthday.
      Gary Margolis. 311
    Building a snowperson. James
      Magorian. 308
    The coming of snow. Haig
      Khatchadourian. 292
    Currents. Mark Vinz. 387
    The eternal snow. Connie Hunt.
      279
    First taste. John Godfrey. 260
    A game of snow. Tom Smith. 368
    Gospel in the drifts. Colette
      Inez. 280
    I follow the snow. Rachel A.
      Hazen. 271
    If I had sorted out. Judson
      Crews. 226
    It's snow fun. Marie Daerr
      Boehringer. 210
    Making angels in Chicago. Jeanne
      Lohmann. 305
    Narragansett snow dance. Randy
      Blasing. 207
    Onion snow (March) Josephine B.
      Moretti. 324
    Perspective. Debra Bruce. 216
    Shoveling snow in Chicago. J.W.
      Rivers. 354
    Snow. David Shapiro. 363
    Snow patterns. Mitchell Howard.
      276
    Snow warning. Norman Andrew
      Kirk. 293
    "Snow." Larry Eigner. 237
    Snowfall. Joyce Carol Oates. 336
    The snowfall. Greg Kuzma. 300
    Snowflakes. David Wagoner. 390
    Sough and sift. James R. Rhodes.
      352
    Warm snow. Alice Joyce Davidson.
      227
    "Whipped cream." Sally Love
      Saunders. 358
    The winter without snow. Carol
      Frost. 249
Snow as sorrow. Marieve Rugo. 356
Snow in April. Anneliese Wagner.
    389
Snow owl. Dave Smith. 367
Snow warning. Norman Andrew Kirk.

293
Snow-dunk in Ontario. Joyce Carol
    Oates. 336
Snow at evening. Charles Olson.
    337
Snow image. Robert Peters. 343
Snow patterns. Mitchell Howard.
    276
Snow, snow. Marge Piercy. 346
Snow-time success. Marie Daerr
    Boehringer. 210
"Snow.". Larry Eigner. 237
Snowbanks north of the house.
    Robert Bly. 209
Snowblind to the banquet. Paul
    Violi. 388
Snowfall. Joyce Carol Oates. 336
The snowfall. Greg Kuzma. 300
Snowflakes. David Wagoner. 390
Snowman. James A. Emanuel. 239
Snowpit in Switzerland. James A.
    Emanuel. 239
Snowshoe hare. Aileen Fisher. 244
Snowshoes. Debra Bruce. 216
So born. May Miller. 320
So clear the flight. May Miller.
    320
So far away. Jacques Sollov. 370
So graven. Josephine Miles. 319
So I lie. Carolyn Stoloff. 376
So it happened. Judson Crews. 226
So lightly she must be air.
    Cathryn Hankla. 268
So little time. James R. Rhodes.
    352
"So many good things." Sally Love
    Saunders. 358
So many others. Rod McKuen. 316
"So many times." Robert A. Sears.
    362
"So muggy/in the thread." Larry
    Eigner. 237
"So often/she seemed to speak too
    quickly." Theta Burke. 218
So powerfully silent. Robert L.
    Wilson. 401
So sassafras. Charles Olson. 337
So still the dawn. Elsa Gidlow.
    254
So what else is new? Harlan
    Usher. 386
So when he leaves, fr. The day of
    the body. Carol Frost. 249
"So you are thinking of
    principles to go on."
    Josephine Miles. 319
Soapbox speech for Kennedy.
    Thomas McGrath. 315
Soaring. Jeanne Lohmann. 305
Sobered. Elsa Gidlow. 254

Social Problems
    Dream dogs. Andrei Codrescu. 223
Social Problems = United States
    Diplomatic relations with
        America. Ray Fleming. 247
    For the furies. Marge Piercy.
        346
    Game talk. Rose Basile Green.
        265
    Memorial Day. Josephine Miles.
        319
    Monoculture. Kirk Lumpkin. 306
    The music of the curbs. John
        Godfrey. 260
    The pledge of a human animal, of
        a bloody smiling fool. Kirk
        Lumpkin. 306
Society. Rosa Bogar. 211
Socrates
    Footnote to the classics. Royal
        Murdoch. 330
    Unwritten. David Shapiro. 363
Soda fountain. Mark Vinz. 387
Soil pipe madonna. Lyn Lifshin.
    303
Soldier. Royal Murdoch. 330
Soldier home. Roy Marz. 312
The soldier-poet. Jocelyn Hollis.
    274
Soldier. Edwin Honig. 275
The soldier's poem. Robert
    Pawlowski. 341
The soldier. A. Dovichi. 233
Soldiers
    Bluebird houses. James Tate. 379
    Driver. Robert Pawlowski. 341
    Elegy for an soldier in any war,
        fr. Elegy and epitaph. Everett
        A. Gillis. 258
    Elegy for soldiers. Anne Bailie.
        199
    Fresco:departure for an
        imperialist war. Thomas
        McGrath. 315
    A man of plastic. Jocelyn
        Hollis. 274
    Privates. Robert A. Sears. 362
    Putting an end to the war
        stories. Larry Moffi. 322
    The smallest soldier. Rachel A.
        Hazen. 271
    The soldier. A. Dovichi. 233
    "Some day when you are picked
        up." Ernest Hemingway. 272
    "There was Ike and Tony and
        Jacque and me." Ernest
        Hemingway. 272
    To Chink whose trade is
        soldiering. Ernest Hemingway.
        272

Water, blood, and desire. C.D.
    Wright. 402
We are not Achilles. Jocelyn
    Hollis. 274
Yet are you wounded, soldier?
    Jocelyn Hollis. 274
Soley. Marc Hudson. 277
Solitude. Evelyn Golden. 263
Solitude. Connie Hunt. 279
Solitude
    "Alone is the consitions of
        bliss." Da Free Jonn. 284
    Alone on a blanket. Lyn Lifshin.
        303
    Angelus. Haig Khatchadourian.
        292
    Being somebody. Edwin Honig. 275
    The biographers of solitude.
        Irving Feldman. 242
    A broken house. Marc Kaminsky.
        288
    "Can you remember beginning?"
        Edwin Honig. 275
    Dark. Greg Kuzma. 300
    Empty harbor. Rod McKuen. 316
    Flying solo. Brenda Marie Osbey.
        340
    Garden song. Rod McKuen. 316
    The great adventure. Rod McKuen.
        316
    "I need to be." Sally Love
        Saunders. 358
    In the face of solitude. Marilyn
        Kallet. 287
    Lines to a girl 5 days after her
        21st birthday. Ernest
        Hemingway. 272
    Reassurance: what gets done.
        Mary Gilliland. 257
    Receiver. William Stafford. 373
    The sense of solitude. Rod
        McKuen. 316
    Sleepless, reading Machado. Mark
        Vinz. 387
    Solitude. Evelyn Golden. 263
    Solitude. Connie Hunt. 279
    Solitude's my home. Rod McKuen.
        316
    Someday. Stephen Knauth. 295
    Une semaine de silence. Robert
        Kelly. 289
    Unfinished song. Carol Frost.
        249
    We live alone. Haig
        Khatchadourian. 292
Solitude's my home. Rod McKuen.
    316
Sollov, Jacques
    Alexander. 370
    Ballet. 371

Beautiful stranger. 370
Beauty queen. 370
The blue light. 370
Bonaparte. 370
Brahman. 371
Celestial destiny. 371
Christ. 371
Christ within. 370
Cleopatra. 370
Come back home. 371
Come closer. 371
The crown. 371
The cup. 371
Dalila. 370
Ecstatic moment. 370
El Cid. 370
Eternal friendship. 371
Eternal peace. 370
The eyes of a girl. 370
Faith. 370
First love. 370
Garden of my life. 370
The golden eagle. 370
The golden fish. 370
The golden lamp. 370
The golden plate. 371
The healer. 371
Hidden desire. 370
I dream. 370
I want to be your everything.
    371
If I had a crown. 370
If you must go. 371
The kingdom shore. 370
Language of flowers. 370
The last tie. 371
The light bearer. 371
Listen to me. 370
Little angel. 371
Little butterfly. 371
Little giant. 370
Little one. 370
Lord thank you. 371
Love thought. 370
Luminous jewel. 370
Magic secret. 370
The magician. 371
Mirage. 371
Mother. 371
My dogs. 370
My heart is bleeding. 371
Nefertiti. 370
Nightingale. 370
Opera. 371
The poet of love. 371
The poet. 371
Police woman. 370
The prospector. 371
The pure light. 371
The purple sun. 371

Ramses II. 370
Real love. 370
Red rose. 371
Remember. 371
Sneba. 370
So far away. 370
Soul in distress. 371
The spaceman. 371
Spaceship. 370
Spiritual sun. 371
The star of my destiny. 371
Sunrise - moonset. 370
Supreme knowledge. 370
The tenor. 370
Thank you. 371
There is a kingdom. 370
The throne. 371
The triangle of love. 370
Walking with the Lord. 371
The wedding garment. 371
White angel. 371
The white bird. 371
White dove. 370
White rose. 370
Why must I leave you. 371
The wise man. 371
Wonderful moments. 370
The world that lives in me. 370
Solo. Josephine Miles. 319
Solo. James Torio. 281
A solo for Charles Munch. Norman
    Andrew Kirk. 293
Solstice. Louise Gluck. 259A
Sombreros
    Purchase of hat to wear in the
    sun. Josephine Miles. 319
Some beneficial rays. James Tate.
    379
Some day when it is dark. Cathryn
    Hankla. 268
"Some day when you are picked
    up." Ernest Hemingway. 272
Some flowers. Stephen Sandy. 357
Some further observations. Paul
    Violi. 388
Some gnomic verses. Marc Hudson.
    277
Some good news. Charles Olson.
    337
Some lines finished just before
    dawn... Miller Williams. 399
Some nasty business. Mitchell
    Howard. 276
Some night again. William
    Stafford. 373
Some prince of the Trojans here.
    Robert Kelly. 289
Some pure heart saying. Paul
    Davis. 228
Some springs. Marie Daerr

Boehringer. 210
Someday. Connie Hunt. 279
Someday. Stephen Knauth. 295
Someone else's children. Robin
    Becker. 202
Someone ought to cry. Patsie
    Black. 206
"Someone would say/we are
    responsible." Theta Burke. 218
"Someone's in touch." Madison
    Morrison. 327
"Someone, an engineer, told a
    confab of wires." Josephine
    Miles. 319
Something. Jim Simmerman. 365
Something in the hunter. James R.
    Rhodes. 352
Something more. Harry Humes. 278
"Something that I." Madison
    Morrison. 327
Sometime something. Norman Andrew
    Kirk. 293
Sometimes. Thomas McGrath. 315
"Sometimes I feel like a caged
    animal." Michael Robert Pick.
    345
"Sometimes I get lost." Michael
    Robert Pick. 345
"Sometimes I wish I was a hawk."
    Michael Robert Pick. 345
"Sometimes it's creative." Sally
    Love Saunders. 358
Sometimes we say it is love.
    Carol Frost. 249
A sometimes wondering. Rachel A.
    Hazen. 271
Somewhere. Patsie Black. 206
Somewhere to go? Rachel A. Hazen.
    271
"Somewhere/in some yesterday."
    Theta Burke. 218
Sommerset. Rod McKuen. 316
Son. Josephine Miles. 319
Son. James A. Emanuel. 239
A son's commencement day. Rose
    Basile Green. 265
The son's lullaby for the mother.
    Roy Marz. 312
A son. May Miller. 320
Sonata. Rod McKuen. 316
The sonata in D minor. Phillips
    Kloss. 294
Song. Thomas McGrath. 315
Song. Ralph J., Jr. Mills. 321
Song. Keith Wilson. 400
Song ("He has gunpowder on his
    breath.") Robert Peters. 343
Song ("Observe the cautious
    toadstools.") W.D. (William De
    Witt) Snodgrass. 369

Song ("Sweet beast, I have gone prowling.") W.D. (William De Witt) Snodgrass. 369

A song ("When a man loves a woman.") David Shapiro. 363

Song after midnight. David Wagoner. 390

The song and dance of. Charles Olson. 337

Song for a march. May Miller. 320

Song for Guenevere. Elsa Gidlow. 254

A song for May. John Reed. 338

Song for Thantog. Joy Harjo. 269

A song for the queen. Jeanne Lohmann. 305

Song like a thin wire. Marge Piercy. 346

Song of a dark pine morning. Maria Gillan. 256

Song of Aeterna 27 over Los Angeles. James Schevill. 360

Song of praise. Maria Gillan. 256

A song of rain. Tefke Goldberger. 262

Song of the infidel. Erin Jolly. 285

Song of the retired senior citizen. Sam Fishman. 246

Song of the snrubs. Anne Bailie. 199

Song of whales. Gerard Malanga. 310

Song to hug by. Mary Gilliland. 257

Song, Cathy
    Beauty and sadness. 372
    Birthmarks. 372
    Blue and white lines after O'Keefe. 372
    Blue lantern. 372
    Chinatown. 372
    A dream of small children. 372
    Easter: Wahiawa, 1959. 372
    Father and daughter. 372
    For A.J.: on finding she's on her boat to China. 372
    For my brother. 372
    From the white place. 372
    Girl powdering her neck. 372
    Hoolehua. 372
    Hotel Geneve. 372
    Ikebana. 372
    January. 372
    Leaving. 372
    Lost sister. 372
    A pale arrangement of hands. 372
    Picture bride. 372
    Primary colors. 372
    The seamstress. 372
    Seed. 372
    Spaces we leave empty. 372
    Stray animals. 372
    Tribe. 372
    Untouched photograph of passenger. 372
    The violin teacher. 372
    Waialua. 372
    The white porch. 372
    The youngest daughter. 372

Song/for Franklin Brainard. Ralph J., Jr. Mills. 321

Song: a new poem of war. Cynthia Grenfell. 266

Song: to--. Edgar Allan Poe. 347

Song:Miss Penelope Burgess, balling the jack. Thomas McGrath. 315

The song. Michael Akillian. 193

The song. David Wagoner. 390

Songport. Rose Basile Green. 265

Songs and Singing
    Above Moraine Park. Marc Hudson. 277
    Augusta's 'Think-positive' song. Carolyn Stoloff. 376
    Blind singer. Betty Adcock. 192
    Don't talk, sing! Alice Spohn Newton. 332
    "Evening, wedged in the door like a grand piano..." Carolyn Stoloff. 376
    Finale. Rachel A. Hazen. 271
    Folk music of Tibet. Robert Kelly. 289
    "Hymns to me." Da Free John. 284
    Intermezzo at Vendemmia. Rose Basile Green. 265
    Isle unforgotten. Alice Spohn Newton. 332
    It goes like this. Susan Stock. 375
    Joy's song. S. Bradford Williams (Jr.). 398
    Love motiff: a girl's song. Keith Wilson. 400
    Nightclub. James Iorio. 281
    Ordinary song. Phyllis A. Tickle. 382
    A poem for Claire of London. James A. Emanuel. 239
    Round valley songs. William Oandasan. 335
    Song after midnight. David Wagoner. 390
    The tenor. Jacques Sollov. 370

The songs of Maximus. Charles Olson. 337

Songs of the only child. Ghita Orth. 339

Songs of transmutation. Ghita
    Orth. 339
Sonnet ("An afternoon splashed
    all grapefruit...") John
    Godfrey. 260
Sonnet ("Eyes to no awesome wind,
    bred.") John Godfrey. 260
Sonnet ("Harbor open your eyes.")
    John Godfrey. 260
Sonnet ("Ice over time.") David
    Shapiro. 363
Sonnet ("In the sunniness of the
    particular noon.") John
    Godfrey. 260
Sonnet ("Ragamuffins as all
    outdoors.") John Godfrey. 260
Sonnet ("Snow falls exclusively
    for the voice to mount.") John
    Godfrey. 260
Sonnet ("Where was that lazy
    river?...") John Godfrey. 260
Sonnet - to Zante. Edgar Allan
    Poe. 347
Sonnet ("Seldom we find...").
    Edgar Allan Poe. 347
Sonnet for a writer. James A.
    Emanuel. 239
Sonnet upon three kings' day.
    Mitchell Howard. 276
Sonnet: to science. Edgar Allan
    Poe. 347
Sons. See Daughters and Sons

Soon. Jim Simmerman. 365
Sooner or later, a close=up.
    James A. Emanuel. 239
Sorrow. Josephine Miles. 319
Sorrow
    After the war (II). John Yau.
    404
    And nobody cries. Rachel A.
    Hazen. 271
    Blue lantern. Cathy Song. 372
    The boa-constrictor. Erin Jolly.
    285
    A broken house. Marc Kaminsky.
    288
    Canto. Patsie Black. 206
    Committal day. James R. Rhodes.
    352
    Contrition. Ernesto Galarza. 252
    Coping with the news. Jeanne
    Lohmann. 305
    The dancing women. John Reed.
    350
    Danny. John F. Barker. 201
    The day the sassafras shed.
    Robert L. Wilson. 401
    Dewato. Marc Hudson. 277
    Discovery under Lenten

waterstorm. Gene Detro. 230
Dolor. Josephine Miles. 319
Each day. Sister Maura. 313
Excursion from grief. May
    Miller. 320
Fall through air. Eileen
    Silver-Lillywite. 364
Go from regret to the magic
    worlds. Kirk Lumpkin. 306
Grey morning. Elsa Gidlow. 254
Grief. Martha Janssen. 283
"Grief dry the/council." Larry
    Eigner. 237
"He has not been burned."
    Madison Morrison. 327
"Hearing it wake, we feel."
    Edwin Honig. 275
Heart's needle. W.D. (William De
    Witt) Snodgrass. 369
"I cry with no tears." Michael
    Robert Pick. 345
I put my trust in the river.
    Jacqueline Frank. 248
Late harvest. Joyce Carol Oates.
    336
Lying in sadness. James L.
    White. 396
A matter of minutes. Rachel A.
    Hazen. 271
Metamorphosis. Patsie Black. 206
The midwinter death of Olivia
    Stroud. Stephen Knauth. 295
The mourning. Joyce Carol Oates.
    336
The outer reaches of the heart.
    Rod McKuen. 316
Passes for Nicanor Parra. Edwin
    Honig. 275
Pieta. Roy Marz. 312
A poem for Sarah's tears. James
    A. Emanuel. 239
Poemgatherers following a giant
    roller from one highway...
    James Magorian. 309
Refuge. Thomas R. Sleigh. 366
The saturday afternoon blues.
    Wanda Coleman. 225
Sea maiden. James R. Rhodes. 352
"Seek out the far capillaries."
    Robert Kelly. 289
Snow as sorrow. Marieve Rugo.
    356
Sorrow. Josephine Miles. 319
Stopping places. Joan Colby. 224
Van Gogh. Sam Fishman. 246
The walk. Norman Andrew Kirk.
    293
The whitewashed wall. Marilyn
    Kallet. 287
"You must be hurting inside."

Michael Robert Pick. 345
Sough and sift. James R. Rhodes.
    352
Soul. Lucien Stryk. 377
Soul
    Ah, my soul. Patsie Black. 206
    "The chemical, high and low." Da
        Free John. 284
    Curvature of sound. Robert
        Kelly. 289
    A difficult demand. Carolyn
        Stoloff. 376
    "Fidelity to one's soul." Theta
        Burke. 218
    Fourth dimension. Anne Bailie.
        199
    Just a thought. Sam Fishman. 246
    Redemption. Josephine Miles. 319
    Soul. Lucien Stryk. 377
    Soul music. James R. Rhodes. 352
    Spiritual exercises. Thomas
        McGrath. 315
    To the prisoner. James R.
        Rhodes. 352
    "When the soul reaches the
        level." Theta Burke. 218
Soul in distress. Jacques Sollov.
    371
The soul in the valley of Kidron.
    Susan Tichy. 381
Soul music. James R. Rhodes. 352
The soul of intercourse. Clayton
    Eshleman. 240
The soul of Spain with McAlmon
    and Bird the publishers.
    Ernest Hemingway. 272
Souls looking for bodies. Andrei
    Codrescu. 223
Sound arithmetic. Carolyn
    Stoloff. 376
Sound of summer. Josephine B.
    Moretti. 324
"The sound.". Larry Eigner. 237
"Sounded like." Larry Eigner. 237
Soundifferously. Norman Andrew
    Kirk. 293
Sounds
    Romanian stones. Keith Wilson.
        400
"Sounds/quiet.". Larry Eigner.
    237
Soundscape. Rose Basile Green.
    265
The source. David Wagoner. 390
Sources. Adrienne Rich. 353
South (United States)
    A moment in time at Culpepper
        plantation. J.W. Rivers. 354
    Sir Gander-Puller of the low
        country. J.W. Rivers. 354

Sources. Adrienne Rich. 353
The south. John F. Barker. 201
Southland drive-in. James
    Applewhite. 198
South woods in October, with the
    spiders of memory. Betty
    Adcock. 192
South Yuma River, Summer 1971.
    Jim Everhard. 241
The south. John F. Barker. 201
"A southern/morning light."
    Madison Morrison. 327
Southland drive-in. James
    Applewhite. 198
Southside. Mark Vinz. 387
Souvenir. Ghita Orth. 339
The sow's head. Robert Peters.
    343
Sowing. See Seed

The spa of the posthumous : Pearl
    Karsten speaks. Sandra
    McPherson. 317
Space. Joan Colby. 224
Space. Joseph Penzi. 342
Space and Space Travel
    Cape Canaveral. Michael Gizzi.
        259
    "Comets clash." Michael Robert
        Pick. 345
    Man in progress. May Miller. 320
    The moon and the beautiful
        woman. James Schevill. 360
    On astronauts who lost their
        lives when their rocket...
        Cornel Lengyel. 302
    Public notice. Cornel Lengyel.
        302
    Return to the world. Albert
        Goldbarth. 261
    The spaceman. Jacques Sollov.
        371
    Starlight. William Oandasan. 335
"Space and time..." Charles
    Olson. 337
Space souffle. Andrei Codrescu.
    223
The spaceman. Jacques Sollov. 371
Spaces we leave empty. Cathy
    Song. 372
Spaceship. Jacques Sollov. 370
Spaceship earth. Patsie Black.
    206
Spaghetti O's. David Wann. 394
Spaghetti westerns and the cult
    of cowboy blood. Harrison
    Fisher. 245
Spain
    As though I didn't know. Carolyn
        Stoloff. 376

The austere place. Carolyn
    Stoloff. 376
Her mornings and evenings.
    Carolyn Stoloff. 376
The soul of Spain with McAlmon
    and Bird the publishers.
    Ernest Hemingway. 272
This Spain. Carolyn Stoloff. 376
Through infinite points. Carolyn
    Stoloff. 376
A Spanish painting. David
    Shapiro. 363
Spanish succession. Richmond
    Lattimore. 301
Sparrows
    For now. Robert Gibb. 253
    Mithuna. Stephen Sandy. 357
    "Sparrows gather on the
        chimney." Larry Eigner. 237
"Sparrows gather on the chimney."
    Larry Eigner. 237
The sparrows that fell. Cornel
    Lengyel. 302
Spas. See Health Resorts

Spatial relations. Robert Anbian.
    194
"Speak not to others." Theta
    Burke. 218
Speaker. Josephine Miles. 319
Speaking and reaching, sels.
    Theta Burke. 218
Speaking to myself. Anthony
    Petrosky. 344
"A special spirit in your birth."
    Robert A. Sears. 362
Speciality barber in beast-heads.
    James Schevill. 360
Spectacles
    Rose-colored glasses. Charles
        Edward Eaton. 236
Speech. Edwin Honig. 275
Speed. Josephine Miles. 319
Speed limit. Josephine Miles. 319
Speedway. Ruth Lisa Schechter.
    359
Spell against weather. Joan
    Colby. 224
Spencer's mountains. Rod McKuen.
    316
The spheres of October. Harry
    Humes. 278
Sphinx skin. David Shapiro. 363
Spider flight. Everett A. Gillis.
    258
"A spider web." Sally Love
    Saunders. 358
Spider's way. Barry Wallenstein.
    393
Spiders

On contemplating the speed of a
    tiny red spider. James Torio.
    281
"A single spider web." Sally
    Love Saunders. 358
Spider flight. Everett A.
    Gillis. 258
"A spider web." Sally Love
    Saunders. 358
Spider's way. Barry Wallenstein.
    393
"When a spider begins/to spin
    his web." Theta Burke. 218
Spikenard and roses. Erin Jolly.
    285
Spinner. Jim Simmerman. 365
Spinsters
    Burning leaves: the spinster.
        Tom Smith. 368
"spirit is not the flesh." Joan
    Walsh Anglund. 197
"The spirit is still." Joan Walsh
    Anglund. 197
"The spirit is the unseen
    circle/within." Joan Walsh
    Anglund. 197
"The spirit that speaks through
    you/is as the light." Joan
    Walsh Anglund. 197
Spirits of the dead. Edgar Allan
    Poe. 347
Spiritual exercises. Thomas
    McGrath. 315
The spiritual hunt. Clayton
    Eshleman. 240
Spiritual sun. Jacques Sollov.
    371
The splash of being. David Wann.
    394
Spleen. Marilyn Kallet. 287
Spleen: Geneva, New York. Marilyn
    Kallet. 287
The split end with average speed.
    Ray Fleming. 247
Splurge. Paul Violi. 388
The sport of kings. Ernest
    Hemingway. 272
Spotlight. Rachel A. Hazen. 271
Spring. Roy Marz. 312
Spring. Joseph Penzi. 342
Spring. Roy Marz. 312
Spring
    Almaden road. Ernesto Galarza.
        252
    Another spring. Maria Gillan.
        256
    April. Ralph J., Jr. Mills. 321
    Arrival. Marie Daerr Boehringer.
        210
    Belated spring. John F. Barker.

201
Captive. Marie Daerr Boehringer. 210
Civic diasters. Charles Olson. 337
"Constellations collapse." James Torio. 281
Day in February. Marie Daerr Boehringer. 210
Early spring green. William Oandasan. 335
Easter season. Louise Gluck. 259A
Encore. Marie Daerr Boehringer. 210
Evensong. Marie Daerr Boehringer. 210
Feast of all fools. Mark Vinz. 387
Four springs, sels. Edwin Honig. 275
Green April. Marie Daerr Boehringer. 210
Greening song. James R. Rhodes. 352
Initimations of spring. Robert L. Wilson. 401
Letter 9. Charles Olson. 337
Love blows in the spring. Dave Smith. 367
Mutual chord of wonder. Alice Spohn Newton. 332
The Nine1910 street car. James Magorian. 309
Oxfordshire spring. Ray Fleming. 247
The perfect fool. Mitchell Howard. 276
Phenomenon. Marie Daerr Boehringer. 210
Primary colors. Catny Song. 372
Primavera. James A. Emanuel. 239
Pursuit of happiness. Robert L. Wilson. 401
Renewal. Marie Daerr Boenringer. 210
Santa Clara spring. Ernesto Galarza. 252
Serenity. Marie Daerr Boehringer. 210
Snow, snow. Marge Piercy. 346
Some springs. Marie Daerr Boehringer. 210
Spring fever. Aileen Fisher. 244
Spring song. Marie Daerr Boenringer. 210
Spring was begging to be born. James Tate. 379
Spring's song. S. Bradford Williams (Jr.). 398

A stalled spring. Ralph J., Jr. Mills. 321
Summit meeting in the spring. May Miller. 320
"This morning." James Torio. 281
Triumph. Marie Daerr Boehringer. 210
Unholy spring. John Godfrey. 260
Vernal equinox. Kirk Lumpkin. 306
Weather insurance. Marie Daerr Boehringer. 210
Spring '44. Josephine Miles. 319
Spring afternoon. Martha Janssen. 283
Spring cleaning. Debra Bruce. 216
Spring dirge. Ernesto Galarza. 252
Spring fever. Aileen Fisher. 244
Spring four, sels. Edwin Honig. 275
Spring in the industrial park. Miriam Goodman. 264
Spring journal: poems, sels. Edwin Honig. 275
Spring lunch. Colette Inez. 280
Spring one, sels. Edwin Honig. 275
Spring song. Marie Daerr Boehringer. 210
Spring song. Cornel Lengyel. 302
Spring storm. James Torio. 281
Spring storm over gotham. Royal Murdoch. 330
Spring three, sels. Edwin Honig. 275
Spring two, sels. Edwin Honig. 275
Spring was begging to be born. James Tate. 379
Spring's song. S. Bradford Williams (Jr.). 398
"Spring.". Michael Robert Pick. 345
Springs
"I told the woman." Charles Olson. 337
Springtime in David Wann. David Wann. 394
The spy. Royal Murdoch. 330
Square hole day. Mary Gilliland. 257
"A square poetess." Madison Morrison. 327
"The squeeking noise replaced the awful." Michael Robert Pick. 345
The squirrel. J.W. Rivers. 354
Squirrels
The front-yard squirrel. Rod

McKuen. 316
The squirrel. J.W. Rivers. 354
SRO. Robert Pawlowski. 341
Ssh. Albert Goldbarth. 261
St. Augustine's prayer to God,
    the Father. Franz Schneider.
    361
St. Barnabas, fr. Friday night
    quartet. David Shapiro. 363
St. John and the angel. Anne
    Bailie. 199
St. Paul's Union Church and
    cemetery, Seiberlingsville,
    Pa. Robert Gibb. 253
The stable. Gary Margolis. 311
The stable. Roy Marz. 312
Stacking the straw. Amy Clampitt.
    222
Stafford, William
    Absences. 373
    Acoma mesa. 373
    After arguing against the
        contention that art... 373
    Anticipating. 373
    Around you, your house. 373
    At the falls: a birthday
        picture. 373
    A cameo of your mother. 373
    A catechism. 373
    Child in the evening. 373
    A child's face in a small town.
        373
    Class reunion. 373
    The color that really is. 373
    Confessor. 373
    A course in creative writing.
        373
    Dark wind. 373
    A day to remember. 373
    An event at Big Eddy. 373
    Fiction. 373
    Finding out. 373
    Friends. 373
    Friends, farewell. 373
    Friends: a recognition. 373
    From Hallmark or somewhere. 373
    From our balloon over the
        provinces. 373
    A glass face in the rain. 373
    A glimpse in the crowd. 373
    Glimpses. 373
    Hanging tough. 373
    Having the right name. 373
    How it all began. 373
    How it is. 373
    How to get back. 373
    If I could be like Wallace
        Stevens. 373
    In a corner. 373
    Incident. 373

Journey. 373
Knowing. 373
The late flight. 373
A late guest. 373
Later. 373
Learning to like the new school.
    373
A letter not to deliver. 373
Letting you go. 373
Little night stories. 373
Looking across the river. 373
Maybe. 373
A message from space. 373
Much I have traveled. 373
Murder bridge. 373
My life. 373
My mother was a soldier. 373
Not very loud. 373
Now wait-. 373
An old pickerel in Walden Pond.
    373
On the road last night. 373
Once in a dream. 373
Once in the 40's. 373
One time. 373
Our cave. 373
Our kind. 373
Passing a pile of stones. 373
Pegleg lookout. 373
Places with meaning. 373
Receiver. 373
Remembering. 373
Remembering brother Bob. 373
Revelation. 373
Rover. 373
Ruby was her name. 373
Sabbath. 373
Salvaged parts. 373
A scene. 373
School days. 373
Seeing and perceiving. 373
Sending these messages. 373
Smoke signals. 373
Some night again. 373
Survivor. 373
A tentative welcome to readers.
    373
There is blindness. 373
They say. 373
Things I learned last week. 373
Things that come. 373
Torque. 373
A touch on your sleeve. 373
Troubleshooting. 373
Tuned in late one night. 373
Watching a candle. 373
We interrupt to bring you. 373
What ever happended to the
    beats? 373
What I'll see that afternoon.

373
    When you go anywhere. 373
    Why I say adios. 373
    Why we need fantasy. 373
    With neighbors one afternoon.
        373
    Yellow cars. 373
    Yellow flowers. 373
    Yucca flowers. 373
Stage Fort Park. Charles Olson.
    337
Stage sounds. Norman Andrew Kirk.
    293
Stages of chilhood. Anne Bailie.
    199
Stags and salmon. Carol Frost.
    249
Staircase. Miriam Goodman. 264
Stairs
    The circular staircase. Charles
        Edward Eaton. 236
The staked woman. Clayton
    Eshleman. 240
A stalled spring. Ralph J., Jr.
    Mills. 321
Stalling for time. Harry Humes.
    278
Stamp madonna. Lyn Lifshin. 303
"Stamping/considered...". Madison
    Morrison. 327
Standing close to greatness.
    Miller Williams. 399
"Standing in a hole." Michael
    Robert Pick. 345
Standing in Barr creek. David
    Wagoner. 390
Standing under the mystery. Mary
    Gilliland. 257
Stanford University
    My fellow at Stanford think
        tank. Tefke Goldberger. 262
    View from the hill. Tefke
        Goldberger. 262
Stanley the Archer. Andrei
    Codrescu. 223
Stanzas. Edgar Allan Poe. 347
Stanzas. Robert Kelly. 289
Stanzas (to F.S.O.). Edgar Allan
    Poe. 347
"Star light, star bright." Jan
    Ormerod. 338
Star of life. Maurice W. Britts.
    215
The star of my destiny. Jacques
    Sollov. 371
Star storm. Alice Spohn Newton.
    333
Star-eyed boy. James R. Rhodes.
    352
The star-splitter. Robert Frost.

    250
Star? Of what? Harlan Usher. 386
Starlight. William Oandasan. 335
Stars
    Al Aaraaf. Edgar Allan Poe. 347
    Definition. Josephine Miles. 319
    Evening star. Edgar Allan Poe.
        347
    Figure. Josephine Miles. 319
    Nothing falls down. Rachel A.
        Hazen. 271
    Patterns in the sky. Jeanne
        Lohmann. 305
    The satin star. Rachel A. Hazen.
        271
    Star storm. Alice Spohn Newton.
        333
    The star-splitter. Robert Frost.
        250
    "The stars." Sally Love
        Saunders. 358
    "We are all made of star stuff."
        Connie Hunt. 279
"The stars.". Sally Love
    Saunders. 358
Startalk in the Greek
    luncheonette. Colette Inez.
    280
Starting. George Eklund. 238
The starting point of we. Norman
    Andrew Kirk. 293
Starting the hostilities. Edwin
    Honig. 275
Starting up. Rod McKuen. 316
State of Maine. Robert A. Sears.
    362
State of the economy. Mark Vinz.
    387
State of women. Richard Blessing.
    208
Stateside. Gary Margolis. 311
A static population, dynamic
    civilization. Phillips Kloss.
    294
The station. James Applewhite.
    198
Statues
    Three apparitions. Carol Frost.
        249
The status of the monk. Andrei
    Codrescu. 223
Statute. Josephine Miles. 319
Staying. Susan Tichy. 381
Steadying the lanscape. Jeanne
    Lohmann. 305
The steamer trunk. James Torio.
    281
Steel blurs. Sally Love Saunders.
    358
Steele, Timothy

An aubade. 374
Coming now. 374
In the king's rooms. 374
Near Olympic. 374
Old letters. 374
The question of identity. 374
The sheets. 374
The shortcut. 374
Summer. 374
Toward Calgary. 374
Waiting for the storm. 374
Steer strait. Marie Daerr
    Boehringer. 210
Stein, Gertrude
    Portrait of a lady. Ernest
    Hemingway. 272
Stems. Robert Gibb. 253
The **stepchild.** Sam Fishman. 246
Stephen the Great. Keith Wilson.
    400
Stephen the Great, Prince of
    Moldova
    Stephen the Great. Keith Wilson.
    400
Stephen's monkey. Wanda Coleman.
    225
"Stepping over stepping stones,
    one, two, three." Jan Ormerod.
    338
Stepping-stone. Alice Joyce
    Davidson. 227
Steps. Maurice Kenny. 291
Steps
    The green step. Kenneth Koch.
    297
The **steps** : mother once in the
    '40's. Sandra McPherson. 317
Steps taken in a debris of day
    lilies. Charles Edward Eaton.
    236
Sterling Mountain. Stephen Sandy.
    357
Stern warning. Margaret Key
    Biggs. 205
Steubenville, Ohio
    Steubenville: "Home of quality
    flat-rolled products." Mary
    Gilliland. 257
Steubenville: "Home of quality
    flat-rolled products." Mary
    Gilliland. 257
Stevens song. Charles Olson. 337
Stevens, Wallace
    Wallace Stevens at ease with
    marble cake. James Schevill.
    360
Stevens, Wallace (about)
    If I could be like Wallace
    Stevens. William Stafford. 373
Stevenson. Ernest Hemingway. 272

Stevenson and James at
    Skerryvore. Donald Revell. 351
Stevenson, Robert Louis
    Stevenson. Ernest Hemingway. 272
    Stevenson and James at
    Skerryvore. Donald Revell. 351
Stiffening, in the Master
    Founders' wills. Charles
    Olson. 337
"Still early morning,the wind's
    edge." Josephine Miles. 319
Still I hear the silence. Alice
    Spohn Newton. 332
Still lives. Albert Goldbarth.
    261
Still waters. James R. Rhodes.
    352
Still waters. Marge Piercy. 346
A **still.** Andrei Codrescu. 223
Stillness. Connie Hunt. 279
Stillness around me. Rachel A.
    Hazen. 271
Stock report. Andrei Codrescu.
    223
Stock, Susan
    Early morning through the door.
    375
    For Stan Getz. 375
    It goes like this. 375
    'It is for me to know what I
    fear.' 375
    Jay. 375
    Jolly sane. 375
    Lone girl at the bus stop. 375
    The machine stop. 375
    Mary. 375
    Mindy. 375
    "My heart hastens." 375
    My similar eyes. 375
    Papa. 375
    Pete. 375
    Poem to a friend. 375
    Portrait of a juvenile
    delinquent. 375
    Predators from a branch of the
    blackthorned sloe. 375
    Rock. 375
    Sleep. 375
    To a you. 375
    Voice. 375
    The yum-yum song. 375
Stockbrokers (satire)
    Little Jack. Harlan Usher. 386
    Lulla - "Buy!"...'Bye!' Harlan
    Usher. 386
Stocks and Bonds
    Market report on cotton gray
    goods. Josephine Miles. 319
Stoloff, Carolyn
    The archaeologist. 376

Arrival at St. George. 376
As the hand goes. 376
As though I didn't know. 376
At night in the high mountains.
    376
At the Woodstock cemetery. 376
Attempting to make lyrics of my
    lovers. 376
Augusta at the shore. 376
Augusta berates a wayward moon.
    376
Augusta discusses carrots, their
    meaning and use. 376
Augusta discusses some of her
    best known roles. 376
Augusta receives a communication
    concerning a bill. 376
Augusta speaks about the first
    manifestation of the dead...
    376
Augusta summons Easter. 376
Augusta tells how she chose a
    profession. 376
Augusta tells the milkman. 376
Augusta thinks through a
    definition. 376
Augusta's 'Think-positive' song.
    376
Augusta's confrontation with her
    landlady. 376
Augusta's little nose song. 376
Augusta's morning meditation.
    376
The austere place. 376
Bearing it. 376
"Because a sailor's pockets."
    376
Behind the starched light. 376
Bermuda notebook. 376
Beyond the parallel lines. 376
Black shoes. 376
The bureau. 376
A cat screams. 376
Chair. 376
Concerning the idea of vase. 376
Delphi. 376
A difficult demand. 376
Dinner time. 376
Doors and keys. 376
"Drawers open and winter
    escapes." 376
Dying of it. 376
"Evening, wedged in the door
    like a grand piano..." 376
Every apartment faces a
    pentagon. 376
Exercise: to hope to invite to
    continue. 376
For an electric man. 376
"A fox and a girl meet among

stars." 376
From a snapshot of the poet. 376
From this ledge. 376
"Garbo's knees are gateposts to
    violets and chateaux." 376
He's packing I hear. 376
Her chronicle. 376
Her mornings and evenings. 376
Her yellow roses. 376
"Hours knock in the wrists of
    gypsies." 376
How can a child hope along
    avenues. 376
I see three fish in the bowl of
    water. 376
I will not go to Mikonos. 376
If he bucks. 376
In the blind. 376
In the Chinese death house. 376
"In the half light summits
    rise." 376
In the red meadow, sels. 376
In transit. 376
Intersection. 376
Is this the place? 376
Last summer's bones. 376
Leaning. 376
"Leaves sail in the shadow of a
    pond." 376
Let's smash. 376
The lifeline. 376
"Light pecks the lilacs..." 376
List. 376
"Locusts older than alphabets."
    376
Looking for buttons. 376
Looking through trees into
    holes. 376
Love me or not. 376
Martinete. 376
Morning come. 376
My mother. 376
My pole. 376
No sitting duck. 376
Notes on an early room. 376
Nothing like a razor. 376
Odyssey of the hair. 376
On the train. 376
Opposites. 376
Outside Avila's walls. 376
"Over a forest of coffins
    morning rings." 376
Past closing time. 376
Pictures. 376
The plant on my table had seven
    leaves. 376
Poet in town. 376
The potter. 376
The reading. 376
Report on the times. 376

"Roads slide across towers." 376
Self=exiled. 376
September night. 376
"Settling on tongues, owls close
    their claws." 376
The shaman. 376
Shopping for shoes. 376
Short subjects. 376
Sister of the rocks. 376
So I lie. 376
Sound arithmetic. 376
"Stone tears loosen, they gallop
    into the canyon." 376
The story-maker and her husband.
    376
Summer rental. 376
Sunday. 376
"Teeth break against clouds."
    376
This Spain. 376
Through infinite points. 376
Through the arch. 376
To the north. 376
Today. 376
The turning. 376
Twilight. 376
Under the flame tree. 376
Under the sun. 376
View of Hydra, Greece. 376
Walking through Naples. 376
We will walk by the trail. 376
The weaver. 376
"When crumbs from light's black
    bread sink in the water." 376
When lonely. 376
Whose was it. 376
Why the question of
    reincarnation doesn't concern
    me. 376
"Will the poems take off their
    garments." 376
Wind and earth. 376
Wool-gathering. 376
"Wounds sing in the red meadow."
    376
Years after. 376
Stompin'.. Norman Andrew Kirk.
    293
A stone and I. Evelyn Golden. 263
The stone of all souls. Mitchell
    Howard. 276
The stone orchard. Joyce Carol
    Oates. 336
Stone roses. Keith Wilson. 400
"Stone tears loosen, they gallop
    into the canyon." Carolyn
    Stoloff. 376
A stone wall in Providence.
    Robert Kelly. 289
The stone, fr. The green step.

Kenneth Koch. 297
Stone, paper, knife. Marge
    Piercy. 346
Stoned by the Lord. Mitchell
    Howard. 276
Stones. See Rocks

Stopped for a beer in Charleston,
    West Virginia. George Eklund.
    238
Stopping places. Joan Colby. 224
Stores. See Shops and Shopping

Stories
    The story. Robert Kelly. 289
    This story, fr. The green step.
        Kenneth Koch. 297
    Two kinds of story-telling. John
        Yau. 404
Stories of three summers. Thomas
    Hornsby Ferril. 243
Storm. Robert Pawlowski. 341
Storm clouds. Wanda Coleman. 225
A storm of sand. Judson Crews.
    226
Storm-felled tree at Eagle
    Bridge. Stephen Sandy. 357
The storm. Debra Bruce. 216
The storm. Erin Jolly. 285
Storms
    Animals in groups. Barry
        Wallenstein. 393
    The fury of a midwestern
        thunderstorm. James Schevill.
        360
    History. Thomas McGrath. 315
    Ice storm remembered. Paul
        Davis. 228
    Island storm. Edwin Honig. 275
    "The sea's/boiling..." Charles
        Olson. 337
    Snow. Robert Frost. 250
    Storm. Robert Pawlowski. 341
    The storm. Erin Jolly. 285
    Waiting for the storm. Timothy
        Steele. 374
A story as wet as tears. Marge
    Piercy. 346
"A story of success and." Madison
    Morrison. 327
The story of what happens.
    Mitchell Howard. 276
The story-maker and her husband.
    Carolyn Stoloff. 376
A story of a memory and his man.
    Miller Williams. 399
The story. Miller Williams. 399
The story. Robert Kelly. 289
The storyteller. David Wagoner.
    390

Storyville, New Orleans
    Storyville, the painted, the
        pure. Norman Andrew Kirk. 293
Storyville, the painted, the
    pure. Norman Andrew Kirk. 293
Strada Petru Gorza 45. Keith
    Wilson. 400
Strain. Roy Marz. 312
Stranded. Marieve Rugo. 356
Strange duality. Evelyn Golden.
    263
Strange lady. Maurice W. Britts
    215
Strange move. Alice Spohn Newton.
    333
Strange tongues, other languages.
    Joan Colby. 224
Strange vision after divorce.
    Gene Anderson. 195
Strange woman. Alice Spohn
    Newton. 333
Stranger. Gayl Jones. 286
Stranger in the night. Robert L.
    Wilson. 401
This stranger. Iefke Goldberger.
    262
Strangers in a photograph.
    Everett A. Gillis. 258
Straw
    Stacking the straw. Amy
        Clampitt. 222
Straw flowers. Keith Wilson. 400
Strawberries
    Looking up and beyond. William
        Oandasan. 335
Stray animals. Cathy Song. 372
Streams. See Brooks and Streams

Street. Josephine Miles. 319
The street cleaner. Erin Jolly.
    285
Street corner signals. James
    Schevill. 360
Street dance. Robert Pawlowski.
    341
Streetlight: the wedding
    photograph. Anthony Petrosky.
    344
Streets. See Roads and Trails

"Strength feels/babies..." Larry
    Eigner. 237
Stripper madonna. Lyn Lifshin.
    303
Striptease
    Backwards stripping madonna. Lyn
        Lifshin. 303
    Jealousy. Lyn Lifshin. 303
    Stripper madonna. Lyn Lifshin.
        303

"Strod the water's edge..."
    Charles Olson. 337
Stroke. Josephine Miles. 319
Strolling on the giant woman.
    Mary Gilliland. 257
Struggle. Martha Janssen. 283
Struggle at the sanctum. Rose
    Basile Green. 265
Stryk, Lucien
    Cherries. 377
    The city: a cycle. 377
    Classroom. 377
    Dawn. 377
    Dirge. 377
    Elm. 377
    Exterminator. 377
    The great exception. 377
    Grief. 377
    I.M. Eugenio Montale. 377
    In our time. 377
    Juggler. 377
    Machines. 377
    Nomads. 377
    November. 377
    Old folks home. 377
    Savants. 377
    Siberia. 377
    Soul. 377
    Waking up in Streator. 377
    Watching war movies. 377
    Where we are. 377
    Willows. 377
    The word. 377
    You must change your life. 377
Stud-farms of cooked shadows.
    Clayton Eshleman. 240
Student. Josephine Miles. 319
A student of tragedy. Norman
    Andrew Kirk. 293
Studies from life. Robin Becker.
    202
Study. Josephine Miles. 319
Studying the light. Harry Humes.
    278
Stumbling out of the Prado. Edwin
    Honig. 275
Stump speech. David Wagoner. 390
Subdivision. Josephine Miles. 319
Subject. Josephine Miles. 319
Submarines
    The death of a submarine.
        Jocelyn Hollis. 274
The substitute bassist. C.D.
    Wright. 402
Subtraction. Richard Blessing.
    208
Suburban rebellions. Mitchell
    Howard. 276
Suburbs
    Suburban rebellions. Mitchell

Howard. 276
Subways
The city is a battery. Barry
Wallenstein. 393
In a station of the Metro. Ezra
Pound. 235
New York subway rush hour. James
Schevill. 360
Song of the retired senior
citizen. Sam Fishman. 246
Times Square water music. Amy
Clampitt. 222
Success. James R. Rhodes. 352
Success
The bird. Greg Kuzma. 300
High school reunion. James
Magorian. 308
Mines, explosions. Josephine
Miles. 319
Nobody cares. Maurice W. Britts.
215
Potential. Connie Hunt. 279
Psalm of success. Ernesto
Galarza. 252
"A story of success and."
Madison Morrison. 327
Success. James R. Rhodes. 352
To the future. Gerard Malanga.
310
Such an alliance. Robin Becker.
202
Such sweet sorrow. Royal Murdoch.
330
Sudden death overtime. Ray
Fleming. 247
Sudden departure. Bill Knott. 296
Sudden thaw. Anneliese Wagner.
389
"Suddenly out of the hedge."
Edwin Honig. 275
Sue Hilton's dog. Josephine B.
Moretti. 324
Suffering does not ennoble. Haig
Khatchadourian. 292
Suicide. Robert Pawlowski. 341
Suicide
Albert. Robert Peters. 343
Billy "balloon" Laura Boss. 213
Broke up. Wanda Coleman. 225
The dancer. Jeanne Lohmann. 305
Dreams are not in season. Robert
Pawlowski. 341
Drowing horses. Joy Harjo. 269
The embrace. Marc Kaminsky. 288
For Heidi. Robert Pawlowski. 341
"The hotel room." Madison
Morrison. 327
Reconstruction. Deborah Tall.
378
Suicide. Robert Pawlowski. 341

The suicide. Deborah Tall. 378
The suicide. Joyce Carol Oates.
336
The suicide runner. James
Schevill. 360
The suicide. Deborah Tall. 378
The suicide. Joyce Carol Oates.
336
Suit of lights. Charles Edward
Eaton. 236
"The suitors do the." Madison
Morrison. 327
Sullivan, George
Three moments for George
Sullivan. Edwin Honig. 275
The sum of its parts. Miller
Williams. 399
The sumac in Ohio. James Wright.
403
Summer. Josephine Miles. 319
Summer. Timothy Steele. 374
Summer
Among wild oats. Ernesto
Galarza. 252
Balloon sleeves and velvet, the
century turned. Colette Inez.
280
Behind: the summer. Anne Bailie.
199
Convinced. Marie Daerr
Boehringer. 210
English summer. Paul Davis. 228
Fever in August. Joan Colby. 224
Liberty Avenue. Anthony
Petrosky. 344
A little life in a summer room.
George Eklund. 238
The non sequiturs of summer.
Charles Edward Eaton. 236
North summer. Maurice Kenny. 291
The question of personnel.
Andrei Codrescu. 223
Sonata. Rod McKuen. 316
Summer. Timothy Steele. 374
The summer Bruce died. Eileen
Silver-Lillywite. 364
Summer idylls. Franz Schneider.
361
Summer meadows. Keith Wilson.
400
Summer nights. Ralph J., Jr.
Mills. 321
Summer rental. Carolyn Stoloff.
376
Summer song. Cynthia Grenfell.
266
Sweet summer of our years.
Everett A. Gillis. 258
Theriot cove. Donald Revell. 351
Victory. Marie Daerr Boehringer.

210

The **summer** Bruce died. Eileen Silver-Lillywite. 364

Summer games. Rod McKuen. 316

Summer idylls. Franz Schneider. 361

Summer insomnia. Franz Schneider. 361

The **summer** kitchen. Sandra Gilbert. 255

Summer litany. Robert Peters. 343

Summer lullaby. Robert L. Wilson. 401

Summer marathon. Paul Davis. 228

Summer marriage. Keith Wilson. 400

Summer meadows. Keith Wilson. 400

Summer mountains. Stephen Sandy. 357

Summer news. James L. White. 396

Summer night. James Tate. 379

Summer nights. Ralph J., Jr. Mills. 321

Summer rental. Carolyn Stoloff. 376

Summer sequence. Rod McKuen. 316

Summer shower. Sally Love Saunders. 358

Summer song. Cynthia Grenfell. 266

Summer storm: Alpe di San Benedetto. Franz Schneider. 361

Summer sun. Robert L. Wilson. 401

Summer was ending. James Applewhite. 198

Summer, Aeneas Valley. Marc Hudson. 277

Summer: small town. Marie Daerr Boehringer. 210

Summertree sketch. Rochelle DuBois. 234

Summit meeting in the spring. May Miller. 320

Sumptuous siesta. Charles Edward Eaton. 236

Sun
   Eight minutes from the sun. Colette Inez. 280
   Feeding the sun. Bill Knott. 296
   Summer sun. Robert L. Wilson. 401
   "The sun spilling everywhere." Sally Love Saunders. 358
   "Sun/right in my eye." Charles Olson. 337
   Sunsong. Colette Inez. 280
   Tie dye. Gerard Malanga. 310
   Under the sun. Carolyn Stoloff. 376

Sun and amiable air. Eve Triem. 383

"The **sun** solid." Larry Eigner. 237

"The **sun** spilling everywhere." Sally Love Saunders. 358

The **sun** underfoot among the sundews. Amy Clampitt. 222

Sun watcher. Phillips Kloss. 294

(**Sun**, sea, rain)(rain season)(Port Townsend, Washington). Bill Knott. 296

Sun-truths. Joyce Carol Oates. 336

"**Sun/right** in my eye." Charles Olson. 337

"**Sun/upside** down." Charles Olson. 337

Sunbeam. Alice Joyce Davidson. 227

Sunday. George Eklund. 238

Sunday. Carolyn Stoloff. 376

Sunday. Greg Kuzma. 300

Sunday
   Near the underground railroad. Dave Smith. 367
   Sunday. George Eklund. 238
   Sunday snow. James L. White. 396

Sunday afternoon. James Torio. 281

Sunday lunch at grandpa's. Phyllis A. Tickle. 382

Sunday morning sandlot football. J.W. Rivers. 354

Sunday morning: Celia's father. Dave Smith. 367

Sunday morning:migrant labor camp. Sister Maura. 313

Sunday music. Amy Clampitt. 222

Sunday picnic: Veteran's anniversary day. Ruth Lisa Schechter. 359

Sunday School
   Young man on a Sunday. Robert Peters. 343

Sunday sermon. Andrei Codrescu. 223

Sunday snow. James L. White. 396

Sunday, January 16, 1966. Charles Olson. 337

Sunday. See also Sabbath

Sundews
   The sun underfoot among the sundews. Amy Clampitt. 222

Sundown song. Randy Blasing. 207

Sundowner. Richard Blessing. 208

Sunflower. Stephen Todd Booker. 212

The **sungod** Huitzilopochtli.

Phillips Kloss. 294
Sunrise - moonset. Jacques
   Sollov. 370
Sunset
   Fairfield Harbor at New Bern,
      N.S. August 22, 1982. Rochelle
      DuBois. 234
   Sunday, January 16, 1966.
      Charles Olson. 337
   Sunset and stars. Maurice W.
      Britts. 215
   Sunset on mission bay. Ray
      Fleming. 247
Sunset and stars. Maurice W.
   Britts. 215
Sunset on mission bay. Ray
   Fleming. 247
Sunsong. Colette Inez. 280
Superstition
   Seeing it. Sharon Bryan. 217
Supreme knowledge. Jacques
   Sollov. 370
Supreme power. Alice Joyce
   Davidson. 227
Suprise atonement. James
   Magorian. 309
Suprised by a flock of Canada
   geese... Robert Gibb. 253
The **surf** of joy pounding. Marge
   Piercy. 346
Surfacing. Gary Margolis. 311
Surgery. Joan Colby. 224
Surgery
   The operation. W.D. (William De
      Witt) Snodgrass. 369
   The wasp. Joyce Carol Oates. 336
Surprise party. Mitchell Howard.
   276
Surprise! Surprise! Alice Spohn
   Newton. 333
Surrender. Marc Kaminsky. 288
Surrender
   The art of surrender. David
      Wagoner. 390
   Poems of submission. James L.
      White. 396
The **surrender** of a skunk. Alice
   Spohn Newton. 333
Survival. Ernest Tedlock. 380
Survival. Martha Janssen. 283
Survival
   After the war (IV). John Yau.
      404
   "Among a hundred mirrors."
      Michael Robert Pick. 345
   The British in Africa. Albert
      Goldbarth. 261
   Contraband. James Torio. 281
   A doctor of the soul. Iefke
      Goldberger. 262

Hagiography. Jim Simmerman. 365
   I will survive. Maurice W.
      Britts. 215
   In a 3-way mirror. Ruth Lisa
      Schechter. 359
   Inflammable abodes. Joan Colby.
      224
   The kill. Clayton Eshleman. 240
   Phoenix. Tom Smith. 368
   Poem to heal David. Mary
      Gilliland. 257
   Struggle. Martha Janssen. 283
   Survival. Martha Janssen. 283
   Survival blue. Maurice W.
      Britts. 215
   Survivors. Paul Davis. 228
   Thinking of Darwin. Herbert
      Morris. 326
   Volcano. Martha Janssen. 283
   A votive offering. Richmond
      Lattimore. 301
   When January slipped away.
      Robert L. Wilson. 401
   Yellow flowers. William
      Stafford. 373
Survival blue. Maurice W. Britts.
   215
Survival manual. Mark Vinz. 387
Survivals, sels. Edwin Honig. 275
Surviving the jungle. Marieve
   Rugo. 356
Surviving the wreck. Betty
   Adcock. 192
Survivor. William Stafford. 373
Survivor, walking. Stephen Sandy.
   357
Survivors. Scott Chisholm. 221
Survivors. Paul Davis. 228
Sutter, John August
   At Sutter's grave: Lititz, PA.
      Robert Gibb. 253
Swallows
   The Belfast swallows. Roy Marz.
      312
   Our two birds. Roy Marz. 312
Swan. Wanda Coleman. 225
The **swan** story. Betty Adcock. 192
Swans
   Wild swan singing. Elsa Gidlow.
      254
Swarming into autumn. Eileen
   Silver-Lillywite. 364
Swastikas
   Maximus, to himself, as of
      "Phoenicians." Charles Olson.
      337
Swearing. Kirk Lumpkin. 306
Sweat, and reflections at the
   symphony. Paul Davis. 228
Sweatshops

Noon. John Reed. 350
Sweeping the room. Edwin Honig.
    275
Sweet Mama Wanda tells fortunes
    for a price (2). Wanda
    Coleman. 225
Sweet memories. Alice Joyce
    Davidson. 227
"Sweet salmon." Charles Olson.
    337
Sweet singing blues. Everett A.
    Gillis. 258
Sweet summer of our years.
    Everett A. Gillis. 258
"The sweetness of breath."
    Michael Robert Pick. 345
A swell idea. Steve Kowit. 299
Swift current. Cathryn Hankla.
    268
"A swift current." Sally Love
    Saunders. 358
The swim. Jenne Andrews. 196
A swimmer in the sea. Sam
    Fishman. 246
Swimming and Swimmers
    A broken lake. James Applewhite.
    198
    Dream of the long distance
    swimmer. Ruth Lisa Schechter.
    359
    For Bonnie, my swim teacher.
    Anneliese Wagner. 389
    "I was bold, I had courage, the
    tide tonight." Charles Olson.
    337
    "In the public/bath..." Madison
    Morrison. 327
    "My mother swimming." Sally Love
    Saunders. 358
    "Nothing much left." Edwin
    Honig. 275
    Return to the light. Richmond
    Lattimore. 301
    Rosecap. Colette Inez. 280
    Still waters. Marge Piercy. 346
"Swimming through the air..."
    Charles Olson. 337
The swinging door. Erin Jolly.
    285
"Swirling tinsel veils." Rokwaho.
    355
Switchboard operator fond of
    using analogies to make...
    James Magorian. 309
The sword dance. John Reed. 350
Swords
    Excalibur. Robert Kelly. 289
    The sword dance. John Reed. 350
Sydney, Australia
    Spencer's mountains. Rod McKuen.

316
Symbiosis. Gene Anderson. 195
Symbiosis. Connie Hunt. 279
Symbols
    Discoveries mid-letter. Sandra
    McPherson. 317
Symmetry. Andrei Codrescu. 223
Sympathetic fallacy. John
    Godfrey. 260
The sympathizers. Josephine
    Miles. 319
Sympathy
    Center piece. Andrei Codrescu.
    223
    "The pains of life and love."
    Theta Burke. 218
Syphilis prior to penicillin.
    James L. White. 396
Syrenyu, sels. William Oandasan.
    335

The T-shirt phenomenon in
    Minnesota on the Fourth of
    July. James Schevill. 360
"Ta meteura/meteor things"
    Charles Olson. 337
Table Cloths
    Crocheted table cloth. James
    Magorian. 309
Table manners. James Magorian.
    309
Table song. Cornel Lengyel. 302
A table with people. Marc
    Kaminsky. 288
The table. Jacqueline Frank. 248
Tableau in a Lutheran church.
    Robert Peters. 343
Tachycardiac seizure. Joyce Carol
    Oates. 336
The tackle, fr. Athletic verse.
    Ernest Hemingway. 272
Take it in your hands. Anneliese
    Wagner. 389
"Take the earth in under a single
    review." Charles Olson. 337
"Take the stillness with you."
    Connie Hunt. 279
Taken to a room. James L. White.
    396
Takeoff. Deborah Tall. 378
Taking off. Barry Wallenstein.
    393
Taking off. William Oandasan. 335
Taking the train to grandpa's.
    Alice Spohn Newton. 333
Talent. Rosa Bogar. 211
Tales from the father of history.

Richmond Lattimore. 301
Tales of Hoffmann. Richmond
    Lattimore. 301
Talismanic ceremony for Lucian,
    March 9, 1971... Andrei
    Codrescu. 223
Talk show. Mark Vinz. 387
Talk to me. Rachel A. Hazen. 271
Talk. See Conversation
                . .
Talking from Inverness. Susan
    Tichy. 381
Talking to Fernando. Irving
    Feldman. 242
Talking with my brother, who came
    to visit. George Eklund. 238
Talking with my wife. Anthony
    Petrosky. 344
"Tall is the fort." Charles
    Olson. 337
The tall Toms. Edwin Honig. 275
Tall trees by still waters. James
    Tate. 379
Tall, Deborah
    Anima. 378
    Anniversary. 378
    Another view. 378
    Bishop's rock. 378
    Crossing. 378
    Dawn, ruins on Lake Inchiquin.
        378
    Day of judgment. 378
    December field. 378
    Deirdre of the sorrows. 378
    A dream of heaven. 378
    Evidence. 378
    The exit. 378
    Grainne. 378
    Initiation. 378
    Landscape with ascet ic. 378
    The little mermaid. 378
    Making hay. 378
    Manhunt. 378
    Memorabilla. 378
    Mooring. 378
    Natural selection. 378
    Our garden. 378
    Reconstruction. 378
    Scheherezade. 378
    Sectarian murder victim. 378
    The suicide. 378
    Takeoff. 378
    Three anecdotes. 378
    The top of a mountain. 378
    The town of the summer palace.
        378
    Vigil. 378
    Wishes. 378
    Yearning. 378
Tally. Josephine Miles. 319

Tamalpais, Mount
    "Looking over toward Tamalpais."
        Josephine Miles. 319
Tamburlaine. John Reed. 350
Tamerlane. Edgar Allan Poe. 347
Tamerlane (Tamburlaine)
    Tamburlaine. John Reed. 350
    Tamerlane. Edgar Allan Poe. 347
A tangential death. Marge Piercy.
    346
Tangerine dawn. Clayton Eshleman.
    240
Tantara! Tantara! Thomas McGrath.
    315
Tantrik X-ray. Clayton Eshleman.
    240
"Tantrist." Charles Olson. 337
Taos lightning. Phillips Kloss.
    294
Tape recorder. Christopher Bursk.
    219
Tapestries
    Blue tapestry. Ruth Lisa
        Schechter. 359
Tapestry. Patsie Black. 206
Taps. James A. Emanuel. 239
Tarantulas on the lifebuoy.
    Thomas Lux. 307
Tarascan names. Robert A. Sears.
    362
Tarascans
    Tarascan names. Robert A. Sears.
        362
    Tzin-tzun-tzan. Robert A. Sears.
        362
Targets. Roy Marz. 312
Targets. Harry Humes. 278
Tartiglia. Robert A. Sears. 362
Taste and Tasting
    Reasons for living. Debra Bruce.
        216
Tasty triumph. Marie Daerr
    Boehringer. 210
Tate, Allen (about)
    The utter stranger. Thomas R.
        Sleigh. 366
Tate, James
    Blue spill. 379
    Bluebird houses. 379
    Brother's unfinished business.
        379
    Constant defender. 379
    Cook's voyage. 379
    Detective Shoes. 379
    The dream of returning to school
        and facing the oral exam. 379
    Earthworks. 379
    Five years old. 379
    The horseshoe. 379
    If it would all please hurry.

379
Interruptions. 379
It wasn't me. 379
A jangling yarn. 379
Jelka. 379
Land of little sticks, 1945. 379
Lousy in center field. 379
Memo to the dark angel. 379
The mink cemetry. 379
The motorcyclists. 379
Mystic moment. 379
Nausea, coincidence. 379
Nobody's business. 379
Odiumto the dark angel. 379
Old photographs of the author. 379
On the world's birthday. 379
Paint 'til you faint. 379
Poem for the sandman. 379
Poem to some of my recent poems. 379
Red bricks and camphor trees. 379
Some beneficial rays. 379
Spring was begging to be born. 379
Summer night. 379
Tall trees by still waters. 379
Tell them. 379
Tending the sheep at big baas flip. 379
To Fuzzy. 379
Toward Saint Looey. 379
Tragedy's greatest hits. 379
The wild cheese. 379
Yellow newspaper and a wooden leg. 379
Yonder. 379
Taxes
Of hidden taxes. Marge Piercy. 346
Simon. Harlan Usher. 386
Tchaikovsky, Peter Ilyich
Tschaikowsky. John Reed. 350
Teach me, dear sister. Irving Feldman. 242
Teacher. Josephine Miles. 319
Teacher's prayer. Josephine B. Moretti. 324
Teaching and Teachers
Academic fowl. Cornel Lengyel. 302
Alain LeRoy Locke. May Miller. 320
April inventory. W.D. (William De Witt) Snodgrass. 369
Assistant professor of juxtapositions granted tenure... James Magorian. 309
Death of a teacher. James
Schevill. 360
An exercise in futility. David Shapiro. 363
The method. Miriam Goodman. 264
P.S. Norman Andrew Kirk. 293
Paying some slight attention to his birthday... Miller Williams. 399
A poem for my teacher. Sandra McPherson. 317
Preliminary to classroom lecture. Josephine Miles. 319
Professor emeritus. James Magorian. 308
Readers. Josephine Miles. 319
A short history of the teaching profession. Sister Maura. 313
Small college athletic director. James Magorian. 309
Student. Josephine Miles. 319
Teacher. Josephine Miles. 319
Third-grade teacher. Martha Janssen. 283
A valentine for my teacher. Jack Prelutsky. 348
Volunteer English department. James Magorian. 309
What to answer. Sharon Bryan. 217
"A team is a machine." Madison Morrison. 327
Teapots
"I'm a little teapot." Jan Ormerod. 338
Tears. Martha Janssen. 283
The tears of Christ pulled inside out. Clayton Eshleman. 240
Tears of white jade. Kirk Lumpkin. 306
Tears so long. Rachel A. Hazen. 271
Techniques. Martha Janssen. 283
Tedlock, Ernest
Dogs in weather. 380
Dogs of the city. 380
For Bill. 380
The hills at Cambria School. 380
A horse lost. 380
A lost friend. 380
Love and the father. 380
On the warm side. 380
Return to the loss. 380
Survival. 380
To Thomas Hardy. 380
Told by the weather. 380
Yesterday's slaughter. 380
Tee-Pee living. Larry Moffi. 322
Teeth
3/4 time t. Larry Eigner. 237
"Teeth break against clouds."

Carolyn Stoloff. 376
Teethering. Edwin Honig. 275
Tehachapi (mountains), California
   Tehachapi south. Josephine
   Miles. 319
Tehachapi south. Josephine Miles.
   319
The **telephone** mashers. James A.
   Emanuel. 239
Telephones
   I live my life by three minute
   phone calls. Laura Boss. 213
   "It cools the booth." Madison
   Morrison. 327
   Quiet office. Josephine B.
   Moretti. 324
   Switchboard operator fond of
   using analogies to make...
   James Magorian. 309
   The telephone mashers. James A.
   Emanuel. 239
The **telesphere.** Charles Olson.
   337
Television
   Talk show. Mark Vinz. 387
   Triptych. Paul Violi. 388
   Untitled: "Our behavior is
   redundant nonadaptive" Kirk
   Lumpkin. 306
   We interrupt to bring you.
   William Stafford. 373
Television story. Wanda Coleman.
   225
Tell me a rainbow of sacrifice.
   Patsie Black. 206
Tell me a rainbow of celebration.
   Patsie Black. 206
Tell them was here. James Tate.
   379
A **telling.** Jenne Andrews. 196
The **telling.** Sam Fishman. 246
The **tempest.** John Reed. 350
Ten days leave. W.D. (William De
   Witt) Snodgrass. 369
Ten dreamers in a motel.
   Josephine Miles. 319
Ten thousand years. Greg Kuzma.
   300
10:30.   Madison Morrison. 327
10 A.M.   Rochelle DuBois. 234
10:29.   Toi Derricote. 229
Tending the lamp. Scott Chisholm.
   221
Tending the sheep at big baas
   flip. James Tate. 379
Tennis
   "The apron off the." Madison
   Morrison. 327
The **tennis** match. Michael
   Akillian. 193

Tennyson, Alfred Lord = Parody
   The charge of the political
   brigade. John Reed. 350
The **tenor.** Jacques Sollov. 370
A **tentative** welcome to readers.
   William Stafford. 373
Tepoztlan. Amy Clampitt. 222
Tepoztlan, Mexico
   Tepoztlan. Amy Clampitt. 222
Teresa's garden. Cornel Lengyel.
   302
Teresa, Saint. See Theresa

The **term's** end. Anne Bailie. 199
The **terminal** patient to his wife.
   Franz Schneider. 361
Terminal sickness. Anne Bailie.
   199
The **terminal.** James Applewhite.
   198
The **terrace** at Hotel du
   Centenaire. Clayton Eshleman.
   240
Terrestrial. Clayton Eshleman.
   240
Terror hiding in glossy sexy
   magazines. Mitchell Howard.
   276
Terrorism and Terrorists
   The terrorist. James Schevill.
   360
The **terrorist.** James Schevill.
   360
Teshuvah. Jeanne Lohmann. 305
Tessarae. Charles Olson. 337
The **test.** Roy Marz. 312
Testing. testing. Andrei
   Codrescu. 223
Tete-a-tete. Andrei Codrescu. 223
Tete-a-tete. Edwin Honig. 275
Teton Range
   This view of things. Judson
   Crews. 226
Texas
   In Texas we got persimmons.
   Judson Crews. 226
A **textual** recording. Andrei
   Codrescu. 223
Thalassa. Robert A. Sears. 362
"Thank God." Charles Olson. 337
Thank you. Rod McKuen. 316
Thank you. Jacques Sollov. 371
Thank you. Steve Kowit. 299
Thanks giving. Alice Joyce
   Davidson. 227
Thanksgiving. Louise Gluck. 259A
Thanksgiving
   "I am living life full and
   long." Michael Robert Pick.
   345

Prayer No. 2. Rochelle DuBois.
    234
Remember me? Alice Joyce
    Davidson. 227
Showers of blessings. Alice
    Joyce Davidson. 227
"Thank God." Charles Olson. 337
Thanksgiving Day
    Kyle Canyon, Thanksgiving 1978.
        David James. 282
    Targets. Harry Humes. 278
    Wild celebration. Robert L.
        Wilson. 401
That boy, in winter or rain.
    George Eklund. 238
That family. Robert Peters. 343
That idea of visiting places in
    dreams. Cathryn Hankla. 268
"That island/floating in the
    sea." Charles Olson. 337
That moment. David Wagoner. 390
"That there was a woman in
    Gloucester..." Charles Olson.
    337
That which is. James Applewhite.
    198
"That's all figures." Larry
    Eigner. 237
That's Karl, my husband. Phillips
    Kloss. 294
"That's/the combination of the
    ocean." Charles Olson. 337
Their bodies. David Wagoner. 390
Their fire. David Wagoner. 390
Their shelter. David Wagoner. 390
Them capybaras of alabac. Stephen
    Todd Booker. 212
Theme. Rose Basile Green. 265
Then. Robert Kelly. 289
Then the children came. Judson
    Crews. 226
A theory of wind. Albert
    Goldbarth. 261
Thera, Greece
    Santorini: stopping the leak.
        James Merrill. 318
Therapeutic. Robert L. Wilson.
    401
Therapist. Martha Janssen. 283
Therapy for Esterhazy in the
    temple of Asklepios. J.W.
    Rivers. 354
There are northern lakes... Joyce
    Carol Oates. 336
"There are twice as." Madison
    Morrison. 327
"There are two ways." Da Free
    John. 284
"There is a force of loneliness
    around my heart." Da Free

John. 284
There is a kingdom. Jacques
    Sollov. 370
"There is a legend about a
    piano..." Albert Goldbarth.
    261
There is an orange happening.
    Norman Andrew Kirk. 293
"There is an orange rotting on
    the table." Andrei Codrescu.
    223
There is blindness. William
    Stafford. 373
"There is no community." Larry
    Eigner. 237
"There is no question." Joan
    Walsh Anglund. 197
"There was a cold pig from North
    Stowe." Arnold Lobel.
"There was a fair pig from
    Cohoes" Arnold Lobel. 304
"There was a fast pig from East
    Flushing." Arnold Lobel. 304
"There was a fat pig from
    Savannah." Arnold Lobel. 304
"There was a light pig from
    Montclair." Arnold Lobel. 304
There was a loud pig. Arnold
    Lobel. 304
"There was a pale pig from
    Spokane." Arnold Lobel. 304
"There was a plain pig, far from
    pretty," Arnold Lobel. 304
There was a poor pig. Arnold
    Lobel. 304
There was a rich pig. Arnold
    Lobel. 304
"There was a rude pig from
    Duluth." Arnold Lobel. 304
"There was a sad pig with a
    tail." Arnold Lobel. 304
There was a salt-works at Stage
    Fort. Charles Olson. 337
"There was a shy pig by a wall."
    Arnold Lobel. 304
"There was a sick pig with a
    cold." Arnold Lobel. 304
"There was a slow pig from
    Decatur." Arnold Lobel. 304
"There was a small pig who wept
    tears." Arnold Lobel. 304
"There was a small pig from
    Woonsocket." Arnold Lobel. 304
"There was a smart pig who was
    able." Arnold Lobel. 304
"There was a stout pig from Oak
    Ridge." Arnold Lobel. 304
"There was a strange pig in the
    park." Arnold Lobel. 304
"There was a tough pig from Pine

Bluff." Arnold Lobel. 304

"There was a warm pig from Key West." Arnold Lobel. 304

"There was a wet pig from Fort Wayne." Arnold Lobel. 304

"There was a young pig from Schenectady." Arnold Lobel. 304

"There was a young pig from Chanute." Arnold Lobel. 304

"There was a young pig who, in bed," Arnold Lobel. 304

"There was a young pig by a cradle." Arnold Lobel. 304

"There was a young pig from Moline." Arnold Lobel. 304

"There was a young pig whose delight." Arnold Lobel. 304

"There was a young pig from Nantucket." Arnold Lobel. 304

"There was an old pig from West Wheeling." Arnold Lobel. 304

"There was an old pig with a clock." Arnold Lobel. 304

"There was an old pig from New York." Arnold Lobel. 304

"There was an old pig in a chair." Arnold Lobel. 304

"There was an old pig with a pen." Arnold Lobel. 304

There was an old pig. Arnold Lobel.

"There was another world." A. Dovichi. 233

"There was Ike and Tony and Jacque and me." Ernest Hemingway. 272

"There was this deer standing." Rocnelle DuBois. 234

There were estuaries. Jenne Andrews. 196

There were other places. Judson Crews. 226

There would be large cuttings of flowers. Edwin Honig. 275

"There'll be times in life." Michael Robert Pick. 345

"There's a certain button." Sally Love Saunders. 358

"There's a lonely part," Theta Burke. 218

There's a train. Eileen Silver-Lillywite. 364

"There's movies." Larry Eigner. 237

"There's no such thing as/identical!" Larry Eigner. 237

There's someone I know. Jack Prelutsky. 348

There's this man, see... Harlan Usher. 386

"There's to be." Madison Morrison. 327

Theresa of Avila, Saint
The life on film of St. Theresa. Andrei Codrescu. 223

Theriot cove. Donald Revell. 351

"These are alternating." Madison Morrison. 327

These are lives. Herbert Morris. 326

"These are not." Madison Morrison. 327

"These bricks, moss-covered now." Robert A. Sears. 362

These faces I see. James R. Rhodes. 352

These many loves. Alice Spohn Newton. 332

"These old houses." Madison Morrison. 327

These people sat right out my window too. Charles Olson. 337

"These public halls." Madison Morrison. 327

"These stairways." Madison Morrison. 327

"These stones if they spoke." Edwin Honig. 275

These three. Ruth Lisa Schechter. 359

"These trees stand very tall under the heavens." W.D. (William De Witt) Snodgrass. 369

Theseus. Maria Gillan. 256

They. Irving Feldman. 242

They all made peace - what is peace? Ernest Hemingway. 272

They are looking for Che Guevara. Steve Kowit. 299

"They brawled in the streets..." Charles Olson. 337

They call them 'The Starlings.' Paul Violi. 388

They drove them out. Judson Crews. 226

They say. William Stafford. 373

They tell me I am lost. Maurice Kenny. 291

They used to have a homecoming day. Richmond Lattimore. 301

They will remember. Rose Basile Green. 265

Thin snow. David Shapiro. 363

The thing king. Charles Edward Eaton. 236

A thing like stone. Jacqueline Frank. 248

Things I learned last week.
    William Stafford. 373
"Things more or less" Larry
    Eigner. 237
Things that come. William
    Stafford. 373
Things to know. Gerard Malanga.
    310
Things you should know. Paul
    Violi. 388
Think of it: the river. Maria
    Gillan. 256
Thinking. Aileen Fisher. 244
Thinking of Darwin. Herbert
    Morris. 326
Thinking of her. Sam Fishman. 246
Third day of the baseball
    playoffs. Mitchell Howard. 276
The third thaw. Mary Gilliland.
    257
Third variation on Corpse and
    mirror. John Yau. 404
Third-grade teacher. Martha
    Janssen. 283
3rd letter on Georges, unwritten.
    Charles Olson. 337
Thirst. Marilyn Kallet. 287
Thirteen. Martha Janssen. 283
Thirteen lines. Jacqueline Frank.
    248
13 vessels, and David Pearce's.
    Charles Olson. 337
Thirty-six. Martha Janssen. 283
The thirty-six master poets.
    James Torio. 281
This and that. James Wright. 403
This chill air. Stephen Sandy.
    357
"This day/is almost done." A.
    Dovichi. 233
This dream. Marilyn Kallet. 287
This hill. Marie Daerr
    Boehringer. 210
"This is the dark." Madison
    Morrison. 327
This is the day. Alice Joyce
    Davidson. 227
"This is the toughest." Madison
    Morrison. 327
"This living hand..." Charles
    Olson. 337
'This magazine of ours.' John
    Reed. 350
This moment. Evelyn Golden. 263
This moment. Anneliese Wagner.
    389
This morning. Jeanne Lohmann. 305
This morning. Tefke Goldberger.
    262
"This morning." Robert A. Sears.
    362
"This morning." James Torio. 281
This side of the window. Marilyn
    Kallet. 287
This Spain. Carolyn Stoloff. 376
This story, fr. The green step.
    Kenneth Koch. 297
This time of year. Marie Daerr
    Boehringer. 210
"This town." Charles Olson. 337
This view of the meadow. Robert
    Gibb. 253
This view of things. Judson
    Crews. 226
This will kill that. Gerard
    Malanga. 310
Thistle down. James R. Rhodes.
    352
Thistles
    Thistle down. James R. Rhodes.
        352
Thor (Norse mythology)
    Thor's home. Rodney Nelson. 331
Thor's home. Rodney Nelson. 331
    The thoroughgoing. Josephine
        Miles. 319
Those I have loved. Elsa Gidlow.
    254
Those spines. Judson Crews. 226
Those that dance to the music.
    Rachel A. Hazen. 271
"Those times when I can feel no
    hope." Theta Burke. 218
"Those who are beautiful." Robert
    Kelly. 289
"Those who despise me love me in
    secret." Da Free John. 284
Those who must stay indoors, fr.
    Friday night quartet. David
    Shapiro. 363
"Though you and I." Madison
    Morrison. 327
Thought
    "I am lost/in the graveyard." A.
        Dovichi. 233
    It thinks. Thomas Lux. 307
    The peacock in the bed. Charles
        Edward Eaton. 236
    Proem. Haig Khatchadourian. 292
A thought. Maurice W. Britts. 215
Thoughts at York Cathedral. Paul
    Davis. 228
Thoughts during Mozart. Paul
    Davis. 228
The thrall. Royal Murdoch. 330
Thread. Josephine Miles. 319
Thread. Alberta Turner. 384
The threat. Andrei Codrescu. 223
Three (number)
    Couvet. Michael Gizzi. 259

Three A.M. Jacqueline Frank. 248
Three anecdotes. Deborah Tall. 378
Three apparitions. Carol Frost. 249
Three definitions of poetry. Robin Morgan. 325
Three Easters. Alberta Turner. 384
Three Florentines summoned. Franz Schneider. 361
Three horses. Thomas R. Sleigh. 366
Three loser's poems. Marge Piercy. 346
Three moments for George Sullivan. Edwin Honig. 275
The three of them. Cynthia Grenfell. 266
Three pieces. Ralph J., Jr. Mills. 321
The three pilgrims. Roy Marz. 312
Three poems for Li Shang-yin. John Yau. 404
3/4 time. Larry Eigner. 237
Three salt sonnets to an incidental lover. Robin Morgan. 325
Three stages. Josephine Miles. 319
Three ways of a river. David Wagoner. 390
Three with a boat on Pine Lake. Iefke Goldberger. 262
The three-toed sloth. Jack Prelutsky. 349
"Three in the afternoon." Madison Morrison. 327
"Three tall unicycle rides." Madison Morrison. 327
Three times. Royal Murdoch. 330
"Three times life size." Madison Morrison. 327
Threshing in my mother's arms. Mary Gilliland. 257
3 fears in triptych. Anne Bailie. 199
Thrift
    Towards a pure economy. Dennis Hinrichsen. 273
Thrift shop. Marieve Rugo. 356
The throne. Jacques Sollov. 371
Through all the San Joaquin area. Judson Crews. 226
Through Breuil's eyes. Clayton Eshleman. 240
"Through his entrance." Madison Morrison. 327
Through infinite points. Carolyn Stoloff. 376

Through the arch. Carolyn Stoloff. 376
Through the gate. Gene Anderson. 195
Through the ice tree. Harry Humes. 278
"Through the inside dark," Theta Burke. 218
"Through the intersection." Madison Morrison. 327
Through the searching, sels. Theta Burke. 218
Through you. Edwin Honig. 275
The throwaway woman. Rochelle DuBois. 234
"Throwing his liofe away." Josephine Miles. 319
Throwing the apple. Scott Chisholm. 221
"Throwing watermelons." Michael Robert Pick. 345
"A thump on/the porch..." Madison Morrison. 327
Thunder
    Salute. Thomas McGrath. 315
Thunderbolt island. Phyllis A. Tickle. 382
Thurs Sept 14th 1961. Charles Olson. 337
Thursday. Patsie Black. 206
Tiburon, Mexico
    Barge. Josephine Miles. 319
Tichy, Susan
    Altitude. 381
    Artillery. 381
    At dawn. 381
    At the Wailing Wall. 381
    Bargaining. 381
    Benediction. 381
    Consecration. 381
    Defenses. 381
    Dream I am St. Augustine. 381
    Dreams of a man without children. 381
    "During siesta..." 381
    Florida Scott-Maxwell helps recite my grandmother's life. 381
    For Allan. 381
    For Avraham. 381
    For Gaby. 381
    "From now on..." 381
    Gaby at the U.N. observation post. 381
    Geology of the Huleh. 381
    The hands in exile. 381
    The hours. 381
    Identity card. 381
    In an Arab town. 381
    In Kiryat Shmona. 381

Irrigation. 381
Kovah Tembel. 381
Life cycle of the Pacific
    mermaid. 381
Lying on my coat. 381
Mare. 381
A meditation in Perthshire,
    Scotland. 381
No matter. 381
October. 381
Painting the fence. 381
"The rich don't have children."
    381
Sauna. 381
Shabbat morning. 381
Shabbat, matah. 381
"A smell of gunpowder..." 381
The soul in the valley of
    Kidron. 381
Staying. 381
Talking from Inverness. 381
To an Irgun soldier. 381
To part of myself. 381
Travel. 381
Tropical storm. 381
Two cities, three loves. 381
Volunteers. 381
What they say about us. 381
"When I stop work..." 381
Why we don't sleep. 381
Work. 381
"Writing on scraps..." 381
Zen. 381
Tickle, Phyllis A.
After an illness. 382
Afternoon social. 382
All Hallows in Lucy. 382
American genesis. 382
Anniversary song. 382
Aubade. 382
The bull snooter. 382
Burglary. 382
Christopher's pond. 382
The cranes. 382
An Easter apology to my guineas.
    382
For Rebecca on a Sunday morning
    in the spring. 382
For Robert Hollabaugh, M.D. 382
For Wade. 382
The fundamentalist. 382
The Ge poems, sels. 382
Hope, Arkansas. 382
Interstate 40. 382
Kohoutek. 382
Lent. 382
Lucy at dusk. 382
The Lucy poems, sels. 382
Michaelmas in Lucy, TN. 382
Miscarriage. 382

My mother's parlor. 382
The Natalie Bartlum poems, sels.
    382
Old woman. 382
Ordinary song. 382
Ringnecks return. 382
Sunday lunch at grandpa's. 382
Thunderbolt island. 382
To a daughter on her wedding
    day. 382
To her daughters. 382
Upon receiving, after her death,
    my mother's earrings... 382
The wake. 382
Woman at midnight. 382
Ticks (parasites)
So it happened. Judson Crews.
    226
The ticks. George Eklund. 238
The ticks. George Eklund. 238
Tide. Josephine Miles. 319
Tie dye. Gerard Malanga. 310
Tiger cat. Robert A. Sears. 362
Tiger sparrow. Norman Andrew
    Kirk. 293
Tigers
The Bengal tiger. Jack
    Prelutsky. 349
Tigers, tygers, and tigres.
    Stephen Todd Booker. 212
Till time gives out. Alice Spohn
    Newton. 332
Time. Frances Mayes. 314
Time
Abstraction no. 1. James Torio.
    281
Against the weather. Marilyn
    Kallet. 287
Along with youth. Ernest
    Hemingway. 272
An ambassador from the future.
    Mitchell Howard. 276
And melancholy. Charles Olson.
    337
Aspects of time. Richmond
    Lattimore. 301
"At ten of six I plead." Madison
    Morrison. 327
Breathless interlude. Ernesto
    Galarza. 252
Burlesquer's song. Bradford
    Morrow. 329
Burningly cold. Norman Andrew
    Kirk. 293
The casino at Constanta. Keith
    Wilson. 400
Certain months for years. Larry
    Eigner. 237
The clock outran the mouse.
    Norman Andrew Kirk. 293

Clockmaker with bad eyes. C.D. Wright. 402

Coming now. Timothy Steele. 374

Complaint against time. Cornel Lengyel. 302

Consent. Erin Jolly. 285

A crippled girl's clothes. Norman Andrew Kirk. 293

Days pass overhead like birds. Rod McKuen. 316

Death wish. Mark Vinz. 387

Discovering it is too late. Robert L. Wilson. 401

The dream. Keith Wilson. 400

Ebb of time. Alice Joyce Davidson. 227

The elusive rose. Rochelle DuBois. 234

"Every day when she came to the steps that led." Josephine Miles. 319

Fifty, fifty-one. Maurice Kenny. 291

Foreshadowing. Thomas Hornsby Ferril. 243

405.F. Steve Kowit. 298, 299

The future now. Gerard Malanga. 310

Glimpses. William Stafford. 373

"Good and bad/time goes." Larry Eigner. 237

"Great Washing Rock..." Charles Olson. 337

Gymnopedie: the exhibition. Donald Revell. 351

The hands of time. Robert L. Wilson. 401

Here comes yesterday. John Godfrey. 260

Home. Richmond Lattimore. 301

Hoolehua. Cathy Song. 372

Hour minute hands seconds. Larry Eigner. 237

Hunter's moon. Erin Jolly. 285

"I am a little boy sometimes." Michael Robert Pick. 345

"I like running gentle streams." Michael Robert Pick. 345

"I would have/om another day." A. Dovichi. 233

The ideal photo. Barry Wallenstein. 393

"If only time was a fantasy." Michael Robert Pick. 345

Imitation. Edgar Allan Poe. 347

In a minor key. Haig Khatchadourian. 292

"In his ordinary world." Edwin Honig. 275

In hot pursuit. Robert L. Wilson. 401

In the home stretch. Robert Frost. 250

In the present we take refuge from the past. Haig Khatchadourian. 292

Leavings. Maria Gillan. 256

Letter to the outside. Mark Vinz. 387

Life is what we make of it. Robert L. Wilson. 401

"Life/night." Larry Eigner. 237

"Lovers should take time from the misery." Michael Robert Pick. 345

The manuscript collection. Charles Edward Eaton. 236

A meeting. Cornel Lengyel. 302

Memoir for a year. Keith Wilson. 400

Metamorphosis. James Torio. 281

No matter. Susan Tichy. 381

No moment. Donald Revell. 351

Not chaos but. Cynthia Grenfell. 266

Now. Marieve Rugo. 356

Now. Robert Peters. 343

The old things. Maurice W. Britts. 215

On the midway. Mitchell Howard. 276

"One hour." Michael Robert Pick. 345

Out of love's timeless egg. Elsa Gidlow. 254

"Perhaps,/upon another day." A. Dovichi. 233

Poem from memory. Keith Waldrop. 392

Praise/complaint. Albert Goldbarth. 261

The present tense. Joyce Carol Oates. 336

Quest. Edwin Honig. 275

Recess. Dave Smith. 367

Regret. Sam Fishman. 246

Remembering the typo. Albert Goldbarth. 261

Roads of quicksand time. Colette Inez. 280

Rock. Miller Williams. 399

Romance, sels. Edgar Allan Poe. 347

Santa Fe, New Mexico, 1970. Maria Gillan. 256

A sirvente for Augusto Trujillo Figueroa. Thomas McGrath. 315

"Slownesses/which are an/amount." Charles Olson. 337

Snow at evening. Charles Olson.

337
Solstice. Louise Gluck. 259A
Some day when it is dark.
  Cathryn Hankla. 268
Speed. Josephine Miles. 319
Stalling for time. Harry Humes.
  278
Tapestry. Patsie Black. 206
Ten thousand years. Greg Kuzma.
  300
This moment. Evelyn Golden. 263
Time laps. David Wann. 394
Time's fabled sanctuary. Everett
  A. Gillis. 258
Time-line. Mitchell Howard. 276
Timelapse. Rochelle DuBois. 234
To the sea=side girls passing
  by. Norman Andrew Kirk. 293
Token stones. Brenda Marie
  Osbey. 340
Traffic with time is a terrible
  thing. Haig Khatchadourian.
  292
The valley Nis (the valley of
  unrest). Edgar Allan Poe. 347
Walking on water. Randy Blasing.
  207
"We see but part/of the circle."
  Joan Walsh Anglund. 197
What it takes. Joan Colby. 224
What the king saw. Ray Fleming.
  247
What time is it? James R.
  Rhodes. 352
"What time is/it day." Larry
  Eigner. 237
Where time exploded. Robert L.
  Wilson. 401
Why we are late. Josephine
  Miles. 319
Winter mountain. Stephen Sandy.
  357
With thanks to time. Marie Daerr
  Boehringer. 210
Worlds. Albert Goldbarth. 261
Year's turn. Marie Daerr
  Boehringer. 210
The year. Everett A. Gillis. 258
Yellow leaves. Anne Bailie. 199
"Yet the closing episode."
  Madison Morrison. 327
Time beyond time, fr. Mirror
  suite. Everett A. Gillis. 258
Time enough for grass. Paul
  Davis. 228
The time express. Robert L.
  Wilson. 401
Time laps. David Wann. 394
Time lapse. David Wann. 394
Time to die or fly. Paul Davis.

228
Time zones. Thomas McGrath. 315
Time's fabled sanctuary. Everett
  A. Gillis. 258
Time-line. Mitchell Howard. 276
"Time is slow for the hungry."
  Michael Robert Pick. 345
A timebomb inside. Rochelle
  DuBois. 234
Timelapse. Rochelle DuBois. 234
Times gone by. Rod McKuen. 316
Times Square water music. Amy
  Clampitt. 222
Timeshare anyone? Rochelle
  DuBois. 234
Tin can madonna. Lyn Lifshin. 303
The tingles. Alice Spohn Newton.
  333
Tiresia's drinking. Clayton
  Eshleman. 240
Tiresias. Mitchell Howard. 276
'Tis morning makes mother a
  killer. Wanda Coleman. 225
Tis pity. Alberta Turner. 384
A tisket, a tasket. Josephine B.
  Moretti. 324
Titian (Tiziano Vecelli)
  Titian: lady in a mirror. Franz
    Schneider. 361
Titian: lady in a mirror. Franz
  Schneider. 361
To a child. Roy Marz. 312
To a child who shot a robin.
  Larry Moffi. 322
To a daughter on her wedding day.
  Phyllis A. Tickle. 382
To a farmer who hung five hawks
  on his barbed wire. David
  Wagoner. 390
To a friend in wake of a
  ballyhoo. Bradford Morrow. 329
To a ghost. Dennis Hinrichsen.
  273
To a lady cottontail. Aileen
  Fisher. 244
To a metaphysical amazon.
  Josephine Miles. 319
To a Negro pitcher. James A.
  Emanuel. 239
To a tragic poetess. Ernest
  Hemingway. 272
To a you. Susan Stock. 375
To a young exile. David Shapiro.
  363
To Alice Notely. Marilyn Kallet.
  287
To an idea. David Shapiro. 363
To an Irgun soldier. Susan Tichy.
  381
To an old lover at a distance.

Elsa Gidlow. 254

To be. S. Bradford Williams (Jr.). 397

To be. James R. Rhodes. 352

To Beata. Rachel A. Hazen. 271

To become. James R. Rhodes. 352

To begin. Donald Revell. 351

To break the hold. Marilyn Kallet. 287

To Celia, beyond the yachts. Dave Smith. 367

To Charles, Duke of Orleans. Richmond Lattimore. 301

To Chink whose trade is soldiering. Ernest Hemingway. 272

To crazy Christian. Ernest Hemingway. 272

"To find/the weight." Larry Eigner. 237

To fish. Carol Frost. 249

To focus somewhere. Paul Davis. 228

To Fuzzy. James Tate. 379

"To get out of here." Madison Morrison. 327

To good guys dead. Ernest Hemingway. 272

To Heather. Rachel A. Hazen. 271

To her daughters. Phyllis A. Tickle. 382

To industry. David Shapiro. 363

To John Reed. Max Eastman. 350

To kick an epic tail. Stephen Todd Booker. 212

To live. S. Bradford Williams (Jr.). 397

To love. S. Bradford Williams (Jr.). 397

To make a summer. Josephine Miles. 319

To make perspective. May Miller. 320

To market. George Eklund. 238

To Milly on our thirty-fifth wedding anniversary. Sam Fishman. 246

To Monica and Liz. Rachel A. Hazen. 271

To mother. Alice Joyce Davidson. 227

To my birthday girl. Maurice W. Britts. 215

To my father, killed in a hunting accident. Betty Adcock. 192

"To my friends when I am eighty-five." Robert Kelly. 289

To my grandchildren. Evelyn Golden. 263

To my heart. Andrei Codrescu. 223

To my married friends. Sally Love Saunders. 358

To one afraid. James R. Rhodes. 352

"To open your ears." Larry Eigner. 237

To painting. David Shapiro. 363

To part of myself. Susan Tichy. 381

To pulse a jubilee. Paul Davis. 228

To reach me. Gary Margolis. 311

To remove mountains. Alice Spohn Newton. 332

"To resist one's self." Theta Burke. 218

"To see the ocean." Larry Eigner. 237

To settle awhile. Paul Davis. 228

To Sue. Rachel A. Hazen. 271

To Sylvia, grown daughter. Betty Adcock. 192

To the dead. David Shapiro. 363

To the deepest level. Evelyn Golden. 263

To the earth. David Shapiro. 363

To the future. Gerard Malanga. 310

To the media. Rose Basile Green. 265

To the mother republic. Rose Basile Green. 265

To the north. Carolyn Stoloff. 376

To the other. Thomas R. Sleigh. 366

To the page. David Shapiro. 363

To the preacher's son paddled for dropping his pants... Larry Moffi. 322

To the prisoner. James R. Rhodes. 352

To the sea-side girls passing by. Norman Andrew Kirk. 293

To the unknown goddess. Elsa Gidlow. 254

To the virgin as she now stands to the monk after a... Andrei Codrescu. 223

To Thomas Hardy. Ernest Tedlock. 380

To touch a star. Alice Spohn Newton. 332

"To travel Typhon" Charles Olson. 337

To Uncle Oscar, dead of lung cancer. J.W. Rivers. 354

To what's-her-name. Irving Feldman. 242

To whom our praise is due. Alice
    Joyce Davidson. 227
To Will Davies. Ernest Hemingway.
    272
To you in particular. Jim
    Simmerman. 365
To-- ("Should me early life
    seem"). Edgar Allan Poe. 347
To-- ("The bowers whereat, in
    dreams, I see"). Edgar Allan
    Poe. 347
To--("I would not lord it o'er
    thy heart"). Edgar Allan Poe.
    347
To -- ("Sleep on, sleep on...").
    Edgar Allan Poe. 347
To be alive be bold. Edwin Honig.
    275
To Elizabeth (To F-s O-d). Edgar
    Allan Poe. 347
"To enter into their bodies."
    Charles Olson. 337
To Florida. Louise Gluck. 259A
To Francis S. Osgood. Edgar Allan
    Poe. 347
["To get the rituals straight..."
    Charles Olson. 337
"To have the bright body of sex
    and love." Charles Olson. 337
To Helen ("Thy beauty is to me").
    Edgar Allan Poe. 347
To Helen (I saw thee once...).
    Edgar Allan Poe. 347
To her whose name is written
    below. Edgar Allan Poe. 347
"To make those silent vessels
    go..." Charles Olson. 337
To Marie Louise. Edgar Allan Poe.
    347
"To market, to market." Jan
    Ormerod. 338
To Mrs. M.L.S.--. Edgar Allan
    Poe. 347
To my mother. Edgar Allan Poe.
    347
"To my Portuguese..." Charles
    Olson. 337
To restore a dead child, sels.
    Edwin Honig. 275
To the last. Robert Pawlowski.
    341
To the river. Edgar Allan Poe.
    347
Toad dreams. Marge Piercy. 346
Toast. Larry Moffi. 322
A toast to the ancestors. Rose
    Basile Green. 265
A toast. James R. Rhodes. 352
The toast. Royal Murdoch. 330
The toaster. Greg Kuzma. 300

Today. Stephen Todd Booker. 212
Today. Alice Joyce Davidson. 227
Today. Carolyn Stoloff. 376
Today and tomorrow. Anthony
    Petrosky. 344
"Today I started lunching in the
    cheater's corner." Robert A.
    Sears. 362
Today, no hour. Norman Andrew
    Kirk. 293
Today, the pigeons fly. Robert L.
    Wilson. 401
Toddler under glass. Clayton
    Eshleman. 240
Together. Norman Andrew Kirk. 293
Together again. Rosa Bogar. 211
"Together in our lives." Michael
    Robert Pick. 345
Togetherness
    Acrophobia. Ghita Orth. 339
    All is one. Connie Hunt. 279
    Aloning. James R. Rhodes. 352
    And. Albert Goldbarth. 261
    The annealing. Marge Piercy. 346
    Anniversary. Deborah Tall. 378
    Antiquing. Robert A. Sears. 362
    "At the fish market we walked
        back and forth." Kenneth Koch.
        297
    Auguries. Robert Kelly. 289
    "Before we could begin our
        life." Robert A. Sears. 362
    Borders. Marieve Rugo. 356
    Cambria. Robert A. Sears. 362
    Cigarette smoke, afterward.
        Keith Wilson. 400
    Constancy. Phillips Kloss. 294
    The essence of things. Ernesto
        Galarza. 252
    Holding on. Colette Inez. 280
    Honeymoon. Joyce Carol Oates.
        336
    "I want to tell you." Robert
        Kelly. 289
    "In you arms." Sally Love
        Saunders. 358
    "It's so nice to be with you."
        Sally Love Saunders. 358
    Language is a chain. Maria
        Gillan. 256
    Late verbs. Marieve Rugo. 356
    Locus solus. Michael Gizzi. 259
    Now, before the end, I think.
        Edwin Honig. 275
    On Boscovich's law that bodies
        can never actually...contact.
        Bradford Morrow. 329
    Opposites. Carolyn Stoloff. 376
    Pen point. Erin Jolly. 285
    Proposal. Alice Joyce Davidson.

227

Pud and I. Robert L. Wilson. 401

Riddle. W.D. (William De Witt)
    Snodgrass. 369

River road. Herbert Morris. 326

Sleep. Anneliese Wagner. 389

Slow dance. Eileen
    Silver-Lillywite. 364

Stanzas. Robert Kelly. 289

The starting point of we. Norman
    Andrew Kirk. 293

Stranger. Gayl Jones. 286

"Through the inside dark," Theta
    Burke. 218

Together. Norman Andrew Kirk.
    293

"Together in our lives." Michael
    Robert Pick. 345

Two love birds. Sally Love
    Saunders. 358

Volar. Rachel A. Hazen. 271

"We are as a rose." Michael
    Robert Pick. 345

"We are two shoes." Sally Love
    Saunders. 358

"Winter's melting snow." Michael
    Robert Pick. 345

With Janice. Kenneth Koch. 297

"You cry for me in your love for
    life." Michael Robert Pick.
    345

"Your smile erases all my pain."
    Michael Robert Pick. 345

Token. Erin Jolly. 285

Token stones. Brenda Marie Osbey.
    340

Tokens. Donald Revell. 351

Told by the weather. Ernest
    Tedlock. 380

Tolerance
    "Release/...and you will
    receive." Joan Walsh Anglund.
    197

Tolls
    The cut. Charles Olson. 337
    My carpenter's son's son's will,
    Lt William Stevens, 1701...
    Charles Olson. 337

Tom and Henry, camping out.
    Stephen Sandy. 357

Tomatoes
    Green tomatoes. Anneliese
    Wagner. 389
    Tasty triumph. Marie Daerr
    Boehringer. 210

The tomb of the unknown poet.
    James Magorian. 308

Tombs. See Cemeteries

Tommy McQuaker. Robert Peters.

343

Tomorrow. James A. Emanuel. 239

Tomorrow. James R. Rhodes. 352

Tonight I feel content. Evelyn
    Golden. 263

Tonight is the coldest night of
    the year. Laura Boss. 213

Tonsillectomy. J.W. Rivers. 354

Too bloated to boogie. Mitchell
    Howard. 276

The top of a mountain. Deborah
    Tall. 378

The top of Pike's Peak. Alice
    Spohn Newton. 333

Topsail island. Betty Adcock. 192

Tornado warnings, fourth night.
    George Eklund. 238

Tornado watch. Sister Maura. 313

Tornados
    Diagrams. Albert Goldbarth. 261
    Tornado warnings, fourth night.
    George Eklund. 238
    Tornado watch. Sister Maura. 313

Torque. William Stafford. 373

Tortoises. See Turtles

Total eclipse. Gary Margolis. 311

Totems (I). Thomas McGrath. 315

Totems (II). Thomas McGrath. 315

Totems (III). Thomas McGrath. 315

Totems (IV). Thomas McGrath. 315

Totems (V). Thomas McGrath. 315

Totems (VI). Thomas McGrath. 315

Toucans
    Toucans too. Jack Prelutsky. 349

Toucans too. Jack Prelutsky. 349

Touch. John Godfrey. 260

Touch. Marge Piercy. 346

A touch of love. Alice Joyce
    Davidson. 227

The touch of something solid.
    Cathryn Hankla. 268

A touch on your sleeve. William
    Stafford. 373

"Touched by my ignorance of
    victory." Michael Robert Pick.
    345

Tough decision. Josephine B.
    Moretti. 324

Tough hide. Alice Spohn Newton.
    332

Toulouse - jocs florals. Michael
    Gizzi. 259

Toulouse-Lautrec, Henri de
    On an unconceived painting by
    Lautrec. Jim Simmerman. 365

Tour guide: La Maison des
    Esclaves. Melvin Dixon. 231

The tourist on the towers of
    vision. James Schevill. 360

Tourists. Roy Marz. 312
Tourists. Josephine Miles. 319
Tourists
    "Our tourist group." Madison
        Morrison. 327
    The tourist on the towers of
        vision. James Schevill. 360
Tourists in Italy. Robin Becker.
    202
Tourists. See also Travel

Tours. C.D. Wright. 402
Toward Calgary. Timothy Steele.
    374
Toward I. Josephine Miles. 319
Toward II. Josephine Miles. 319
Toward integrity, sels. Theta
    Burke. 218
Toward paradise. Thomas McGrath.
    315
Toward Saint Looey. James Tate.
    379
Toward Senesqua. Ruth Lisa
    Schechter. 359
Toward the end of 1969. Andrei
    Codrescu. 223
Towards a pure economy. Dennis
    Hinrichsen. 273
The tower, fr. Fresh air. Irving
    Feldman. 242
Town characters, fr. Noastalgia
    poems. Robert A. Sears. 362
Town meeting. Gary Margolis. 311
The town of the summer palace.
    Deborah Tall. 378
Towns
    Along the way. Mark Vinz. 387
    Among many to decide. Paul
        Davis. 228
    At an open window. George
        Eklund. 238
    Little Compton. Randy Blasing.
        207
    Nut-brown bird. Mitchell Howard.
        276
    Summer: small town. Marie Daerr
        Boehringer. 210
    "This is the toughest." Madison
        Morrison. 327
    Town characters, fr. Noastalgia
        poems. Robert A. Sears. 362
Toy trains in the landlord's
    house. Dave Smith. 367
Toys
    First London conference in the
        American campaign... James
        Schevill. 360
    "Smiling girls, rosy boys." Jan
        Ormerod. 338
Trace. Cynthia Grenfell. 266

Tracing. James R. Rhodes. 352
Tracking. Gerard Malanga. 310
Tract. Josephine Miles. 319
Trade center. Josephine Miles.
    319
Traffic Signals
    'At the corner of Muck and
        Myer.' Paul Violi. 388
Traffic with time is a terrible
    thing. Haig Khatchadourian.
    292
Tragedy's greatest hits. James
    Tate. 379
"The tragic hero." Madison
    Morrison. 327
A trail of sparkle. Alice Spohn
    Newton. 332
Train wheels. Josephine B.
    Moretti. 324
The train, fr. The green step.
    Kenneth Koch. 297
The training of a fighter. J.W.
    Rivers. 354
Training session for insurance
    adjusters. James Magorian. 309
Training the dog to come. Robin
    Becker. 202
Trains. Andrei Codrescu. 223
Trains Wrecks. See Railroads

The Tramontane sonata. Paul
    Violi. 388
Tranquilizers. Josephine B.
    Moretti. 324
Trans-American express. Steve
    Kowit. 299
Transcendentalism
    The last New England
        transcendentalist. James
        Schevill. 360
Transition. Toi Derricote. 229
Transition. Connie Hunt. 279
Translating. Jacqueline Frank.
    248
Translation. Marieve Rugo. 356
Translation. Ghita Orth. 339
Translations and Translators
    Crossing the river. Steve Kowit.
        299
    Translating. Jacqueline Frank.
        248
Translations from the Esquimaux:
    there are seasons. Ernest
    Hemingway. 272
A transport fo children. Cornel
    Lengyel. 302
Transpose. Norman Andrew Kirk.
    293
Transvestites
    "Do queens have." Madison

Morrison. 327
Transylvania: a heartland. Keith
    Wilson. 400
Transylvanian set piece. Keith
    Wilson. 400
Trapped. Rachel A. Hazen. 271
Trappers and Trapping
    Recipe. Tom Smith. 368
Trasimene. Amy Clampitt. 222
Trasmiene (lake), Italy
    Trasimene. Amy Clampitt. 222
Travel. Susan Tichy. 381
Travel. Greg Kuzma. 300
Travel
    Anthropology. David James. 282
    Armchair traveler. Josephine B.
        Moretti. 324
    "At that price." Madison
        Morrison. 327
    Boredom. Joyce Carol Oates. 336
    Brochure. Paul Violi. 388
    Change of territory. Melvin
        Dixon. 231
    Charter line. Mark Vinz. 387
    Continuing. Ghita Orth. 339
    Cross-country, & motif appears.
        Albert Goldbarth. 261
    Deception pass, fr. Salt Air.
        Sharon Bryan. 217
    Ecstasy of motion. Joyce Carol
        Oates. 336
    Far beyond distance, fr.
        Voyages. Everett A. Gillis.
        258
    Forseeing the journey. James
        Applewhite. 198
    A friend starts west on
        Melville's birthday. Robert
        Gibb. 253
    Gossip. Marc Kaminsky. 288
    Hard travellin'. Thomas McGrath.
        315
    Have kids, will travel.
        Josephine B. Moretti. 324
    Her yellow roses. Carolyn
        Stoloff. 376
    Honeymoon. Ghita Orth. 339
    Launched. Herbert Morris. 326
    Much I have traveled. William
        Stafford. 373
    Night journey. Thomas R. Sleigh.
        366
    Place to place. Larry Eigner.
        237
    Places are not where we are.
        Marieve Rugo. 356
    Postcards. Mark Vinz. 387
    The sketchbook. Robin Becker.
        202
    Toward Saint Looey. James Tate.

        379
    Travel. Susan Tichy. 381
    Travel. Greg Kuzma. 300
    Travel plan. Jeanne Lohmann. 305
    Travel poem. Ernest Hemingway.
        272
    Travel songs. Colette Inez. 280
    The traveler of lavishness.
        James Schevill. 360
    "Traveling is fine." Sally Love
        Saunders. 358
    Trip. Josephine Miles. 319
    Wanderlust. John Reed. 350
    "We'll be off to Europe."
        Madison Morrison. 327
    White houses and black roads.
        Marieve Rugo. 356
    "You ride for some hours." Larry
        Eigner. 237
Travel plan. Jeanne Lohmann. 305
Travel poem. Ernest Hemingway.
    272
Travel songs. Colette Inez. 280
Travel. See also Air Travel,
    Tourists

The **traveler** of lavishness. James
    Schevill. 360
The **traveler**. John Reed. 350
Travelers. Josephine Miles. 319
Traveling art exhibit. James
    Magorian. 308
"**Traveling** is fine." Sally Love
    Saunders. 358
Traveling, 1950. Betty Adcock.
    192
The **treason** of the clerks takes
    many forms. Herbert Morris.
    326
"**Treasures** and pains." Theta
    Burke. 218
"**Tree** frogs busily singing."
    Sally Love Saunders. 358
The **tree** house. Louise Gluck.
    259A
The **tree** inside us. Maria Gillan.
    256
The **tree** of life. Connie Hunt.
    279
The **tree**. Ezra Pound. 235
Trees
    At last, the secret. Alice Spohn
        Newton. 332
    Autumnal. Josephine Miles. 319
    A bit of me. Rachel A. Hazen.
        271
    Brooklyn Botanic Garden. Michael
        Gizzi. 259
    Buying the Brooklyn Bridge.
        James Magorian. 308

Death of the old orange orchard.
Gene Anderson. 195
Elegy spoken to a tree. Dennis
Hinrichsen. 273
Fire lookout playing with
matches. James Magorian. 309
"The 5 and 1/2 million."f. Larry
Eigner. 237
Flower studies: brown-eyed
Susan. Tom Smith. 368
Green morning, full summer.
Marieve Rugo. 356
"In the trees." Larry Eigner.
237
"In winter in the woods." Robert
Frost. 250
The man who grew trees from his
hands. Everett A. Gillis. 258
Morning in branches. Josephine
Miles. 319
Old trees. Robert A. Sears. 362
"One tree/holds/a hundred
birds." Joan Walsh Anglund.
197
The painter studying trees
without leaves. James
Schevill. 360
Perennial necessity. Marie Daerr
Boehringer. 210
Poplars. Ralph J., Jr. Mills.
321
Rock creek fall. Ernesto
Galarza. 252
Seascape. Joseph Penzi. 342
Second-growth trees. Robert
Pawlowski. 341
A shade-lending tree. Alice
Spohn Newton. 332
"Shadowy." Larry Eigner. 237
Storm-felled tree at Eagle
Bridge. Stephen Sandy. 357
Stump speech. David Wagoner. 390
The tree. Ezra Pound. 235
The white birches. Robert Gibb.
253
"Trees." Larry Eigner. 237
The trembling of the veil. Thomas
McGrath. 315
"A tremendous night-/time
robbery..." Madison Morrison.
327
"Tremendous rains." Madison
Morrison. 327
Tremorhands. Stephen Todd Booker.
212
Trento. Robert A. Sears. 362
Trespass. Miriam Goodman. 264
The triangle of love. Jacques
Sollov. 370
Tribe. Cathy Song. 372

Triem, Eve
The four o'clocks. 383
Going by jet. 383
Homage to Plotinus. 383
Midsummer rites. 383
My another road. 383
One memory of Rose. 383
Sun and amiable air. 383
Us to the untouchable ends. 383
The waitress. 383
Trilogy. Michael Akillian. 193
Trinc. Thomas McGrath. 315
Trinidad. Michael Gizzi. 259
Trinity. Randy Blasing. 207
Trio. Cynthia Grenfell. 266
Trip. Josephine Miles. 319
Trip wire. Miriam Goodman. 264
Triptych. Paul Violi. 388
Triptych. Colette Inez. 280
Triptych. James Torio. 281
Triumph. Marie Daerr Boehringer.
210
Tromp l'oeil. Marieve Rugo. 356
Tropical storm. Susan Tichy. 381
"A trot, a canter." Jan Ormerod.
338
Troubleshooting. William
Stafford. 373
Troy
Approaching Troy. Randy Blasing.
207
The truant officer's helper.
David Wagoner. 390
The truck. Greg Kuzma. 300
Trucks
Mannerly memo. Marie Daerr
Boehringer. 210
True accounts from the imaginary
war. C.D. Wright. 402
Trust. Rochelle DuBois. 234
Trustworthiness
Anticipating. William Stafford.
373
Coda: "bringing up baby" Gerard
Malanga. 310
Easy to remember. Jeanne
Lohmann. 305
Trust. Rochelle DuBois. 234
Truth. Alberta Turner. 384
Truth
The black cottage. Robert Frost.
250
"Can one be good." Da Free John.
284
Canto. Marilyn Kallet. 287
Consummation. Norman Andrew
Kirk. 293
Conversation with the giver of
names. Harry Humes. 278
Down at the bottom of things.

Marge Piercy. 346
Evangel. Josephine Miles. 319
Fishing License. James Magorian. 308
"Forehead, breath, and smile." Da Free John. 284
"I have heard and seen enough. You cannot imagine." Da Free John. 284
"I have two ways." Da Free John. 284
Icicles. Ray Fleming. 247
In defense of uncertainty and disarray. Miller Williams. 399
"Is it possible/for one to come unto." Theta Burke. 218
Messages in the wind. Rosa Bogar. 211
"My room is slanted." Da Free John. 284
The new science. Stephen Knauth. 295
Night owl. Wanda Coleman. 225
"Oh spirit locked within." Connie Hunt. 279
Peace. Connie Hunt. 279
"Peace, infinity's plot." Michael Robert Pick. 345
Poem from memory. Keith Waldrop. 392
Relief. Martha Janssen. 283
The restless mind. Sam Fishman. 246
Rumors. John Yau. 404
Runes with variations. Cornel Lengyel. 302
Some pure heart saying. Paul Davis. 228
"There is no question." Joan Walsh Anglund. 197
The thing king. Charles Edward Eaton. 236
'This magazine of ours.' John Reed. 350
To-- ("The bowers whereat, in dreams, I see"). Edgar Allan Poe. 347
To be. James R. Rhodes. 352
"Truth does not change." Connie Hunt. 279
The truth. James R. Rhodes. 352
Tuned in late one night. William Stafford. 373
Ultimately. Ernest Hemingway. 272
Voice of truth. Connie Hunt. 279
"The waters teach us/the sands teach us/the winds speak." Joan Walsh Anglund. 197
What if? Elsa Gidlow. 254

"When I know the Truth and the world becomes." Da Free John. 284
"Within the spinning of events/...which is time." Joan Walsh Anglund. 197
"Within you/lie the answers." Theta Burke. 218
You are. James R. Rhodes. 352
"Truth does not change." Connie Hunt. 279
The truth is. Jeanne Lohmann. 305
The truth of mirrors. Marieve Rugo. 356
A truth-teller's complaint. Cornel Lengyel. 302
The truth. James R. Rhodes. 352
Try it on. Sister Maura. 313
Trying. Albert Goldbarth. 261
Trying. Miller Williams. 399
Trying to attract your attention without being too obvious. Marge Piercy. 346
Trying to drive away from the past. James Applewhite. 198
Trysts
  Amabo, mea dulcis ipsithilla. Steve Kowit. 299
  "If dawn would only quiet me the host." Robert Kelly. 289
  Three times. Royal Murdoch. 330
  Waialua. Cathy Song. 372
  Weekend. James Torio. 281
Tschaikowsky. John Reed. 350
Tucson, Arizona. Frances Mayes. 314
Tumor. Richard Blessing. 208
Tune. Robert Kelly. 289
Tuned in late one night. William Stafford. 373
Tuneless wand'rings. Rachel A. Hazen. 271
A tunnel to the moon. Cathryn Hankla. 268
Turkey
  Anatolia. Paul Violi. 388
  Blues are American haikus. Andrei Codrescu. 223
  Last day in Istanbul. Randy Blasing. 207
  Waverly. Paul Violi. 388
Turn on. Laura Boss. 213
"Turn out your." Charles Olson. 337
Turn-of-the-century house. Dave Smith. 367
Turner, Alberta
  The angel of - 384
  Arch. 384
  Before meat. 384

Bliss. 384
Brace. 384
Choosing a death. 384
Clenching. 384
Cloth. 384
Creep. 384
The devil. 384
Die. 384
Drift. 384
Fond. 384
Forgive. 384
Four fears. 384
From a dictionary of common
     terms, sels. 384
Gold? Chick? Food? 384
Good. 384
In love with wholes. 384
Keeping. 384
Knees. 384
Knowing. 384
Leosan. 384
Making old bones. 384
Paradise. 384
Press. 384
The prudence of Nan Corbett. 384
Shetland. 384
Short commons. 384
Skirt. 384
Smoke. 384
Thread. 384
Three Easters. 384
Tis pity. 384
Truth. 384
Wear. 384
Turner, Thomas Noel
     Hillbilly night before
          Christmas. 385
Turner, Tina
     The fourth confrontation with
          Tina Turner. David James. 282
     The second confrontation with
          Tina Turner. David James. 282
Turning. Marilyn Kallet. 287
The turning. Carolyn Stoloff. 376
Turnips. Sandra Gilbert. 255
Turnips
     Turnips. Sandra Gilbert. 255
The turtle. Jack Prelutsky. 349
Turtles
     Beaded turtle. Maurice Kenny.
          291
     The turtle. Jack Prelutsky. 349
Twain, Mark
     Mark Twain's torch song. Stephen
          Knauth. 295
Twelfth Street. Roy Marz. 312
Twelve. Martha Janssen. 283
12 midnight.   Rochelle DuBois.
     234
"23 School and 16 Columbia."

Charles Olson. 337
Twentieth anniversary. Betty
     Adcock. 192
Twentieth Century
     Au bout du temps. Andrei
          Codrescu. 223
Twenty 26:vii:79 nyc. Gerard
     Malanga. 310
"Twenty days of leave." Michael
     Robert Pick. 345
Twenty-five panchos. J.W. Rivers.
     354
Twenty. Robert Kelly. 289
Twenty poems, sels. Kenneth Koch.
     297
Twilight. Carolyn Stoloff. 376
Twilight
     Another. Joyce Carol Oates. 336
Twilight path. Cynthia Grenfell.
     266
Twin circles. Alice Joyce
     Davidson. 227
Twindream. Colette Inez. 280
The twist. Charles Olson. 337
Two at the fair. James
     Applewhite. 198
Two by two. Robin Morgan. 325
Two cities, three loves. Susan
     Tichy. 381
Two come to mind. Gary Margolis.
     311
Two eastern places. John Godfrey.
     260
Two for Mother Goose, sels. Tom
     Smith. 368
The two goldfish. Greg Kuzma. 300
Two horses. Joy Harjo. 269
Two in June. Ralph J., Jr. Mills.
     321
Two kinds of language. John Yau.
     404
Two kinds of song. John Yau. 404
Two kinds of story-telling. John
     Yau. 404
Two kinds of trouble. Josephine
     Miles. 319
Two legends: a birthday party.
     Tom Smith. 368
Two legends: nails. Tom Smith.
     368
"The two lights in/unison..."
     Larry Eigner. 237
Two love birds. Sally Love
     Saunders. 358
Two mediations on Guanajuato.
     John Yau. 404
Two peach trees. Marge Piercy.
     346
Two photographs for a
     non-existent album. Robert

Anbian. 194

Two poems. Ralph J., Jr. Mills. 321

Two poems on definitions of pitch. Sandra McPherson. 317

Two poems/Toward silence. Carol Frost. 249

Two postcard poems. William Oandasan. 335

The two rings' lesson. Ghita Orth. 339

Two scenes. Cynthia Grenfell. 266

Two sides of a three-sided figure. Marieve Rugo. 356

Two tramps in mud time. Robert Frost. 250

Two versions of the Lord's Prayer, sels. R. Buckminster Fuller. 251

Two weeks ago today. Robert L. Wilson. 401

The two white horses. Roy Marz. 312

Two women sleeping on a stone. C.D. Wright. 402

Two words. Betty Adcock. 192

The two-horned black rhinoceros. Jack Prelutsky. 349

"The two-room/apartment...". Madison Morrison. 327

"Two attendants." Madison Morrison. 327

"Two hornets feast upon my plate." James Torio. 281

Two poems on the New Year. Erin Jolly. 285

Two rooms. John Reed. 350

Two stars in a row. Alice Spohn Newton. 332

2 P.M. Rochelle DuBois. 234

Twoborn. Rokwaho. 355

Twoborn (...prelude). Rokwaho. 355

Twoborn Atataho. Rokwaho. 355

Twoborn shaman star dancer. Rokwaho. 355

Typewriters
    Mitrailliatrice. Ernest Hemingway. 272

Typhoid Fever
    Prairie miracle. Alice Spohn Newton. 333

Typhon (mythology)
    "To travel Typhon" Charles Olson. 337

Tyrannosaur. X.J. Kennedy. 290

Tyre
    Later Tyrian business. Charles Olson. 337
    "128 a mole." Charles Olson.
337

Tyrian businesses. Charles Olson. 337

Tzin-tzun-tzan. Robert A. Sears. 362

Ubiquist. Robert Kelly. 289

Uccello. Thomas R. Sleigh. 366

Uccello, Paolo
    Uccello. Thomas R. Sleigh. 366

UFO scenarios. Harrison Fisher. 245

UHFO. Harrison Fisher. 245

The Ukiah arcade/p.o. box 3838. Stephen Todd Booker. 212

Ulalume - a ballad. Edgar Allan Poe. 347

Ultimate aloneness. Elsa Gidlow. 254

Ultimately. Ernest Hemingway. 272

Umbrian plain. Roy Marz. 312

The unbeliever dreams. George Eklund. 238

Unbiased geneticist visiting a wax museum. James Magorian. 309

Uncertainty
    "One reached out/in her need." Theta Burke. 218

Uncle Aubrey. Stephen Knauth. 295

Uncle Louie. Martha Janssen. 283

Uncle Max leaves for Rumania. J.W. Rivers. 354

Uncle Max steeps young Culpepper... J.W. Rivers. 354

Uncles. Robert Peters. 343

Uncles
    The bad uncle. David Wagoner. 390
    Car trip. Robert Peters. 343
    Mackey. Anthony Petrosky. 344
    Mon oncle. Bradford Morrow. 329
    Poor Bill. Maurice W. Britts. 215
    Uncle Aubrey. Stephen Knauth. 295
    Uncle Louie. Martha Janssen. 283

The undead: a pentacle of seasons. Robin Morgan. 325

The undead. Keith Wilson. 400

Under. Roy Marz. 312

Under arrest. Wanda Coleman. 225

Under arrest (2). Wanda Coleman. 225

Under capricorn. Rod McKuen. 316

Under Snaefellsjokull. Marc Hudson. 277

Under the eaves. Stephen Sandy. 357

Under the flame tree. Carolyn Stoloff. 376

Under the mushroom. Margaret Key Biggs. 205

Under the patronage of the moon. Joan Colby. 224

Under the raven's nest. David Wagoner. 390

Under the sun. Carolyn Stoloff. 376

Under Virgo. John Godfrey. 260

Underground literature. James Magorian. 308

"Undo buttons." Jan Ormerod. 338

The undressing. Carol Frost. 249

Une semaine de silence. Robert Kelly. 289

Unemployment
    "An unemployment office." Madison Morrison. 327

"An unemployment office." Madison Morrison. 327

Unexplained absences. Sandra McPherson. 317

Unfinished song. Carol Frost. 249

The unfitted passage. Bradford Morrow. 329

Unforgettable games. James Torio. 281

Unholy spring. John Godfrey. 260

Unicorns
    8 P.M E. Rochelle DuBois. 234

Unicycles
    "Three tall unicycle rides." Madison Morrison. 327

Unidentified Flying Objects
    UFO scenarios. Harrison Fisher. 245

Uninvited. Alice Joyce Davidson. 227

Union Square, San Francisco. Paul Davis. 228

Unique. Iefke Goldberger. 262

Unitarian Easter. Sandra McPherson. 317

Unitarianism
    Unitarian Easter. Sandra McPherson. 317

United States
    AI nostri. Rose Basile Green. 265

    America. Alice Joyce Davidson. 227

    America 1918. John Reed. 350

    America, all singing. Rose Basile Green. 265

    Anthem. Rose Basile Green. 265

    As of Parsonses or Fishermans

    Field... Charles Olson. 337

    Brooklyn, Iowa, and west. Josephine Miles. 319

    Can you see us? Ruth Lisa Schechter. 359

    Capt Christopher Levett (of York). Charles Olson. 337

    Confessions of an American visitor of the large screen. James Schevill. 360

    December 18th. Charles Olson. 337

    The decline of the wasp? Rose Basile Green. 265

    Dreaming America. Joyce Carol Oates. 336

    Elegy for America. Eileen Silver-Lillywite. 364

    An ethnic-American crying. Rose Basile Green. 265

    Ethnic-Americans. Rose Basile Green. 265

    Fatta l'America. Rose Basile Green. 265

    Geopolitics. David Wann. 394

    "Having descried the nation." Charles Olson. 337

    I am an American. Alice Joyce Davidson. 227

    I like Americans. Ernest Hemingway. 272

    In lieu of a love poem for America. Steve Kowit. 298, 299

    Invitation. Rose Basile Green. 265

    It happened that my uncle liked to take my hand in his. Thomas Lux. 307

    It is new to you too. Norman Andrew Kirk. 293

    Jenni's love. Rose Basile Green. 265

    Lars Italica. Rose Basile Green. 265

    Letter 16. Charles Olson. 337

    Look at us. Ruth Lisa Schechter. 359

    Minority. Rose Basile Green. 265

    New marching song. Rose Basile Green. 265

    A new world, fr. Fresh Air. Irving Feldman. 242

    No landing. Rose Basile Green. 265

    Obsessive American sight. James Schevill. 360

    On the midway. Stephen Knauth. 295

    One ethnic-American. Rose Basile Green. 265

Pro patria. Rose Basile Green.
    265
Rediscovery. Rose Basile Green.
    265
Reprise. Rose Basile Green. 265
Revolutionary song. Thomas
    McGrath. 315
Right wing mag: a found poem.
    Marge Piercy. 346
Samsen at the sin and flesh
    pond. James Schevill. 360
The scene. James Applewhite. 198
Science fiction: dizzying
    changes in America. James
    Schevill. 360
Selavie. Andrei Codrescu. 223
"7 years..."S. Charles Olson.
    337
Songport. Rose Basile Green. 265
Theme. Rose Basile Green. 265
West from Ithaca. Josephine
    Miles. 319
Where we were in the 1960s.
    James Schevill. 360
United States. See also Social
    Problems

Universe. See Cosmos

Universities. See Colleges

Unless love die. Edwin Honig. 275
Unlimited timeouts. Ray Fleming.
    247
Unpitying Aphrodite. Elsa Gidlow.
    254
Unroofed. Joan Colby. 224
Unsafe. Iefke Goldberger. 262
The unseen. Larry Moffi. 322
Untic...ov tic. W.D. (William De
    Witt) Snodgrass. 369
Until.... Rod McKuen. 316
Untitled. May Miller. 320
Untitled. Joy Harjo. 269
Untitled: "Our behavior is
    redundant nonadaptive" Kirk
    Lumpkin. 306
Untitled: "walking up/down
    mountains" Kirk Lumpkin. 306
Untitled:"In the place that is my
    self" Kirk Lumpkin. 306
Untitled:"Is it my art" Kirk
    Lumpkin. 306
Untitled:"Love the questions"
    Kirk Lumpkin. 306
Untouched moment. Evelyn Golden.
    263
Untouched photograph of
    passenger. Cathy Song. 372
Unwritten. David Shapiro. 363

Up is down. Evelyn Golden. 263
"Up the steps, along the porch"
    Charles Olson. 337
"Up to the wooden hill." Jan
    Ormerod. 338
Up, liberation! Royal Murdoch.
    330
Up-tight. James R. Rhodes. 352
Upon cutting a flower for my
    mistress. Robert Pawlowski.
    341
Upon graduation. Rachel A. Hazen.
    271
Upon looking into Ethel Waters'
    'La vie en blues.' Bradford
    Morrow. 329
Upon receiving, after her death,
    my mother's earrings...
    Phyllis A. Tickle. 382
Upon twelve. Josephine Miles. 319
Uppsala. Michael Gizzi. 259
Upstate. Paul Violi. 388
Upward mobility. Connie Hunt. 279
Urban Ode. Sandra McPherson. 317
 Urban society. Rose Basile Green.
    265
The urges. Andrei Codrescu. 223
Us. Stephen Todd Booker. 212
Us. Andrei Codrescu. 223
Us to the untouchable ends. Eve
    Triem. 383
Use capricious in a sentence.
    Sharon Bryan. 217
The usefulness. Charles Olson.
    337
The uses of New York. Mitchell
    Howard. 276
The uses of sunday's music. Jenne
    Andrews. 196
Uses of the lost poets. Thomas
    McGrath. 315
Usher, Harlan
    Bah! Sheep! 386
    Biographical note on Ms Goose.
        386
    Boy blue. 386
    'Bye, Baby Bun-ting! 386
    Collitch bread. 386
    Computers ● those "in" things.
        386
    Dedication. 386
    George E. 386
    Happy what, author? 386
    Hot tubbers. 386
    Humpty who? 386
    Im-poet-ent. 386
    Indoor sports. 386
    Jack & Jill. 386
    Little Jack. 386
    Lulla - "Buy!"...'Bye!' 386

Marx. 386
Mary Lams. 386
Merry Xmas, author! 386
Ms Hubbard. 386
Ms Mary. 386
Ms Muffet. 386
Old King Cool. 386
Simon. 386
Six pence, and more! 386
So what else is new? 386
Star? Of what? 386
There's this man, see... 386
Why it's poro. 386
Work? Who, me? 386
Utamaro, Kitagawa
Beauty and sadness. Cathy Song.
    372
Girl powdering her neck. Cathy
    Song. 372
Utrecht. Michael Gizzi. 259
The **utter** stranger. Thomas R.
    Sleigh. 366

V.A. hospital. Anthony Petrosky.
    344
Vacancies, occupancies. Bill
    Knott. 296
Vacation
August. Gary Margolis. 311
Cabin opening. Robert Pawlowski.
    341
The first day of spring at the
    cabin... Anthony Petrosky. 344
"God is away for the summer."
    Ernest Hemingway. 272
Holiday. Josephine Miles. 319
Incidental gift catalog love
    song poem. Colette Inez. 280
Vacation: an extended postcard.
    Albert Goldbarth. 261
Vermont cabin: late summer. Dave
    Smith. 367
Vacation: an extended postcard.
    Albert Goldbarth. 261
Vacuum. Josephine Miles. 319
Valdarno. Franz Schneider. 361
Valediction cparicen. David
    Shapiro. 363
Valentine. Ernest Hemingway. 272
Valentine. J.W. Rivers. 354
Valentine and the birds. Roy
    Marz. 312
A **valentine** for my best friend.
    Jack Prelutsky. 348
A **valentine** for my teacher. Jack
    Prelutsky. 348
Valentine's Day

I made a giant valentine. Jack
    Prelutsky. 348
I only got one valentine. Jack
    Prelutsky. 348
"If my Valentine you won't be."
    Ernest Hemingway. 272
It's Valentine's Day. Jack
    Prelutsky. 348
Valentine. J.W. Rivers. 354
Words and magic hands. Rachel A.
    Hazen. 271
Valentines. Rod McKuen. 316
Valkyries
Valkyrs. John Reed. 350
Valkyrs. John Reed. 350
The **valley** Nis (the valley of
    unrest). Edgar Allan Poe. 347
Valley with girls. Elsa Gidlow.
    254
Valleys
Summer, Aeneas Valley. Marc
    Hudson. 277
Winter, Aeneas Valley. Marc
    Hudson. 277
Vallombrosa. Franz Schneider. 361
"**Valorem** is." Charles Olson. 337
Vampires
The best fullback in
    Transylvania. James Magorian.
    309
Van Gogh. Sam Fishman. 246
Van Gogh's "The Starry Night"
    Anne Bailie. 199
Van Gogh, Vincent
Again, Van Gogh. George Eklund.
    238
Copy from an old master. Ernesto
    Galarza. 252
Self portrait. James Torio. 281
Van Gogh's "The Starry Night"
    Anne Bailie. 199
Vancouver, George
George Vancouver's death dream.
    Marc Hudson. 277
Vanish. C.D. Wright. 402
Vanity. See Pride and Vanity

Variation on Corpse and mirror.
    John Yau. 404
Variations. Jeanne Lohmann. 305
Variations on a poem of Stefan
    George. Robert Kelly. 289
Variations on a theme by a
    sycamore. Ernesto Galarza. 252
Variations on some stirrings of
    Mallarme. Robert Kelly. 289
A **variety** show. Rachel A. Hazen.
    271
The **varnish** of their days.
    Mitchell Howard. 276

The **vase**. Franz Schneider. 361
Vases
    Concerning the idea of vase.
        Carolyn Stoloff. 376
Vatican, The
    A quiet day at the vatican.
        James Magorian. 309
"The **vault**/of heaven." Charles
    Olson. 337
VD-stricken college presidents.
    James Magorian. 309
"**Veda** upanishad edda than."
    Charles Olson. 337
Vedi Napoli e muori. Ray Fleming.
    247
Veins. John Godfrey. 260
Venereal Disease
    Syphilis prior to penicillin.
        James L. White. 396
    VD-stricken college presidents.
        James Magorian. 309
Venetian blinds. David Shapiro.
    363
Venice, Italy
    Notes on Venice. Anne Bailie.
        199
Venus. Roy Marz. 312
Venus. John Godfrey. 260
Venus (mythology)
    Venus. Roy Marz. 312
Verbatim I. Cynthia Grenfell. 266
Verbatim II. Cynthia Grenfell.
    266
Verbatim III. Cynthia Grenfell.
    266
Verdict. Josephine Miles. 319
Vermont
    Finished country. Stephen Sandy.
        357
    Northway tanka. Stephen Sandy.
        357
Vermont cabin: late summer. Dave
    Smith. 367
Vermont/January. Robin Becker.
    202
Vermont: passing the time. Sharon
    Bryan. 217
Vernal equinox. Kirk Lumpkin. 306
Veronica's veil. Sister Maura.
    313
Versailles - Galerie des Glaces.
    Michael Gizzi. 259
Versailles - le hameau. Michael
    Gizzi. 259
Verse/re-verse mantra. Kirk
    Lumpkin. 306
Versus. Stephen Todd Booker. 212
The **very** end. Thomas R. Sleigh.
    366
Very late July. Marge Piercy. 346

Very late thoughts. Mitchell
    Howard. 276
Vespers. Robert Gibb. 253
The **vestal** in the Forum. James
    Wright. 403
Veterans
    Cook's voyage. James Tate. 379
    "Moments stop my sight." Michael
        Robert Pick. 345
    Rehabilitation. Ruth Lisa
        Schechter. 359
    "Sad man returns from war."
        Michael Robert Pick. 345
    "We died." Michael Robert Pick.
        345
Veterans Day
    Ceremonial. Robert A. Sears. 362
Victim. Martha Janssen. 283
Victoriano Huerta. J.W. Rivers.
    354
Victory. Marie Daerr Boehringer.
    210
Vienna, Austria
    Esterhazy's Vienna stopover,
        1973. J.W. Rivers. 354
Vietnam. Evelyn Golden. 263
Vietnam
    Stateside. Gary Margolis. 311
Vietnam War
    The age of silence... James
        Schevill. 360
    All wars are holy. Andrei
        Codrescu. 223
    At Penn's Landing, Philadelphia,
        Pa. Jocelyn Hollis. 274
    The Dahlia Gardens. Amy
        Clampitt. 222
    The end of a war (Jan.1973).
        Rodney Nelson. 331
    Guests of the nation. Steve
        Kowit. 298, 299
    In the jungle in Vietnam.
        Jocelyn Hollis. 274
    In the name of the children.
        Jocelyn Hollis. 274
    Prayer in Vietnam. Jocelyn
        Hollis. 274
    September night. Carolyn
        Stoloff. 376
    Vietnam. Evelyn Golden. 263
    War zone 1961-1975. Jocelyn
        Hollis. 274
The **view** - July 29, 1961. Charles
    Olson. 337
View from a balloon. Charles
    Edward Eaton. 236
View from a tower. James
    Applewhite. 198
View from the hill. Tefke
    Goldberger. 262

View   354

View of Hydra, Greece. Carolyn
    Stoloff. 376
View of the corporation lady in
    bughouse square, Chicago.
    James Schevill. 360
"View" : fr tge Orontes. Charles
    Olson. 337
Viewing the body. Sharon Bryan.
    217
Views from Gettysburg. Josephine
    Miles. 319
Views to see Clayton from.
    Josephine Miles. 319
Vigil. Deborah Tall. 378
Vigil. Marieve Rugo. 356
The vigil. James Torio. 281
The vigilances of evening. Bill
    Knott. 296
Vigils. Josephine Miles. 319
Vigils
    Vigils. Josephine Miles. 319
The Viking's horn at Sogne. Ray
    Fleming. 247
Village cemetery Sunday morning.
    Jeanne Lohmann. 305
Village Life
    The rustle of the dark. Keith
        Wilson. 400
    Village square: July. Marie
        Daerr Boehringer. 210
Village night. Anneliese Wagner.
    389
Village square: July. Marie Daerr
    Boehringer. 210
Village wizard. Albert Goldbarth.
    261
Vince and Joe. George Eklund. 238
Vinebrook Plaza demolition.
    Miriam Goodman. 264
Vinegar. James L. White. 396
Vinegarroon. X.J. Kennedy. 290
Vinegarroons
    Vinegarroon. X.J. Kennedy. 290
Vinz, Mark
    Along the way. 387
    Anthropologist. 387
    Bedtime story. 387
    Business as usual. 387
    Ceremonial. 387
    Changing the guard. 387
    Charter line. 387
    Climbing the stairs. 387
    Collection. 387
    Contingency plan. 387
    Currents. 387
    Death wish. 387
    Deja vu. 387
    Discount shopping. 387
    Dream house. 387
    A dream of fish. 387

    A dream of snow. 387
    Endangered species. 387
    Exploring the natural history
        museum. 387
    Feast of all fools. 387
    Festival of light. 387
    First light. 387
    The funeral. 387
    Genesis. 387
    A harvest. 387
    Holiday Inn. 387
    Hometown blues. 387
    Householder. 387
    Hunter. 387
    In a drought year. 387
    Indian corn. 387
    Insomniac. 387
    Into the dark. 387
    Journey. 387
    Junta. 387
    Keeping in touch. 387
    A kind of victory. 387
    Letter to the outside. 387
    Life of the party. 387
    Line storm. 387
    A matter of angels. 387
    Midcontinent. 387
    Missing person. 387
    Music lesson. 387
    North Dakota Gothic. 387
    Patriarch. 387
    Poet, seeking credentials... 387
    Postcards. 387
    Proposition. 387
    The prowler. 387
    Quilt song. 387
    Recluse. 387
    Resolution. 387
    Revolutionary. 387
    Ripoff artist. 387
    Sleepless, reading Machado. 387
    Sleepwalking. 387
    Soda fountain. 387
    Southside. 387
    State of the economy. 387
    Survival manual. 387
    Talk show. 387
    The world's greatest two-piece
        band. 387
Violence. Gerard Malanga. 310
Violence
    "An adolescent room." Madison
        Morrison. 327
    Crescendo. C.D. Wright. 402
    "Deep currents foam on the
        surface." Michael Robert Pick.
        345
The violence and glory of the
    American spirit. James
    Schevill. 360

355   Voice

Violets. Josephine Miles. 319
Violets
   Teresa's garden. Cornel Lengyel.
   302
   Violets. Josephine Miles. 319
Violi, Paul
   Anatolia. 388
   'At the corner of Muck and
   Myer.' 388
   Big daddy. 388
   Brochure. 388
   Cheeseburger serenade. 388
   The Chiclets paragraphs. 388
   Concordance. 388
   Dry spells. 388
   Exacta. 388
   Index. 388
   Melodrama. 388
   Montauk. 388
   One for the monk of Montaudon.
   388
   Outside Baby Moon's. 388
   Phenakistes urges his crew
   onward. 388
   Probe and brood. 388
   Puddles on ice. 388
   Rifacimento. 388
   Scattered remains. 388
   Shadow royal. 388
   Silencer. 388
   Slump. 388
   Snowblind to the banquet. 388
   Some further observations. 388
   Splurge. 388
   They call them 'The Starlings.'
   388
   Things you should know. 388
   The Tramontane sonata. 388
   Triptych. 388
   Upstate. 388
   Voice. 388
   Waverly. 388
   Whalefeathers. 388
   With Ann on Cape Breton. 388
The violin teacher. Cathy Song.
   372
Violins
   Irish violin. James R. Rhodes.
   352
   Letter from Cremona. Jeanne
   Lohmann. 305
Viper Sunday. Stephen Knauth. 295
Virginity
   Virgins at one time. Norman
   Andrew Kirk. 293
Virgins at one time. Norman
   Andrew Kirk. 293
Viris illustribus. Harrison
   Fisher. 245
Virtue

Saint. Everett A. Gillis. 258
Virtue. See also Fidelity

The visceral arts. Stephen
   Knauth. 295
Vishniac, Roman
   The scientist surveys the
   protozoa. James Schevill. 360
Vision. Joy Harjo. 269
A vision of Abraxas. Evelyn
   Golden. 263
A vision. Mitchell Howard. 276
Visionary adventures of a wild
   dog pack. Joyce Carol Oates.
   336
Visions
   Circuit of the intruder. Cathryn
   Hankla. 268
   Passing through. Mitchell
   Howard. 276
   "There is an orange rotting on
   the table." Andrei Codrescu.
   223
Visions of the city. Thomas
   McGrath. 315
Visions of the fathers of
   Lascaux. Clayton Eshleman. 240
Visit. Frances Mayes. 314
Visit. Josephine Miles. 319
Visit. Robert Pawlowski. 341
A visit from the ex. Marge
   Piercy. 346
Visit on the beach. Cynthia
   Grenfell. 266
"A visit to the dead." Madison
   Morrison. 327
The visit. Gary Margolis. 311
Visiting Emily Dickinson's grave
   with Robert Francis. Robert
   Bly. 209
Visiting hour. Josephine Miles.
   319
The visiting hour. Toi Derricote.
   229
Visiting hours. Ruth Lisa
   Schechter. 359
Visiting the Farallones. Robert
   Bly. 209
"Visiting yesterday/today
   burying." Larry Eigner. 237
The visitor. James Applewhite.
   198
"The visitors/walk...". Madison
   Morrison. 327
Viva la libertad! Royal Murdoch.
   330
Vocation. Rochelle DuBois. 234
Vocation. Martha Janssen. 283
Voice. Susan Stock. 375
Voice. Paul Violi. 388

Voice of truth. Connie Hunt. 279
The voice. Kirk Lumpkin. 306
Voices
    "Saying/is elegy." Robert Kelly.
    289
    Who. Edwin Honig. 275
Voices overheard on a night of
    the Perseid shower. Marc
    Hudson. 277
Volar. Rachel A. Hazen. 271
Volcano. Frances Mayes. 314
Volcano. Martha Janssen. 283
Volcanos
    Volcano. Frances Mayes. 314
Volume 13: Jirasek to
    lighthouses. Cathryn Hankla.
    268
Volunteer English department.
    James Magorian. 309
Volunteers. Susan Tichy. 381
Voodoo mambo: to the tourists.
    Melvin Dixon. 231
Voss, William
    The local genius. Amy Clampitt.
    222
Vote. Josephine Miles. 319
A vote for Harold. Steve Kowit.
    298, 299
Voter. Josephine Miles. 319
A votive offering. Richmond
    Lattimore. 301
Voyage. Josephine Miles. 319
Voyage to last August. Roy Marz.
    312
Voyages, sels. Everett A. Gillis.
    258
The voyeur directs an ending.
    Larry Moffi. 322
Vulgarity
    That family. Robert Peters. 343

Wagner, Anneliese
    Absence. 389
    Benediction for my daughters.
    389
    Birthday. 389
    Club for elders. 389
    Count to ten. 389
    Covenant beyond sorrow. 389
    Family. 389
    For Bonnie, my swim teacher. 389
    Green tomatoes. 389
    Hand work. 389
    The hat. 389
    I play with his son. 389
    Jonah's house. 389
    Karen. 389

    Leaving him. 389
    Letter from my grandmother
        interned in France. 389
    Liebe mutter. 389
    Mad Agnes scrubs the parapet...
        389
    Man with purple beard. 389
    Monday morning. 389
    The net. 389
    Oblique. 389
    Odor. 389
    On seeing a page of Virginia's
        Woolf's diary. 389
    Our stories. 389
    Painter. 389
    Postmark Miami. 389
    Prehistoric coffins in Provence.
        389
    Reckoning. 389
    Refugee, 1940. 389
    Report from the Jewish Museum.
        389
    She-goat at puck fair. 389
    The sign for the sun. 389
    Sleep. 389
    Snow in April. 389
    Sudden thaw. 389
    Take it in your hands. 389
    This moment. 389
    Village night. 389
    Walking together, ducking
        branches. 389
    Your shroud, papa. 389
Wagoner, David
    Aerial act. 390
    After the high school
        graduation, 1944. 390
    The art of surrender. 390
    Author of 'American ornithology'
        sketches a bird... 390
    The author says goodbye to his
        hero. 390
    Backtracking. 390
    The bad uncle. 390
    The best slow dancer. 390
    Bitter cherry. 390
    Breath test. 390
    By starlight. 390
    Canticle for Xmas Eve. 390
    The caterpillar. 390
    Danse macabre. 390
    Earthbird. 390
    Elegy for my mother. 390
    Elegy for the twenty-four
        shelves of books. 390
    Elephant ride. 390
    The escape from monkey island.
        390
    Feeding. 390
    First light. 390

The flower. 390
For a fisherman who dynamited a
  cormorant rookery. 390
For a woman sitting by a creek.
  390
The gardener's dream. 390
Getting away. 390
Golden retriever. 390
A guide to the field. 390
Her dream and the awakening. 390
His dream. 390
The horsemen. 390
The illusionist. 390
In love. 390
In the booking room. 390
In the Plaza de Toros. 390
Jack and the beanstalk. 390
Kingfisher. 390
The land behind the wind, sels.
  390
Lifesaving. 390
Loons mating. 390
Making camp. 390
March for a one-man band. 390
Medusa's love. 390
Moss campion at the snow line.
  390
My father in the basement. 390
The naval trainees learn how to
  jump overboard. 390
Octopus. 390
The open staircase. 390
The other house. 390
Our blindness. 390
Pandora's dream. 390
Peacock display. 390
Poem about breath. 390
A remarkable exhibition. 390
Replanting a garden. 390
The rules. 390
Seeing the wind. 390
The shape. 390
The shocking machine. 390
Sleeping alone. 390
Sleeping Beauty. 390
Snowflakes. 390
Song after midnight. 390
The song. 390
The source. 390
Standing in Barr creek. 390
The storyteller. 390
Stump speech. 390
That moment. 390
Their bodies. 390
Their fire. 390
Their shelter. 390
Three ways of a river. 390
To a farmer who hung five hawks
  on his barbed wire. 390
The truant officer's helper. 390

Under the raven's nest. 390
Waking up in a garden. 390
Walking into the wind. 390
Walking on the ceiling. 390
Washing a young rhinoceros. 390
The water lily. 390
Winter wren. 390
A woman feeding gulls. 390
A woman standing in the surf.
  390
Writing an elegy in my sleep.
  390
A young girl with a pitcher full
  of water. 390
A young woman found in the
  woods. 390
Your fortune: a cold reading.
  390
Wagons
  Wheel songs, fr. Nostalgia
    poems. Robert A. Sears. 362
Waialua. Cathy Song. 372
Wailing Wall, Jerusalem
  At the Wailing Wall. Susan
    Tichy. 381
Wainscott. Gerard Malanga. 310
The **wait.** Wanda Coleman. 225
Waiters and Waitresses
  Cleveland summer of nickel tips.
    Colette Inez. 280
  Meditations on an old waiter of
    some distinction. James Torio.
    281
Waiting. Miriam Goodman. 264
Waiting. Eileen Silver-Lillywite.
  364
Waiting. James R. Rhodes. 352
Waiting. Robert Peters. 343
Waiting
  "The blues and lights." Da Free
    John. 284
  Don't wait for me. Andrei
    Codrescu. 223
  "For so long you've." Sally Love
    Saunders. 358
  4 P.M.   Rochelle DuBois. 234
  The lady in the single. Louise
    Gluck. 259A
  The long waiting. Haig
    Khatchadourian. 292
  Never to wait again. Robert L.
    Wilson. 401
  There's a train. Eileen
    Silver-Lillywite. 364
  Waiting. Miriam Goodman. 264
  Waiting. Eileen
    Silver-Lillywite. 364
  Waiting for Marguerite. Herbert
    Morris. 326
  Waiting for you. Jacqueline

Frank. 248

"Your love comes in phases."
Sally Love Saunders. 358

Waiting for an Alaskan moose.
Sally Love Saunders. 358

Waiting for Marguerite. Herbert
Morris. 326

Waiting for the storm. Timothy
Steele. 374

Waiting for the warden. Stephen
Sandy. 357

Waiting for you. Jacqueline
Frank. 248

Waiting in paradise for Adam to
come back from the city. Jenne
Andrews. 196

Waiting out November. Scott
Chisholm. 221

Waiting their turn. Gary
Margolis. 311

Waitingroom. Christopher Bursk.
219

The waitress. Eve Triem. 383

The wake. Phyllis A. Tickle. 382

The wake. Robert L. Wilson. 401

Wakening
The black room. Joy Harjo. 269

Waking in Jordan. Larry Moffi.
322

Waking in the endless mountains.
Dave Smith. 367

Waking up in a garden. David
Wagoner. 390

Waking up in Streator. Lucien
Stryk. 377

Wakoski, Diane
The lady who drove me to the
airport. 391

The Walden Pond caper. James
Magorian. 309

Waldrop, Keith
The chances of magic. 392
Elegy. 392
Poem from memory. 392

Wales
Welsh song. John Reed. 350

Walk by a cemetery wall. Michael
Akillian. 193

A walk in early winter. Rodney
Nelson. 331

A walk in the woods. Evelyn
Golden. 263

A walk into the Cumner Hills. Ray
Fleming. 247

"Walk North on the/rock..."
Madison Morrison. 327

A walk to school. Alice Spohn
Newton. 333

A walk with my children. Gene
Anderson. 195

The walk. Norman Andrew Kirk. 293

Walking. Barry Wallenstein. 393

Walking
"Can you walk on tiptoe." Jan
Ormerod. 338

An evening walk. Cornel Lengyel.
302

February woods. Harry Humes. 278

"I often think of buying a
cane." Da Free John. 284

"I turn directly West." Madison
Morrison. 327

"I've taken a balder walk..."
Madison Morrison. 327

Into the dark. Mark Vinz. 387

The invalid. Thomas R. Sleigh.
366

My daily walk. Evelyn Golden.
263

November streets. Dennis
Hinrichsen. 273

"The visitors/walk..." Madison
Morrison. 327

"Walking along in barefoot
shoes." Michael Robert Pick.
345

Walking in the path of the moon.
Cathryn Hankla. 268

Walking in the redwoods. Sally
Love Saunders. 358

Walking into the wind. David
Wagoner. 390

Walking on the ceiling. David
Wagoner. 390

Walking on water. Randy Blasing.
207

Walking Sticks
Bedtime story. Mark Vinz. 387

Walking through Naples. Carolyn
Stoloff. 376

"Walking through old haunts."
Michael Robert Pick. 345

Walking to Dewato. Marc Hudson.
277

Walking together, ducking
branches. Anneliese Wagner.
389

Walking with the Lord. Jacques
Sollov. 371

Wallabies
The wallaby. Jack Prelutsky. 349

The wallaby. Jack Prelutsky. 349

Wallace Stevens at ease with
marble cake. James Schevill.
360

Wallenstein, Barry
Animals in groups. 393
Ant. 393
At night. 393
Autumn music. 393

The careful bump. 393
City eyes. 393
The city is a battery. 393
The city rat. 393
Coming to town. 393
Deception. 393
Dressed to the last. 393
Fantastic. 393
Heartbreak. 393
Hero's song. 393
The ideal photo. 393
Not the darkness. 393
The park beckons. 393
Roller coaster kid. 393
Spider's way. 393
Taking off. 393
Walking. 393
White. 393
Why a poem? 393
Woodsplitting. 393
The wrench of love. 393
Wallpaper
Can you? Josephine B. Moretti.
324
Wallpaper hanger squashing an ant
with his thumb. James
Magorian. 309
Walls. Paul Davis. 228
Walls
Mending wall. Robert Frost. 250
Wainscott. Gerard Malanga. 310
Walpurgis. Erin Jolly. 285
The **walrus.** Jack Prelutsky. 349
Walruses
The walrus. Jack Prelutsky. 349
Walt Whitman. Edwin Honig. 275
Wanda and Steve. Wanda Coleman.
225
Wanderer in his thirtieth year.
C.D. Wright. 402
The **wanderer** to his heart's
desire. John Reed. 350
Wandering Navajo weavers. James
Schevill. 360
Wanderlust. John Reed. 350
Wanderlust. See Travel

Wang Wei
For Wang Wei. Marc Hudson. 277
Wann, David
A priori. 394
Afternoon. 394
Alley. 394
Atoms unlimited. 394
Barefoot realiization. 394
Breakfast. 394
Can. 394
Down at the plant. 394
Falling fast, clutching dogma.
394

53 slaughtered in Mid-East
skirmish. 394
Fourth grade. 394
From herewhere? 394
The future of jazz. 394
Gardener in March. 394
Geopolitics. 394
If you're here now, you win. 394
Interception. 394
Je suis un orange. 394
Killer credit card still at
large. 394
Lust. 394
Misfortunes: uncreated
lifetimes. 394
Missing them. 394
New Year's Day walk. 394
Now let us examine the almond.
394
Nutmeet rose bud. 394
Of course it is. 394
Planetary childhood. 394
Responsibility occurence. 394
Scenario for a species. 394
The secret life of plants. 394
"See what a fine job." 394
The sirens. 394
Spaghetti O's. 394
The splash of being. 394
Springtime in David Wann. 394
Time laps. 394
Time lapse. 394
"When the wind." 394
With apologies to Scientology.
394
Wrong suspect raped in
Sacramento rape case. 394
Wanted - sensuous woman who can
handle 12 inches of man. Steve
Kowit. 299
The **wanting.** Sam Fishman. 246
Wapa club. Robert A. Sears. 362
War
At the tomb of the unknown
soldier. Robert Pawlowski. 341
The bone walkers, post world war
three underground dream.
Colette Inez. 280
"Breaking through trees."
Michael Robert Pick. 345
"Brilliance/shooting stars
erupt." Michael Robert Pick.
345
Camp-songs. Anne Bailie. 199
Casualty report. John F. Barker.
201
Champs d'honneur. Ernest
Hemingway. 272
The chooser and the chosen.
Robert Kelly. 289

"Churchbells/years ago." Larry
  Eigner. 237
Civilian. Josephine Miles. 319
Communique on cork. Gary
  Margolis. 311
Conquistador. Steve Kowit. 299
Epilogue. Jocelyn Hollis. 274
Every apartment faces a
  pentagon. Carolyn Stoloff. 376
Exchanging prisoners. Gary
  Margolis. 311
53 slaughtered in Mid-East
  skirmish F. David Wann. 394
Finale - to my country. Rose
  Basile Green. 265
"Hours line gray streaks in a
  warrior's face." Michael
  Robert Pick. 345
How it is. William Stafford. 373
I am ordered to go and say so
  long. Gary Margolis. 311
"I think now of all the wars."
  Michael Robert Pick. 345
"I weep for you brothers of
  war." Michael Robert Pick. 345
"If the war is over." Michael
  Robert Pick. 345
Killed. Ernest Hemingway. 272
"Killing, taking a man's
  life..." Michael Robert Pick.
  345
Leosan. Alberta Turner. 384
Let's smash. Carolyn Stoloff.
  376
Lies. Christopher Bursk. 219
Morning come. Carolyn Stoloff.
  376
Munich. Sam Fishman. 246
"My brothers, two." Michael
  Robert Pick. 345
My double in a drama filmed in
  France. Herbert Morris. 326
Octagon. Erin Jolly. 285
On a loved one going to war.
  Jocelyn Hollis. 274
Order of battle. Marieve Rugo.
  356
"Our bombs can now kill all."
  Michael Robert Pick. 345
Palm Sunday debriefing. Jenne
  Andrews. 196
Perhaps a prayer. James
  Schevill. 360
Pictures of the people in the
  war. Louise Gluck. 259A
Poem ("The only man I ever
  loved.") Ernest Hemingway. 272
Poem for the sandman. James
  Tate. 379
The poet of the prison

Isle:Ritsos against the
  colonels. Thomas McGrath. 315
Proof mark. James Torio. 281
Purple lilacs, blue water.
  Charles Edward Eaton. 236
The quilt. John F. Barker. 201
"Rages/strain." Charles Olson.
  337
"Readied in tradition." Michael
  Robert Pick. 345
Sangar. John Reed. 350
Shock troops. Ernest Hemingway.
  272
"A smell of gunpowder..." Susan
  Tichy. 381
Soldier. Edwin Honig. 275
The soldier's poem. Robert
  Pawlowski. 341
Song: a new poem of war. Cynthia
  Grenfell. 266
Starting the hostilities. Edwin
  Honig. 275
Sunday picnic: Veteran's
  anniversary day. Ruth Lisa
  Schechter. 359
Through the arch. Carolyn
  Stoloff. 376
"Time is slow for the hungry."
  Michael Robert Pick. 345
Tropical storm. Susan Tichy. 381
True accounts from the imaginary
  war. C.D. Wright. 402
Under the flame tree. Carolyn
  Stoloff. 376
Vote. Josephine Miles. 319
War and evolution. Jocelyn
  Hollis. 274
War is a wonderful thing. Kirk
  Lumpkin. 306
Watching war movies. Lucien
  Stryk. 377
"We're caught in an ambush."
  Michael Robert Pick. 345
What does war do to men? Michael
  Robert Pick. 345
What ever happended to the
  beats? William Stafford. 373
You're dead! James R. Rhodes.
  352

War = Nuclear
"Alone now/together." A.
  Dovichi. 233
"And/so it ends/quickly." A.
  Dovichi. 233
Introduction. A. Dovichi. 233
"Not even/the width of oceans."
  A. Dovichi. 233
Petition. Cornel Lengyel. 302
Town meeting. Gary Margolis. 311

War and evolution. Jocelyn
    Hollis. 274
War bride. Robert A. Sears. 362
War games in the bath.
    Christopher Bursk. 219
War is a wonderful thing. Kirk
    Lumpkin. 306
War zone 1961-1975. Jocelyn
    Hollis. 274
Warden. Josephine Miles. 319
Wards Island. Ruth Lisa
    Schechter. 359
"The warehouse.". Madison
    Morrison. 327
Warehouses
    "The warehouse." Madison
        Morrison. 327
Warm snow. Alice Joyce Davidson.
    227
Warm, friendly creatures.
    Mitchell Howard. 276
Warning. Rod McKuen. 316
Warning. Josephine Miles. 319
A warning. Evelyn Golden. 263
Warren, Robert Penn
    Chief Joseph of the Nez Perce.
    395
Warren, Robert Penn (about)
    Lines on a poet's face. Betty
    Adcock. 192
Warrior daughters. Colette Inez.
    280
Washing a young rhinoceros. David
    Wagoner. 390
"Washing between the buildings."
    Larry Eigner. 237
The washing machine cycle. James
    Schevill. 360
Washington D.C. too. Rachel A.
    Hazen. 271
Washington's man. Paul Davis. 228
Washington, D.C.
    Capitol. Josephine Miles. 319
Wasp conscious. Rose Basile
    Green. 265
The wasp. Joyce Carol Oates. 336
The watch of the live oaks. James
    Schevill. 360
"Watch-house.". Charles Olson.
    337
The watch. Marge Piercy. 346
The watchdogs. Robert Peters. 343
Watches. See Clocks

Watching a candle. William
    Stafford. 373
"Watching the immense self
    scattering ocean." Edwin
    Honig. 275
Watching war movies. Lucien

Stryk. 377
Water
    Bodies of water. Charles Edward
        Eaton. 236
    The dispute over bodies in
        water. Cathryn Hankla. 268
    It is not Golgotha. Judson
        Crews. 226
    Melting song. Edwin Honig. 275
    The water is the skin of the
        river. Cathryn Hankla. 268
    A young girl with a pitcher full
        of water. David Wagoner. 390
Water burning wills away. Cathryn
    Hankla. 268
Water color. Haig Khatchadourian.
    292
Water color II. Haig
    Khatchadourian. 292
Water is air to the kingfisher.
    Mary Gilliland. 257
The water is the skin of the
    river. Cathryn Hankla. 268
The water lily. David Wagoner.
    390
Water pie: tonight, 12/11/72.
    Albert Goldbarth. 261
Water we walked on. Larry Moffi.
    322
Water's edge. Michael Akillian.
    193
Water, blood, and desire. C.D.
    Wright. 402
Waterbug. Thomas Hornsby Ferril.
    243
Watercolor. Jeanne Lohmann. 305
Watercolors. Martha Janssen. 283
Watergate dreams of success.
    James Schevill. 360
"The waters teach us/the sands
    teach us/the winds speak."
    Joan Walsh Anglund. 197
Waters, Ethel
    Upon looking into Ethel Waters'
        'La vie en blues.' Bradford
        Morrow. 329
Watersking
    The mad waterskier on the cold
        edge of spring. James
        Schevill. 360
Wave of unreason. Erin Jolly. 285
Waverly. Paul Violi. 388
Waves. Stephen Todd Booker. 212
Waves. Richmond Lattimore. 301
Waves
    From the shore. Jeanne Lohmann.
        305
    Waves. Stephen Todd Booker. 212
    Waves. Richmond Lattimore. 301
Waves hump their backs and then.

Sally Love Saunders. 358
The **way** I feel. Rosa Bogar. 211
The **way** it is. Ernesto Galarza. 252
"The **way** waits/... and we must walk it." Joan Walsh Anglund. 197
The **way** we love. Rose Basile Green. 265
The **wayfarer**. Erin Jolly. 285
Ways and means. Gerard Malanga. 310
The ways of love. Alice Joyce Davidson. 227
We. Miller Williams. 399
"We all have to die..." Michael Robert Pick. 345
"We are all made of star stuff." Connie Hunt. 279
"We are as a closed eye/...that will not see." Joan Walsh Anglund. 197
"We are as a rose." Michael Robert Pick. 345
"We are each/a piece of a great puzzle." Theta Burke. 218
"We are liken to animals." Michael Robert Pick. 345
"We are looking at each other." Sally Love Saunders. 358
We are not Achilles. Jocelyn Hollis. 274
We are sisters. Maria Gillan. 256
We are so far apart. Rosa Bogar. 211
"We are two shoes." Sally Love Saunders. 358
"We are waiting for something to happen to this." Da Free John. 284
We ate green apples. Judson Crews. 226
We both know. James R. Rhodes. 352
"We came across the desert." Michael Robert Pick. 345
"We cling to/and espouse a creed." Theta Burke. 218
"We died." Michael Robert Pick. 345
"We drive to the." Madison Morrison. 327
"We have the generation which carries something new..." Josephine Miles. 319
"We have/nearly finished..." Madison Morrison. 327
We hear the whisper of the perfect. Jenne Andrews. 196
We interrupt to bring you.

William Stafford. 373
We live alone. Haig Khatchadourian. 292
"We live in the body/... but we are not of the body." Joan Walsh Anglund. 197
We live in this room. Eileen Silver-Lillywite. 364
"We make heroes of some." Theta Burke. 218
"We open the lid." Madison Morrison. 327
"We see but part/of the circle." Joan Walsh Anglund. 197
"We shall overcome" : a smile for the 1960's. James A. Emanuel. 239
"We sit about." Madison Morrison. 327
"We sit on the curb and." Madison Morrison. 327
"We walked out of time." Edwin Honig. 275
We will walk by the trail. Carolyn Stoloff. 376
"We'll be off to Europe." Madison Morrison. 327
"We're caught in an ambush." Michael Robert Pick. 345
"We've weathered many storms." Michael Robert Pick. 345
We, ethnics, had the dream. Rose Basile Green. 265
We, the churches. Kirk Lumpkin. 306
"We/are being devoured." A. Dovichi. 233
Wealth
     Doing without. Mitchell Howard. 276
     There's this man, see... Harlan Usher. 386
Wealth = Satire
     'Bye, Baby Bun-ting! Harlan Usher. 386
Wealth. See also Property

Wear. Alberta Turner. 384
Weary. Mitchell Howard. 276
Weasels
     Don't ever seize a weasel by the tail. Jack Prelutsky. 349
Weather
     Be nice to Bonny. Alice Spohn Newton. 332
     Change. Anthony Petrosky. 344
     Change of climate. Marie Daerr Boehringer. 210
     Distant weather. Mitchell Howard. 276

Motions of weather. Cathryn
    Hankla. 268
Told by the weather. Ernest
    Tedlock. 380
Weather report. Thomas McGrath.
    315
The weather's criminal. Edwin
    Honig. 275
Weather report. Thomas McGrath.
    315
The weather's criminal. Edwin
    Honig. 275
Weather-wise. Marie Daerr
    Boehringer. 210
Weather insurance. Marie Daerr
    Boehringer. 210
Weaver star. Marilyn Kallet. 287
The weaver. Carolyn Stoloff. 376
Weavers. Ghita Orth. 339
Weavers
    The weaver. Carolyn Stoloff. 376
    The zigzag means lightning.
        David James. 282
The web we spin. Evelyn Golden.
    263
The web. Norman Andrew Kirk. 293
Wedding dance. Cornel Lengyel.
    302
The wedding garment. Jacques
    Sollov. 371
Wedding photograph with clock.
    Jim Simmerman. 365
Wedding portrait. Keith Wilson.
    400
Wedding prayer. Alice Joyce
    Davidson. 227
The wedding ring. John Reed. 350
Weddings. See Marriage

Weed. Josephine Miles. 319
Weeds. Robert Gibb. 253
Weeds
    Bitter cherry. David Wagoner.
        390
    "It lifts my spirits." Sally
        Love Saunders. 358
Weekend. James Torio. 281
Weeping for a man in the brown
        chair legless, with a cane.
        Scott Chisholm. 221
Weeping. See Crying

Weight of days. Colette Inez. 280
The weight. Marge Piercy. 346
Weightlifting
    Muscle collecting. James
        Magorian. 308
Weird terminations. David James.
    282
Weiss, Arlene

Vigil. Deborah Tall. 378
Wejack. Maurice Kenny. 291
Welfare
    The wait. Wanda Coleman. 225
Well of love. Alice Joyce
    Davidson. 227
Well-meaning. Martha Janssen. 283
The well. Albert Goldbarth. 261
Wells
    Of the parsonses. Charles Olson.
        337
Welsh song. John Reed. 350
Welsh, Mary (Mrs. Ernest
    Hemingway)
    First poem to Mary in London.
        Ernest Hemingway. 272
    Poem to Miss Mary. Ernest
        Hemingway. 272
Were you there? James R. Rhodes.
    352
Werenskiold's portrait of Henrik
    Ibsen. Ray Fleming. 247
Wes Turley. Norman Andrew Kirk.
    293
West (United States)
    Glancing behind. Alice Spohn
        Newton. 333
    Western ways. Richmond
        Lattimore. 301
West from Ithaca. Josephine
    Miles. 319
West Gloucester. Charles Olson.
    337
The west is the best and the
    future is near. Andrei
    Codrescu. 223
The west main book store
    chickens. Marge Piercy. 346
West-running brook. Robert Frost.
    250
The west. John Reed. 350
Western ways. Richmond Lattimore.
    301
Wet feathers. Alice Spohn Newton.
    333
Wet nurse. Ghita Orth. 339
The wetbacks. Ernesto Galarza.
    252
Whalefeathers. Paul Violi. 388
The whaler's landfall: Sandwich
    Islands. Franz Schneider. 361
Whales. Harry Humes. 278
Whales and Whaling
    Whales. Harry Humes. 278
What a giraffe eats. Albert
    Goldbarth. 261
What a tribal unit is. Albert
    Goldbarth. 261
What am I to do? Rosa Bogar. 211
What are the most unusual things

you find in garbage cans?
James Schevill. 360
What chance ignorance. Norman
Andrew Kirk. 293
What changes, my love. Edwin
Honig. 275
"What damp paper." Larry Eigner.
237
"What deceptive means do
politicians weave." Michael
Robert Pick. 345
What do you do with a wasted
life? Maurice W. Britts. 215
"What do you think caused the
disaster here." Josephine
Miles. 319
'What does bankruptcy mean to
you.' David Shapiro. 363
What does war do to men? Michael
Robert Pick. 345
What ever happended to the beats?
William Stafford. 373
What followed. Josephine Miles.
319
What goes on inside. Judson
Crews. 226
What goes us. Marge Piercy. 346
What happened. Marieve Rugo. 356
"What happened, Pa." Michael
Robert Pick. 345
What happens when it rains.
Mitchell Howard. 276
What he is. Wanda Coleman. 225
What hit me in the newspaper
article. Laura Boss. 213
What I have I give. Rachel A.
Hazen. 271
What I need to hear. Jeanne
Lohmann. 305
What I should have said. Joy
Harjo. 269
What I want. Joan Colby. 224
What I'll see that afternoon.
William Stafford. 373
What if? Elsa Gidlow. 254
What is Christmas? Alice Spohn
Newton. 332
What is it. Roy Marz. 312
"What is life for knotted lives."
Michael Robert Pick. 345
What is love? Maurice W. Britts.
215
What is wrong with this picture?
Jim Simmerman. 365
What it takes. Joan Colby. 224
What John Dillinger meant to me.
Robert Peters. 343
What keeps us. Anthony Petrosky.
344
What music. Joy Harjo. 269

What must be. Erin Jolly. 285
What she found in the river.
Robert Kelly. 289
What the fox agreed to do. Robert
Bly. 209
What the heart can bear. Robert
Gibb. 253
What the king saw. Ray Fleming.
247
What the sky holds. Marilyn
Kallet. 287
What they say about us. Susan
Tichy. 381
What time is it? James R. Rhodes.
352
"What time is/it day." Larry
Eigner. 237
What to answer. Sharon Bryan. 217
What to say. Sharon Bryan. 217
What to wear. Josephine B.
Moretti. 324
What will become of the fat and
slow performing woman? Carol
Frost. 249
What you remember of me. Joan
Colby. 224
What's that smell in the kitchen?
Marge Piercy. 346
What's wrong? James Schevill. 360
"What/to study with." Larry
Eigner. 237
Whatever broken thing you have.
James A. Emanuel. 239
Whatever our final fate. Phillips
Kloss. 294
Wheel songs, fr. Nostalgia poems.
Robert A. Sears. 362
Wheel zeal. Josephine B. Moretti.
324
The wheel. Sandra McPherson. 317
"Wheels walk, never talk."
Michael Robert Pick. 345
When. Gary Margolis. 311
"When a spider begins/to spin his
web." Theta Burke. 218
"When a teenager." Madison
Morrison. 327
When April. Stephen Sandy. 357
"When burly men." Madison
Morrison. 327
"When crumbs from light's black
bread sink in the water."
Carolyn Stoloff. 376
"When do poppies bloom..."
Charles Olson. 337
When dreams are dreams. Rachel A.
Hazen. 271
When friends leave. Robin Becker.
202
"When I am heard." Da Free John.

284
"When I am lost I like to."
   Michael Robert Pick. 345
"When I am not." Theta Burke. 218
"When I fear to speak." Theta
   Burke. 218
"When I know the Truth and the
   world becomes." Da Free John.
   284
When I read of the rose of
   Dachau. James A. Emanuel. 239
"When I stop work..." Susan
   Tichy. 381
"When I telephoned a friend, her
   husband told me." Josephine
   Miles. 319
"When I was a little man."
   Michael Robert Pick. 345
"When I was eight,I put in the
   left-hand drawer." Josephine
   Miles. 319
"When I was just a boy." Michael
   Robert Pick. 345
"When I was lost and needed
   growth for life." Michael
   Robert Pick. 345
"When I was young." Michael
   Robert Pick. 345
"When I'm lost and alone." Theta
   Burke. 218
"When is the year when I was
   ten." Michael Robert Pick. 345
"When Jack's a good boy." Jan
   Ormerod. 338
When January slipped away. Robert
   L. Wilson. 401
When lonely. Carolyn Stoloff. 376
When love becomes a stranger.
   Elsa Gidlow. 254
When love is gone. Rosa Bogar.
   211
When love leaves. Sam Fishman.
   246
"When moons peek through clouds."
   Michael Robert Pick. 345
When my times comes. Wanda
   Coleman. 225
"When one acts toward another."
   Theta Burke. 218
When rain doesn't fall. Mary
   Gilliland. 257
"When Sanders brings feed to his
   chickens,some sparrows."
   Josephine Miles. 319
"When September tells the."
   Madison Morrison. 327
When she is absent. Elsa Gidlow.
   254
"When she is moved by her man..."
   David James. 282

When the bars close. Rod McKuen.
   316
"When the brokers were raining on
   Wall Street." Robert Kelly.
   289
When the cook's not hungry.
   Josephine B. Moretti. 324
When the deer will flee.
   Jacqueline Frank. 248
"When the fire is low." Theta
   Burke. 218
When the silence becomes too much
   to bear. Herbert Morris. 326
"When the soul reaches the
   level." Theta Burke. 218
When the sun came, the rooster
   expanded to meet it. Josephine
   Miles. 319
"When the wind." David Wann. 394
When the world was steady. David
   James. 282
"When things have left him." Da
   Free John. 284
"When you don't know it." Michael
   Robert Pick. 345
When you don't speak to me. John
   Hawkes. 270
When you find love. Alice Joyce
   Davidson. 227
When you go. James R. Rhodes. 352
When you go anywhere. William
   Stafford. 373
When you have faith. Alice Joyce
   Davidson. 227
"When you win, they are." Michael
   Robert Pick. 345
When you're away. Mary Gilliland.
   257
Where are the lovers? Ray
   Fleming. 247
Where are the wise. Alice Spohn
   Newton. 332
Where are you going?, fr. The day
   of the body. Carol Frost. 249
"Where can a man go." Michael
   Robert Pick. 345
Where he is. Wanda Coleman. 225
Where is Mercy Street? Ruth Lisa
   Schechter. 359
Where is she now? Tom Smith. 368
Where it all ends. Alice Spohn
   Newton. 332
Where love is still. Elsa Gidlow.
   254
Where nothing grows. Marge
   Piercy. 346
Where the dying live and the
   living die. Robert L. Wilson.
   401
"Where the hell is my life?"

Michael Robert Pick. 345

Where time exploded. Robert L.
   Wilson. 401

Where we are. Lucien Stryk. 377

Where we were in the 1960s. James
   Schevill. 360

Where you first saw the eyes of
   coyote. Linda Noel. 334

Where you have been. Gary
   Margolis. 311

Whether awe or loss. Paul Davis.
   228

Whether they feared or whether
   they loved. Roy Marz. 312

While gardens grow their roses.
   Alice Spohn Newton. 332

While I stay. Ruth Lisa
   Schechter. 359

"While on/Obadiah Bruen's Island,
   the Algonquins" Charles Olson.
   337

"Whipped cream." Sally Love
   Saunders. 358

Whiskers and moon. John Godfrey.
   260

Whispering harps. James R.
   Rhodes. 352

Whistler, James McNeill
   The butterfly and the scorpion:
   James McNeill Whistler. James
   Schevill. 360

The whistling woo. Rachel A.
   Hazen. 271

White. Barry Wallenstein. 393

White. Joseph Penzi. 342

White (color)
   Mounted policemen. Robert Kelly.
   289
   White. Barry Wallenstein. 393

White angel. Jacques Sollov. 371

White bear. Joy Harjo. 269

The white birches. Robert Gibb.
   253

The white bird. Jacques Sollov.
   371

"White clouds in the sky." Larry
   Eigner. 237

White clown. Charles Edward
   Eaton. 236

White dove. Jacques Sollov. 370

A white dress. Gerard Malanga.
   310

White Flower Farm. Michael Gizzi.
   259

The white grave. Rachel A. Hazen.
   271

A white horse. Cathryn Hankla.
   268

White houses and black roads.
   Marieve Rugo. 356

White lady. Norman Andrew Kirk.
   293

White lake. James Applewhite. 198

White night. David Shapiro. 363

The white porch. Cathy Song. 372

White rose. Jacques Sollov. 370

White shutters. C.D. Wright. 402

White Sound. Robin Morgan. 325

White summer, museum piece,
   Montague Street in winter.
   Cathryn Hankla. 268

"The white ticket." Madison
   Morrison. 327

White water. Judson Crews. 226

White woman with the Navajos.
   James Schevill. 360

The white writing of Mark Tobey.
   James Schevill. 360

White, James L.
   The arc-welder's blue. 396
   The clay dancer. 396
   a colored girl. 396
   Dying out. 396
   The first time. 396
   Gatherings. 396
   I'd trade these words. 396
   Lying in sadness. 396
   Making love to myself. 396
   Naming. 396
   An ordinary composure. 396
   Oshi. 396
   Overweight. 396
   Poems of submission. 396
   Returning. 396
   The salt ecstasies. 396
   Skin movers. 396
   Summer news. 396
   Sunday snow. 396
   Syphilis prior to penicillin.
   396
   Taken to a room. 396
   Vinegar. 396

"A whitened fist." Theta Burke.
   218

The whitewashed wall. Marilyn
   Kallet. 287

Whitman stock-taking,
   cataloguing. James Schevill.
   360

Whitman, Charles
   The Austin tower. Stephen Sandy.
   357

Whitman, Walt
   The carpenter of Brooklyn. Royal
   Murdoch. 330
   The death of Whitman. Stephen
   Knauth. 295
   Walt Whitman. Edwin Honig. 275
   Whitman stock-taking,
   cataloguing. James Schevill.

360

Whittling
   The man who carves whales. Harry
      Humes. 278
Who. Edwin Honig. 275
Who am I? Rosa Bogar. 211
Who are we? Evelyn Golden. 263
"Who are you sir." A. Dovichi.
   233
"Who called brought to my mind
   the name of power." Josephine
   Miles. 319
Who can know God? Evelyn Golden.
   263
Who do you accuse? Marilyn
   Kallet. 287
Who has the chair. Josephine B.
   Moretti. 324
"Who is my inheritor?" Da Free
   John. 284
Who scans the meadow. Aileen
   Fisher. 244
"Who shall we raise up, who
   glorify-our wounded."
   Josephine Miles. 319
Who sit watch in daylight. C.D.
   Wright. 402
Who was killed in the car. Greg
   Kuzma. 300
Who will it be? Rosa Bogar. 211
Who will listen. Connie Hunt. 279
Who's afraid of Maurice Schwartz?
   Ruth Lisa Schechter. 359
"Who's intelligent." Larry
   Eigner. 237
Who, me? I'm fine. Marie Daerr
   Boehringer. 210
Who?. James R. Rhodes. 352
"Wholly absorbed." Charles Olson.
   337
"Whoppers whoppers whoppers!"
   Larry Eigner. 237
Whose was it. Carolyn Stoloff.
   376
Why. Connie Hunt. 279
Why a poem? Barry Wallenstein.
   393
Why birds sing. Tom Smith. 368
"Why did the tragic hero."
   Madison Morrison. 327
"Why do I keep on writing love
   songs?" Robert A. Sears. 362
Why do I love you? Maurice W.
   Britts. 215
"Why do white/women..." Madison
   Morrison. 327
"Why fear death?" Joan Walsh
   Anglund. 197
Why I never left Saccarappa.
   Robert A. Sears. 362

Why I say adios. William
   Stafford. 373
Why in Toronto? Marge Piercy. 346
Why it's here. Harlan Usher. 386
"Why light, and flowers? Paul
   Oakley." Charles Olson. 337
Why man? Sam Fishman. 246
Why must I leave you. Jacques
   Sollov. 371
Why the question of reincarnation
   doesn't concern me. Carolyn
   Stoloff. 376
Why this loving is better. Jenne
   Andrews. 196
Why we are late. Josephine Miles.
   319
Why we don't sleep. Susan Tichy.
   381
Why we need fantasy. William
   Stafford. 373
Why write. Andrei Codrescu. 223
Why you don't hear from me.
   Thomas McGrath. 315
Why?. Sam Fishman. 246
Widening the road. Robert Gibb.
   253
Widow's poem. Anthony Petrosky.
   344
A widowhood. Judson Crews. 226
Widows and Widowers
   In memoriam. James Torio. 281
   The mourning. Paul Davis. 228
   Old woman. Phyllis A. Tickle.
      382
Wiedersehen. Miller Williams. 399
Wife. Edwin Honig. 275
Wife Mary. Paul Davis. 228
Wild celebration. Robert L.
   Wilson. 401
The wild cheese. James Tate. 379
The wild creatures of my
   childhood. Kirk Lumpkin. 306
Wild figs and secret places. Gayl
   Jones. 286
Wild garden. Marie Daerr
   Boehringer. 210
The wild grasses. Sandra Gilbert.
   255
Wild swan singing. Elsa Gidlow.
   254
A wilderness of light. Cathryn
   Hankla. 268
Wildies of Burnett Lane. Maurice
   Kenny. 291
"Will she be aware." James Torio.
   281
"Will the poems take off their
   garments." Carolyn Stoloff.
   376
William Carlos Williams and T.S.

Eliot dancing... James
Schevill. 360
"William Stevens." Charles Olson.
337
Williamette. John Reed. 350
Williamette (river), Oregon
Williamette. John Reed. 350
Williams (Jr.), S. Bradford
And the songs of life's joy...,
sels. 398
As I live and I feel. 398
Brad and Tade's song. 398
Connie's song. 398
Dad's song. 398
Devotion's song. 398
God's song. 398
I mature and I grow. 398
Joy's song. 398
Life's song. 398
Love's song. 398
"Never quit searching." 397
Spring's song. 398
To be. 397
To live. 397
To love. 397
Williams, Miller
Aesthetic distance. 399
Birth of the blues. 399
Children's games. 399
Documenting it. 399
The firebreathers at the Cafe
Deux Magots. 399
For Victor Jara. 399
Going. 399
In a gradually moving car
somewhere in Calcutta. 399
In another town. 399
In defense of uncertainty and
disarray. 399
In Nashville, standing in the
wooden circle... 399
Inference. 399
Learning. 399
Learning to read. 399
Letters. 399
Living on the surface. 399
Logos. 399
Lost in Ladispoli. 399
The man who believes in five.
399
The muse. 399
A newspaper picture of
spectators at a hotel fire.
399
Normandy beach. 399
Paying some slight attention to
his birthday... 399
People. 399
Rebecca at play. 399
Remembering the man. 399

Rock. 399
Rubaiyat for Sue Ella Tucker.
399
Running into things. 399
A short play. 399
Sir. 399
Some lines finished just before
dawn... 399
Standing close to greatness. 399
A story of a memory and his man.
399
The story. 399
The sum of its parts. 399
Trying. 399
We. 399
Wiedersehen. 399
The young lt. col. 399
Williams, William Carlos
William Carlos Williams and T.S.
Eliot dancing... James
Schevill. 360
Williamsburg. Michael Gizzi. 259
Willows. Lucien Stryk. 377
Wills and Testaments
Preparing the will, three
generations. Sandra McPherson.
317
Wilson, Alexander
Author of 'American ornithology'
sketches a bird... David
Wagoner. 390
Wilson, Edmund
"Little Mr. Wilson." Ernest
Hemingway. 272
Wilson, Keith
The American literary
conference. 400
The casino at Constanta. 400
Casino royale. 400
The Celt in me. 400
Child's tale. 400
A Christmas card from Romania.
400
Cigarette smoke, afterward. 400
Concerning Tsiganes. 400
The dream. 400
A fashioner of stone roses. 400
The father. 400
The floods of spring. 400
Flowers of shadow. 400
From a conversation in a street.
400
Gypsy bears. 400
Hebrew stones. 400
The house of lions. 400
In the Piastsa of Matei Corvin.
400
Lacul Gilaului. 400
Languages. 400
Legends. 400

Love motiff: a girl's song. 400
Memoir din Cluj. 400
Memoir for a year. 400
The minaret at Constanta. 400
Monk's song. 400
A mother's stone. 400
The old cemetery in Cluj. 400
Old tomb carving: the nameless
     prince. 400
One rose of stone. 400
The park at Cluj. 400
Peasant song. 400
A prayer for rivers. 400
Reg gypsy wagon, with flowers.
     400
A registry of graves. 400
The road of kings. 400
Romanian classroom. 400
A Romanian embroidery. 400
Romanian song. 400
Romanian still life. 400
Romanian stones. 400
Romanian tale. 400
Romanian thoughts. 400
Romanian village. 400
Romanian village II. 400
The rustle of the dark. 400
Seadream. 400
Secret agent. 400
Sheepherder's song. 400
Sketch of a peasant man. 400
Song. 400
Stephen the Great. 400
Stone roses. 400
Strada Petru Gorza 45. 400
Straw flowers. 400
Summer marriage. 400
Summer meadows. 400
Transylvania: a heartland. 400
Transylvanian set piece. 400
The undead. 400
Wedding portrait. 400
A Yugoslav circus. 400
Wilson, Robert L.
    The aliens. 401
    Among dark hills. 401
    Arkansas night. 401
    Attempted kidnapping. 401
    Autumn dancers. 401
    Autumn plea. 401
    Benumbed. 401
    Big bird seen hanging with blue
       legs... 401
    A breath of winter. 401
    Captured. 401
    Cat and I. 401
    Celebration. 401
    Commoners. 401
    Communion with the dead. 401
    The day the sassafras shed. 401

Desensitized. 401
Discovering it is too late. 401
Don't let the dreams die out, my
    friend. 401
Entombment. 401
The fact of the matter is. 401
Fall. 401
Going back. 401
Grave discovery. 401
Green April. 401
Grim, dark morning. 401
The guise is all the difference.
    401
The hands of time. 401
Holding on. 401
Hope no more. 401
The house next door. 401
In hot pursuit. 401
In search of yesterday. 401
Initimations of spring. 401
Last blast. 401
The last chapter. 401
Life is what we make of it. 401
Little old red schoolhouse. 401
Lonely heart and heavy. 401
Making it. 401
Me. 401
My electric cat. 401
Never to wait again. 401
Night whispers. 401
No two hands the same. 401
November leaves. 401
Now, going on eternity. 401
The path that separates. 401
The poem not recorded. 401
Practicing for death. 401
Prelude to autumn. 401
The price of freedom. 401
Pud and I. 401
Purely psychological. 401
Purification rite. 401
Pursuit of happiness. 401
Recollection. 401
Revelation and return. 401
Roots among these rocks. 401
Searching. 401
Shadows. 401
Silence broken. 401
So powerfully silent. 401
Stranger in the night. 401
Summer lullaby. 401
Summer sun. 401
Therapeutic. 401
The time express. 401
Today, the pigeons fly. 401
Two weeks ago today. 401
The wake. 401
When January slipped away. 401
Where the dying live and the
    living die. 401

Where time exploded. 401
Wild celebration. 401
Wind poems. 401
Winter song I. 401
Winter song II. 401
The worth of being less. 401
The winch. Charles Edward Eaton. 236

Winckelmann, Johann Joachim
Dialogues: Johann Joachim
Winckelmann and Joseph Busch.
Albert Goldbarth, 261
Wind. Robert Gibb. 253

Wind
The beaten one. Rachel A. Hazen. 271
"Begin a/mid things." Larry Eigner. 237
The breeze and the day. Maurice W. Britts. 215
For the wind. James R. Rhodes. 352
Sea:wind. Josephine Miles. 319
Seeing the wind. David Wagoner. 390
A seldom wind. John F. Barker. 201
Shaking in the autumn wind. Mary Gilliland. 257
A theory of wind. Albert Goldbarth. 261
Two in June. Ralph J., Jr. Mills. 321
Walking into the wind. David Wagoner. 390
"When I was young." Michael Robert Pick. 345
"When the wind." David Wann. 394
Wind. Robert Gibb. 253
Wind at my window. Maurice W. Britts. 215
A wind dies. Edwin Honig. 275
Wind poems. Robert L. Wilson. 401
Wind and earth. Carolyn Stoloff. 376
Wind at my window. Maurice W. Britts. 215
A wind dies. Edwin Honig. 275
The wind in the orchard. Gary Margolis. 311
Wind is my friend. Tefke Goldberger. 262
Wind is the wall of the year. Marge Piercy. 346
Wind poems. Robert L. Wilson. 401
The wind. Eileen Silver-Lillywite. 364
Windmill valley. Alice Spohn Newton. 333

Windmills
Primping the windmill pump. Alice Spohn Newton. 333
Window dressing. Josephine B. Moretti. 324
Windows
Glimpsed. Ralph J., Jr. Mills. 321
Shut windows. Maurice W. Britts. 215
Variations on a poem of Stefan George. Robert Kelly. 289
Window dressing. Josephine B. Moretti. 324
Windows of the world. Patsie Black. 206
Windows to scenes divine. Alice Spohn Newton. 332
The **winds** blow long, fr. Voyages. Everett A. Gillis. 258
The **winds** of March. Maurice W. Britts. 215
"The **winds** of my passion." Sally Love Saunders. 358
"The **windy** urban street scene." Madison Morrison. 327
Wings. John Godfrey. 260
Wings. Albert Goldbarth. 261
Wings and seeds. Sandra McPherson. 317
The **winning** thing. Charles Olson. 337
Winter. Larry Eigner. 237
Winter. George Eklund. 238
Winter. Jacqueline Frank. 248
Winter. Joseph Penzi. 342
Winter
Air for air. Stephen Sandy. 357
The aliens. Robert L. Wilson. 401
Berkshire County journal. Robin Becker. 202
Bird feeder. Harry Humes. 278
Breakage. Ghita Orth. 339
A breath of winter. Robert L. Wilson. 401
A bribed referee. James Magorian. 309
Brief thaw. Ralph J., Jr. Mills. 321
Camp field: icicle river. Franz Schneider. 361
Chiaroscuro. Marge Piercy. 346
Cold frame. Carol Frost. 249
"Deceived by winter thaw." James Torio. 281
"Drawers open and winter escapes." Carolyn Stoloff. 376
11/80. Ralph J., Jr. Mills. 321

The fact of the matter is.
    Robert L. Wilson. 401
Fourteen men stage head winter
    1624/5. Charles Olson. 337
Good hours. Robert Frost. 250
Illinois winter. Robin Becker.
    202
In the wind before a storm.
    Stephen Knauth. 295
In winter. Michael Akillian. 193
January morning. J.W. Rivers.
    354
Last blast. Robert L. Wilson.
    401
More that winter ends than
    spring begins. Marge Piercy.
    346
No consolation. Larry Moffi. 322
November. Gary Margolis. 311
Orphan leaves. Rodney Nelson.
    331
A prayer in winter. Franz
    Schneider. 361
Puritania. Albert Goldbarth. 261
Return to the woods. Anthony
    Petrosky. 344
Season. Jacqueline Frank. 248
Skeleton of winter. Joy Harjo.
    269
Snow-time success. Marie Daerr
    Boehringer. 210
Snowshoes. Debra Bruce. 216
Talking with my wife. Anthony
    Petrosky. 344
The third thaw. Mary Gilliland.
    257
The wake. Robert L. Wilson. 401
Water color. Haig
    Khatchadourian. 292
Wind is the wall of the year.
    Marge Piercy. 346
Winter. Jacqueline Frank. 248
Winter. Joseph Penzi. 342
Winter land. Sam Fishman. 246
Winter song I. Robert L. Wilson.
    401
Winter song II. Robert L.
    Wilson. 401
Winter sonnet. Phillips Kloss.
    294
Winter wait. Marie Daerr
    Boehringer. 210
Winter weeds. Harry Humes. 278
Winters. Ralph J., Jr. Mills.
    321
Winterset. James Torio. 281
Xmas day with Miss Universe.
    Randy Blasing. 207
Winter bouquet. W.D. (William De
    Witt) Snodgrass. 369

Winter combat. Paul Davis. 228
Winter in Istanbul. Andrei
    Codrescu. 223
Winter in Lincoln Park
    Conservatory. Robin Becker.
    202
Winter in Norfolk, Virginia.
    Debra Bruce. 216
Winter land. Sam Fishman. 246
Winter moon. Roy Marz. 312
Winter mountain. Stephen Sandy.
    357
Winter night. John Reed. 350
Winter Park, Florida
    The great Winter Park sinkhole.
    Ruth Lisa Schechter. 359
Winter return. Richmond
    Lattimore. 301
Winter roads. Thomas McGrath. 315
Winter rose. William Oandasan.
    335
A winter run. John Reed. 350
Winter solstice-Christ mass poem.
    Kirk Lumpkin. 306
Winter song I. Robert L. Wilson.
    401
Winter song II. Robert L. Wilson.
    401
Winter sonnet. Phillips Kloss.
    294
Winter stream. Harry Humes. 278
The winter the Gen. Starks was
    stuck. Charles Olson. 337
Winter voyage. Anne Bailie. 199
Winter wait. Marie Daerr
    Boehringer. 210
Winter weeds. Harry Humes. 278
The winter without snow. Carol
    Frost. 249
Winter wren. David Wagoner. 390
"Winter's melting snow." Michael
    Robert Pick. 345
Winter, Aeneas Valley. Marc
    Hudson. 277
Winter, your father's house. Jim
    Simmerman. 365
Wintering. George Eklund. 238
Winters. Ralph J., Jr. Mills. 321
Winterset. James Torio. 281
Winthrop, John
    Stiffening, in the Master
    Founders' wills. Charles
    Olson. 337
Wisconsin
    Eagle River, Wisconsin: 1930.
    Robert Peters. 343
Wisconsin village. Anne Bailie.
    199
Wisdom. James R. Rhodes. 352
Wisdom

Anagoge for an island. Thomas
Hornsby Ferril. 243
Complaint against time. Cornel
Lengyel. 302
Gordu wisdom. Kenneth Koch. 297
"I'll wear a wig." Da Free John.
284
The proverbs of clowns. Cornel
Lengyel. 302
The time express. Robert L.
Wilson. 401
Wisdom. James R. Rhodes. 352
The wise man. Jacques Sollov. 371
Wishes. Deborah Tall. 378
Wishes and Wishing
"Star light, star bright." Jan
Ormerod. 338
The witch of Coos. Robert Frost.
250
Witch of the sea. Phillips Kloss.
294
Witch trial, transcript. Albert
Goldbarth. 261
Witchcraft
The witch of Coos. Robert Frost.
250
Witch of the sea. Phillips
Kloss. 294
Witch trial, transcript. Albert
Goldbarth. 261
Witches' winter. Debra Bruce.
216
A witches brew. Alice Spohn
Newton. 333
Witches' winter. Debra Bruce. 216
"With a heavy heart." Theta
Burke. 218
With Ann on Cape Breton. Paul
Violi. 388
With apologies to Scientology.
David Wann. 394
With child. Rosa Bogar. 211
With family below Albion Basin.
Sharon Bryan. 217
With Janice. Kenneth Koch. 297
With neighbors one afternoon.
William Stafford. 373
"With no love to feel." Theta
Burke. 218
With thanks to time. Marie Daerr
Boehringer. 210
"With the bill of a cap." Madison
Morrison. 327
With the tide. May Miller. 320
With this to come back to.
Phillips Kloss. 294
With you. Lyn Lifshin. 303
Within our choosing. Alice Joyce
Davidson. 227
"Within the spinning of

events/...which is time." Joan
Walsh Anglund. 197
"Within you/lie the answers."
Theta Burke. 218
"Within/our letting go/is the
seed/of our receiving." Joan
Walsh Anglund. 197
Without. Marilyn Kallet. 287
"Without asylum they." Madison
Morrison. 327
Without love. Edwin Honig. 275
Without thirst. John Godfrey. 260
Witness. Josephine Miles. 319
Witness. Betty Adcock. 192
Wittgenstein, Ludwig
The picture of Wittgenstein.
David James. 282
Wives. See Marriage

Woken. Ralph J., Jr. Mills. 321
Wolf. Mary Gilliland. 257
"The wolf/slinks off." Charles
Olson. 337
Wolves
Later. William Stafford. 373
Sacrifice. Maurice Kenny. 291
The woman and the man, fr. The
green step. Kenneth Koch. 297
A woman at middle age. Marieve
Rugo. 356
Woman at midnight. Phyllis A.
Tickle. 382
Woman at the mirror. Erin Jolly.
285
Woman at window. Everett A.
Gillis. 258
The woman chained to the shore
unchains herself. Marilyn
Kallet. 287
A woman feeding gulls. David
Wagoner. 390
Woman from Sacramento in
Westchester. Ruth Lisa
Schechter. 359
The woman hanging from the
thirteenth floor window. Joy
Harjo. 269
The woman in black. Charles
Edward Eaton. 236
The woman in the woods. Phillips
Kloss. 294
Woman on a park bench. James R.
Rhodes. 352
Woman song. Maria Gillan. 256
A woman standing in the surf.
David Wagoner. 390
A woman staring through a
telescope at Alcatraz. James
Schevill. 360
Woman untouched. Margaret Key

Biggs. 205

The **woman** who buries. Lyn
   Lifshin. 303

The **woman** who collects boxes. Lyn
   Lifshin. 303

The **woman** who loved wool. Harry
   Humes. 278

"The **woman** who said she went out
   every Sunday." Charles Olson.
   337

"A **woman** with a basket was
   walking." Josephine Miles. 319

Woman's dream of man thinking of
   his woman. Tefke Goldberger.
   262

Woman's liberation. Sister Maura.
   313

Womb and city. Andrei Codrescu.
   223

Women

   After Villon: the dead ladies.
      Tom Smith. 368

   Anima. Deborah Tall. 378

   Annanda's talk with Buddha. Gary
      Margolis. 311

   Aranjuez. Michael Gizzi. 259

   Ariel view. Robin Morgan. 325

   Ascending scale. Marge Piercy.
      346

   Ashes, ashes, all fall down.
      Marge Piercy. 346

   Augusta discusses some of her
      best known roles. Carolyn
      Stoloff. 376

   Bad grounds. C.D. Wright. 402

   Bald woman needs no title. Mary
      Gilliland. 257

   Ballad of Claudine. Sam Fishman.
      246

   Brief lives. Sister Maura. 313

   Caddy and Annie and these and
      thee. Gene Detro. 230

   Calendar days, yellow page
      nights. Laura Boss. 213

   Celestial timepiece. Joyce Carol
      Oates. 336

   Chanukah madonna. Lyn Lifshin.
      303

   Chorus for Neruda #2. Thomas
      McGrath. 315

   The common living dirt. Marge
      Piercy. 346

   A creed for a free woman. Elsa
      Gidlow. 254

   Deep rivers. C.D. Wright. 402

   The depressed woman. Rochelle
      DuBois. 234

   The discarded. Marge Piercy. 346

   Distorted views. Rochelle
      DuBois. 234

Divorce. Marge Piercy. 346

Divorced women. Debra Bruce. 216

Documentary. Robin Morgan. 325

Dogtown-Ann. Charles Olson. 337

A dream of fair women. Harrison
   Fisher. 245

The drive. Marilyn Kallet. 287

Elaine. Marilyn Kallet. 287

Elena. Irving Feldman. 242

Episodes. Miriam Goodman. 264

Escape. Rochelle DuBois. 234

Ethnic-American woman. Rose
   Basile Green. 265

Excavating hardpan. Mary
   Gilliland. 257

Fata morgana. Charles Edward
   Eaton. 236

The fefe women. Brenda Marie
   Osbey. 340

Few thing about B-Girl. Harrison
   Fisher. 245

For a gifted lady, often masked.
   Elsa Gidlow. 254

For Marg so she could... Andrei
   Codrescu. 223

"From centuries your line."
   Robert A. Sears. 362

From the womanflower. Margaret
   Key Biggs. 205

Gathering fire. Mary Gilliland.
   257

George E. Harlan Usher. 386

"Gods no matter how huge."
   Stephen Todd Booker. 212

Grammarian thumbing an old text.
   Edwin Honig. 275

The hermit-woman. Gayl Jones.
   286

Hymn to a mystery. Elsa Gidlow.
   254

In praise of difference. Rod
   McKuen. 316

In the blind. Carolyn Stoloff.
   376

In this story. Jeanne Lohmann.
   305

"The Italian counts." Madison
   Morrison. 327

Jill in the box. Marge Piercy.
   346

Kate. Wanda Coleman. 225

The La Jolla ladies. Ray
   Fleming. 247

The ladie's locker room at the
   Concord. Laura Boss. 213

Lady Charisma. Charles Edward
   Eaton. 236

The lady poets with foot notes.
   Ernest Hemingway. 272

The lady who drove me to the

airport. Diane Wakoski. 391
The laughter of women. Elsa
    Gidlow. 254
The learned lady. Roy Marz. 312
Learning the elements. Sharon
    Bryan. 217
Let wisdom wear the crown: hymn
    for gaia. Elsa Gidlow. 254
Like Ester. Stephen Todd Booker.
    212
Lubbock tune. Gene Detro. 230
Mad Agnes scrubs the parapet...
    Anneliese Wagner. 389
Madhouses. Brenda Marie Osbey.
    340
Malmaison. Michael Gizzi. 259
Melisande. John Reed. 350
The momentary glimpses of women
    through the windows. James
    Schevill. 360
The motorcyclists. James Tate.
    379
My Maggie machine. Robert
    Pawlowski. 341
The no-name woman in San
    Francisco. James Schevill. 360
Old country. Jeanne Lohmann. 305
On board the QE2 Laura Boss. 213
On the street after hours.
    Norman Andrew Kirk. 293
Original women. Robert Kelly.
    289
Our lady. John Godfrey. 260
Pack rat sieve. Mei-Mei
    Berssenbrugge. 203, 204
Pedestal madonna. Lyn Lifshin.
    303
Poem for Kyra. Andrei Codrescu.
    223
Poems from the river Aurelia
    (sels.) Andrei Codrescu. 223
Postcard from a voyage. Robert
    Anbian. 194
Prehistoric coffins in Provence.
    Anneliese Wagner. 389
Ragged ending. Marge Piercy. 346
Ramona Veagis. Brenda Marie
    Osbey. 340
Rebecca at play. Miller
    Williams. 399
Rite. Jacqueline Frank. 248
Rose's poem. Robin Becker. 202
Seascape: woman on the beach.
    Haig Khatchadourian. 292
The shapes our searching arms.
    James Schevill. 360
Sheet rock madonna. Lyn Lifshin.
    303
Sisters. Tom Smith. 368
Slug nmadonna. Lyn Lifshin. 303

So lightly she must be air.
    Cathryn Hankla. 268
Some beneficial rays. James
    Tate. 379
Song:Miss Penelope Burgess,
    balling the jack. Thomas
    McGrath. 315
Sources. Adrienne Rich. 353
Stamp madonna. Lyn Lifshin. 303
Stern warning. Margaret Key
    Biggs. 205
Stripper madonna. Lyn Lifshin.
    303
The swim. Jenne Andrews. 196
A table with people. Marc
    Kaminsky. 288
The throwaway woman. Rochelle
    DuBois. 234
Tin can madonna. Lyn Lifshin.
    303
To the virgin as she now stands
    to the monk after a... Andrei
    Codrescu. 223
Triptych. Colette Inez. 280
"Turn out your." Charles Olson.
    337
Two women sleeping on a stone.
    C.D. Wright. 402
2 P.M.   Rochelle DuBois. 234
Warrior daughters. Colette Inez.
    280
We ate green apples. Judson
    Crews. 226
We hear the whisper of the
    perfect. Jenne Andrews. 196
Who has the chair. Josephine B.
    Moretti. 324
Wind and earth. Carolyn Stoloff.
    376
The woman chained to the shore
    unchains herself. Marilyn
    Kallet. 287
Woman song. Maria Gillan. 256
The women of Huanuni. Ernesto
    Galarza. 252
The women study in workshop
    together. Miriam Goodman. 264
Would she vanish, kissed? Elsa
    Gidlow. 254
Writing the words. Brenda Marie
    Osbey. 340
Yellow dresses. C.D. Wright. 402
You clasped your hands. Judson
    Crews. 226
"The young ladies." Charles
    Olson. 337
Women = African
Fulani girl. Robert A. Sears.
    362
Palm wine. Robert A. Sears. 362

Women = Black
   Beauty. Irving Feldman. 242
   Ceremony for Minneconjoux.
      Brenda Marie Osbey. 340
   A design of choice. Maurice W.
      Britts. 215
   Doctor's report. Wanda Coleman.
      225
   Fiction study. Gayl Jones. 286
   Fingering the jagged grains.
      Melvin Dixon. 231
   Flight of the California condor.
      Wanda Coleman. 225
   I see me. Rosa Bogar. 211
   Lady on a bus. Jeanne Lohmann.
      305
   The machete woman. Gayl Jones.
      286
   Matrix. Stephen Todd Booker. 212
   A new kind of man. Rosa Bogar.
      211
   Pretty face. Wanda Coleman. 225
   Wild figs and secret places.
      Gayl Jones. 286
Women = Housewives
   The day after Christmas.
      Josephine B. Moretti. 324
   Her chronicle. Carolyn Stoloff.
      376
   I sweat I mop I stink. Wanda
      Coleman. 225
Women = Indians of America
   Leaving. Joy Harjo. 269
   What music. Joy Harjo. 269
   The woman hanging from the
      thirteenth floor window. Joy
      Harjo. 269
Women = Korean
   Picture bride. Cathy Song. 372
   "Women aren't supposed." Sally
      Love Saunders. 358
Women at the lakeside. Elsa
      Gidlow. 254
Women in love. Robin Becker. 202
   The **women** of Huanuni. Ernesto
      Galarza. 252
   The **women** study in workshop
      together. Miriam Goodman. 264
Women's Rights
   The disturbance. Marge Piercy.
      346
   Feminist writers. Rochelle
      DuBois. 234
   "Glenn's definition of
      equality." Sally Love
      Saunders. 358
   Ms Muffet. Harlan Usher. 386
   State of women. Richard
      Blessing. 208
   The watch. Marge Piercy. 346

   What's that smell in the
      kitchen? Marge Piercy. 346
Women's Rights = Satire
   Ms Mary. Harlan Usher. 386
Wonderful moments. Jacques
      Sollov. 370
"**Wonis kvam.**" Charles Olson. 337
Wood
   Woodsplitting. Barry
      Wallenstein. 393
The **wood-pile.** Robert Frost. 250
The **woodchuck.** Robert Gibb. 253
Woodchucks
   The woodchuck. Robert Gibb. 253
Woodcock. Maurice Kenny. 291
Woodcocks
   Woodcock. Maurice Kenny. 291
The **woodlot.** Amy Clampitt. 222
Woodpile whistler. Ernesto
      Galarza. 252
Woods. Robert Peters. 343
Woods. See Forests

Woodsplitting. Barry Wallenstein.
      393
Woody's wool. Marge Piercy. 346
Wool-gathering. Carolyn Stoloff.
      376
Woolf, Virginia
   Homage to Virginia Woolf. Joyce
      Carol Oates. 336
   On seeing a page of Virginia's
      Woolf's diary. Anneliese
      Wagner. 389
The **word** for it. May Miller. 320
The **word** man. Larry Moffi. 322
Word songs. Colette Inez. 280
"The **word/has** been spoken/why
      need we speak it/again?" Joan
      Walsh Anglund. 197
The **word.** Lucien Stryk. 377
The **word.** Phillips Kloss. 294
Words
   Abattoir. Frances Mayes. 314
   About our lips. Mary Gilliland.
      257
   "All the stories never told."
      Theta Burke. 218
   Cambridge. Michael Gizzi. 259
   Changes on the organ theme. Roy
      Marz. 312
   The columnist listening to "you
      know" in the park. James
      Schevill. 360
   Conversation. Josephine Miles.
      319
   The death of a word. Alice Spohn
      Newton. 333
   The doorway. Mitchell Howard.
      276

The echolaliac. Robin Becker.
  202

Fantastic. Barry Wallenstein.
  393

Games with some. Tefke
  Goldberger. 262

He motioned for the words. John
  Hawkes. 270

Hearing. Jeanne Lohmann. 305

I packed my trunk for Albany.
  David Shapiro. 363

Language. Paul Davis. 228

Little night stories. William
  Stafford. 373

Logos. Miller Williams. 399

"'Man' and 'woman', these are
  horrid words..." Andrei
  Codrescu. 223

November twenty seventh. David
  Shapiro. 363

Powerful words. Martha Janssen.
  283

Private moments only. Gerard
  Malanga. 310

Rifacimento. Paul Violi. 388

Snowblind to the banquet. Paul
  Violi. 388

Two words. Betty Adcock. 192

The word man. Larry Moffi. 322

Word songs. Colette Inez. 280

The word. Lucien Stryk. 377

You speak. Gerard Malanga. 310

Words and magic hands. Rachel A.
  Hazen. 271

"Words penetrate a poem." Kenneth
  Koch. 297

Words rising. Robert Bly. 209

Words to a former musician.
  Thomas R. Sleigh. 366

Words to persons who find
  themselves feeling small.
  Mitchell Howard. 276

Work. Andrei Codrescu. 223

Work. Susan Tichy. 381

Work

  Bah! Sheep! Harlan Usher. 386

  Cheating on company time. Miriam
    Goodman. 264

  Day into night. Rosa Bogar. 211

  Life's work. Connie Hunt. 279

  Lunch at the desk with the news.
    Miriam Goodman. 264

  9 A.M.   Rochelle DuBois. 234

  Signal-to-noise. Miriam Goodman.
    264

  Staircase. Miriam Goodman. 264

  Two tramps in mud time. Robert
    Frost. 250

The work of the soul. Michael
  Akillian. 193

Work. See also Employment, see
  Labor

Work? Who, me? Harlan Usher. 386

Worker. Wanda Coleman. 225

The worker. Ernest Hemingway. 272

Working for peace. Alice Joyce
  Davidson. 227

Working on our masters in
  communications. Joan Colby.
  224

Working woman. Josephine B.
  Moretti. 324

The working writer. Marge Piercy.
  346

World. Josephine Miles. 319

World

  Al Aaraaf. Edgar Allan Poe. 347

  Animaux. Donald Revell. 351

  Ars poetica. Everett A. Gillis.
    258

  "Astride/the Chabot/fault."
    Charles Olson. 337

  "The blow is creation." Charles
    Olson. 337

  "The condition of the light from
    the sun." Charles Olson. 337

  "Does the world look like a park
    to you?Yes,almost..."
    Josephine Miles. 319

  "The Earth is not a place for
    me." Da Free John. 284

  Einstein in the orchard. Harry
    Humes. 278

  F-. Joyce Carol Oates. 336

  From our balloon over the
    provinces. William Stafford.
    373

  The green tide. Mitchell Howard.
    276

  "Heaven as sky is made of
    stone..." Charles Olson. 337

  Helluva big neighborhood.
    Mitchell Howard. 276

  "The history/of earth..."
    Charles Olson. 337

  "It is difficult/for me." A.
    Dovichi. 233

  Let us gather at the river.
    Marge Piercy. 346

  Lockdance. Mitchell Howard. 276

  Mareoceanum. Charles Olson. 337

  [Maximus, from Dogtown-IV].
    Charles Olson. 337

  The myth of Cancer. Mitchell
    Howard. 276

  "On the earth's edge..." Charles
    Olson. 337

  On the face of my words. Ray
    Fleming. 247

The pier dwellers. Stephen
   Knauth. 295
Planetary childhood. David Wann.
   394
Poem 143. The festival aspect.
   Charles Olson. 337
Same day, later. Charles Olson.
   337
Scenario for a species. David
   Wann. 394
School's out. Colette Inez. 280
Sea sickness. Andrei Codrescu.
   223
Some night again. William
   Stafford. 373
Song to hug by. Mary Gilliland.
   257
Spaceship. Jacques Sollov. 370
Spring four, sels. Edwin Honig.
   275
Stroke. Josephine Miles. 319
"That's/the combination of the
   ocean." Charles Olson. 337
There is blindness. William
   Stafford. 373
To a metaphysical amazon.
   Josephine Miles. 319
To the earth. David Shapiro. 363
The unfitted passage. Bradford
   Morrow. 329
Winter night. John Reed. 350
World. Josephine Miles. 319
The world before it became a
   poem. Ray Fleming. 247
The world comes back like an old
   cat. Marge Piercy. 346
The world before it became a
   poem. Ray Fleming. 247
The world comes back like an old
   cat. Marge Piercy. 346
The world in the year 2000. Marge
   Piercy. 346
"World is endlessly allowed to
   be." Da Free John. 284
The world of expectations. Albert
   Goldbarth. 261
The world that lives in me.
   Jacques Sollov. 370
World War II. Jacqueline Frank.
   248
World War, First
   April 7, 1967 John F. Barker.
      201
   "Arsiero, Asiago." Ernest
      Hemingway. 272
   At the Chateau de Villegenis
      that summer. Herbert Morris.
      326
   Memorial Day 1933. Robert
      Peters. 343

To good guys dead. Ernest
   Hemingway. 272
Uncles. Robert Peters. 343
World War, Second
   The anniversary. Amy Clampitt.
      222
   Dec. 7, 1941. Josephine Miles.
      319
   Defense of Luxembourg. Ernest
      Hemingway. 272
   Elegy for cliches. Debra Bruce.
      216
   First poem to Mary in London.
      Ernest Hemingway. 272
   The gardener's letter from
      Stalingrad. Franz Schneider.
      361
   The Hague, 5 May 1945. Tefke
      Goldberger. 262
   Limited service in World War II.
      James Schevill. 360
   May 1945. Edwin Honig. 275
   Memories of World War II: The
      decision. Tefke Goldberger.
      262
   My father & World War Two.
      Evelyn Golden. 263
   Normandy beach. Miller Williams.
      399
   One-eye and the German prisoners
      of war in Colorado. James
      Schevill. 360
   Poem to Mary. Ernest Hemingway.
      272
   Poetry. Ernest Hemingway. 272
   World War II. Jacqueline Frank.
      248
World without end: a Japanese
   screen. Charles Edward Eaton.

The world's greatest two-piece
   band. Mark Vinz. 387

The world. Kenneth Koch. 297
Worlds. Albert Goldbarth. 261
"Worlds are an exclamation of my
   names." Da Free John. 284
"The worlds fall out of my right
   hand." Da Free John. 284
"The worlds/likes and dislikes."
   A. Dovichi. 233
Worms
   Bloodworms. J.W. Rivers. 354
   Sea mouse. Amy Clampitt. 222
   Williamsburg. Michael Gizzi. 259
Worship
   Breakthrough. Paul Davis. 228
   Come back home. Jacques Sollov.
      371

The cup. Jacques Sollov. 371

Dawn to dusk. Alice Joyce
  Davidson. 227

Ecstatic moment. Jacques Sollov.
  370

Fellowship. Alice Joyce
  Davidson. 227

The golden fish. Jacques Sollov.
  370

"Holding hands/we are a
  circle/...of the spirit." Joan
  Walsh Anglund. 197

The kingdom shore. Jacques
  Sollov. 370

Legacy. Alice Joyce Davidson.
  227

The light bearer. Jacques
  Sollov. 371

Little one. Jacques Sollov. 370

Love glow. Alice Joyce Davidson.
  227

Loving heart. Alice Joyce
  Davidson. 227

"The One who crawled me off His
  knee." Da Free John. 284

Partnership. Alice Joyce
  Davidson. 227

The poet of love. Jacques
  Sollov. 371

The poet. Jacques Sollov. 371

The prospector. Jacques Sollov.
  371

Quiet place. Alice Joyce
  Davidson. 227

Rama holds an orgy. Mitchell
  Howard. 276

Sabbath. William Stafford. 373

Tell me a rainbow of sacrifice.
  Patsie Black. 206

Tell me a rainbow of
  celebration. Patsie Black. 206

These faces I see. James R.
  Rhodes. 352

To whom our praise is due. Alice
  Joyce Davidson. 227

"The word/has been spoken/why
  need we speak it/again?" Joan
  Walsh Anglund. 197

Worshipping Kali in the San
  Bernardino Mountains. Gene
  Anderson. 195

The worst poems make the best
  "poems" Andrei Codrescu. 223

The worth of being less. Robert
  L. Wilson. 401

Would she vanish, kissed? Elsa
  Gidlow. 254

The wound. Louise Gluck. 259A

Wounds
  "From inner battle he has come."
  Theta Burke. 218

"Wounds sing in the red meadow."
  Carolyn Stoloff. 376

Wreck. Josephine Miles. 319

Wrecking for the freeway. James
  Schevill. 360

The wrench of love. Barry
  Wallenstein. 393

Wrens
  The canyon wren. Phillips Kloss.
  294

  Winter wren. David Wagoner, 390

Wright, C.D.
  Alla breve loving. 402

  Bad grounds. 402

  The beautiful urinals of Paris.
  402

  Bent tones. 402

  Blazes. 402

  Boss of darkness. 402

  Clockmaker with bad eyes. 402

  Crescendo. 402

  Deep rivers. 402

  Drift. 402

  Falling beasts. 402

  Fascination. 402

  Fields. 402

  Foretold. 402

  Jazz impressions in the garden.
  402

  Landlocked, fallen, unsung. 402

  Libretto. 402

  Listening to a brown-eyed man
  play it for somebody else. 402

  Livelihoods of freaks and poets
  of the western world, sels.
  402

  The night before the sentence is
  carried out. 402

  Obedience of the corpse. 402

  Pontoons. 402

  Run for the roses. 402

  The secret life of musical
  instruments. 402

  Smoke rings. 402

  The substitute bassist. 402

  Tours. 402

  True accounts from the imaginary
  war. 402

  Two women sleeping on a stone.
  402

  Vanish. 402

  Wanderer in his thirtieth year.
  402

  Water, blood, and desire. 402

  White shutters. 402

  Who sit watch in daylight. 402

  Yellow dresses. 402

Wright, James
  Come, look quietly. 403

A dark moor bird. 403
Entering the temple in Nimes. 403
Leaving the temple in Nimes. 403
Notes of a pastoralist. 403
Old Bud. 403
The sumac in Ohio. 403
This and that. 403
The vestal in the Forum. 403
Wright, James (about)
For James Wright rom a dream, 1978 Ralph J., Jr. Mills. 321
Totems (II). Thomas McGrath. 315
Wright, Richard
Richard, Richard: American fuel. Melvin Dixon. 231
Richard, Richard: an American hunger. Melvin Dixon. 231
Writ on the back of an airline barf bag. Gene Detro. 230
Writer's blues. Tefke Goldberger. 262
Writing an elegy in my sleep. David Wagoner. 390
Writing and Writers
Alchemy. Joseph Penzi. 342
American baroque. Mitchell Howard. 276
"And everything the author knows." Ernest Hemingway. 272
A course in creative writing. William Stafford. 373
Creative writing. Robin Becker. 202
An example of work. David Shapiro. 363
Extinctions, schedule of. Bill Knott. 296
For Robt Duncan, who. Charles Olson. 337
Happy what, author? Harlan Usher. 386
Horizon. Rachel A. Hazen. 271
Ice fishing. James Magorian. 309
Jelka. James Tate. 379
"Little drops of grain alcohol." Ernest Hemingway. 272
The lookout's report. Cornel Lengyel. 302
Luncheon 2 Josephine Miles. 319
Makers. Josephine Miles. 319
Men and publishers. Lyn Lifshin. 303
Merry Xmas, author! Harlan Usher. 386
Montana syndrome not far from where General Custer perished. James Magorian. 308
On an unpublished author. Cornel Lengyel. 302

Poem, 1928. Ernest Hemingway. 272
Sequel. Ernest Hemingway. 272
Shining star. David James. 282
658.386/B 972.S. Christopher Bursk. 219
"Sometimes it's creative." Sally Love Saunders. 358
"There was an old pig with a pen." Arnold Lobel. 304
Things to know. Gerard Malanga. 310
To Marie Louise. Edgar Allan Poe. 347
Underground literature. James Magorian. 308
The white writing of Mark Tobey. James Schevill. 360
Why write. Andrei Codrescu. 223
The working writer. Marge Piercy. 346
Writer's blues. Tefke Goldberger. 262
Writing in bed. David Shapiro. 363
Writing in bed. David Shapiro. 363
"Writing on scraps..." Susan Tichy. 381
Writing poems on graph paper. James Magorian. 309
Writing poetry in the woods. Tefke Goldberger. 262
Writing the words. Brenda Marie Osbey. 340
Writing to a prisoner. Sandra McPherson. 317
Written at Mule Hollow, Utah. Robert Bly. 209
Wrong suspect raped in Sacramento rape case. David Wann. 394
"Wrote my first poems." Charles Olson. 337
Wyeth, Andrew
Her room. Gary Margolis. 311

X wives. Harrison Fisher. 245
X-rays
Doctor Dionysus. Charles Edward Eaton. 236
Xerox. Miriam Goodman. 264
Xiphosuran. X.J. Kennedy. 290
Xmas day with Miss Universe. Randy Blasing. 207
Xochicalco. Steve Kowit. 299

Yadkin Valley sketchbook. Stephen
    Knauth. 295
The yak. Jack Prelutsky. 349
Yaks
    The yak. Jack Prelutsky. 349
Yams
    Conversation on a yam. Irving
    Feldman. 242
Yarmalong
    The road to Yaramalong. Rod
    McKuen. 318
Yau, John
    After the war (I). 404
    After the war (II). 404
    After the war (III). 404
    After the war (IV). 404
    Any day now you will return. 404
    Aztec love song. 404
    Brief item. 404
    Broken off by the music. 404
    Chinese villanelle. 404
    Corpse and mirror (I). 404
    Corpse and mirror (II). 404
    Corpse and mirror (III). 404
    The dream life of a coffin
    factory in Lynn,
    Massachusetts. 404
    For Alexander Pope's gardens.
    404
    January 18, 1979. 404
    Late night movies. 404
    The lost colony. 404
    Missing pages. 404
    Nantucket. 404
    Off to the side. 404
    Parallel lives. 404
    Persons in the presence of a
    metamorphosis. 404
    The pleasures of exile. 404
    The reading of an ever-changing
    tale. 404
    Rumors. 404
    Scenes from the life of Boullee.
    404
    Second variation on Corpse and
    mirror. 404
    Shanghai shenanigans. 404
    Shimmering pediment. 404
    Third variation on Corpse and
    mirror. 404
    Three poems for Li Shang-yin.
    404
    Two kinds of language. 404
    Two kinds of song. 404
    Two kinds of story-telling. 404
    Two mediations on Guanajuato.
    404
    Variation on Corpse and mirror.
    404
Yea and nay. Mitchell Howard. 276
A year from now. Rachel A. Hazen.
    271
Year of the dog. Gene Anderson.
    195
Year's turn. Marie Daerr
    Boehringer. 210
The year. Everett A. Gillis. 258
Yearning. Deborah Tall. 378
Years
    Light year. Josephine Miles. 319
Years after. Carolyn Stoloff. 376
Yeats, William Butler
    Mary Conway. Paul Davis. 228
    On the great wheel. Anne Bailie.
    199
Yellow. Ralph J., Jr. Mills. 321
Yellow (color)
    Yellow. Ralph J., Jr. Mills. 321
Yellow cars. William Stafford.
    373
Yellow dresses. C.D. Wright. 402
Yellow flowers. William Stafford.
    373
Yellow leaves. Anne Bailie. 199
Yellow newspaper and a wooden
    leg. James Tate. 379
The yes log. Andrei Codrescu. 223
"Yes, I will meet him." Madison
    Morrison. 327
"Yes/there must have been." Wanda
    Coleman. 225
"Yesterday evening as the sun set
    late." Josephine Miles. 319
Yesterday's slaughter. Ernest
    Tedlock. 380
Yet are you wounded, soldier?
    Jocelyn Hollis. 274
"Yet leaving here a name..."
    Albert Goldbarth. 261
"Yet the closing episode."
    Madison Morrison. 327
Yi, yi, the sky. David James. 282
The Yolorai dance. Stephen
    Knauth. 295
Yom Kippur War (1973)
    Gaby at the U.N. observation
    post. Susan Tichy. 381
Yonder. James Tate. 379
York, England
    By the gate at York. Paul Davis.
    228
    Walls. Paul Davis. 228
Yorkminster, England
    Thoughts at York Cathedral. Paul
    Davis. 228
Yost, Merlen (Mert)
    O lifting wings of laughter.
    Alice Spohn Newton. 332

You and I. Martha Janssen. 283
"You and I make." Madison
    Morrison. 327
"You and I." Madison Morrison.
    327
You are. James R. Rhodes. 352
"You are like the crescent moon-"
    Sally Love Saunders. 358
"You are the sort of." Madison
    Morrison. 327
You bastard. Norman Andrew Kirk.
    293
"You beat them all." Robert A.
    Sears. 362
You can't f*** with mother
    nature. Jim Everhard. 241
You can't ignore a bagpipe.
    Robert A. Sears. 362
You clasped your hands. Judson
    Crews. 226
"You come home to." Madison
    Morrison. 327
"You cry for me in your love for
    life." Michael Robert Pick.
    345
You don't understand me. Marge
    Piercy. 346
"You drew the space in." Charles
    Olson. 337
You fed me well. Rosa Bogar. 211
"You get a cold." Theta Burke.
    218
"You must be hurting inside."
    Michael Robert Pick. 345
You must change your life. Lucien
    Stryk. 377
"You never know." Larry Eigner.
    237
"You poor helpless creature of
    power." Michael Robert Pick.
    345
"You ride for some hours." Larry
    Eigner. 237
You said. Debra Bruce. 216
You say. Elsa Gidlow. 254
You seemed so poised and tender
    tonight. Haig Khatchadourian.
    292
You speak. Gerard Malanga. 310
"You went/with me..." Madison
    Morrison. 327
You your voice departing. Joseph
    Penzi. 342
"You're a large wooden treasure
    chest." Sally Love Saunders.
    358
You're dead! James R. Rhodes. 352
You've touched me. Connie Hunt.
    279
Young black man teaching Italian

to middle-class white... Ray
    Fleming. 247
Young eyes. Rosa Bogar. 211
A young girl with a pitcher full
    of water. David Wagoner. 390
"The young ladies." Charles
    Olson. 337
The young lt. col. Miller
    Williams. 399
Young man on a Sunday. Robert
    Peters. 343
Young man with infant. Stephen
    Sandy. 357
Young secretaries. Josephine B.
    Moretti. 324
A young woman found in the woods.
    David Wagoner. 390
Young Yorick's confession. Cornel
    Lengyel. 302
"The younger man." Madison
    Morrison. 327
The youngest daughter. Cathy
    Song. 372
Your Christmas present. Dave
    Smith. 367
Your fantastic outlines. Andrei
    Codrescu. 223
Your fortune: a cold reading.
    David Wagoner. 390
Your friend. Rosa Bogar. 211
"Your hair/is not the most
    beautiful." Jim Everhard. 241
"Your love comes in phases."
    Sally Love Saunders. 358
"Your love." Theta Burke. 218
"Your love." Sally Love Saunders.
    358
Your phone call at 8a.m. Joy
    Harjo. 269
Your shroud, papa. Anneliese
    Wagner. 389
"Your smile erases all my pain."
    Michael Robert Pick. 345
"Your sweetness was in my hand."
    Michael Robert Pick. 345
Youth
    An adolescent girl. Carol Frost.
        249
    Album. Josephine Miles. 319
    The American girl. Harrison
        Fisher. 245
    At the record hop. Wanda
        Coleman. 225
    Bitter orange village. Randy
        Blasing. 207
    Blazes. C.D. Wright. 402
    Circle without end. Mitchell
        Howard. 276
    Fourteen. James A. Emanuel. 239
    Guess what was ripped out of the

wall today? Mitchell Howard.
276
Hey, young folks. Rosa Bogar.
211
"Hitchhiking in blinding storm."
Michael Robert Pick. 345
"The innocence of youth."
Michael Robert Pick. 345
It was your song. Steve Kowit.
299
Lesley. Josephine B. Moretti.
324
Lines to a girl 5 days after her
21st birthday. Ernest
Hemingway. 272
Lookin' for gas at the youth
guidance center. James
Schevill. 360
Ms. Livvy's boy. Brenda Marie
Osbey. 340
Paracelsus in Puerto Rico.
Charles Edward Eaton. 236
Personal history. Robert Peters.
343
A poem. Stephen Todd Booker. 212
Sex education. Martha Janssen.
283
Shorth poem, long story. Jeanne
Lohmann. 305
Sommerset. Rod McKuen. 316
Star-eyed boy. James R. Rhodes.
352
Tommy McQuaker. Robert Peters.
343
Valley with girls. Elsa Gidlow.
254
What goes on inside. Judson
Crews. 226
"When a teenager." Madison
Morrison. 327
Winter. Larry Eigner. 237
"You are the sort of." Madison
Morrison. 327
Young Yorick's confession.
Cornel Lengyel. 302
"The younger man." Madison
Morrison. 327
Youth and Age
Betrayal. Eileen
Silver-Lillywite. 364
A dream from Hokusai. Charles
Edward Eaton. 236
Progressive dinner. Michael
Akillian. 193
Yr amanuensis. Bradford Morrow.
329
Yucca flowers. William Stafford.
373
Yucca moth. Phillips Kloss. 294
A Yugoslav circus. Keith Wilson.
400
Yugoslavia
Antonic Gomic (at Monument Park
in Yugoslavia). James A.
Emanuel. 239
The yum-yum song. Susan Stock.
375

Zapata's sister speaks. J.W.
Rivers. 354
Zapata, Emilio
The stable. Gary Margolis. 311
Zapata's sister speaks. J.W.
Rivers. 354
The zebra. Jack Prelutsky. 349
Zebras
The zebra. Jack Prelutsky. 349
Zen. Susan Tichy. 381
Zenith. Randy Blasing. 207
The zigzag means lightning. David
James. 282
Zion
Sources. Adrienne Rich. 353
Zodiac
The pulse of the zodiac puzzle.
Rochelle DuBois. 234
Zoo doings. Jack Prelutsky. 349
Zoological Gardens
A report to an academy. Joyce
Carol Oates. 336
Zoo doings. Jack Prelutsky. 349
Zora Neale Hurston. Melvin Dixon.
231
Zurich - the hidden patient.
Michael Gizzi. 259
Zurich, Switzerland
Sidewalk cafe. Jeanne Lohmann.
305
Zzzzz. X.J. Kennedy. 290
Zzzzzzzzzzzzz. Andrei Codrescu.
223

A & W PUBLISHERS
95 Madison Ave
New York, NY 10016

ABINGDON PRESS
201 8th Ave S
Nashville, TN 37202

ACADEMY CHICAGO LTD
425 N Michigan Ave
Chicago, IL 60601

ADASTRA
101 Strong St
Easthampton, MA 01027

ADVENT
141 E 44th St, Ste 511
New York, NY 10017

AHSAHTA PRESS
Dept of English, Boise State U
Boise, ID 83725

ALEMBIC PRESS
1744 Slaterville Rd
Ithaca, NY 14850

ALICE JAMES BOOKS
138 Mt Auburn St
Cambridge, MA 02138

ALLEN & UNWIN
9 Winchester Terrace
Winchester, MA 01890

ALLY PRESS
Box 30340
St Paul, MN 55175

ALPHA PRINTING
6301-B Central Park NW
Albuquerque, NM 87105

AMERICAN INDIAN STUDIES CENTER
Univ of California
3220 Campbell Hall
Los Angeles, CA 90024

AMERICAN POETRY PRESS
Box 634
Claymont, DE 19703

AMPERSAND EDITIONS
765 Sunset Pkwy
San Francisco, CA 94947

AMPERSAND PRESS
Roger Williams College
Bristol, RI 02809

AMS
56 E 13th St
New York, NY 10003

APPLEZABA PRESS
PO Box 4134
Long Beach, CA 90804

ARCSOFT PUBLISHERS
Box 132
Woodsboro, MD 21798

ARDIS PUBLISHERS
2901 Heather Way
Ann Arbor, MI 48104

ARK
Box 332, Times Sq Sta
New York, NY 10108

ARK & ARBOR PRESS
Box 901
Little Compton, RI 02837

ARKHAM HOUSE PUBLISHER
Box 346
Sauk City, WI 53583

ART DIRECTION BOOK CO
10 E 39th St
New York, NY 10016

ASHOD PRESS
PO Box 1147, Madison Sq Sta
New York, NY 10159

ATHENEUM PUBLISHERS
597 Fifth Ave
New York, NY 10017

ATLANTIC MONTHLY PRESS
8 Arlington St
Boston, MA 02116

AUGUST HOUSE
Box 3201
Little Rock, AR 72203

AVATAR
Box 16703
Raytown, MO 64133

AVON BOOKS
959 8th Ave
New York, NY 10019

BARNES & NOBLE BOOKS
PO Box 327
Totowa, NJ 07511

WILLIAM L. BAUHAN
Old Counbtry Rd
Dublin, NH 03444

BEACON PRESS
25 Beacon St
Boston, MA 02108

BEARSTONE PUBLISHING CO
PO Box 324
Farley, IA 52046

BKMK PRESS
5725 Wyandotte St
Kansas City, MO 64113

BLACK SPARROW PRESS
Box 3993
Santa Barbara, CA 93105

BLIND BEGGAR PRESS
735 Magenta St, Apt 9-E
Bronx, NY 10467

BLUE CLOUD QUARTERLY
Marvin, SD 57251

BLUE GIANT PRESS
47A Dana St
Cambridge, MA 02138

BOSS BOOKS
Box 370, Madison Sq Sta
New York, NY 10159

BRADBURY PRESS
2 Overhill Rd
Scarsdale, NY 10583

BRANDEN PRESS
Box 843
Brookline, MA 02147

GEORGE BRAZILLER INC
1 Park Ave
New York, NY 10016

BRIGADOON PUBLICATIONS
3911 Richmond Ave
Staten Island, NY 10312

BURNING DECK
71 Elmgrove Ave
Providence, RI 02906

CADMUS EDITIONS
PO Box 4725
Santa Barbara, CA 93103

CALLALOO POETRY SERIES
University of Kentucky
Lexington, KY 40505-0276

CAMBRIDGE UNIV PRESS
32 E 57th St
New York, NY 10022

CAPRA PRESS
PO Box 2068
Santa Barbara, CA 93120

CARNATION PRESS
Box 101
State College, PA 16801

THE CAROLINA WREN PRESS
300 Barclay Rd.
Chapel Hill, NC 27514

CARPENTER PRESS
Rte 4
Pomeroy, OH 45769

CELESTIAL ARTS
231 Adrian Rd
Millbrae, CA 94030

CHANTRY PRESS
PO Box 144
Midland Park, NJ 07432

CHERRY VALLEY EDITIONS
2314 Georgian Woods Pl
Silver Spring, MD 20902

CITY LIGHTS BOOKS
261 Columbus Ave
San Francisco, CA 94133

CLEIS PRESS
Box 8281
Minneapolis, MN 55408

CLEVELAND STATE UNIV POETRY CENTER
Cleveland, OH 44115

COMPTON PRESS
301 W 108th St, #4B
New York, NY 10025

CONTACT II PUBLICATIONS
Box 451, Bowling Green Sta
New York, NY 10004

CONTINUING SAGA PRESS
1822 Mason St
San Francisco, CA 94133

COOPER BEECH PRESS
PO Box 1852, Brown Univ
Providence, RI 02912

THE COOPER ORCHID PUB CO
1966 Westbrook Dr
Jackson, MI 49201

COPPER CANYON PRESS
PO Box 271
Port Townsend, WA 98368

CORNWALL BOOKS
440 Forsgate Dr
Cranbury, NJ 08512

COUNTRYMAN PRESS
Box 175
Woodstock, VT 05091

COWARD, McCANN & GEOGHEGAN
200 Madison Ave
New York, NY 10016

COYOTE/BUSSARD
Box 10233
Eugene, OR 97440

CREATIVE WRITING PROGRAM
Univ of Nebraska at Omaha
Omaha, NE 68182

THE CROSSING PRESS
Box 640
Trumansburg, NY 14886

THOMAS Y CROWELL
10 E 53rd St
New York, NY 10022

CROWN PUBLISHERS
1 Park Ave
New York, NY 10016

D & S PUBLICATIONS
6334 St Andrews Circle
Ft Meyers, FL 33907

DALMAS & RECOUR
6322 Cool Shade Dr
Fayetteville, NC 28303

DAMASCUS ROAD
6271 Hill Rd
Wescosville, PA 18106

THE DAWN HORSE PRESS
PO Box 3680
Clearlake, CA 95422

DELACORTE PRESS
1 Dag Hammarskjold Plaza
New York, NY 10017

DELAFIELD PRESS
Suttons Bay, MI 49682

DELAWARE VALLEY POETS
PO Box 6203
Lawrenceville, NJ 08648

THE DIAL PRESS
245 Park Ave
New York, NY 10016

DIANA'S BIMONTHLY PRESS
71 Elmgrove Ave
Providence, RI 02906

DODD, MEAD & CO
79 Madison Ave
New York, NY 10016

DOMINA BOOKS
16455 Tuba St
Sepulveda, CA 91343

DOUBLEDAY & CO
245 Park AVe
New York, NY 10167

DRAGON GATE
508 Lincoln St
Port Townsend, WA 98368

DRAGON'S TEETH PRESS
El Dorado National Forest
Georgetown, CA 95634

DRYAD PRESS
15 Sherman Ave
Takoma Park, MD 20012

DUCK DOWN PRESS
Box 1047
Fallon, NV 89406

THE ECCO PRESS
18 W 30th St
New York, NY 10001

ELL ELL DIVERSIFIED INC
Santa Rosa, CA

EMPIRE BOOKS
Box 29388
Los Angeles, CA 90027

ERASMUS BOOKS OF NOTRE DAME
PO Box 661
Notre Dame, IN 46556

FABER & FABER
99 Main St
Salem, OH 03079

FARRAR, STRAUSS & GIROUX
19 Union Sq West
New York, NY 10003

FOLKORICA
301 E 47th St
New York, NY 10017

FORIS PUBLICATONS
703 Cornell Ave
Cinnaminson, NJ 08077

FORTRESS PRESS
2900 Queen Lane
Philadelphia, PA 19129

FULL COURT PRESS
138-140 Watts St
New York, NY 10013

GAY SUNSHINE PRESS
Box 40397
San Francisco, CA 94140

DAVID R GODINE
306 Dartmouth St
Boston, MA 02116

THE GOLDEN QUILL PRESS
Avery Rd
Francestown, NH 03043

THE GREENFIELD REVIEW PRESS
Rd 1, Box 80
Greenfield, NY 12833

GREENWILLOW BOOKS
105 Madison Ave
New York, NY 10016

GREENWOOD PRESS
88 Post Road West
Westport, CT 06881

GREYWOLF PRESS
PO Box 142
Port Townsend, WA 98368

GROSSET & DUNLAP
200 Madison Ave
New York, NY 10016

GROVE PRESS INC
196 W Houston St
New York, NY 10014-9983

GUILD PRESS
PO Box 22583
Robbinsdale, MN 55422

GUSTO PRESS
Box 1009
Bronx, NY 10465

HADRIAN CREATIVE BOOKS
47 Hyde Blvd
Ballston Spa, NY 12020

G.K. HALL & CO
70 Lincoln St
Boston, MA 02111

HANGING LOOSE PRESS
231 Wyckoff St
Brooklyn, NY 11217

HARBINGER PRESS
347 Willow Ave
Corte Madera, CA 94925

HARCOURT, BRACE, JOVANOVICH
1250 Sixth Ave
San Diego, CA 92101

HARPER & ROW
10 E 53rd St
New York, NY 10022

HARVARD UNIV PRESS
79 Garden St
Cambridge, MA 02138

HEINEMAN EDUCATIONAL BOOKS
4 Front St
Exeter, NJ 03833

THE HEYCECK PRESS
27 Patrol Court
Woodside, CA 94062

HOLIDAY HOUSE INC
18 E 53rd St
New York, NY 10022

HOLMANGERS PRESS
Star Rte, Shelter Cove
Whitethorn, CA 95458

HOLT, RINEHART & WINSTON
521 Fifth Ave
New York, NY 10175

HORIZON PRESS
156 5th Ave
New York, NY 10010

HOUGHTON MIFFLIN CO
1 Beacon St
Boston, MA 02107

IMPACT PUBLISHERS
PO Box 1094
San Luis Obispo, CA 93460

INDIANA UNIV PRESS
Tenth & Morton Sts
Bloomington, IN 47405

THE IRON PRESS
Franklin, MI 48025-0176

IRVINGTON PUBLISHERS INC
551 5th Ave
New York, NY 10176

ISIS PRESS
1516 Morton Ave
Ann Arbor, MI 48104

ITHACA HOUSE
108 N Plain St
Ithaca, NY 14850

JARGON SOCIETY
Box 106
Frankfort, KY 40602

THE JOHNS HOPKINS UNIV PRESS
Baltimore, MD 21218

KHANIQAHI-NIMATULLAHI
306 W 11th St
New York, NY 10014

ALFRED A KNOPF INC
201 E 50th St
New York, NY 10022

KONGLOMERATI PRESS
Box 5001
Gulfport, FL 33737

KULCHUR FOUNDATION
888 Park Ave
New York, NY 10021

J B LIPPINCOTT CO
10 E 53rd St
New York, NY 10022

LITTLE, BROWN & CO
34 Beacon St
Boston, MA 02106

LOGBRIDGE-RHODES
Box 3254
Durango, CA 81301

LONGMANS INC
19 W 44th St
New York, NY 10036

LOTHROP, LEE & SHEPARD BOOKS
105 Madison Ave
New York, NY 10016

LOTUS PRESS
PO Box 21607
Detroit, MI 48221

LOUISIANA STATE UNIV PRESS
Baton Rouge, LA 70803

LOYOLA UNIV PRESS
3441 N Ashland Ave
Chicago, IL 60657

THE LUNCHROOM PRESS
PO Box 36027
Grosse Pt Farms, MI 48230

LYNX HOUSE PRESS
PO Box 800
Amherst, MA 01104

MACMILLAN, INC
866 3rd Ave
New York, NY 10022

MARXIST EDUCATIONAL PRESS
Anthropology Dept, Univ MN
215 Ford Hall, 224 Church SE
Minneapolis, MN 55455

McBOOKS PRESS
106 N Aurora
Ithaca, NY 14850

McGRAW-HILL BOOK CO
1221 Avenue of the Americas
New York, NY 10020

THE EDWIN MELLEN PRESS
PO Box 450
Lewiston, NY 14092

MEMPHIS STATE UNIV PRESS
Memphis, TN 38152

MESA VERDE PRESS
144 Mesa Verde St
Sante Fe, NM 87501

METACOM PRESS
31 Beaver St
Worcester, MA 01603

MOJAVE BOOKS
7040 Darby Ave
Reseda, CA 91335

MOMO'S PRESS
45 Sheridan St
San Francisco, CA 94103

MONTEMORA FOUNDATION
Box 336, Cooper Sta
New York, NY 10276

WILLIAM MORROW & CO
105 Madison Ave
New York, NY 10016

MOUNTAIN STATE PRESS
University of Charleston
2300 Mac Corkle Ave SE
Charleston, WV 25304

MULTNOMAH PRESS
10209 SE Division St
Portland, OR 97266

NAIAD PRESS
Box 10543
Tallahasse, Fl 32302

NAVAL INSTITUTE PRESS
Annapolis, MD 21402

NEW AMERICAN LIBRARY
1633 Broadway
New York, NY 10019

NEW DIRECTIONS PUBLISHING CORP
80 Eighth Ave
New York, NY 10011

NEW RIVERS PRESS
1602 Selby Ave
St Paul, MN 55104

NIGHT HORN BOOKS
495 Ellis St
San Francisco, Ca 94102

W W NORTON & CO
500 5th Ave
New York, NY 10110

OHIO UNIV PRESS/SWALLOW
Scott Hall 143
Athens, OH 45701

ONTARIO REVIEW PRESS
SEE PERSEA

OVERLOOK PRESS
667 Madison Ave
New York, NY 10021

OXFORD UNIV PRESS
200 Madison Ave
New York, NY 10016

PATRICE PRESS
Box 42
Gerald, MO 63037

PELICAN PUBLISHING CO
PO Box 189
Gretna, LA 70053

PERSEA BOOKS
225 Lafayette St
New York, NY 10012

PICES PRESS
PO Box 4075
Lubbock, TX 79409

PIZZUTO, LTD
San Gabriel, CA

PRENTICE-HALL INC
Englewood Cliffs, NJ 07632

PRINCETON UNIV PRESS
Princeton, NJ 08540

PULSAR PUBLICATIONS
PO Box 714
Lafayette, CA 94549

RANDOM HOUSE
201 E 50th St
New York, NY 10022

FLEMING H REVELL CO
184 Central Ave
Old Tappan, NJ 07675

RIVERSTONE PRESS
809 15th St
Golden, CO 80401

RRP PUBLISHERS
12 W 17th St
New York, NY 10011

SATURDAY PRESS, INC
PO Box 884
Upper Montclair, NJ 07043

SCARECROW PRESS INC
52 Liberty St
Metuchen, NJ 08840

SCHOCKEN BOOKS INC
200 Madison Ave
New York, NY 10016

THE SEA HORSE PRESS
307 W 11th St
New York, NY 10014

THE SEAL PRESS
312 S Washington St
Seattle, WA 98104

HAROLD SHAW
Box 567
Wheaton, IL 60187

SIMON & SCHUSTER
1230 Avenue of the Americas
New York, NY 10020

SLOW LORIS PRESS
923 Highview St
Pittsburgh, PA 15206

SOL PRESS
2025 Dunn Pl
Madison, WI 53713

SOUP
545 Ashbury
San Francisco, CA 94114

SPARROW PRESS
103 Waldron St
West Lafayette, IN 47906

SPOON RIVER POETRY PRESS
Illinois Arts Council
PO Box 1443
Peoria, IL 61655

ST LUKE'S PRESS
1407 Union
Memphis, TN 38104

ST MARTIN'S PRESS
175 5th Ave
New York, NY 10010

STAR GARDEN POETS COOPERATIVE
24721 Newhall Ave
Newhall, CA 91321

STATE STREET PRESS
67 State St
Pittsford, NY 14534

STATE UNIV PRESS OF NEW YORK
State Univ Plaza
Albany, NY 12246

STATION HILL PRESS
Station Hill Rd
Barrytown, NY 12507

STEMMER HOUSE
2627 Caves Rd
Owings Mills, MD 21117

STERLING PUBLISHING CO
2 Park Ave
New York, NY 10016

STONE COUNTRY
PO Box 132
Menemsha, MA 02552

STRAWBERRY PRESS
Box 451, Bowling Green Sta
New York, NY 10004

LYLE STUART INC
120 Enterprise Ave
Secaucus, NJ 07094

SUN
347 W 39th St
New York, NY 10018

SUN & MOON PRESS
4330 Hartwick Rd
College Park, MD 20740

SUBURST PRESS
Box 6
Portland, OR 97215

SUNSTONE PRESS
Box 2321
Sante Fe, NM 87501

SUTTER HOUSE
Box 212
Lititz, PA 17543

SYLVAN PUBLICATIONS
7104 NE Hazel Dell Ave
Vancouver, WA 98665

THE SYMPOSIUM
1620 Greenfield Ave
Los Angeles, CA 90025

DIRECTORY OF PUBLISHERS

TEMPORAL ACUITY PRESS
1535-121 Ave SE
Bellevue, WA 98005

TENDRIL MAGAZINE
PO Box 512
Green Harbor, MA 02041

TEXAS TECHNICAL UNIV PRESS
Box 4240
Lubbock, TX 79409

THORP SPRINGS PRESS
803 Red River St
Austin, TX 78701

THREE CONTINENTS PRESS
1346 Connecticut Ave, Ste 1131
Washington, DC 20036

THUNDER'S MOUTH PRESS
242 W 104th St
New York, NY 10025

TODD & HONEYWELL INC
10 Cuttermill Rd
Great Neck, NY 11021

TOOTH OF TIME BOOKS
Box 391
Gradalupita, NM 87722

TOOTHPASTE PRESS
Box 546
West Branch, IA 52358

TUCSON PUBLIC LIBRARY, FRIENDS
PO Box 27470
Tucson, AZ 85726

TWAYNE PUBLISHERS
70 Lincoln St
Boston, MA 02111

UNICORN PRESS
Box 3307
Greensboro, NC 27402

UNIV OF ALABAMA PRESS
Box 2877
University, AL 35486

UNIV OF ARKANSAS PRESS
201 Ozark St
Fayetteville, AR 72701

UNIV OF CALIFORNIA PRESS
50 E 42nd St, Rm 513
New York, NY 10017

UNIV OF CHICAGO PRESS
5801 Ellis Ave
Chicago, IL 60637

UNIV OF GEORGIA PRESS
Athens, GA 30602

UNIV OF ILLINOIS PRESS
Box 5081, Sta A
Champaign, IL 61820

UNIV OF IOWA PRESS
Graphic Srvs Bldg
Iowa City, IA 52242

UNIV OF MASSACHUSETTS PRESS
Box 429
Amherst, MA 01004

UNIV OF MICHIGAN PRESS
PO Box 1104
Ann Arbor, MI 48106

UNIV OF MISSOURI PRESS
200 Lewis Hall
Columbia, MO 65211

UNIV OF NEW MEXICO PRESS
Journalism Bldg
Albuquerque, NM 87131

UNIV OF NOTRE DAME PRESS
Notre Dame, IN 46556

UNIV OF PENNSYLVANIA PRESS
3933 Walnut St
Philadlephia, PA 19104

UNIV OF PITTSBURGH PRESS
127 N Bellefield
Pittsburgh, PA 15260

UNIV OF TEXAS PRESS
Box 7819
Austin, TX 78712

UNIV OF UTAH PRESS
101 USB
Salt Lake City, UT 84112

UNIV OF WASHINGTON PRESS
Box 85569
Seattle, WA 98105

UNIV PRESS OF AMERICA
4720 Boston Way
Lanham, MD 20706

UNIV PRESS OF NEW ENGLAND
Box 979
Hanover, NH 03755

UNIV PRESSES OF FLORIDA
15 NM 15th St
Gainesville, FL 32603

UNIVERSITY PRESS OF AMERICA
PO Box 19101
Washington, DC 20036

UTAH STATE UNIV PRESS
UMC 95
Logan, UT 84322

VEGTUNES ENTERTAINMENT CO
Box 450W, N Baldwin St
Baldin, NY 11510

VIKING PENGUIN INC
625 Madison Ave
New York, NY 10022

WAMPETER PRESS
Box 512
Green Harbour, ME 02041

FREDERICK WARNE & CO, INC
2 Park Ave
New York, NY 10016

**WASHINGTON WRITERS'
PUBLISHING HOUSE**
Box 50068
Washington, DC 20003

WAYNE STATE UNIV PRESS
5959 Woodward Ave
Detroit, MI 48202

WESLEYAN UNIV PRESS
110 Mt Vernon St
Middletown, CT 06457

WEST OF BOSTON
PO Box 2, Cochituate Sta
Wayland, MA 01778

WESTERN PUBLISHING CO
850 3rd Ave
New York, NY 10022

THE WHITE EAGLE PUBLISHER
PO Box 1332
Lowell, MA 01853

WINDFLOWER PRESS
Box 82213
Lincoln, NE 68501

WINGS PRESS
Box 325
Belfast, ME 04915

WINSTON-DEREK PUBLISHERS
PO Box 90883, Pennywell Dr
Nashville, TN 37209

WINSTON PRESS
430 Oak Grove
Minneapolis, MN 55403

**WOODBRIDGE PRESS
PUBLISHING CO**
Box 6189
Santa Barbara, CA 93111

WORKING WEEK PRESS
420 E. Eufaula St
Norman, OK 73069

WYNAUD PRESS
3005 Ronna
Las Cruces, NM 88001

YALE UNIV PRESS
92A Yale Sta
New Haven, CT 06520

YELLOW MOON PRESS
1725 Commonwealth
Brighton, MA 02135